D0327840

CHARLESTON & SAVANNAH

MIKE SIGALAS WITH MELISSA BIGNER

CHARLESTON AND THE
SOUTH CAROLINA LOWCOUNTRY

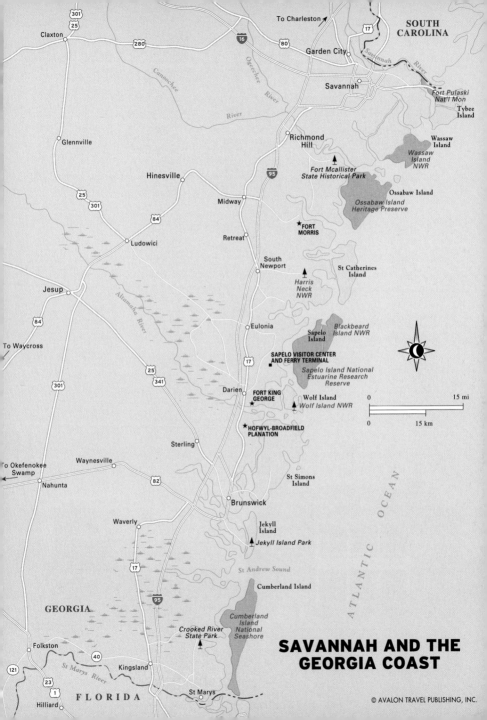

SAVANNAH AND THE
GEORGIA COAST

DISCOVER CHARLESTON & SAVANNAH

Gone With the Wind's Scarlett O'Hara saw Charleston and Savannah as sister cities of mythical but faded antebellum beauty and vitality. Her construct is still helpful today, as it remains easier to see each city's subtle differences by comparing one to the other.

Most of the differences come down to age: Charleston was founded in 1670, and is thus 63 years older than her younger sister. Play along, and Charleston could be the Queen Elizabeth of the pair: the older, primmer, more serious, and more responsible. (Charleston, after all, was the first established British colony south of Virginia; and truthfully, Savannah came about initially to buffer Charleston from the Spanish.)

Continue with the sister royals game, and Savannah is the lighter-hearted, dance-'til-dawn Princess Margaret. And while lil' Margie was getting drunk off the fruits of her cotton boom, tinkering with

Drayton Hall is one of Charleston's original plantation houses.

steamships and wrought-iron balustrades, Charleston acted the big sister and stood up to Northern pressures and demands. Through the leadership of Senator John C. Calhoun, and the solidarity of her Confederate-minded citizens, Charleston became the face, voice, and heart of the region. Given that both cities suffered under the North's hand during those prewar days, it was still Charleston who finally slapped the Union's face, demanding a divorce via secession.

When the war came, Savannah was unprepared for and (according to Robert E. Lee) unenthusiastic about its self-defense. Big sis' Charleston, however, beat the Yankees back from Fort Sumter, and kept the Confederacy alive with its blockade runners. When the fort finally surrendered, Savannah smiled shrewdly at Sherman, fluttered her mossy eyelashes, and gave herself up for occupation. Charleston, however, bit her lip defiantly, and weathered the longest siege and bombardment of any city during the war. When all fighting ended, Savannah's occupying Northerners helped launch that city on its

Kayak to wild and barren Lowcountry barrier islands.

second cotton boom, while Charlestonians dug through the rubble of their streets.

Today you can still see those differences of old. In the mid-1990s, the last vestiges of old Charleston dug in their heels as they attempted (and failed) to keep women from attending The Citadel Military College, that nursery room of the Ideal Southern Male. But southward? Savannah made money hand-over-fist leading amused outsiders on guided tours, answering impolite questions about her con artists, drag queens, and murderers, all thanks to John Berendt's true-crime tell-all, *Midnight in the Garden of Good and Evil*.

These days, both sisters have curtsied to progress and recognize that tourism and an influx of outsiders have been their mixed-blessing salvation. For visitors, that means the cities rose to the occasion and blossomed into national-caliber shopping and dining destinations: Each claims design districts that appeal to antique aficionados and label hounds both; each has put Southern cuisine — nouveau and classic comfort food — on the international epicurean map; and

Cool off at Waterfront Park along the Charleston Harbor.

each is lauded for luxe accommodations that revive the best of Old South decadence.

And as for lingering stereotypes? Savannahians like to say that "in Charleston, they ask you who your great grandfather was…in Savannah, they ask you what you want to drink." But the common joke is utter nonsense. Lineage still has its place in both towns, and the same class of people who are snobs in Charleston are snobs in Savannah. Further, nearly since its inception, Charleston was known for its liberal attitudes toward religious dissenters, free blacks, and heavy drinkers, and earned a reputation for materialism and hedonism long before Savannah. "Wicked Charleston" (as it was called centuries ago) was as short on licentiousness then (and now) as Savannah is short on Old Money arrogance. The roaming visitor, however, could easily miss such undercurrents, seeing the majority of locals for what they most obviously are: Jovial Southerners living it up in typically convivial waterfront towns.

Outside the sister cities, roam the Lowcountry and Golden Isle coast and the offerings are a mixed bag. Sure, you can kayak your

Sullivan's Island is home to occasional eccentricity.

© SEAN SLINSKY

way through undisturbed marshes of the ACE Basin, and you can hike all over undeveloped barrier islands like Cumberland, but it's just as possible to play a round on a world-class golf course at Kiawah, or attend a tennis camp at one of the country's top resorts on Hilton Head. And while you can still buy boiled peanuts on old Savannah Highway 17, get fresh 'maters from a roadside stand, and pit-cooked, sweet-mustard-sauced pork from a shabby barbecue joint, chain USA is seeping in...and even thick, rich Gullah accents are beginning to get watered down. So pack your bags now. This culturally wealthy and still-distinct region, anchored by two aged beauties, and offering so much to so many varied interests, is changing; rarely can you sample the Old South and New South in such proximity.

In Savannah, getting lost is a detour into good urban design.

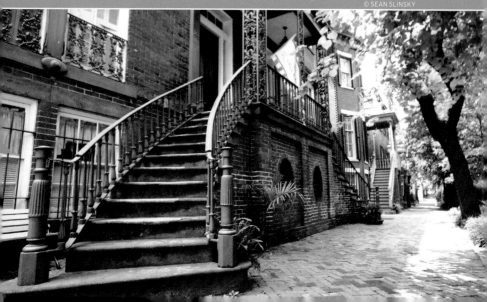

Contents

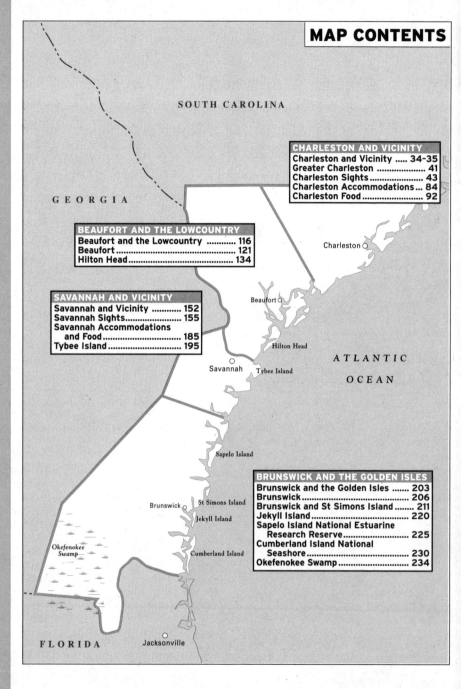

12

MAP CONTENTS

SOUTH CAROLINA

GEORGIA

Charleston

Beaufort

Hilton Head

ATLANTIC

OCEAN

Savannah   Tybee Island

Sapelo Island

St Simons Island
Brunswick
Jekyll Island

Okefenokee
Swamp

Cumberland Island

FLORIDA   Jacksonville

The Lay of the Land

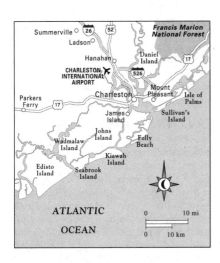

CHARLESTON AND VICINITY

The greater Charleston area is the northern-most region covered by this book. The city itself sits on a peninsula jutting southward, and is hugged by the Cooper River to the east and the Ashley River to west. These rivers spill out into the Charleston Harbor, then into the Atlantic Ocean. Along Charleston's nearby coastal shore, scores of barrier islands—some populated, some still wild—mix with marshes and tidal plain rivers for miles upon winding miles. This span of land and water is mostly linked by bridges and begins what's known as the Lowcountry of South Carolina, which spreads from here southward to the Georgia border. The main barrier islands that congregate near Charleston include Isle of Palms, Sullivan's Island, and Folly Beach—and it's on these beaches where locals get their sand fix. It's that pairing, of Charleston (a Colonial and antebellum town infused with great shopping, dining, and historical sights and plantations), plus the outlying towns and beach islands (with their outdoor and small-town appeal), that makes this area a top draw for vacationers who want to sample the rural and urbane South in one bite.

BEAUFORT AND THE LOWCOUNTRY

This region begins barely north of Beaufort (about an hour and a half south of Charleston), and continues southward to the Georgia border, encompassing Hilton Head (about 45 minutes south of Beaufort) along the way. Still considered the Lowcountry—it's got the requisite mix of low-lying waterfront towns, marshes, barrier islands, and rivers—this area offers something of a schizophrenic experience. Those who head only to Beaufort will get a small-town water-font vacation, complete with vintage Main Street–style shopping, and a historic preserved area with quaint cottages, antebellum manses, and Colonial vestiges. With the nearby ACE Basin (a marsh and wooded wilderness rife

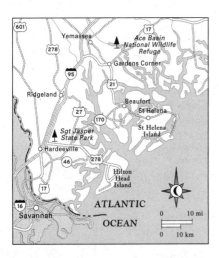

with black-water and tidal rivers prime for paddling), the Beaufort portion of this region gives visitors a quiet, slow-paced retreat, where things moves about as fast as a Southern drawl. Visit Hilton Head, with its golf courses, resorts, tennis camps, outlet shopping, and you've got an escape of a different sort. The bonus is that because of these two towns' proximity (and because Savannah's just 35 miles from Hilton Head), you can sculpt a vacation here that truly has it all.

SAVANNAH AND VICINITY

Since land formations tend to disregard state borders, the stew of islands, marshes, fishing villages, and port cities continues past the South Carolina border along down the Georgia coastline. Savannah, perched inland on the Savannah River, comes first after Hilton Head, and mostly counts on barrier island Tybee for its beaches. While Charleston wears more of a smiley, pastel countenance and has the feel of a city that added on streets as the town overflowed, Savannah is a little more reigned in, with her vast Southern charms and sublime urban development. The city was laid out on a practical grid with refined details, such as the huge Forsyth Park, scores of lushly landscaped squares, and wide sidewalks linking it all together. The squares are surrounded by townhomes, museums, galleries, cafés, restaurants, and shops, which creates a vivacious mix of commercial and residential action, and thus makes the historic area a truly walkable, lively place at (nearly) all hours. When you consider the array of architecture—a wonderful mix of Victorian, deco, and antebellum buildings—it's stunning. And toss in the hipster-cool vibe that the Savannah College of Art and Design students lend to the place, plus the city's proximity to the laid-back beach town of Tybee, Savannah, like Charleston, is another national must-see.

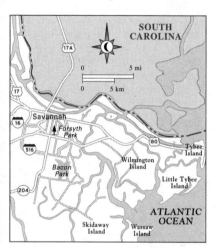

BRUNSWICK AND THE GOLDEN ISLES

This region comprises the most rural and small-town-riddled portion of the coast, plus it offers the most untamed outdoor experiences. It appeals to escape artists and wanderers who want to get away from the hustle of destination cities and resort-laden islands. Explore this area, and you opt instead for small Southern towns linked by winding roads, and beach-rimmed islands that, while they are long-since discovered and getting developed, still retain the local flavors, accents, shops, and pace that first drew people to them. Brunswick is a shrimping city begun in 1771 that's perched on the mainland, and is about 80 miles south of Savannah. Along its coast, you'll find the so-called "Golden Isles"—St. Simons, Jekyll, Sea Island, and Little St. Simons—where you can find quiet or rowdy beaches, fine dining or barbecue, chain hotels or tiny locally owned inns, plus historic sites that stretch back to Colonial settlements and wars. Continue south to St. Marys (about an hour and a half away), and you can either hop the ferry to camp on the wild-horse-laden Cumberland Island National Seashore, or head to nearby Folkston, where the Okefenokee awaits folks who want to paddle alongside gators in the vast swamp. Those looking to get a "Florida: Been there, done that" patch can stick their big toe into one of the more charming and historic Sunshine state experiences: Amelia Island and its Fernandina Beach is a mere 35 miles south of St. Marys. While this region may not have the flash and urbanity of its northern counterparts, it surely has the soul of the South and then some.

Planning Your Trip

This book covers the Sea Islands coastline from Charleston, South Carolina, south to Fernandina Beach, at the northernmost tip of Florida. Given that this distance—not including side trips—takes about seven hours to span via the old Atlantic Coastal Highway (almost half that if you take the interstate), most people vacationing here on limited time tend to pick one sister city (that's Charleston or Savannah), park it downtown for a few days, and then hit the closest beach for a few more days, or vice versa.

Of course, there are also those who want to bypass urbanity, to hug trees, splash in the waves, and muck about the swamps as much as possible, and that's another viable vacation option in these parts. And there are still others with the time (a week, perhaps) and stamina to cover *both* Charleston and Savannah, *and* the loads of tidbit towns and activities in between.

The great thing about this corner of the world is that it's all up for grabs: You've only got to concoct your dream setup, which is where this chapter's itineraries come into play. Check out the suggested ones on the following pages to see what works for your interests, budget, schedule, and speed. Meanwhile, here are some tips that might help inform your decision.

WHEN TO GO

Locals will tell you that the best times to see the area are in autumn or spring. (In fact, some inns consider midsummer and winter to be off-season.) And there's sense to this. In autumn, the crops are in—meaning roadside stands are packed with fresh fruits and vegetables—and the temperature and humidity are down. In fact, in Georgia and South Carolina, most state and county fairs are held in the fall (rather than in midsummer), to capitalize on the more merciful weather. And while fall is also hurricane season, the season's beautiful cool days are still too tempting to miss.

In the spring, the dogwood and azalea blossoms are out and the weather is a blessed mix: not too cold, not too hot, but just right.

But even in this age of air-conditioning, local summers are just too hot and humid for many people. Temperatures rise to over 100°F, with humidity above 50 percent (and usually much higher). And while 100°F temperature with 100 percent humidity is about right for a hot shower, it stinks for a vacation.

Still, though, summer on the Sea Island Coast has its own likable nuances. The ocean waters are warm and swimmable. The kids are out of school and fill the playgrounds. And there is something to be said for being able to say you've experienced the South's legendary humidity at its high-water mark.

It's also true that a midsummer lightning storm over the marshes and harbors are experiences not to be missed. And, too, those looking to understand the heart of Southern culture have only to live through a hot week in August to understand where the region's slow speech and languid pace comes from. When it's that hot and that humid—when just getting out of bed coats your back with sweat—sitting out on the shady porch with a pitcher of sweet tea sounds like the only reasonable thing to do. So if you're planning a lot of sightseeing, think twice before visiting between June and September.

Winter along this part of the coast is much milder than in other eastern states, where average January temperatures hover in the mid-40s. Even still, a visit at this time of year has its own appeal: The Atlantic is too cold to swim, but surfers still brave it with wet suits. The lush look is gone, but the high number of evergreen pines, palmettos, and live oaks keeps the place pretty green year-round. And come Christmas, Charleston and Savannah turn on the Dickensian charm big-time, with horse-drawn carriages decked out in garlands, trees and row houses dressed in twinkling lights, and carolers singing in nearly every church. The experience is a genuine treat.

WHAT TO TAKE

Packing for the Sea Island Coast depends entirely on when you're visiting and what you plan to do on your time off. First and foremost, dress for the weather and temperatures typical for the time of your visit. That means lightweight cotton shorts and skirts in the summer; long pants, mid-weight sweaters and jackets in the winter, and gloves for the faint of heart. During spring and fall, opt for transition wear, and know that layers are best as the days evolve from cool mornings to warm days to cool nights again, and layers let you adjust to your comfort level.

As for style? The Gapification of America has happened in this corner of the world, just like so many other regions. But add that to Savannah and Charleston's casual approach to the good life, and it means that dining out in even the finest restaurants rarely means more than a pair of khakis and an oxford or Polo for men, and a low-key getup (skirt and top or slacks and blouse) for women. To stereotype, Charleston is a bit more frilly for women. You'll run into a fair share of Lily Pulitzer fans here, and skirts galore; but the latter's just as much function as fashion as skirts are literally the coolest thing to wear in the heat and humidity. In Savannah, thanks to the local coffeehouse scene and Savannah College of Art and Design (SCAD) students, you'll see more thirtysomethings and younger decked out in all black. Both towns have their fair share of old-school, Old South seersucker, Bucks, and "No white before Labor Day" types, plus couture label snobs, the khaki-uniformed, a rash of flip-flop addicts, and a smattering of Euro-chicsters. Outside the cities? Think generic USA.

When it comes to comfort, opt for it. Bring shoes appropriate to what you plan on doing. In the cities you will walk and walk and walk: Aim for cushioned, nonblistering shoes with soles that make sense on knobby cobblestone streets and magnolia-root-cracked sidewalks. In the wilds, loads of thorns border even the most civilized path, and oyster shells along the marsh banks will slice your feet like a deli meat saw: Water-safe sports sandals and hiking boots make the most sense. On the beach, fire-hot sand and burrs are not your friends: Wear flip-flops. In the water, those who don't like stepping where they can't see what's on the bottom should bring water slippers.

As you are entering a tropical area where flash storms can easily interrupt a day (or take it over), clear forecasts or not, pack an umbrella and a raincoat. If you are planning on being outside any time other than winter, for any length of time, bring insect repellant. While everyone is best off with basic sunscreen all year-round, it's a must here in the summer. And for those who are especially sun sensitive, a hat and sunglasses should take care of you. Last, bring a day bag, something that can carry your water and a snack if you're in town, and any loot you might buy along the way.

Explore Charleston and Savannah

THE SOUTHERN SAMPLER TOUR

Southern comfort food is often offered as a buffet, where meat, seafood, veggies, and desserts all line up side-by-side. Take that same approach to touring the region and opt for the all-you-can-eat vacation platter, where shopping, home and garden tours, outdoor sports, and more are all back-to-back. To explore the entire region from Charleston, South Carolina, to St. Marys, Georgia, let the skinny, old Atlantic Coastal Highway (usually Highway 17) lead you through gorgeous marshlands, live-oak forests, and tiny towns. At times you'll be tempted to hop on I-95, which merges with Highway 17 here and there, but don't (unless time necessitates it). The longer route only takes about seven hours from end to end—without side trips—and is more scenic and uniquely Southern. Begin in Charleston, and then head south.

LEG ONE: CHARLESTON AREA

DAY 1

Spend the day getting the lay of the land. Take a **carriage tour,** and shop the **Old City Market,** where slaves shopped but were never sold. Then hit the **King Street shops.** Start at Lower King where the big-ticket antique shops are, then work your way north. Middle King runs from Market to Calhoun streets, with scores of local and chain shops. Upper King gets more funky with one-of-a-kind boutiques, a comic store, and mod house goods. If shopping's not your bag (or if it's rainy), visit the **Gibbes Museum of Art** for a history of Lowcountry artists, and the **Charleston Museum,** or take the kids to the **Children's Museum of the Lowcountry.** Get breakfast at The Baker's Café, lunch at SNOB, and dinner at FIG.

DAY 2

Stick to downtown again, this time checking out the gardens, homes, and architecture.

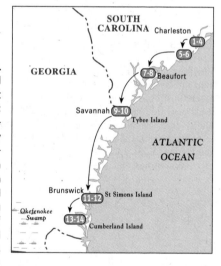

Wander the **South of Broad** neighborhood, and the **French Quarter** around St. Philip's Episcopal Church; following Church Street from St. Philip's to the water affords some of the best gaping. Explore one of the many house museums and walk **The Bat-**

tery, **White Point Gardens,** and **Waterfront Park,** to take in the harbor-front view and gawk at the multimillion-dollar historic homes that dwell within site of **Fort Sumter.** Or take a walking tour based on your own interests: African American history, the Civil War, architecture, ghosts. Try breakfast at Hominy Grill, lunch at Jestine's Kitchen, and a fancy dinner at McCrady's or Charleston Grill.

DAY 3

Head to **Plantation Row** via Highway 17 to West Ashley, then Highway 61. There, visit **Middleton Place** for its amazing landscaping and restaurant specializing in Southern comfort foods. Then visit **Drayton Hall** to see the only still-standing original plantation house in the greater Charleston area. If you have kids, opt for the ever-blooming **Magnolia Plantation and Gardens,** where a tram ride past the swamps and old rice fields introduces them to gators at close range. Getting out to the string of neighboring plantations takes about 45 minutes from downtown in light traffic, so it's generally a day or half-day affair depending on how much you explore and if you take the available tours.

DAY 4

Hit the beach. If you've got a family or want a low-key experience, try **Sullivan's Island** or **Folly Beach County Park** at the west end of Folly. If you're into water sports (surfing, kiteboard, windsurfing), try **Isle of Palms** or Folly's mid to east end. For those staying in places with kitchenettes, pick up fresh shrimp on the way back to town to boil up some local fare. Others should hit the seafood shacks: Bowen's Island for Folly folk; The Wreck for Sully's and Isle of Palmers.

LEG TWO: EDISTO AND THE ACE BASIN

DAYS 5-6

Make the hour drive from Charleston to **Edisto** via Highway 17 then Route 174, and stop at roadside stands for produce, boiled peanuts, and an earful of Gullah and other Lowcountry accents. Rent an Edisto Beach State Park cabin or an oceanfront cottage for two nights in the tiny, quiet waterfront community of Edisto. There are no chain stores or restaurants here, and no hotels, just families and mellow types doing their own mellow thing. Spend your time kayaking the nearby **ACE Basin** solo or with guided tours, collecting shells at the state park beach, or touring the old country churches. Pack a beach book (like the Savannah-based *Midnight in the Garden of Good and Evil* or one of Pat Conroy's Lowcountry-placed tomes) and board games for kicks at night. Buy shrimp off the docks and boil it yourself. If you'd rather eat out, try breakfast at Ruby's Seahorse, lunch at Po' Pigs Bo-B-Q, and dinner at the Old Post Office Restaurant.

LEG THREE: BEAUFORT AND ST. HELENA ISLAND

DAY 7

Rejuvenated post-Edisto, get back out on Highway 17 and drive about 1.5 hours south to the waterfront fishing town of **Beaufort** (on Highway 21). Stay in one of the many B&Bs, like the über-fancy antebellum Beaufort Inn, where your breakfast is an award-winning one, or at the Rhett House Inn, where the columns will blow you away. Spend the day shopping the local mix of galleries, bookstores, and gift shops on **Bay Street,** and stroll the historic district's neighborhoods. Take a carriage ride, if time permits or your feet get worn out, then wrap up the day with a white-linen dinner at Saltus River Grill.

DAY 8

If you're a military enthusiast, head to **Parris Island** to tour the **marine base** and check out the **Parris Island Museum.** Those into Gullah and African American history should aim for **St. Helena Island** and the **Penn Center Historic District,** where some of the country's first freed slaves went to school, and later where leader Martin Luther King Jr. convened annually with supporters to further the nation's civil-rights agenda. Get a shrimp burger at the Shrimp Shack on Lady's Island on the way in to St. Helena, and dine on nouveau Lowcountry entrées at Bateaux on the way back downtown.

LEG FOUR: SAVANNAH

DAY 9

Take Route 170 from Beaufort toward Highway 17 and **Savannah,** and follow signs into downtown. As in Charleston, your first day in Savannah is best spent learning your way around town. Take an open-air trolley tour of the **historic district,** earmarking any churches, squares, and manors you want to visit later. Other than those along Broughton Street and centered around the City Market, the shops, restaurants, and galleries are spread throughout the historic area, mixed in with coffeehouses, tea rooms, museum homes, and private residences. Wander as much as you can the first day (Bull Street at Johnson Square on down to Forsyth Park is a great route), and pick up the missed scraps of interest the next day.

You can't go wrong meandering in this city – it was laid out for just that reason more than 200 years ago. Get lunch at the Soho South Café, and dinner at Sapphire Grill or The Olde Pink House.

DAY 10

Start with breakfast at the original Clary's Café. Then visit the **Telfair Museum of Art,** which comprises three buildings: the 1819 gallery-laden **Telfair Academy of Arts and Sciences;** the 1819 **Owens-Thomas House,** a well-heeled landmark residence; and the 2006 **Jepson Center for the Arts,** a modern art museum with galleries and hands-on exhibits. Make a point of having tea or coffee in a locally owned café, like the Gryphon Tea Room or The Gallery Espresso, then get lunch at the community-dining favorite: Mrs. Wilkes' Boarding House. If art doesn't appeal, visit the domineering **Fort Pulaski** or **Old Fort Morris** (both just out of town on the way to Tybee); each saw service in the Civil War and earlier. Those left with a spare afternoon would do well with a ride east of downtown to **Bonaventure Cemetery** to walk among the tombstones with the ghosts. Come sundown, get the heck out of there and dine at 45 Bistro, or go lowbrow for 'cue at Johnny Harris Restaurant.

LEG FIVE: THE GOLDEN ISLES

DAY 11

Hit the road again, following, you guessed it, Highway 17 to **Brunswick and The Golden Isles.** Pick your temporary home-base island of choice based on what you crave: **St. Simons** has its pier, lighthouse, and surrounding village area with local shops and restaurants. It's perfect for those looking for family-friendly or low-key offerings. **Jekyll Island** has the ocean lapping at its 10 miles of beach, the 1886 Jekyll Island Club Hotel complex, and homes that once belonged to the Rockefellers and their ilk back in the early 1900s. **Sea Island** has The Cloister at Sea Island, an iconic Southern hotel with its spa, golf course, horseback riding, and skeet shooting. No matter where you land, spend your first day settling in and exploring the island.

DAY 12

Hit the beaches in the morning or play a round of golf at one of the top courses in the country, the Sea Island Golf Club on St. Simons. On a rainy day shop, and head to nearby Brunswick on the mainland to wander its antique shops and revitalized downtown, focusing on the area around Newcastle and Gloucester streets. Have dinner at Cargo Portside Grill in Brunswick.

LEG SIX: CUMBERLAND ISLAND NATIONAL SEASHORE AND THE OKEFENOKEE SWAMP

DAYS 13-14

If you're happy where you are and prefer your outdoor experiences tame, stay put. If, however, you want to hike an undeveloped barrier island accessible by ferry only, or explore the country's largest swamp refuges (accessible by canoe or johnboat only), get back in the car.

Head south down Highway 17 toward St. Marys, and just before getting on I-95 (it's tolerable here because it's got great views), stop off at The Georgia Pig for barbecue. Those up for the barrier island (have your hiking and camping gear ready), take Route 40 East off I-95 to St. Marys and hop the ferry to **Cumberland Island National Seashore.** Spend a night or two out there under the stars, playing Survivor and tracking the wild horses. Paddleheads take Route 40 West and head to Folkston, and Route 2 to **The Suwannee Canal Recreation Area Visitor Center.** Get a guide there who will outfit you properly and lead you on an overnight tour deep into **Okefenokee Swamp,** where bellowing gators have eyes that glow red in the beam of a flashlight, and campers sleep on wooden platforms. Whether you go island or swamp, pack heavy-duty sunscreen and hard-core insect repellant, and explore this wild corner of the Sea Island coastline.

THE COLONIAL, REVOLUTIONARY, AND CIVIL WAR HISTORY TOUR

While it's true that America was first settled by Europeans wishing to celebrate religious freedoms and opportunities afforded in the New World, let's not forget what "opportunities" really meant: the potential to earn big bucks. Back in the day, in these parts big bucks came two ways, via plantations—some of the most profitable of which were in this Sea Island area—and via shipping. Considering that Charleston and Savannah were founded in 1670 and 1733 respectively, and had long represented the two major ports along the East Coast, this stretch of early settled waterfront was one of the most contested parts of the country during both the Revolutionary and Civil wars, and during Colonial times as well. Throughout the region, flags still fly over the old forts, and yes, reenactors still rage mock battles from both wars. To peek at the past with soldiering, Colonial, and antebellum living in mind, try this tour.

DAY 1

Start at the beginning with a trip off the peninsula to the **Charles Towne Landing State Historic Site,** where Charleston's first settlement was situated. While scouts decided on the best location for the Colonial city, they set up temporary homes, gardens, and lives here. Since you're in the West Ashley area, head up Route 61 and visit **Middleton Place Plantation.** Those who saw Mel Gibson's *The Patriot* might recognize the elaborate landscaping, but will wonder where the house went – for the answer, ask Grant's guys. Check out the plantation (and Colonial) stable yard, blacksmith shop, and slave cabin before returning to town for the night. (Eat at the Middleton Place restaurant if the timing's right for dinner.)

DAY 2

Spend your second day in town South of Broad Street. Start with **Jack Thompson's Civil War Walking Tour,** by far the most vivid around, especially with the prewar, postwar, and present-day photos he shares of the very route you take. Next, head down to the Battery and wander through the **Edmonston-Alston House;** here, it's said, General P. G. T. Beauregard watched the battle for Fort Sumter from its second story. Residents of this street watched from their rooftops. If you have time, head to the **CSS Hunley** in North Charleston to see the submarine used by Confederates in 1864 to sink a Union ship–the first such maneuver by a sub in naval warfare. If you can't make it to North Chucktown, see the replica downtown outside the **Charleston Museum.** Pop in there to catch even more Colonial and antebellum history and artifacts.

DAY 3

The last day in Charleston means its time to hit the water. Take the boat (there's only one operator) over to **Fort Sumter,** where Confederates first attacked Union troops and ignited the nightmare between the states. When you're back on the mainland, drive out to Sullivan's Island and **Fort Moultrie.** Here, the Colonial army won an early battle of the Revolutionary War, trounced the Yanks, and gave the Revolution a vital jump start. (If you're in town in November, Boone Hall Plantation hosts an annual reenactment battle.)

DAYS 4-5

Savannah's collection of nearby forts were initially intended to ward off foreign threats during pre-Revolutionary War times, but did service during the Civil War as well. Spend the morning driving from Charleston to Savannah via Highway 17, settle in, then head off to explore the moated and monumental **Fort Pulaski,** 14 miles out of town off Highway 80 just before Tybee Island, where the future General Lee first worked as an engineer. Today, the fort has been restored

from its past battles and has drawbridges, barracks, and more. The first half of day two is best spent three miles out of town at the exhibit-laden **Old Fort Jackson,** the oldest fort in the state, which weathered the War of 1812 and saw Confederate duty as well. Afterward, come back into the city to visit Sherman's onetime office quarters back downtown, the **Green-Meldrim House.** As you move on toward St. Simons, take I-95 to the 144 Spur, and visit **Fort McCallister,** the best originally preserved fort of those in the area.

DAY 6

Before it became super quaint, St. Simons was super bloody. In fact, one historical site marks where the Battle of Bloody Marsh (between the Spanish and the English) took place in 1742. Visit that charming chapter of history, then head over to **Fort Frederica National Historic Site.** Here, ruins of the original 1736 settlement and a short film and artifacts tell the story of the colony, and how they made the most out of living in the boonies with pesky troubles from mosquitoes, the Spanish, and more.

THE HISTORIC PRESERVATION AND CITY PLANNING TOUR

Between the two, Charleston and Savannah have weathered earthquakes and hurricanes (minor and major), massive fires, wars, military occupation, the Depression, and another stretch of lean times during the mid-to-late 20th century. Given the trials, it's truly stunning that either town has any postcard-worthy points of interest left. But, thanks in part to those rough times—the local catchphrase "preserved through poverty" partly explains why so many old buildings remain, rather than having been torn down and replaced—and thanks to the country's first historic preservation groups and first protected historic districts, the sister cities are international examples of how to meld the past and present. In fact, Prince Charles toured Savannah and its riverfront district to see rehab done right. To sample the Sea Island Coast from a preservation perspective, try this trip.

DAY 1

Stay in a historic B&B downtown (like the John Rutledge House Inn or the Governor's House Inn), or at the Embassy Suites on Meeting Street, which is in the old, fortresslike Citadel building on Marion Square. Stop by the Charleston Visitors Center building – it was once a railroad depot and was successfully re-purposed into its latest incarnation. Wander south down Anson Street, over to Church Street,

then down to Whitepoint Gardens and East Battery, and circle back to Tradd Street to sample the best mix of Colonial, antebellum, and Victorian architecture. Then head over to Meeting and Broad streets, where you'll find the beautifully restored Old Main Post Office, City Hall, and Charleston County Courthouse, as well as the 1761 St. Michael's Episcopal Church, the oldest standing church building in town. Swing by the 1703 Old Power Magazine on Cumberland Street, the oldest remaining public building in Charleston. Take tours of the Aiken-Rhett House and Nathaniel Russell House in town. Eat dinner at Basil, Coast, or Rue de Jean to see how the Upper King design district is wearing the town's latest urban renewal.

DAY 2

Take one day to head 45 minutes out of town (Highway 17 to Route 61/Ashley River Road) to the 1740s Drayton Hall Plantation. A Historical Landmark, it's the oldest preserved Georgian-style structure of its kind in the country. Aim to wrap up your tour there close to dinnertime, and make reservations at Middleton Place Plantation, just up the road.

SOUTH CAROLINA — Charleston 1-3

GEORGIA

4 Beaufort

5 Hilton Head

6-7 Savannah

ATLANTIC OCEAN

Brunswick 8

DAY 3

Drive to the Hampton Park neighborhood just north of the Historic District at Ashley Avenue and Moutrie Street, and see the 1922 **Citadel Military College,** set in an early-1900s suburb. Last, head over the new Arthur Ravenel Jr. Bridge (Highway 17) and check out **Old Village** in Mount Pleasant, where Charlestonians used to summer. Get dinner at the aptly named The Wreck, a seafood shack on the docks on the outskirts of the neighborhood, or at The Old Village Post House. (If you're in town in the spring or fall, look what house tours and lectures the preservation groups are offering.)

DAY 4

Take Highway 17 to Highway 21 to **Beaufort** to see how the heart of this once-tiny waterfront village has held onto its buildings and slow-paced charm since its inception in 1710. The walkable **historic district** is a neighborhood mix of historic bungalows and columned manses, all centered around **Bay Street,** which fronts the harbor. "Downtown" is a still-vibrant collection of shops, restaurants, bars, and galleries that draws locals, in spite of the encroaching developments that edge along the roads into the historic area. Spend the night in one of the more historic antebellum inns (like the Rhett House Inn or Beaufort Inn), and visit the **Beaufort Museum** and the 1790s **John Mark Verdier House Museum.** Have dinner out at Bateaux, set on a former plantation on Lady's Island. (If you're in town during the spring or fall get tickets to the local home tours.)

DAY 5

If you're interested in development and planning, swing by the resort-laden **Hilton Head** on your way to Savannah (Route 170 from Beaufort is the most scenic, but I-95/Highway 17 will do; either way take Highway 278 onto the island). To see Hilton Head's "before" side, take Route 46 to **Old Bluffton** (off Highway 278). Once an 1825 fishing town north of the area's wilds and plantations, its historic bungalows and general store have transformed into an artist community, with galleries, antiques shops, and studios filling the old buildings. Get lunch at Pepper's Porch, and then continue down Highway 278 to the **Sea Pines Resort,** wending your way around to the Harbourtown marina. This was the first resort on the island, built back in the 1960s by Charles Fraser, who paved the way for the style of resort community that now claims most of the Sea Island Coast barrier islands: playgrounds that attempt to integrate themselves into the environment rather than claim it totally. Leave Hilton Head and continue to Savannah for the night.

DAY 6

In **Savannah,** stay at another historic inn, like the 1873 Hamilton-Turner Inn. Eat dinner at the 1700s Olde Pink House while you're in town, and be sure to pop in to the Gryphon Tea Room to see how a turn-of-the-20th-century pharmacy was re-purposed into a café with many of the original trappings in place. Savannah, unlike Charleston, was fully planned out from its inception to be a grid of residential and commercial streets interrupted by public park squares. Wander the stretch from Johnson Square down Bull Street to Forsyth Park to best soak up the benefits of this smart city planning. Catch a show at the restored 1921 **Lucas Theatre for the Arts,** and tour the tabby, 1819 **Owens-Thomas House,** touted by historians as the greatest example of a Regency-style home in the country. And be sure to check out the 1820 **Isaiah Davenport House,** too. Last in town, visit the stunning 1839 **Cathedral of St. John the Baptist,** and the 1878 **Temple Mickve Israel,** the only Gothic synagogue in the country.

DAY 7

Get a box of pralines on **River Street,** and see how the once-dead riverfront now thrives. Then head out of town to the nearby **Isle of Hope** and turn onto Skidaway Road for the tabby ruins and living history area at the Colonial-era **Wormsloe Plantation.** If you have the time, head the **Starland District** at Desoto Avenue, Bull and 37th streets, the next up-and-coming part of town that's getting its own hipster makeover. Here you'll find a smattering of shops, an arts center, a coffeehouse, and lofts. (If you are in town in March, get tickets to the annual homes and gardens tours. Otherwise, take an architecture-themed walking tour.)

DAY 8

Brunswick (about an hour and a half south of Savannah off I-95), and its **Old Town** area are undergoing a wonderful revitalization. Visit the port town's "Main Street" at Newcastle and Gloucester streets to see how new shops and restaurants are replacing empty or rarely frequented storefronts; pop in the restored **Old City Hall,** too. The entire area, with its parks, neighborhoods, and shopping area, was originally laid out in 1771 based on Savannah's plan.

THE GULLAH AND AFRICAN AMERICAN HISTORY TOUR

Sullivan's Island (just outside Charleston) was called the Ellis Island for slaves brought to America before the Civil War, as it was where stolen Africans were quarantined before they were auctioned off in the downtown marts and shipped throughout the Confederate states. Being such a major hub for so many African tribes, and being the country's center for the slave trade left an indelible cultural mark on Charleston and the greater Sea Island Coast, once rich in plantations large and small. To communicate with one another, the slaves created a new language, Gullah, which was an amalgam of various African tribal dialects. The term "Gullah" went on to represent the greater African American culture, and today you can still hear the rich, rollicking accents, and trace nuances of Lowcountry cuisine to its sometime-African roots.

DAY 1

Spend half your time in Charleston in town, and half of it off the peninsula. Downtown, take a **bus tour** (either Gullah Tours or the Sites & Insights tour) to cover the city's less-often-touted past. Drivers, many of whom speak Gullah, give the best overview of African American Charleston, and show you hidden African American graveyards, reputed slave rebellion leader Denmark Vesey's house (now a private residence), and the **Old Slave Mart** on Chalmers Street, among many other sites. After the tours, visit **Gallery Chuma** for prints by Gullah artist Jonathan Green. Later, get another history lesson at the College of Charleston's **Avery Research Center for African American History and Culture,** where freed people of color earned teaching certificates after the Civil War. Watch their history movie and take a tour of the old schoolroom. For dinner, eat at Hominy

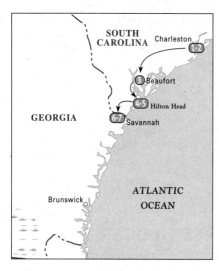

Grill or Jestine's Kitchen for a taste for Gullah-inspired cooking.

DAY 2

Follow Highway 17 over the bridge into **Mount Pleasant** to visit **Boone Hall Plantation.** Here you'll find the region's best examples of original slave quarters. Next, head back toward town and stop at one of the outdoor **sweetgrass basket stands.** The craft, its weaving methods, and designs have been traced back to plantation days, and to Africa before that. Try the red rice, okra, and gumbo at Gullah Cuisine on your way back to town. (Also, if you come in late September or early October, take in the MOJA Arts Festival, the city's only African American festival.)

DAY 3

Take Highway 17, then Highway 21 to **Beaufort,** and on into **Helena Island,** home of the **Penn Center Historic District.** Initially one of the first schools for freed blacks after the Civil War, it was also where Dr. Martin Luther King Jr. met annually with the Southern Christian Leadership Conference. Visit the **York W. Bailey Museum** there, and stop by the **Red Piano Too Art Gallery,** where local folk artists sell their work; check out the one-room Gullah museum inside – it's worth a peek. Tour lovers get the best overview of the area with Gullah-n-Geechie Mahn Tours or by visiting the Gullah Festival, held every May. Wrap up the history lessons with dinner at Bateaux, set on the grounds of a former island plantation.

DAY 4

Take Route 170 from Beaufort toward **Hilton Head,** then Highway 278 onto the island proper. Before it became resort- and retiree-central, Hilton Head was a mix of one-time plantations and heirs' property – land that had been given to freed slaves as retribution, then parceled out among subsequent generations. Since the first resort didn't appear until the 1960s, the Gullah culture here is still rich, though many of the sights themselves are in ruin or signified by marker only. Given that, the best way to soak up the story is with a tour from **Gullah Heritage Trail Tours.** Let them lead you to old churches, graveyards, and where the country's first freedman village, the 1862 **Mitchelville,** once stood. While on Hilton Head, stop by De Gullah Creations to shop for handmade quilts, sweetgrass baskets, and other collectibles, and at The Gullah Bookstore.

DAY 5

Take one of several tours to **Daufuskie Island,** the site of Pat Conroy's novel, *The Water Is Wide.* On the island (accessible only by ferry), you'll see the **Old Daufuskie Schoolhouse,** the 1855 **First Union African Baptist Church,** and more, and get a feel for how isolated the barrier island was for its tiny, Gullah-populated community well into the 1970s. (If you come in June, check out Daufuskie Day there, or in February, head to Hilton Head's Native Islander Gullah Celebration.)

DAYS 6-7

Take Route 170 toward **Savannah** and follow signs into downtown. Once there, make the **King-Tisdell Cottage Museum of Black History** your first stop. There, you'll get an overview of African Americans' role in U.S. history, and can partake of the city's best "school" for the subject at hand: **The Negro Heritage Trail Tour.** If you don't opt for the guided tour, which covers Colonial to modern times and includes a stop at **The Beach Institute,** be sure to visit the latter on your own – it's where the city's freed slaves were educated after the Civil War. These days, it's a gallery of African American arts and crafts. To explore a major stop on the Underground Railroad, visit the **First African Baptist Church** near the City Market. Last, wind down your immersion in Gullah and Sea Island African American history with the exhibits at the **Ralph Mark Gilbert Civil Rights Museum.**

THE WATER-RAT AND TREE-HUGGER TOUR

Fly into either the Savannah or Charleston airport and it's stunning how green this region appears from the air. While locals rightly lament the development that's taken over much of the coastline and barrier islands, it is still entirely possible to lose yourself in the solitude of the marshes, refuges, rivers, and protected lands here. For those who go on vacation to get lost, the Sea Island Coast offers loads of unique exploration experiences, and even better, if it rains or gets too dang hot, there are plenty of cool small towns (and two big ones) in which to salvage your precious time off the clock.

DAY 1

Stay in the **James Island County Park** cabins, or camp out at the **Palmetto Islands County Park** in **Mount Pleasant** to get your green fix and nighttime peace and quiet. Then set up your first day trip of the week with the folks from Coastal Expeditions. Either rent their kayaks and get maps and route advice from them, or, even better, take their daylong guided tour through the back rivers of the area, which wind past old plantation grounds and the remains of antebellum docks and rice trunks.

DAY 2

The next day, drive north of town via Highway 17 to the **Seewee Visitors Center,** where you catch the ferry that takes you into **Cape Romain National Wildlife Refuge.** The ferry takes you to wild **Bull Island;** stick with the guide and you'll get a naturalist tour, or explore on your own for the half day.

DAYS 3-4

For your last two days in town, pull on your bathing suit (or wet suit) and gear up for your choice of wave riding – surfing, windsurfing, bodysurfing, kiteboarding, or boogie boarding – and hit the water at **Sullivan's Island, Isle of Palms,** or **Folly Beach.** Local outfitters offer rentals, lessons, and tips on the prime spots of the day.

DAYS 5-6

If the Charleston area was a little too populated for your taste, you'll be happier with the head count south of town. Take Highway 17, then Route 174 to **Edisto,** where there's nary a hotel, motel, chain shop, or restaurant, just cottages, seafood shacks, and plenty of marsh-front camping. Book one of the cabins (or camp) at the **Edisto Beach State Park,** and spend your days beach-combing there, or rent kayaks and hit the **ACE Basin,** where the Ashepoo, Combahee, and Edisto rivers form a huge, waterlogged wilderness.

DAYS 7-8

To get really, really rural, drive up Route 64 (off Highway 17 at Jacksonboro) to Highway 15 to find **Canadys.** Let the folks at Carolina Heritage Outfitters gear you out with canoes, and send you down the **Edisto River** to one of their two waterfront tree-house bed-and-breakfasts. Paddle to your home for the night, light up the tiki torches on the porch, grill whatever you brought for supper, and count the fireflies from the rocking chairs.

DAYS 9-10

Your next move depends on how far south you ultimately want to go and how deep your pockets are. The well-heeled outdoor enthusiast should book a night at the remote **Little St. Simons,** where the only thing going on the island is the luxe lodge and its outdoor entertainment. The cash-strapped environmentalist will get just as cool an experience by going groovier at Brunswick's 30-year-old **The Hostel in the Forest,** a combo of bare-bones geodesic domes, tree houses, and a sweat lodge.

  Those who want to make it all the way to Georgia's southernmost state line can forgo this part of the trip, and opt instead for a similar experience at **Cumberland Island National Seashore.** Take Highway 17 South to I-95 South, and exit at Route 40 for St. Marys. Take the ferry over from "downtown" if you are planning to camp out on the nearly barren, no-cars-for-tourists island, where wild horses roam. Noncampers can take the

high-rent route and book nights at the Greyfield Inn, where guests make tame forays into the island's wilderness and 17.5 miles of beaches.

DAYS 11-12

If you've never been to the **Okefenokee Swamp,** go. One of the (if not *the*) largest such refuges of its kind in the country, it's as massive and wild as anything can get along this stretch of the Southeast, and the best way to experience it is to immerse yourself on an overnight trip. It's easy to get wicked lost out here, so opt for a guided overnight trip with an outfitter, who will provide the boats and gear, and reserve the camping platforms you'll call home for as many nights as you can take. With the lily ponds, the fishing, the gators, and the otherwordly vastness of the place, it's definitely not to be missed. At least, that is, if you're the tree-hugging, water-rat type. Take Route 40 toward Folkston, then Route 2 to **The Suwannee Canal Recreation Area Visitor Center.**

CHARLESTON AND VICINITY

Travel writer John Milton Mackie puts his finger on one of Charleston's greatest charms: "It was pleasant to find an American city not wearing the appearance of having all been built yesterday," he writes. "The whole town looks picturesquely dingy, and the greater number of buildings have assumed something of the appearance of European antiquity." Few who have visited here would disagree. What makes Mackie's opinion interesting is that he wrote these words over 140 years ago, in 1864. Even then, Charleston was already closing in on its bicentennial. Founded in 1670, this is about as old an American city as you'll find.

Charleston's nickname, the "Holy City," refers to the number of cathedral peaks that tower over its streets, not to any especial piety in the populace. The city is the gem of the state in many ways, as it's part laid-back waterside town, part blue-collar port city, part urban shopping and dining destination, and part Southern time capsule. And while not just *anything* goes here, it's definitely the most liberal area in South Carolina.

Charleston is a noted player on the international arts scene: The annual Spoleto Festival draws hundreds of thousands of art enthusiasts from around the world. Charleston also overflows with culture of the more organic variety: African, Greek, and Irish-American festivals (among others), Gullah basket-weaver stands, Civil War reenactments, black-tie-only debutante balls for the daughters of SOBs (wealthy Charlestonians living South of Broad Street), and shrimp boils held by fifth-generation shrimpers. And Charleston has the Citadel,

HIGHLIGHTS

◖ The Battery and White Point Gardens: Charleston's mega mansion row is a series of pastel-colored antebellum homes from which residents once watched the first shots of the Civil War (page 40).

◖ Waterfront Park: This stretch of waterfront fountains, benches, swings, and trimmed lawns gives a tremendous view of Charleston Harbor and introduces visitors to a cross section of the city's population. It's what the best in the urban-renewal public-spaces dream-to-be (page 42).

◖ King Street: Charleston's prime shopping street shows another great face of urban renewal and offers shopping for every taste (page 42).

◖ Old City Market: Slaves once frequented this open-air market to buy vegetables and meats for their owners; now vendors sell souvenirs and sweetgrass baskets here (page 45).

◖ St. Michael's Episcopal Church: The oldest church structure in town, Confederate soldiers once used its tower as a lookout (page 48).

◖ Old Exchange and Provost Dungeon: Charleston's port business was conducted in this present-day museum (page 48).

◖ Edmondston-Alston House: This East Bay Street mansion is part of The Battery's promenade of multi-million-dollar homes, and is part museum, part residence. The tours give a fantastic overview of the city history (page 49).

◖ Drayton Hall: A National Historic Landmark, this Georgian home is the best-preserved original plantation house in the Lowcountry (page 50).

◖ Middleton Place: The sprawling grounds of this onetime rice plantation exemplify the grandeur of pre–Civil War life. Visit for the gardens, living history exhibits, and the restaurant (page 52).

◖ Fort Sumter National Monument: Fort Sumter, just off The Battery in Charleston Harbor, was where the Civil War began (page 60).

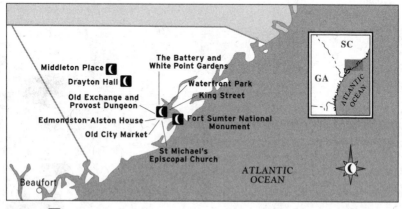

LOOK FOR ◖ TO FIND RECOMMENDED SIGHTS, ACTIVITIES, DINING, AND LODGING.

perhaps the most distinctively Southern—and South Carolinian—place left on the planet.

Charleston's history is as worthy of veneration as that of any American city: The first decisive American victory of the Revolutionary War was won over at Sullivan's Island in 1776; the first shot of the Civil War was fired here. A lot of people through the years have chided Charleston as a city that worships the past, but all of Charleston's careful primping and long-sighted preservation have paid off; in 1997, *Travel and Leisure* magazine named Charleston the 24th-best city in the world and 6th-best in the United States, handily besting such traveler's favorites as Seattle, Portland, Miami, Las Vegas, Austin, Atlanta, Savannah, Washington, D.C., Philadelphia, and Los Angeles. Of other Southern cities, only New Orleans made the top 25. In 2000 the magazine named Charleston on of the world's top 10 cities for value.

Readers of *Southern Living* magazine have named Charleston the "Premier Shopping Area," "Most Romantic Getaway," "Favorite Dream Getaway," "Favorite Weekend Destination," and "Most Historic Travel Destination in the South."

Condé Nast Traveler readers have named it a top 10 domestic destination for years. In 2000, they ranked it number three, following only San Francisco and New Orleans. Chicago and New York City squeaked in front of it in 2001, moving it back to the number five position, but it was still the only small American city to make the top 10, and the only top-ranked city to also rank high in "friendliness factor." The **Charleston Place Hotel, Planters Inn,** and **John Rutledge House Inn** were all cited for distinction, as was the **Woodlands Resort & Inn.**

National Geographic Traveler named Charleston as one of its "Top 50" must-sees in the United States. In 2001, *Family Fun* magazine named Charleston the third-best city in the southeast for family vacations. And it goes on and on; *Bride's* tapped the Charleston area as a top honeymoon destination; *Travel and Leisure* named it as one of "10 Great Places to Spend Christmas," sharing rank with Bali, Munich, London, Padua, and other international destinations.

Perhaps most telling is the compliment given Charlestonians by Marjabelle Young Stewart, nationally renowned etiquette expert. Over the past 20 years, Charleston has never failed to make her list of the United States' most mannerly cities. And in 12 recent years, Charleston has ranked number one. In fact, in 2001, the city tied for first with New York City, still recovering after the September 11 attacks. Although the Big Apple and the Holy City have never been particularly fond of each other, Mayor Joe Riley was so gracious about sharing the award with the traumatized giant that news networks played his remarks worldwide for days. If you're looking for the Old South, you won't find a better urban expression of it than Charleston.

PLANNING YOUR TIME

Charleston makes a simple one-stop shop for those ready to soak up the charms of Southern culture, the tastes of Lowcountry cuisine, the relics Colonial and Civil War history, the unique outdoor offerings afforded by the area's barrier islands and surrounding marshes. While the itineraries at the beginning of this book can give you a feel for themed ways to explore this region (based on history, architecture, outdoors, Gullah influences, and more), most people heading solely for the Holy City prefer to sample a little of all the offerings.

To get the best, most varied experience, start with a walk of the downtown Battery area, where you'll spot the huge pre–Civil War mansions weighed down with ironwork and piazzas. Fort Sumter is off in the harbor, and Folly Beach sits to the west, Mount Pleasant to the immediate eastern shore, and Sullivan's Island poking out from behind it. Take a carriage ride to get the history and your bearings, and return to any museum houses or other significant sights that piqued your interest along the way. Shop King Street, and dine out at one of the many fabulous restaurants on the peninsula. Then spend a day exploring one of the many

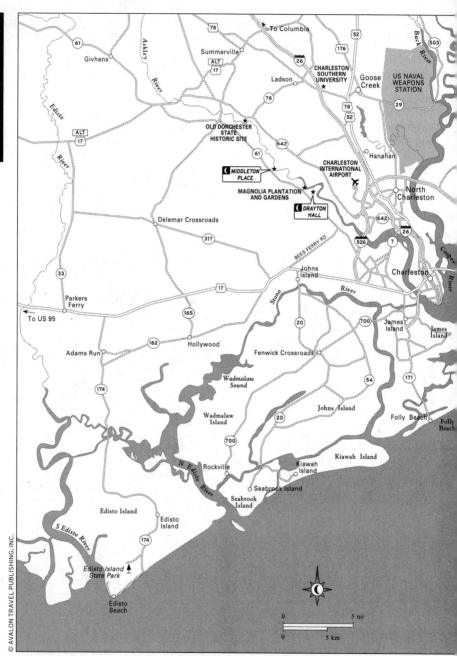

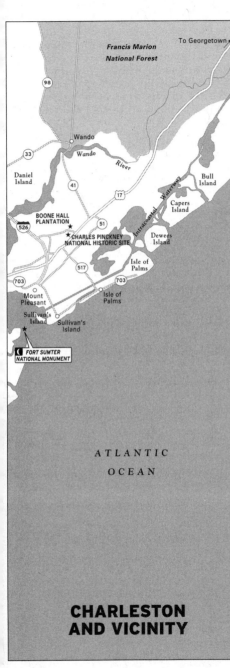

CHARLESTON AND VICINITY

plantations along Route 61 in the West Ashley area. Last, play outside either on the beaches of the nearby islands, on the golf greens of the many neighboring resorts, on the boats that ply the Gulf Stream offshore, or on the kayaks that meander along the countless rivers. With such a roundup (great any time of the year, but at peak in spring and fall), you'll get the most out of your time here.

ORIENTATION

Charleston stands on a peninsula lying between the Ashley and Cooper rivers, a tongue of land pointed at the Old World. Here, Charlestonians like to say, the Ashley and Cooper rivers meet to form the Atlantic Ocean.

At the southernmost point of the peninsula stands White Point Gardens and The Battery, where pirates were left hanging in the coastal breezes to scare off their scurvy brethren, and where guns fired upon British ships during the War of 1812.

Although the peninsula points southeast, Charlestonians have traditionally seen their city as the center of the world and thus have decided that the area above old Charleston is north; northeast of the Cooper, by Mount Pleasant, becomes "East Cooper"; the islands to the other side are "West Ashley"; and southwest of The Battery is "South." And White Point Gardens is due south.

Thus, the region to the northeast of the Cooper River is called simply "East Cooper," which encompasses the major town of Mount Pleasant as well as the buffer Sea Islands of Sullivan's Island and Isle of Palms. The area southwest of the peninsula, on the other side of the Ashley, encompassing James Island, John's Island (where slaves composed the hymn that would become the civil-rights anthem "We Shall Overcome"), and Folly Beach is called simply "West Ashley." The Charleston Neck region and farther northwest are now called "North Charleston."

HISTORY

History is as palpable in Charleston as the scent of the wood-pulp factories, which old-timers

© SEAN SLINSKY

Look for earthquake bolts on the sides of homes along The Battery.

base in St. Augustine was not all that far away. Neither did it help that the colonists kept running across the overgrown remains of Spanish forts on Santa Elena Island; they knew well that the Spaniards had massacred French Huguenot settlers in the past, and this low-lying site, surrounded on three sides by woods, was hard to defend. All this made the British wary. To top it off, the local Edisto Indians weren't really showing them much Southern hospitality (it hadn't been invented yet).

Fortunately, soon after they had landed, the leader of the Kiawah Indians, based north in the present-day Charleston region, sent word that the English would be welcome in the Kiawah land farther north: They could help the Kiawah fight against the hated Spanish and the Westo Indians, the latter of whom the Kiawah described as "a ranging sort of people reputed to be man-eaters." Joined by some Edisto Indians and led by the *cassique* (chief), the settlers sailed for the region now called West Ashley, just south of Charleston peninsula. There, in early April, on the shores of the Ashley River at Albemarle Point—site of present-day Charles Towne Landing—they founded Charles Town, named after their king.

As rice and later indigo became important local crops, and as Barbadians and Europeans, drawn by the reports drifting back from Carolina of cheap land and high profits, sailed into Charles Town Harbor, the city grew and prospered. By 1700, Charles Town had become inarguably the crown jewel of England's North American colonies.

The bulk of Europeans who immigrated to South Carolina in the early Colonial period came as indentured servants or slaves to work for those already living in the colony. With so much land, and a rice economy that required a great amount of labor, indentured servants and slaves soon poured by the boatload into Charleston to be bought by planters who were building plantations among the coastal Sea Islands and up the rivers.

By 1680 the settlers had decided that the Albemarle Point spot was too unhealthful and hard to defend; some settlers began moving

still call "bread and butter." In 1855, back before most other American cities had even *begun* their histories, Charleston's elites decided to form the South Carolina Historical Society, which today maintains a collection of books, letters, plantation histories, and genealogical records. Several local TV and radio stations even start off their newscasts with, "And now, from America's *most historic city*. …"

Colonial Powerhouse

South Carolina's first permanent European settlement, Charleston was founded at its current peninsular site only after the original colonists changed their minds twice. Their first choice was Port Royal, site of the former failed French and Spanish colonies and thus the best-documented site for 17th-century European travelers. But when the English colonists under Governor William Sayle arrived at Port Royal on March 15, 1670, they were greeted by Spanish-speaking Indians—a disheartening reminder that the Spanish still considered Carolina their land, and that the Spaniards' over to Oyster Point, site of the present-day Charleston Battery. The white-shell-covered point at the end of a narrow-necked peninsula was much easier to defend—there was no question about which direction a ground attack might come from—and planters both north and south of the port city could easily transport their goods from plantation to town using the natural currents of tidal creeks. In May 1680 the lords proprietors formally instructed the governor and his council to resettle Charles Town at Oyster Point.

Meanwhile, the English-African-Indian mix was becoming even more diverse. French Huguenot Protestants began arriving in Charleston by the boatloads in 1680. French King Louis the XIV's 1685 repeal of religious freedoms for non-Catholics accelerated this process. European Jews, enticed by the colony's tolerant policies on religious freedom, poured in as well; by the end of the 18th century, Charleston had the second-largest Jewish population in the country.

In 1686, although the Spanish had resigned themselves to the idea of an English settlement at Charles Town, they forbade further encroachment to the south. Nonetheless, the increased population of Charles Town required planters to move out away from the city to find enough land for their plantations.

By 1690, the gradual movement of Charles Town to Oyster Point was officially completed. By now the city's population was estimated at around 1,200 people, making Charles Town the fifth-biggest city in all North America. By 1695, Charles Town citizens (or rather, their slaves) had built thick stone walls and six bastions, making the city into an armed fortress.

In 1700, the city established a tax-supported free library, possibly the first in America. On September 2, 1706, joint French and Spanish units attacked Charles Town during Queen Anne's War, but the Carolinian forces captured a French vessel and sent the papists packing. The Powder Magazine at 79 Cumberland Street and the Pink House Tavern at 17 Chalmers were built in 1710, and the Rhett Mansion went up at 54 Hasell Street in 1712. The city

served as a refuge for survivors of the initial Yamassee attacks in Beaufort and the Lowcountry plantations, and in the years leading up to the American Revolution, Charleston served as the Southern center of patriot sentiment.

Although it held off the British Navy at the Battle of Sullivan's Island in 1776, the city was captured by the British in 1780 and remained in British hands until they withdrew at war's end. Charleston was the state's capital until 1788 and served as one of the nation's most important ports, exporting Southern cotton and rice in the early part of the 19th century until protective tariffs ended the trade. In 1830, to compete with Savannah, which received produce from eastern Carolinian farmers who floated their goods down the Savannah River, a group of Charlestonians built America's first commercial railroad, stretching from Charleston to the newborn Savannah River town of Hamburg (near modern-day North Augusta). When the "Best Friend of Charleston" began taking this run, it was the longest railroad in the world.

The War Between the States

In 1860, after being chased out of Columbia by an epidemic, South Carolina leaders passed their Ordinance of Secession here, a major step toward the beginning of the Civil War. The first armed conflict of the war began here the following April, with the Confederates firing upon the Union garrison holed up inside Fort Sumter.

During the War Between the States, Charleston saw little action after Fort Sumter, although Union boats quickly sealed off the port to all but the most stealth blockade-runners. Union forces, including the famed African American 54th Massachusetts, attempted to take Fort Wagner to the south of the city, but Confederate forces successfully defended it. The world's first "successful" military submarine—the CSS *Hunley*—sailed out from Breach Inlet between Sullivan's Island and Long Island (Isle of Palms) and sank the USS *Housatonic* before sinking itself, with all hands. The war in Charleston ended as Confederate troops fled and the black 55th Massachusetts

CHARLES TOWN'S OWN PIRATES

A final note to Charles Town's pirate era came in late October 1820, when a British Navy sloop swept up beside a boatload of drunken pirates captained by Calico Jack Rackham. The captain and most of his crew, who were too inebriated to fight, promptly fled to the hold of their ship and tried to hide. But two pirates stayed on deck to fight. They fired their pistols and flailed away with cutlasses and axes. In desperation, one of them started shooting at the drunks in the hold, trying to stir up some ambition. When that failed, the British sailors took the vessel. To their shock, they found that the wildcats with the cutlasses were two women: Mary Read, of England, and Anne Bonny, of Charles Town.

Born in Ireland of an extramarital affair between her lawyer father, William Cormac, and the family maid, Anne came to America with her scandal-dodging parents. Cormac made a fortune as a merchant in Charles Town, and Anne soon had her suitors, although her reputation for physical violence deterred not a few. Eventually, her eye fell to James Bonny, who by all accounts had even less character than he had money. The two married and left for rough-and-tumble New Providence in the Bahamas. Having married Mr. Wrong, Anne now abandoned him for Mr. More Wrong, in the form of Calico Jack Rackham, a noted pirate who'd taken the royal pardon and was trying, half-heartedly, to live within the law. Unfortunately, adultery and spousal abandonment went outside of these laws. Rather than risk flogging, Anne and Jack took to the seas to raid and pillage their troubles away.

But despite the memories the couple shared over the next months – the sailors speared, the evocative sprong and splash after a victim had walked the plank, Anne's heart – or, well, something – could not stay true. She became enamored with a fresh-faced Dutch sailor who had been captured and pressed into service. When she finally made her move, she discovered that the cute little Dutch boy was not only not Dutch, but was also not a boy.

Mary Read, it seemed, had been born out of wedlock as well and had been raised in boys' clothes after the death of her brother. She'd worked as a cabin boy and went on to fight as a foot soldier, and later as a dragoon, at the Battle of Flanders during the War of the Spanish Succession. There she fell in love with her tent mate, and the two married and settled down. She dressed as a woman for the first time and was beginning to sort through some deep-seated identity issues when her beloved husband up and died. Not sure how to proceed in a skirt but very comfortable in pantaloons, Read signed on as a sailor and headed out to sea on a Dutch vessel. And that's where she had been working when Rackham took her ship. Anne and Mary became such fast friends that Calico Jack challenged Mary to a fight – only then did Anne reveal her friend's gender to him.

Although the historical record is silent on the issue, it's likely that Calico Jack and Anne next did what any couple would do – they set to fixing Mary up. One imagines them cruising the high seas, keeping an eagle eye out for eligible sailors. Finally, they captured a ship and impressed some of the crew, and Mary fell head over boots for one of them. The prisoner, perhaps shrewdly, returned her affections. By the time the British navy captured the ship, both women on Captain Jack's Love Cruise were pregnant.

In a Jamaica courtroom, the women told the judge, "We plead our bellies." The judge delayed the executions until after the children were delivered. As would-be-father Calico Jack shuffled off to the gallows, he paused for a last moment with his wife. "Had you fought like a man," she reminded him, "you need not have been hanged like a dog."

Although Mary's beau, having been forced into service, was released to raise their child, Mary died in prison before she could give birth. Nobody's ever been able to prove that Anne Bonny eventually went to the gallows. Some speculate that her wealthy father in Charles Town arranged her release, on the grounds that his grandchild needed a mother.

marched through the streets, shocking white citizens and bringing emancipation to the city's black slaves.

After the War

The city had been ravaged by long-term bombardment, and it took a long time to recover. The discovery of nearby phosphate deposits brought some life back into the local economy, but the severe "shake" of 1886—an earthquake of an estimated 7.7 on the Richter scale—left 60–92 dead and caused an estimated $23 million damage.

By dredging Charleston Harbor to make room for large transatlantic freighters, the city improved its shipping activity.

Around this time, several savvy Charlestonians began to think that perhaps all the postwar poverty had actually been a blessing in disguise because by impoverishing Gilded Age business interests it had prevented them from initiating new projects, for which the city's historic buildings would have been torn down. In the early 1920s, Charleston devoted itself to expanding its tourism industry, leading to building both the Fort Sumter Hotel—now the Fort Sumter House—and the newly revitalized Francis Marion Hotel. With its harbor, and with the construction of the Charleston Naval Yard (spearheaded by North Charleston–raised Chief of the U.S. Armed Services Committee Mendel Rivers), Charleston became an important military installation during both world wars. Although many places shut their doors with the base closures at the end of the Cold War, by then tourism had become the city's chief industry. Today, tourism complements the city's production of paper and wood pulp, asbestos, clothing, cigars, rubber products, fertilizer, and other items.

One of the best things that's happened to Charleston over the past quarter century has been the reign of Citadel graduate Joseph P. Riley as mayor. First elected in 1975, Riley has focused on stimulating new development and restoration of historic downtown Charleston, starting by planting high-end projects—1986's Charleston Place, for instance—in run-down neighborhoods, and then watching as the adjacent neighborhoods rejuvenated themselves. He spearheaded the annexation of Daniel Island and numerous other areas so that Charleston's physical size—and, thus, the size of its tax base—has exploded from 16.7 square miles in 1975 to nearly 105 square miles by 2005. The River-Dogs' classy riverfront stadium—lovingly named Joseph P. Riley Jr. Stadium (or "The Joe") in the mayor's honor—is one of Riley's more recent accomplishments, along with the forward-looking, pedestrian-friendly development of Daniel Island and the new South Carolina Aquarium, placed amid what had been a fairly ugly and certainly not tourist-friendly part of town.

Avid fans or foes of planned developments will want to see Daniel Island off I-526 North. Long an agricultural island farmed by poor blacks (including famed Charleston blacksmith Philip Simmons), Daniel Island is now being reborn as Riley's dream city, a re-creation of the classic Charleston neighborhoods of yesteryear. Charleston's popular soccer team, the Charleston Battery, now plays here, and the Family Circle Cup women's tennis tournament moved from Hilton Head to a stadium on Daniel Island in 2001. In the late 1990s Charleston's venerable Catholic high school, Bishop England, moved into a beautiful facility on the island, and in 2004, a top-of-the-line preschool opened here. A combination elementary and middle school is in the design phase. The island, at first only a cluster of neighborhoods built around parks, is growing a walkable, brick-front downtown, which should make living on Daniel Island more attractive to the less adventurous. Many residents claim that living on the island is like living in a small town, but with all the amenities of Charleston a short drive away.

Base and Clinton-era shipyard closures put some 19 percent of Charleston's workforce out of jobs. Fortunately, city leaders worked together to find industries to fill the projected shortfall, and within three years, some $1.2 billion in capital investment had created more than 8,000 new jobs. Today, as retiring baby boomers and other sunseekers pour into the region, the biggest threats facing Charleston are leapfrogging home prices—which are driving many natives up north to Awendaw or west to Summerville, replaced by part-time owners from Charlotte, Atlanta, and points north—and cultural homogenization.

At deadline, Mayor Joe Riley and crew were planning on building a Slavery Memorial and Museum in Charleston. This would be fitting because most of the slaves imported into North America entered via Charleston.

Finally, although it will be decided by the time this book reaches the shelves, at press time, Charleston, Mount Pleasant, and North Charleston were all vying to be allowed to permanently display the CSS *Hunley* in their towns.

Sights

To understand Charleston's logistics, think "parallels." Parallel rivers—the Ashley to the west and the Cooper to the east—separate the peninsula from the mainland. The primarily suburban area west of the Ashley is called **West Ashley,** which includes **James Island, Folly Beach, Johns Island, Kiawah Island,** and **Seabrook Island.** East of the Cooper is called **East Cooper,** which includes **Mount Pleasant, Sullivan's Island,** and the **Isle of Palms.** And the area immediately north of Charleston is called **North Charleston.** Who needs Rand McNally? Farther north lay the booming suburbs of **Hanahan, Ladson, Goose Creek,** and **Summerville.**

Parallel Highways 78 (King Street) and 52 (Meeting Street) thread the peninsular spine one block apart from each other. A couple of blocks east of Meeting, East Bay Street (Highway 52 Spur) follows the southward plunge, turning to East Battery Street after Broad. Over toward the Ashley side of the peninsula, Ashley and Rutledge streets provide the main artery for traffic, and similarly end up at the south end of the peninsula.

Because the city of Charleston was founded from the tip of the peninsula and spread its way up, you'll find the very oldest and most historic sections in the southern half of the peninsula. The visitors center on Meeting Street is a good starting point for southbound walking tours, although the Citadel and a few other historic sites north of this point are certainly worth viewing. But if you see nothing else in the area, see downtown Charleston.

First off, you'll want to notice certain things. For instance, you'll see a few streets still paved with stones, but there just aren't a whole lot of stones sitting around in the Charleston soil. In fact, most of the stones in the streets were imported as ballast from English ships.

Charleston city planners, along with commercial and neighborhood associations, have broken up the downtown area into various subdistricts, but in practice, all you need to know to successfully navigate downtown Charleston are a handful of landmarks, and a few districts anchored by street names.

◖ THE BATTERY AND WHITE POINT GARDENS

The Battery is the name for the tip of the Charleston peninsula; to the west is the Ashley River, to the east is the Cooper River. These rivers join to form the Charleston Harbor, which spills out into the Atlantic Ocean. Along the eastern side of The Battery, there's a wide, slate walk along a water wall that affords a tremendous view of the water, and some of the city's most postcard-perfect pastel mansions. If you're looking for a quick fix of columns and piazzas, head here. (Out in the harbor, you can spot Fort Sumter, as well.) The walkway continues around the peninsula to the west and parallels White Point Gardens, so named by Colonial settlers because it was white from its long-ago piles of bleached oyster shells.

A lot of pirates used to hang around here—literally. In 1718, Stede "The Gentleman Pirate" Bonnet and 21 of his men were allowed

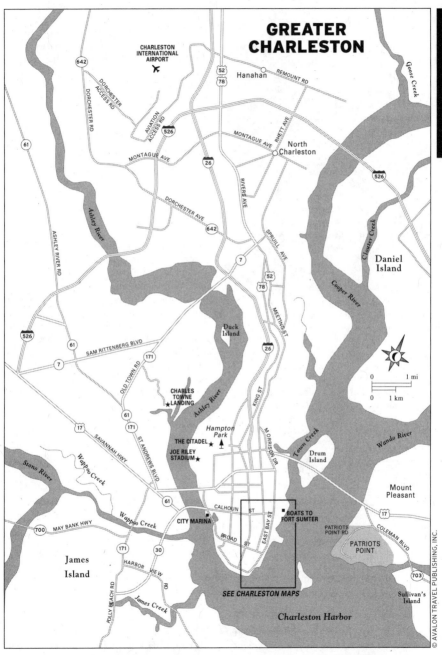

GREATER CHARLESTON

© SEAN SLINSKY

Towering mansions on The Battery are staples of any visit to Charleston.

to hang for quite a while, so that their corpses' ghastly presence could send a message to other would-be pirates. But the city long ago cleaned up all the bodies, so don't let this keep you from visiting; however, to keep the same general demeanor of tension in the place, the city has neglected to put any bathrooms here, so plan ahead.

This area got its nickname when it housed guns protecting Charleston Harbor during the War of 1812. The northeast side of The Battery is also called "High Battery." No one's been executed here in many years, but a lot of couples take advantage of the natural beauty here and get married in the gazebo.

In 1923 the city donated land on The Battery for the Fort Sumter Hotel (now the Fort Sumter House, the condo building at One Meeting Street). John F. Kennedy and a Danish woman who was apparently a Nazi spy spent some passionate nights here in February 1942.

Now the gardens are host to a quaint bandstand (host to wedding ceremonies aplenty), arthritic live oaks and shaggy palmettos, scores of Charleston benches, and a host of cannons that show how the area earned its Battery moniker during wartimes. After a stroll, it's the best place to catch a spot of shade and watch the local and tourist activity that converges on this area. Get here by heading south on East Bay to East Battery, or follow Murray Boulevard till it hits East Battery.

◖ WATERFRONT PARK

To see how a one-time swampy Colonial wharf area can transform into a gem of city park planning, head to Waterfront Park, which runs along the East Cooper and Harbor area from Exchange Street to Vendue Range. Like The Battery and White Point Gardens, this area—a piece of longtime Mayor Joe Riley's vision to invigorate downtown—is a hotbed of local and tourist traffic. Couples stroll the pebble paths, kids play in the huge fountains, seniors rock in the swinging benches on the dock, and fishermen catch supper wading in the outlying marsh grass. The park has plenty of shade and sunshine seating, a great view of the **USS Yorktown**, and is home to the free, modern Waterfront Park City Gallery. Plaques explain the historical layout of the city, and give a great grounding for first-timers.

Head north of the park two blocks and you come to the **Old City Market,** or "the Market" in local jargon. This is the nucleus of Charleston's tourist scene, and many popular clubs, restaurants, and shops orbit around the area from North and South Market streets, from East Bay to Meeting streets. It's also where many of the carriage tours leave.

Charleston Place, the hotel whose opening kick-started the revival of Old Charleston, is at the west end of The Market, and squats between Market, Meeting, and King streets. It's host to a ground-floor interior mall of upscale shops.

◖ KING STREET

Speaking of shopping, King Street is the hub of commerce in town, as there are no malls on the peninsula. The area can be broken down

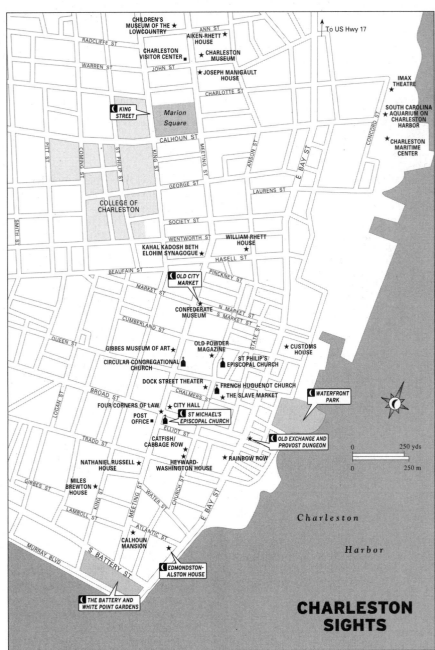

CHILDREN'S MUSEUM OF THE ★ LOWCOUNTRY

RADCLIFFE ST

AIKEN-RHETT ★ HOUSE

ANN ST

To US Hwy 17

CHARLESTON VISITOR CENTER ■

★ CHARLESTON MUSEUM

WARREN ST

JOHN ST

★ JOSEPH MANIGAULT HOUSE

IMAX THEATRE

CHARLOTTE ST

SOUTH CAROLINA AQUARIUM ON ★ CHARLESTON HARBOR

☾ KING STREET

Marion Square

★ CHARLESTON MARITIME CENTER

CALHOUN ST

PITT ST

ST PHILIP ST

KING ST

COMING ST

MEETING ST

ANSON ST

E BAY ST

CONCORD ST

GEORGE ST

LAURENS ST

COLLEGE OF CHARLESTON

SOCIETY ST

SMITH ST

WENTWORTH ST

WILLIAM RHETT HOUSE ★

KAHAL KADOSH BETH ELOHIM SYNAGOGUE ★

HASELL ST

BEAUFAIN ST

PINCKNEY ST

☾ OLD CITY MARKET

MARKET ST

CONFEDERATE ★ MUSEUM

N MARKET ST

S MARKET ST

CUMBERLAND ST

QUEEN ST

GIBBES MUSEUM OF ART ★

OLD POWDER MAGAZINE

STATE ST

★ CUSTOMS HOUSE

CIRCULAR CONGREGATIONAL ⛪ CHURCH

⛪ ST PHILIP'S EPISCOPAL CHURCH

DOCK STREET THEATER

CHALMERS ST

⛪ FRENCH HUGUENOT CHURCH

BROAD ST

★ THE SLAVE MARKET

LOGAN ST

FOUR CORNERS OF LAW

CITY HALL

☾ WATERFRONT PARK

POST OFFICE ■

⛪ ☾ ST MICHAEL'S EPISCOPAL CHURCH

ELLIOT ST

TRADD ST

CATFISH/ CABBAGE ROW

★ ☾ OLD EXCHANGE AND PROVOST DUNGEON

NATHANIEL RUSSELL ★ HOUSE

HEYWARD-WASHINGTON HOUSE

★ RAINBOW ROW

0   250 yds

MILES BREWTON ★ HOUSE

GIBBES ST

KING ST

MEETING ST

WATER ST

CHURCH ST

E BAY ST

0   250 m

LAMBOLL ST

Charleston

MURRAY BLVD

ATLANTIC ST

CALHOUN MANSION ★

S BATTERY ST

☾ EDMONDSTON-ALSTON HOUSE

Harbor

☾ THE BATTERY AND WHITE POINT GARDENS

CHARLESTON SIGHTS

into three parts: Lower King (South of Market Street to Broad Street), where high-end antique shops cluster; Middle King (North from Market Street to Calhoun Street), where chain and local clothing, home-goods, and specialty shops reign; and Upper King (North of Calhoun Street to Cannon Street), where there's a mix of funky boutiques, interior-design shops, and longtime local staples. There are restaurants and bars peppered along the way. Lower King has fine dining; Middle King has coffee shops, cafés, and college hangouts. Upper King is the home of hipster eats and bars.

Along the King Street corridor, you'll come across **Francis Marion Square,** which sits right between King and Meeting streets and is home to many of the city's public events, including the farmers market held every Saturday from March to December. Just north of here you'll find the **Charleston Visitor Center** one block off King at Meeting Street.

King Street continues past Cannon Street and crosses over **Highway 17/The Crosstown,** which cuts across the neck of the peninsula. North of the Crosstown, you'll find **Joe Riley Stadium, The Citadel,** and **Hampton Park.**

THE CHARLESTON VISITOR CENTER

The **Charleston Visitor Center** (375 Meeting St., 843/853-8000, www.charlestoncvb.com) is at the corner of John and Meeting streets, two blocks north of Calhoun Street. It's a great place to stop in and get some background and a bagful of brochures, maps, and coupon books. The folks here will also plan out your stay and call hotels to find you a room. They are very helpful and, except on extremely busy days during Spoleto, they provide good, fast service. A bookstore also provides some worthwhile titles you may want to read around the pool or on the balcony of your room. They also offer tickets for an in-house audiovisual show, the 24-minute *Forever Charleston,* which tells the city's story. Admission is charged. Viewing this film is not a bad first step if this is your first visit and you're trying to get an overview of what all's here.

FROM CALHOUN STREET TO BEAUFAIN/HASELL STREETS
College of Charleston

The College of Charleston (66 George St., 843/805-5507, www.cofc.edu) is simply one of the most beautiful and historic campuses in America. Situated as it is near the bright lights of downtown Charleston, it's no surprise that the COC has long had a reputation as a party school; even back in the early 1800s, famed pioneer, Mexican War commander, and later U.S. presidential candidate John C. Frémont was booted from the college rolls for his tendency to show up for classes with a hangover—if he showed up at all. You may recognize the school buildings from the Alexandra Ripley miniseries, *Scarlett,* parts of which were filmed here.

Founded in 1770, chartered in 1785, opened in 1790, and made a municipal college in 1837, this is the oldest municipal college in America. Attendance used to be free to Charleston students: It was considered a natural extension of

CHARLESTON COURTESY IN ACTION

A friend was visiting and my wife and I joined her, with our two young sons, in a horse-drawn carriage tour of the city. Our guide had no sooner finished boasting about Charleston's legendary good manners when a car began racing beside us, honking angrily in an attempt to pass us on the narrow street. Finally, after a full block, the car was able to pull beside our carriage. At this point, the driver rolled down his window, and we all braced for an angry earful. Instead, he thrust a hand out the window, holding a toddler's sneaker in his fingers.

It was my son's. Unknown to us, it had dropped off his foot and tumbled out of the carriage two blocks back, and this quick-thinking motorist had pulled over, snatched it up, and chased us for two blocks. We thanked the driver profusely, and, needless to say, Charleston's reputation for courtesy was left unblemished.

the K–12 free education. It's a wonderful place to walk around, although the area can get a little dicey at night.

The College of Charleston's impressive and modern-faced 2004 **Addlestone Library** (201 Calhoun St., 843/953-5530) is open varying hours throughout the year. **The Avery Research Center** (125 Bull St., 843/953-7609, www.cofc.edu/avery) is open Mon.–Sat. noon–5 PM; it opens before noon by appointment only.

Kahal Kadosh Beth Elohim Synagogue

Over on Hasell Street you'll find the large, 1840 Greek Revival Kahal Kadosh Beth Elohim Synagogue (90 Hasell St., 843/723-1090, www.kkbe.org), the second-oldest synagogue in the nation (founded 1749) and the oldest in continuous use. More important, in 1824 this became the birthplace of Reform Judaism in the United States. It's worth making a visit; archives are available. Open Mon.–Fri. 10 AM–noon, Sun. 10 AM–3:45 PM.

St. Mary of the Annunciation Catholic Church

If you're feeling ecumenical, head across the street to St. Mary of the Annunciation Catholic Church (89 Hasell St., 843/722-7696, www.catholic-DOC.org/saintmarys), the first church in the Carolinas and Georgia. Built in 1839, the church building contains several beautiful paintings. Open Mon.–Fri. 9:30 AM–3:30 PM; Mass Sun. 9:30 AM.

FROM BEAUFAIN/HASELL STREETS TO BROAD STREET
[C] Old City Market

The 1841 Old City Market on Market Street between Meeting and East Bay, continues today as Charleston's beating heart. A good place to start your visit, it features small shops, restaurants, and a flea market atmosphere. You'll find vendors for everything from special homegrown hot rice recipes ("So good you'll double-smack your lips!" brags one sign) to professional photographs of the city.

© SEAN SLINSKY

Sweetgrass baskets, made by local African American women, are sold at the Old City Market.

The Confederate Museum

The Confederate Museum (Meeting and Market Sts., 843/723-1541) above the Old City Market is run by the Daughters of the Confederacy and includes war memorabilia like uniforms, swords, guns, cannons, and flags mostly from the area. Open Tues.–Sat. 11 AM–3:30 PM. Rates are $5 adults, $3 children, those under six free.

Old Powder Magazine

In the wake of Indian attacks, early Charles Town residents built the square, low-lying 1703 Old Powder Magazine (79 Cumberland St., 843/722-9350, www.powdermag.org), as part of the city's fortifications near the northwest bastion. Today, it's the oldest remaining public building in Charleston. Post restoration, it is scheduled to reopen for tours in 2006.

St. Philip's Episcopal Church

St. Philip's Episcopal Church (142 Church St., 843/722-7734, www.stphilipschurchsc.org)

was built 1835–1838 by Joseph Hyde, although Edward Brickell White later added a tall octagonal steeple. This steeple once held a light for seamen, but this made it a target during the Union bombardment of the city. This church congregation is the first Anglican parish south of Virginia. According to local legends, barristers questioned Reverend White's credibility because he had in 1682 drunkenly christened a young bear. White went on to remain a pastor for many years, but the bear apparently drifted from the faith.

If you'd like to attend a service in this magnificent structure—and many traveling visitors do—services are held Sun. at 8:15 AM and 10:30 AM, and Wed. at 10 AM and 6 PM.

Declaration of Independence signer Edward Rutledge and John C. Calhoun lie buried out in the church's graveyard, along with Colonel William Rhett, capturer of pirate Stede Bonnet. Both Christopher Gadsden, the maverick revolutionist, and Charles Pinckney, four-time

© SEAN SLINSKY

Prominent figures in local and early American history worshipped at St. Philip's Episcopal Church.

governor and drafter and signer of the Federal Constitution, are also said to be buried here in unmarked graves.

Huguenot Church

Although the current Gothic Huguenot Church (136 Church St., 843/722-4385, www.firstfrenchchurch.org), is "only" 150-plus years old, it was built on the walls of its predecessor. French Huguenots have worshiped on this site since as early as 1687. Until the early 1900s, the service was conducted in French on certain Sundays, but now it's English only, save for one special weekend in April. Call for hours, as they vary. Service is Sun. at 10:30 AM.

Circular Congregational Church

The Circular Congregational Church (150 Meeting St., 843/577-6400, www.circular-church.org), a huge brick Romanesque structure, was built in 1891 for a congregation founded way back in 1681. The church began with a group of non-Anglican Calvinists from several nationalities and was originally known as the Church of Dissenters. Architects designed the present church in the aftermath of the 1886 earthquake, using circular logic. Dr. David Ramsay (1749–1815), author of the definitive early South Carolina history, *History of South Carolina (1789),* and an important early biography of George Washington, is buried among others in the churchyard. Today the church building continues in use for the local congregation of the United Church of Christ. Services are Sun. at 10:15 AM in the summer and 11 AM the rest of the year.

Dock Street Theater

The historic Dock Street Theater (135 Church St., 843/720-3968), is the latest iteration of the original 1736 Dock Street Theater—the first building in America designed for purely theatrical purposes—and the 1809 Planters Hotel, both of which were located here. The Dock Street Theater (on then–Dock Street, which was later renamed Queen Street) opened on February 12, 1736, with a performance of *The Recruiting Officer* by George Farquhar. After a few successful seasons, the theater burned. But Charleston had caught footlight fever, and a second theater opened on the same site on October 7, 1754. Theater became wildly popular with the powdered wig set before the Revolution, so much so that the proprietors built a new, grander theater to replace this second theater on nearly the same site, opening in 1773. Unfortunately, although the theater miraculously survived the heavy bombardments during the Revolution, it burned to the ground shortly thereafter.

In the last decades of the 18th century, theater productions were banned in Charleston under a particularly harsh blue law because thespians were officially condemned as antithetical to decent, upright living. But this era was short-lived, and shortly thereafter, productions were taking place in various spots around Charleston, although the Dock Street Theater still lay in ruins. In 1809, a business concern built the **Planters Hotel** around the ruins of the theater. In 1835, to meet popular demand, the hotel was remodeled to include a theater, so that by the theater's centennial, the Dock Street Theater was again up and running. The theater was closed by the Civil War, but the Works Progress Administration (WPA) during the Depression got the theater refurbished and open in time for its bicentennial on February 12, 1936.

Charleston-born actor Thomas Gibson ("Greg" of TV's *Dharma and Greg*) performed with the Footlight Players here in the 1970s before moving on to the College of Charleston, and later Julliard, *Chicago Hope,* and Greg-dom. Today, the Dock Street Theater continues to offer first-rate theatrical performances through the Charleston Stage Company, the state's largest theater company, producing more than 120 performances a year. If you just want to poke your head inside to take a look around this historic building, stop by during business hours, Mon.–Fri. 9 AM–5 PM. To inquire about shows, contact the box office (843/965-4032 or 800/454-7093) Mon.–Fri. 10 AM–5 PM or the troupe (www.charlestonstage.com). When running, shows are held Thurs., Fri., and Sat. at 8 PM, Sun. at 3 PM.

The Old Slave Mart Museum

The Old Slave Mart Museum (6 Chalmers St., 843/958-6467, osmm@ci.charleston.sc.us), is one of the many places in this neighborhood where slaves were sold during the days of the slave trade. The museum is set to reopen in summer 2006 after renovations, but the facade and location itself is interesting nonetheless.

BROAD STREET

Broad Street bisects the downtown peninsula andencompasses the first commercial and governmental portion of the city, dead-ending at the once-vital Old Exchange and Provost Dungeon. At the corner of Meeting and Broad streets, St. Michael's Episcopal Church is another handy landmark because you can see its steeple for many blocks.

Four Corners of Law

The intersection of Broad and Meeting streets is known as the Four Corners of Law because the buildings on each corner represent a different sort of law. On the northeast corner stands City Hall, circa 1801, at Meeting and Broad streets, representing city law. The Charleston County Courthouse, representing legal law, stands on the northwest corner. On the southwest corner, the U.S. Courthouse and old main Post Office represent Federal law. Directly across Broad you'll find St. Michael's Episcopal Church holding down the southeast corner, representing divine law. On most days, the traffic on Meeting Street represents the law of perpetual motion.

Charleston City Hall (80 Broad St., 843/724-3799), on Meeting and Broad streets, was built circa 1801; the City Council Chamber contains valuable works of art, including the John Trumbull portrait of George Washington, dated 1791. The tower above is topped by an Indian weather vane; the Indian is supposed to be King Haigler, a Catawba chief and savior of the Camden Quakers in 1753. He fought with the Carolinians against the Cherokee in 1759 but was killed by a Swanee ambush in 1765. The town bell was cast in Philadelphia in 1824. It used to ring out every night at nine o'clock, marking the beginning of curfew hours for slaves. At press time, the Hall was closed to the public for restoration work, but is scheduled to reopen in fall of 2006 for tours.

◖ St. Michael's Episcopal Church

St. Michael's Episcopal Church (71 Broad St., 843/723-0603, www.stmichaelschurch.net), circa 1761, is the oldest church building in South Carolina. During Colonial days, this was the second Anglican church built south of Virginia. The clock toward the top of the 186-foot tower/steeple has kept time for Charlestonians since 1764. Inside the church is grand, with box pews; wealthy Charlestonians would rent these to assure themselves the best—and hence, most prestigious—seats possible on Sundays. How they reconciled this kind of privilege with the teachings of a peasant rabbi who spent most of his time around the downtrodden is beyond me. The graveyard beside the church is worth visiting for its many ornate and affecting tombstones. The bells overhead were stolen by the British during the Revolution and carried back to England in 1784, although they came back to Charleston. In 1862, they were shipped to Columbia for safekeeping from Federal shells and stored in a shed on the grounds of the State House—as if that wasn't a target. When the State House was burned in 1865 by Sherman's troops, the bells were partially destroyed. Preservation-minded folks sent the fragments that remained to England in 1866, and they were recast in the original molds. Then the bells made their fifth trip across the Atlantic, landing in Charleston in 1867.

St. Michael's stands on the corner of Broad and Meeting streets, where the first church in Charleston—St. Philip's—was built 1681–1682. When the growing parish was divided in 1751, the lower half was named St. Michael's. George Washington and Lafayette both worshipped here, and the first vested boys' choirs in the country began here. During the Revolutionary period, Reverend Robert Cooper was forced out of the pulpit—and out of the country—for offering prayers for the king of England. Because the church's steeple provided the highest viewpoint in Charles Town, Peter Timothy, editor of the *Charles Town Gazette,* climbed up there with a spyglass to watch the approaching British troops before the American loss of the town in 1780. Timothy had taken over the paper from his mother, the first woman publisher in the United States and a business partner of Benjamin Franklin. To make the steeple less of a target for British guns, Continental Commodore Abram Whipple proposed that someone should paint it black to make it less obvious to the eye. But once it was painted black, against the blue sky, it stuck out far more than before. Open Mon.–Fri. 9 AM–4:30 PM, Sat. 9 AM–noon. Donations accepted. Sun. services are at 8 AM, 10:30 AM, and 6 PM.

◖ Old Exchange and Provost Dungeon

The Old Exchange and Provost Dungeon (122 E. Bay St., 843/727-2165, www.oldexchange.com) stands on the site of the original British Court of Guards, built in 1680. In 1767 the current exchange and customs house was built right on top of the old building, preserving the basement down below. Admission is $7 adults, $3.50 kids, free for those six and under. The building is open daily 9 AM–5 PM.

Today you can visit the basement dungeon, where Stede Bonnet, the pirate, was imprisoned in 1718. Audio-animatronic characters, including a parrot, explain the site's history. The building once stored the tea taken during Charleston's version of the Boston Tea Party. When the British had the Carolinians bottled up in the city in 1780, General William Moultrie hid 10,000 pounds of gunpowder in a secret room behind a false wall in the basement. Although the British moved in and took over the city and the building, they never did find the hidden powder.

In 1791, George Washington stood on the steps of this building to watch a parade given in his honor. That night, Washington tripped the light fantastic at a ball and governor's dinner in the Exchange Hall.

SOUTH OF BROAD STREET

The area South of Broad Street is much more than a neighborhood—it's an entity unto itself. Thanks to the high-ticket home prices, the residents here were long ago nicknamed by the tag South of Broad—S.O.B. for short—a joke and jab that's stuck around even after millionaire house prices have spread all over the peninsula. And while this area is made up of mostly private residences, it's a great place to stroll and see fine architecture, amazing gardens, and the appeal of Charleston's good life. Here are some places worth noting from the sidewalk, and some S.O.B. house museums that welcome visitors.

Cabbage/Catfish Row

You'll come to Cabbage/Catfish Row at 89–91 Church Street, the model for DuBose Heyward's Catfish Row in his novel *Porgy,* the basis for George Gershwin's opera *Porgy and Bess.* Vendors once peddled produce along the street here (hence the name Cabbage Row). In the novel, Heyward relocated *his* row over to East Bay Street to place it closer to the waterfront (hence catfish). Not that you'll find many catfish in Charleston Harbor. (It's interesting to note that although it was based on a novel written by a native son, and set in the city, *Porgy and Bess* was not performed in Charleston until 1970. The interracial cast required to stage the show would have violated segregationist city codes.)

Heyward-Washington House

Farther south along Church Street you'll come to the Heyward-Washington House (87 Church St., 843/722-0354, www.charleston-museum.org), circa 1772, which was the home of Thomas Heyward Jr., whose name you may remember from the bottom portion of the Declaration of Independence. George Washington lived here a while in Charleston in 1791. The original kitchen building is still there, as well as Charlestonian furniture and a formal garden abloom with plants available in Charleston in the 18th century. Open Mon.–Sat. 10 AM–5 PM, Sun. 1–5 PM; tours every half hour till 4:30 PM. Admission is $9 adults, $4 kids under 12. This home is owned by the Charleston Museum, and they offer an $21 combination ticket that will get you into the Heyward-Washington House, the **Joseph Manigault House** (350 Meeting St., 843/723-2926), and the **Charleston Museum** (360 Meeting St., 843/722-2996, www.charlestonmuseum.org). You don't have to see them on the same day, either. If any two of these would be enough for you, you can purchase a two-attraction ticket for $16. Call the Charleston Museum for information.

Nathaniel Russell House

The Nathaniel Russell House (51 Meeting St., 843/724-8481, www.historiccharleston.org) was built for a local prosperous merchant in 1808, the year before Abraham Lincoln was born, and stands amid a large, lush garden. A great example of the Federal style popular after the Revolution, this rectangular three-story mansion has a three-story octagonal bay on one side, a freestanding spiral staircase, Adams-style furnishings, and ornate moldings. Guided tours Mon.–Sat. 10 AM–5 PM, Sun. 2–5 PM. Last tour begins 4:40 PM. Closed Thanksgiving, Christmas Eve, Christmas. Admission is $10 adults, kids under six free. You can get a combo ticket to visit the Russell house and the refurbished Aiken house for $16. (A Charleston Heritage Passport—$55.95—will allow you to see the Nathaniel Russell House, Drayton Hall plantation, the Edmondston-Alston House, the Gibbes Museum of Art, and Middleton Place. Buy one at the Charleston Visitor Center.)

◖ Edmondston-Alston House

If you're only going to take one home tour, you may want to make it the circa-1828 Edmondston-Alston House (21 E. Battery, 843/722-7171, www.middletonplace.org). For one thing, this is one of those beautiful mansions on The Battery that overlook the harbor. It's also a great example of the "golden era" for Charleston antebellum society. Originally built for Charles Edmondston, a wealthy Scottish-born merchant and owner of a lucrative wharf, the home has been owned by Alston family members since 1838. Because members of the Alston family still live here, your 30-minute guided tour ($10 adults, children under six free) will cover only the lower two floors of this stately three-floor Greek Revival. Open Tues.–Sat. 10 AM–5 PM (last 30-minute tour starts at 4:30 PM), Sun.–Mon. 1:30–4:30 PM.

Calhoun Mansion

The Calhoun Mansion (16 Meeting St., 843/577-1100, www.jmccharleston.com), a 24,000-square-foot Victorian baronial manor house, circa 1876, features a 75-foot domed ceiling with stairwell. John C. Calhoun never lived here, but a kinsman did. The house is filled with antiques and surrounded by a lavish formal garden. Open Tues.–Fri. 11 AM–3:30 PM (closed Thanksgiving–Feb. 1). Admission is $15.

PLANTATIONS, GARDENS, AND PARKS

Most South Carolinians, even at the height of antebellum society, never owned a slave. Only a relative handful owned, much less lived on, plantations. In fact, more African Americans lived on plantations than European Americans ever did, and they lived as slaves, which means that most people who lived on the famed Southern plantations, with their stately buildings that nearly every new house built in South Carolina seems to emulate, did so unwillingly.

Even still, most non-Southerners don't feel that they've visited the "real" South until they tour a plantation. And if you're seeking antebellum excess, you've come to the right place. Coastal South Carolina in particular was one of the wealthiest plantation areas in antebellum times, and Charleston was the hub of antebellum Carolinian life—as it is today, in many ways—so you'll find many old plantations here, some of them open to the public.

◖ Drayton Hall

Drayton Hall (3380 Ashley River Rd./Rte. 61, 843/769-2600 or 888/349-0588, www.draytonhall.org) is a redbrick Georgian-Palladian

Find Colonial-era graveyards on plantations, on the outskirts of cities, and flanking in-town and rural churches.

© SEAN SLINSKY

home, and one of the finest examples of early-Georgian architecture in the United States. Reputed to not be the nicest guy, original owner John Drayton was, however, a rich man, and the owner of 500 slaves at his death.

Completed in 1742, the house was used as a smallpox hospital during the War Between the States, which allowed it to be the only authentically Colonial structure along the Ashley River to survive Shermanization. Just keep in mind that this was the—ahem—"smaller" house of the Draytons. There's no furniture here, which makes it easier to appreciate the architecture, moldings, and flooring. Open daily Mar. 1–Oct. 31, 9:30 AM– 4 PM; Nov. 1–Feb. 28, 9:30 AM–3 PM; tours on the hour. Admission is $12 adults, $8 children 12–18), $6 children 6–11, children 5 and under free. Access to the grounds only is $5.

Magnolia Plantation and Gardens

Of all the Charleston plantations, **Magnolia Plantation and Gardens** (3550 Ashley River

Rd./Rte. 61, 843/571-1266 or 800/367-3517, www.magnoliaplantation.com) is my personal favorite—and that's saying something. John Drayton's daddy, Thomas Drayton, lived on Magnolia Plantation in the main house, where he was born in 1708. Thomas Drayton Jr., Thomas's father, built the original house in the 1680s. He came here with a group of Barbadian planters in 1671, with (later governor) John Yeamans.

Drayton's great-great-grandson, Reverend Dr. John Drayton, apparently treated his slaves quite well, educating them in reading, writing, and math skills—all illegal—while providing them religious instruction. Sherman and Co. Remodelers burned the Magnolia Plantation house to the ground and strung up Adam Bennett, the top-ranking slave, from a nearby (still-standing) tree because he refused to tell them where he'd buried the family treasure. Fortunately, the Boys in Blue remembered at the last moment that they were, after all, supposed to be "God's Truth Marching On," and they cut poor Bennett down. After the war was over, Bennett traveled 250 miles on foot to Flat Rock, North Carolina, where Reverend Drayton was hiding out in one of the Draytons' summer homes, having heard that the freed slaves had seized control of the plantation and "taken [it] for their own." Bennett told Drayton everything was ready for his return. Drayton later disassembled his Summerville house and floated it downriver to the plantation, where it stands today on the foundation of the Shermanized house. House tours are available; admission is $7, children six and under not permitted.

The good reverend planted his informal gardens in the 1840s and opened them to the public in 1870 as a way of paying for the upkeep of the plantation; the magnificent gardens today include a **Biblical Garden,** featuring most of the plant species mentioned in the Old and New Testaments (unfortunately, the Tree of Eternal Life from Genesis is missing); an herb garden; a Barbados tropical garden; a wildlife refuge; and a petting zoo.

If you feel that your own family tree could stand a little thinning, you might be interested in bringing the brood over to the quarter-mile *Camellia sasanquas* maze. Perhaps most impressive is Magnolia's latest addition, the 60-acre **Audubon Swamp Garden.** For $7 per adult, you can take the "Nature Train"—a tram, to be more accurate—for an interesting tour of the grounds, but you should take the Swampwalk (also $7) as well. If you were at the drive-ins in the late 1970s, you saw these swamps featured in the Adrienne Barbeau epic *The Swamp Thing.* Many years before Barbeau slogged these waters, trailing a residue of acting greatness, no less a personage than John J. Audubon, the famed ornithological artist, wandered the same area, sketchbook in hand, as a guest of the Reverend Dr. Drayton.

Open Mon.–Sat. 8 AM–5 PM; prices vary according to which of Magnolia's attractions you want to tour, but basic admission to the grounds and garden run $14 adults, $8 children six and older, free for children five and under. Senior citizens save a dollar on most

© SEAN SLINSKY

Magnolia Plantation and Gardens offers the most lavish and romantic plantation grounds in the area.

admissions. Some of the trails are paved and wheelchair accessible.

◖ Middleton Place

Here you get an idea of Charleston's abundance of floral beauty: Drop Middleton Place (4300 Ashley River Rd./Rte. 61, 843/556-6020 or 800/782-3608, www.middletonplace.org) into the middle of nearly any other region in the country and it would attract visitors from hundreds of miles away. But then, I suppose Middleton Place does that already, and it's just four miles past Magnolia Plantation.

And well they *should* come, for Middleton Place holds the nation's oldest landscaped gardens, begun back in the 1740s. Arthur Middleton, signer of the Declaration of Independence, grew up here. A lot of locals prefer Middleton for its lack of hype; a visit here is more like visiting an actual plantation than is a visit to, say, Magnolia, which has been opened for—and shaped by—the demands of paying customers since Reconstruction. Although only a staircase and foundation remain of the main house, for a couple of bucks extra you can tour the "flanker" house, where the Middletons lived after the war. Don't even think about taking a camera inside—the folks at Middleton have gone so far as to construct a row of lockers on the house's front porch, where you may (must) leave your camera before entering the house. Mel Gibson and company were treated a little differently when they visited; they used Middleton Place as the location for Lord Corwallis's party in 2000's *The Patriot*. Then again, I suspect Mel paid more than $20 for the privilege.

Remarkable gardens are featured here as well, of a more formal, French variety. Unlike Magnolia, these aren't particularly impressive outside of spring—go in June and you'll be mainly touring rows of shrubs. You can also take a tour of the authentically appointed guest (now main) house, walk amid a small slave graveyard, or visit an authentic working stable yard. Open daily 9 AM–5 PM. Admission to the garden and stables is $20 adults, $5 children. If you want to tour the remaining house, the additional charge is $10.

You'll also find the good Southern-style **Middleton Place Restaurant** here with impeccable atmosphere and surprisingly moderate prices. The three-course, prix fixe lunch, with choices like she-crab or African peanut soup, fried chicken or barbecue, pecan pie or Huguenot torte, is especially affordable ($14.95), while dinner, which is especially romantic, goes upscale with offerings that range from alligator tail appetizers to osso bucco, pork, and roast duckling entrées ($27–29). Lunch 11 AM–3 PM with admission to the gardens. Dinner Sun., Tues., Thurs. 6–8 PM; Fri.–Sat. till 9 PM with no admission surcharge; reservations required.

You'll also find the **The Inn at Middleton Place** (4290 Ashley River Rd./Rte. 61, 843/556-0500 or 800/543-4774, www.theinn-atmiddletonplace.com), a flagrantly "modern" design that won the coveted American Institute of Architects (AIA) Honor Award in (shudder) 1975. Yes, I've read Ayn Rand's *Fountainhead*, too, but with all the Colonial splendor about—which is, after all, what draws tourists out here—the architects might have just *gone* with the theme. Instead, what we have is what the inn's marketing folks, 30 years later, assure us is an "exciting counterpoint" to the traditional architecture of Middleton Place. Ask about their Middleton Inn Restaurant package deals, which include dinner for two with your room charges, which range $139–450 a night.

Cypress Gardens

Up north along the Cooper River, in Moncks Corner, you'll find 170 acres of azaleas, dogwoods, daffodils, wisteria, and dark waterways at Cypress Gardens (3030 Cypress Gardens Rd., Moncks Corner, 843/553-0515, www.cypressgardens.info). Two nature trails offer you good chances to look for wildlife: river otters, woodpeckers, owls, and, of course, our friend the alligator. Springtime is bloom time, and fall is also quite pretty. Summertime is pretty, too—pretty hot, and a pretty good time to bring repellent. Take the glass-bottom boat ride, or canoe yourself and a significant other around. From Charleston, head north on I-26

© SEAN SLINSKY

Paddle through Cypress Gardens just outside Charleston.

to Exit 208; follow Highway 52 North and look for the signs to Cypress Gardens. Open daily (except major holidays) 9 AM–5 PM. Admission is $10 adults, $9 children 6–12, children under 6 admitted free.

Boone Hall Plantation

Closest to downtown Charleston is Boone Hall Plantation (1235 Long Point Rd. 843/884-4371, www.boonehallplantation.com), lying along the Wando River in Mount Pleasant. Although its main plantation house is a 1935 reconstruction of the original, Boone Hall is worth visiting because (1) it allows you to see what a plantation looked like when it was relatively new; (2) it contains nine original slave cabins, which tell more about slave conditions than all the interpretive exhibits in the world; (3) if you're looking for the type of plantation you may have seen in the TV miniseries *North and South,* Boone Hall Plantation *is* where that miniseries and several others were filmed; and (4) rumor has it that Margaret Mitchell's Tara is mod-

eled after the place—down to the gauntlet of moss-dripping oaks at the entrance (*Gone With the Wind* was published in 1936, a year after Boone Hall's renaissance). Battle reenactments are performed here in the summer, filling the grounds and mansion with period-dressed soldiers and belles (nobody seems to want to come dressed as a slave). For the Civil War buff, there's nothing like it. Boone Hall Plantation is at Highway 17 and Long Point Road. Open Apr. 1–Labor Day, Mon.–Sat. 8:30 AM–6:30 PM; Sun. 1–5 PM. Otherwise open Mon.–Sat. 9 AM–5 PM, Sun. 1–4 PM. Admission is $14.50 adults, $7 children 6–12, children under 6 admitted free.

From separate nearby entrances on Long-point Road and off Highway 17 North, Boone Hall Farms (843/856-5366) allows you to pick peaches, strawberries, and tomatoes in season from the plantation's grounds. In October, the plantation sells U-pick pumpkins. This is a fun way to spend a few hours with the kids. The "jumpy house" and a lengthy tractor-drawn hayride beneath the moss-strewn oaks are free.

HELL HOLE SWAMP

Several stories circulate about how Hell Hole Swamp got its name. The most probable one concerns General Francis Marion, the French-American partisan fighter known as "The Swamp Fox." Legend has it that British troops chasing Marion during the Revolutionary War watched him disappear into the swamp. After hours of slogging through the muck, they couldn't find him. One of the soldiers marveled, "That's a helluva hole." And so the area got its name as Hell Hole Swamp.

While folks often refer to the towns of Jamestown, Huger, Bethera, and Shulerville as being set in Hell Hole Swamp, the name technically refers only to an area of the Francis Marion National Forest — 2,000 acres of wilderness, uninhabited by anything but swamp critters. But Hell Hole Swamp is more than a physical locale — it's a mythical place, "'its whereabouts always designated as 'just a piece down the road,'" as the 1941 Works Project Administration (WPA) guide put it. Here, far from the eye of the law, and equipped with souped-up automobiles for racing over the crude dirt and mud roads to and from hidden stills, bootleggers ruled the swamp, churning out the Prohibition-era "liquid corn" that was not only tippled in the blind tigers of Charleston and from front-porch stoops of Berkeley County, but was also sold across the country. Like today's drug lords, rival bootleggers battled over turf — two competitors shot it out on Moncks Corner's Main Street one day in 1926. Al Capone is said to have visited Hell Hole Swamp once, to check on the production

end of his illegal whiskey empire. Sometimes illegal whiskey would also be brought up from Cuba, along the Santee River, and stored in Hell Hole Swamp until it was smuggled aboard trains bound for Chicago.

The Hell Hole brand of shine even advertised its low iodine content with the proud slogan "Not a Goiter in a Gallon." The moonshine industry continued strong even after FDR's revocation of Prohibition, providing cheap (because untaxed) and powerful intoxicants for the rural poor.

Mendel Rivers, St. Stephen — born chairman of the House Armed Services Committee, liked to boast that he was a member of the "Hell Hole Swamp Gang," a group of Berkeley County boys who had gone on to gain national or state political prominence, including Governor Robert E. McNair, State Senator Rembert Dennis, and Columbia Mayor Lester Bates.

Not long ago, when local counties decided to pitch in and create a high school for students of St. Stephens and surrounding towns, one of the first names suggested would have established Hell Hole High. The idea was quickly voted down.

But the average folks around here (if not the average school-board member) remain powerfully proud of the Hell Hole name. Each May, Jamestown holds the annual **Hell Hole Swamp Festival** (Jamestown, 843/257-2233, www.festivalnews.info) featuring a tobacco-spitting contest, 10K Gator Run, parade, pig cook-off, beauty contest, softball tournament, and other events.

Angel Oak Park

Don't make a special trip for this sight, but if you're over on rural-but-developing John's Island—say, on the way to Kiawah—you'll find **Angel Oak** (3688 Angel Oak Rd., 843/559-3496), a massive live-oak *(Quercus virginiana)* tree just 65 feet tall but 25.5 feet in circumference and providing some 17,000 square feet of shade. Because live oaks tend toward heart rot, making core samples useless in determining age, nobody knows for sure how old the Angel

Oak is, although some estimates based on the large limbs stretching out up to 89 feet from the trunk and measuring 11.25 feet around put it at possibly 1,400 years old.

Incidentally, although some have waxed poetic about the way the Angel Oak spreads its angelic, "winglike" branches to the ground, the name comes from Justis Angel, who owned the tree and its land in the early 1800s. The South Carolina Agricultural Society rented the tree for one dollar a year from the Mutual Land

and Development Corporation from 1959 to 1964 until another private owner bought the tree and surrounding site. He opened the land to the public, but vandalism and other problems forced him to build a fence around it and start charging a viewing fee.

In 1991, the City of Charleston acquired the Angel Oak and the surrounding property and opened Angel Oak Park to the public in 1991. People use the grounds here for picnics, family reunions, weddings, and other special events. Permits are required for large events and for the use of alcoholic beverages. Open Mon.–Sat. 9 AM–5 PM, Sun. 1–5 PM. Free admission.

Charles Towne Landing State Historic Site

I'm excited about the future of this park, which for years was one of Charleston's most overlooked and underdeveloped assets, the kind of destination that was ignored in the city's tourism brochures. After a $19-million renovation, **Charles Towne Landing State Historic Site** (1500 Old Towne Rd., off Hwy. 171, 843/852-4200, www.southcarolinaparks.com) is poised to return to the top strata of area attractions. It's Charleston's answer to Manteo, North Carolina's popular Roanoke Island Festival Park.

One thing the Landing has going for it is location. Off Highway 171 about three miles northwest of downtown Charleston, it rests on the original site of Charles Towne—the spot the founders abandoned when they decided it was safer and healthier to move over to White Point. Because this land has been largely left alone for the past 330 years as the peninsula developed, a visit here truly feels like a step back to the first days of English settlement in the Carolinas. The historic recreations, including a British settler's homestead and the *Adventure,* a full-scale replica of a 17th-century trading vessel, contribute to this illusion (both are undergoing continuing restoration).

Like the rest of the park, the ship was born in the heady days of the late 1960s, when Charleston, which had just finished with its Civil War centennial celebrations, prepared

to celebrate both the city's tricentennial (in 1970) and the nation's bicentennial all within a six-year span. No doubt, the geodesic dome convention center and the interpretive center got the job done, but before Nixon reached the end of his first reel of tape, they had grown dated. The site's Colonial motif and its "modern" structures clashed worse than the Carolinians and the Spanish ever did; it was enough to make you want to head to the Home for Retired Architects with an interrogator's lamp and a squirt gun to get some answers. Mercifully, the renovations have replaced the dated buildings with even more modern—yet thematically appropriate—structures.

Generations of Charleston schoolchildren today remember Charles Towne Landing fondly as one of the region's inescapable field trip destinations, and it's upon this grateful constituency that the park's restoration has been dedicated.

There really is a lot of ground to cover here, and if you'll be visiting the Animal Forest, you'll do plenty of walking. Or you can rent a bike by the hour ($3 deposit, $3 per hour), available at the information center.

Highlights of the park include the aforementioned *Adventure.* The 53-foot craft is a reproduction of the sorts of boat the early settlers used to sail up and down the coast when trading with other settlements. It's not a transoceanic vessel, simply because it couldn't have taken enough goods across to make it worth the while. The restoration process is worth inspection, just as much as the finished product will be.

To get to the dock site of the *Adventure,* you'll have to pass through the original **Fortified Area** with its reconstructed wooden palisade walls and earthen fortifications built against Spanish and Indian attack.

The nearby **Crop Garden** shows the sorts of crops that the settlers experimented with, including indigo, cotton, sugar cane, and food crops. Here you'll also see the **Horry/Lucas Ruins,** remains of a late-18th-century mansion that burned in this area, preserving all sorts of goodies for today's archaeologists.

As you walk through the extensive Animal Forest habitat area—the closest thing Charleston has to a zoo—you'll see the same animals the settlers would have seen in 1670, including bison, pumas, bears, wolves, alligators, and bobcats. The displays here were designed by Georgia-born naturalist Jim Fowler, the guy who used to wrestle alligators while Marlin Perkins hovered overhead in a helicopter on *Mutual of Omaha's Wild Kingdom,* and who has appeared more recently on the Animal Planet cable channel.

Unlike the original Charles Towne settlement, almost everything here is wheelchair accessible. Admission is $5 for 16 and older, $3.25 seniors, $3 children 6–15, free for those under 6. Open daily 8:30 AM–5 PM.

James Island County Park

This park (861 Riverland Dr., James Island, 843/795-7275, www.ccprc.com) is a 640-acre facility with boardwalks, bike and hiking trails, a fishing/crabbing dock, lagoons, pedal boat and kayak rentals, a climbing wall, a playground, picnic sites, a campground, rental cabins, and the **Splash Zone** water park, featuring a 200-foot slide, a lazy river, and other attractions. Open year-round, 8 AM–dusk. Splash Zone open seasonally 10 AM–6 PM. Park admission is $1 per person; Splash Zone $10 adults, $7 kids 42 inches and shorter, free for those age two and under.

Palmetto Islands County Park

This beautiful park (444 Needlerush Pkwy., Mount Pleasant, 843/884-0832, www.ccprc.com) on Long Point Road in Mount Pleasant features marsh boardwalks, trails, a mile-long canoe trail, a playground, a water park, an observation tower, bicycle paths, and fishing docks. Park open year-round, 9 AM–dusk. Splash Island open seasonally 10 AM–dark. Park admission is $1 per person; Splash Island $7 adults, $5 kids 42 inches and shorter.

Folly Beach County Park

A neat park with beach access, Folly Beach (W. Ashley Ave. at the westernmost tip of Folly Beach, 843/588-2426) offers 2,500 feet of oceanfront and 200 feet of riverfront beach. Lifeguards are on duty during the high season. Plenty of parking is available, as well as dressing areas, showers, public restrooms, and picnic tables. Open daily summer 9 AM–7 PM, otherwise 10 AM–dark. Admission is $5 per car.

Francis Marion National Forest

Francis Marion comprises 250,000 acres of forest north of Charleston, offering picnicking and camping sites; boat ramps; fishing; and horseback, bicycle, and motorcycle trails. Head north on Highway 17 and look for the signs.

Seewee Visitor and Environmental Education Center

This outpost (5821 Hwy. 17 N, 843/928-3368, www.fws.gov/seeweecenter) serves as the visi-

© SEAN SLINSKY

Marking the site of a major Civil War battle between black Union infantry and Confederate rebels, Morris Island Lighthouse still stands just off Folly Beach.

tors center for the immense Francis Marion National Forest and the sprawling Cape Romain Wildlife Refuge. The center focuses on the natural history of the Lowcountry, featuring hands-on displays, and a red wolf education area. The huge preserved tracts include miles of trails, some for hiking, some for biking. Camping ($15–20, plus $5 gate fee) is available at the Buck Hall Recreation Area (843/887-3257) on the Intracoastal Waterway. Open Tues.–Sun. 9 AM–5 PM.

Caw Caw Interpretive Center

Run by the Charleston County Park and Recreation Commission, **Caw Caw Interpretive Center** (5200 Highway 17 S, 843/889-8898, www.ccprc.com/cawcaw.htm) is just about 20 minutes from downtown, and definitely worth a trip, especially if you're looking to entertain outdoor-loving kids. Once part of a rice plantation, its 654 acres include woodlands, and the remnants of the onetime fields, now home to deer, otter, and all manners of birds. There are more than seven miles of trails that cover the area, and there's a 1,200-foot boardwalk, too. But the best part of Caw Caw are the Lowcountry history, culture, and science programs it offers. Guided morning walks teach participants about local herbs and medicinal plants, once used by Gullah folk; nighttime walks uncover gators and owls; workshops teach basket weaving and rice harvesting; and the list goes on. To see what's available when you're in town, call or check the website. Open Wed.–Fri. 9 AM–3 PM, Sat.–Sun. 9 AM–5 PM, other times depending on special events. Admission is $1; special programs cost nominal additional fees.

MUSEUMS, HISTORY, AND ART
Charleston Museum

You can't miss this museum (360 Meeting St., 843/722-2996, www.charlestonmuseum.org), as you head south toward the Market and Battery off Highway 17 or I-26 along Meeting Street; it's on the east side of the street, a modern-looking brick building fronted by a large

model of the CSS *Hunley*. The oldest museum in all of North America, this is one of the best, first places to stop and get a handle on Lowcountry culture and history. Kids will enjoy the interactive "Discover Me" room upstairs, and history buffs will enjoy the collection of small-press historical books in the gift shop downstairs. The museum also operates the historic Heyward-Washington and Joseph Manigault houses. No flash photography is permitted. Open Mon.–Sat. 9 AM–5 PM, Sun. 1–5 PM. Admission to any one of the museum's sites (the museum or either house) is $10 adults, $4 ages 3–12; admission to two sites is $16 adults, $8 children; admission to all three is $21 adults, $12 children.

Children's Museum of the Lowcountry

Since it opened in 2003, this 10,000-square-foot, dynamic museum (25 Ann St., 843/853-8962, www.explorecml.org) has saved many a parent in Charleston on a rainy or otherwise blah day. Bring kids up to 12 years old here to play in the interactive exhibits and they'll leave knowing loads about the Lowcountry—it truly is an all-ages affair. One of most popular rooms finds juniors donning rubber boots and raincoats, and then smashing buttons to start stimulated storms over a model of the city. While they get to splash about with model boats and more, they learn how water cycles from cloud to rain to river. Another room is taken over by a shrimp boat, complete with radios, scales, and nets for the haul. Kids climb all over the boat (and the castle in another room), and while supervision is attentive, attendants truly let them play like real kids—boisterous and vivacious. There's an arts-and-crafts room, too, with its own set of programs, and other special workshops and fun days are offered year-round, plus summer camps. Open Tues.–Sat. 10 AM–6 PM, Sun. 1–6 PM. Admission is $5 per person.

Joseph Manigault House

Head to John Street and visit this house (350 Meeting St., 843/723-2926), a National Historic Landmark built in 1803 by amateur architect Gabriel Manigault, and considered to be the premier example of Adams-style architecture in the country. Open daily, $9 adults, $4 children. This home is owned by the Charleston Museum, which offers an $21 combination ticket that will get you into the Heyward-Washington House, the Joseph Manigault House, and the Charleston Museum. You don't have to see them on the same day, either. Or you can purchase a two-attraction ticket for $12. Call the Charleston Museum for information: 843/722-2996. Open Mon.–Sat. 10 AM–4:30 PM, Sun. 1–4:30 PM.

Aiken-Rhett House

And since you're in the neighborhood, take in the Aiken-Rhett House (48 Elizabeth St., 843/723-1159), which was begun in 1817. This is the former home of Governor William Aiken Jr., son of the first president of the South Carolina Canal and Railroad Company. This unique three-story home also served as headquarters for C. S. A. General P. G. T. Beauregard during the war. This house has been preserved pretty much as it was during the Aiken-Rhett days, with the original wallpaper, paint colors, and many of the original furnishings still there. Ask the staff at the museum for directions to the house. Admission to the Aiken-Rhett house is $10; admission to the Aiken-Rhett and the Nathaniel Russell House is $16 adults. Open Mon.–Sat. 10 AM–5 PM, Sun. 2–5 PM (last tour at 4:15).

The Confederate Museum

Above the Old City Market, the Daughters of the Confederacy run this museum (843/723-1541) in the restored monolith Market Head building. It includes war memorabilia like uniforms, swords, guns, cannons, and flags, mostly from the Lowcountry area. Open Tues.–Sat. 11 AM–3:30 PM. Rates are $5 adults, $3 children, those under six free.

Gibbes Museum of Art

This museum (135 Meeting St., 843/722-2706, www.gibbesmuseum.org) has presented outstanding collections of American art to the public since 1905, with an emphasis on portraits relating to Southern history. Artists represented include Benjamin West, Thomas Sully, and Rembrandt. The museum also includes Japanese wood-block prints and one of the world's best collections of miniatures, with more than 10,000 pieces. Each year, the Gibbes presents dozens of exhibitions by regional, national, and internationally known artists.

If you come for nothing else, come for the local artwork; Alice Ravenel Huger Smith, Anna Heyward Taylor, and other Lowcountry artists have created an impressive body of work focused on the Holy City. The museum also offers films, lectures, videos, talks, and symposia on the works and on the arts in general. Art classes for all ages are also held here quarterly, in case viewing all this fine work makes your palette hand twitch.

Allow yourself time to browse the museum shop as well. The building was erected as a memorial to James Shoolbred Gibbes; it's Charleston's best example of beaux arts architecture. Open Tues.–Sat. 10 AM–5 PM, Sun. 1–5 PM. Admission is $7 adults, $6 seniors, $4 children 6–18. Parking garages are on nearby Queen and Cumberland streets. All facilities are handicapped accessible.

Avery Research Center for African American History and Culture

Even if the College of Charleston weren't one of the most beautiful college campuses in America, the Avery Research Center (125 Bull St., 843/953-7609, www.cofc.edu/avery) would make it worth a visit. The research center, set in the restored 1868 Avery Normal School for freed persons, is a research center for documenting and preserving the history and culture of Lowcountry African Americans. It includes the Johns Island Collection of historical photographs and taped gospel music, a reading room, and archives. Until the African American heritage museum opens (sometime in 2007), Avery is your best place to learn about Lowcountry African American history. Open Mon.–Sat. noon–5 PM. Walk-in tours are of-

THE STONO UPRISING

Just as the fruits of leisure began to bloom in Charles Town, adversity struck again. Constantly trying to weaken the English colony in Carolina, Spain sent out operatives who made it known that the country offered freedom to any Carolinian slaves who could reach St. Augustine.

On September 9, 1739, at Stono Creek, a large number of African American slaves broke open a store from which they took weapons. They killed 21 whites, including women and children, and marched southward, killing every white in their path, encouraging other slaves to come with them, and burning numerous houses along the road. At 11:00 the next morning, Governor William Bull, riding back to Charles Town from Granville County with four other men, saw this fireball of human rage barreling down the road. Fortunately for him, he spotted them far enough away that he was able to hide until they had passed.

It's unfortunate for the slaves that they hadn't stolen horses as well as guns. Governor Bull rode to give notice to the Charles Town mi-

litia, which rode after the walking mob, catching up with them by four o'clock and shooting and hanging 44 of them. The surviving rebels escaped into the dense woods but were hunted down over the following weeks.

The uprising understandably frightened white Carolinians. "If such an attempt is made in a time of peace," Bull wondered, "what might be expected if an enemy should appear upon our frontier with a design to invade us?"

Over the next year, several minor insurrections arose across the colony and were put down. Numerous other plots for rebellion were uncovered, and no doubt many slaves and free blacks were unjustly implicated and tried for plans dreamed up only in the minds of anxious slave owners. Eventually, a law was passed requiring white men to go armed to church, in preparation for slave uprisings.

The slave code became stricter after the Stono uprising, but – talk about your thin silver linings – so did laws against the brutal maltreatment of slaves, which white Charlestonians saw as a factor in the rebellion.

fered Mon.–Fri. 2–4 PM, Sun. noon–5 PM. Donations requested.

American Military Museum

Here (360 Concord St., 843/723-9620, www.americanmilitarymuseum.org) you'll find uniforms and other artifacts from every branch of the service, collected from the American Revolution to the present. Admission is $6 adults, $2 children 12 and younger, free for military persons in uniform. Open Mon.–Sat. 10 AM–6 PM, Sun. 1–5 PM.

Patriots Point Naval and Maritime Museum

Among the exhibits here (40 Patriots Point Rd. Mount Pleasant, 843/884-2727 or 866/831-1720, www.patriotspoint.org), across the harbor from the city, you'll find a little thing called the aircraft carrier **USS Yorktown.** Those fascinated by things nautical can also

tour a submarine, a destroyer, and a re-creation of a Vietnam naval support base.

Clanging your way around these ships can be fascinating, although you should note that most of the tours are inaccessible to wheelchairs, and anyone may find the climbing from deck to deck something of a challenge, especially on a hot day. Also, claustrophobes should think twice before descending into the *Clagamore* submarine.

On the hangar deck of the USS *Yorktown,* you'll find the **Congressional Medal of Honor Museum** (40 Patriots Point Rd., Mount Pleasant, 843/884-8862), headquarters of the Congressional Medal of Honor Society. The Medal of Honor is the highest award for valor in action that the United States awards to service personnel. The museum is divided up into the nine eras of U.S. military history: the Civil War, Indian Campaigns, Wars of American Expansion, Peacetime, World War I, World

War II, Korea, Vietnam, and the Iraq war. Some of the recipients' names you'll probably recognize—Audie Murphy, Sergeant Alvin York—while others you may not, such as Marcario Garcia, who single-handedly assaulted two German machine-gun emplacements during World War II, and Brent Woods, one of the African American Indian fighters dubbed "buffalo soldiers" by their foes. Open daily 9 AM–6:30 PM. Admission is $14 adults, $7 kids 6–11.

⬛ Fort Sumter National Monument

Set on a man-made island begun in 1829, this fort had only recently been completed when U.S. Major Robert Anderson withdrew all the Federal troops from Sumter's hard-to-defend mainland sister forts (including Fort Moultrie on Sullivan's Island) and holed up out here in the middle of Charleston Harbor, awaiting relief from the North. When word came that Lincoln was sending a flotilla to supply the soldiers, the Southerners who had taken over the mainland forts fired the first shots of the Civil War. After getting bombed for 34 hours straight—a feat not duplicated until some Citadel upperclassmen on weekend leave did it in 1959—Anderson surrendered. Just two years later, Union troops working their way north from the landing at Hilton Head took over the Morris Island guns and returned the favor, bombarding the fort for two years—one of the longest sieges on the books. The Confederates finally evacuated in February 1865, and Charleston fell immediately afterward.

Today, to go out and tromp around this important American landmark you'll need to take a 2.5-hour boat tour either from Patriots Point in Mount Pleasant or from the terminal and Visitor Education Center at Liberty Square (360 Concord St.) beside the aquarium. (Handicap accessibility is provided at Liberty Square.) There is also a 90-minute tour that passes by the fort without stopping. Either way, call **Fort Sumter Tours** (360 Concord St., 843/722-2628 or 800/789-3678, www.spiritlinecruises.com). Admission is $13

HERMAN MELVILLE AND THE "STONE FLEET"

In December 1861, at the start of the Civil War, the U.S. government sent 16 old ships loaded with granite ballast up from newly captured Port Royal to the blockade line outside Charleston Harbor. There, the old ships were sunk to block the harbor from below. One Northern newspaper account crowed, "before two days are past it will have made Charleston an inland city."

Some Northerners called the move heartless on humanitarian grounds. To *Moby Dick* author Herman Melville of New York, it was a waste of good sea vessels. In "The Stone Fleet: An Old Sailor's Lament," he bemoans in particular the sinking of the *Tenemos*, a whaler in which he had sailed as a young man around Cape Horn. He calls the ships' scuttling "a pirate deed," and chides those in charge for the deed's futility, since ultimately it had no effect on Southern blockade-running:

And all for naught. The waters pass – Currents will have their way; Nature is nobody's ally; 'tis well; The harbor is bettered – will stay. A failure, and complete, Was your Old Stone Fleet.

---

adults, $12 seniors, $6 kids 6–11. Boats depart from Liberty Square daily at 9:30 AM, noon, and 2:30 PM; and they leave Patriots Point at 10:45 AM, 1:30 PM, and 4 PM. Arrive 30 minutes before departure for tickets and boarding.

Charles Pinckney National Historic Site

Take Highway 17 North through Mount Pleasant proper, pass the Isle of Palms Connector, and you'll come to Long Point Road, and the striking Christ Church, a Colonial-era, still-active Episcopal church that dates to the 1840s.

Turn left, follow the brown National Park Service (NPS) signs for about a mile or so, and you'll arrive at Charles Pinckney National Historic Site (1254 Long Point Rd., 843/881-5516), a 28-acre spot preserved from the former 715-acre Snee Farm, a plantation owned by Charles Pinckney (1757–1824), framer of the U.S. Constitution, four-time South Carolina governor, and U.S. Ambassador to Spain under President Jefferson, 1801–1805. Pinckney is one of those guys in the background of all the famous historical paintings like Louis S. Glanzman's *Signing of the Constitution,* where you can see Pinckney rubbing elbows with George Washington, James Madison, and other varsity squad Founding Fathers.

One of the things about historic sites like this one—and Fort Moultrie across the marshes on Sullivan's Island—is that they are not nearly as imposing as most NPS properties tend to be. It's a good spot to spend a couple of hours, though; George Washington did so back in 1791, while making his triumphant presidential tour of the South. Although no standing structures remain from the Pinckney era, the folks in the NPS have

turned a circa-1820 Lowcountry home into a nice visitors center and museum. It includes a display of the archaeological work going on here (more than 150,000 artifacts have been recovered thus far), as well as exhibits showing the efforts of the African American slaves (and, later, sharecroppers) who made Snee Farm successful. Self-guided walking tours. Open daily 9 AM–5 PM. Free admission, but donations appreciated.

The South Carolina Aquarium

This 93,000-square-foot marvel (100 Aquarium Wharf, 843/720-1990, www.scaquarium.org) features some 10,000 living organisms, representing 500 species indigenous to the state. The aquarium's more than 60 exhibits focus on the state's water life, beginning on the top floor with the Blue Ridge ecosystems of the northeast, then moving on to include life forms found in the state's rivers, swamps, and salt marshes (kids will love the otters), and off its shores (they'll love the sharks, too). The aquarium actually sticks some 200 feet out over the Cooper River, reinforcing the aquatic theme

© SEAN SLINSKY

The first shots of the Civil War took place at Fort Sumter.

ELIZA LUCAS PINCKNEY

When Charleston's Eliza Lucas Pinckney died of cancer in Philadelphia in 1793, President George Washington – at his own request – served as one of her pallbearers. This was a fitting finale to the life of one of America's most accomplished 18th-century women.

Born in the West Indies around 1722, Eliza came to Carolina with her family in 1738, at the age of 15. Her father, Major George Lucas, owned a large plantation overlooking Wappoo Creek "seventeen miles by land and six by water" from Charleston. The Lucases owned other plantations around the colony. In 1739, the political conflicts between Spain and England required the elder Lucas to return to his military post in Antigua. With her brothers attending school in England and her mother an invalid, Eliza was left to supervise the 600-acre Wappoo plantation (including its 20 slaves) and to maintain correspondence with the overseers who managed the plantations on the Combahee and Waccamaw.

Because many of the rice markets were unavailable now that they were at war with Spain, at her father's suggestion Eliza began methodically experimenting with raising indigo. In 1740, 1741, and on through 1744 she experimented with raising a promising grade of indigo. By the end of 1744 she had impressed the British government, which wanted the dark blue dye for their uniforms.

By 1745, the Lucases were making a large income from the crop. The sales saved the family's Wappoo plantation. In 1744 Eliza married Charles Pinckney, South Carolina's first native lawyer, a widower more than twice her age. He built her a home in Charleston overlooking the harbor, and they also lived on the Belmont Plantation on the Cooper River. Eliza bore four children, three of whom lived to adulthood; her daughter, Harriet, ended up marrying into the Horry family of Hampton Plantation and competently managed that plantation after her husband died. Eliza's two sons, Charles Cotesworth and Thomas, became important Ameri-

can leaders during the Revolutionary period. After spending five years living in England, the family returned to the colonies in 1758, whereupon the elder Charles was struck immediately with malaria. He died in Mount Pleasant and is buried in St. Philip's churchyard.

Eliza survived her grief and went on to take care of the family's long-neglected Belmont Plantation, along with the islands they owned near Hilton Head (today known as Pinckney Island), the Pinckney Plains plantation west of the upper Ashley, the 1,000-acre Auckland tract on the Ashepoo River, and several others. She also oversaw two homes on East Bay Street in Charleston.

During the Revolution, Eliza's slaves deserted the plantation for the British camps, where they were promised freedom, although smallpox broke out there immediately and many died. Charles Cotesworth Pinckney became a brigadier general by war's end and was elected to the General Assembly in 1782. He was named one of South Carolina's delegates to the national Constitutional Convention in 1787. That same year Thomas had been elected governor of the state, and the following year he presided at the State Convention that ratified the Constitution. Both men were national candidates for the Federalist party; when President Washington made a tour of the South in 1791, he stopped at Hampton Plantation for breakfast with the Pinckneys and Horrys.

Just a year later, Eliza journeyed to Philadelphia to consult a doctor famous for cancer cures. She died there on May 26, 1793, and was buried the next day, with President Washington as one of her pallbearers. She was 70 years old.

The Letterbook of Eliza Lucas Pinckney includes a fascinating collection of letters, most from her indigo-experimenting years, but spanning in all 1739–1762. You can pick up a copy in almost any South Carolina library, as well as from Sandlapper Publishing.

and giving guests the chance to spot the dolphins who frequent the waters.

Built in a former industrial area—part of it a federal Superfund site—the aquarium is the centerpiece of Joe Riley's master plan for this part of the Cooper River. Next door, at the newly lain Liberty Square, is the new Visitor Education Center and boats to Fort Sumter. The total improvement to the area cost more than $100 million (the aquarium itself cost $47 million), but the project has boosted Charleston's already high ratings as a desirable vacation and relocation destination. The aquarium is pleasant, built for lingering rather than filing-through in a hurry; be sure to take in the ocean breezes out on the rocking chairs on the second-floor balcony, overlooking the harbor.

Admission is $15 adults, $13 seniors, $8 kids 3–11, free for kids 2 and under and students. Open daily mid-Apr.–mid-Aug., 9 AM–6 PM; otherwise 9 AM–5 PM. Closed major holidays.

While you're down here, you might want to see what the current offering is next door at the **Charleston IMAX Theatre** (360 Concord St., 843/725-4629, www.Charlestonimax.com). Tickets for a standard (i.e., 2-D) IMAX film are $8.50 adults, $7.50 children 3–11; slightly more if you add another dimension.

The Citadel

North of the Crosstown in the heart of Hampton Park, the Citadel Military College (171 Moultrie St., 843/953-6726 or 800/868-3294, www.citadel.edu) moved over here to the banks of the Ashley River in 1922, after 80 years at Marion Square. The Old Citadel building was originally built in 1822 after the reputed Vesey conspiracy was uncovered, as a place for whites to hole up in the event of another slave uprising. Although this first building originally kept a standing army of professional soldiers—as did the Arsenal, now the Governor's House, in Columbia—Governor Peter Richardson suggested in 1842 that it would be cheaper and smarter to replace the professional soldiers with young men who could both provide protection and receive military and "practical" training.

By 1861, the two schools merged into the single South Carolina Military Academy.

On January 9, 1861, Citadel cadets stationed on Morris Island fired the first shot of the War for Southern Independence, firing on the Union steamer *Star of the West* as it attempted to reprovision the Union soldiers garrisoned at Fort Sumter. After the war, Union soldiers occupied the old campus until 1881, after which the South Carolina Military Academy reopened under the state's jurisdiction and quickly became the training ground for the state's business and political leaders. In 1919, the City of Charleston donated the present 200-acre site to the college, which was in need of expansion.

When you get there, just tell the cadet at the gate to direct you to the museum. You'll find the **Citadel Museum** (171 Moultrie St., 843/953-6846) on the third floor of the Daniel Library, the first building to your right inside the main gate. The museum features the history of the Citadel, with photographs highlighting exhibits that attempt to document the military, academic, social, and athletic aspects of cadet life. Open Sun.–Fri. 2–5 PM, Sat. noon–5 PM. Closed major holidays. Free.

Next to the library is the Summerall Chapel. If you go inside, walk quietly—the poor harassed first-year cadets ("knobs") sometimes sneak in here to take a nap on a pew. If it's Christmastime, ask around and see when they've scheduled the candlelight service (sometime the first week in December), a memorable spectacle that you'll want to catch, if possible.

Of course, the most famous Citadel graduate of the past 50 years is novelist Pat Conroy, who drew on his experiences here to write two of his earliest books: 1970s' *The Boo,* a nonfiction biography of Thomas Nugent "The Boo" Courvoisie, the Commandant of Cadets during Conroy's time there, and 1980s' fictional *The Lords of Discipline,* also set at the Citadel. In *Lords,* Conroy changes the school's name to "The Institute" and changes The Boo's name to "The Bear." Folks at the Citadel don't generally take to the latter book, which revolves

UPON THIS TAINTED HAM...

When cadet Pat Conroy attended the Citadel in the late 1960s, he spent most of his time in Capers Hall (home of the English Department), named for one of the most distinguished graduates of the Citadel, Confederate General, Episcopal Bishop, and Sewanee Chancellor Ellison Capers, class of 1857.

Apparently, Capers was always a man of deep spiritual devotion. The following prayer is attributed to him while he was a cadet here. Tom Law, one of Capers' fellow cadets, recorded the prayer thus:

Lord of love
Look from above
Upon this tainted ham;
And give us meat
That's fit to eat
For this ain't worth a damn.

around corruption in the ranks of the cadets and the school administration. In fact, when *Lords* was made into a movie, the filmmakers had to film the campus scenes at an institute up north. Since then, Conroy and his alma mater have made amends, and his last Dawg-centric book (*My Losing Season*), a nonfiction account of his senior year on the college basketball team, is a popular read for alumni and students alike.

Despite the media scrutiny of the mid-1990s over the school's single-sex status, the Citadel has educated and awarded degrees to female students for decades through its evening programs. Now, however, a few female cadets are members of the Corps of Cadets; on weekends it's common to see them in their gray uniforms, browsing with male cadet friends amid the shops of King Street.

Some male cadets express resentment at having been forbidden the single-sex educational experience they wanted; others say that as long as female cadets are held to the same standard,

they'll be happy. Fortunately for all concerned, after the Shannon Faulkner debacle, the bulk of subsequent female cadets have more than held their own.

At Mark Clark Hall, where you'll find a canteen and gift shop, both open to civilians. Guided tours of the college are available during the school year; a self-guided tour brochure is available at the school public safety office.

EAST COOPER AREA
Mount Pleasant

The East Cooper area includes beautiful antebellum Mount Pleasant, fun-and-sun Isle of Palms, and historic Sullivan's Island. Mount Pleasant is a subtly beautiful Lowcountry town founded in 1680. Erase the cars parked on the sides of the narrow streets in the historic district and you can well imagine that it's 1859 here. Not surprisingly, even many island dwellers consider a move inland to Mount Pleasant a move "up." Novelists Bret Lott and Josephine Humphries and former Milwaukee Brewers star Gorman Thomas all call the town home.

Other than the Patriots Point Naval and Maritime Museum, and Boone Hall Plantation, one of the best things to do in Mount Pleasant is to walk around the Old Village.

Development has taken its toll, particularly north of town, but the Mount Pleasant Commercial Design Review Board has had some effect on curtailing the madness. Credit them with the walkable **Mount Pleasant Towne Centre** (on Hwy. 17, just south of the Isle of Palms Connector), a well-landscaped and -configured outdoor mall featuring homey touches like summer block parties and holiday carriage rides.

Isle of Palms and Sullivan's Island

On the north lip of Charleston Harbor, Sullivan's Island is a beautiful southern beach retreat, home of Fort Moultrie, which was the site of a famous Revolutionary battle, the burial place of great Seminole chief Osceola (who died while incarcerated here), and sometime home of Edgar Allan Poe (who, while stationed here, found the settings for such famous stories as *The Gold Bug,* and, some argue, *Fall of the House of Usher*), and Lieutenant (later General) William Tecumseh Sherman. Along with Fort Wagner on the southern side of the harbor, Fort Moultrie was designed to work in unison with Fort Sumter in providing protection for Charleston Harbor. Hence it's doubly ironic that Moultrie's guns were used for firing on the Union-held Sumter at the start of the Civil War.

The Breach Inlet between Isle of Palms and Sullivan's Island has made the history books twice. First, during the American Revolution, British General Cornwallis landed a regiment of troops on Isle of Palms and tried to sneak them south across the shallow inlet and onto the north end of Sullivan's Island. They hoped to rear-surprise the Americans holding down the palmetto-log fortress on Sullivan's southern tip, but unfortunately for Cornwallis, the inlet proved treacherous. While attempting to march across its swift currents, dozens of his men drowned or were picked off midstream by American sharpshooters. The British retreated.

In the 1860s Confederate soldiers launched the *Hunley*—claimed by some as the world's first successful submarine—from Breach Inlet's shore. Pedaled by one man and steered by another, the sub slipped southward around Sullivan's Island and successfully planted and exploded a bomb on one of the Union ships blockading Charleston Harbor, but sank itself (with all hands) in the process. The wreck of this pioneer sub was finally discovered in 1995 by a team headed by popular novelist Clive Cussler. It turned out to be much smaller than historians had believed. After much debate over whether the ship should be raised, it was—in the summer of 2000, right about the time the Confederate battle flag came down from the capitol in Columbia.

Today, besides some great kiteboarding, Sullivan's Island is best known for its unpretentious but expensive homes (some built in former military bunkers), a handful of nice seafood restaurants, and Fort Moultrie, now

© SEAN SLINSKY

One of the most expensive zip codes in the country, Sullivan's Island is home to a mix of cottages, giant beach houses, and the occasional bunker-turned-home.

THE BATTLE OF SULLIVAN'S ISLAND

With war erupting in and around Boston, the British decided that their best strategy was to take advantage of the strong loyalist support in the Southern colonies, beginning a military drive from the Carolina coast – at either Wilmington or Charles Town – that might sweep through the South Carolina Upcountry, gathering men, and then on through North Carolina and Virginia to sandwich Washington in the north.

Realizing this, the Continentals sent English professional soldier General Charles Lee down to Charles Town to oversee the town's defense. After inspecting the palmetto log fort at the southern tip of Sullivan's Island, protecting the mouth of the harbor, and after noting that its isolation left its defenders no avenue of retreat, he declared it a "slaughterhouse" and ordered it closed. The stubborn Colonel William Moultrie said he and his men could hold the fort, even if the British guns blasted away the earthworks and the Americans had to hide behind the piles of rubble to await the landing party. On this advice, South Carolina President Rutledge refused to evacuate it. And so it was that on June 18, 1776, as British troop ships sailed to Charles Town, prepared to first seize Sullivan's Island and then the town, they found the fort expertly manned by Colonel William Moultrie and a garrison of men who fought as though their lives depended on it.

Having found Wilmington firmly in patriot hands, Sir Henry Clinton continued south and landed 2,000-3,000 men on Long Island (now Isle of Palms), just a narrow inlet to the north of Sullivan's. The plan was that at the same moment the nine British ships began shelling the fort, these trained soldiers would rush across the shallow Breach Inlet, overtake the Americans guarding the opposite shore, and proceed southward down the island to overtake the fort.

Unfortunately for the plan, the Breach Inlet was five feet deeper than British intelligence had said it was. The Brits could not "rush" across, but would have to be ferried across by longboat. The extra time it would take to row versus wade would slow down the process considerably because there were only boats enough for 600 redcoats to cross at once, and because 780 Americans under Colonel William Thomson had dug into reinforcements on the opposite shore to prevent just such an attack.

Communication broke down. The infantry on Long Island were as surprised as the Ameri-

---

part of Fort Sumter National Monument. The Sullivan's Island Lighthouse, at Station 18½ on Middle Street, is the most modern lighthouse in the United States. Built in 1962, it's 140 feet tall, shines a light that can be seen 26 miles out to sea, and features an elevator. It's closed to the public.

Isle of Palms was developed relatively recently—around the turn of the 20th century—and for a long time was accessible only by ferry. In the early 1900s it became a tourist destination, with a giant pavilion and the second-largest Ferris wheel in the world spinning high overhead. Hurricanes inspired renovation of the town's layout, and today the Isle of Palms, while still a tourist destination, largely serves as the beach for East Cooper residents and is home to a favorite dinner destination

for Charlestonians—The Boathouse at Breach Inlet. The north part of the island, which was untouched jungle until the 1970s, is now the home of the Wild Dunes Resort, a megaplex of jungle condos, bungalows, and golf courses. Wild Dunes is a popular destination for people boating the East Coast along the Intracoastal Waterway.

Fort Moultrie (1214 Middle St., Sullivan's Island, 843/883-3123, www.nps.gov/fomo) is officially a part—the larger part—of Fort Sumter National Monument, and features a visitors center where you should take time to watch the short but worthwhile film that gives the history of the fort. The present-day Fort Moultrie is, in a sense, the third fort to occupy the south end of Sullivan's. The first was the palmetto-log fort that took a beating cans when the British ships swooped in closer and opened fire. Uncertain about what exactly the navy had in mind, and facing severe losses if they tried the assault, the infantry decided to wait until the ships had silenced the Carolinian guns before attempting the crossing. A captain of the British 37th regiment assigned to Long Island wrote: "Very fortunately for us it was not attempted, for in the opinion of all present, from what we have since learned, the first embarkations must have fallen a sacrifice."

Around 11 AM, the British ships continued on to a point 300 yards (900 yards, according to one British source) from shore, dropped anchor, and opened fire. Moultrie and his 400-plus South Carolinians had little powder and had to ration their shots, but to everyone's surprise, including the relieved Carolinians, the spongy palmetto logs absorbed the British salvos. Still, some shots got through, eventually killing 11 Carolinians and wounding 50 more.

"I never experienced a hotter fire," General Charles Lee, who visited the fort midbattle, later wrote General Washington. But his description reveals that despite 12 hours of this unrelenting barrage, Moultrie's men were brave:

The noble fellows who were mortally wounded conjured their brethren never to abandon the standard of liberty. Those who lost their limbs deserted not their posts. Upon the whole, they acted like Romans in the third century.

No one's quite sure why the British decided they needed to overtake Sullivan's Island first before taking Charleston; possibly they feared entering the harbor and thus exposing themselves to both the guns set up on the southern side of the harbor as well as Moultrie's. Presumably, had they won Sullivan's Island, they would have established a base of operations on the relatively secure site, from which they might begin taking Charleston.

When the British troops on Long Island awoke the next day, they saw that their British boats had disappeared. In truth, the British ships had lost hundreds of men. A few weeks later, complaining that "The heat of the weather now is almost become intolerable," the sweltering Brits were picked up by British naval vessels and taken north to other perils. This key victory caused the British to rethink their strategy and abandon the South for nearly three years.

but held during a fierce June 28, 1776, battle against nine British warships. The current fort, its 15-foot walls encompassing 1.5 acres, was completed in 1809, although improvements, including radar, continued on through World War II. During the Civil War, Fort Moultrie held some 40 guns and 500 Confederate soldiers, who weathered a 20-month siege that began in 1863. In 1947, when new technological advances made the fort obsolete, Fort Moultrie was deactivated, after 171 years of service. Since its adoption as a national park site in 1961, the interior of the fort has been restored with various weapons and fortifications spanning from the 1820s through World War II.

Private Edgar Allan Poe pulled sentry duty on these walls in the 1820s. Ten years later,

Lieutenant William T. Sherman served here as well, developing an affection for the city that would serve it well at the end of the Civil War.

Out in front of the fort on Middle Street, you'll see the small, fenced grave of Osceola, leader of the Seminole resistance to President Andrew Jackson's relocation of all Native American tribes to the west side of the Mississippi. U.S. troops caught Osceola in 1837 and brought him north to Fort Moultrie, where he was by most accounts given reasonable freedoms (for a prisoner) and treated with respect by his captors. Famed American artist George Catlin hurried here and captured Osceola on canvas, finding him "ready to die. . . cursing the white man. . . to the end of his breath." That end came shortly thereafter: Osceola died here in 1838, far from his beloved Florida homeland.

A major outcry arose here in 1999 when, while nobody was looking, a developer threw up a row of condos an arm's length from Fort Moultrie. Fortunately, The Trust for Public Lands, a private, nonprofit organization in Washington, D.C., stepped in to buy the land, demolish the houses, and preserve the views. Fort Moultrie is open daily 9 AM–5 PM. Closed major holidays. Partially wheelchair accessible. No fee is charged to tour the visitors center, but a small fee—$3—is charged to enter the fort.

Stella Maris Catholic Church (1204 Middle St., 843/883-3108, www.catholic-DOC.org/stellamarris.org), near the fort, is an interesting and quaint old church, which, rather than featuring a large crucifix above the altar, features a statue of Mary holding the baby Jesus. Mass Sat. 5:30 PM; Sun. 8 AM, 9:30 AM, 11:30 AM, 5:30 PM; Mon., Tues., Wed., Fri. 8 AM; Thurs. 7 PM.

One other thing to see before you leave the island: Down on I'On Street you'll see some interesting homes, but by far the most interesting ones are those built in the old bomb-proof artillery installations. To see one of these, head over the north tip of island and I'On Street. There's a group of three battery homes here, but since they are private property be sure to stay on the street.

Entertainment and Events

Check free indie weekly *Charleston City Paper* (www.charlestoncitypaper.com) or *Preview*, the free weekend insert from the *Post and Courier* (www.charleston.net), for the latest goings-on. Both are available at area bars and restaurants.

FESTIVALS

Historic Charleston Foundation's **Annual Festival of Houses and Gardens** (108 Meeting St., 843/722-3405, www.historiccharleston.org) runs mid-March to mid-April, and gives you the chance to visit privately owned historic sites. The monthlong program includes afternoon and evening walking tours and special programs and events. Call well in advance for tickets ($45).

The Preservation Society of Charleston (147 King St., 843/722-4630, www.preservationsociety.org) founded in 1920, runs the **Annual Fall Candlelight Tours of Homes and Gardens** in October. For nearly six weeks, visitors are welcomed into well-heeled homes and gardens in the historic district. Call well in advance for tickets ($45).

Spoleto Festival U.S.A.

This world-famous international arts festival—begun in historic, aesthetically blessed Spoleto, Italy—chose similarly blessed Charleston when establishing its America-based counterpart festival in 1977. For 17 days each late May and early June, Charleston's streets, parks, auditoriums, and stages are taken over with experimental and traditional works by artisans from China, Europe, Russia, Africa, and beyond. The festival's finger-on-the-international-pulse producers pack more than 130 groundbreaking dance, music, opera, and theater performances into these truly exhilarating two-plus weeks. The sheer volume and variety of shows means there's truly something for everyone (chamber music or classical one-ring circus, anyone?); and because the smorgasbord usually means 4 or 5 events daily during the week and up to 12 per day on the weekends, even the most Faustian traveler can satiate their cultural appetite. With rickshaws scooting ticket-holders off to shows, and every restaurant buzzing with the audience members recounting their most recently attended events, the Spoleto experience is not to be missed. Contact the Spoleto Festival USA (14 George St., 843/722-2764, www.spoletousa.org) or box office (843/579-3100) starting in November for more information.

Piccolo Spoleto Festival

Piccolo Spoleto (843/554-6060, www.piccolospoleto.com) runs concurrently with Spoleto, and offers regional and national talent at low to free admission prices. Some of the most enthusiastically attended free events include: the open-air reggae Block Party and Charleston Symphony orchestra shows at the Customs House by Waterfront Park; the Marion Square art-and-crafts festival; and the children's parade and shows. With bluegrass and jazz bands playing outdoors, singer-songwriters and gospel choirs performing in local churches, indie theater troupes and comedians on stage everywhere, it's a dynamic counterpart to its big-sister festival. Call the City of Charleston Office of Cultural Affairs (843/724-7305) for a schedule.

MOJA Arts Festival

Talk about taking a lemon and making lemonade: Charleston served as the port of entry for most of the slaves imported to the United States; from this grim historical fact each fall arises this joyous early-fall festival (843/724-7305, www.mojafestival.com) focusing on the area's rich African American and Caribbean heritages. The festival's name is appropriate, considering that it's dedicated to unity (*moja* is the Swahili word for "one"). Contact the Charleston Office of Cultural Affairs for schedules and ticket information.

CONCERT VENUES

The 2,300-seat **North Charleston Performing Arts Center** (5001 Coliseum Dr. N., 843/529-5050, www.colesiumpac.com) catches most of the big rock and country acts these days, as well as ice shows, Broadway plays, and various other events. Tickets to Coliseum events are available at the Coliseum Ticket Office (843/529-5000) and at all Ticketmaster (843/554-6060) outlets.

The **Music Farm** (32-C Ann St., 843/853-3276 or 843/722-8904, www.musicfarm.com) is legendary in the area for giving local bands a place to open for traveling college-circuit bands, and for attracting nationally known acts. **Cumberland's** (301 King St., 843/577-9469, www.cumberlands.net) and **Windjammer** (1008 Ocean

LOWCOUNTRY SPIRITUALS

The Lowcountry has produced some of America's most popular spirituals. "We Shall Overcome," the anthem of the Civil Rights Movement in the 1960s, began as a Johns Island folk song. The even better known (and much-recorded) "Michael Row Your Boat Ashore" had its beginnings in Beaufort. Northern teachers and missionaries present in Beaufort during the Civil War heard the song belted out by African Americans as they rowed the ferryboats from the landing at the foot of Beaufort's Carteret Street across the Beaufort River to the opposite shore of Lady's Island, now known as Whitehall Landing. Some of the missionaries wrote down the words and music, and the song appeared for the first time in the 1867 book *Slave Songs of the United States:*

Michael Row the Boat Ashore
Michael row the boat ashore, hallelujah,
Michael boat a Gospel boat, hallelujah.
Michael boat a music boat, hallelujah,
Gabriel blow the trumpet horn, hallelujah.
O you mind your boastin' talk, hallelujah,
Boastin' talk will sink your soul, hallelujah.
Jordan stream is wide and deep, hallelujah,
Jesus stand on th' other side, hallelujah.

Common wisdom has it that the "Michael" of the song is the archangel mentioned in the Bible. Whether he ever worked in the Beaufort area as a boatman is unknown. Why Michael has to row while Gabriel gets to play his horn is also unknown.

Blvd., 843/886-8596, www.windjammer.com) are other major places to find live acts, although they're certainly not the only ones. Check the free indie weekly *Charleston City Paper* (www.charlestoncitypaper.com) or *Preview,* the free weekend insert from the *Post and Courier* (www.charleston.net), to find out who's playing where.

NIGHTLIFE

Charleston's after-dark offerings are as varied as its population: There are bars for prepsters, hangouts for college students, lounges and wine bars for the chic-inclined, pubs for beerhounds, sports bars for scorekeepers, dance clubs for Travolta-ites, a cigar club for puffers, and meat markets for conventioneers. Intermingling is more than welcome, so check out the following list of best picks. While these mostly center on the action-oriented downtown, there are other spots in the greater area; check outlying area dining listings for the best spots, as the bars there usually piggyback on those restaurants. Finally, last call is usually at 1:30 AM, because downtown bars close at 2 AM.

Clubs with Music

Love the nightlife? Got to boogie? One of the best places to catch live acts downtown is also the one of the oldest: the aforementioned small and smoky **Cumberland's** (301 King St., 843/577-9469, www.cumberlands.net). If you're lucky, you'll be here for Monday metal karaoke night; or for the annual Lowcountry Blues Society Blues Jam emceed by DJ Shrimp City Slim. **Mistral Restaurant** (99 S. Market St., 843/722-5708), a cozy little French restaurant with a bar, features live blues and jazz Mon.–Thurs. and a terrific Dixieland Jazz band Fri–Sat.

The previously mentioned **Music Farm** (32-C Ann St., 843/853-3276 or 843/722-8904, www.musicfarm.com), is run by a young duo who book the nationally popular alt acts that attract locals and college kids alike. Ticket prices vary but range from free to $20. They are available Mon.–Fri. noon–4 PM at the box office window (32-C Ann St.); cash only, or online (www.etix.com).

In West Ashley, **J. B. Pivots Beach Club** (1662 Hwy. 17, 843/571-3668, www.pivots-beachclub.com) sits just behind Shoney's and offers a Shag Night on Tues., with beginner lessons. Sat. usually features live entertainment.

At the **Windjammer** (1008 Ocean Blvd., 843/886-8596, www.windjammer.com), it's always spring break. Downstairs there's a fenced-in outdoor area with volleyball courts, where various professional volleyball tournaments are held. Live music is played here most nights; Hootie and the Blowfish have been known to try out new music here; and sometimes the club even hosts local theater.

Over on the Isle of Palms, **Coconut Joe's** (1120 Ocean Blvd., 843/886-0046) is a great place to sit up top and listen to reggae on the roof with crashing waves in the background.

Trio Club & Lounge (139 Calhoun St., 843/965-5333) is a half-breed: Upstairs it's a DJed hip-hop dance club; downstairs it's a crowded live R&B band venue. It's a two-great-tastes-that-taste-well-together combo for a wide-range demo.

For pure dancing downtown, DJs, pulsing bass, and flashing lights included, head to **City Bar** (192 E. Bay St., 843/577-7383) in your best strut-wear. There's a dress-well code at the front door, and the scene is usually twenty- to thirty-something hotties trying to score each other's digits. For 1980s and 1990s mixes that attract those wanting first to shake their money makers, and *then* check out the opposite sex, head to the similar demographic at **213 Top of the Bay** (213 E. Bay St., 843/722-1311). The most cross-pollinated age-wise of the DJed group is **Bar 145** (145 Calhoun St., 843/853-6687).

Lounges, Wine Bars, and Cocktails

Just as the tapas scene has come to town, so has the lounge, wine bar, and martini culture arrived. These spots are for those who have dollars to spare and prefer a see-and-be-seen crowd. Though of-the-moment fashions and bubbly talk is the general order, there's room for more laid-back types, too, as it's still equal-opportunity Charleston. Some of the best downtown: Upper King's cool **Chai's Lounge & Tapas** (462 King St., 843/722-7313); the smokey, puffer-haven **Club Havana** (177 Meeting St., 843/853-5008, www.clubhavana.com), upstairs from the Tinder Box cigar shop; the velvet-laden, hookah pipe–populated **Torch** (545 King St., 843/723-9333); the local young professional and gourmand hot spot **McCrady's Wine Bar and Lounge** (155 E. Bay St., 843/577-0025).

Also, several downtown restaurants—**FIG** (232 Meeting St., 843/805-5900, www.eatatfig.com), **39 Rue de Jean** (39 John St., 843/722-8881, www.39Ruedejean.com), and **The Pavilion Rooftop Bar** (22 E. Bay St., 877/440-2250, www.marketpavilion.com), for instance—have hopping bars with great drinks and eats and scenesters, as well, without some of the pretense of the other spots. Last, **The Rooftop Bar and Restaurant** (23 Vendue Range, 843/577-7970, www.vendueinn.com) is on the top floor of The Library Restaurant at Vendue Inn; head here for a (slightly obscured) view across Charleston Harbor, live music, a covered deck, and open-air wining and dining in the most casual setting of this category.

Neighborhood Hangouts and Pubs

The Blind Tiger (38 Broad St., 843/577-0088), attracts one of the most varied aged crowds in town, and tends to be more local and khakied than other bars near the College, Old City Market, and Upper King Street area. There's a rambling outdoor courtyard worth hiding out in.

Tommy Condon's (160 Market St., 843/577-3818, www.tommycondons.com) may be in the touristy Old City Market area, but it's still a winner among visitors and residents both, thanks to the festive live Irish music bands that play five days a week. **Vickery's Beaufain Street Bar and Grill** (15 Beaufain St., 843/577-5300, www.vickerys.com) is just hidden enough at Beaufain and Archdale streets to remain mostly local and definitely mellow for all ages; its outdoor patio stays full nearly year-round.

If luck deserts and you're still unaccompanied (or hungry for a burger) when the disco balls stop spinning, stumble to the Upper King Street area and this small, smoky, late-night dive: **AC's Bar and Grill** (467 King St., 843/577-6742); it's a Charleston last-call standard.

Gay and Lesbian

Gays and lesbians are welcome at any clubs mentioned here, and others in the Charleston area as well, but gay-specific spots downtown include **Dudley's** (42 Ann St., 843/723-2784) and **Club Pantheon** (28 Ann St., 843/577-2582, www.clubpantheon.com). Beyond downtown, West Ashley's **Patrick's** (1377 Ashley River Rd., 843/571-3435, www.patrickspub.net) is popular; as is North Charleston's cozy **Deja Vu II** (4628 Spruill Ave., 843/554-5959, www.dejavuii.com).

Brewpubs

Southend Brewery and Smokehouse (161 E. Bay St., 843/853-4677, www.southendbrewery.com) features handcrafted microbrewed beers, smoked ribs and chicken, and a third-floor cigar lounge, with billiard tables. I never pass up a chance to ride in a glass elevator, so up I went to the third floor, tracing the brass path of the steam vent of one of the brewing tanks as we rose. Up on the third floor they have TVs tuned to sporting events and a nice view of the entire restaurant. It's really a wonderful location and a good place to watch the game. Expect to spend $7–18 for some worthy burgers, pizza, pasta, and "brew-b-cue." Southend has become so popular that today you can find sister locations up in North Carolina in Charlotte and Raleigh.

THEATER VENUES

The **Charleston Stage Company** the state's largest theater company, offers first-rate theatrical performances at the historic Dock Street Theater, producing more than 120 performances a year. To learn about shows, contact the box office (843/965-4032 or 800/454-7093) Mon.–Fri. 10 AM–5 PM or the troupe (www.charlestonstage.com).

The HaveNots! (280 Meeting St., 843/853-6687, www.thehavenots.com) comedy improv company plays Sat. nights at 8 PM in Theatre 99, located above a bicycle shop downtown. Other gut-splitting shows run throughout the week, and the group also runs an annual comedy festival in January. Tickets range $8 –12.50.

The **Footlight Players Theatre** (20 Queen St., 843/722-7521 or 843/722-4487, www.footlightplayers.com) is in the quaint French Quarter near the Dock Street Theater and offers a wide range of shows regularly; box office hours are Mon.–Fri. noon–5 PM, or until curtain on performance days.

Pure Theatre (701 E. Bay St., Ste. 1017, 843/723-4444, www.puretheatre.org) is the youngest of the mix, and offers contemporary, cutting-edge, provocative, and often new works by local and national playwrights.

CINEMAS

Calling the **Charleston IMAX Theatre** (360 Concord St., 843/725-4629, www.charlestonimax.com), a "cinema" is a bit like calling Charlestonians a tad nostalgic, but it does show films, of the five-story-high and often 3-D variety.

For a multiscreen suburban theater, head over to Mount Pleasant for **Movies at Mt. Pleasant** (963 Houston Northcutt Blvd., 843/884-4900, www.easternfederal.com) or the even nicer **Palmetto Grande 16** (1319 Theatre Dr., 843/216-8696, www.movietickets.com). Indie and foreign film fans head to James Island for **The Terrace** (1956 Maybank Hwy., 843/762-9494, www.terracetheater.com).

COFFEE SHOPS AND CAFÉS

While Charleston does have its fair share of coffee shops, Savannah's lesser-numbered offerings tend to have better all-hours ambience. Still, though, the Charleston variety have their charm. **East Bay Coffeehouse** (159 E. Bay St., 843/723-3446) is the best in town, and has live music, couches and tables, and a mellow vibe. In addition to light eats, they serve alcohol as well. Open daily 7 AM–11ish PM; bar open later, depending on customer flow.

Kaminsky's Most Excellent Café (78 N. Market St., 843/853-8270) in the Old City Market, is one of the best places to get dessert in Charleston—that is, if you have a sweet tooth as big as their giant desserts and can weather the tourist fray and the usual line. Beautiful dark-wood paneling, incredibly indulgent desserts, and a wide selection of wine add to the experience. Open daily, noon–2 AM.

Port City Java is a small chain of coffeehouses with several Charleston locations. Two of the best are downtown, one at the Francis Marion Hotel (387 King St., 843/853-5282), and one next to MUSC hospital (261 Calhoun St., 843/937-9352). Both serve coffeehouse cuisine including the usual baked goods, paninis ($6.75), wraps ($6.50), and salads ($4.25–8.95), along with its smooth espressos and other coffees and teas. Open daily 6:30 AM–8 PM.

Like nearly every other American town with a stoplight, Charleston now has its share of **Starbucks.** Both lower downtown locations—one on King Street (239 King St., 843/805-8007) and one on Calhoun (168 Calhoun St., 843/805-8005) by the College of Charleston—are worth visits, as the first is in an old bank, and the second is in a tiny house that for years was the area's local breakfast diner. The most generous hours of any in the chain are at the King Street location: Open Sun.–Thurs. 6 AM–10 PM, Fri.–Sat. 6 AM–midnight.

Shopping

King Street

King Street is the single best shopping street in Charleston and residents separate it into three main districts: Lower King, from Broad to Market streets; Middle King, from Market to Calhoun streets; and Upper King, from Calhoun to Cannon streets. Each has a unique flavor and personality and dividing and conquering according to your interests is the best approach. (A few must-mentions here are one or two streets off King, but in the same basic district.)

Lower King sports the highest price tags in town, and is home to the finest antique and home stores, plus the best clothiers (outside Charleston Place's interior mall, where Gucci and St. Johns sit). You can't go wrong browsing here, but be sure to stop in at **South of Market** (173 King St., 843/723-1114, www.southof-market.biz) for French country home accessories; **Livingstons' Antiques** (163 King St., 843/556-6162) for 200-year-old English

finds; **George C Birlant & Co.** (191 King St., 843/722-3842) for silver and chandeliers; and **Queen Charlotte Antiques** (61 Queen St., 843/722-9121) for stone garden decor.

In the Middle King area, chain retail clothing stores show up to make the area an outdoor mall with the requisite Gap, Banana Republic, Abercromie & Fitch, J. Crew, Urban Outfitters, Pottery Barn, Willims-Sonoma, and on. Peppered in between these, you'll find some local gems, from boutique dress shops to home goods and music stores. This part of King is most frequented by college students and the general population, tourists and locals alike. Don't miss the outdoor lover's **Halfmoon Outfitters** (280 King St., 843/853-0990, www.halfmoonout-fitters.com); the kitchen nut's **Fred** (237 King St., 843/723-5699, www.fredstore.com); the saucy card addict's **Metropolitan Deluxe** (164 Market St.; 843/722-0436 or metropolitan-deluxe.com.); the interior design snob's **ESD Designs** (314 King St.,843/577-6272); the

© SEAN SLINSKY

King Street is the backbone of Charleston shopping.

bargain outlet lover's **Oops** (326 King St., 843/722-7768); the indie music lover's **52.5** (75 Wentworth St., 843/722-3525 www.corporaterocksucks.com). . . or the more mainstream (but still locally owned) **Millennium Music** (372 King St., 843/853-1999).

The Upper King district is an evolving area with once low but increasingly rising rents that give an eclectic mix of shops. Here, you'll find Waterworks, the gourmet bath chain, and the locally owned **Dwelling** (474 King St., 843/723-9699), a modern furniture and art store; **Lulan Artisans** (69 King St., 843/722-0118), a shop for fine, imported, handwoven Asian fabic; **English Rose Antiques** (436 King St., 843/722-7939), a deal mecca for old things; **Magar Hatworks** (557.5 King St., 843/577-7740, www.magarhatworks.com); and **Whatcha Like Gospel** (449 King St., 843/577-9786)—all neighbored up in the same stretch.

Artists' Galleries

While you can find scores of galleries from Broad Street to East Bay Street and northward, there are several off the beaten path worth a visit. Here are some of the most unique. (Most all are closed on Sundays.)

Showcasing the work of more than 50 local craftspersons, **Charleston Crafts** (Hasell St., 843/723-2938, www.charletsoncrafts.org) is a fun place to browse for baskets, pottery, glasswork, jewelry, paper, photos, wood, and more. At the more intellectual end of crafts, **Nina Liu and Friends** (24 State St., 843/722-2724) sells contemporary ceramic, fiber, glass, and more. Set in a three-story onetime home on State Street, it makes for terrific exploring.

Like Nina Liu, the neoclassical **Anne Long Fine Art** (12 State St., 843/577-0447), the Southern-themed **Charleston Renaissance Gallery** (103 Church St., 843/723-0025), and the abstract **Eva Carter** (132 E. Bay St., 843/722-0506) are members of the Charleston Fine Art Dealers Association (www.cfada.com). Look for orange CFADA flags and stickers to differentiate the better galleries from the fray. An enclave of such galleries are at Church and State streets.

In the Upper King Street area, **Redux Contemporary Art Center** (136 St. Philip St., 843/364-2958, www.reduxstudios.org) is part studio, part art school, and part gallery for locally innovative (and underfunded) artists. You can visit the exhibitions gallery there Wed.–Sat. noon–5 PM.

Gallery Chuma/African American Art Gallery (43 John St., 843/722-7568, www.gallerychuma.com), features—you guessed it—works created by African American artists. Occupying both floors of a historic building, covering a total of some 2,900 square feet, Chuma claims to be the largest African American gallery in the South. Gullah artist Jonathan Green's works are a permanent fixture, as are those of several other renowned artists. Open Mon.–Sat. 10 AM–6 PM, or Sun. by appointment.

With all the great birding in the area, it's only proper that you'll find **The Audubon Gallery** (190 King St., 843/853-1100, www.audobonart.com), which offers exhibits of wildlife art by regional artists, and features the work of Vernon Washington, as well as prints by Old Man Audubon, who was no stranger to Charleston.

Farmers Markets

Charleston's Farmers Market (843/724-7305, www.ci.charleston.sc.us) is held in Marion Square (King, Calhoun, and Meeting streets) Mar.–Dec., Sat. 8 AM–1 PM, and features fresh local produce, jams, jellies, handmade soaps and crafts, plus artwork, face painting, and a crepe stand. **Mount Pleasant's Farmers Market** (645 Coleman Blvd., 843/884-8517, www.townofmountpleasant.com) is more of an outdoor grocery, with mostly produce, seafood, herbs, gourmet prepared foods, and superb barbecue, cooked as you wait in line. Add live bluegrass and a canopy of live oaks overhead and it's the real deal. Open Apr.–Oct., Tues. 4 PM–dark.

Antiques

Charleston is so old that people throw away items (declaring them "too modern") that would be antiques anywhere else in the country. See the King Street shopping section for downtown shops, but head over the bridges for the best booth malls and real steals. Mount Pleasant has a few great places to wander: **Page's Thieves Market** (1460 Ben Sawyer, 843/884-9672); **Hungryneck Antique Mall** (401 Johnnie Dodds Blvd., 843/849-1733); and the **Antiques Market** (634 Coleman Blvd., 843/849-8850). And in West Ashley, **Junk & Jive Retro Mart** (827 Hwy. 17, 843/225-5483) and **Architectural Antiques & Garden Elements** (1011 St. Andrews Blvd., 843/571-3389) are tops.

Bookstores

For new books downtown, the **Waldenbooks** (120 Market St., 843/853-1736) in the Charleston Place mall is the only game in town. In addition to their stellar collection of Carolina- and Charleston-related titles. If you see my book there, please make a show of reading from it and murmur approvingly in earshot of the staff. Open daily. Independent and locally owned, **The Ravenous Reader** (520 Folly Rd., 843/795-2700) sits just at the other side of the James Island Connector bridge, which links downtown to Folly Road. It's got a small but good stock of new books.

For used books, the only remaining store downtown is **Boomers Books & Collectibles** (420 King St., 843/722-2666); thank goodness it has an enormous meandering collection, even though you'd never guess as much from its demure Upper King storefront. Open daily till 6 PM.

If all you want is a paperback for beach reading, stop by **Trade-a-Book** (1303-3 Ben Sawyer Blvd., 843/884-8611) on your way to Sullivan's Island or Isle of Palms.

Flea Markets and Auctions

For a bizarre mix of yard-sale-flavor second-hand goods and new items from knives and CDs to velvet paintings, visit the **Coastal Carolina Flea Market** (165 Market Rd., Ladson, 843/797-0540), 20 minutes north of Charleston via I-26 in Ladson. Held Sat.–Sun., 8 AM–5 PM.

To get your antiques at auction, check in with **Page's Thieves Market** (1460 Ben Sawyer, 843/884-9672) in Mount Pleasant, as they have about two Sat. auctions a month. Or visit Roumilatt's Antiques and Auctions (2241 Hwy. 17, 843/766-8899), where they have auctions the first and third Sat. of each month.

Sports and Recreation

BEACHES

My favorite beach in this region is Isle of Palms, but then, I never pack a lunch, so being close to some good lunch spots is important to me. If you're looking for a beach-beach, meaning bikini shops, hamburger stands, and board rentals, then you'll want to hit either Isle of Palms (right around the Isle of Palms County Park at the end of the Isle of Palms Connector) or Folly Beach.

Isle of Palms

One of the reasons Isle of Palms (IOP) is now so easy to reach—via the 1994 Isle of Palms Connector—is because the owner of the Windjammer bar campaigned to get the road built with tax dollars, and then immediately began broadcasting to all the young party animals of Charleston how easy it was to get out to Isle of Palms. When he was the first person mugged

Surrounded by barrier islands, Charleston has plenty of beach for all.

© SEAN SLINSKY

by unsavory youth drawn by the "easy access" and good times, a lot of people had a hard time feeling sorry for him. All that aside, Charleston County has built a nice recreational facility on the water here, the **Isle of Palms County Park** (1–14 Aves., Isle of Palms, 843/886-3863). This spot is for the loud, tan, bikini crowd; it's a great place to join a pickup game of volleyball or watch one of the recurring tournaments. And it's tops for kite or old-school surfing. Visit IOP for the action, its hamburger shops, and beach bars right there on the water. Since the main downtown strip was redone in 2004, the boardwalk is much more family-friendly.

Sullivan's Island

Named for Captain Florence O'Sullivan, captain of the *Carolina,* Sullivan's today has some of the better surf in the area, right down by 21st Street. This area has become one of the pricier addresses in the Charleston area; if you can't afford to buy on The Battery, you might just have to settle for oceanfront on Sullivan's. The challenge of going to the beach here is the lack of a parking lot; just park on a residential street, but make sure no signs forbid it. At the south end of the island (down by Fort Moultrie), swimming is prohibited. And a good thing, too, because it's dangerous there. But don't let that stop you from heading down after a day at the beach to visit Fort Moultrie and walk along the beach, where you'll have a great view of Fort Sumter and, if you're fortunate, a huge ship that passes by like a city block on water.

Folly Beach

Folly Beach has always had great bumper stickers. It calls itself "The Edge of America." After Hurricane Hugo (1989), when most of the beach's famed white sands were swept away, a new bumper sticker began to appear: "Where's the Beach?" Now with beach renourishment programs, the beach is back, although no one thinks it will stick around very long. Better see it while you can.

THE BATTLES FOR FORT WAGNER

Folly Island first appears on history's radar during the Civil War, when Union troops stationed at Hilton Head waded through waist-high water onto the south end of Folly Beach as part of their attempt to capture Fort Wagner, the nearly impregnable Confederate fort on Morris Island, north of Folly Beach. Once it captured Fort Wagner, the Union planned to turn the fort's guns on Fort Sumter, the island fortress in the midst of Charleston Harbor – the disabling of which Northerners saw as the key to capturing Charleston. Capturing Charleston, in turn, was the key to crippling Southern importation and shipment of arms and supplies to its armies throughout the South.

First, however, the Yanks had to capture the southern end of Morris Island, just across Lighthouse Inlet from them. From April 7 to July 6, 1863, the Union soldiers spent their time building up earthworks to protect their gun batteries and constructing barges for an amphibious assault. When the battle actually began, the hard-pressed Confederates holding down the south end of the island eventually ran for the safety of Fort Wagner, leaving 17 dead, 112 wounded, and 67 missing. The Union, although it suffered similar losses, had won the south end of the island.

The next day the Union assaulted Fort Wagner and suffered terrible casualties. A week later, as immortalized in the movie *Glory*, the black 54th Massachusetts Volunteer Infantry, led by Colonel Robert Shaw, attempted to take the fort and was bloodily repulsed, costing 40 percent of the 54th's lives. More than 1,500 men were lost in both attacks. The fort was never taken; however, the men stayed on Little Folly Island, and the black 55th Massachusetts and 1st North Carolina landed on Folly on August 3rd. The Northern army believed, apparently, that the African Americans could naturally work better than whites in the extreme heat and humidity. Unfortunately, nature had no such preconceptions, and the men started dropping like flies as they dug trenches, cut timber, built wharves, loaded and unloaded goods, and hauled heavy guns to the front on Morris Island. Most of this work was done under heavy Confederate fire. As if this weren't enough, the Northern whites took advantage of their black cohorts, using them to police and lay out the white camps. In the first seven weeks on Folly, 12 members of the 55th Massachusetts died; 23 had perished by December.

Eventually the Southerners withdrew from Wagner to defend Charleston itself, and the Northerners quickly moved in and turned their guns onto Sumter, which nonetheless hung in there until reduced to rubble. Eventually, the surviving members of the 55th Massachusetts would get the honor of marching into Charleston to bring the Day of Jubilee to the African-Americans of Charleston.

Folly Beach has served many roles in its history: from a Civil War killing field to a Southern Coney Island, from an archaeological excavation site to a countercultural refuge, and, increasingly, to upscale Charleston oceanfront suburb.

The island first appears on history's radar during the Civil War, when Union troops stationed at Hilton Head waded through waist-high water onto the south end of Folly Beach as part of their attempt to capture Fort Wagner, the nearly impregnable Confederate fort on Morris Island, north of Folly Beach. In the 1930s and 1940s, the Folly Pavilion provided great dancing; an amusement park drew the kids. Ira Gershwin stayed here to pick up local flavor while writing the score to *Porgy and Bess*. But tide, time, and storms have taken all of those away from Folly, although a fishing pier still draws anglers, and the Holiday Inn remains a favorite place for local shaggers.

If Hurricane Hugo had a good side, it is that in passing through it ripped open the sands enough to expose some long-hidden archaeological remnants from the Union encampments on Folly Island. Five months after the storm, several Folly residents and beachcombers called to report that they'd found bones on the beaten-up island. Archaeologists raced out and quickly identified the bones as cattle bones. Big deal.

Fortunately, Rod O'Conner, a former Folly Beach police officer, shortly thereafter notified the Charleston Museum that he'd found not just bones, but leather remnants. Local members of the Underwater Archaeological Division, South Carolina Institute of Archaeology and Anthropology, headed out to the scene, collected what they could, and got the U.S. Coast Guard, which controlled the land, to allow a dig to take place immediately. Time was running out because the sand in which the artifacts lay was being lost to the ocean daily.

From April 24 through November, archaeologists removed as many artifacts as they could, while the ocean ate away at the dig site. By November, the remaining land yielded little. The site was officially closed.

Two years later, when the Coast Guard prepared to relinquish control of the property, Federal laws required them to commission an archaeological survey of the entire area. A private archaeological firm located remnants of the assault batteries and other important occupation-era features on the island. They recommended that the land be preserved as an historic park, and most of it has been acquired by the Department of Parks, Recreation and Tourism, which has plans to preserve it as a park.

Partly because it had had some of the tackiest pre-Hugo buildings, Folly took one of the worst hits from the storm and took the longest to recover. You could walk here for years after Hugo and find telephones and food processors still buried in the sand. But when the buildings finally went back up, they began reflecting the increased value of the oceanfront property. As *The Post and Courier* reporter Linda L. Meggett reported, prices had begun to climb significantly by early 1998. A vacant lot assessed for $45,400 in 1993, for example, sold for $100,000 in March 1996. The starting sale price of the villas in the new 96-unit complex on West Arctic Avenue opened at $169,000 in 1997. By early 1998, it had climbed to $240,000. For a villa, mind you—essentially a condo.

The dreadlocks seem to be headed out and the dread yuppies are on their way in, paying too much for houses and thus pushing up everyone's assessments and property taxes. But if the surf stays great at The Washout and elsewhere on the east end, the scene can't ever get too tame.

Kiawah's Beachwalker Park

The only public beach on Kiawah Island, Beachwalker Park (Beachwalker Dr., Kiawah, 843/768-2395) is a beautiful stretch of beach—about 450 feet worth—with restrooms, dressing areas, outdoor showers, a snack bar, a picnic area, and parking. It's on the west end of the island. Unfortunately, the rest of the island is privately owned, so beach access is limited to home owners or resort guests.

IN AND ON THE WATER
Surfing

The single best, most dependable surf spot in the Charleston area, if not in the entire state, has long been **The Washout,** halfway to the end of East Ashley Avenue on Folly Beach. At press time, Folly's beach renourishment project had been taking its toll on Washout surf condition, but locals in the know feel a few big (and inevitable) storms should set things back to normal. Regardless, you might try **10th Street,** where you can count on smaller but often cleaner—and less-crowded—waves. Beside the Holiday Inn at East Atlantic Avenue, the **Edwin S. Taylor Fishing Pier** (101 E. Artic Ave., 843/588-3474, www.follyfishingpier.com), AKA The Pier, sometimes offers clean waves and long rides, but you'll need to keep an eye out for The Law: Although not always enforced, it's illegal to surf within 200 feet of the pier.

Over in East Cooper, a lot of folks like the surf from 25th down to Wild Dunes, if the wind is blowing out of the northeast, especially. Or you may try **Bert's** at Station 22, Sullivan's Island; named in honor of the venerable nearby bar, it's one of the best places to surf at low tide.

Founded in 1965, **McKevlin's Surf Shop** (8 Center St., 843/588-2247, www.mckevlins.com) has a 24-hour surf report (843/588-2261), which is updated several times throughout the day. Tim McKevlin sells and rents new and used boards and bodyboards and has the most knowledgeable and courteous counter folk in the area. The Charleston *Post and Courier* offers its own **InfoLine Surf Report** (843/937-6000, ext. 7873), updated a minimum of three times per day.

Kitesurfing

Charleston's waves and wind doesn't always allow for primo surfing, but it's ideal for kitesurfers. If you've never seen the sport, walk any beach in these parts and you'll spot the adrenaline junkies catching serious air, dangling from chutes like puppets, and jetting across waves crests, size be damned. Folly, Isle of Palms, and Sullivan's each feature kitesurfers. To find out the best spots du jour, buy gear, or take lessons, contact either **Halfmoon Outfitters** (425 Coleman Blvd., 843/881-9472, www.halfmoonoutfitters.com) or **Air** (753 Coleman Blvd., 843/388-9300, www.catchsomeair.com).

Waterskiing

Tidal Wave Water Sports (69 41st Ave., 843/886-8456, www.tidalwavewatersports.com) operates out of the Isle of Palms Marina, and offers waterskiing trips as well as a waterski school. Open daily Apr.–Sept.

Sailing

AquaSafaris (Patriots Point Marina, 843/886-8133, www.aqua-safaris.com) offers chartered sailboats, while **Ocean Sailing Academy** (24 Patriots Point Rd., 843/971-0700, www.oceansail.com) runs sailing schools for all levels of experience.

Jet Skis and Parasailing

Tidal Wave Water Sports (69 41st Ave., Isle of Palms Marina, 843/886-8456, www.tidalwavewatersports.com) rents Jet Skis by the half hour and hour, and runs parasailing trips, too.

Kayaking and Canoeing

The **Bohicket Boat Adventure and Tour Company** (2789 Cherry Point Rd., Wadmalaw Island, 843/559-3525, www.bohicketboat.com) offers a three-hour guided kayak tour along the remote salt marsh adjoining the North Edisto River. They'll also take you by boat out among the dolphins and on to remote sea islands. Once there, you can either decide to relax on the beach or head out for more explorations via kayak. Rates for both excursions runs about $40.

Over in Mount Pleasant, **Coastal Expeditions** (514-B Mill St., 843/884-7684, www.coastalexpeditions.com), next to the Shem Creek Bar and Grill at the Shem Creek Maritime Center, is the best place to rent a kayak or canoe, or to sign up for a guided tour of the Lowcountry's barrier islands, the cypress swamp, and Charleston Harbor. Because you'll be paddling a sea kayak, which is larger and much more stable than other kayaks, you don't need prior training for most of these trips. Half-day trips ($58) cover Shem Creek and Morgan Creek behind Isle of Palms. Full-day tours ($85) are six hours long; one is a trip to undeveloped Capers Island, which is accessible only by boat. Overnight trips to Capers Island State Wildlife Refuge are also available.

If you'd like to get over to Bull Island in the Cape Romain National Wildlife Refuge, Coastal Expeditions sends a ferry over there that you can catch. Call for rates and schedule. If you don't need no stinking tour leader, rent a single kayak ($38 half day, $48 full day) or double kayak ($48 half day, $58 full day). Open daily Mar.–Oct.; Dec.–Feb. by appointment only.

Boat Rentals

The **Bohicket Boat Adventure and Tour Company** (2789 Cherry Point Rd., Wadmalaw Island, 843/559-3525, www.bohicketboat.com) offers everything from little johnboats to speedboats, 15-foot Boston whalers, and 22-foot Catalina sailboats. Rental for a full-size boat runs around $100–200 half day, $150–350 full day. Open Mar.–Dec.

Diving

With history comes shipwrecks; off the coast you'll find great wreck diving. If you're here in the winter, beware that rough, cold waters can make offshore diving pretty inhospitable between October and April or May. But people dive in the historic rivers year-round; one Low-country favorite is the Cooper River, which is filled with fossilized giant shark teeth, bones, mammal teeth, and Colonial and prehistoric artifacts. Expect water temps in the 50s.

Contact **Charleston Scuba** (335 Hwy. 17, 843/763-3483, www.charlestonscuba.com) for equipment, classes, and tours.

Cruises

One of the best possible ways to spend a night in Charleston is to take a dinner and dancing cruise on the three-deck *Carolina* that **Spiritline Cruises** (360 Concord St., 843/722-1691, www.spiritlinecruises.com) operates. Tickets ($41.23 weekdays, $45.23 Fri.–Sat.) include an excellent dinner and a live band (on a covered, air-conditioned deck).

The **Bohicket Boat Adventure and Tour Company** (2789 Cherry Point Rd., Wadmalaw Island, 843/559-3525, www.bohicketboat.com) offers sunset and ecotour cruises, and tours of the ACE Basin. Open Mar.–Dec.

Fishing

If you get to South Carolina and realize you forgot to bring your yacht, don't panic—it happens to all of us. Fortunately, several companies specialize in getting fisherfolk out to where the deep-sea fish are biting. Most will also rent you the tackle you left back home as well. Out in the Gulf Stream you can fish for marlin, sailfish, tuna, dolphin, and wahoo. Closer in, you can still hope to land mackerel, blackfin tuna, cobia, and shark. The **Bohicket Boat Adventure and Tour Company** (2789 Cherry Point Rd., Wadmalaw Island, 843/559-3525, www.bohicketboat.com) offers dolphin watching, sunset cruises, barrier island shelling, powerboat rentals, and family fishing in the North Edisto River.

The **Bohicket Boat Adventure and Tour Company** (2789 Cherry Point Rd., Wadmalaw Island, 843/559-3525, www.bohicketboat.com) offers in-shore fishing trips and offshore fishing trips on a fleet of six passenger boats, running 25–55 feet in size. Open Mar.–Dec.

For tackle and charters, try **Barton and Burwell Fishing Supplies** (47 S. Windemere Blvd., 843/766-3220, www.bartonandbarwell.com) in West Ashely. Open daily.

Shrimping and Crabbing

The **Bohicket Boat Adventure and Tour Company** (2789 Cherry Point Rd., Wadmalaw Island, 843/559-3525, www.bohicketboat.com) offers crabbing and shrimping outings. Open Mar.–Dec.

Water Parks

Splash Island in Palmetto Islands County Park in Mount Pleasant and **Splash Zone** in James Island County Park are open every weekend in the summer 10 AM–6 PM (or dark). Cost is about $8 for Charleston County residents, $10 for noncounty residents. These fees are in addition to the $1 park entrance fee. Call 843/795-4386 for information.

HIKING

Just north of Awendaw, you'll find The Francis Marion National Forest and the trailhead for the 27-mile **Swamp Fox Passage of the Palmetto Trail.** The Palmetto Trail connects with the **Lake Moultrie Passage.** Believe it or not, you could have walked through some parts of this area just after Hurricane Hugo and been the tallest thing in the forest. Today, you'll find lots of pine trees, some Carolina bays, the famous insect-gulping pitcher plant, and cypress swamp. Pack insect repellant and a lot of water because the primitive campgrounds won't provide any. Don't do this hike in the summer, unless as some type of penance—the humidity, heat, and insects will take most of the fun out of the excursion. Bikers use this trail as well, but most of the time you should have it to yourself.

The **Seewee Center** (5821 Hwy. 17 N, 843/928-3368, www.fws.gov/seeweecenter) serves as the visitors center for the forest, and camping ($15–20, plus $5 gate fee) is available at the **Buck Hall Recreation Area** (843/887-3257). Open Tues.–Sun. 9 AM–5 PM. Also, the **Palmetto Conservation League** (864/948-9615, www.palmettoconservation.org) has loads of info on the area, especially farther north.

BIKING

If you want to bike around downtown Charleston, check out **The Bicycle Shoppe** (280 Meeting St., 843/722-8168). They are the only rental agency on the peninsula. Call for rates.

Of course, no one says you have to keep your rental bike confined to downtown. One of the joys of Carolina beaches is that the flat landscape allows the ocean to creep up quite a ways along the beach, leaving a cement-hard, flat surface behind, perfect for long bike rides. It's possible to park on Isle of Palms at the county park and ride all the way to the north end of the island, giving you a look at the Wild Dunes boardwalk. Or you can head south, take the bridge across Breach Inlet to Sullivan's Island, and check out some of the unique houses there. Stop at Dunleavy's or Sullivan's for lunch, and turn back. You can also mountain-bike the 27-mile **Swamp Fox Trail.** Off the peninsula, try **Mike's Bikes & Backwoods** in Mount Pleasant (704 Coleman Blvd., 843/884-5884) or on the way to Folly Beach (808 Folly Rd., 843/795-3322). Rates run $5 hourly, $15 daily, $40 for an entire week.

GOLF

The South Carolina coast played home to the first golf course in America, which should be no surprise. Way back in 1786, when the manufacture of white polyester was only a pipe dream, Charlestonians created Harleston Green and organized the South Carolina Golf Club, also the nation's first. Through the years, Charlestonians have continued to golf

with style. In 1998, *Links* magazine named Kiawah Island Resort and Wild Dunes as 2 of the top 100 golf resorts in North America. More recent rankings by *Golf Magazine* place them in the top 50 resorts in country.

The first thing a duffer will want to do is stop in at the Charleston Visitor Center and pick up a *Charleston Area Golf Guide,* an annual publication by **Charleston Golf, Inc.** (800/774-4444, www.charlestongolf-guide.com), a nonprofit organization dedicated to promoting the Charleston area as a golf destination. Contact these people and they'll help you arrange your golf outings on your next visit. They will also give you a listing and ranking of every course in the area.

Charleston boasts courses by Pete Dye, Tom Fazio, Arthur Hills, Jack Nicklaus, Rees Jones, and Robert Trent Jones Sr., among others. Dye's **The Ocean Course** at Kiawah Island has been ranked by *Golf Magazine* as one of the top 100 courses in America, and *Golf Digest* has dubbed it "America's Toughest Resort Course," as well as one of its "100 Greatest Courses." Taking up more than two miles of oceanfront beach dunes, this is one of the most beautiful courses in the world. Local hotels offering golf packages include Francis Marion Hotel, Hampton Inn, Holiday Inn: Riverview, Kiawah Island Resort, the Mills House, Seabrook Island Resort, and Wild Dunes Resort. See *Accommodations* listings for addresses and phone numbers.

TENNIS

If you're looking for tennis, try the public **Charleston Tennis Center** (19 Farmfield Rd., West Ashely, 843/769-8258, www.charlestoncity.info) with its 15 lighted courts; the award-winning tennis programs at **Wild Dunes Resort** (5757 Palmetto Dr., 843/886-2113, www.wilddunes.com), where courts are for lessons and resort guests only; or **Kiawah East and West Beach Tennis Center** (843/768-2838, www.kiawahresort.com), which offers tennis clinics for adults and kids in it two tennis complexes with 23 clay courts and 3 hard courts.

MORE RECREATION

You can shoot **pool** at the **Southend Brewery and Smokehouse** (161 E. Bay St., 843/853-4677, www.southendbrewery.com).

Classic Golf (1528 Ben Sawyer Blvd., Mount Pleasant, 843/881-3131) is just before the bridge to Sullivan's Island. This place is humble compared to Myrtle Beach's towers of stucco, but it still does the trick and then some, thanks to the little bar and restaurant on the premises. Open Mon.–Fri. 4 PM–2 AM, Sat.–Sun. noon–2 AM.

For the excitement that is indoor bowling, try **Twin River Lanes** (613 Johnny Dodds Blvd., Mount Pleasant, 843/884-7735).

PROFESSIONAL SPORTS

Sports Illustrated selected Charleston as the 24th of the top 25 "sports towns" in the United States. The honor was all the better because Charleston was the only town in the top 25 without a major-league franchise.

Baseball

Charleston has long hosted some estimable minor-league ball teams, dating back to the Southern League's Charleston Seagulls, who first took the field in 1886. Later, major-league brothers Sandy Alomar Jr. and Roberto Alomar played minor-league ball in Charleston before making the bigs, as did Carlos Baerga, Kevin Seitzer, Willie Randolph, Pascual Perez, Danny Jackson, David Cone, and John Candelaria. Nowadays, the RiverDogs are affiliated with the Tampa Bay Devil Rays.

But they haven't been called the River-Dogs for all that long. In the late 1980s and early 1990s, the team played as the Charleston Rainbows, a name that not only featured some pretty goofy-looking logos but also made it rather hard to cheer with conviction as the team battled tough-sounding squads like the Hickory Crawdads or Capital City Bombers. It just never felt right bolting to your feet in a late inning, beer in your fist, and shouting, "Go Rainbows!"

Today, the mercifully renamed **RiverDogs** (360 Fishburne St., 843/577-3647, www.riverdogs.com) play Class A ball at the 1997 Joseph P. Riley Park, which was named for the city's innovative and generally beloved mayor. If you want to see a game at this fine, old-timey-styled stadium—designed by the same folks who created Baltimore's famed Camden Yards—head down to "the Joe" and buy tickets ($4–8) in person. The great thing about parks this small is that there really aren't any bad seats; 10 or so rows may be the only difference between high-end and low-end tickets. The highest-priced seats feature wait service, which could be helpful if you're physically disabled. Most games start at 7:05 PM. If you can't make the game, ESPN (950 AM) provides the play-by-play commentary.

Hockey

The **South Carolina Stingrays** (3300 W. Montague Ave., Ste. B302, North Charleston, 843/744-2248, www.stingrayshockey.com) play Oct.–May in the North Charleston Coliseum as members of the East Coast Hockey League. They won the 1996–1997 and 2000–2001 Kelly Cup and have posted winning records every season since their inception in the mid-1990s. They also average more than 6,000 fans a game. If you have never caught a live hockey game, give it a try. It's a fun time, even if you haven't watched a hockey game since the 1980 Winter Olympics. You'll find Stingrays games on the radio at 910 AM. Most games start at 7:05 PM. Tickets start at $10.

Soccer

The **Charleston Battery** (1990 Daniel Island Dr., Daniel Island, 843/971-4625, www.charlestonbattery.com) do battle at Blackbaud Stadium over on Daniel Island (right off I-526), Apr.–Sept. in the United Soccer League. The games are broadcast on news radio WSC730 AM.

Accommodations

Charleston is full of charming places to stay, from quaint B&Bs to world-class hotels, from seaside cottages to beautiful campsites overlooking the undulating golden salt marshes. There are also several cheaper, more practical motels for those who would rather spend their money at the restaurants and clubs than at the hotel desk.

The listings here are necessarily incomplete; I've given you a sampling of the different types of lodgings available, but feel free to stop into the Charleston Visitor Center on the way into town and browse the racks of pamphlets for the many different businesses offering a place to sleep in the Holy City. If you stumble on a really first-rate place I've failed to mention, drop me a line about it so we can tip off other folks who would appreciate the things it has to offer. This way you can be more sure it will still be around next time you come to town.

There are a couple of different ways you might approach lodging in Charleston. One

is to find somewhere quiet off in the wilderness not 25 minutes away from the downtown historic district. Another approach is to grab a room at one of the local beaches, making daily or nightly trips into the Holy City for sightseeing and entertainment. Approach number three is to find a cheaper place on the outskirts, in Summerville or North Charleston, or maybe over in West Ashley. The upside of this is that you can save some money. The downside is that you probably won't save *that* much money from the better-value downtown spots, and you'll be spending your evenings staring at the glare of a Shoney's or Waffle House sign rather than the quaint flickering gaslights of the historic district.

Which brings me to approach number four, which is to stay downtown as cheaply as possible. This is usually my strategy. There's just nothing like waking up early and strolling down Market or King until the smell from some coffeehouse or bakery lures you in. And if

© SEAN SLINSKY

Bed-and-breakfasts fill the "Holy City"; John Rutledge House Inn is one of the best.

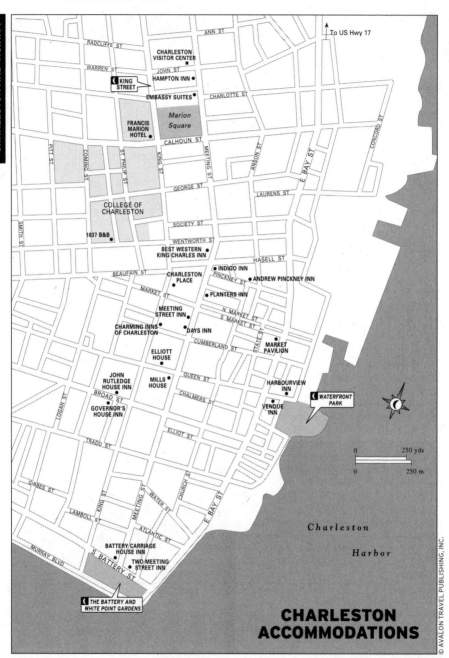

RADCLIFFE ST
ANN ST
To US Hwy 17
WARREN ST
CHARLESTON VISITOR CENTER
JOHN ST
KING STREET
HAMPTON INN
EMBASSY SUITES
CHARLOTTE ST
FRANCIS MARION HOTEL
Marion Square
CALHOUN ST
PITT ST
COMING ST
ST PHILIP ST
KING ST
MEETING ST
ANSON ST
E BAY ST
CONCORD ST
GEORGE ST
LAURENS ST
COLLEGE OF CHARLESTON
SOCIETY ST
SMITH ST
1837 B&B
WENTWORTH ST
BEST WESTERN KING CHARLES INN
HASELL ST
INDIGO INN
BEAUFAIN ST
CHARLESTON PLACE
PINCKNEY ST
ANDREW PINCKNEY INN
MARKET ST
PLANTERS INN
MEETING STREET INN
N MARKET ST
S MARKET ST
CHARMING INNS OF CHARLESTON
DAYS INN
CUMBERLAND ST
STATE ST
MARKET PAVILION
ELLIOTT HOUSE
JOHN RUTLEDGE HOUSE INN
MILLS HOUSE
QUEEN ST
HARBOURVIEW INN
BROAD ST
CHALMERS ST
GOVERNOR'S HOUSE INN
LOGAN ST
VENDUE INN
WATERFRONT PARK
ELLIOT ST
TRADD ST
GIBBES ST
KING ST
MEETING ST
WATER ST
CHURCH ST
E BAY ST
LAMBOLL ST
ATLANTIC ST
MURRAY BLVD
BATTERY CARRIAGE HOUSE INN
S BATTERY ST
TWO MEETING STREET INN
THE BATTERY AND WHITE POINT GARDENS

Charleston

Harbor

0   250 yds
0   250 m

CHARLESTON ACCOMMODATIONS

it's possible to fall in love with a city, I can pinpoint the moment I fell in love with Charleston for the first time: It was 7 AM, and I stumbled downstairs from the King Charles Inn and sat out in front of Fulford and Egan (since moved) on Meeting Street, sipping a mocha as the dawn stretched over the weathered storefronts and wet, deserted streets.

Approach number five is paying whatever it costs to stay wherever you want in the quaint spots downtown. This isn't normally an option for me, but if it's an option for you, skip ahead to the *$200 and Higher* section that follows.

One note: High season for many Charleston lodgings are spring and fall, meaning that after Spoleto, you'll find low-season rates (with price reductions of up to 50 percent) in the heat of summer, as well as in the chill of winter. And winter is not always that chilly either. December temperatures often sneak up into the 70s.

Spoleto Festival, which runs for two weeks in May and June, is the highest season of all. The rates quoted as follows, as with all others in this book, reflect double-occupancy low rates during the high season. If you come in low season, rates may be considerably lower.

HISTORIC DISTRICT
Under $25

You know a city's got the "it" factor when the hostels appear. **Charleston's Not So Hostel** (156 Spring St., 843/722-8383, www.notso-hostel.com) has been around a few years thanks to a local COC grad who never left town. The hostel is a small compound of slouchy 1840s Charleston single houses, with porches and hammocks aplenty, and an air of Southern hospitality–meets–laid-back-groover. The front house holds the dorms, and the back houses have single private rooms, which can be rented for long stretches. Free high-speed Internet; air-conditioning; a large, stocked kitchen (free waffles); coin laundry; bike rentals; and a camping platform are all available. The only downside is the enclave's location: near the hospitals in a "transitional" neighborhood five blocks north of the college. To get to the best touring spots in town, you'll need

to ride a bike or to hop on a CARTA bus. But with rates at $19 per night ($15 per night for three or more nights), a five-block displacement is easy to get over.

$100-200

For some reason, the ◖ **Andrew Pinckney Inn** (40 Pinckney St., 843/937-8800 or 800/505-8983, www.andrewpinckneyinn.com) remains a terrific secret on the lodging front. Go figure, as it's one block from the Old City Market, right around the corner from terrific restaurants, and about two blocks from prime King Street shopping. Add that its rooms are top-rate, the complimentary breakfast on the rooftop terrace includes biscuits and gravy, and rates start at $89 in December and January, and the mystery continues. Average room rates hover at about $139 throughout the year, but can get as high as $279 for suites.

The same folks who run the well-heeled John Rutledge House Inn and the even-better-heeled Wentworth Mansion run a group of three smaller and more modest inns in the Lower King Street antique area. All are set in 100-plus-year-old buildings, well restored and dressed in antiques, and offer light breakfasts, great views, and fine service; some have courtyards, fountains, and fireplaces. A stay at any one is like getting the best of a bed-and-breakfast setting (without the frilly trappings) and the service of a fine hotel (without the cookie-cutter rooms). Rates start at $120 and go up to the high $200s for suites in high season. **Kings Courtyard Inn** (198 King St., 843/723-7000 or 800/845-6119); **Victoria House Inn** (208 King St., 843/720-2944 or 800/933-5464); **Fulton Lane Inn** (202 King St., 843/720-2600 or 800/720-2688) all fall under the apt Charming Inns of Charleston (www.charminginns.com) moniker.

I like the **Best Western King Charles Inn** (237 Meeting St., 843/723-7451, www.king-charlesinn.com) right downtown andwithin walking distance of the Old City Market. Sure, your balcony (if you get one) probably doesn't look out over much, but it's an excellent base to head out from and return to each day, and the rooms are spacious and reasonably priced. Because a lot of business travelers stay here, you can sometimes get pretty good rates on the weekends. The inn underwent a major renovation that entailed replacing the entire eastern facade with a stucco surface, adding a secondary lobby, and enlarging the guest rooms. Now it fits into the neighborhood even better than before. Rates start at $129.

One of the most intimate spots in Charleston is the **Elliott House Inn** (78 Queen St., 843/723-1855, www.elliotthouseinn.com), with a charming, fully enclosed courtyard, built on the site of original buildings designed by Robert Mills. It's in the antique district of Lower King, and fittingly, the rate-included continental breakfast is served on silver. Rates run about $85–185. Expect to pay less during the summer and winter, and more in the fall and spring. Room rates here include use of the hotel's many bikes, which are perfect for exploring the nooks and crannies of the historic district.

When I'm not feeling particularly wealthy or adventurous, I usually find Days Inns to be a safe bet. If you're looking for a clean bed and decent service, you might want to head over to **Days Inn: Charleston Historic District** (155 Meeting St., 843/722-8411 or 800/329-7466, www.daysinn.com) The facility here looks like a revamped motel, but you can't beat the location, right next door to the Meeting Street Inn. Both spots are snug in the heart of downtown's shopping and historic areas. Rates range $99–249.

For my money—or, for that matter, for your money—**(Meeting Street Inn** (173 Meeting St., 843/723-1882 or 800/842-8022, www.meetingstreetinn.com) is one of the most romantic spots to stay in the city. It features a nice courtyard with fountains and tables, and large, beautiful Charleston single-house-style rooms with four-poster rice beds (in most rooms), armoires, and wood shutters on the windows. Ask for a room on the ground floor so your view will look out into the courtyard and not over the courtyard wall and into the Days Inn parking lot. If no first-floor rooms are

available, then ask for a room on an upper floor (there are four) in the high numbers—you'll be able to step out onto your back balcony and see the main entrance to Charleston Place, which is beautifully lit at night. A stellar staff provides service here, and room rates include continental breakfast and an afternoon wine-and-cheese reception. Rates range $109–249.

Battery Carriage House Inn (20 S. Battery, 843/727-3100 or 800/775-5575, www.battery-carriagehouseinn.com) is right down on The Battery, and has 11 rooms with four-poster beds, hardwood floors, quilted bedspreads, and so on. Continental breakfast only, which is slightly unfortunate, as down here on The Battery it's not like you can walk around the corner and get shrimp and grits. Rates range $79–279.

The very romantic 18th-century **Vendue Inn** (19 Vendue Range, 843/577-7970 or 800/845-7900, www.vendueinn.com) features fireplaces in some rooms, a beautiful restaurant, and a rooftop bar. This building was once home to a print shop financed by Benjamin Franklin; when the printer, Lewis Timothy, died, his widow took over and capably managed the business, becoming the first female publisher in the United States. She later handed over the business to her son, Peter Timothy, who daringly used to climb up into the bell tower of St. Michael's and spy on the British troops camped over at James Island. Rates range $130–299 during the off-season.

$200 and Higher

The **Hampton Inn: Charleston Historic District** (345 Meeting St., 888/754-4001 or 843/723-4000, www.charleston-hotels.net) sits across from the Charleston Visitor Center, a reasonable walk from the Market area, although you can take one of the DASH trams, which are always heading down into the historic district. Although it's relatively new, this place seems like it's been here forever; it features antique reproductions in the rooms and lobby and offers a nice, gated pool and an exercise room. This might be perfect for you if you're interested in being out of the Market tourist fray, but up for exploring the nearby Charleston Museum, Upper King shops, and this area's hipster restaurant scene. Rates range $99–269.

Rooms at the **Indigo Inn** (One Maiden Ln., 843/577-5900 or 800/845-7639, www.indigoinn.com) face an interior courtyard with a fountain. While the location's sweet—just a bit over a block from the Market and King Street's most dense shopping—the space is a bit uninspired. Rates range $99–235.

The four-story circa-1844 **Planters Inn** (112 N. Market St., 843/722-2345 or 800/845-7082, www.plantersinn.com) offers 62 rooms and several suites with fireplaces and whirlpool baths. A Relais & Chateaux property, it's a well-heeled joint that is also home to one of the city's two best high-end restaurants—the highly nationally acclaimed Peninsula Grill. Rates range $250–600.

Farther up the peninsula, at Marion Square you'll find the **Francis Marion Hotel** (387 King St., 843/722-0600, www.francismarioncharleston.com), built in 1924 as part of a push to turn Charleston into a tourism center. The Francis Marion was hit hard by Hurricane Hugo and underwent a major $12-million renovation by the Westin Company in the 1990s as part of Mayor Joe Riley's effort to bring a renaissance to this stretch of King Street. The plan worked, and the hotel offers some of the best views of downtown as it's one of the tallest structures in the historic district. Rates range $89–319.

The **Mills House Hotel** (115 Meeting St., 843/577-2400 or 800/874-9600, www.millshouse.com) is a fine reconstruction of a famed antebellum inn, right downtown at the corner of Queen and Meeting streets, at the foot of one of the few remaining cobblestone streets—Chalmers—in town. It's furnished in antebellum antiques; Robert E. Lee and Teddy Roosevelt both raved about it. It's old-school Charleston, with a wonderfully old-school restaurant that is all about dressy Southern favorites, linen tablecloths, and manners. Rates hover around $200.

Of course, if Bob and Teddy aren't big enough names, you might want to head over to the 🅒 **John Rutledge House Inn** (116 Broad St., 843/723-7999 or 866/720-2609, www.johnrutledgehouseinn.com), where no less than George Washington once sat down to breakfast. Traveling writers take note: The former owner, John Rutledge, brainstormed on a little thing called the U.S. Constitution in one of the inn's rooms. Wine and sherry are offered each evening in the ballroom. Rates range $250–600.

A newish spot situated in the nighttime quiet by Waterfront Park is the appropriately named **HarbourView Inn** (Two Vendue Range, 843/853-8439 or 800/853-8439, www.harbourviewcharleston.com). Rooms on the Concord Street side overlook the harbor, as does the communal sitting room area. With the Market less than a block away, Charleston's only waterfront restaurant (Fleet Landing) just down the street, and the Waterfront Park City Gallery nearby, it's a primo location, still surprisingly off the radar. Rates range $159–409.

In the Upper King area, while the Francis Marion Hotel was under refurbishment during the 1990s, another exceptional renovation took place about the same time across Marion Square in the original Citadel Building. After months of work, the **Embassy Suites** (337 Meeting St., 843/723-6900 or 800/362-2779, www.embassysuites.com) emerged, offering elegant 2-room units, 12 rooms with whirlpools, and a complimentary full breakfast. Thanks to its historic exterior, the place looks something like a castle, and its interior courtyards are truly stunning. Rates range $110–269.

A luxurious boutique hotel at the foot of the Old City Market, suited bellhops greet **Market Pavilion** (22 E. Bay St., 877/440-2250, www.marketpavilion.com) guests and other visitors who dine at the upscale steak house (Grill 225) on the hotel's first floor, or upstairs at its Pavilion Rooftop bar and cascading pool area. Rooms are decorated uniquely in fine Lowcountry furniture, with chandeliers, and fireplaces in some cases. If you're honeymooning or otherwise celebrating, their suites are tremendous; some include balconies and marble baths. The location is terrific, and the

JFK AND THE SPY WHO LOVED HIM

FBI files released in 1998 revealed that in 1942, when John Fitzgerald Kennedy was a 24-year-old naval lieutenant working in the Atlantic fleet's intelligence office at 29 East Battery, Charleston, he enjoyed two visits from tall, blonde Inga Arvad Fejos, a former Miss Denmark. But Fejos was also a Nazi sympathizer with ties to Hitler, Goebbels, and Goering. Kennedy was of interest to the Nazis because of his father, Joseph Kennedy, who was the former ambassador to England.

President Franklin Delano Roosevelt's attorney general knew of Fejos's background and had set the FBI on her case. When she rented a room at the Fort Sumter Hotel, the FBI promptly bugged it. Apparently, the lovers set the bug wires aglow with their passionate carryings on. In between, Kennedy was recorded spilling the beans to Fejos about his future military assignments.

Instead of taking the evidence to the Navy, which would probably have resulted in JFK receiving an assignment swabbing decks, the attorney general unaccountably took it to Joseph Kennedy himself. The elder Kennedy, to save his son's political future, had him shipped off to PT boat duty in the Pacific theater. The rest of the story is, as they say, history: Kennedy captained *PT-109*, which was rammed and sunk, but managed to save his crew, which made him a hero, igniting his political career and eventually leading to the White House. So there it is – incontrovertible evidence that Charleston's romantic ambience led to JFK's election as president.

---

service is impeccable yet personal. Rates range $225–395.

Before ◖ **Charleston Place** (205 Meeting St., 843/722-4900 or 800/611-5545, www.charlestonplacehotel.com) opened up in 1986, the Old City Market and the nearby portion of King Street were not frequented by polite society, shall we say. Another Joe Riley project, this development and its upscale interior mall (Gucci, Godiva, St. John, etc.) was the shot in the arm that transformed the historic district into a tourist mecca. Today, the hotel is run by the famous Orient Express group. Thanks to the staff's impeccable service; the facility's extravagant suites, ballrooms, and concierge floor; lavish public spaces besot with enormous chandeliers and towering floral arrangements; and the presence of the region's finest gourmet restaurant, the hotel is luxury's standard bearer—in the States and abroad. *Condé Nast Traveler* counts Charleston Place as one of *the world's* best stays year after year; *Travel and Leisure* also named it as one of the best hotels in the world, plus ranked its new spa as the best city spa in the country. (The accolades placed the hotel above such also-rans as New York's Ritz-Carlton, London's The Ritz, Los Angeles's Hotel Bel-Air, and the Four Seasons hotels in Boston, New York, and London.) Rates range considerably, $509–1,800.

Bed-and-Breakfasts

Charleston overflows with historic bed-and-breakfasts. If you come to town without a place to lay your head, stop by the Charleston Visitor Center, and pop over to their Lowcountry Reservation Service. It's a free, walk-in-only service that will book you a room nearly anywhere in town based on your preferences, bed-and-breakfasts included. Otherwise, try the **Historic Charleston Bed & Breakfast** (60 Broad St., 843/722-6606) group, for reservations throughout the historic district. Here are some of the more interesting and diverse options.

If you'd like to stay in an authentic Charleston Single House, the **1837 Bed and Breakfast** (126 Wentworth St., 843/723-7166, www.1837bb.com) gives you just that opportunity. This place is a bit off the beaten path but still in the old, historic part of Charleston. There are nine rooms in all, including some in the carriage house. Rates range $79–165.

◖ **The Governor's House Inn** (117 Broad St., 843/720-2070 or 800/720-9812, www.governorshouse.com) is a magnificent 1760s home with a huge garden and wide porches that also happens to be a National Historic Landmark. The antiques-laden interior, with its towering ceilings and mile-high windows, is so spectacular magazines use it for fashion photo shoots, and wedding receptions are commonplace. Situated in the heart of the historic district, afternoon tea, evening sherry, and a light breakfast are offered. Rates range $179–495, the latter being a high-season suite.

Two Meeting Street Inn (2 Meeting St., 843/723-7322, www.twomeetingstreet-inn.com) is a favorite of deep-pocket travelers, and celebs looking for a hyper-romantic setting. A pretty Queen Anne Victorian down on The Battery, facing White Point Gardens, it wears million-dollar-plus Tiffany stained-glass windows, and a rambling porch. Afternoon tea and sherry, as well as continental breakfasts, are served. Rates range $195–305.

Over in the Old Village section of Mount Pleasant **The Old Village Post House** (101 Pitt St., 843/388-8935 or 800/549-7678, www.old-villageposthouse.com) is set in an 1888 home with six large rooms/suites with private whirlpool baths, telephones, TVs, and continental breakfast. Besides its handy location in the Village's charming tiny downtown strip with its shops and old-school pharmacy, the inn also benefits from the fantastic Post House restaurant downstairs. Rates range $115–185.

Isle of Palms

When we lived in Columbia, my wife and I used to come down to the Isle of Palms and stay at the **Ocean Inn** (1100 Pavilion Dr., 843/886-4687, www.ocean-inn.com), just one block off the ocean. Now it's gone condo, but you can still get a nice room here. It's a small place with a laid-back ambience and a little pathway running back to the convenience store out on Palm Boulevard where you can get late-night munchies. Rooms feature kitchenettes, which would be a good idea considering all the shrimp you're going to catch here. Rates range $110–165.

The 51-room **Seaside Inn** (1004 Ocean Blvd., 888/999-6516 or 843/886-7000, www.seasideinniop.com) stands right on the waterfront, amid the bars and beach traffic, but also right on the sand. You'll find a microwave and refrigerator in every room and a free "grab-and-go" breakfast downstairs. Free parking is available here, which will mean something to you if you're coming during the busy warm-weather months. Rates range $89–279.

Another catacomby way to go is to rent one of the **Sea Cabins** right beside the county park. These are small and not exactly private, but staying here *does* give you access to private tennis courts, a pool, and a fishing pier. They also (unlike the condos down at Wild Dunes) put you within walking distance of the island's restaurants and shops. Choose between one-or two-bedroom villas. Contact Island Realty (843/886-8144 or 800/707-6429, www.island-realty.com) to get a nice, thick brochure that includes the cabins and other rentals on nearby islands. Sea Cabins rates average about $1,000 per week in the summer.

For the upper-crust way to experience this area, try **The Boardwalk Inn** (5757 Palm Blvd., 843/886-2260 or 800/845-8880, www.wild-dunes.com) at Wild Dunes. They've painted the exterior in pastel colors as an homage to downtown's colorful Rainbow Row. If you want to golf while in Charleston, this is the place to stay because it includes the world-ranked Wild Dunes Links, as well as the Harbor Course.

There's also the Wild Dunes seaside Grand Pavilion, with its mock early-1900s boardwalk, but without the rides and carnies. It's charming, nicer, and cleaner than it could be if it were not part of a resort, which I guess is the point. Rates range $100–380.

Mount Pleasant

If your goal is to be within walking distance of the Towne Centre Mall megacomplex, and a bridge away from the Isle of Palms, then the **Hampton Inn & Suites** (1104 Isle of Palms Connector, 843/856-3900, www.hamptoninn.com), right at the foot of the Isle of

Palms Connector on Highway 17 in Mount Pleasant, is your best bet. It sports a tropical, sugarcane-plantation look, with Bermuda shutters; Canary Island date palms; hardwood, stone, or woven matted floors; and teak, mahogany, and rattan furniture. Forty of the 121 rooms are 2-room suites that include a full kitchen. Rates range $109–179.

At present, Mount Pleasant's only bed-and-breakfast is **Longpoint Bed and Breakfast** (1199 Long Point Rd., 843/849-1884, www.charleston-longptn.com). The five-room inn looks like a log cabin from the outside, but inside it's furnished with antiques and blessed with marsh views. It's just up the road from the Charles Pinckney National Monument and Boone Hall Plantation, and just south of Palmetto Islands County Park. Rates range $99–179.

If a little bit of city bustle goes a long way with you, consider staying at the **Charleston Harbor Resort Patriots Point** (20 Patriots Point Rd., 843/856-0028, www.charleston-harborresort.com). This deluxe resort offers a great across-the-harbor view of Charleston's steepled skyline and blinking lights. Although swimming in the harbor is forbidden (not to mention a bad idea) because of harbor-mouth currents, the resort has pools and a nice sand beach to relax on. You're also a cart-ride away from the Patriots Point Golf Course. One more additional bonus is that you can watch the big freight ships pass by your window, something like watching a New York City street slide by. Rates range $89–799.

On the other side of the lot next to the Harbor Resort are 10 cottages camouflaged by lush tropical plantings. The enclave makes up the **Belvidere Club & Resort** (16 Patriots Point Rd., 843/884-3342, www.belvidereclub.com), another of the Charleston area's best-kept lodging secrets. The two-bedroom cottages are crisply decorated in an elegant Lowcountry palette, and have full kitchens, washers and dryers, cable, DVD, Bose stereos, faxes, and high-speed Internet, plus screened porches that overlook the harbor, Fort Sumter, and Charleston's Battery homes. With the ad-

vent of the Ravenel Bridge, Belvidere is just a short scoot over Highway 17 to all the action downtown, though on-site you feel like you're islands away. Golf privileges come via the RiverTowne Country Club and neighboring Patriots Point Links. Check into their pre-arrival grocery stocking service, and pack a swimsuit for the harbor-front pool or heated outdoor spa. Rates range $325–525 during high season, but keep in mind that (thanks to sleeper sofas and three full baths per cottage) each one sleeps six people comfortably.

West Ashley

Please see *Middleton Place* in the *Sights* section for information on staying at the **The Inn at Middleton Place.**

The renovated **Holiday Inn: On the Beach** (One Center St., 843/588-6464, www.holiday-inn.com), is one of several nice Holiday Inn locations. Shag dancing is the norm here, and yes, they give lessons. Rates range $149–249. Another quirky Holiday Inn is on Highway 17—the round **Holiday Inn: Riverview** (301 Hwy. 17, 843/556-7100, www.holiday-inn.com/charleston-riverview). Right on the Ashley River it's a short hop over the West Ashley bridges to downtown. Rates range $79–154.

Rental Houses

You'll find rental houses aplenty in the beach cities. Contact **Resort Quest** (www.resortquest.com) for a free 28-page guide on one of the Charleston area's many beach resorts, offering information on lodging rates, golf packages, tours, and more. Call 800/346-0606 for Isle of Palms, Wild Dunes, or Sullivan's Island. Call 800/845-3911 for Kiawah Island, and 800/845-2233 for its neighbor, Seabrook Island. Another major player for Kiawah and Seabrook homes is **Beachwalker Rentals** (3690 Bohicket Rd., Ste. 4-D, 843/768-1777 or 800/334-6308, www.beachwalker.com).

Good places to find a rental on the Isle of Palms or Sullivan's Island include **Carroll Realty** (103 Palm Blvd., 843/886-9600 or 800/845-7718, www.carrollrealty.com); **Dunes**

Properties of Charleston (1400 Palm Blvd., 843/886-5600 or 888/843-2322, www.dunes-properties.com); and **Island Realty** (1304 Palm Blvd., 843/886-8144 or 800/476-0400, www.islandrealty.com).

If you're thinking about staying on Folly Beach, contact **Fred Holland Realty** (50 Center St., 843/588-2325, www.fredholland.com); **Sellers Shelters** (104 W. Ashley Ave., Folly Beach, 843/588-2269); or **Dunes Properties of Charleston** (31 Center St., 843/588-3800, www.dunesproperties.com).

Campgrounds

Unlike most major cities, Charleston offers several fine campgrounds within 20 minutes of downtown. As long as it's not high summer, so that you won't be essentially camping in a bug-infested sauna, if you're trying to save your money for the restaurants rather than for your bed, you might want to give it a try. Of area campgrounds, **The Campground at James Island County Park** (871 Riverland Dr., 843/795-7275, www.ccprc.com) is a neat campground at a nice park, with 125 RV sites, full hookups, 24-hour security, an activity center, the **Splash Zone** water park for the kids, and a round-trip shuttle service to the historic district and Folly Beach. Reservations are recommended. Rates range from $28 for sites with full hookup, to $26 for water and electricity, and $16 for tent sites. It also offers 10 modern vacation cottages overlooking the Stono River marsh. Each sleeps up to eight and includes a kitchen, TV, and telephone. Rates for the cottages are $122 per night, $732 per week. There's a two-night minimum and a two-week maximum stay, and they rent only by the week Memorial Day through Labor Day. (Prices do not include tax.)

In East Cooper, in Mount Pleasant along Highway 17, the **KOA Mt. Pleasant-Charleston** (3157 Hwy. 17 N, 843/849-5177, www.koa.com) is a beautiful spot surrounded by pines, set on a pond, and located next door to a golf course. Of course, like most KOAs, it's managed to mow down every semblance of a shade tree in the midst of the campground itself, but this one's definitely better than most, while still offering the KOA standard features that have made them so popular: a swimming pool, playground, pond, boat rentals, and so on. A cute little camp store there will keep you from having to run into town for hot cocoa and such, and there are plenty of nearby restaurants to satiate you, too. Rates range, depending on if you are in a tent ($20–28), RV ($28–45), or cabin ($45–139).

Food

CHARLESTON PROPER

Charleston is one of the best restaurant cities in the United States; believe it or not, this a *narrowed-down* list of personal favorites. You won't go wrong if you eat from any of these, but if you hit one of the tourist joints off the list, you might be disappointed, as some may be big on hype, but fall short in taste, atmosphere, and local authenticity. Instead, stick to my tried-and-true for the best experiences.

Southern and Lowcountry

On the soulful side of the Lowcountry map comes **◖ Jestine's Kitchen** (251 Meeting St., 843/722-7224). Here, fried chicken, seafood, veggies, and classic Southern desserts (cola cake) carry the day. One of the most reasonable meals on Meeting Street, dinnertime prices top out at $14. Open daily for lunch and dinner.

◖ Hominy Grill (207 Rutledge Ave., 843/937-0930, www.hominygrill.com) shares the same homey ethic as Jestine's, but cranks the recipes up a notch from Southern-flavored blue-plate fare to add a little more of a gourmand's flair. While it is set in a whitewashed old building with pressed-tin ceilings, creaky wooden floors, and chalkboard menus, there is

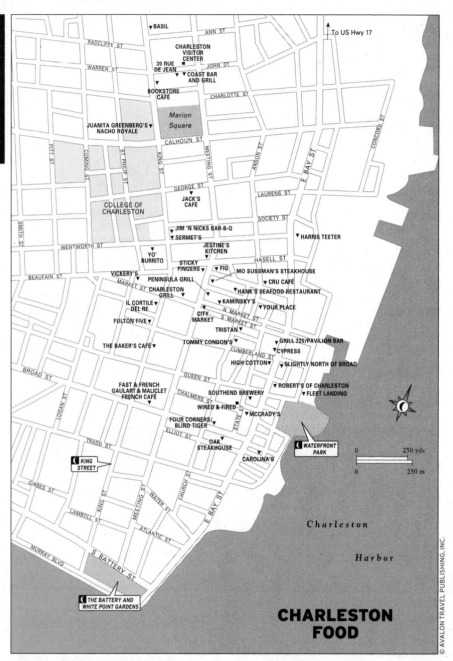

To US Hwy 17

BASIL
RADCLIFFE ST
ANN ST
CHARLESTON VISITOR CENTER
WARREN ST
39 RUE DE JEAN
JOHN ST
COAST BAR AND GRILL
BOOKSTORE CAFÉ
CHARLOTTE ST
Marion Square
JUANITA GREENBERG'S NACHO ROYALE
CALHOUN ST
PITT ST
COMING ST
ST PHILIP ST
KING ST
MEETING ST
GEORGE ST
LAURENS ST
E BAY ST
CONCORD ST
ANSON ST
COLLEGE OF CHARLESTON
JACK'S CAFÉ
SOCIETY ST
SMITH ST
JIM 'N NICKS BAR-B-Q
SERMET'S
HARRIS TEETER
WENTWORTH ST
YO' BURRITO
JESTINE'S KITCHEN
HASELL ST
STICKY FINGERS
FIG
MO SUSSMAN'S STEAKHOUSE
BEAUFAIN ST
VICKERY'S
PENINSULA GRILL
CRU CAFÉ
MARKET ST
CHARLESTON GRILL
HANK'S SEAFOOD RESTAURANT
IL CORTILE DEL RE
KAMINSKY'S
YOUR PLACE
FULTON FIVE
CITY MARKET
N MARKET ST
S MARKET ST
TRISTAN
THE BAKER'S CAFÉ
TOMMY CONDON'S
GRILL 225/PAVILION BAR
CYPRESS
CUMBERLAND ST
HIGH COTTON
SLIGHTLY NORTH OF BROAD
BROAD ST
LOGAN ST
QUEEN ST
ROBERT'S OF CHARLESTON
FAST & FRENCH GAULART & MALICLET FRENCH CAFÉ
FLEET LANDING
CHALMERS ST
SOUTHEND BREWERY
TRADD ST
WIRED & FIRED
STATE ST
MCCRADY'S
FOUR CORNERS/ BLIND TIGER
ELLIOT ST
OAK STEAKHOUSE
WATERFRONT PARK
KING STREET
CAROLINA'S
CHURCH ST
E BAY ST
GIBBES ST
0   250 yds
0   250 m
LAMBOLL ST
KING ST
MEETING ST
WATER ST
ATLANTIC ST
Charleston
MURRAY BLVD
S BATTERY ST
Harbor
THE BATTERY AND WHITE POINT GARDENS

CHARLESTON FOOD

© AVALON TRAVEL PUBLISHING, INC.

a range of offerings: pimiento cheese with okra pickles and toast; okra and shrimp beignets; pinto bean cakes with roasted green tomato sauce, sweet onion relish, jasmine rice, and cilantro sour cream; grilled duck with fried eggplant and sautéed greens. Breakfast and brunch (shrimp, mushroom, and bacon over cheese grits; buttermilk pancakes; and more) are standards for Charlestonians. And since Hominy's, a short car or rickshaw ride from the historic district, it's usually locals only. Dinner entrées top out at $20, lunch $10. Open for lunch and breakfast Mon.–Fri.; brunch Sat.–Sun.; dinner Mon.–Sat.

◖ FIG (232 Meeting St., 843/805-5900, www.eatatfig.com) stands for "Food Is Good," and here, in a sublime bistro setting with sublime flavors, it is. The young owners believe that food that tastes good together grows together, meaning the menu features dishes based on the daily harvest from nearby farms, and the catch local fishermen haul in as well. Think roast suckling pig with sautéed rapini, new potatoes, and grain mustard; roasted vine-ripe heirloom tomatoes with black olives and goat cheese; and warm shrimp-and-radicchio salad with pancetta, and you've got the idea. Entrées are about $20, and the restaurant (and hopping bar) are open Mon.–Sat. for dinner.

Sharing the same neighborhood hangout vibe, but set in a quaint and cheery yellow Charleston single house, a block off the Old City Market, **Cru Café** (18 Pinckney St., 843/534-2434, www.crucafe.com) has a wide range of offerings that range from orange sherbet cake and grape Nehi drinks to fine wines, espresso, chin-wiping four-cheese macaroni, poblano and mozzarella fried chicken, seared duck with duck confit wonton, and Thai seafood risotto, among many others. Even stranger than the assortment itself, is that it all makes sense when you're there, and it's all pulled off impeccably. A small plate and loaded salad makes a full meal without annihilating your wallet ($13), and dinner entrées range $13–20. Open for lunch and dinner Tues.–Sat.

Cypress (167 E. Bay St., 843/727-0111, www.magnolias-blossom-cypress.com) offers

classic Lowcountry cuisine (prices range $18–36) with a modern twist in an upscale atmosphere that's more New York than typical of Charleston. An extensive wine list is offered. Open nightly for dinner.

◖ Slightly North of Broad (192 E. Bay St., 843/723-3424, www.mavericksouthernkitchens.com)—aka **SNOB**—has the best shrimp and grits in town, and aside from the lunchtime fried chicken liver plate, it generally offers relatively healthful fare, with plenty of creative seafood and meat entrées. The atmosphere is casual, festive good dining; dinner runs about $16–28 per plate. Open daily for lunch and dinner.

Another local favorite, **Carolina's** (10 Exchange St., 843/724-3800, www.carolinasrestaurant.com) is set in a pre–Revolutionary War–era wharf building in between Waterfront Park and nearby Rainbow Row. The tucked-away location makes it more of a locals' restaurant, and patrons come to the hideaway

Try the Maverick Grits with shrimp and sausage at Slightly North of Broad (aka SNOB).

© SEAN SLINSKY

for sautéed jumbo lump crab cakes with red rice; green tea leaf–smoked pork chops with a sweet-potato cake and sautéed field greens, peach chutney, and pepper gravy; and the macadamia-nut-fried Carolina quail with collard greens, jalepeñno tasso, and corn bread. It's casual but white-linen fare; entrées range $10–25. Open nightly for dinner.

When Bradley O'Leary wrote his *Dining By Candlelight: America's 200 Most Romantic Restaurants,* he named ❰ **Charleston Grill at Charleston Place** (224 Market St., 843/577-4522, www.charlestongrill.com) South Carolina's most romantic restaurant. And rightly so: It is a beautiful, intimate, and elegantly formal spot, looking out on Charleston Place's courtyard. Dinner entrées average around $30, but the price is worth it if you're tired of conventional Lowcountry fare. It regularly wins a Mobil Four Star rating. Open nightly for dinner. Reservations are suggested.

Peninsula Grill (112 Market St., 843/723-0700, www.peninsulagrill.com) is Charleston Grill's main rival in the Lowcountry goes über-gourmet and über-fantastic in an über-elegant setting. It, too, has been one of the city's long-standing award winners on the national gourmand scene. Think loud and festive folks surrounded by velvet walls, and a menu of cracklin' pork osso buco with lemon-thyme potato pie, sweet onion arugula, and jus; pan-roasted jumbo scallops with yellow tomato cobbler, steamed spinach, and lobster-tomato butter; and benne-crusted rack of lamb in a coconut mint pesto. Get the coconut cake for dessert (*really*) and go when you either want to impress your dining companions or celebrate an event. Dinner entrées average about $30. Open nightly for dinner. Reservations are suggested.

Seafood

While nearly every restaurant in town serves seafood, a few places specialize in it particularly. Of those, **Fish** (442 King St., 843/722-3474, www.fishrestaurant.net) is a very low-key, warmhearted spot in the Upper King area that serves such dishes as blue crab–stuffed tuna, mahimahi, and wreckfish, each for around $17.

During warm months, try the shrimp cocktail with its Bloody Mary sorbet, or the lobster gazpacho if you opt to dine outdoors in the small intimate courtyard. Open for lunch Mon.–Fri., and dinner Mon.–Sat.

Just around the corner from Fish is **Coast Bar and Grill** (39-D John St., 843/722-8838, www.coastbarandgrill.com), set in a cavernous brick warehouse off an alley, which makes it easy to miss. That's a mixed blessing in that if you *can* find it, you can often get a last-minute table. Come here for the ambience, part seafood shack, part tiki hut gone upscale; the blowfish lamp bar; and the freshest, healthiest seafood offerings in town. Try the seviche, Baja fish tacos, grilled soft-shell crab, paella, or your-pick fish and sauce cooked over open flames in the oak-wood grill. Entrées range $15–30. Open nightly for dinner.

❰ **Fleet Landing** (186 Concord St., 843/722-8100, www.fleetlanding.net) is one of Charleston's youngest restaurants, destined for continued popularity because it's the only waterfront restaurant on the downtown peninsula. A onetime Depression-era ferry-shuttle depot, and later a Navy fleet-landing building, the space was vacant from 1970 until 2004, when the insides were gutted and turned into today's mod-nautical themed restaurant. Here, a half block south of Waterfront Park, cement floors and beams share space with life jackets as wall art, and kids are just as welcome in the boat-vinyl booths as happy-hour types are at the open-air bar. The building juts out over the marsh and above the water; sit outside and you can watch the dolphins and pelicans feed. Try the fried-seafood platters, fresh catch of the day as you like it, the fried-green-tomato stack with blue-crab salad, and the slaw. Open daily for lunch and dinner; lunches average $8, dinners $20.

Hank's Seafood Restaurant (109 Hayne St., 843/723-3474, www.hanksseafood.com) rounds out this seafood category as the priciest and most boisterous of the group. Expect huge portions, a rowdy community table, and butcher paper–covered two- and four-top tables, set with heavy cutlery and pillars of real sea salt. Try the Lowcountry bouillabaise (fish, clams, oysters, mussels, shrimp, and scallops in tomato, leek, and garlic broth) for $22; the seafood à la Wando (sautéed shrimp, scallops, and fish with sherry-finished crabmeat and button mushrooms in shellfish saffron cream with fried grit cakes) for $20; or the seafood platter #2 (crab cake, crumb-fried shrimp, french-fried sweet potatoes, and coleslaw) for $18. It's run by the same people behind Peninsula Grill. Open nightly for dinner.

Continental

Long considered one of the most *interesting* dining experiences in Charleston, the tiny **Robert's of Charleston** (182 E. Bay St., 843/577-7565, www.robertsofcharleston.com) is run by owner/chef Robert Dickson and his wife. Robert sings as well as he cooks, so you're treated to operatic selections and songs from Broadway musicals as you dine on the finely rendered prix fixe fare; expect to pay $83 per person, not including tax and tip. You needn't worry about what to order; Robert decides that for you. As you might guess, you need reservations. Seating is at 7:30 PM, Thurs.–Sat.

Fast & French/Gaulart & Maliclet French Café (98 Broad St., 843/577-9797, www.fast-andfrench.org) is a very unique, very *narrow*, very French restaurant that feels like a quick trip to the Continent. Locals comes for the community tables, no-fuss (but authentic and tasty) French fare, and fabulously unstuffy service. Thursday night is fondue night, and the gazpacho and carrot cake are the best in the city. Open daily for breakfast and lunch; dinner Tues.–Sat. Prices range $5–12.

39 Rue de Jean (39 John St., 843/722-8881, www.39Ruedejean.com) looks and feels exactly like a brasserie in Paris, down to the waiters dressed in white shirtsleeves and black aprons. The food is fresh with a mostly French influence, although you'll find a pretty extensive sushi menu. Mussels are also an excellent specialty here with six recipes to choose from. The outside café-style seating is very popular in the fall and spring. A plat du jour is featured daily, with entrées such as braised rabbit,

coq au vin, and cassoulet. The kitchen is open until midnight, and the wine list is extensive. Open daily for lunch and dinner. Dinner prices range $17–25.

The most upscale French fare downtown is served in the artfully funk-meets-swank space at **Tristan** (55 S. Market St., 843/534-2156, www.tristandining.com). If it's chilly, try the Kobe oxtail soup with toasted pearl barley, horseradish, wild mushrooms and truffles in Kobe beef broth. And the langoustines (lobster-and-chervil stuffing fried with Kataifi pastry, over fingerling potatoes and seabean mushrooms, with lemon aioli and fried candied lemon slices) is another wild ride. *Woah* right here! Find Tristan, one of the most unmobbed best restaurants in town, in the Old City Market area. Lunch entrées are about $12; dinner entrées range $17–39. Open daily for lunch and dinner, and Sun. for brunch.

And because it considers itself to be "contemporary American with a French flair," I'm including █ **McCrady's** (2 Unity Alley, 843/577-0025, www.mccradysrestaurant.com). Set in the city's oldest tavern (circa 1778), McCrady's is of the same caliber as top dogs Peninsula and Charleston Grill, but is a little more Frenchie than Southern, and a little hipper, too, though no less well-heeled. The rock shrimp crepes with truffle sauce, and the venison with micro potatoes, apples, celery root, and truffle caramel sauce are ridiculously fantastic. There's an adjoining wine bar with a tapas menu. Come here to celebrate, to dig into the award-winning, extremely deep wine list, and to eat at one of the country's most acclaimed restaurants. Entrées range $25–34. Open nightly for dinner.

Italian

If you've been bustling about the historic district all day and can use a little tranquillity, head over to **Fulton Five** (5 Fulton St., 843/853-5555), one of the most intimate restaurants in town. Tucked back off King Street south of Market, Fulton Five offers fine northern Italian cuisine, like braised lamb shank with oven-roasted zucchini, mushroom, and

Parmesan polenta cake, with a caramelized sweet onion and marsala reduction. Dine outside on the tiny, second-story courtyard, or inside in the cozy, low-ceilinged living room. Dinners range $15–32. Reservations are suggested. Open Mon.–Sat. for dinner. (The owners close the place sometime in mid-Aug. when it gets too hot and open again in early Sept.)

Right up King Street, you'll find another Italian classic, **Il Cortile del Re** (193 King St., 843/853-1888). With the city's best dining courtyard, its warm-colored and softly lit dining space and wine bar (all long, skinny rambling spaces), and its Italian owners who specialize in nonpretentious fare, it's another favorite hangout among locals. Try the Cinghiale con Fagioli e Polenta (traditional slowly stewed wild boar with cannellini beans and polenta in tomato sauce). Prices range $12–25. Open for dinner Mon.–Sat.

Over in the more-populated Old City Market area **Cintra** (16 Market St., 843/377-1090) serves more nouveau Italian fare in a hipster setting alongside an extensive martini menu. Lowcountry flavors show up in some of the entrées, like the shrimp-and-calamari Sicilian Fregula stew with pine nuts, caper berries, and currants, and the triggerfish piccata with rapini and Anson Mills polenta. Prices range $16–32. Open nightly for dinner.

Steak and Ribs

On the dressed-down end, locally owned **Sticky Fingers** (235 Meeting St., 843/853-7427, www.stickyfingers.com) opened in 1992, and regularly wins awards for its ribs and barbecue. As it's one of two barbecue spots downtown, it's a little more touristy than off-the-path, but that doesn't stop countless celebs from stopping in and leaving their head shots and autographs. Try the Memphis-style ribs with bourbon barbecue sauce. Open daily for lunch and dinner. Prices range $15–20.

On the dressed-up end, there are a few major players on the meat-eating scene. The newest of the bunch is **Oak Steakhouse** (17 Broad St., 843/722-4220, www.oaksteakhouserestaurant.com), located in the thick of the action on

Broad Street in an 150-year-old building. The inside's as classic as the Italian-tinged menu of veal (offered four ways), steaks, lamb, pork chops (offered with a variety of sauces), and more, and features huge windows that open onto the streets, three levels of intimate dining rooms with hardwood floors, fireplaces, and fine oil paintings. Prices range from $17 for a burger to $54 for the 28-ounce prime porterhouse. Open for dinner Mon.–Sat.

Another relative newbie is **Mo Sussman's Steakhouse** (Meeting St., 843/958-8887, www.mosussmansstakhouse.com). Here, the sirloin strips are dry aged for 26 days, the burgers are of Kobe beef, and steak and eggs means Kobe flat-iron steak with local Mepkin Abbey organic eggs. Try the potato pancakes as a side. Prices range $18–41. Open for dinner Mon.–Sat.

The last of this white-linen group is the Market Pavilion Hotel's **Grill 225** (225 E. Bay St., 843/266-4222, www.grill225.com). This open, airy, light-filled space is the city's only 100 percent USDA Prime steak house, meaning it serves the most tender and juicy beef of the bunch. Add its luxury boutique hotel service, and giant wine list, and it's the fairest of them all on the gussied-up front. Prices top out at $39. Open daily for lunch and dinner, Sun. for brunch as well. Casual but nice clothing is the standard at each of these, and reservations are recommended.

Barbecue

Downtown, you'll find barbecue at the aforementioned Sticky Fingers, and as of 2005, at **Jim 'N Nick's Bar-B-Q** (288 King St., 843/577-0406, www.jimnnicks.com) in the heart of King Street shopping district. Though the small Southern chain has Birmingham roots, the 'cue is just as good as other local offerings, even if the meat (pork, chicken, turkey, Angus beef, pork link sausage) is a little different: Hickory smoked in brick pits, it's crispy on the outside, juicy on the inside, and served with their signature sweet-and-spicy tomato-based sauce. It's good stuff, and definitely worth repeat visits. Sides like homemade cheese biscuits, creamed spinach, and collard greens, and mile-high pies (lemon ice box, chocolate cream, pecan, coconut) round out the meal. Their family reunion value meals feed from 4 to 18 people and are great for beach picnics. Most dinner run about $10, but Jim's Deluxe Combo (a half rack of ribs, three barbecued meats, and four sides) goes for $30 and a heart attack. Open daily for lunch and dinner.

For old-school, homegrown barbecue joints, you'll need to leave the Charleston peninsula, but it's well worth the trip. One of the oldest (1946) and most revered spots is **Bessinger's BBQ and Burgers** (1602 Hwy. 17, 843/556-1354, www.bessingersbbq.com) in West Ashley, run by Thomas Bessinger. Featuring his own variation-on-a-theme mustard-based sauce, expect tried-and-true barbecue items with Southern sides. Open Mon.–Sat. for lunch and dinner; and Sun. for buffet-style lunch and dinner. Lunch averages about $8, dinner about $15, and the buffet is $11.50.

Another Bessinger brother runs **Melvin's Barbecue** from two locations, one on James Island (538 Folly Rd., James Island, 843/762-0511, www.melvinsbbq.com), and another in Mount Pleasant (925 Houston Northcutt Blvd., 843/881-0549, www.melivinsbbq.com). These are probably my favorite barbecue spots in the Charleston area, and Melvin's been holding court down here for some 50 years. Much to the surprise of loads of folks, *Playboy* magazine voted Melvin's hamburgers the best in all of the United States back in 1999, and Emeril more recently said Melvin's has the best cheeseburgers in the country. But I'd still go for the barbecue—it's that good. Open Mon.–Sat. for lunch and dinner. Prices range from $3 for a hotdog to $15.99 for the "killer" South Carolina barbecue combo plate.

Some swear that **Momma Brown's Bar-B-Que** (1471 Ben Sawyer Blvd., 843/849-8802) is the best in the area, but they must be North Carolinians—so is Momma. Whereas Melvin and Thomas Bessinger excel with their father Joe's legendary South Carolina hickory mustard and hickory red sauces, Momma's $8 buffet features a North Carolina–like pepper-and-vin-egar sauce along with such Southern favorites as macaroni and cheese, hash, and banana pudding. They'll sell it to you by the sandwich, the plate, or in bulk ($4 per pound). Open Tues.–Sat. for lunch and dinner; Sun. for lunch.

Burgers

While the previously called-out Rue de Jean, a few of the barbecue joints, and all the steak houses offer some fine gourmet and down-home burgers, there are two places in town that specialize in the American passion. **Bodacious Burgers** (102 N. Market St., 843/720-4737) lets you pick your patty: beef, lamb, tuna, black bean, buffalo, ostrich, crab, turkey veal, venison, duck, and on and on), your roll (six kinds), your cheese (eight types), your veggies (nine varieties), and extras (avocado, fried egg, mango chutney, and more). Served in a smoky sports-bar atmosphere, it's definitely a testosterone zone, and a college hangout. A loaded burger averages $10. Open daily for lunch and dinner. At the other end of the spectrum is the local longtime favorite, **Your Place** (6 N. Market St., 843/722-8360), recently relocated inside the Rainbow Shops at the Old City Market, at North Market and State streets. With its graffitied tables, dollar bills on the wall, old vinyl stools and booths, Your Place is as dressed down as they come, just like the menu. Your patty (hand-formed, beef only), comes on a bun with lettuce, tomato, onion, and mayo, and extras like cheese, jalepeño, or bacon. So why the following among Charlestonians? The burgers are that good, big, juicy, and how you'd wish they'd taste at home, for about $5, with a pickle and chips on the side. Open Mon.–Sat. 10 AM–4 PM. Cash only.

Mexican and Southwestern

For a little taste of Austin, Texas–style digs and laid-back Tex-Mex fare, head to **Juanita Greenberg's Nacho Royale** either downtown (439 King St., 843/723-6224) or on James Island en route to Folly Beach (967 Folly Rd., 843/576-6224). Try the especially good chicken quesadillas ($5.70). Open daily for lunch and dinner. As of press time, the best burrito spot in town was opening anew, and locals were counting the days. **Yo' Burrito** (77 Wentworth St., 843/853-3287, www.yo-burrito.com) is part groover bar, part college and neighborhood hangout, and part the place where homemade salsa addicts and mahi burrito lovers get their fix. The beer's cheap, the lemonade's fresh-squeezed, and the shrimp, chicken, and pork quesadillas are plain wicked. Burritos are about $6.50, quesadillas $7.

Pub Grub

Make no mistake: Charleston is just as much a drinkin' town as it is an eatin' town. That means there are scads of places to get a good bite along with your pint. For starters, **Tommy Condon's** (160 Market St., 843/577-3818, www.tommycondons.com) is one of my favorite places to catch a Notre Dame game. It's a quintessential Charleston eating bar, owned by the pillarlike (and verifiably Irish) Condon family, and the kind of neighborly place that other chains try to emulate. Come to hear live Irish music Wed.–Sun. nights. The food—featuring local seafood and some Irish standards—is good, but the main reason to eat here is that it's one of the last-standing locally owned institutions in the Market area. Open daily for lunch and dinner (till 1 or 2 A.M.). Prices average about $10.

Next up is the easy-to-miss local hideout, **Vickery's Beaufain Street Bar and Grill** (15 Beaufain St., 843/577-5300, www.vickerys.com), which is lodged discreetly between King and Archdale streets. The interior, like the menu, has a Cuban-slash-Lowcountry look. The worn-in bar, booths, and wooden tables and chairs accommodate the usual amiable crowd of mostly downtown residents. As for food, the jerk-roasted chicken with black beans and rice is a favorite. Lots of light meals, black beans, and salads are offered, too, and best enjoyed on the relaxed outdoor patio. Open daily (except Christmas) for lunch and dinner (till 2 A.M.). Prices range $10–16. Another seriously local bar with eats is the **Blind Tiger Pub** (38 Broad St., 843/722-9601, www.btpub.com). The menu's limited but serves its beer-buddy

or Bloody Mary–partner purpose: burgers, wings, and seven paninis to choose from, plus weekend brunch with frittatas, omelets, and bananas Foster French toast. Open daily for lunch and dinner. Expect to pay about $10 for any meal.

One last spot worth mentioning here is in a class of its own: **Pavilion Bar** (225 E. Bay St., 843/266-4222, www.grill225.com). While other fine hotel restaurants in town have terrific bar menus (Peninsula Grill and Charleston Grill, for example), the rooftop Pavilion excels not only in its offerings—smoked chicken and plantain pizza, rum-spiced baked brie, Kobe beef or USDA Prime sirloin burgers—but also in its unparalleled view. Located in the rooftop pool area of the city's only true boutique hotel, the umbrella-covered tables look out over the city, the harbor, and the new bridge with nary an obstruction. Dishes range $10–15. Open daily for lunch and dinner.

Asian

If you like your seafood raw, as in sushi style, Rue De Jean has a great selection, but **Sushi Hiro** (298 King St., 843/723-3628) specializes in the stuff. Not quite a hole in the wall, but not a bit flashy or fussy, either, it's where sushi fans head for authenticity and low prices: six-piece rolls for $3.75; or two sashimi pieces for $3.50. There are drink and daily specials, too. Open Mon.–Sat. for dinner. If Thai food's your thing, you've got two solid options. **Little Thai Too** (350 King St., 723-4990, www.littlethaihouse.com) typically has a short wait, is not a scenester place, and sits in the heart of the middle King Street shopping area. With a huge selection (green-curry salmon and red-curry duck are tops), custom "secret recipe" sauces to choose from, and a booklet of choices for about $11 or less, it's a winner. Open for lunch Mon.–Fri.; open nightly for dinner. Little Thai's older cousin is in the Upper King Street area, just north of the visitors center. **Basil** (460 King St., 843/724-3490) is the rowdier of the pair, and given its proximity to some of the hipper, local-frequented bars in town (plus, of course, its great food), it tends to be packed with cool folk. If that's what you're looking for, put your name on the list and mingle at the bar till your table's ready. (Try for a kitchen seat, as it's got a great view of the chef-magicians, and tends to open up faster than other spots in this first-come place.) The menu's a one-page affair, but the offerings range from a great Pad Thai to their perfect fried duck, with lots of roaming in between. Lunch plates are about $8, and dinner runs $11–21. Open Mon.–Fri. for lunch and dinner.

Mediterranean

If you are shopping the King Street strip and need a lunch spot that appeals to the whole crew, there are two places that would well do the trick. (Save dinner out, though, for one of the other places mentioned here, as these are not necessarily Charleston-unique.) **Olde Towne Seafood** (229 King St., 843/723-8170) has been around since 1972, which is astounding in a city that's weathered so much change in the last 30 years. It's all taverna, dark, wooden booths, chickens on a rotisserie spit, and the smells of fried potatoes and garlic. The Greek fare is the best (moussaka, spanakopita, souvlaki sandwich), but the alternatives (hamburgers, seafood po'boys, chicken fingers) do the trick as well. Kids meals are about half the price of adult fare. Open daily for lunch (about $7–8) and dinner (about $10–17). For more of a café experience, with windows that look out onto the bustling King Street, try **Sermet's** (276 King St., 843/853-7775). The grilled salmon with red wine–poached pears, gorgonzola, mixed greens, and kiwi apple vinaigrette ($12) is a satisfying but light lunch, and the crab burger with aioli and sweet-potato fries ($9) is awesome. There are panini and pastas, too, with small and regular portions offered at both lunch and dinner. Kids can get burgers, pasta, and grilled cheese.

Tapas

For a region that used to be more inclined toward all-you-can-eat buffets, the greater Charleston area has seen a recent explosion in the number of tapas restaurants. The ones downtown are equal parts restaurant, lounge, wine bar, and local bar.

The first on the scene was **Chai's Lounge & Tapas** (462 King St., 843/722-7313), and it's swank central with earth-toned walls and murals, and earthy mod lamps and lanterns casting a soft glow about. For $7 apiece, try the quesadilla (crawfish, smoked Gouda queso, peppers, roasted tomato, and corn relish); the crispy rock shrimp (a huge portion in a Chinese to-go box); and the mini Angus burgers. Open nightly, with live music and DJs. Just up the street in the same Upper King part of town, **Raval** (453 King St., 843/853-8466) is all about atmosphere, and has a Goth-wine-cellar look about it. Huge community bar-top tables fill the tiny seating area, but with candlelight and loads of wine-by-the-glass options, it all has a rosy, cozy, relaxed look. As for food, it's more appetizer fare (beet-and-egg salad, ham-and-cheese plates, chorizo and piperade, squid salad), but here less is more, thanks to artful combos packed with flavor. Just as you taste the wines, you taste the tapas ($7 average). Open for dinner Mon.–Sat.

Diner Food

A classic locals' breakfast spot in town is **Jack's Café** (41 C George St., 843/723-5237) featuring top-notch waffles, grits, homemade (from scratch) biscuits, home fries, decent coffee, eggs, and of course, Jack himself, at the grill as he has been since 1972. Also, the burgers are just as rocking as the breakfast. Open for breakfast and lunch Mon.–Fri. 6:30 AM–3:30 PM. You'll pay about $6 or less here for either meal. The **Marina Variety Store Restaurant** (17 Lockwood Dr., 843/723-6325, www.citymarina.com) is another great greasy spoon downtown open daily for all three meals, starting at 6:30 AM. Come here for awesome views of the Ashley River, ancient wooden booths, and a menu that's got basic diner fare, plus bonuses like fried grits, alligator tails, and shrimp-stuffed omelets. Expect to pay about $6 for breakfast, $8 for lunch, and $12 for dinner.

Breakfast and Brunch

Aside from Jack's, there are two other worthwhile restaurants serving solely breakfast and lunch downtown. **The Baker's Café** (214 King St., 843/577-2694, www.bakerscafe.com) is one, and offers frittatas and 11 kinds of poached eggs, topped with everything from artichoke hearts, smoked salmon, crumbled bacon, and cheddar, to sausage, onions, mushrooms, cream, and hot sauce for breakfast. It's located in the Lower King area and is a great place to start a day of shopping or exploring historic sites. Prices are about $9. Open Mon.–Fri. 8 AM–2 PM, Sat.–Sun. 9 AM–2 PM.

The other worthwhile restaurant, owned by members of the same family, is the **Bookstore Café** (412 King St., 843/720-8843, www.bookstorecafecateringandevents.com), open for breakfast at 9 AM weekdays and 8 AM on weekends. It features unique twists on tried-and-true Lowcountry eats. Try the "Southern Benedict," with fried green tomatoes, bacon, and eggs on croustades with hollandaise sauce ($9.25), or the simpler "Keith's Breakfast Special" ($9.95): eggs and fried green tomatoes, topped with country ham, gravy, and grits ($8.95). They also offer 10 different $9 Island Potato Casseroles: a bed of home fries, grilled onions, peppers, and mushrooms topped with eggs and (depending on whether you choose a "Dewees," "Seabrook," "Kiawah," "Wadmalaw," or "Goat") an assortment of other toppings. Lunch brings salads, soup, and sandwiches, including the roasted-pork-and-fried-green-tomato sandwich ($8.95) and a Monte Cristo (also $8.75). The restaurant, which wears bookshelf wallpaper inside, is just north of Marion Square.

And a quick word about brunch: It's a local institution, thanks to the late-Saturday-night proclivities of residents and visitors alike. Charleston Grill, Peninsula Grill, Tristan, Hominy Grill, Fleet Landing, Carolina's, Grill 225, and ◖ **High Cotton** (199 E. Say St., 843/724-3815) all excel in exemplary brunches. Call ahead for reservations.

OUTLYING AREAS
Folly Beach

On the way out to Folly Beach is **Bowen's Island** (1870 Bowen Island Rd., 843/795-

2757). You may not believe that this shabbiest of shacks has good food when you first see it, but actually, it isn't all that hard to believe because the Lowcountry is full of such hovels. What's hard to believe is that this is one of the best spots in the Lowcountry to eat authentic South Carolina seafood—oysters especially. Open for dinner Tues.–Sat. Prices range $9–19 for local oysters roasted seasonally in burlap sacks. Cash or local check only.

On Folly Beach proper, most restaurants cluster around the main drag—Center Street. There's a mix of dive bars and fried-seafood places, plus a few standout restaurants. On the fried end of the spectrum, **The Crab Shack** (24 Center St., 843/588-3080) here is the best location of the local chain. There's a wild outdoor porch, where swing chairs meet tables piles with buckets and baskets of food. Plastic forks and knives help families tear into standard local seafood platters, and other Lowcountry fare like shrimp-and-crab casserole, deviled crabs, and shrimp cakes. Prices average about $14. Open for lunch and dinner daily. Another similarly laid-back and family-friendly spot is **Snapper Jack's** (10 Center St., 843/588-2362), where all 17 of their hot and cold sandwiches are less than $9; and where the ribs and fish have a Cajun kick. Dinner entrées average $20. Another super-casual spot is **Woody's** (39 Center St., 843/588-0088), which specializes in pizza, subs (all $6.95), and beer. Try the $14–18 White Pizza (parmesan, reggiano, ricotta, provolone, mozzarella, spinach, garlic, and tomato). Open daily for lunch and dinner.

For finer dining fare, you've got three options on Folly. First, there's **RJ's Seashell Restaurant** (41 Center St., 843/588-9001), where you can get fried, broiled, or grilled local seafood, served with sweet-potato fries, coleslaw, and hush puppies, and Southern favorites like fried-green-tomatoes salad with black-eyed-pea relish and blue cheese, shrimp and grits, and buttermilk fried chicken with black pepper gravy, collard greens, and garlic mashed potatoes. Dinner entrées average $17. Open for lunch and dinner daily, plus brunch on weekends. And the local tapas craze has spread all the way out here, too, in the form of **11 Center Street Wine & Gourmet** (11 Center St., 843/588-9898). Downstairs is a wine and gourmet food shop, where you can buy bottles to go with your meal. Outside there's a fireplace and candlelit patio, while upstairs is an open-aired, covered deck with great views and live, mellow music, tables, and sofas. The sea bass wrapped in prosciutto with olives and basil cream sauce ($10) is a good pick, as are the spinach and chicken spring rolls, sautéed with bacon, corn, and mozzarella, then wrapped in a wonton and fried ($8). Open for lunch and dinner daily. Last is the gently worn, but still reigning grand dame of nice dining in these parts: **Café Suzanne** (4 Center St., 843/588-2101). Come here for a quiet place where older family members and those seeking a little below-radar intimacy can try gourmet dishes. Entrées run the gamut from oven-roasted duck breast with apple-raisin chutney to shrimp, sausage and spinach in basil tomato sauce with gnocchi, and chicken schnitzel and dressing. Dinner entrées average $17. Open for lunch and dinner Tues.–Sat., and for brunch Sun.

Speaking of breakfast food, the **Lost Dog Café** (13 A Center St., 843/588-9669) serves it up all day. Offering everything from cinnamon rolls and pancakes to lox, cream cheese, tomatoes, and capers on a bagel, plus coffees galore, it's the best everyday wake-up out here. Their Thai wrap and chicken salad on a croissant are great lunch options, too. Most meals are $6 or less. Open daily 6:30 AM–3 PM.

West Ashley

This part of town has gotten a bad rap for years. But thanks to the funky Avondale commercial strip, with Junk & Jive Retro Mart, great thrift and antique stores, and Poe's Studio, the restaurants that have sprung up here make it a sometime destination for downtowners tired of downtown prices. Head here to eat if you want to get out of the fray on the peninsula, or if you find yourself shopping and starved. The finest dining in these parts is at **Al Di La** (25 Magnolia Rd., 843/571-2321),

where the northern Italian fare is gourmet and tenderly rendered. The bread's made in-house and will undo you, and pastas include ricotta and mascarpone gnocchi with shrimp, grape tomatoes, and basil. The pan-roasted chicken breast, wrapped in prosciutto and stuffed with torn bread, gold raisins, and fontina cheese in an onion sauce ($14.50) is another favorite, though the menu changes daily. Entrées range from $9 for a small pasta plate, to $15. Open for dinner Tues.–Sat. **Voodoo** (15 Magnolia Rd., 843/769-0228) is part swank-meets-retro-funk bar, and part tiki tapas lounge. The pupu platter ($18) is an array of peanut-sesame chicken satays, crab rangoon, coconut-banana shrimp, Szechwan beef egg rolls, and red chili barbecue ribs. Their gourmet tacos run $6 for two, and small plates are all less than $10. The kitchen's open Mon.–Fri. 4 PM–1:30 AM, Sat.–Sun. 5:30 PM–1:30 AM.

Those with a serious need for Indian food are in luck here, as the city's only two India restaurants call Avondale home. The one within easiest walking distance of the shops is **Taste of India** (851 Hwy. 17, 843/556-0772, www.tasteofindia.biz). The $6.99 daily lunch buffet is the best deal, but nighttime means you score, too, since there are pages of offerings featuring traditional favorites. Open daily for lunch and dinner.

Please see *Middleton Place* in the *Sights* section for information on dining at **Middleton Place Restaurant.**

Shem Creek

There's some good eating to be done out on Shem Creek in Mount Pleasant. My favorite is the casual, creek-side **Shem Creek Bar and Grill** (508 Mill St., 843/884-8102, www.shemcreekbarandgrill.com). Local restaurant icon John Avenger and company make some mean milk shakes, especially the Dreamsicle (vanilla ice cream, orange juice, amaretto) and the Oreo (vanilla ice cream, Oreo cookies, kahlua), for $5.95. But the true star here is the seafood; every day brings new specials, but you won't go wrong with the basic fried shrimp dinner ($12.99), served with creek shrimp and vegetables.

Arrive by boat if you like, and stay for the sunset. At night have a drink down on the dockside bar, and try an oyster from the raw bar, too. Open for lunch and dinner nightly.

Back in 1999, **Vickery's Bar and Grill**—they of downtown fame—opened a Shem Creek location (1313 Shrimpboat La., 843/884-4440, www.vickerys.com). With the double martinis, seafood, Cuban theme, and the best sunset view of the marshes and shrimp boats in the whole Charleston area, it has the broadest appeal for bar rats, families, locals, and tourists-in-the-know. Prices range $10–16. Open daily for lunch and dinner (till 1 A.M.).

Rivaling the aforementioned old-timers for creek-side bar action is newcomer **Red's Icehouse** (98 Church St., 843/388-0003, www.redsicehouse). Once a true dockside icehouse, Red's galvanized sides now houses the youngest, liveliest scene in these parts, where the waterside view lets diners see who caught what out at sea that day. Beer comes in buckets, and food-wise, the steamed oysters, Lowcountry boil, and Baja shrimp tacos are good bets. Most meals run about $10, with scores of po'boys below that. Check in about the weekly sunset cruises, with food, drinks, and live music. Open daily for lunch and dinner.

If you're aiming for super-casual, try out ◖ **The Wreck (of the Richard and Charlene)** (106 Haddrell St., 843/884-0052). This truly used to be a restaurant that no one but a handful of locals knew about, but once everybody else heard about this great undiscovered place in a run-down icehouse with big portions, reasonable prices, boiled peanuts for appetizers, and fried grits as a side, The Wreck became, well, *discovered*. But that doesn't mean it's not still wickedly good. Deep-fried shrimp and fish are the specialties. Aim for the shack at the end of a dirt lot between two wholesale seafood operations, and you've got the right place (there's no sign). Open Tues.–Sun. for dinner. Prices range $12–18. Cash and local checks only.

Mount Pleasant

People in the Mount Pleasant area used to have to cross a bridge to find a good restaurant. Not anymore: With the rapid growth of the area east of the Cooper River, there is no shortage of great dining. Although there's no reason to take it this far, you could even spend an entire vacation hereabouts and not have to head downtown to eat.

Its strip-mall location is not initially promising, but **Locklear's Lowcountry Grill** (320 W. Coleman Blvd., 843/884-3346, www.locklears.com) serves some of my favorite seafood and Southern fare in the Lowcountry. Try the luscious Rockville shrimp and hominy with its spicy Cajun crème sauce ($15), and a cup or bowl of their award-winning she-crab soup. Lunch is less than $10, and dinner runs about $16 a plate. Open daily for lunch and dinner, and Sun. for a great brunch. In the same complex is **Niko's Café** (320 Coleman Blvd., 843/216-7785), a Greek restaurant serving wonderful spanakopita, marinated roast pork, and lamb. The herb-roasted potatoes are tremendous. Tell them you were sent by a Greek-American travel writer, and maybe they'll slip you some free baklava—but don't count on it. Lunch is less than $7, while dinner prices range $7–18. Open Tues.–Sat. for lunch and dinner.

Down the road just a bit, the reasonably priced **Boulevard Diner** (409 Coleman Blvd., 843/216-2611) serves great fresh fish, along with diner food with a creative, gourmet twist. For $7 apiece, the chicken potpie and country fried steak are great, and the fried eggplant, tomato, and blue-cheese sandwich is crave-worthy. Open Mon.–Sat. (starting at 7 A.M.) for breakfast, lunch, and dinner. It's not surprising that Boulevard is owned by the same folks who run The Mustard Seed, just down the road. Speaking of **The Mustard Seed** (1036 Chuck Dawley Blvd., 843/849-0050), it's a friendly, heartfelt local favorite that you might well miss if you aren't looking for it. Vegetarians and health-conscious folks with big appetites fare well with the moderately priced offerings, including mounds of sweet potatoes and shrimp, lemon, and basil cakes. Every entrée is under $11. Open Mon.–Sat. for lunch and dinner.

For seriously authentic Lowcountry eats, try ◖ **Gullah Cuisine** (1717 Hwy. 17 N,

843/881-9076) where lunch entrées go for about $10, and the $6.45 lunch buffet features Southern church supper–style offerings (red rice, fried chicken, candied yams, and on). Dinner plates (about $16),such as crab cakes, shrimp and grits, and seafood casserole, go well with the okra gumbo and she-crab soup. Open Mon.–Sat. for lunch and dinner; Sun. 11 AM–3:30 PM.

For a better-than-average country breakfast in a roadside-diner-dive setting, try **Billy's Back Home** (794 Coleman Blvd., 843/881-3333). My wife swears that Billy's has the best country-fried ham in the business. Open Mon.–Sat. 6 AM–3 PM. Everything is under $10.

For a lighter breakfast, **Bagel Nation** (1909 Hwy. 17 N, 843/881-1462), in the Bi-Lo complex next to Towne Centre, serves wonderful, boiled bagels (the owner's Jersey accent suggests she knows her stuff) Single bagels are $0.79 or 13 for $7.99, and bagel sandwiches are $6.

For a quick bite (in a prime spot on Coleman Boulevard if you're coming or going from Sullivan's Island), **So-Cal Burritos** (440 W. Coleman Blvd., 843/216/0708) wraps superior steak, fish, fried, Thai or fajita chicken, and shrimp burritos. Try the tacos, too, like the crab cake BLT, or the beer-battered mahimahi tacos with cabbage and Baja sauce. Families are welcome, and flip-flops dominate here. Also, because it's also a surfer-themed bar, they serve beer and frozen drinks. Most burritos are $7. Open daily for lunch and dinner. Another place for a quick—and potentially healthful—bite is the **Whole Foods Market** (923 Houston Northcutt Blvd., 843/971-7240) hot-and-cold food bar. Think organic fare, some ethnic, some gone Southern, like North Carolina–pulled pork barbecue, sweet potatoes with honey, tofu stir fry, wood-oven pizzas, roasted veggies, and loads more. Everything's by the pound in the food bar; expect to pay about $9 for a fully loaded plate. Open daily.

While everywhere mentioned in Mount Pleasant thus far is not necessarily "fancy," there are a handful of great places in this area

to get downtown-caliber food *and* ambience. Head to these if you have a special event and just can't make it over the bridge. **Coco's** (863 Houston-Northcutt Blvd., 843/881-4949, www.cocoscafe.net) is the real French deal. Like most of the places in Mount P, you have to disregard the strip-mall location, but once you get over the exterior trappings, it's a quirky, dark little bistro all the way inside. The homemade duck paté ($6.25), and Escargots de la Bourgogne baked in garlic butter ($6.25) are old favorites, and the panfried flounder in brown butter ($16.95) is fantastic. Dinner entrées average $17. Lunch is a $11 prix fixe affair with selections changing daily, often the most popular dinner meals with a soup or salad, glass of wine or beer. Open for lunch Mon.–Fri., for dinner Mon.–Sat. **Langdon's Restaurant and Wine Bar** (778 S. Shellmore Rd., 843/388-9200) is another hidden gem, this one tucked away off Johnnie Dodds Boulevard by the Bi-Lo shopping center near I'On. Come here for Lowcountry dishes served in a white-linen atmosphere; try the crispy grouper over brie grits with apple-wood-smoked bacon in chardonnay-basil cream ($28); or the pork rib chop candied with a hoisen-honey glaze, served with citrus-seared sweet potatoes and collard greens ($19). Open for dinner Mon.–Sat. Last up is **Zinc Bistro and Bar** (28 A Bridgeside Blvd., 843/216-9330, www.zincbistroandbar.com). Set in the bottom floor in one of the law office towers out at Patriots Point, it looks the most like a downtown restaurant with it's mile-high ceilings, winding bar, sprawling outdoor patio, and crowd of beautiful people. But if the latter's a turnoff, get over it. Otherwise you'll miss an amazing, one-of-a-kind view of the harbor, Ravenel Bridge, and Charleston Battery, not to mention the supreme food as well. The grilled veal chop with local polenta, fava beans, and truffle butter ($28) is no joke; and the nicoise-style tuna tartare appetizer ($10) ain't no slouch, either. Taste the peanut butter chocolate mousse teardrop ($7) for dessert and you'll weep. Entrées average $25. Open for dinner Mon.–Sat. Get reservations at any of these three finer dining spots.

If you head up Chuck Dawley Boulevard toward I-526 and away from Coleman Boulevard, turn right on Bowman Road (at the Jack Flash car wash), and take a quick left on Stuart Engals Boulevard. One-half block up on your left, you'll come to the out-of-the-way **Olde Colony Bakery** (1391 Stuart Engals Blvd., 843/216-3232, www.oldecolonybakery.com), which used to be operated downtown on King Street. As King Street became more popular with cookie-buying tourists—and less so with cake-buying locals—the bakery's owners decided to move over here where they could get more baking done without all the distractions. Even so, they keep a little bakery shop here, selling traditional Lowcountry benne wafers, an authentic Charleston cookie derived from West Africa and named after the Bantu word for sesame seeds, from which the crisps are made. You also might try the Pecan Pinches and especially the Benne Cheese Zingers.

Sullivan's Island

Atlanticville Restaurant and Café (2063 Middle St., 843/883-9452, www.atlanticville.com) is set in and above what used to be a fairly unassuming produce stand here on the island. The restaurant has live music on Tues. and Fri., and serves contemporary American cuisine made from local seafood and produce. It's the dressiest joint on the island, with decor and prices to match. Dinners average $22. Open for dinner Mon.–Sat., and brunch Sun. 10 AM–2 PM.

Bert's Bar (2209 Middle St., 843/883-3924, www.berts-bar.com) is everybody's favorite secret place on Sullivan's Island. It's more an enigma than a secret, really—a *total dive* is what it is. And we're all darned glad to have a dive out here among the multimillion-dollar homes. This is a place where if you came often enough, everybody really would know your name. Sandwiches (deli meats and fixings, fried flounder, BLTs, grilled cheese) and baskets of chicken tenders and corn dogs make up the daily menu, where only one item goes over $6; and Friday nights means it's fish-fry time. Open from lunch till 2 AM daily.

Dunleavy's Pub (2213 A Middle St., 843/883-9646) is a great family bar where you can eat fairly cheaply out on the island. The hot dogs (served six ways, each for about $6) are stellar; and the shepherd's pie and roast beef with provolone are good, too. Open Sun.–Thurs. from lunch till 1 AM; and till 2 AM otherwise. Prices are less than $10.

If there's a scene on Sullivan's, which typically shies away from that, it's at **Poe's Tavern** (2210 Middle St., 843/883-0083, www.poestavern.com), so-named because Edgar Allen once was stationed here as a soldier. The no-fuss place, a mix of tables, bar, patio, and the liveliest porches on Middle Street, offers gourmet burgers and chicken sandwiches as the main event (plus a few super fish tacos and salads as sideshows). Choose your toppings based on their combos, then pick your meat, and you've got a masterpiece on the way. One winner: the Amontillado (guacamole, jalapeño Jack cheddar, pico de gallo salsa, and chipotle sour cream). Everything they offer makes great takeout, too. Prices average $9. Open daily for lunch and dinner.

High Thyme (2213-C Middle St., 843/883-3536) is the daintier, quiet, dressed-down café of the Sully bunch. Gourmet palates fare well here, with dishes like gnocchi, smoked salmon, and chorizo over spinach in brown butter; and benne-seed-crusted tilapia over Napa slaw with ginger sauce and wonton crisps. Lunch averages $8, and dinner runs about $19. Open Mon.–Sat., and for Sun. brunch.

Isle of Palms

My favorite place on Isle of Palms is still **Banana Cabana** (1130 Ocean Blvd., 843/886-4361). Even if you don't hear it playing while you're here, you'll leave singing Jimmy Buffet. The bar area itself, when you first walk in, is small and friendly, but walk on through to the enclosed porch and outside patio, where you'll find good seating and wonderful ocean views. Order the Macho Nachos ($8.99), the drink of your choice, and enjoy. Open daily for lunch and dinner.

Right upstairs from the Cabana, you'll find the pricier **One-Eyed Parrot** (1130 Ocean

Blvd., 843/886-4360), serving fresh seafood, Caribbean style. The Rasta fried grit cake with shrimp and scallops ($16.99) rocks, as does the Jerk Seafood Spectacular ($19.99). Open daily for dinner. A few yards down the beach, you'll find **Coconut Joe's** (1120 Ocean Blvd., 843/886-0046), which is popular for its great ocean views, its rooftop bar—often with reggae playing—and its fresh fish. If you come with a child, be sure to ask for a complimentary sea dollar. The coconut shrimp are supposed to be an appetizer, but they make a good, if slightly greasy, meal. Dinners average $18. Open daily for lunch and dinner; breakfast also Sat.–Sun. 8:30 AM–10:30 PM.

The other great restaurant on Isle of Palms is **The Sea Biscuit Café** (21 J. C. Long Blvd., 843/886-4079), which has great grits, great biscuits, and an exemplary collection of hot sauces. This is another one of those superior secret places that everybody knows about; if you get here late for breakfast on the weekend, bring or buy a paper, sit down outside, and prepare for a (worthwhile) wait. Open for breakfast and lunch Tues.–Fri. 6:30 AM–2:30 PM; breakfast only Sat.–Sun. 7:30 AM–1 PM. Prices average $6.

I always have to blink to think that the former greasy spoon that attracted bikers and boaters and looked and smelled like an old boathouse over at Breach Inlet has been revitalized into a fancy restaurant called **The Boathouse at Breach Inlet** (101 Palm Blvd., 843/886-8000, www.boathouserestaurant.com). Apparently Charlestonians have become accustomed to the face of this culinary Eliza Doolittle: Time and again local newspaper readers vote the Boathouse Charleston's "Best Waterfront Dining," thanks to the marsh and inlet view, the immaculately shipshape interior, and gourmet seafood like lobster and crab cakes with Tabasco sauce and fried onions ($28). Prices range $13–26. Open for dinner nightly, and also for Sun. brunch 11 AM–2 PM.

For take-out fare, try Coconut Joe's, or these two other options. **Ooh…La La's Gourmet Market** (1503 Palm Blvd., 843/216-3456, www.oohlalas.com) adds a twist to Southern standards and ethnic fare. Their casseroles are great for families renting beach digs with a kitchenette; try the seafood casserole with shrimp, scallops, and mushrooms in white wine sauce ($16 for a small, $42 for a large); or the daily single plates like chicken satay with peanut sauce or crab cake on a croissant. Prices vary greatly depending on how many you're feeding. Open Tues.–Fri. 10 AM–7 PM, Sat. 9:30 AM–5:30 PM. At the other end of the spectrum, **Fat Jack's Café** (1101 Ocean Blvd., 843/886-4445) delivers their pizzas, burgers, seafood baskets and more. As for the pizzas, try the ($18) Cajun with andouille sausage, crawfish tail, peppers, onions, and mushrooms. Most items are $10 or less. Open daily for lunch and dinner.

Daniel Island

On the quickly developing, neo-traditional Daniel Island, pirate buffs should visit **Queen Anne's Revenge** (160 Fairchild St., 843/216-1724, www.qarevenge.com). The restaurant is designed to look like the inside of Blackbeard's storied flagship, the *Queen Anne,* which in real life was discovered sunken off Beaufort, North Carolina. Pirate and 18th-century nautical displays decorate the walls. Kids love it, and the food, specifically the steaks and seafood, are first-rate. Prices range $15–25. Open for lunch and dinner daily.

Also tucked away on the island is one of the Charleston area's best restaurants: **Sienna** (901 Island Park Dr., 843/881-8820, www.siennadining.com). It's a cozy, airy place, with a friendly front bar frequented by the prepster folk who live and work in these parts, booth alcoves, and an earth- and jewel-toned decor that adds a classy flair to the down-to-earth vibe. As for the food, it's outstanding: For starters, try the endive salad with fried grapes, dolce gorgonzola gelato, and 25-year-old balsamic; as a main course, treat yourself to the olive oil–poached snapper with trophie pasta, shrimp, and pesto broth; for dessert, try the pineapple carpaccio or chilled nectarine soup with almond semifrio, wild huckleberries, and white peach sorbetto. Tasty as they sound, the descriptions fall short, as the magic is in the execution. Come here for yourself, for all the service and nationally acclaimed fare of a downtown restaurant without a bit of the pretense you sometimes stumble into over the bridge. Entrées range $16–28. Open for dinner Mon.–Sat.

Farther North on Highway 17

A wonderfully authentic place out on Highway 17 North is **Seewee Restaurant** (4808 Hwy. 17 N, 843/928-3609) a homey, tasty spot, set in a circa-1920s general store. Owner Mary Rancourt opened it up as a restaurant in 1993, but didn't—thank goodness—remove the red tin roof, old shelving, worn flooring, and tongue-and-groove paneling. Most dinners include a fish, three sides, and hush puppies. The fried fish is excellent. The roast pork loin is great as well, and if you've been saving up your fat intake, now is the time to splurge

and get the country fried steak—you won't find better. Make sure one of your sides is the spicy fried green tomatoes. If you've never tried them, you won't find a better example.

The seafood is wonderfully (and simply) prepared. Each piece of fish is so fresh that its next of kin have yet to be notified. It's as casual as the house of a country uncle (a popular country uncle—it gets very crowded most nights, so you might want to head out there for a late lunch or early dinner). The lunch buffet usually runs about $6. For dessert, try the pineapple cake or the peanut butter pie.

Unfortunately, the front steps aren't particularly amenable to wheelchairs, and there's no ramp. But call ahead and maybe Miss Mary can work something out for you—even if it's just a carryout. Open Mon.–Thurs. 11 AM–9 PM, Fri. 11 AM–10 PM, Sat. 8 AM–10 PM, Sun. 11 AM–3 PM.

Information and Services

Tourist Offices and Visitors Centers

The **Charleston Visitor Center** (375 Meeting St., 843/853-8000, www.charlestoncvb.com) is the best place to stop in and get some background information and a bagful of brochures and coupon books. Open daily, except major holidays, Apr.–Nov. 8:30 AM–5:30 PM, Nov.–Mar. 8:30 AM–5 PM.

Kiawah Island visitors will want to call the **Kiawah Island Visitor Center** (22 Beachwalker Dr., Kiawah Island, 800/774-0006, www.charlestoncvb.com). You'll find the **Mt. Pleasant/Isle of Palms Visitor Center** (311 Johnnie Dodds Blvd., Mount Pleasant, 800/774-0006, www.charlestoncvb.com) on Highway 17 North at McGrath Darby Boulevard. Both have the same hours as the downtown branch.

Hospitals, Police, Emergencies

The largest hospital on the peninsula is the **Medical University of South Carolina**

Hospital (171 Ashley Ave., 843/792-2300, www.muschealth.com), but you are also in good hands at **Roper Hospital** (316 Calhoun St., 843/402-2273, www.roperhospital.com), or **Charleston Memorial Hospital** (326 Calhoun St., 843/792-2300, www.muschealth.com). In North Charleston, call **Trident Medical Center** (9330 Medical Plaza Dr., 843/797-7000, www.tridenthealthsystem.com). In Mount Pleasant, call **East Cooper Regional Medical Center** (1200 Johnnie Dodds Blvd., www.eastcoopermedctr.com); and in West Ashley, call **Bon Secours St. Francis Hospital** (2095 Henry Tecklenburg Ave., 843/402-2273, www.ropersaintfrancis.com).

In an emergency, reach the police, fire department, and ambulances by dialing **911.** The **Poison Control Center 24-Hour Help Line** is 800/222-1222.

The police can be reach for nonemergencies as well: In Charleston, West Ashley, and James Island, call 843/577-7434; in Mount Pleasant, call 843/884-4176.

Child Care

Vee's Sitter Service (13 Elmwood Ave., 843/722-2203 or 800/242-0685, www.vees-sitter.com) offers professionally trained, CPR-certified, insured and bonded sitters who will watch kids or seniors.

Post Office

You'll find the old main post office downtown (83 Broad St., 843/577-0690, www.usps.com) and another on East Bay Street (557 E. Bay St., 843/722-3624, www.usps.com).

Public Libraries

Find the **Charleston County Public Library Main Branch** (68 Calhoun St., 843/805-6801, www.ccpl.org). Or track down the **Edgar Allan Poe Library** (1921 I'On Ave., Sullivan's Island, 843/883-3914)—the coolest little branch library—on I'On Avenue on Sullivan's Island, built into an old defense bunker.

Newspapers

The Post and Courier (www.charleston.net) is the paper of record in Charleston, as it has been for many years. Every Thursday, it includes an insert called the *Preview*, which provides current movie, play, and music listings. The *Charleston City Paper* (www.charlestoncitypaper.com) is the free independent paper that covers the greater Charleston area; new editions come out Wednesdays and are widely available.

Radio Stations

96 WAVE is the big "alternative" station here; you'll see its bumper stickers stuck to everything that's not tied down, including traffic signs. It's a good place to hear local rock. **WEZL, "The Weasel,"** is one of the better country stations in the state, playing a good mix of old and new hits. **WSCI FM 89.3** is the local NPR affiliate, full of regional music shows. If it's talk you want, listen to **WTMA 1250 AM** in the mornings to get a sense of the workings of the city. Chicago-born transplant "Rocky D" grapples with local political issues on WTMA 1250 during the afternoon drive home. Midday is filled with the usual syndicated talk shows.

Transportation

GETTING THERE
Airlines

Charleston International Airport (5500 International Blvd., 843/767-1100, www.chs-airport.com) is host to Continental (800/525-0280, www.continental.com); Delta (800/221-1212, www.delta.com); discount carrier Independence Air (800/359-3594, www.flyi.com); US Airways (800/428-4322, www.usairways.com); and United Express (800/241-6522, www.ual.com).

GETTING AROUND

One word of advice: Walk. My motto for enjoying downtown Charleston is to PASAP (park as soon as possible). Rain or no rain, you don't want to drive around downtown Charleston any longer than you have to, especially if you're a first-time visitor. Charleston was designed to be walked, not driven.

The city has several public and private parking lots, most of which are reasonably priced. A good place to stop on your way downtown is the **Charleston Visitor Center** (375 Meeting St., 843/853-8000, www.charlestoncvb.com), right across from the Charleston Museum. Here, ask the person at the information window for a *Visitors' Guide Map*, which clearly labels the places where you can legally park your car. If you want to play it safe, just leave your car there at the center and take one of the tourist trolleys farther down the peninsula.

DASH

The Downtown Area Shuttle (DASH) is just one segment of the City of Charleston's public transportation system. DASH buses look like trolleys, and they're really pretty nice ways to get from one end of the peninsula to another. You'll notice DASH shelters, benches, and trolley stop signs located throughout the city. These are the only places you'll be able to get on or off a trolley; DASH drivers aren't allowed to make any special stops. One-way fares are $1.25 (exact change only, kids under 6 free, 55 and over $0.60 one way during nonrush hour trips), but the best deal is a $4 one-day pass, available from the **Charleston Visitor Center** (375 Meeting St., 843/853-8000, www.charlestoncvb.com). You can also purchase passes and get DASH schedules at all city-owned downtown parking garages. As of press time, the routes, hours, and further details were in flux as the system is being overhauled; visit www.ridecarta.com or call the visitors center for current details.

Another way to get around is by rickshaw: the **Charleston Rickshaw Company** (22 Society St., 843/723-5685) provides human-powered service Mon.–Thurs. 6 PM–midnight, Fri.–Sat. 6 PM–2 AM, and Sun. 5–11 PM. The cost is $4.50 per 10 minutes per person, or $45 per hour per bike. This is a great, cheap way to see downtown without having to hunt for parking. Call ahead for reservations if you'd like, or simply flag down drivers who congregate at the Old City Market and scoot by nearly every tourist spot.

ORGANIZED TOURS
Walking Tours
Charleston Strolls (843/766-2080, www.charlestonstrolls.com), and **Jack Thompson's Civil War Walking Tours** (17 Archdale St., 843/722-7033, www.civilwartours.com), both offer organized walking tours, for about $17 per person. Tours leave from the Mills House hotel and kids 12 and under are free. The folks from *The History Channel* got a kick out of **The Pirates of Charleston** tour from the folks at **Tour Charleston** (E. Bay St., Ste. 103, 800/854-1670, www.tourcharleston.com). Tickets are $15 adults, $13 kids 13–18, and $10 for those 12 and under. Janice Kahn leads **Chai Y'all** (843/556-0664) tours of Charleston, which explores the

city's Jewish roots—after all, this area was once the center of Jewish Colonial life. Walking tours, car tours, or step-on minibus tours are available; call to customize yours.

Carriage Tours
One fun way to learn the history of the historic buildings of Old Charleston without having to walk around, nose-in-book, is to take one of the city's many carriage tours. And here's a tip—the folks who run these tours love to know they have customers lined up in advance, so all the ones mentioned here will likely give you a lower price for reserving spots ahead of time. Look for them near the Old City Market. **Palmetto Carriage** (40 N. Market St., 843/723-8145, www.palmettocarriagecompany.com) offers one-hour tours daily from 9 AM till about 4:30 PM. Offering more unnecessary e's than any other company in town is the **Olde Towne Carriage Company** (20 Anson St., 843/722-1315, www.oldetownecarriage.com). **Old South Carriage Tours** (14 Anson St., 843/723-9712, www.oldsouthcarriage.com) also runs tours. Generally speaking, tours last about an hour and cost $20 adults, $10 children 4–12, with those under 3 riding free.

Minibus Tours
For all the romance of the horse-drawn carriage, there are days in Charleston when you feel the town is best seen from the inside of an air-conditioned vehicle. **Talk of the Towne** (843/795-8199, www.talkofthetowne.com) boasts of being able to take you past 250 historic buildings in just two hours. And that's not including all the nonhistoric buildings thrown in as gimmes. All tours (three daily) leave from the Charleston Visitor Center. The tour company offers complimentary pickup at downtown hotels, inns, and the Old City Market by special arrangement. Fares for the shorter, 75-minute tour run $17 for adults, $10 children 12 and under. The two-hour tour includes a visit to either the 1808 Nathaniel Russell House or the 1828 Edmondston-Alston House. Fares are $26 adults, $16 children.

Sites & Insights (843/762-0051, www.sitesandinsights.com) focuses on African American history, offering daily tours of points of interest, downtown, on the outlying islands, and a combo tour that covers both. Rates range $10–23, depending on age and the length of the tour. **Gullah Tours** (843/763-7551, www.gullahtours.com) is another well-loved African American–themed tour of downtown, where guide Alphonso Brown baffles riders by speaking a little of the old Lowcountry slave language. Tickets cost $18 adults, $15 middle and high school students, $12 elementary students. Tours are Mon.–Sat. Each bus tour suggests reservations; call for times.

Harbor Tours

For a memorable tour of Charleston Harbor, contact **Charleston Harbor Tours** (196 Concord St., 843/722-1691, www.charlestonharbortours.com) for maritime history tours; **Sandlapper Tours** (Charleston Maritime Center, Concord St., 843/881-7337) for nature or ghost tours; or **Spiritline Cruises** (360 Concord St., 843/722-2628 or 800/789-3678, www.spiritlinecruises.com) for a dinner cruise. Boat type, prices, dates, and trip lengths range greatly so contact the tour groups for specifics.

Beyond Charleston

NORTHWEST ON I-26
Summerville

Summerville's quiet, old-resort-like feel, with its meandering azalea- and pine-shaded streets, is no accident: This burg of 22,000 used to be a place where Lowcountry planters and Charleston residents would hide from the summer fevers. Apparently the distance from the coast and the "high" elevation (75 feet) kept down the mosquitoes.

Summerville is home to author Effie Wilder, whose manuscript was discovered in the slush piles of *Peachtree Press.* This longtime resident of the Presbyterian Home of Summerville became a first-time novelist at age 85 in 1995 with *Out to Pasture: But Not Over the Hill,* and tossed out two other novels (*Over What Hill: Notes from the Pasture,* and *Older But Wilder: More Notes from the Pasture—My Final Short Novel*) before she was 88. She's retired again. For now.

One good place to stay here is the **Bed and Breakfast of Summerville** (304 S. Hampton St., 843/871-5275), set in a one-room cottage in a garden behind the 1865 **Blake Washington House,** on South Hampton Street. Emmagene and Dusty Rhodes's place features a pool, a grill, and bicycles for touring the town. This place is privacy incarnate. Infants are okay, but pets are not. Rates range $70–90. Reservations are a must.

While in town, you may want to visit the **Summerville-Dorchester Museum** (100 E. Doty Ave., 843/875-9666), which features exhibits on Dorchester County and Summerville history, with an emphasis on medical, natural, and plantation history. Open Thurs.–Sat. 10 AM–2 PM.

At **Colonial Dorchester State Historic Site** (Hwy. 642/Dorchester Rd., about a quarter mile north of Old Trolley Road and six miles south of Summerville, 843/873-1740), you'll find the spot where, in 1697, Massachusetts Congregationalists founded a bluff-top town overlooking the Ashley River. Most of them moved on to the town of Midway, Georgia, by the 1750s, but the British soldiers retreating after their evacuation of Charleston took out their wrath on what remained of Dorchester in the 1780s. Today, you'll still find the bell tower of St. George's Church and the tabby walls of the old town fort. Open daily 9 AM–6 PM. Onsite archaeological excavation takes place every Saturday, weather permitting.

SOUTHWEST ON HIGHWAY 17
Charleston Tea Plantation

The only tea plantation (6617 Maybank Hwy., 843/559-3791 or 800/443-5987, www.americanclassictea.com) in America is on Wadmalaw Island. Home to American Classic Tea; here you learn about the process of tea making during a one-hour tour that includes a short trip to the fields and the plantation's unique harvester in action. Sample teas and benne wafers in the gift shop and stock up on tea bargains or special gift baskets that are not available in stores. Closed for years, the plantation should open again in April 2006, with tram rides and tours of the new factory. Call for hours and (nominal) fees.

Kiawah Island

This 10,000-acre island features some 10 miles of beautiful beach, although only the area at Beachwalker County Park is accessible to those not staying in one of the island's resort villages. *Family Fun* magazine ranked **Kiawah Island Resort** (12 Kiawah Beach Dr., 843/768-2121 or 800/576-1570, www.kiawahresort.com) as the number two Family Resort in the southeast. The resort features five championship golf courses and is popular with the tennis crowd. Pampered types lap up the newest addition, the megaluxe oceanfront hotel, spa, restaurant and bar enclave dubbed The Sanctuary at Kiawah ($275–675 per night). Ice-skaters like it, too, apparently: 1998 Olympic gold medalist Tara Lipinsky and her family own a house here on the island. Book island stays through the resort, or try **Resort Quest** (800/845-3911, www.resortquest.com) for a free guide that includes Kiawah and offers information on lodging rates, golf packages, tours, and more.

Seabrook Island Resort

Seabrook (115 Fresh Fields Dr., 843/768-0880), is located next to Kiawah, 23 miles off Highway 17 at Main Road. It's similar to its neighbor in that it's all villas and a beach club with swimming pools, restaurants, lounges, tennis courts, two golf courses, an equestrian center, trails, fishing gear, sailboats, and bicycles. Contact **Resort Quest** (800/777-8660, www.resortquest.com) for rentals and more information.

EDISTO ISLAND

In 1861, as South Carolina's statesmen gathered in Charleston to debate whether to secede from the Union immediately or wait for other Southern states to come along, the delegate from Edisto Island leaped to his feet and shouted that if South Carolina didn't vote to secede from the Union immediately, then by God, Edisto Island would secede by itself. This anecdote gives you a little insight into the independent, the-hell-with-y'all feel of this little Sea Island. Coming out here for a vacation stay is a little like seceding from the rest of the world.

Archaeologists have found numerous sites used by Edisto Indians in the centuries before the Europeans arrived. In 1674, the British bought the island off the tribe for a few tools, cloth, and some really neat trinkets. Indigo and Sea Island cotton plantations covered the island for quite a while, but after the boll weevil plague in 1920, the land was reduced to mostly small farming and, near the water, tourism.

The island could call itself "The Last Unresort"—it remains largely resortless, and most of the locals seem committed to keeping it that way. The Edisto Island Historical Preservation Society opened up the Edisto Island Museum in 1991 to combat encroachment. Edisto is a great spot to rent a beach house or camp and just relax. The waves can be pretty decent, the handful of restaurants are perfectly decent and sometimes quite good, and the people are friendly.

Edisto Island Museum

On your way into town, keep a sharp eye out on your right for the Edisto Island Museum (8123 Chisholm Plantation Rd., 843/869-1954, www.edistomuseum.com). They've done a wonderful job there with a small building, presenting several exhibits interpreting the unique ingredients of Sea Island life. A few books and old posters are for sale here, and very helpful workers will assist you. Admission is $3 adults, $2 students, free for those under 10.

Zion Baptist Church

The oldest home still standing on the island was built around 1735, but most seem to have been built in the 1950s through 1970s, before land prices raced upward. The Zion Baptist Church you pass on your left as you enter Edisto Beach was founded in 1810 by Hepzibah Jenkins, a strong-willed woman raised by her family's slaves after her mother died and her father was imprisoned during the American Revolution. So grateful was she to these people that she built this church for them in 1810.

Edisto Beach State Park

Edisto Beach State Park (8377 State Cabin Rd., 843/869-2756, www.southcarolinaparks.com) may just be the best shelling beach in South Carolina. My wife and I once scored about a dozen conch shells (pronounced "conk" here) in a 20-minute walk; however, the no-see-ums are equally legendary here: Bring Avon's Skin-So-Soft and Deep Woods OFF! and you should be okay. Better yet, pick up one of those screened-in tents to put around the picnic table. Of course, if you're at one of the sites that faces the ocean and not the marshes, you'll be better off, but these are usually reserved in advance, so call ahead.

The number of shells in the sand at Edisto is incredible. But look a little closer and you might realize that some of them are actually fossils; their presence in this area is attributed by some to the theory that this area was once under the Atlantic Ocean. Back then, Upcountry rivers and streams poured directly into the ocean, depositing the shark teeth, horse, and mastodon bones found here today. Open daily. Admission is $4 adults, $1.50 children.

Events

The Edisto Island Historical Preservation Society's **Tour of Historic Plantation Houses, Churches, and Sites** is held on the second Saturday in October. Contact the Edisto Island Museum (8123 Chisholm Plantation Rd., 843/869-1954, www.edistomuseum.com) for information. Since the area's plantation homes are private, the only way to tour them is to visit during the fall tour, or to take the Pink Van Tour with **Island Tours & T'ings** (843/869-1110, www.pinkvantour.com).

Shops, Rentals, Charters

Island Bikes and Outfitters (140 Jungle Rd., 843/869-4444, www.islandbikesoutfitters.com) rents four-wheel bikes, Island Cruisers, 17-foot rental boats, kayaks, canoes, and surfboards, plus all the umbrellas, beach chairs, crab traps, fishing rods, rafts, tubes, strollers, and pull carts you'll ever need for a good time on the beach. You can rent by the hour, by the half day, full day, three days, and by the week. Reserve ahead if you can. The young entrepreneur owner, Tony Spainhour, says he'll deliver weekly rentals. **Edisto Watersports & Tackle** (3731 Docksite Rd., 843/869-0663) leads kayak tours of the area, charters deep-water fishing boats, sells bait, and rents fishing gear.

Cap'n Jimmy Bell's Edisto Shrimp Boat Charters (843/869-2726 or 843/607-5347) leads motorboat eco water tours of the area, plus shrimping trips on which you can catch your dinner.

In recent years, a tiny collection of shops have sprouted up on Jungle Boulevard near Highway 174. The best of the bunch is the **Fish or Cut Bait Gallery** (142 Jungle Rd., 843/869-2511), where you'll find regional arts and crafts.

On the right as you come into Edisto, you come across Karen Carter's **The Edisto Bookstore** (547 Hwy. 174, 843/869-1885, www.theedistobookstore.com), tucked into a roadside building with a smattering of other stores. Karen's a friendly, helpful person who keeps her shelves well stocked with both new and used books, local guidebooks, nautical charts, and an Internet station for $6 per hour.

Accommodations

If you're not camping, at one of the many sites at the park, reserve one of their six air-conditioned cabins ($72–124). Contact Edisto Beach State Park (8377 State Cabin Rd., 843/869-2756, www.southcarolinaparks.com). Generally, you need to book these up to six months in advance, but you might get lucky. Otherwise, the traditional way to stay on Edisto Island (practically the only way, given the determined lack of hotels and motels) is to rent one of the hundreds of beach houses lining the shore.

Several rental companies service the island. Here are a few: **Edisto Sales and Rentals Realty** (1405 Palmetto Blvd., 800/868-5398, www.edistorealty.com); **Fairfield Ocean Ridge** (1 King Cotton Rd., 843/869-2561 or 800/845-8500, www.efairfield.com).

One warning: Rent a house too far south on the island and the water nearest your house will contain inlet currents that make it unsafe to enter. Which means you'll need to hop in the car every time you want to go swimming—not everyone's idea of a relaxing week at the beach.

Food
On the way into Edisto, you'll find a few great places to eat. First, there's **Po' Pigs Bo-B-Q** (2410 Hwy. 174, 843/869-9003), in the same building as the Island Express gas station. Don't let the unassuming exterior throw you: The award-winning, nationally acclaimed barbecue is some of the best in the state. Choose from four sauces, all South-Carolina specific, and get the $8.50 buffet, which features hash (regular and liver), pork skins, limas and ham, red rice, turnip greens, corn, casseroles, slaw, and much more. Get it to go or eat in. Open for lunch and dinner Wed.–Sat.

Next up is the **Old Post Office Restaurant** (1442 Hwy. 174, 843/869-2339), which specializes in "New Lowcountry," and is something of a institution for islanders and visitors. The fish, grits, and sausages are what people talk about here. Open for dinner Mon.–Sat.

Farther down, stop at **Main's Market** (1084 Hwy. 174, 843/869-1337) for a down-home church potluck-flavored meal in a former roadside grocery. Try the shrimp and grits with brown gravy ($8) for breakfast; the homemade pimiento cheese sandwich ($5) or the tarragon chicken salad wrap ($7) for lunch; or the

buffet with ribs, fried chicken and fish, okra gumbo, tomato pie, squash casserole, corn pies, and bread or banana pudding for lunch ($7) or dinner ($8). Open daily for all meals, and Sun. for lunch only.

On Edisto Beach proper, the **Pavilion** (102 Palmetto Blvd., 843/869-3061) sits at the corner of Highway 174 and Palmetto Boulevard and is an old, old local spot, where you can get good fried fare and an amazing view. Order the all-you-can-eat shrimp. Prices range $9–25. Open Wed.–Mon. for lunch and dinner.

On the other side of the island, facing the marshes, you'll find **Dockside Restaurant** (3730 Dock Site Rd., 843/869-2695), featuring fresh shrimp, hush puppies, crab, shrimp, and shrimp. Dishes range $15–20. Open Mon.–Sat. for dinner.

The Seacow Eatery (145 Jungle Rd., 843/869-3222) serves three meals daily in a family-friendly, tiny, and jam-packed house. Build-your-own omelets include shrimp, sausage, ham, bacon, and veggies; lunch includes fresh, healthful salads, sandwiches, and wraps flavored with local seafood, pork, and deli meats; and dinner dishes are home-style meals that change daily. Main entrées average $7. Open daily starting at 7 AM.

Last, to join islanders for huge burgers and fries in a basket on a back porch, head to the shack known as **Ruby Seahorse** (108 Jungle Rd., 843/869-0606). If you've packed antacids, try the pimiento chili burger ($5.50) all the way. Prices average $5. Open for lunch and dinner daily.

Information
For more information on this unique little island, contact the **Edisto Chamber of Commerce** (430 Hwy. 174, or P.O. Box 206, Edisto Beach, SC 29438, 843/869-3867, www.edistochamber.com).

BEAUFORT AND THE LOWCOUNTRY

A couple decades ago, residents of the Low-country around Beaufort used to have an arduous time traveling around from island to island, much less from island to mainland. To get from Beaufort to Savannah, a 45-minute trip today, used to require a drive from Beaufort to Sheldon, Sheldon to Ridgeland, Ridgeland to Garden City, Georgia, and then on to Savannah, taking up the good part of a day. Add this to the fact that not many Sea Islanders owned a car in the first place, and it's no wonder that many people in Beaufort never set foot in Savannah, and vice versa. People living on the smaller islands traveled even less, and some part of nearly any trip they *did* take was sure to involve a boat. In the late 1960s when Pat Conroy taught there, Daufuskie Island was so isolated from the mainland that the Gullah children Conroy took across on Halloween to trick-or-treat in Port Royale came away believing that on the mainland, all one had to do to get candy was knock on a door.

Today, in the world of satellite television, car phones, and pagers, you'd be hard-pressed to find anyone that innocent down here. But while the modern world of air-conditioning and cappuccino has found the Sea Islands, their character is imbedded enough that it will never wash away entirely—at least not until the last shrimp boat has been beaten into a golf cart.

Despite the bridges that connect most of the islands now, the Lowcountry is still a land where, what with all the shrimping, crabbing, and fishing to be done, boats are considered essential equipment. As Jackie Washington of the little village of Broad River puts it: "If

© SEAN SLINSKY

HIGHLIGHTS

☾ Beaufort Historic District: With it's Bay Street shops and restaurants, and the surrounding neighborhood with historic homes and inns, this is the village heart of this growing waterfront town (page 120).

☾ Beaufort Museum: This small museum is set in a former Colonial rampart, and gives a great overview of the modest but historic town (page 120).

☾ Penn Center Historic District: Once the site of a school where freed slaves were taught after the Civil War, the Penn Center went on to be the annual retreat location for Dr. Martin Luther King Jr. and his Southern Christian Leadership Conference (page 126).

☾ Harbour Town: With its landmark lighthouse and marina, Harbour Town—in the middle of Sea Pines Resort—shows how Hilton Head began (page 133).

☾ Old Bluffton: Just before you get to Hilton Head, make a side trip to see how the island was before it became overwhelmed by resorts. This little town is now a funky enclave of artist galleries and studios based in historic cottages (page 143).

☾ Ernest F. Hollings ACE Basin National Wildlife Refuge: Three major rivers feed into this one area near Beaufort, offering hundreds of miles of pristine paddling for outdoor lovers (page 145).

☾ South Carolina Artisans Center: To see the present-day face of art in the Lowcountry, visit this gem of a gallery in the tiny, inland town of Walterboro (page 146).

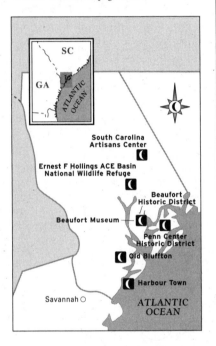

LOOK FOR ☾ TO FIND RECOMMENDED SIGHTS, ACTIVITIES, DINING, AND LODGING.

you don't own a boat around here, you're living half a life."

PLANNING YOUR TIME

How you tackle this area truly depends on your mood and inclinations. If you're into small-town escapes, aim for Beaufort, and stay in one of the many historic bed-and-breakfasts, set in antebellum and Victorian mansions in the town's historic downtown neighborhood. This neighborhood includes Bay Street, a sweet little main-street stretch of shops, restaurants, and galleries that runs along a waterfront park. Several of the bars and dining patios look out over the water to take in the Lowcountry view.

Day trips from here usually include jaunts to the historic Penn Center on St. Helena Island, and outdoor forays into the nearby ACE Basin, where three rivers feed into a vastly undeveloped marsh and coastal woodland. On the flipside, Hilton Head offers guests some of the country's most popular golf courses, tennis camps, beaches, and family resorts. Stay at one of these, and spend sporty family time together; there are movie theaters, kid-friendly restaurants, and outlet shopping in neighboring Bluffton to keep everyone entertained. For those wishing to tap into the local scene, there's nearby Old Bluffton and Daufuskie Island, accessible only by boat. Of course, you can split your trip to try a little of each town on for size. And you can also opt to pair a Hilton Head visit with a Savannah one, or a Beaufort visit with a Charleston one, to toss a little port-city action into the mix.

Beaufort and Vicinity

Some 65 islands make up Beaufort County. Named after one of Carolina's lords proprietors, Henry, Duke of Beaufort, the town of Beaufort (pronounced "BYOO-fert") is the county seat, its 12,000 residents making it the biggest town on Port Royale, one of the biggest islands in the county.

A scene in *The Big Chill* captures the town of Beaufort beautifully: Kevin Kline and William Hurt jog-walk down Bay Street in the early morning fog, longtime friends reunited after years, middle-aged men in T-shirts drenched with the humidity, and with their efforts to remain potent into old age. Old business blocks lean over the men's shoulders like kindly merchants of a 1950s childhood. Dawn gleams from the dewy asphalt of the narrow street. The scene's visuals perfectly illustrate the film's thematic issues: the postwar generation's search for renewed hope and vital community. And these things seem to draw baby boomers to Beaufort, even today.

Beaufort is a quiet, romantic poem of a town, a town best absorbed, rather than "done." It's a historic town—second oldest in

© SEAN SLINSKY

The Beaufort Museum now calls this 1700s tabby-and-brick building home.

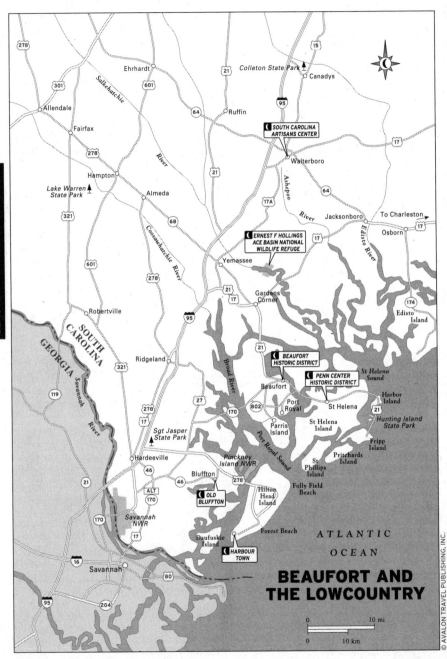

BEAUFORT AND THE LOWCOUNTRY

0   10 mi

0   10 km

© AVALON TRAVEL PUBLISHING, INC.

the state, founded in 1710, only 40 years after Charleston. And because it sits far from the heavily trafficked path beaten flat by the 20th century, Beaufort remains a town where many of the differences between 1840 and 2000 seem trivial somehow, and the visitor immediately feels either desperately out of place or home at last.

HISTORY

Six flags—or eight, counting the flagless Westoes' and Yamassees' earlier claims to the land—have flown over the people living their lives out in this location: The French, Spanish, English, Scottish, American, and Confederate flags have all waved overhead. Although the French and Spanish both failed to successfully

GULLAH CULTURE OF THE SEA ISLANDS

On the quiet Sea Islands south of Charleston, a centuries-old culture is passing away. Like most African Americans in the state, the Gullah people are descendants of West Africans who made the horrific passage to South Carolina as slaves. (The name of both the people and their language, "Gullah," was long thought to be a derivation of "Angola." Today, many believe it evolved from the words Gola and Gora, both tribal names in modern-day Liberia.) Yet even from the first, the Sea Islander slaves lived lives that were notably different from those of their enslaved contemporaries. For one thing, most Sea Islanders lived on isolated plantations where one could commonly find 100 or more Africans for every white person; a Gullah field worker might go months without coming into contact with a European. Consequently, Sea Islanders retained their West African language, culture, and crafts much more coherently than those slaves who lived on the mainland.

After the outbreak of the Civil War, Federal ships swept down upon the Sea Islands, establishing the area as a base of operations as they set about shutting down Southern ports. Sea Island slave owners fled, leaving their rice, cotton, and indigo plantations to their slaves. Although President Andrew Johnson nullified General William T. Sherman's order setting aside the Lowcountry for former slaves, many former white planters did not reclaim their lands, and after several deadly hurricanes hit in the late 1890s, many remaining whites left the islands. Few black Sea Islanders interacted at all with whites, and many had never even been to the mainland in their lifetimes. The truth was, despite the hardships their isola-

tion brought them, the Sea Islanders knew they had a good thing.

Things might have stayed like this indefinitely if mainlanders hadn't woken up to the fact that the islands featured some of the best beaches on the East Coast. The Fraser family from Georgia had bought up much of Hilton Head Island for logging, but then one of them got the idea of turning some of the cheap farmland into golf courses. Snowbirds from places like New Jersey and Pennsylvania – as sick of Florida as they were of flurries – flocked to the "new" paradise. As quickly as you could say "Please remove your golf shoes," Hilton Head Island became a Northern beachhead in the area – for the second time in a century.

Land prices for the remaining Sea Islanders on Hilton Head and surrounding islands shot up from around $100 an acre in the 1940s to over $100,000 for some oceanfront acres today. In the intervening years, many of those who didn't want to move have found that they can't keep up with the higher property taxes and have been forced to sell. Many of those who have somehow remained have discovered that they aren't adequately trained for the higher-paying jobs the resorts had brought to the islands. Consequently, while mainlanders from around the country move in to take many of the managerial and technical positions, the lower-paid service positions have fallen to the Sea Islanders. For many, these become lifelong jobs.

And yet, while native Gullah islanders are losing much of their physical and spiritual world to encroaching resorts, network television, and the public schools, the culture lives on, preserved in the still-strong extended families and church-based community.

settle the area, Scottish subjects pouring into already crowded Charleston in the late 1600s asked the lords proprietors if they could try to settle the bad-luck region and were given permission. Thus, in 1684, Lord Cardross founded the city as a haven for Scottish immigrants. Two years later, Cardross and his fellow settlers were all dead, murdered by an army of Spaniards and Westoes.

The Yamassee

As early as 1684, the Yamassee Indians of Georgia, who had had trouble getting along with the Spanish, asked for asylum in Carolina. The Carolinian settlers granted the Yamassees' request, figuring that it couldn't hurt to have this warlike tribe who hated the Spanish between St. Augustine and themselves. In the next decades, 10 different Yamassee towns were founded between the Savannah River and Charleston. In 1711, Yamassee warriors joined with British troops under Colonel Barnwell in aiding North Carolinian settlers in their fight against the Tuscarora Indians.

But by this time the Spanish threat had fairly subsided, and the town of Beaufort had already been laid out in 1710, to become home to some seasoned Barbadian planters, along with other immigrants who had arrived in Charles Town to find all of the best land there already purchased. Unfortunately, the new settlers' homesteads infringed on the lands granted earlier to the Yamassee, and worse, some of the British Indian traders cheated the Native Americans and allowed them to run up oppressive amounts of credit that gave them every reason to want to do whatever it took to be free from their debts.

Thus it was that when Beaufort was just five years old, Yamassee Indians wiped out almost everybody in the town, in fact, almost everybody south of Charles Town. But after the Yamassee and other hostile tribes were chased away and killed (many ran south and joined the defiant Seminole confederation in Florida), settlers came back to the old Second City and began settling here again. The British conquered and occupied the town during the Revolution.

The War Between the States

In the War of 1812, English gunboats sailed into range but found the port city too strongly fortified to attack, but 50 years later, during the Civil War, the Union Army was not so intimidated. And they had little reason to be because most of Beaufort's fighting men had already left town to join the Confederate Army elsewhere. The Yankees attacked the Sea Islands in early November 1861, beginning with an amphibious landing at Hilton Head; they took Beaufort, the wealthy planters' town, on November 7.

The women and children, horrified at the rapacious Northern men bursting into their homes, fled the city, leaving only one white citizen of Beaufort—a pro-Union Northerner who'd moved down just before the war. Although some slaves left with their white owners' families, many thousands of field hands were left behind. Some acquired plots of land subdivided by the Northern Army for farming; some acquired the huge empty houses in town. The Penn School was opened on St. Helena Island by Quaker missionaries from Pennsylvania to educate the former slaves.

After the War

When the railroad came to town, Beaufortians insisted it be built one mile away from downtown, to reduce the noise and soot. As the 19th century wound down, the strong Northern presence in the area refused to fade. By 1940, one-third of the taxable land of Beaufort County had been purchased by Northerners for hunting preserves. Today, in new "Old South" developments like Newpoint on St. Helena Island, many of the residents are emigrated Northerners, many living in large mock plantation homes modeled after those owned by the slaveholders their ancestors came to undermine during the Civil War.

In the 1960s and 1970s, Beaufort gained a bit of renown as the hometown of Smokin' Joe Frazier, heavyweight boxing champion of the world. And then Beaufort native Pat Conroy started broadcasting the town's beauties,

ROBERT SMALLS: BEAUFORT'S SAVIOR SLAVE AND UNION WAR HERO

In 1862, Confederates dismantled an old fort on the southern end of Folly Island to take the guns to another fort that needed them. They loaded the Confederate guns onto the CSS *Planter*, piloted by African American slave Robert Smalls. That night while the others slept ashore, Smalls loaded his family and a group of other slaves aboard and slipped the Confederate ship past rebel guns, through the mines he and his crewmates had helped place, and delivered the boat to the Union soldiers in Charleston.

Smalls's heroism made him an instant cause célèbre for the North. He was given a reward for "capturing" an enemy craft and sneaking it through the mined harbor and sent north to meet with President Lincoln and Secretary of State Edwin Stanton, where he pleaded for the arming of black troops. Upon his return to the South, Smalls continued to serve aboard the *Planter*. In 1863, while plying the waters of Folly River, the ship came under such heavy fire from Confederate guns that the ship's captain abandoned the wheelhouse and hid in the coal storage. Smalls — who faced certain death as a traitor if captured — took over the ship and sailed her clear of the enemy's guns. For this he was named captain of the *Planter*. He served the Union forces for the duration of the war, providing the Federals with invaluable information about the Lowcountry coast. His service also included a stint with the Beaufort Light Infantry, during which he was stationed in the Beaufort Arsenal, which is now the Beaufort Museum.

After the war, the Union honored Smalls by asking him to take part in the ceremonies at the re-raising of the Union flag over Fort Sumter. He was later voted the United States' first African American congressman, and he purchased the home of his former owner. Smalls served in the South Carolina house of representatives, the state senate, and eventually the U.S. Congress. Although he was convicted of taking a bribe and removed from office, Smalls was later pardoned by Governor Wade Hampton III.

Smalls was appointed collector of the Port of Beaufort by the Republicans and served almost continuously in this position from 1889 until 1913. In 1895, he served as a delegate at the South Carolina Constitutional Convention, where he attempted — unsuccessfully — to stop the disenfranchisement of African Americans. Here, in response to the charge that he was a Confederate deserter, Smalls testified:

I stand here the equal of any man. I started out in the war with the Confederates; they threatened to punish me and I left them. I went to the Union army. I fought in 17 battles to make glorious and perpetuate the flag that some of you trampled under your feet.

Until his death in 1915, Smalls lived in his former master's home in Beaufort. The Robert Smalls Parkway and Beaufort's Robert Smalls Junior High School are both named for this remarkable man.

foibles, and sins to the world via such novels as *The Great Santini, The Prince of Tides,* and *Beach Music.*

Southern Archetype

Today, Beaufort is a beautiful antebellum town, something of an archetype for Southern splendor, given the town's high profile in a host of movies set in the South, including film versions of Conroy's novels and *The Big Chill,*

Forrest Gump, and *Something to Talk About.* In fact, *The Big Chill*'s Tom Berenger liked it here so much that he bought a home on the Okatie River for himself.

Many South Carolinians come here to visit Hunting Island State Park, preserved for decades by a hunters' collective and later grabbed by the state and reserved for public use. Here you'll see subtropical flora at its best. Speaking of Hollywood, Hunting Island was used (along with Fripp Island) as the location for Disney's live-action version of *The Jungle Book.*

SIGHTS

You'll probably want to stop in the **Visitors Information Center** (1006 Bay St., 843/524-3163, www.beaufortsc.org) for tour maps, information on lodging and dining, and plenty of brochures. The historic downtown district is called "Old Point." The reason you see so many old buildings still standing here is that Union troops occupied this region early in the Civil War, meaning that it was already Union-held for more than three years by the time Bill Sherman and his 8,000-man incineration squad came to the Carolina coast.

(Beaufort Historic District

On the drive into Beaufort along Highway 21, you may wonder what's the big deal about this place, after all, the road in is lined with the same tired strip malls that plague many a developing small town. But have patience and

One of the best things to do in Beaufort is simply wander the historic area.

head to the old historic portion (bordered by the water, and Bay, Boundary, and Adventure streets). There you'll find a strollable mix of commercial and residential buildings, antebellum manses and 1950s storefronts, picket fences and live oaks, and sidewalks that link everything together. It's charm personified and walking the area is a must to get a feel for Beaufort's soul, even if you don't read a single historic plaque.

(Beaufort Museum

The brick-and-tabby arsenal building (713 Craven St., 843/379-3331, www.historic-beaufort.org) looks like a small-town satellite campus of The Citadel. The two brass guns outside were captured from the British in 1779 and seized by Union soldiers after the fall of Fort Walker in 1861. They were returned to Beaufort in 1880. This 1798 building—rebuilt in 1852—makes a great place for a museum, albeit this one is on the small side. Granted, the sheer amount of history in the town seems to deserve a grander reckoning, but the museum does a fine job of documenting day-to-day life in the early days of the Sea Islands. In Barbra Streisand's *The Prince of Tides,* this building doubled as a Greenwich Village loft for the dinner party scene. Open Mon.–Sat. 11 AM–4 PM. Admission is about $3, free for those under six.

St. Helena's Episcopal Church

Founded in 1712 and built in 1724, this church (505 Church St., 843/522-1712), has seen a lot of history. It survived the Yamassee War in 1715, the Revolution in the 1770s and 1780s, and even the Civil War—when army doctors performed surgeries using the churchyard's flat tombstones as operating tables. Open daily 10 AM–4 PM.

National Cemetery

Right on Highway 21 in Beaufort, you'll come upon the National Cemetery (1601 Boundary St., 843/524-3925), established by Abraham Lincoln in 1863 for burying the Northern Army's victims of its war against the South. Some

© SEAN SLINSKY

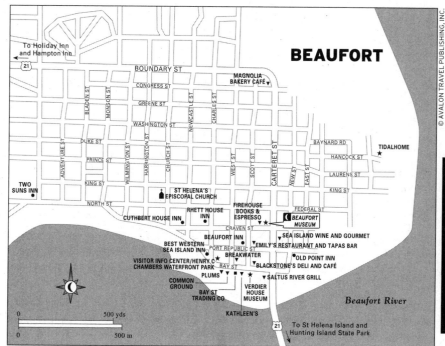

BEAUFORT AND THE LOWCOUNTRY

9,000 Union boys lie here, along with 122 Southerners who died defending their homeland from the Northern invaders. Relatively recently, in 1989, 19 Union soldiers from the African American Massachusetts 54th Infantry were reburied here after having been discovered on Folly Island in the wake of Hurricane Hugo. Open daily dawn–dusk.

John Mark Verdier House Museum

Over on Bay Street, John Mark Verdier, a wealthy merchant, built this Federal-style home (801 Bay St., 803/379-6335, www.historic-beaufort.org) in the 1790s. In 1825, when the Marquis de Lafayette visited town on his triumphant return tour of the United States, he was welcomed here as a houseguest. Union soldiers received a less-cordial welcome, but nonetheless, they made this home their headquarters during the Northern occupation of

Beaufort during the Civil War. Who can blame them? Each of the eight guest rooms has its own fireplace. Open Mon.–Fri. 10:30 AM–3:30 PM. Admission is $6 adults, $3 students. Or you can purchase a combination ticket for the Verdier House and Beaufort Museum: $8 adults, $4 students.

Henry C. Chambers Waterfront Park

Concerts take place all the time on the outdoor stage, and weekdays find mothers and nannies sitting on the porch swings while their children play on the mock-Victorian jungle gym. This park is a pleasant place to bring a snack and have an impromptu picnic.

Tidalholm

Sam and Sarah Cooper (Kevin Kline and Glenn Close) lived in this 1856 home in *The Big Chill;* apparently they bought it from the

Santini family after Bull Meachum (Robert Duvall) crashed his plane off the coast at the end of *The Great Santini*. The real-life, current owners have signs up to remind you that Bull, Sam, and Sarah can't come out to play—this is a private home. But for fans of these films, it can be fun to peer through the gates to see where Kline, Jeff Goldblum, Tom Berenger, and Meg Tilly played football during half-time for the Michigan game, or the porch where Duvall sat reading the paper and cussing out Fidel Castro.

Tidalholm actually carries with it a wonderful story. James Fripp owned the house at the outbreak of the Civil War. When he returned from battle at war's end, he found it occupied by a Frenchman and in the process of being auctioned off to pay his estate's back taxes. Fripp watched as the French stranger outbid the others and purchased the home. Then the Frenchman, who had dwelled in the abandoned home during the war, walked over to Fripp, kissed him on both cheeks, handed him the deed to the house, and walked away forever.

Tours

Carolina Buggy Tours (1002B Bay St., 843/525-1300), provide you with a narrated history of the city and historic Old Point neighborhood. Cost is $18 adults, $7 kids. For tours focused specifically on the Gullah culture, try **Gullah-n-Geechie Mahn Tours** (P.O. Box 1248, St. Helena Island, 843/838-7516 or 843/838-3758, www.gullahngeechie-tours.net).

ENTERTAINMENT AND EVENTS
Nightlife

By and large, this is a casual town where there are lots of places to have a couple of drinks with friends, and not many places to boogie down and get rowdy. That said, **Plum's** (904.5 Bay St., 843/525-1946, www.plumsrestaurant.com) is one of the best places to catch live music from time to time, or to hang out after dinner until the wee hours. Open daily for lunch, din-

ner, and drinks. Saltus River Grill has a particularly lively bar scene for the khaki set. And The Beaufort Inn caters to that crew as well.

Cinema

One of the last around, the **Hiway 21 Drive-In** (55 Parker Dr., 843/846-4500, www.beaufort-online.com) still shows movies out under the stars. Call to hear what's showing. Admission is $6 adults, $1 kids 3–13.

Events

On a weekend in March, St. Helena's Episcopal Church offers its self-guided **Spring Tours** (507 Newcastle St., 843/522-1712, www.sthelenas1712.org) of the city's gorgeous Colonial homes and plantation estates, a tradition since the 1950s. Prices are $30 for the candlelight tour and $40 for the plantation bus tour, which includes a box lunch. In May, the annual **Gullah Festival** (843/525-0628, P.O. Box 83, www.gullahfestival.net) features dances, live music, storytelling, and art displays in an all-out celebration of the Sea Island's unique African American culture.

If you missed the Spring Tours, then maybe you can make the late-October **Fall Festival of Homes and History** (801 Bay St., 803/379-6335, www.historic-beaufort.org) sponsored by the Historic Beaufort Foundation and featuring home tours, lectures, and special events. Cost ranges greatly depending on the event. Over on St. Helena Island, every second weekend in November brings the annual **Heritage Days Celebration** (16 Penn Center Circle W., St. Helena Island, 843/838-2432, www.penncenter.com) a three-day festival celebrating African American Sea Island culture.

SHOPPING

The great thing about a small town is that they are so conveniently compact. Here, that means that most of the shops worth browsing are all within walking distance and center around Bay Street and the waterfront park. These are some of the best: I can never stop into Beaufort without browsing through **Bay Street Trading Company/The Book Shop** (808 Bay

Beaufort's Bay Street shopping and dining area

St., 843/524-2000, Mon.–Fri. 10 AM–5:30 PM, Sat. 10 AM–5 PM, Sun. noon–4 P.M.), which offers plenty of rare, locally written books and wonderful souvenirs. Open daily. **McIntosh Book Shoppe** (917 Bay St., 843/524-1119, Mon.–Sat. 10 AM–5 PM (closed for lunch around noon), Sun. 1–5 PM) practically across the street sells new, used, and rare books as well, and specialize in South Carolinian lit, the Civil War, architecture, and Gullah themes. Open daily.

There are scores of galleries in town (13 in the local guild), and several line Bay Street. Wander into the ones that pique your interest, but be sure to stop in **The Gallery** (802 Bay St., 843/470-9994, www.thegallery-beaufort.com, Mon.–Sat. 10 AM–5 PM, and otherwise by appointment). Because they represent a host of artists who work in several different media, it's a great cross section at decent prices. Also worth a peek, **Longo Gallery** (407 Carteret St., 843/522-8933, Mon.–Sat. 10 AM–5 PM) is run by a husband-and-wife team whose colors and styles bring their space alive vividly.

When it comes to whip-smart gifts and random home goods, **Lulu Burgess** (917 E. Bay St., 843/524-6457, Mon.–Sat. 10 AM–6 PM, Sun. noon–5 PM) has an amazing array of stuff, from shopaholic mints to bizarre pillows and witty stationery. Open daily. For hand-painted furniture, garden accessories and decor, hop in the car and stop at **Camden Field at Home** (902 Boundary St., 843/986-1006, www.camden-field.com) on your way out of town, if nothing else. Scads of national magazines have featured Camden's tables, armoires, and more, and it's a neat place to poke around, as it's set in an old gas station. Open Mon.–Sat. 10 AM–6 PM.

ACCOMMODATIONS
Motels and Hotels
The **Best Western Sea Island Inn** (1015 Bay St., 843/522-2090, www.bestwestern.com) enjoys a great location downtown across from the water. Rates range $109–139 and include a continental breakfast. Most other chains cluster out along Boundary Street, including a **Ramada Inn** (2001 Boundary St., 843/524-2144). Rates range $59–79. You'll also find a very nice **Hampton Inn** (2342 Boundary St., 843/986-0600). Rates rage $94–114.

Inns and Bed-and-Breakfasts
You just know a cute town immortalized in the baby-boomer classic *The Big Chill* is going to have its share of bed-and-breakfasts.

Named by *American Historic Inns* as one of the "Top Ten Inns in the Country," the **Beaufort Inn** (809 Port Republic St., 843/521-9000, www.beaufortinn.com), offers 27 units, $149–285, breakfast included. Rooms have private baths and most have private balconies. Even if you're staying elsewhere, poke your head in to see the unique atrium wrapped by a curving stairway. In fact, if you're not staying here, consider eating here at the restaurant, named by *Country Inns Magazine* as one of the top 10 restaurants in the country. Breakfast, lunch, and dinner daily. (Closed Sat. for lunch.)

The Rhett House Inn (1009 Craven St., 843/524-9030 or 888/480-9530, www.rhetthouseinn.com) offers 17 rooms, each

The Rhett House Inn plays host to visiting celebrities.

featuring its own mini-library to complement a larger one downstairs. "Fire-eater" Robert Barnwell Rhett is said to have written a draft of the Ordinance of Secession here, which led to the Civil War. Nick Nolte and champion of the underprivileged Barbra Streisand stayed here in these regal furnishings during the filming of *Prince of Tides*. Owners Stephen and Marianne Harrison hail from Manhattan originally, so perhaps it's understandable why Babs felt at home here. Rates range $145–245.

Other bed-and-breakfasts include the seven-unit, 200-year-old **Cuthbert House Inn** (1203 Bay St., 843/521-1315 or 800/327-9275, www.cuthberthouseinn.com), where General Sherman once stayed. It is a lavish, grand space. Rates range $155–265. The **Old Point Inn** (212 New St., 843/524-3177, www.oldpointinn.com) was built in 1898 and has five nicely appointed rooms. Rates range $95–$150).

At the fully accessible, five-room **Two Suns Inn Bed & Breakfast** (1705 Bay St., 843/522-1122 or 800/532-4244, www.twosunsinn.com),

each room in the 1917 manor features a view of the bay and salt marsh. Rates start at $130.

Camping

The place to camp in the Beaufort area is **Hunting Island State Park** (2555 Sea Island Pkwy., 843/838-2011, www.hunting-island.com), where there are also beachfront cabins to rent. The S. C. State Park Service (866/345-7275, www.reserveamerica.com) books reservations starting March 1. You can camp at **Point South KOA** (I-95 Exit 33 & Hwy. 17 interchange, Yemassee, 843/726-5733, www.koa.com) for $22–50; it's a half hour out of town. **Tuck in de Woods** (22 Tuc In De Wood Ln., Saint Helena Island, 843/838-2267) has 74 sites and shares the same island as the Penn Center.

FOOD
Coffee

For coffee and baked goods, you won't find a better spot than **Firehouse Books and Espresso Bar** (706 Craven St., 843/522-2665) which is set, as you might guess, in an old firehouse. The quaint brick building is a short stroll from Boundary Street, and offers sandwiches, espresso, flavored coffees, muffins, and other coffeehouse favorites. A very good book selection is available upstairs. Outdoor sipping is available. In Waterfront Park, **Common Ground** (102 West St., 843/524-2326) offers smoothies as well as espresso.

Breakfast

For those not staying at a bed-and-breakfast, the long-time place to get morning meals (all day long) has been **Blackstone's Deli and Café** (205 Scott St., 843/524-4330), a festively raucous restaurant with two stories of dining space, usually filled to the gills with families on weekends and working folk on weekdays (WiFi is available). Try the shrimp and grits, or eggs as you like 'em. And if you dig the scene, stop by later for lunch, as the $5 deli sandwiches are loaded with fresh meats, a host of Southern salads, and even liverwurst, if you're into it. Prices are less than $10. Open daily 7:30 AM–2 PM.

On the quiet end of the spectrum, **Kathleen's** (822 Bay St., 843/524-2500) is mainly a lunch joint specializing in fried green tomato and seafood, but they do a fine breakfast as well, with $0.99 à la carte items that allow you to build your own plate. Open for breakfast Sat.–Sun. 7 AM–11 AM, and otherwise for lunch and dinner Mon.–Sat. starting at 11 AM.

Casual Eats

Magnolia Bakery Café (703 Congress St., 843/524-1961) is right next to the visitors center, and specializes in light lunches and fresh-baked desserts. If you're in a hurry, get lunch in a bag ($8): your choice of chicken Dijon, tuna, or ham salad, or deli meats, on a roll or croissant with coleslaw or chips and a cookie. If you have time to enjoy the water view, try the daily special, like lump crab cakes with lime-caper tartar sauce, and a slice of apple-caramel pie. Prices average about $6. Open Mon.–Sat. 9 AM–5 PM.

Belle's (911 Boundary St., 843/986-1185) is a much less frilly joint, but they nonetheless serve up great blue-plate Southern fare in a low-key environment; if you want fried chicken, collard greens, cheese biscuits, and Calabash fried shrimp, come for the lunch buffet ($8). Open Mon.–Fri. 11 AM–2:30 PM.

To skip the Southern route altogether, head to **Sea Island Wine and Gourmet** (403 Cateret St., 843/524-9463). A short walk just around the corner from the Bay Street action, the fare is worth the sidetrack: Try The Davinci (Genoa salami, sopressata, capicola, provolone, onions, tomatoes, greens, olive oil, herbs; $8) or a handmade, flat-bread pizza, like the Pinot Bianco (roasted garlic olive oil, provolone, gorgonzola, and mozzarella; $6.50). It's a grocery and wine cellar with a handful of bistro tables. Open Mon.–Sat. 10 AM–6 PM.

Outside downtown, along Highway 21 on St. Helena Island, you'll run across the famous (**Shrimp Shack** (1925 Sea Island Pkwy., St. Helena Island, 843/838-2962), a place that keeps getting written up in major national magazines but somehow manages to retain its casual-meal-on-the-back-porch charm. Fried shrimp is king of the menu, but they offer shrimp cooked other ways, and other types of seafood, chicken, and steaks that contain no shrimp whatsoever. But when in Shrimp Shack, eat shrimp. My favorite is the shrimp burger.

Of course there are the typical fast-food joints on the way into town. But there's an alternative: Cook your own food. To buy the freshest shrimp around, take Highway 21 to Helena Island and you'll come across **Gay Fish Incorporated** (1948 Sea Island Pkwy., 843/838-2763), owned by a guy named Charlie Gay, who will sell you fresh shrimp by the pound.

Lowcountry and Fancy Eats

The (**Beaufort Inn** (809 Port Republic St., 843/521-9000), draws crowds, accolades, and media attention galore. The *Atlanta Constitution* pronounced it "a MUST dining experience," AAA gave it Four Diamonds, and still, the dress style is only "nice casual." Beaufort's like that. People like to come here for the elegant atmosphere, fine wine list, and fresh seafood. It'll cost you quite a bit to eat here, but you won't forget the experience anytime soon. Closed Sat. for lunch, otherwise open daily for breakfast, lunch, and dinner. Reservations suggested.

(**Saltus River Grill** (802 Bay St., 843/379-3474, www.saltusrivergrill.com) is the swankiest, and most metro-appointed of all dining spots in town, but thanks to the locals who frequent the place, it still manages to be casual, in spite of its deco metal and wood decor, and sublime chocolate and blue color palette. Sushi? Check. Raw bar? Check. Extensive wine list? Check. And how about the entrées? Delicious and then some. Try the Lowcountry Style Flounder, stuffed with rock shrimp and crab stuffing, fried capers, crumbled bacon, baby green beans, and buerre blanc sauce. Pretty people, pretty food. Open daily for dinner. Reservations recommended.

Breakwater (205 West St., 843/524-4994), is a notch or two toward the casual end of dial, but is still elegant, hip, and polished, and serves a great mix of small- and entrée-portion dishes. The shrimp and grits (with yellow stone-ground grits, fresh local shrimp, tasso ham gravy, and homemade biscuits) are particularly good. Prices range $14–33. Open for dinner Mon.–Sat.

Emily's Restaurant & Tapas Bar (906 Port Republic St., 843/522-1866) has been around since 1989, and thanks to its longevity and off-Bay-Street location is more of a locals hangout than tourist destination. But tourists who are in town for more than a night would do well to swing by. With its long bar, glossy black piano, and $8 tapas menu (shrimp done six ways, soft-shell crab, crabmeat rangoon, crab cakes, and on), it's a great way to sample your way through Lowcountry fare in a dressy setting with a friendly, Lowcountry attitude. Entrées are about $20. Open for dinner Mon.–Sat.

For a more rurally located Southern experience, take the bridge from Beaufort to Lady's Island, take the first sharp right at Whitehall Drive, and turn right into the grounds of **C Bateaux** (27 Whitehall Landing, 843/379-0777, www.bateauxrestaurant.net). Set on a one-time plantation, the casual building hides a terrific menu that puts a gourmet twang to local favorites. The crisp fried buttermilk oysters are served with corn jus, chive-oil, and horseradish semifreddo ($6); and the Shrimp Papardelle (house-made pasta with local sautéed shrimp, roasted tomato sauce, zucchini ribbons, and roasted crème fraîche, $14) are particularly good. Average dinner entrées are about $20. Open for lunch and dinner Mon.–Fri., and dinner only on Sat. Reservations suggested.

The Original Steamer Oyster and Steakhouse (168 Sea Island Pkwy., Lady's Island, 843/522-0210) on Lady's Island is another pricey but tasty place for seafood. The Frogmore Stew ($15.95) is quintessentially Lowcountry. Rumor has it that Nick Nolte favored this place while filming *Prince of Tides* here in town. Open daily for lunch and dinner.

Barbecue
In this part of the state, it seems like the best barbecue joint in just about every town is a Duke's. This **C Duke's Barbecue** (1509 Salem Rd., 843/524-1128) features a large all-you-can-eat buffet and a half-mustard, half-tomato-based sauce. Open Fri.–Sat. 11 AM–9 PM.

INFORMATION
For more information on the Beaufort area, contact the **Greater Beaufort Chamber of Commerce** (1006 Bay St., 843/524-3163, www.beaufortsc.org).

ST. HELENA ISLAND
Frogmore
Frogmore is a tiny town—officially part of St. Helena—intersected by Highway 21. You can't miss it if you're headed in from Beaufort. Also unavoidable is the **Red Piano Too Art Gallery** (870 Sea Island Pkwy., 843/838-2241, www.redpianotoo.com), where folk art rules. A great place to pick up a one-of-a-kind (literally) souvenir, including painted furniture, mobiles, regional landscapes, and books written in Gullah, they also have a one-room Gullah museum inside. Closed Sun. during the winter, otherwise open daily.

If you're in town for the Gullah Festival or some other Penn Center event, head across the intersection from the Red Piano Too (left across from the park), and check out the Africa-themed clothing and knickknacks that roadside vendors sell during special-event weekends.

In the late 1980s, islanders voted to restore the old Spanish name "St. Helena" to the island, although the island had been called "Frogmore"—after a former plantation owner—for years. It was a controversial, politically motivated attempt to refocus the history of the island, and some locals disagreed vehemently: For a time, islanders' produce was refused at mainland farmers markets, and a noose was even hung at the park outside the Penn Center as a warning. But now the St. Helena name seems to have grown (back) on folks.

C Penn Center Historic District
Here on Martin Luther King Drive stands one of the first schools established for the recently

freed slaves of the South. The Penn School (16 Penn Center Circle W, St. Helena Island, 843/838-2432, www.penncenter.com) was founded by two white Quaker women, Laura Towne and Ellen Murray, and supported by the Freedman's Society in Philadelphia, Pennsylvania. Later that year, African American educator Charlotte Forten joined the team. In the early 1900s, Penn began to serve as a normal (teachers'), agricultural, and industrial school. The school graduated its last class in 1953.

Every January, 1963–1967, Dr. Martin Luther King met here with the biracial Southern Christian Leadership Conference to plan strategies for overturning segregation and Jim Crow laws. The **Retreat House,** which still stands at the end of a dirt road on the waterfront, was built for Dr. King in 1968, but he was assassinated before he could stay there. For years, the Peace Corps trained many of its tropics-bound volunteers here. Angela Brown, an East Los Angeles schoolteacher who trained here in 1987 before heading off to Cameroon, says the similarities between Gullah and the pidgin English she heard in Cameroon were striking.

Today, the 50-acre, 19-building center continues as something of a spiritual homeland for those devoted to civil rights in general and the betterment of African Americans in particular. Its mission statement says that the Penn Center's purpose is to "preserve the Sea Island's history, culture, and environment." Ironically, the school built for the movement of Gullah blacks into mainstream American society has become something of a shrine to the unique African American culture the original Northern teachers came down here to "educate" out of the freed persons.

The center, deemed a National Historic Landmark district in 1974, consists of some 19 buildings. The first one to visit is the **York W. Bailey Museum** (Cope Industrial Bldg., Penn Center, 843/838-2432, www.penncenter.com) on the right side of Land's End Road as you come in from Highway 21. This is one of the world's major centers of information on the Gullah culture and the connections between West Africa and the Sea Islands. Be sure to peek into the bookshop, where you'll find several hard-to-find books, including a couple penned by Penn Center alumni. You'll also find recordings by the **Hallelujah Singers,** the gospel group featured in *Forrest Gump* and renowned throughout the country for their powerful vocal harmonies. The singers are based here at Penn Center and perform frequently in the area. Open Mon.–Sat. 11 AM–4 PM. Admission is $4 adults, $2 senior citizens and children.

To get to the Penn Center, take Highway 21 South through Beaufort to St. Helena Island. Take a right on Martin Luther King Jr. Drive, and continue until you see signs for the Penn School Historic District.

LUKE 9:23-25 IN GULLAH

23. Jedus tell um all say, "Ef anybody want fa folla me, e mus don't do jes wa e want fa do no mo. E mus cyah e cross an be ready fa suffa an die cause ob me, ebry day. 24. Anybody wa da try fa sabe e life, e gwine loss e true life. Bot anybody wa loss e life cause ob me, e gwine habe de true life. 25. Wa good e do a man ef e own ebryting een de whole wol an gone ta hell wen e ded? E done loss e true life, ainty?"

23. And he said to them all, "If any one will come after me, let him deny himself, and take up his cross daily, and follow me. 24. For whosoever will save his life shall lose it: but whoever will lose his life for my sake, the same shall save it. 25. For what is a man advantaged, if he gain the whole world, and lose himself, or be cast away?"

From *De Good Nyews Bout Jedus Christ Wa Luke Write,* 1995

EXPERIENCING GULLAH CULTURE

Perhaps the best-known craft to the casual Carolina visitor is **basket weaving.** In the Charleston Market and along Highway 17 north of Mount Pleasant, Gullah women sit in their stands making and selling their wares, the products of a tradition passed down from African ancestors and carried across the Atlantic in the minds and hands of women locked in the holds of slave ships. Most of the baskets you'll see for sale bear European influences as well – the relatively lightweight baskets found for sale are for show, not for carrying clothing, food, or babies, as are the heavier "work" baskets, which are more uniformly African in origin.

Both the "show" and "work" baskets, which are woven from the Lowcountry's sweetgrass, pine straw, bulrushes, and palmetto leaves, contain patterns and designs similar to those found in Nigeria, Ghana, Togo, and Benin. Both boys and girls learn basket making at a young age, although primarily women continue weaving as adults.

Another celebrated element of the Gullah culture is the **storytelling** tradition passed down from time eternal. Many of the traditional Gullah stories (still told today) appear to have African parallels. One popular series features "Brer Rabbit," a wily rabbit who stays one step ahead of those who are physically bigger than him through his quick wits. A lot of historians have theorized that this story reflects the slaves' own strategies for outwitting the dominant white class during antebellum times, but as scholar Patricia Jones-Jackson points out in *When Roots Die: Endangered Traditions on the Sea Islands*, Brer Rabbit – like characters abound in West African cultures, suggesting that although slaves may well have found it easy to identify with the Brer Rabbit character, the character itself predates American slavery.

Other common Gullah stories feature Jesus as a character and always contain some sort of moral lesson. Call-and-response relationships between storyteller and audience, in fact, resemble the ones between Gullah preachers and their congregations. Most Sea Island churches tend toward emotive Baptist and Methodist services, with the call-and-response forms found in many African American cultures. One interesting Gullah belief, which is becoming progressively less common, perceives the human as divided into body, soul, *and* spirit. At death, the body dies, the soul travels to heaven or hell, but the spirit is left behind to do either good or harm to people here on Earth.

LANGUAGE

Technically speaking, the Gullah tongue is considered a creole language rather than a dialect like inland Black English or American Southern English. Linguists consider a dialect to be a variant of standard English particular to a specific region or social environment, whereas a true creole descends from a "pidgin," a combination language created by people speaking different languages who wish to communicate with one another. Technically, a pidgin has no native speakers; when because of isolation the pidgin is allowed to become the dominant tongue in a region (as has Gullah on the Sea Islands), the tongue is considered a creole.

Although most Gullah words come from English, some words (one linguist estimates 4,000) derive from African languages, including *gula* (pig); *cush* (bread or cake), *nansi* (spider), and *buckra* (white man).

Jones-Jackson points out several grammatical elements to listen for when conversing with a Gullah speaker; they include pre-marked verbs ("I don shell em" instead of "I shelled them"), verb serialization ("I hear tell say he knows," instead of "I hear it said that he knows"), and adverb-adjective duplication for emphasis ("clean clean"

Newpoint

If the shiny new shopping centers on the Sea Island Expressway are making you feel a bit queasy, it may help to take a walk through the Newpoint development, on Sam's Point Road. When you see the quality craftsmanship on the old-style homes, with their front porches within conversation's distance of the sidewalk, you'll swear that the neighborhood comes from the 1820s, but these homes are generally less than 10 years old.

Interestingly, the folks in the real estate office

rather than "very clean"). All of these characteristics seem to have roots in African languages.

WHERE TO EXPERIENCE GULLAH CULTURE

Near Beaufort: The 49-acre, 16-building Penn Historic Center on St. Helena Island stands as perhaps the world's foremost center of information on Gullah culture and on the connections between West Africa and the Sea Islands. The first place to visit is the **York W. Bailey Museum** (Cope Industrial Bldg., Penn Center, 843/838-2432, www.penncenter.com), on the right side of Land's End Road as you come in from Highway 21. Open Mon.–Sat. 11 AM–4 PM. Admission is $4 adults, $2 senior citizens and children.

If you can make it here in November, you may get to take part in the **Heritage Days Celebration** (16 Penn Center Circle W, St. Helena Island, 843/838-2432, www.penncenter.com), a three-day festival celebrating African American Sea Islands culture.

Right at the intersection of Highway 21 and Land's End Road, you'll find the **Red Piano Too Art Gallery** (870 Sea Island Pkwy., 843/838-2241, www.redpianotoo.com), an old plank grocery store, which has reopened as an art gallery for folk artists, with a small museum as well.

For Beaufort-area tours focused specifically on the Gullah culture, call **Gullah-n-Geechie Mahn Tours** (P.O. Box 1248, St. Helena Island, 843/838-7516 or 843/838-3758, www.gullahngeechietours.net).

In May, Beaufort hosts a **Gullah Festival** (St. Helena Island, 843/525-0628, www.gullahfestival.net), with traditional storytelling, music, and other events.

On Hilton Head, visit **The Gullah Bookstore** (148-1 William Hilton Pkwy., 843/342-2002) and **De Gullah Creations** (Shelter Cove Mall, 843/686-5210) for arts, crafts, and books, and more.

Charleston Area: You'll find Gullah basket weavers selling their baskets along Highway 17 north of Mount Pleasant, around the Market area, and sometimes at other known tourist haunts like the visitors center or at Patriots Point, although prices at the latter tend to be more expensive. **The Avery Research Center** (125 Bull St., Charleston, 843/953-7609, www.cofc.edu/avery) at the College of Charleston features a reading room and archives dedicated to documenting and preserving the cultural history of Lowcountry African Americans. **Gallery Chuma/African American Art Gallery** (43 John St., Charleston, 843/722-7568, www.gallerychuma.com) features Gullah artist Jonathan Green's works as a permanent fixture, along with those of several other renowned African American artists. Open Mon.–Sat. 10 AM–6 PM, or Sun. by appointment. **Gullah Tours** (Charleston, 843/763-7551, www.gullahtours.com) of Charleston leave from the gallery daily; call for information. For authentic Sea Island cooking, try **Gullah Cuisine** (1717 Hwy. 17 N, Charleston, 843/881-9076).

MEDIA

Well-regarded books on Sea Island culture and the Gullah tongue include the informative *When Roots Die: Endangered Traditions on the Sea Islands,* Patricia Jones-Jackson (Athens, GA: University of Georgia Press, 1987), which is highlighted by the inclusion of several transcribed Gullah folk tales, sermons, and prayers. South Carolina Educational Television (800/553-7752, www.scetv.org), offers several video titles that touch on Gullah and Sea Island subjects.

The bookstore in the museum at the Penn Center is one of the best places in the state (and the world) to find books, music, and videotapes relating to Sea Island culture.

---

here say that only about one-fifth of Newpoint's population is native South Carolinian. The rest are people looking for the South of their imaginations, who have found that it's easier (and cheaper) to re-create it than to buy into The Point in Beaufort itself. The riverbank here, although fronted by huge multimillion-dollar homes, is a public waterfront, open to all.

The strength of a place like this is that when people move here they are signing on to a code of conduct, to a view of life, and promising to share a set of values—neighborliness, respect for others' property, and privacy—with the rest of their neighbors. The downside? The homes here run $207,000–364,000 and on up to $1.4 million. A lot of others who would love to live in a place with this sort of lifestyle simply can't afford to buy a home here.

Nonetheless, to see a new development done right, head over to St. Helena Island, turn left on the first light onto Sams Point Road (Highway 802), and drive 1.5 miles until you see the brick columns on the left, heralding Newpoint's entrance.

HUNTING ISLAND STATE PARK

Take Highway 21 east of Beaufort for 16 miles and you'll finally reach the ocean at **Hunting Island State Park** (2555 Sea Island Pkwy., 843/838-2011, www.huntingisland.com). Native tribes used to hunt here, and after Europeans moved in, hunters purchased the land and ran the island as a hunting club. To reward them for their preservation efforts, the government snatched up the land and turned it into a park. And what a park it is. This is a subtropical forest. Tell the kids they're going camping where the exteriors for Disney's recent live-action remake of *The Jungle Book* were shot. And let 'em know they can climb the 140-foot 1875 **Hunting Island Lighthouse.**

You can rent a waterfront cabin (866/345-7275, www.southcarolinaparks.com), but do so at least six months in advance. Cabin rates range $89–145 and require a two-night minimum stay. Camping—273 sites—is also available. Rates range $17–25.

Open Mon.–Sun. 6 AM–6 PM; 6 AM–9 PM during daylight savings time. Admission is $4 adults, $2.50 seniors, and $1.50 for children 6–15. Lighthouse admission is $0.50.

FRIPP ISLAND

Captain Johannes Fripp, hero in the British battles against the Spanish, purchased this coastal island between Hunting Island and Pritchard's from the Yamassee Indians, who had come to settle here in the last part of the 1600s. Nowadays it's a developed and controlled-access resort island (843/838-3535 or 800/845-4100, www.FrippIslandResort.com) with more than 200 homes and villas for rent, and plenty of golf and tennis. The **Fripp Island Marina** (843/838-1517) can hook you up with charter fishing boats, as can **Fripp Island Excursions** (843/838-1518).

Things are changing quickly here. How quickly? Remember the Vietnam sequence in *Forrest Gump?* It was filmed here in 1993. Today, "Vietnam" is a golf course.

PARRIS ISLAND

More than one million men and women have trained at Parris Island before being shipped off to do battle elsewhere. During World War II alone, more than 204,000 Marines were prepared for battle on this island—as many as 20,000 at a time. Stop at the gate when you reach base: If you don't, you may be shot. But seriously (and I was serious), stop and ask the guard there to tell you how to get to the **Douglas Visitor's Center** (Bldg. 283, Blvd. de France, Parris Island, 843/228-3650, www.beaufortonline.com/military/). There you can pick up maps and brochures that will guide you through a tour of the remains of some of the earliest European settlements in North America. The visitors center is open Mon.–Wed. 8:30 AM–4:30 PM; Thurs. 7:30 AM–7 PM; Fri. 7:30 AM–4:30 PM; Sat.–Sun. noon–4 PM.

Charles Fort, Fort San Felipe, Santa Elena, and San Marcos

Here in 1564, French settlers under Jean Ribaut attempted to create a settlement they called Charles Fort on the shore of what is today called Parris Island. But after Ribaut was imprisoned during political intrigues on a trip back to France, the suffering Frenchmen left in Charles Fort were miserable, thinking they'd been forgotten. After surviving a while upon the good graces of the local Native Americans, they built a boat—the first ever built in North America for transatlantic travel—and sailed it back to France, and that was the end of French Carolina. In 1566, the Spaniards built Fort San

© SEAN SLINSKY

Beaufort's nearby marine bases remind visitors that this is a military town, too.

Felipe and the village of Santa Elena on the exact same site. Indians destroyed the village in 1576 after the Spaniards fled from their hostility, but a year or so later the Spaniards rebuilt the town, protected by a new, larger fort they called San Marcos. For centuries, the exact location of the Charles Fort site was a mystery, until archaeologists realized that some of the artifacts they were finding at San Felipe were French, not Spanish. Those crazy Spaniards had built right on top of the French foundations, more or less. Behind the base's private golf course clubhouse, **The Sand Trap** (1050 Blvd. De France, Parris Island, 843/228-4578), you'll find the oldest European-style pottery kiln ever found on the continent. Inside the clubhouse itself, you'll find a pretty decent cheese sandwich. Stop by the visitors center before you come out here to get a driving map. Clubhouse open daily 7 AM–5 PM.

Parris Island Museum

If you're a fan of all things military, you're in for a treat at this museum (Bldg. 111, 111 Panama St., 843/228-2951), which celebrates the long history of military life on Parris Island, which I suppose is what you'd expect. One exhibit celebrates women Marines, who have served here since 1943 when they arrived as reservists, filling in jobs vacated by men needed in the Pacific. Another room attempts to help visitors understand the grueling regime of a Marine Corps recruit here at Parris Island. One display allows you to push a button and get an earful of abuse (minus the obscenities) from a mannequin drill instructor.

But perhaps most interesting for civilians are the display cases interpreting local history going all the way back to 1564, when Huguenot pioneer Jean Ribaut arrived with settlers to establish an ill-fated French colony in North America. You'll see some neat artifacts from the 500-person 16th-century Spanish town of Santa Elena, built atop—or so researchers discovered just a couple years back—the former French settlement of Charles Fort. The upper-echelon Spaniards ate off imported Ming dynasty china, shards of which have been recovered in the soil near the 14th green of the Parris Island Golf Course. Open daily 8:30 AM–4:30 PM.

PORT ROYAL

This relatively undiscovered town of 3,000 gives you an idea of what Beaufort was like before *Santini*. Here you can view one of the new but old-looking neighborhoods, along the lines of Newpoint on St. Helena.

A fine seafood spot is **11th Street Dockside** (1699 11th St., 843/524-7433), one of those waterfront restaurants with open-beam ceilings, wooden tables and chairs, and tanned servers running around in shorts and aprons, with the name of the restaurant emblazoned on their Polo shirts. It is, in fact, what many of the places in Murrells Inlet and Shem Creek started out as, and still pretend to be. Good seafood and a relaxed, great atmosphere with a view of the boats out on the river.

The restaurant has been around for years, although new owners bought it in 1995 or so. It draws a lot of visiting parents who come to see their gun-toting children graduate from Parris Island on Fridays. Therefore, you'll want to get here early if you come on Thursday.

Keep heading south along Highway 281 and you'll come across **The Sands** (at Battery Creek and Beaufort River, 843/986-2200, www.portroyal.org), which is where the young folk of Port Royal hang out and play volleyball. Here you'll find a boardwalk leading to an observation tower, which provides a great view of the harbor and the docks of the Port Authority, where the hurricane scene from *Forrest Gump* was filmed.

DAUFUSKIE ISLAND

Hilton Head is a creature unto itself, but hop over it and you'd land here, on Daufuskie.

After more than a century of virtual obscurity as a home for freed slaves who shrimped and farmed on the small island, Daufuskie gained fame as the setting for Pat Conroy's 1972 novel *The Water is Wide*, which later became the Jon Voight movie *Conrack*. Still accessible only by boat, this island remains partially authentic Lowcountry and part generic Golfland, in the form of the **Daufuskie Island Resort and Breathe Spa** (421 Squire Pope Rd., Hilton Head, 843/842-2000 or 800/648-6778, www.daufuskieresort.com).

The island is a nice little half-day trip; you can walk or drive a golf cart around the small village and see the 1934 **Daufuskie Island Elementary School.** Over on the south end, you'll find the 1800s **First Union African Baptist Church** with two front doors—one for women worshippers, and one for men. Down at the end of the dirt road here is the old **Mary Dunn Cemetery** with tombstones dating back to the late 18th century.

During **Daufuskie Day** (800/523-3373, www.hiltonheadisland.org) in late June, storytellers and artists show how life was like on the island in years past, and kids can play all sorts of old-fashioned games, like sack and egg races.

Check with the marinas in Hilton Head for scheduled ferries and tour boats. **Vagabond Cruises** (22D Bow Cr., Hilton Head, 843/363-9026, www.vagabondcruise.com) offers a trip to the island, on which you get a narrated naturalist cruise, plus a guided bus tour, with stops at spots made famous by *The Water is Wide*. Open Mar.–Nov., Thurs. and Sat. 9 AM–noon. Cost is $45 adults, $15 children.

If you'd like to stay overnight, try one of the resort's 200-plus units, which include beach cottages, an inn, luxury vacation homes, and more.

Hilton Head

In his sequel to *Less Than Zero*, Brett Easton Ellis sends one of his overstimulated rich-kid characters to Hilton Head for the weekend. This alone is good proof of the island's emergence as a domestic jet-setter paradise.

Annually, about 2.5 million people visit 42-square-mile Hilton Head Island, the largest Sea Island between New Jersey and Florida. One of the first communities in the United States to bury its phone lines, this planned community is conceptually head and shoulders above the Irvines of the world.

Most visitors come to stay in one of four main resort communities—Palmetto Dunes, Port Royal Resort, Sea Pines Resort, and Shipyard Plantation—to play the area's 40-plus championship golf courses, play tennis on one of the island's 300-plus courts, and relax on its 12 miles of white-sand beaches.

HISTORY

Hilton Head Island contains two ancient Native American shell rings, one located in the Sea Pines Forest Preserve and the other on Squire Pope Road. Nobody knows quite what they were used for, but their presence here argues for the existence of a people who lived here before the Yamassee and even before the earlier Ewascus Indians. British captain William Hilton spotted this island in 1663 while scouting for good sugar and indigo-growing land for his Barbadian employers and advertised in London for settlers, although, because no one in London knew what a "golf villa" was, he didn't get any takers. Nonetheless, the island did eventually develop as an agricultural area, becoming the home of several large plantations in the Colonial period and on up to the Civil War.

During the Civil War, this was the site of an amphibious landing of 13,000 Union troops in November 1861—the largest U.S. amphibious landing until World War II. Despite its use during the Civil War as a major control center and supply base for the Union navy's blockade

of Charleston and Savannah, once the Yanks were gone, Hilton Head returned to its sleepy ways. It remained isolated from the mainland until 1956, when a bridge was built connecting the 12-mile-long island to the mainland.

People didn't catch on immediately. As late as 1961, Hilton Head was home to just 1,000 African Americans and about 50 whites. The only businesses were a liquor store and a gas station. But Hilton Head landowner Charles Fraser had a vision: a Southerner's utopia, where golf courses, coastal breezes, and casual lodgings went side by side. Fraser built and opened **Sea Pines Resort** in the 1960s—the island's first resort complex. **Palmetto Dunes, Shipyard, Forest Beach, Hilton Head Plantation,** and **Port Royal** followed over the years. All have things to recommend them, but stick with Sea Pines, Shipyard, Palmetto Dunes, or Port Royal to be on the ocean.

Hilton Head is a unique place with unique problems, the most inescapable of which is traffic. Nearly all of the different massive "plantations" are de facto large cul-de-sacs, traffic-wise, so all traffic eventually spills onto one of the two main through-roads on the island—Highway 278 (the William Hilton Parkway) and the four-lane Cross Island Parkway ($1 toll), which cuts from Highway 278 near Spanish Wells Road to Sea Pines Circle on the south end of the island.

Today, the island offers 3,000 hotel rooms and 6,000 homes and condos, hosting as many as 65,000 people during a busy spell.

SIGHTS

The island of Hilton Head is divided into various private and public complexes.

◖ Harbour Town

Harbour Pointe Village is on the water at the southwestern tip of the island, deep in The Sea Pines Resort. An odd mix of New England seafront, Mediterranean chateau, and 1970s condo tack, it's where you'll find the famed

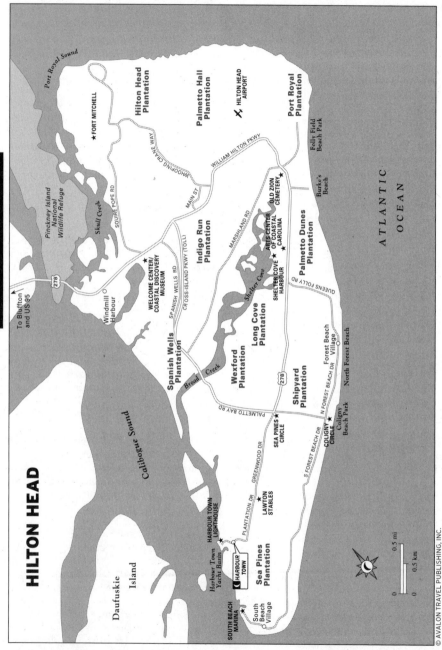

HILTON HEAD

Daufuskie Island

Calibogue Sound

Port Royal Sound

Pinckney Island National Wildlife Refuge

★ FORT MITCHELL

Hilton Head Plantation

Palmetto Hall Plantation

✈ HILTON HEAD AIRPORT

Port Royal Plantation

Skull Creek

Squire Pope Rd

Whooping Crane Way

Main St

William Hilton Pkwy

Folly Field Beach Park

Burke's Beach

ATLANTIC OCEAN

Windmill Harbour

WELCOME CENTER/ COASTAL DISCOVERY MUSEUM ◎

Spanish Wells Rd

Cross-Island Pkwy (Toll)

Indigo Run Plantation

Marshland Rd

ARTS CENTER OF COASTAL CAROLINA ★

OLD ZION CEMETERY ★

Palmetto Dunes Plantation

Shelter Cove

SHELTER COVE HARBOUR ★

Queens Folly Rd

To Bluffton and US-95

278

Spanish Wells Plantation

Broad Creek

Wexford Plantation

Long Cove Plantation

Shipyard Plantation

278

Palmetto Bay Rd

N Forest Beach Dr

Forest Beach Village

North Forest Beach

Harbour Town Yacht Basin

HARBOUR TOWN LIGHTHOUSE ★

◆ HARBOUR TOWN

Plantation Dr

Greenwood Dr

LAWTON STABLES ★

SEA PINES CIRCLE ★

COLIGNY CIRCLE ★

Coligny Beach Park

S Forest Beach Dr

Sea Pines Plantation

SOUTH BEACH MARINA ★

South Beach Village ★

0   0.5 mi

0   0.5 km

© AVALON TRAVEL PUBLISHING, INC.

Harbour Town Lighthouse (149 Lighthouse Rd., 843/671-2810, www.harbortownlighthouse.com). Developer Charles Fraser built the lighthouse in 1970. Although folks laughed at him at the time, he was building the lighthouse not to help lead ships into port, but rather to lead golfers into real estate offices—he knew that camera operators covering the MCI Heritage across the water on the Harbour Town Golf Links would naturally focus in on this red-and-white lighthouse, perched poetically at the entrance to Harbour Town like a Statue of Liberty for the world's affluent:

Bring me your sires, your well-born, Your coddled masses yearning to tan deep...

And of course he was right. The zoom lenses haven't yet pried themselves from the giant candy-cane lighthouse: it's become the internationally recognized symbol of Hilton Head. As you ascend the lighthouse to a gift shop

© SEAN SLINSKY

Sea Pine's 1970 Harbour Town Lighthouse still draws tourists to its shopping village and marina.

and overlook at the top (not wheelchair accessible), you'll find photos and descriptions of the 12 other lighthouses on the East Coast. Open daily 10 A.M.–9 P.M. Admission is $1.50, children under five free.

South Beach Village

South Beach Village is another quaint spot in Sea Pines that plays on the New England–seaside-village-with-exceptionally-warm-weather theme. Last time I was here it was almost 105°F—everyone sat around in the chairs and along the seaside bar drinking and talking. A visit to the **Salty Dog Café** (232 S. Sea Pines Dr., 843/686-2323 or 843/363-2198, www.saltydog.com) restaurant enclave is a must—something like the Hard Rock Cafe, where people who don't even eat there feel compelled to purchase a T-shirt in the gift shop. There are several restaurants in the marina under the same Salty Dog umbrella, and between each, you can dine from 8 A.M. to 11 P.M. daily. **Captain John's Gallery** (232 S. Sea Pines Dr., 843/686-2323 or 843/671-5199, www.saltydog.com) is a decent seafood place; it has a good view but inflated prices.

Audubon Newhall Preserve

If you get weary of the island's calculated charms, the Audubon Newhall Preserve (Palmetto Bay Rd., 843/842-9246 or 843/842-9056, www.hiltonheadaudobon.org) on your left just before you reach the cross-island tollway, is a wonderful place to disappear for a while. Wander the easily traversable trails and you'll see what the island looked like in its natural sublimity, before it was "improved." Open daily dawn–dusk. Free admission.

Old Zion Cemetery

Just after you come down onto the island on Highway 278 from the bridge, to your right (at Mathews Dr. and Folly Field Rd.) is the antebellum Old Zion Cemetery at the **Zion Chapel of Ease,** one of several chapels that served St. Luke's Parish, established in these parts in 1767, back in the days when the Church of England was the state religion and the state was divided into Anglican parishes rather than counties.

Arts Center of Coastal Carolina

Over in the Shelter Cove Marina stands this $10 million complex (15 Shelter Cove La., 843/686-3945 or 843/842-2787, www.artscenter-hhi.org), which hosts art shows and music and theater performances. Contact the center for the latest offerings. Box office open Mon.–Fri. 10 AM–5 PM (and till curtain time show days). Art exhibits open Mon.–Fri. 10 AM–4 PM. No admission charged to view the art gallery.

The Coastal Discovery Museum

You'll find this natural-history museum (100 William Hilton Pkwy., 843/689-6767, www.coastaldiscovery.org) on the second floor of the **Hilton Head Island Chamber of Commerce Welcome Center** (100 William Hilton Pkwy., 800/523-3373, www.hiltonheadisland.org). The museum also features displays on Hilton Head's roles in the American Revolution and the War Between the States. Stop in and see if the folks there have planned any of their tours, which focus on local history, marine life, nearby Pinckney Island, African Americans on the Sea Islands, and the Civil War. Open Mon.–Sat. 10 AM–5 PM, Sun. 10 AM–4 PM. Free admission to museum. Contact the museum for tour dates, times, fees, and reservations.

Pinckney Island National Wildlife Refuge

On Highway 278, just one half mile west of Hilton Head Island, you'll come across the entrance to the 4,000-plus- acre Pinckney Island National Wildlife Refuge (912/652-4415, www.fws.gov/pinckney), which was named after the land's former owners, U.S. Chief Justice and Constitution-framer Charles Pinckney and Declaration of Independence signatory Charles Cotesworth Pinckney. Here you'll find nearly 3,000 acres of salt marsh and small islands, 14 miles of trails to walk or bike, and not a single car beyond the parking lot. Take the 2.9-mile round-trip **Osprey Pond Trail** or, if

you really want to experience the refuge's flora and fauna and have a day to do it in, take the 7.9-mile round-trip **White Point Trail.** Open dawn–dusk. Free admission.

The Coastal Discovery Museum (100 William Hilton Pkwy., 843/689-6767, www.coastaldiscovery.org) offers some tours of the area, and **Water-Dog Outfitter** (Water-Dog Outfitter Kayak, Canoe, and Bike Center, 21 Sea Ln., Broad Creek Marina, 843/686-3554, www.waterdogoutfitter.com) leads water and bike eco-excursions through the refuge.

Tours

Based at Shelter Cove Harbour, **Adventure Cruises** (Ste. G, Harbourside III, Hilton Head, 843/785-4558, www.hiltonheadisland.com/adventure), offers dolphin-watching tours, and even crabbing cruises.

The Coastal Discovery Museum (100 William Hilton Pkwy., 843/689-6767, www.coastaldiscovery.org) offers a large variety of tours of the Hilton Head. **H2O Sports** (149 Lighthouse Rd., Harbour Town Marina, 843/671-4386, www.h2osportsonline.com) offers "Enviro Tours" in a U.S. Coast Guard–certified Zodiac inflatable, specializing in up-close dolphin encounters and bird-watching. Finally, for more than 20 years **Outside Hilton Head** (Ste. H, Shelter Cove Plaza, 843/686-6996, www.outsidehiltonhead.com) has offered a huge variety of powerboat and kayak tours. Check into their fishing trips, Daufuskie excursions, and kayak school.

Gullah Heritage Trail Tours (843/681-7066, www.gullahheritagetour.com) run two-hour bus tours that leave from the Welcome Center and cover the island's tabby plantation ruins, former freedmen village, one-room schoolhouse, and 10 African American communities that have withstood resortification. Get a solid history of life on the island, and the lowdown on Gullah culture. Call to reserve your spot. Tours operate Wed.–Sun. Prices are $20 adults, $10 children under 12.

Gullah-n-Geechie Mahn Tours (P.O. Box 1248, St. Helena Island, 843/838-7516 or 843/838-3758, www.gullahngeechietours.net)

also leads Gullah-based tours of the greater Hilton Head area.

ENTERTAINMENT AND EVENTS
Nightlife
While this is a family place for the most part, the island does like to hang out. The **Brick Oven Café** (Park Plaza, 843/686-2233 or 843/785-7155) is a popular late-night mellow spot. And **The Big Bamboo Café** (Coligny Plaza, 843/686-3443) attracts a crowd to its World War II–era lounge in the Coligny Plaza. For the most concentrated action, hit any bar in the so-called Barmuda Triangle, in the area around Park Plaza near the Sea Pines Circle.

Festivals
Hilton Head being a resort, with scads of people—and retirees—means folks have a lot of free time on their hands. It's no surprise then that some of that free time gets turned toward planning various festivals. The **Winter Carnival** (843/686-4944, www.hiltonheadhospitalityassociation.com), a two-month-long festival beginning in January, is a smorgasbord of arts and cultural events. If you're a Gullah jazz saxophonist with a taste for lasagna, this is really a must. February also means it's time for the seagrass baskets and gospel singing of the **Native Islander Gullah Celebration** (877/650-0676, www.gullahcelebration.com). The third weekend of March brings on **Wine Fest** (843/686-4944 or 800/424-3387, www.hiltonheadhospitalityassociation.com), held the second weekend in March in the Shelter Cove Community Park, and billed as the East Coast's largest tented public wine-tasting event, complete with auctions and live entertainment.

During March, **Springfest** (800/424-3387, www.hiltonheadhospitalityassociation.com), a monthlong event celebrating sports, arts, and food, takes over the island.

The weekend following Augusta's Masters Tournament, the **MCI Heritage** (800/671-2448 or 800/234-1107) is held on Pete Dye's **Harbour Town Golf Links** (32 Greenwood Dr.,

Hilton Head Island, 800/925-4653, www.seapines.com) at Sea Pines Resort. Attend and watch 120 of the world's top duffers battle over $1.4 million in prize money. Call for information on getting in (to see, not play).

The Sunday afternoon closest to Cinco de Mayo (May 5), brings the Arts Center of Coastal Carolina's **Family Fiesta Latina** (888/860-2787, www.artcenter-hhi.org).

Come October, **Beaufort Shrimp Festival** (843/986-5400, www.beaufortshrimpfestival.com) barrels into town for a two-day orgy of all things crustacean. Tour marine exhibits, check out shrimp boats, listen to music, and eat, eat, eat.

SHOPPING
With up to 65,000 folks penned onto an island with discretionary income and lots of leisure time on their hands, you can just see the merchants' register fingers twitching, can't you? There are several shopping centers on the island, including **The Mall at Shelter Cove** (24 Shelter Cove La.), anchored by Belk and Saks Off Fifth, and including Banana Republic, Talbot's, and Coldwater Creek, among others. This is not a bad place to go during a torrential downpour. **The Plaza at Shelter Cove** (Shelter Cove Lane) is the requisite parasite strip plaza near the mall, featuring a T. J. Maxx and Outside Hilton Head, a good sporting-goods store.

Other options include **The Village at Wexford** (1000 William Hilton Pkwy.); **Harbour Town** (on Lighthouse Rd. in Sea Pines Resort); **Northridge Plaza** (435 William Hilton Pkwy.); **Pineland Station** (William Hilton Pkwy.); **Port Royal Plaza** (95 Mathews Dr.), which offers a **Sam's Wholesale Club;** and **Fresh Market Shoppes** (890 William Hilton Pkwy.). You'll find a **Wal-Mart** (Pembrook Dr.) here, perhaps one of the few you needn't feel guilty about visiting because there was no cute old downtown for it to usurp.

The Tanger Outlet Centers (843/837-4339, www.tangeroutlet.com), on Highway 278 at the Gateway to Hilton Head Island in Bluffton, are divided up into two separate malls, but all told, they offer scores of stores, including Nike, The Gap, Book Warehouse, Mikasa, Oshkosh B'Gosh, Eddie Bauer, J. Crew, Samsonite, a frightening-sounding store called Toy Liquidators, and a crazy little joint called Perfumania ("Smellorama" was apparently already taken). It's like a monthful of shopping catalogs come to life. Enter at your own risk.

Beyond the chains and discount shops, check out **The Gullah Bookstore** (148-1 William Hilton Pkwy., 843/342-2002), where you find Gullah arts, crafts, and books. And pop into **De Gullah Creations** (Shelter Cove Mall, 843/686-5210) for quilts, books, collectibles, and more.

SPORTS AND RECREATION
Beaches
At **Coligny Beach Park** off Coligny Circle, **Driessen Beach Park** on Bradley Beach Road, and **Folly Field Beach Park** off Folly Field Road, you'll find parking and public access to some of the most beautiful, pristine white-sand beaches in North America. These beaches don't offer much in the way of waves, though. But bring your bike and you can ride for miles along the hard-packed sand.

Golf
Hilton Head Island is well known as home to the annual **MCI Heritage** (800/671-2448 or 800/234-1107), held on Pete Dye's **Harbour Town Golf Links** (32 Greenwood Dr., Hilton Head Island, 800/925-4653, www.sea-pines.com) at Sea Pines Resort the weekend after the Masters Tournament in Augusta. But the island is also known for the renowned Robert Trent Jones, George Fazio, and Arthur Hills courses inside **Palmetto Dunes Resort** (P.O. Box 5606, Hilton Head Island, 843/785-1161 or 800/845-6130, www.palmettodunes.com). **Shipyard Plantation Golf Club** (45 Shipyard Dr., 843/681-1760, www.shipyardgoldclub.net) has great courses with lower rates.

To choose the best public course for you, call the island-wide **tee time booking service** (843/785-1138 or 800/827-3006) before you visit. Or, for public courses, contact the state's tourism group for the free *Smiles and Places Guide* (800/682-5553, www.discoversouthcarolina.com).

Tennis
With some 300 courts, including clay, hard, and grass surfaces, Hilton Head is as much a tennis mecca as it is a holy land for golfers.

In 2002 **Sea Pines** (32 Greenwood Dr., 843/363-4495 or 800/732-7463, www.sea-pines.com) was named the number two Best Tennis Program by no less than *Tennis Magazine,* and other island resorts regularly make the magazine's top 50.

The **Palmetto Dunes Tennis Center** (6 Trent Jones La., 843/785-1152 or 800/972-0257, www.palmettotennis.com) contains 23 clay, 2 hard, and 6 lighted courts. For tennis lessons, ask at any racquet club—many offer them. Or call the **Van der Meer Tennis University** (19 Deallyon Rd. and 116 Shipyard Dr., 843/785-8388 or 800/845-6138, www.vandermeertennis.com).

Rates and hours vary greatly, so call ahead for details.

Horseback Riding
Lawton Stables (32 Greenwood Dr., 843/671-2586) is based in Sea Pines Resort and runs trail rides three times daily. Rates range from $50 per person eight years old and up, to pony rides for those under eight. Reservations required.

Biking
With the growing traffic on Hilton Head, and with the many fine trails laid out across the island, biking is a good idea. Although the designated paths won't take you far into Hilton Head Plantation or Sea Pines Resort, you can get almost anywhere else in the island by bike. To rent one, you might call **AAA Riding Tigers Bike Rentals** (843/686-5833), **Fish Creek Landing** (843/785-2021), or **South Beach Cycles** (843/671-2453).

Paddling
For on-the-island canoe rentals, you'll want to talk to **Outside Hilton Head** (The Plaza

at Shelter Cove, Ste. H, 843/686-6996 or 800/686-6996, www.outsidehiltonhead.com) or **Water-Dog Outfitter** (Water-Dog Outfitter Kayak, Canoe, and Bike Center, 21 Sea La., Broad Creek Marina, 843/686-3554, www.waterdogoutfitter.com).

If you're thinking about venturing off the island, you'll find canoe paddling tours of the ACE Basin, barrier islands, coastal marshes, and the Edisto River water trails, offered by **Carolina Heritage Outfitters** (Rte. 15, Canadys, 843/563-5051 or 800/563-5053, www.canoesc.com); and kayak tours of the same from **Palm Key** (330 Coosaw Way, Ridgeland, 800/228-8420, www.palmkey.com) or **Beaufort Kayak Tours** (843/525-0810, www.beaufortkayaktours.com).

If at all possible, bring your own canoe or kayak because rentals aren't cheap.

Boating
You'll find powerboats to charter or rent at **Island Watersports of Hilton Head** (232 S. Sea Pines Dr., 843/671-7007) and **Outside Hilton Head** (The Plaza at Shelter Cove, Ste. H, 843/686-6996 or 800/686-6996, www.outsidehiltonhead.com). And **H2O Sports** (149 Lighthouse Rd., Harbour Town Marina, 843/671-4386, www.h2osportsonline.com) rents sailboats.

Parasailing
If you want to be dragged by a speedboat through the Lowcountry sky, **H2O Sports** (149 Lighthouse Rd., Harbour Town Marina, 843/671-4386, www.h2osportsonline.com) will do it.

Charter Fishing and Shrimping
With the Gulf Stream so close by, no doubt the true anglers will want to get out and truly angle for something big enough to cover a wall in the den. **Drifter Excursions** (232 S. Sea Pkwy., 843/363-2900, www.bitemybait.com), **Seawolf Charters** (843/525-1174, www.seawolfcharter.com), and **Bonnie Rae Daily Charters** (843/683-6060 or 843/706-2181) can set you up. Catch a ride aboard the shrimp trawler **Tammy Jane** (843/384-7833) June–Nov. and see how seafood is hauled in with a 40-foot net. Cost is $40 adults, $20 children 12 and under.

ACCOMMODATIONS
Hunting for the best possible room in Hilton Head is like hunting for a bullet casing on Normandy Beach on D-Day plus one; it's easy to become overwhelmed. Most people choose their room based on what they hope to be doing while on the island.

Under $100
Hilton Head Plaza Hotels & Suites (36 S. Forest Beach Dr., 843/842-3100 or 800/535-3248, www.hiltonheadplaza.com), has a luxurious lobby, with five floors in the main building providing scenic views of the island. Several amenities are offered, including a pool and a fitness center. A stay here entitles you to a complimentary membership to Coligny Beach Club. Rooms come with cable, iron, full-sized ironing board, hair dryer, refrigerator, microwave, and coffeemaker. Rates are $59–209.

On the Highway 278 drag, between Shipyard Plantation and Palmetto Dunes, you'll find the humble two-story **Red Roof Inn: Hilton Head** (5 Regency Pkwy., 843/686-6808, www.redroof.com) with 111 rooms that run from $90 per night. Along the same "we're-only-going-to-sleep-there-anyway" lines is Hilton Head's **Motel 6** (830 William Hilton Pkwy., 843/785-2700 or 800/466-8356, www.motel6.com), where rooms range $45–63 and some include kitchenettes.

$100 and Up
As far as specific resorts go, **[Palmetto Dunes** (Hwy. 278, 843/785-1106, www.palmettodunes.com) a 2,000-acre resort with the aforementioned world-class golfing, a tennis center, and miles of white-sand beach. Check into their two hotels or one of their condos, and immediately your biggest worry is choosing where to eat that night; the folks here will take care of everything else. Rooms range

$89–599 (Hilton, 843/686-8000) and $179–349 (Marriott, 843/686-8000); and condos range $900–2,100 per week (800/845-6150).

Disney's Hilton Head Island Resort (22 Harborside La., 407/939-7540 or 843/341-4100, www.disneyvaacationclub.com) offers special activities for kids, but other than that, it's hard to imagine how even Walt's minions can improve on the natural beauty already here. The intricate illusions of nature that seem impressive in downtown Anaheim or Orlando feel a bit unnecessary here, but you might give them a call to hear Mickey's side of it. Rates are $295–710.

Bed-and-breakfasts seem to have a hard time of it on Hilton Head, but in a world of massive resorts, the **Main Street Inn** (2200 Main St., 843/681-3001 or 800/471-3001, www.mainstreetinn.com) seems relatively intimate, offering 32 units, many of which are wheelchair accessible. Nice gardens can be found here, and a Continental breakfast comes with the price of the room, which will run you $169–289.

Vacation Rentals

You'll find villas for $1,000–3,500 per week from **The Vacation Company** (42 New Orleans Rd., 843/785-9050, www.vacationcompany.com). Or call **Resort Quest Hilton Head** (800/845-6132, www.resortquesthiltonhead.com). Ask for the free literature they'll be glad to send you. If you're visiting on a last-minute whim, call the folks at **The Vacation Outlet** (843/836-4990 or 843/422-4291) for specials and discounts all over the island.

FOOD

Hilton Head is crawling with as many restaurants as there are rooms to rent. While it's not hard to find decent places to get meals, it's not exactly easy to get authentic Southern fare, ethnic fare, fine cuisine, or seafood guaranteed to be fresh not frozen and flown in from elsewhere. To help you out, here are some of the best places to eat on the island. And since in these parts *nothing* goes undiscovered, call ahead to get reservations or see about wait times.

© SEAN SLINSKY

Hilton Head locals head to Hudson's on the Docks; the shrimp boats attest to how fresh the catch is.

Southern and Seafood

For fresh-off-the-boat seafood, cooked up like a true fry house, try **⟨ Hudson's on the Docks** (1 Hudsons Rd., 843/681-2772, www.hudsonsonthedock.com). Just off Squire Pope Road and far from the resort scene, this 30-year-old institution is always packed (with locals), but if you're in a hurry, small parties can eat fast up at the bar inside. Otherwise, there's usually a balloon-wielding clown for kids out front, and there's a terrific view of the shrimp trawlers and Skull Creek for everyone else. Favorites are the locally caught shrimp dishes, and anything stuffed with their crabmeat, both served with hush puppies, seven-day slaw, rice, and a salad. Nothing's fancy, but everything's good here. Oh, and if you're here for an extended visit, get the frequent fryer card to score free meals. Prices average $18 an entrée, and a children's menu is available. Open daily for lunch and dinner.

Another family-friendly place, **Scott's Fish Market** (Shelter Cove Harbor, 843/785-7575) also sits on the water. Overlooking the Shelter Cove Marina, it's a lively place, with indoor/outdoor seating, Fiestaware dishes, and a similarly peppy, preppy menu, staff, and clientele. The menu's rather varied, and you can get anything from a batter-fried platter ($21) with jumbo scallops and local shrimp, to rare tuna with greens ($20), or filet mignon ($24). Prices average $20 an entrée, and a children's menu is available. Open daily for lunch and dinner.

While every upscale restaurant here has a fair share of seafood offerings, one longtime favorite is C **Charley's Crab House** (2 Hudsons Rd., 843/342-9066), right next door to Hudson's on Skull Creek. It's another local institution, and bustles with families celebrating events from anniversaries to summer reunions. Dress the kids up and head here so they can show off their good manners to Grandma. There are three floors of dining space, plus loads of outdoor dining, so it's action-central. Try the Carolina rainbow trout with creole mustard crust and lemon rémoulade and Smithfield ham ($19); or the shrimp and grits, served here with sautéed okra blended into smoked bacon garlic grits and topped with fried okra ($17). You can also opt for several types of fresh fish cooked as you like it. Prices range $17–37, with loads of options in the middle range. Open for lunch Mon.–Fri.; dinner nightly; and brunch Sun. Call for reservations.

Contemporary

Red Fish (8 Archer Rd., 843/686-3388, www.redfishofhiltonhead.com) is part gourmet food shop, part wine cellar, and part contemporary restaurant, specializing in seafood. Leave young kids at home for this one, and come for the upscale, white-linen setting and the artful food. Oven-roasted sweet-potato-encrusted catfish comes with a creamy andouille sauce, orzo wild rice, black beans, and fried bananas; ahi tuna and lobster is served with edamame hummus, crispy shiitake mushrooms, and a plum wine reduction; and the burgers defy the norm: there's a Cajun shrimp–and–lobster burger, and Kobe beef burger with foie gras. The award-winning wine list numbers 1,000-plus. Prices range $20–32 an entrée. Open for lunch Mon.–Sat., and dinner nightly. Early-bird specials 5–5:45 PM. Call for reservations.

Two Eleven Park Wine Bar & Bistro (211 Park Plaza, 843/686-5212) has a great lineup of appetizers that will let you sample their flavors, local and from afar: rock shrimp tacos, crab stew, Cajun oysters, bistro pâté, beer-battered lobster tails, and Montrachet goat cheese. And unlike elsewhere, you can tame island prices by opting for a $13 small-plate version of a main entrée, like the cornmeal catfish or smothered shrimp. If seafood's wearing you out, try their crispy curry chicken, or the orange praline duck. It's a casual-chic setting void of pretense. Prices range $13–30. Open nightly for dinner. Call for reservations.

In the same development, just near the Sea Pines Resort gate, **Carolina Grill** (213 Park Plaza, 843/785-3000) is a dark, publike restaurant that serves a wide range of tastes. There's beef goulash with braised sweet-and-sour red cabbage and garlic potatoes; veal osso bucco with herbs, garlic, tomato, carrot, celery, and onion; barbecued baby back ribs with creamy corn polenta, collards, carrots, and a golden raisin slaw. If you're here during the winter, it's a great place for a meal that will both fill you up and warm you up. Prices average $25. Open for dinner Mon.–Sat.

Italian

Di Vino's (5 Northridge Plaza, 843/681-7700) is set in a typically Hilton Head–esque uninspiring shopping plaza. A sign out front reads:

No Pizza No Iced Tea No French Fries

In other words, when you head into this cozy (14-table) restaurant, expect to meet with some serious northern Italian food. Its shrimp-and-fettuccine pesto, seafood, chicken, and pasta makes it one of the island's better restaurants. Expect to spend about $7 for an appetizer, $17 and up for dinner.

Brick Oven Café (Park Plaza, 843/686-2233 or 843/785-7155), on the other hand, does have pizza, and even delivers. The only problem with that is delivery means you miss out on hanging in the laid-back neighborly restaurant. It's more locals than tourist mobs, but all are welcome and come for the huge array of brick-oven-cooked pizzas. Build your own from 30-plus gourmet and standard toppings (including pulled pork), or try the scampi, roasted vegetable, Mexican, or cordon bleu. Pizzas are about $15, sandwiches $7, "tappaetizers" $8, and entrées $18. Open nightly for dinner.

Mexican

San Miguel's Mexican Café (Harborside 3 Bldg., Shelter Cove Marina, 843/842-4555, www.sanmiguels.com) offers a Tex-Mex choices for a good price ($8–15), with a bueno view of Shelter Cover Marina. It's packed with families. Open Mon.–Sat. for lunch and dinner; Sun. dinner only.

For authentic food on paper plates (and low prices), try **Amigo's** (70 Pope Ave., Circle Center, 843/785-8226). Open daily 11 AM–9 PM.

Just as you come onto the island expressway, there's a pair of family-owned-and-operated bilingual restaurants that also serve authentic, fresh Mexican food, popular among the local Hispanic crowd and other residents alike. For a fast and healthy burrito, try **Baja Tacos** (160 Fairfield Sq., 843/689-3325), where your choice of meat include steak, chicken, and pork (plain or barbecued). Prices range $2.25–6. Open daily from 9 AM–9 PM. Just around the parking-lot corner is **MiTerra** (160 Fairfield Sq., 843/342-3409), a real south-of-the-border place imitated by wannabes. Spanish pop and mariachi music pipes throughout the stucco building and entrées include a huge array of traditional fare and seafood (fried platters or chilled, cocktail-style). Prices average $11. Open nightly for lunch and dinner.

Budget and Breakfast

Cheap spots to enjoy good breakfasts on the island are plentiful; the best include the following. The **Palmetto Dunes General Store** (1 Trent Jones La., 843/686-2507), which has

a little kitchen in back where you can buy a basic breakfast for real-world (i.e., *not* Hilton Head) prices ($3.99). Open daily 6 AM–11 PM. Another one of my favorites, especially because it's open 24 hours, is the **Hilton Head Diner** (6 Marina Side Dr., 843/686-2400), where you'll find not only the predictable hamburgers, fries, and shakes, but (oddly) a full bar. So if you've always thought your patty melt would taste better with a screwdriver, here's your chance. Bring change for the jukebox. **Harold's Diner** (641 William Hilton Pkwy., 843/842-9292) is a rarity in these parts: a true greasy-spoon dive where they are grumpy at everyone, and don't care who you are. Why go? The attitude's refreshing in these parts: The eggs, grits, and burgers are great, and you can't beat the rock-bottom prices. And you can sit on the squatty counter stools to watch all the action. Open Mon.–Sat. 7 AM–3 PM.

A polar opposite to the others in this category is **Signe's Heaven Bound Bakery & Café** (93 Arrow Rd., 843/785-9118, www.signes-bakery.com). On the island since 1972, they serve up dishes like all-day breakfast (frittatas and breakfast polenta with fresh fruit on the side, and a great blackberry French toast). With 14 kinds of house-made bread—including squaw bread, pear bread, peach almond, and more—the hot and cold sandwiches are tops. Add in tomato, devilled crab, roasted salmon, or spanakopita tarts, and then consider the cakes, brownies, pies, and cookies, and it's a ridiculous must. Come to eat in, to take out, or to stock your fridge. Breakfast prices are less than $7, sandwiches about $5. Open Mon.–Fri. 8 AM–4 PM, Sat. 9 AM–2 PM.

Brewpubs

When it opened up a few years back, the **Hilton Head Brewing Company** (Hilton Head Plaza, 7-C Greenwood Dr., 843/785-2739, www.hiltonheadbrewingcompany.com) became the state's first brewpub or microbrewery to operate (legally) in South Carolina since Prohibition. The menu features some good brew favorites: baby back ribs, pizza, seafood, steak, and even bratwurst. Open daily for lunch and dinner. The kitchen closes at 10 PM, but the bar stays open till 2 AM.

In the Northridge Plaza, **Mickey's** (435 William Hilton Pkwy., 843/689-9952), re-creates an old-time pub feel: good solid pub menu, televisions blaring sports—the usual. A place where actual locals head to escape the tourists. Open daily for lunch and dinner.

INFORMATION AND SERVICES
Information

For more information on Hilton Head Island, stop by the **Hilton Head Island Chamber of Commerce Welcome Center** (100 William Hilton Pkwy., 843/785-3673, www.hiltonheadisland.org). You can book a room or a tee time there as well. Open daily 9 AM–6 PM.

Child Care

Some resorts offer child care and children's programs, but if you're in an independent villa or hotel and aren't willing to risk taking baby out to a nicer restaurant, call **Companions, Nurses & Nannies** (11 Palmetto Pkwy., 843/681-5011).

GETTING THERE
Driving

Most people drive to Hilton Head Island, plummeting down from the north on I-95 before hanging a left at Highway 278. From anywhere on the South Carolina coast, you'll want to drive down Highway 17 to get here. From almost anywhere else in the state, you'll want to cut over to I-95; from most spots in the Upcountry, you'll want to find I-26 first, then head south on I-95 when you reach it.

Flying

People coming from out of state normally fly into the **Savannah/Hilton Head International Airport** (400 Airways Ave., 912/964-0514, www.savannahairport.com) and drive to the Hilton Head Island. The airport receives flights from AirTran (800/247-8726, airtran.com), American Eagle (800/433-7300, www.aa.com), Continental Express (800/525-0280, www.continental.com), Delta (800/221-1212, www.delta.com), Independence Air (800/359-3594, www.flyi.com), Northwest (800/225-2525), United Express (800/241-6522, www.ual.com), and US Airways (800/428-4322, www.usairways.com). You can also fly into the **Charleston International Airport** (5500 International Blvd., 843/767-1100, www.chs-airport.com), via Continental, Delta, Independence Air, US Airways, and United Express. (Beaufort visitors usually opt for the Charleston route.)

USAir Express (800/428-4322, www.usairways.com), offers daily commuter flights direct to the Hilton Head Island Airport. You'll find taxi service at the **Hilton Head Airport** (120 Beach City Rd., 843/689-5400, www.hiltonheadairport.com) to get you to your hotel.

Train

Oh yeah, right—like they're going to allow a noisy train chugging its way onto the island. You can, however, take **Amtrak** (800/872-7245, www.amtrak.com) to Savannah just 35 miles away, and then take a shuttle from there.

GETTING AROUND

Because so many of the island's highlights are spread far apart on this large island, unless you're just planning to hole up in a specific complex, you'll want to consider either biking or renting a car. There are several rental car companies that serve the airports and have satellite offices. Call or visit websites for details: **Avis** (800/230-4898, www.avis.com); **Budget** (800/527-0700, www.budget.com); and **Enterprise** (800/261-7331, www.enterprise.com).

Taxicab companies include **Yellow Cab** (843/686-6666).

◖ OLD BLUFFTON

Once, when I was 20, I spent a week at Disney World in Florida. About halfway through the week, my friends and I grew so tired of the manicured lawns, overpriced meals, and carefully constructed walkways, spiels, and

© SEAN SLINSKY

Old Bluffton's downtown historic area is a collection of 1800s buildings that are now art studios, galleries, and antique shops.

smiles that we exploded out of Disney airspace just to find a burger joint, talk to the locals, and say we'd actually seen a bit of central Florida.

This same sort of reaction against cultural vacuousness is what seems to propel many Hilton Head guests over the bridge and into Old Bluffton. This tiny antebellum town, founded in 1825, has become something of a day trip for people staying at Hilton Head. Initially established as a summer resort for Lowcountry planters escaping the fevers in the rice fields and swamps, Old Bluffton was home to poet Henry Timrod, "poet laureate of the Confederacy," when he taught here briefly in the 1860s. And lest we forget, Simons Everson Manigault, Holden-Caulfield-on-Sweet-Tea hero of Padgett Powell's *Edisto,* attends school in Bluffton.

During the Northern invasion, Union gunboat bombardment nearly leveled the town, and the church would have burned down if small detachments of boys in gray hadn't arrived to put out the fires in time.

As development kicks in at a rapid pace outside of Old Bluffton's small neighborhood historic district, the older area has undergone a bit of a renaissance in the past few years. On its few streets, lined with bungalows and tiny cottages, an artist colony has sprung up, and studios and antique shops now fill the homes there. To cleanse your palate of resort madness, and to touch a true face of the South, make sure you visit either on the way into town or on the way out.

When you go, be sure to visit **The Store** (56 Calhoun St., 843/757-3855) for antiques and art; it's set in an old-time general store, complete with lounging dog, and has an adjacent wine shop, too. At **Jacob Preston** (10 Church St., 843/757-3084), you'll find groovy pottery in earth and sea tones. And for wacky cartoon-colored paintings and scrap metal yard art, check out **Amos Hummell** (843/290-0507, www.hummellstudios.com) in the aluminum shack on Calhoun Street. All these are open Tues.–Sat.

If you're there at breakfast time, head to the **Sippin' Cow Café** (1230 May River Rd.,

843/757-5051) for their fluffy pancakes (six-plus for $4), biscuits and gravy ($2–4), or the breakfast burrito ($4.50). Open Tues.–Sat. 8 AM–4 PM. For lunch, try the Cow, or head to the 50-plus-year-old **⟨ Pepper's Porch** (1255 May River Rd., 843/757-2295), an ambling barnlike place that serves real Southern home cookin' and seafood to locals. You'll feel 1,000 miles from vacationland, and can get

stuffed on loads of dishes for every budget. The fried chicken, fried okra, and collard greens, with an extra side of cheesy grits, is especially good. Open Mon.–Sat. for lunch and dinner.

To get to Old Bluffton, take Highway 278 toward Bluffton and Hilton Head, turning right onto Route 46 for 1.3 miles. At May River Road, turn right, and park anywhere on Calhoun Street to wander the shops.

Beyond Beaufort

SHELDON CHURCH RUINS

Just south of Beaufort, between Gardens Corner and the town of Yemassee off Highway 17 on Highway 21, you'll pass the ruins of this church. The Sheldon church was first built in 1753, but the British burned it in 1779. It was rebuilt, but in 1865 William Tecumseh Sherman came through and burned it again.

In the dark days of Reconstruction, nobody around here had the money to rebuild the church again. The ruins remain ruins even today, an indictment of the violence of the Northern armies of 1865. Memorial services are held here under the open sky and moss-draped oaks on the second Sunday after Easter.

⟨ ERNEST F. HOLLINGS ACE BASIN NATIONAL WILDLIFE REFUGE

Named for the three rivers draining the basin—the Ashepoo, Combahee, and Edisto—and the venerable senator who championed them, this refuge (8675 Willtown Rd., Hollywood, 843/889-3084, www.fws.gov/acebasin.com) serves as home to American alligators, short-nose sturgeon, wood storks, loggerhead sea turtles, blue-winged teals, and southern bald eagles, along with several other endangered or threatened species. Refuge open daily daylight to dark. Office open Mon.–Fri. 7:30 AM–4 PM. If you'd like to tour the area in a 38-passenger pontoon boat, call **ACE Basin Tours** (1 Coosaw River Dr., Port Royal, 843/521-3099 or 866/521-3099, www.acebasintours.com).

The best way to experience the ACE basin, however, is in a canoe or kayak. For rentals and/or guided tours, call **Carolina Heritage Outfitters** (Rte. 15, Canadys, 843/563-5051 or 800/563-5053, www.canoesc.com); **Outside Hilton Head** (The Plaza at Shelter Cove, Ste. H, 843/686-6996 or 800/686-6996, www.outsidehiltonhead.com); or **Palm Key** (330 Coosaw Way, Ridgeland, 800/228-8420, www.palmkey.com).

YEMASSEE

This town is farther off I-95 than the others on this list, but it's close enough. The main thing it offers—that some of the other highway stops don't—is campsites. **Point South KOA** (I-95 Exit 33 and Hwy. 17 interchange, Yemassee, 843/726-5733, www.koa.com) offers 53 sites, which range $22–50. **The Oaks** (1292 Campground Rd., 843/726-5728, www.koa.com) has 80 more.

Outside of town stands **Auld Brass,** the one and only plantation ever designed by Frank Lloyd Wright. It's owned today by Wright aficionado and Hollywood producer Joel Silver, of *Die Hard* and *Lethal Weapon* fame, and generally closed to the public. Once every other year, the **Open Land Trust** (843/521-2175, www.openlandtrust.com) offers guided tours.

WALTERBORO

Here's a good-looking town with some vision. With just under 6,000 residents and more a-comin', the Colleton County county seat knows it's got enough beautiful old homes and history to draw some bulging pocketbooks on their way down to Hilton Head. A while back, it lobbied for and got the right to open South Carolina's official Artisan's Center here, showcasing (and selling) the best handicrafts from Palmetto State craftspersons.

The story goes that Walterboro's name comes from a tree-felling contest. The rice town, founded in the early 18th century, was first named Ireland Creek, but two prominent citizens, a Mr. Walter and a Mr. Smith, each believed the burg should be renamed after himself, and a tree-felling contest was used to settle the matter. In truth, there were two Walters, Paul and Jacob Walter, Lowcountry planters who carved out a retreat up here just far enough away from the mosquitoes and sand fleas.

Another local legend says that the 1879 tornado that tore through town only knocked over the churches, leaving all the bars standing.

A lot of people like to walk or drive **Hampton Street** for its old houses, the earliest of which were built in 1824. Another site is the (private) **Jones-McDaniel-Hiott House** (418 Wichman St.), where the most famous person who ever lived in the house somehow managed to not be a Jones, McDaniel, or Hiott. Instead, it was Elizabeth Ann Horry Dent, widow of the commander of the USS *Constitution* during 1804's Battle of Tripoli, which later worked its way into the nation's consciousness through the Marine Corps Hymn:

From the halls of Montezuma to the shores of Tripoli, We fight our country's battles In the air, on land and sea.

◖ South Carolina Artisans Center

The South Carolina Artisans Center (334 Wichman St., 843/549-0011, www.southcarolinaartisancenter.org) features original handcrafted jewelry, pottery, baskets, furniture, and more, all made here in South Carolina, and most of it for sale. Getting this state center located in Walterboro was a major boon for the

plucky little city, and finding it is your boon. Open Mon.–Sat. 9 AM–6 PM, Sun. 1–6 PM. No admission charged, but bring buying money.

Colleton Museum

The Colleton Museum (239 Jefferies Blvd., 843/549-2303, www.southcarolinamuseums.org/colleton) is set in a restored 1855 jail. Pop inside—no admission—to check out some of the artifacts reflecting the area's importance during Colonial days as a rice-growing region, along with other displays detailing life in this region. Open Tues.–Fri. 10 AM–5 PM, Sat. noon–4 PM.

Colleton County Courthouse

The Colleton County Courthouse (101 Hampton St., 843/549-5791, www.colleton-county.org) is the site where Robert Barnwell Rhett, the fiery states' rights politician, demanded that South Carolina secede from the United States—way back in 1828, during the Nullification Crisis.

Slave Relic Museum

The Slave Relic Museum (208 Carn St., 843/549-9130, www.slaverelics.org) displays 200-plus-year-old artifacts made and used by Lowcountry slaves. Open Mon.–Thurs. 9:30 AM–5 PM, Sat. 10 AM–3 PM. Admission is $6 adults, $5 for children. Given the region's current dearth of African American museums in the Lowcountry, it's especially well worth a trip.

Tuskegee Airmen Memorial Park

Walterboro was one of the five combat training centers for World War II's sole African American pilots—the Tuskegee Airman—and the only such facility in the Southeast. Pay homage to their efforts at the Tuskegee Airmen Memorial Park (537 Aviation Way, Lowcountry Airport, 843/549-9595, www.tuskegeeairmen.org).

Events

Come to Walterboro any third Saturday of the month (excluding November), when it hosts the **Handmade Day** (334 Wichman St., 843/549-0011, www.southcarolinaartisancenter.org) wherein you can watch artisans creating their works right before your eyes. The last full weekend of April brings out the **Rice Festival** (843/549-1079, www.ricefestival.org), featuring the world's largest pot of rice and a rice-cooking contest.

Practicalities

Walterboro offers several chain hotels up on the interstate. I recommend the $30–35 **Village Inn** (904 N. Jeffries Blvd., 843/549-2581); the two-unit, $100-a-night **Mt. Carmel Farm B&B** (3610 Mt. Carmel Rd., 843/538-5770), where pigs, horses, and other pets are welcome; or the $69–99, four-unit **Old Academy Bed and Breakfast** (904 Hampton St., 843/549-3232, www.oldacademybandb.com).

If you've brought along a tent or have an RV, set up at **New Green Acres RV Park** (396 Campground Rd., 843/538-3450 or 800/474-3450).

As far as eating goes, **Duke's Barbecue** (949 Robertson Blvd., 843/549-1446) uses a mustard-based sauce that has made them a popular outfit. Open Wed.–Sun. 11 AM–9 PM.

Information

For more information on Walterboro, call the **Walterboro-Colleton Chamber of Commerce** (109-C Benson St., 843/549-9595, www.walterboro.org).

COLLETON STATE PARK

If you go left on Highway 17 at Walterboro, you'll end up on Route 15. Before long you'll come to this park (147 Wayside La., Canadys, 843/538-8206, www.discoversouthcarolina.com/stateparks), hidden among the live oaks growing along Edisto River, flowing black and silent like Waffle House coffee (and tasting much the same). This is the headquarters for the **Edisto River Canoe and Kayak Trail,** which covers 56 miles of black water. There are 25 campsites (866/345-7275, www.reserveamerica.com) in the park, each a good place to sleep before slipping off down the river in the

morning. Reach the park rangers in the office 11 AM–noon. Open daily 8 AM–9 PM. Admission is $2 adults, $1.25 seniors, free for those under 16.

Contact **Carolina Heritage Outfitters** (Rte. 15, Canadys, 843/563-5051 or 800/563-5053, www.canoesc.com) to rent a canoe or kayak, or to sign up for a guided tour along the trail.

SAVANNAH NATIONAL WILDLIFE REFUGE

Here (Hwy. 170 and the Savannah River, 921/652-4415, www.fws.gov/savannah), along the South Carolina shore of the Savannah River, 26,295 acres have been set aside as a sanctuary for migratory waterfowl and other birds, as well as other Lowcountry creatures. With all these tasty morsels around, it's no wonder that this is also a good place to see alligators. Open dawn to dusk only; no charge. Off I-95, take Exit 5 to Highway 17 South, take Highway 170.

You'll want to take the **Laurel Hill Wildlife Drive,** where you're likely to spot some gators, and possibly quite a few. Bring a camera, but don't get too close: they may look like logs with legs, but when they're motivated, they can move much faster than a human being for short distances. Now you've probably heard someone say that the muscles an alligator has to open its mouth are very weak, so if necessary you can wait until the gator has its mouth closed and then clamp the mouth shut with your hands. This is true. But if you get to the point where you find yourself holding a whipping, writhing six-foot alligator by the mouth, then you have probably gotten too close in the first place.

Be sure to check out the small plantation cemetery, marked by a millstone that once belonged to a nearby mill. The Laurel Hill Plantation, where most of the cemetery's current residents once spent their vertical days, is no more.

Many people like is to hike or bike along the miles of dikes. Bring insect repellent if you plan either of these activities.

SERGEANT JASPER COUNTY PARK

This relatively new state park (1458 Red Dam Rd., 843/784-5130) on Exit 8 off I-95 north of Hardeeville serves as both a recreational park for local residents and a deluxe rest stop for folks barreling down the interstate to Florida or up to New York. There's an observation deck that overlooks a man-made lake and picnic shelters. The park's name honors the man who raised the Palmetto flag after it was shot down during the battle of Fort Moultrie; he was killed later in the siege of Savannah, and a monument commemorates him. Open daily 9 AM–dark. Admission is $5 adults, $3 those 60 and older, $2 kids.

RIDGELAND

Ridgeland used to be known as something like the Las Vegas of South Carolina—not for its gambling, but for the goggle-eyed (i.e., drunk) Georgians who used to sneak over here and take advantage of South Carolina's relatively lax marriage requirements. Today, Ridgeland is home to the **Frederic R. Pratt Memorial Library** (123-A Wilson St., 843/726-7744), where you'll find 250 rare books on Lowcountry history and culture; and the **Pauline Pratt Webel Museum** (123-B Wilson St., 843/726-8126), which houses Native American artifacts and other historical displays reflecting life in this part of the world. You'll also find several chain motels, along with the **Plantation Inn** (Hwy. 17 N, 843/726-5510). **Duke's Barbecue** (690 Jacob Smarts Blvd., 843/726-6244), offers a large buffet with vegetables and fried chicken, and Duke's fine mustard-based sauce. Open Thurs.–Sat. 11 AM–8:30 PM. Call for directions.

ROBERTVILLE

This little town, a short jog northwest along arcing Highway 652, gets its name from the family of Henry Martyn Robert (1837–1923). The town is proud to claim Robert, who wrote *Robert's Rules of Order,* the world's most pop-

ular handbook on parliamentary procedure. (This in spite of the fact that he, a well-known military engineer, made the social faux pas of fighting for the Union during the war.) So if you've ever "had the floor" or "seconded a motion," you may want to tip your hat to the master as you pass through town.

"WE PAPA": THE LORD'S PRAYER IN GULLAH

Jedus tell um say, "Wen oona pray, mus say:
And he said unto them, When ye pray, say:
We Papa een heaben,
Our Father which art in heaven,
leh ebrybody hona you nyame cause you da holy.
Hallowed be thy name.
We pray dat soon you gwine rule oba all ob we.
Thy kingdom come,
Wasoneba ting you da want, leh um be een dis wol,
Thy will be done,
same like e be dey een heaben.
On earth as it is in heaven.
Gee we de food wa we need dis day yah an ebry day.
Give us this day our daily bread,
Fagibe we fa de bad ting we da do.
And forgive us our sins–
Cause we da fagibe dem people was do bad ta we.
As we forgive those who sin against us.
Leh we don't have haad test wen Satan try we.
And lead us not into temptation,
Keep we from e ebil.
but deliver us from evil.

Translation from *De Good Nyews Bout Jedus Christ Wa Luke Write,* prepared by the Sea Island Translation and Literacy Team, 1995.

SAVANNAH AND VICINITY

Savannah is an elegant city, rightly renowned for its 24 squares, which are reminiscent, to some, of Paris. In fact, in 1989, the Parisian newspaper *Le Monde* named Savannah as "The Most Beautiful City in North America."

And that's certainly not the last high-profile accolade Savannah has received. Savannah was named one of the "Top Three Romantic Getaways" by *Southern Living,* one of the "Top 10 U.S. Cities to Visit" by *Condé Nast Traveler,* one of the "Top 10 Walking Cities," by *Walking,* one of Marjabelle Young Stewart's "Top 10 Best-Mannered Cities in America," and one of the "Top 10 Southeast Cities for Family Vacations" by *Family Fun.* Perhaps most telling, in the midst of all this recognition, Savannah was also named one of the *New York Times'* "Top 12 Trendy Travel Hot Spots in the World."

The city basking in the glow of all these superlatives sits at the mouth of the Savannah River, the slithering brown border dividing Georgia and South Carolina. The city stands at 31 degrees 4 minutes north latitude and 81 degrees 5 minutes west longitude: Head due west of Savannah and you'll eventually end up in San Diego.

Savannah is bigger than Charleston and beautiful in a different way. Much of old Charleston (founded 1670) reflects the influences of the former Barbadian plantation owners who helped settle the region. Savannah, which lost 400 buildings to fires in 1796, and again in 1820, is of newer vintage. The city's troubles with fires led local architects to

© SEAN SLINSKY

HIGHLIGHTS

(Lafayette Square: It's hard to beat this square for historic value. Be sure to visit the Cathedral of St. John the Baptist, where you'll feel as though you are in an ancient European landmark. The towering ceilings and artwork are a testament to the city's early craftsmen…not to mention the local piety (page 160).

(Madison Square: Located on the Bull Street corridor, this square has a great mix of history, shopping, dining, and art, and shows how the city continues to thrive by being relevant to daily life (page 160).

(Forsyth Park: The city's largest green space is populated with fountains, and a great place to stroll under the live oaks. See if there's an outdoor concert here when you're in town (page 162).

(Old Fort Jackson: An 1800s-era relic

with Colonial roots, this brick fortress is just three miles from downtown (page 168).

(Fort Pulaski National Monument: Charleston has its plantations, Savannah has its forts. Visit this one to see a moated wonder that survived from Colonial times (page 169).

(Telfair's Owens-Thomas House: One of the Telfair Academy of Arts and Sciences gems, this gorgeous and decadently decorated house museum gives you a peek into pre–Civil War times (page 172).

(Bonaventure Cemetery: Take a ghost tour of this cemetery, one of the most eerie and romantic places in the South (page 172).

(Tybee Island: Eat at the Crab Shack and North Beach Grill, and hang out on the beach to soak up the laid-back side to the Savannah area (page 194).

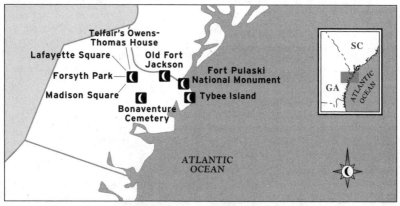

LOOK FOR **(** TO FIND RECOMMENDED SIGHTS, ACTIVITIES, DINING, AND LODGING.

forego flammable wooden exterior railings for wrought iron, which is why Savannah features so much more New Orleans–like scrollwork than its sister city to the north. Its mammoth historic district covers 2.2 square miles and contains 1,286 "historically significant" buildings. Some 300 of those buildings owe their salvation to the Historic Savannah Founda-

tion, which has been helping to keep wrecking balls away around here since 1955.

Savannah's location helps account for its distinct Southerness even as it sits in a state and a region that is rapidly homogenizing into something called the American Sunbelt. The bustling, "progressive" town of Atlanta is four hours away; high-tech mecca Raleigh-Durham is more than five hours away. The sunburns of Miami are more than seven hours south. But Charleston, perhaps the most Southern city in America, lies just 108 miles north on Highway 17.

For many outlanders, Savannah was little more than the name of a (the best) Girl Scout Cookie (discontinued), until the blockbuster novel, *Midnight in the Garden of Good and Evil.* In fact, nowadays, Savannahians commonly refer to the book's publication as a chronological touchstone: To many Savannahians, "Before the Book" and "After the Book" are completely different eras.

The rule holds in Savannah as it does in Charleston: *When you get to Savannah, park as soon as possible.* Oglethorpe designed this town to be walked, not driven. Second, although cobblestone River Street is certainly scenic and worth a visit, walk inland up a perpendicular street—pick Bull if you only have time for one—until you have passed through and explored at least four squares. Then head over a couple of blocks and discover the squares on that street.

Give Savannah a little while to work its charms on you. As one local put it, she's not Las Vegas, grabbing you by the eyes with aggressive glitter; she's a Southern lady rich in hidden allure.

PLANNING YOUR TIME

Thanks to Oglethorpe's vision, Savannah is a terribly easy city to navigate and wander by foot. Still, it's a good idea to get your bearings before you dive in. Catch one of the trolley tours from the visitors center, and you'll get a roundup of the most notable sights in town. Make note of the places that catch your eye and ear, and head back to them by foot, if possible.

Start at the top of Bull Street (at Johnson Square), and work your way south toward **Forsyth Park.** Along the way, you'll see a great mix of shops, Victorian and antebellum homes, museums, inns, and cafeés. While in town, stay at an historic bed-and-breakfast, visit at least one coffeehouse or tearoom, one of the Telfair

Academy of Arts and Sciences buildings (perhaps the house museum or the new modern arts center), and dine in one of the many fine restaurants mentioned in our listings. Next, shop, aiming for the River Street area (sweets), the City Market (souvenirs), the design district along Whitaker (antiques and art), and try to get lunch at Mrs. Wilkes' Boarding House.

For the full Savannah area experience, head out to **Bonaventure Cemetery,** and visit **Fort Pulaski** before continuing on to **Tybee Island.** Unwind by hanging out on the beach, taking a boat or paddling tour, and kicking back at the most mellow bars and restaurants in this region.

HISTORY

The Yamacraw tribe dwelt on the sandy bluff that became Savannah before the English arrived, but only for about 15 years. They were refugees themselves, having come out on the bad side of the 1717–1719 Yamassee war up in Carolina. The Yamacraw asked the British powers in Charles Town if they could relocate south of the Savannah River, and Charles Townians, ever happy to put friends between themselves and the feared Floridian Spanish, agreed. The Yamacraw picked the best, safest site they could find, a spot just south of the Savannah River, which gave them freshwater and fish. But their spot was also up on a bluff, which cut down on the bugs and allowed them the chance to spot any waterborne enemies while they were still a long ways off.

Oglethorpe arrived with his first settlers in 1733, and with the help of the Musgroves, a husband-and-wife trading team, Yamacraw chief Tomochichi agreed to allow the English to settle on the bluff near his tribe. Savannah grew quickly, and despite constant threat of Spanish attack, several plagues of yellow fever, and two devastating fires in 1796 and 1820, the town rode the shoulders of King Cotton to the first rank of American cities before the War Between the States.

After Federal forces established a stronghold at Hilton Head and proceeded to shut off Savannah as a Confederate port, the city's role in the war was minimal. Local interests tried

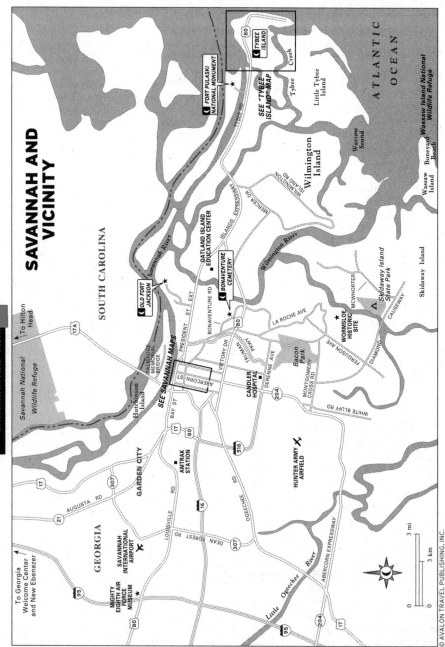

SAVANNAH AND VICINITY

SOUTH CAROLINA

GEORGIA

To Georgia
Welcome Center
and New Ebenezer

To Hilton Head

Savannah National
Wildlife Refuge

ATLANTIC OCEAN

Wassaw Island National Wildlife Refuge

SEE "TYBEE ISLAND" MAP

TYBEE ISLAND

Tybee Creek

Little Tybee Island

Wassaw Sound

Wilmington Island

Wassaw Island

Boneyard Beach

FORT PULASKI NATIONAL MONUMENT

OLD FORT JACKSON

OATLAND ISLAND EDUCATION CENTER

BONAVENTURE CEMETERY

Skidaway Island State Park

Skidaway Island

WORMSLOE HISTORIC SITE

SEE SAVANNAH MAPS

CANDLER HOSPITAL

HUNTER ARMY AIRFIELD

Bacon Park

GARDEN CITY

AMTRAK STATION

SAVANNAH INTERNATIONAL AIRPORT

MIGHTY EIGHTH AIR FORCE MUSEUM

Savannah River

Wilmington River

Hutchinson Island

TALMADGE MEMORIAL BRIDGE

Little Ogeechee River

Ogeechee River

Little Ogeechee River

PRESIDENT ST EXT

BONAVENTURE RD

MERCER DR

ISLANDS EXPRESSWAY

WILMINGTON ISLAND RD

MCWHORTER

FERGUSON AVE

DIAMOND CAUSEWAY

LA ROCHE AVE

VICTORY DR

SKIDAWAY RD

DERENNE AVE

MONTGOMERY CROSS RD

WHITE BLUFF RD

ABERCORN EXPRESSWAY

DEAN FOREST RD

LOUISVILLE RD

AUGUSTA RD

BAY ST

ABERCORN ST

TRUMAN PKWY

95 17 307 21 17A 174 17 80 80 16 516 204 307 204 17 95

3 mi

3 km

SAVANNAH AND VICIN

© AVALON TRAVEL PUBLISHING, INC.

to create armor-clad ships to sink the North's blockade ships but ultimately failed at it. Nonetheless, Savannah, even under siege, never lacked star power. The city began the conflict under the protection of General Robert E. Lee (who, years earlier, had helped design Fort Pulaski) and ended as Union General William T. Sherman's Christmas present to U.S. President Abraham Lincoln, the eastern terminus of one of the most famous military maneuvers in history, the March through Georgia. After the war, Savannah, unravaged by Sherman, rebounded more quickly than other parts of the South.

Preservation

Savannah's Preservation movement officially began in 1955, the same year that Disneyland, the ultimate shrine to American nostalgia, opened in Southern California. Of course, among the citrus groves of Anaheim, the 19th-century streets had to be built from scratch; the sleepy Southern river around Tom Sawyers' Island had to be dug out with bulldozers and dyed green to hide the steamboat tracks. In Savannah, of course, there was no need to conjure up a historical feel: The mythical American past was still standing, if a little wobbly, but it was endangered. Just the year before, local progressives had torn down the beloved City Market. Now they were preparing to bulldoze the historic Davenport House on East State Street, but the preservationists stopped them, and their success built confidence to save other historic structures. The Historic Savannah Foundation would use a revolving fund to buy up old structures and sell them to anybody who would promise to refurbish them. Before long, home values had shot up in the historic district and the previously low-rent Victorian district, which had originally been built as an extension of downtown during the boom days of cotton but which had seen hard times, and middle- and upper-class investors began buying those homes and fixing them up as well.

Midnight Hits Savannah

Perhaps years from now, the impact that New Yorker John Berendt's 1994 blockbuster *Midnight in the Garden of Good and Evil* has wrought on Savannah will seem less significant than it does today, but it's doubtful. Other Savannah-set blockbuster books may have come in the past, but no book has ever hit it so big: *Midnight* spent an unheard-of 100 weeks on the *New York Times* best-seller List, sold 1.25 million copies in America alone, saw translation into more than a dozen foreign languages, and became a major motion picture. At the same time, no other book had ever hit at a time of such massive mobility. Many retired and semiretired baby boomers, as well as multiple-home owners, were financially and technologically able to move south to the town they'd come to know through Berendt's book.

Of course, massive change was inevitable as the town of Savannah filled up with newcomers hoping to live in the town their very arrival had helped to alter. Nowadays, most native Savannahians cannot hope to buy a home in Historic Savannah, where even townhomes can go for a cool million. Some locals fret that Savannah has become more of a tourist attraction and less of a city.

Of course, once they squinted their way through the book and were certain their names weren't mentioned, many other Savannahians were excited about the book, particularly those who owned investment properties or businesses dependent on the tourism trade. Tourism shot up 50 percent after the book was published. Locals enjoyed the skyrocketing property values. Greater Savannah's population, which had grown by 27,000 between 1980 and 1990, nearly doubled the rate of growth. By 2000, the population of the Savannah area had reached over 292,000, up from 257,899 in 1990 and 230,728 in 1980.

Some mourned the town's loss of connection and distinctiveness. Of course, if any city's fabric drips so much color that it could weather a bit of fading, it's probably hyperchromatic Savannah, where, as in Charleston and Seattle, the inherent diversities of a port region have meshed with end-of-the-road cultural inbreeding to make for all sorts of eccentricities.

Sights

Savannah is the sort of town where half the fun comes with just relaxing, blending in, slowing down to the leisurely pace of the city. The town does have its historic sites, from the home where Juliette Low Gordon founded the Girl Scouts of America to the house where Sherman stayed after cutting the back of the Confederacy, not to mention the childhood home of premier Southern scribe, Flannery O'Connor. Other than that, the history here is mostly regional—important to Savannahians and to those interested in the town as an entity unto itself.

Which it certainly is.

As you get oriented to Savannah, keep in mind that the entire town lies south of the Savannah River—meaning that, as you put the river to your back and head "up" Bull Street toward Forsyth Park, you're really heading "down." (Compounding this confusion is the fact that several local Savannah maps face south, which is fine until somebody tells you to head west on Broughton and you head east.) Just remember, the farther you get from the river in Savannah, the farther south you are.

Wherever you're coming from, it's likely that you'll enter the city on Montgomery Street, on the west side of the historic district. Take this to Bay Street, head east, and, unless you get lucky with a spot on the street, you'll want to park either down on River Street or in garages on East Bay/Abercorn or on the west side of Warren Square.

Bull Street is Old Savannah's spine. With the gold-leaf-domed City Hall building at its northern end, Bull Street is the east–west dividing line for addresses.

HISTORIC SQUARES

Savannah's squares define the downtown district, and each individual square helps define that little quarter of the city. For a long while the story has been that of the 24 original squares, 21 are still extant. But that's changing, happily, because the city plans to restore Ellis Square, old site of the City Market, to its former location. This will involve tearing down a beloved parking structure (a new parking lot will go *under* the square), but Savannahians should survive the blow.

The first thing to remember is that monuments mean nothing, at least not when you're trying to figure out what square you're in. The Pulaski monument, which even General Sherman found touching, doesn't stand in the center of Pulaski Square—no sir. It's atop Monterey Square. Sergeant Jasper still waves the flag, but not above his own square—it's in Madison. To explore the squares, you'll want to walk them, but if you need to drive through a square, be sure to yield to the traffic that's already in the square.

Calhoun Square

This square, on Abercorn between Taylor and Gordon, is named after South Carolina statesman, U.S. Vice-President, and champion of Southern

Hanging out in any of the city's lush square gardens is a must.

© SEAN SLINSKY

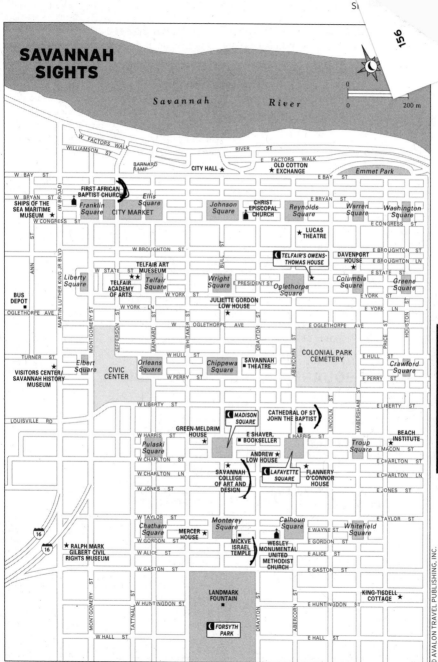

SAVANNAH SIGHTS

Savannah River

W FACTORS WALK
WILLIAMSON ST
RIVER ST
E FACTORS WALK
BARNARD RAMP
CITY HALL ★
OLD COTTON ★ EXCHANGE
E BAY ST
Emmet Park

W BAY ST

SHIPS OF THE SEA MARITIME MUSEUM ★
W BRYAN ST
FIRST AFRICAN BAPTIST CHURCH ★
Ellis Square
Franklin Square CITY MARKET
E BRYAN ST
Johnson Square
CHRIST EPISCOPAL CHURCH
Reynolds Square
Warren Square
Washington Square

W CONGRESS ST
E CONGRESS ST

W BROUGHTON ST
LUCAS ★ THEATRE
E BROUGHTON ST
E BROUGHTON LN

ANN ST
TELFAIR ART MUSEUM ★★
☽Telfair's Owens-Thomas House
DAVENPORT HOUSE ★
E STATE ST

W STATE ST
LIBERTY SQUARE
TELFAIR ACADEMY OF ARTS ★★
Telfair Square
Wright Square
E PRESIDENT ST
Oglethorpe Square
Columbia Square
Greene Square

BUS DEPOT ■
W YORK ST
W YORK LN
E YORK ST
E YORK LN

OGLETHORPE AVE
JULIETTE GORDON LOW HOUSE ★

W OGLETHORPE AVE
E OGLETHORPE AVE

TURNER ST
VISITORS CENTER/ SAVANNAH HISTORY MUSEUM ★
Elbert Square
CIVIC CENTER
W HULL ST
Orleans Square
Chippewa Square
SAVANNAH ■ THEATRE
COLONIAL PARK CEMETERY
E HULL ST
Crawford Square

LOUISVILLE RD
W PERRY ST
E PERRY ST

W LIBERTY ST
E LIBERTY ST
BEACH INSTITUTE ★

☽MADISON SQUARE
CATHEDRAL OF ST JOHN THE BAPTIST ☾

W HARRIS ST
GREEN-MELDRIM HOUSE ★
E SHAVER, ■ BOOKSELLER
E HARRIS ST
Troup Square
E MACON ST

Pulaski Square
ANDREW ★ LOW HOUSE
E CHARLTON ST

W CHARLTON ST
SAVANNAH COLLEGE OF ART AND DESIGN
☽LAFAYETTE SQUARE
FLANNERY O'CONNOR HOUSE ★
E CHARLTON LN

W CHARLTON LN
W JONES ST
E JONES ST

W TAYLOR ST
E TAYLOR ST

Chatham Square
Monterey Square
Calhoun Square
Whitefield Square

MERCER HOUSE ★
E WAYNE ST

W GORDON ST
MICKVE ISRAEL TEMPLE ✡
WESLEY MONUMENTAL UNITED METHODIST CHURCH ✝
E GORDON ST

W ALICE ST
E ALICE ST

★ RALPH MARK GILBERT CIVIL RIGHTS MUSEUM
W GASTON ST
E GASTON ST

LANDMARK FOUNTAIN
KING-TISDELL COTTAGE ★

W HUNTINGDON ST
E HUNTINGDON ST

☽FORSYTH PARK

W HALL ST
E HALL ST

0
0   200 m

SAVANNAH AND VICINITY

© AVALON TRAVEL PUBLISHING, INC.

..ghts John C. Calhoun of South Carolina. Calhoun Square is one of the latest squares, and one of four squares named after South Carolinians (Jasper, Johnson, and Wright being the others). Calhoun is known as home to the 1,000-seat **Wesley Monumental United Methodist Church** (429 Abercorn St., 912/232-0191, www.wesleymonumental.org), built 1875–1890.

Chatham Square

Laid out in 1847, this square was named in 1851 after William Pitt, the Earl of Chatham, who stood as an advocate for the rights of the colonies in the years before the American Revolution. (Georgia wasn't the only grateful colony: He's also the man for whom Pennsylvania's Pittsburgh is named.) The square, located on Barnard Street, between Taylor and Gordon streets, is also known for the **Gordon Row** (101–129 W. Gordon St.), a row of 15 four-story town houses built during the antebellum cotton heydays of 1853 by speculators. The houses' curved entry balustrades make them a Savannah landmark.

Chippewa Square

Located on Bull Street, between Perry and Hull streets, this is where Forrest Gump sat on his bench with his box of chocolates. When the filming was over, the Plexiglas benches (several were made by the prop crew) followed Tom Hanks and company back to Hollywood (although Savannah was able to get one back for display in the History Museum). The fate of the chocolates is lost to history.

Chippewa Square was named to commemorate American valor in the 1814 Battle of Chippewa in Canada, by some accounts the greatest battle in the War of 1812. Chippewa Square has several points of interest predating Gump, however. The bronze statue of Georgia's founder, General James Edward Oglethorpe, graces Chippewa Square. The ironwork around the Atlanta Life building is worth a look. The Romanesque, 1833 **First Baptist Church** (223 Bull St., 912/234-2671, www.fbc-sav.org) is Savannah's oldest surviving church. In the 19th century, Chippewa was popular as home of the William Jay–designed

---

MIKE'S SQUARE-NAMING SCORECARD

For whom were Savannah's squares named, generally? Here's a breakdown of the 24 still-existing squares:

NAMED AFTER FRIENDLY COLONIAL-ERA BRITISH LEADERS
Chatham

NAMED AFTER U.S. MILITARY VICTORIES
Chippewa
Monterey
Orleans

NAMED AFTER PATRIOT REVOLUTIONARY HEROES
Elbert
Greene
Lafayette
Pulaski
Warren

Washington

NAMED AFTER COLONIAL-ERA GOVERNORS
Ellis
Reynolds
Wright

NAMED AFTER SAVANNAHIAN AND GEORGIAN LEADERS
Crawford
Oglethorpe
Telfair
Troup
Whitefield

NAMED AFTER SOUTH CAROLINIANS
Calhoun
Johnson
Wright

Savannah Theatre, where much of the town's live theater took place. After a fire destroyed the theater in 1916, the Savannah was reborn as a cinema. Now the theater has come full circle and has reopened as a live theater. One block north of the square is the **Independent Presbyterian Church** (207 Bull St., 912/236-3346, www.ipcsav.org), founded as a branch of the Church of Scotland in 1755. The current building dates to the 1880s, although you'll notice that the plaques seem to try to hide this fact. Just before the fire that inspired this latest incarnation, the pastor, I. S. K. Axson, married his granddaughter off to another preacher's kid, a bookish but devout young man who had spent much of his youth in Augusta—Thomas Woodrow Wilson, later president of the United States.

Columbia Square

Between 1757 and 1790, when Savannah was walled against the Spanish and Indian invaders, this was Savannah's eastern limit, one of six gates. The square was laid out in 1799 and is located on Habersham Street, between York and State streets. The fountain in the center comes from the Wormsloe Plantation site. The name honors the early-American, pre–Uncle Sam symbol for American freedom, the woman Columbia. The naming of Columbia, South Carolina, and the District of Columbia date from this same period. The Renaissance Revival **Kehoe House** (123 Habersham St., 912/232-1020, www.kehoehouse.com), a 13-room B&B, stands on the corner of Habersham and State streets. William Kehoe was an iron magnate who was proud of his industry; the iron balustrades and railings along the balconies attest to this fact. Here, too, is the **Isaiah Davenport House** (324 E. State St., 912/236-8097, www.davenportsavga.com), which was built during the presidency of James Monroe, and today is a house museum.

Crawford Square

Laid out in 1841, this square is named for William Harris Crawford, a former governor, U.S. Senator (1807–1813), and Secretary of the

NAMED AFTER AMERICAN COLONIAL LEADERS FRIENDLY TO NEW COLONY
Franklin

NAMED AFTER AMERICAN PRESIDENTS
Madison
Washington

NAMED AFTER WOMEN
Columbia (mythological)
Liberty (ditto)
Telfair (named in part for Mary Telfair, heiress and benefactor)

SAVANNAH WOMEN AND MEN OF ACCOMPLISHMENT WHO DON'T HAVE SQUARES
Clarence Thomas
Emma "Lady of 6,000 Songs" Kelly
Flannery O'Connor
Johnny Mercer
Juliette Gordon Low
Peter Tondee

FAMOUS SAVANNAHIANS WHOSE SQUARES WOULD NO DOUBT BE INTERESTING
Joe Odom
Lady Chablis
Stacy Keach

FAMOUS NON-SAVANNAHIANS WHO MADE SO MUCH OFF SAVANNAH THEY COULD PROBABLY AFFORD TO BUY A SQUARE
John Berendt

A BRIEF WALKING TOUR OF SAVANNAH

As you stand on East Bay facing north, you'll have, in order, **Factors Walk** – the 19th-century Wall Street of the Cotton Industry; the shops, restaurants, and pubs of cobblestone **River Street;** the Savannah River; Savannah Harbor – home to The Westin Golf Resort & Spa; and South Carolina. To your left, 18 miles down Highway 80, lies **Tybee Island,** Savannah's main beach. To your right is the airport.

Before you, lies the **Historic District.** Beyond that is the **Victorian District,** and beyond that, Savannah's **Southside.** The Historic District includes all of the city's historic **squares** and runs 14 blocks to **Forsyth Park** at Gaston Street. The Victorian District continues about as far south as the park itself, ending at **Park Street.** After that, you're in **Midtown,** and then the **Southside.** These are where most of us would need to live and shop if we moved to Savannah, but they have limited attractions to the traveler.

When Union General William T. Sherman toured the conquered city during the Civil War, he rode up **Bull Street.** You might want to do the same thing: Bull Street is Savannah's spine. Head southward through Johnson Square, the city's oldest. Jog right along Bryan Street and you'll come to Ellis Square, which was formerly the City Market and is now a parking lot, but soon to be returned to its former glory. This is a worthwhile site to stop at early on in your visit: Because of the destruction of the old City Market for this eyesore in 1954, the new Ellis Square is slated to be built over a subter-ranean parking garage that will replace the present one. The two-block area around here is called **The City Market,** and the former feed stores and warehouses wedged between Barnard, Congress, and Bryan streets have grown into a rather happening part of town, with a couple of the city's most popular restaurants, its best pizza parlor, several music venues, art studios, galleries, and specialty shops, as well as frequent live music outdoors. It's beautiful at night.

Return east along East Congress Street, turn right at Bull, and continue along to Wright Square, Chippewa Square, Madison Square, and Monterey Square. Between Wright and Chippewa, you'll cross over Oglethorpe Avenue, one of the major east–west roads; Liberty Street comes between Chippewa and Madison. At Monterey Square, *Midnight* fans will recognize the **Mercer House,** now owned by Jim Williams' sister. One block after Monterey Square, you'll reach Forsyth Park and the beginnings of the Victorian District. The park's northern edge borders Gaston Street; this is another important marker: just as Charlestonians divide up their peninsula "South of Broad" and "Not South of Broad," Savannahians divide theirs into "North of Gaston" and "Not North of Gaston." Unlike Charleston's all-residential South of Broad area, the area North of Gaston contains all the restaurants, bars, and shops you could hope for. In *Midnight,* Joe Odom argues that all true Savannahians stay "North of Gaston,"

Treasury (1816–1825). Due partly to Crawford's friendship with President Monroe, the very popular president paid a visit to Savannah in 1819. It's located on Houston Street, between Hull and Perry streets.

Franklin Square

Located on Montgomery Street, between Bryan and Congress streets, Franklin Square was laid out in 1790 and originally named "Water Tank" or "Reservoir" Square because this is where the tank stood. Later it was renamed for Founding Father Benjamin Franklin, agent before Parliament for the Colony of Georgia from 1768 to 1775. The square is home to the **First African Baptist Church** (23 Montgomery St. 912/233-2244, www.oldestblackchurch.org), the oldest continuously meeting African American congregation in the United States.

Greene Square

This square is named for Revolutionary War General Nathanael Greene, who was awarded an exiled loyalist's abandoned plantation and while that might be hard to stick to for residents who might occasionally have to run Southside to the Oglethorpe Mall or Lowe's, for visitors this is a fine rule.

The exception, of course, is Forsyth Park itself. The fountain there was a favorite of both Confederate and Union troops during the War Between the States, and it's still the best-known and most-loved fountain in the city.

If time permits, walk around the park, taking in a bit of the Victorian District's charm on the perimeter, and then head east (right) on Gaston until you come to Abercorn, the other major north–south thoroughfare. (In fact, if you headed south here, Abercorn would turn into the Abercorn Expressway and take you through strip malls and chain restaurants of the Southside.)

Heading north on Abercorn, you'll come to Calhoun Square, and then Lafayette Square, home of the Andrew Low House, St. John's Cathedral, Flannery O'Connor Childhood Home, and the Hamilton-Turner House, which is a fine bed-and-breakfast and appeared in *Midnight*.

Continue north and you'll pass the Colonial Park Cemetery, which is worth a walk-through. Most of Colonial Savannah is buried there (except James Oglethorpe, who died back in the Old Country). Speaking of which, you'll come to Oglethorpe Square next. At this point, you may want to head left to Columbia Square, where the spectacular Owens-Thomas House is worth a tour. North along Habersham, you'll hit Warren Square. At this point head right on Congress to Washington Square. The gazebo here looks as if it dates back to the 19th century, but it was built for the filming of the Burt Reynolds film *Gator* in 1973, right when Burt was riding the wave of success after *Deliverance*.

Continue another block east and you'll come to East Broad, which used to be the eastern border of the city (Martin Luther King used to be called "West Broad" before its renaming). This used to be the ragged, shady outskirts of town. The colony's Trustees Garden was here, where the first settlers experimented with various plants to find out what would grow here and what would not. The gardener's shed, considered the oldest extant building in all of Georgia, has been assumed into the former tavern now known as the **Pirate's House,** where shady traders and bona fide pirates used to mingle with sailors to share grog and sing shanties, and where captains desperate for crewmembers were rumored to get patrons drunk, carry them down the tunnels that lead out from below the building, and take them out to the riverfront and onto their ships. One Savannah constable is said to have stopped in for a few drinks and woken up the next day as an involuntary crewmember bound on a long sea voyage. It took him two years to find his way back to Savannah.

Continue north from here, cross East Bay and down onto River Street, where the first thing you'll come to is the **Waving Girl Statue.** Continue on to the shops and restaurants of River Street.

after the war out of gratitude for his services in the Southern Theater of the war. Perhaps the square's naming—it was laid out in 1799—was out of guilt; sunstroke killed the 44-year-old Rhode Island–born general just a few years after moving into his gift plantation. It was while living on Greene's Fatal Plantation as a tutor for the Widow Greene's fatherless children that Eli Whitney invented the cotton gin in 1793. You'll find Greene Square on Houston Street, between York and State streets.

Johnson Square

The center of activity for earliest Savannah, Johnson Square, on Bull Street, was named for Robert Johnson, the Governor of South Carolina. Residents used to draw water from the well here, and Johnson Square was where citizens would post public notices and gather to discuss the colony's grievances against England. In later years, President Monroe visited (1819), and Marquis de Lafayette stopped through on his 1825 visit. Daniel Webster came in 1848. The large obelisk in the middle commemorates the life—and the grave, which is below it—of Revolutionary General Nathanael Greene. The Greek Revival **Christ Church Savannah (Episcopal)** (28 Bull St., 912/232-4131, www.christchurchsavannah.org) stands here on the former "trust lot." Both George Whitefield (founder of Bethesda Orphanage) and John Wesley (founder of Methodism) led the congregation here. In fact, the two men together founded America's first Sunday school here, in 1736.

◖ Lafayette Square

It's hard to beat this square, on Abercorn Street, for historic value. One of the Abercorn squares, Lafayette was laid out in 1837 and named after the Marquis de Lafayette, who visited Savannah in 1825 and stayed at the Owens-Thomas House on Oglethorpe Square. Lafayette is home to the **Andrew Low House** (329 Abercorn St., 912/233-6854, www.andrewlowhouse.com), which hosted both Robert E. Lee and William Makepeace Thackery (twice); the Hamilton-Turner House, which briefly hosted *Midnight in the Garden of Good and Evil*'s Joe Odom; the Gothic **Cathedral of St. John the Baptist** (222 E. Harris St., 912/233-4709, www.savannahcathedral.org); and the **Flannery O'Connor Childhood Home** (207 E. Charlton St., 912/233-6014).

◖ Madison Square

In the DeSoto district, this square was named in honor of James Madison, framer of the Constitution, fourth President of the United States, and husband of Dolly Madison, popular Tar Heel first lady. A statue honoring Sgt. William Jasper, who was killed in 1779 during the Siege of Savannah, stands in the square, in the shadow of the DeSoto Hilton. A granite marker here identifies the southern line of British defense during the siege that took Jasper's life. Savannah's best bookstore, **E. Shaver, Bookseller** (326 Bull St., 912/234-7257), is here. So is the Gothic Revival–style 1853 **St. John's Episcopal Church** (329 Bull St.), beloved by Savannahians for its beautiful chimes. The parish house next door, the **Green-**

Meldrim House (14 W. Macon St.), served as General William T. Sherman's headquarters in Savannah. At this house, Sherman, at the suggestion of a U.S. Treasury agent, wrote his famous telegram to President Lincoln, offering the city as a Christmas present, and here, too, Sherman drafted his Field Order 15, granting land lots on the Sea Islands (of no greater than 40 acres) to former slaves for the duration of the war. This square is located on Bull Street, between Harris and Charlton streets.

Monterey Square

During the Mexican War, the U.S. Army took Monterey, Mexico, in a battle led on the American side by General Zachary Taylor (the future president) and largely fought by Southern troops. The South, after all, was eager to claim new southern lands for the United States, which would presumably use slaves and thus would provide more political power to the beleaguered slave states.

To celebrate this important victory on the way to Manifest Destiny, Savannahians renamed this spot on Bull Street, between Taylor and Gordon streets, as Monterey Square. To the average Savannahian, Monterey is best known as the home of the Pulaski Memorial, a tribute to Count Casimir Pulaski, who suffered fatal wounds during the 1779 battle; or as home to the **Congregation Mickve Israel** (20 E. Gordon St., 912/233-1547, www.mickveisrael.org), the third-oldest Jewish congregation in America (1733), and the only Gothic synagogue in America (1878). The latter houses the oldest Torah in the United States (pre-1733). Both of these landmarks are worth a visit. To the average visitor, Monterey Square is best known as the location of the **The Mercer House Museum** (429 Bull St., 912/236-6352), where Jim Williams and Danny Hansford both met their death in *Midnight in the Garden of Good and Evil*.

Oglethorpe Square

Laid out in 1742, Oglethorpe Square is home to the tabby English Regency **Owens-Thomas House** (124 Abercorn St., 912/233-9743), perhaps the most worthwhile of many worthwhile home museums in Savannah. It was Richard Richardson who, while at a London wedding, met architectural apprentice William Jay and invited him to come to Savannah to design a home for him. Jay's arrival in Savannah, of course, is a celebrated event because it led to the creation of several of the city's most prized architectural landmarks. This square dates back to 1742 and honors the founder of Georgia, General James Edward Oglethorpe. It is on Abercorn Street, between State and York streets.

Orleans Square

This quiet square honors South Carolina–born Andrew Jackson and the heroes of the Battle of New Orleans. The surviving British had hardly crawled out of the "thickets where the rabbits wouldn't go" when the square was laid out in 1815 on Barnard Street, between Hull and Perry streets. In 1989, the German Memorial Fountain was dedicated here to commemorate the contributions of early German settlers to the growth of Georgia.

Pulaski Square

This square was named for the Polish American Revolutionary War hero Count Casimir Pulaski, who died while charging the British at the 1779 Siege of Savannah. The square, laid out in 1837, is located on Barnard Street, between Harris and Charlton streets.

Reynolds Square

Home of **The Olde Pink House** (23 Abercorn St., 912/232-4286), a present-day restaurant, and the John Wesley Monument, Reynolds was originally laid out in 1734 and called Lower New Square. In later years it was renamed for Captain John Reynolds, governor of Georgia in 1754. Back in the colony's earliest days, when the trustees were hoping to establish silk plantations in Georgia, Lower New Square was where the public filature—a reel that drew silk from cocoons—was kept.

The statue of John Wesley is a relatively new fixture, having arrived in 1969 compliments of the Methodists of Georgia. As the nearby plaque explains, it depicts Wesley during his brief Georgia ministry, adorned in Church of England vestments.

Telfair Square

The only square named (in part) for a real (not mythological) woman, Telfair was originally named Saint James but was renamed in 1833 after three-time Georgia Governor Edward Telfair and his daughter, heiress Mary Telfair (1789–1873), who lived here on the square and gave the Telfair house to the city in her will. The striking 1818 William Jay–designed **Telfair Academy of Arts and Sciences** (121 Barnard St., 912/232-1177, www.telfair.org) faces the square.

Before the Regency Telfair House went up, the residence of the royal governors of Georgia stood on this site. Hence it was here, as noted on the plaque outside the museum, that on the night of January 18, 1776, young Major Joseph Habersham, leading a small force of Savannah patriots, strode into the chamber where Governor Wright and his Council were conferring and announced: "Sir James, you are my prisoner." Wright went peacefully but later escaped to a British ship; Habersham, after the war, was named Postmaster General of the United States.

Troup Square

On Habersham Street between Harris and Charleton streets, Troup Square was laid out in 1851, at the peak of the city's antebellum cotton heyday. The armillary sphere—an astronomical model used to display relationships among the principal celestial circles—stands on a slate step-up in the midst of the square, which was named for George Michael Troup, Georgia governor (1823–1827). Follow Charlton Street east and you'll come to eight stucco units at 410–424 East Charlton, built in 1882 and featuring Victorian bay windows and sweeping front steps and iron railings. At 410–424 East Macon Street you'll find Kennedy Row, built in 1885, brick townhomes that have become a local landmark.

Warren Square

Named for Revolutionary General Joseph Warren, president of the Third Provincial Congress, Warren Square was laid out in 1791 on Habersham Street, between Bryan and Congress streets.

Washington Square

Laid out in 1790 on Houston Street between Bryan and Congress streets, this well-landscaped square honors, as you might guess, former General (and then-President) George Washington, who would stop through to inspect the place a few years later. The houses bordering the square have been restored; among them are some of Savannah's oldest homes, duly noted by plaques.

Whitefield Square

Named for the Reverend George Whitefield, founder of the Bethesda Orphanage and early minister at Christ Church, the square was laid out in 1851 and sits on Habersham Street, between Gordon and Taylor streets.

Wright Square

Named after Georgia's third, final, and best Colonial governor, the popular, South Carolina–born Sir James Wright, Wright Square is home to the William Washington Gordon monument. Gordon was an early mayor of Savannah and founder of the Central Railroad of Georgia. The large boulder that's also here was taken from Stone Mountain (possibly from Robert E. Lee's ear) to mark the grave of Tomochichi, the Yamacraw Indian Chief without whom Savannah would have been an unlikely proposition. According to Savannah native Carl Weeks, if you walk around the gravestone three times and knock on it, "Tomochichi will say nothing." Try it. On the east side of the square stands the 1879 **Lutheran Church of the Ascension** (120 Bull St., 912/232-4151). The congregation here was organized in 1741 by Salzburger pastor John Martin Bolzius of Ebenezer. They built their first church here. The church is worth a visit inside, if only to see the Ascension Window behind the window.

Wright Square sits on Bull Street, between State and York streets.

Ellis Square

Laid out in 1733, this square was named after Henry Ellis, the Crown's second, generally unpopular, but not completely ineffectual royal governor. The story goes that Ellis used to walk around summertime Savannah with a parasol and a thermometer dangling underneath, at eye level, so he could meticulously record the hellish temperatures. He concluded that Savannahians breathe the hottest air on Earth.

Ellis Square was located on Barnard Street, between Bryan and Congress streets. The old City Market was located there. Then Progress came knocking—with a wrecking ball, as usual—and the beloved, if dilapidated, market went down and a beautiful white concrete parking garage rose majestically in its place. The plan is now to tear down the parking garage and rebuild the square over the place where the garage was. The new garage will be underground, which is a first for Savannah.

Elbert Square

Created in 1801, this square was named for General Samuel Elbert, a Georgia governor and member of the Provincial Congress. The square sat on Montgomery Street, between Hull and Perry streets, but now you'll just plow straight through on Montgomery.

Liberty Square

The name of this defunct square commemorates the "Sons of Liberty," those pre-Revolutionary rabble-rousers who used to meet at Peter Tondee's Tavern on Broughton Street and mix politics with their ale. The square was laid out in 1799 and was located on Montgomery Street, between State and York streets, until visionaries decided that the road to Progress ran directly through the center of the square.

PLANTATIONS, GARDENS, AND PARKS

◖ Forsyth Park

Laid out in 1851 and named for Governor

John Forsyth, 20-acre Forsyth Park sits on Gaston Street between Whitaker and Drayton streets, marking the end of the historic district proper and the start of the Victorian district. Forsyth features a white fountain (1858), similar to the one in the Place de la Concorde in Paris, France. During the Civil War, first Confederates and then Union soldiers commented on the beauty of the fountain. It's by far the most famous font in town. Nearby stands a monument to the Confederacy, erected in the mid-1870s, after the Yankees pulled out. Inside the railing stand two busts of Confederate generals Lafayette McLaws and Francis S. Bartow. This peaceful park, with its fountain, moss-draped oaks, memorials, and Fragrant Garden for the Blind, was expanded after the war by annexing the former militia parade ground.

Emmett Park

Located at the intersection of East Bay and East Broad streets, Emmett Park is named after Irish patriot Robert Emmett. The park is home to a fountain honoring three different ships, which carried the name "Savannah," as well as the Vietnam-shaped Vietnam Veterans Memorial. The park also features old harbor lights. During the Revolution, the British intentionally sank ships in the harbor to cause havoc with French and American vessels using the port of Savannah. Savannahians used these lights to warn sailors of the scuttled ships lurking beneath the waters.

Wassaw National Wildlife Refuge

Accessible only by boat, seven-mile-long Wassaw Island provides its few visitors with that rarity of East Coast treasures—undeveloped oceanfront. The 10,070-acre refuge for migratory birds (912/652-4415, www.fws.gov/wassaw) consists almost exclusively of the barrier island itself, along with two small inshore islands (known, together, as Little Wassaw Island) and some hammocks. This is a great place for bird-watching, and it's only 14 miles from downtown Savannah. If you are boatless, Joe Dobbs (912/598-0090, CAPTJ-DOBBS@aol.com) offers charters to the refuge. Call for prices and information.

Isle of Hope and Wormsloe State Historic Site

Isle of Hope features several attractive old homes dating to the first part of the 19th century, perched on a high shell bluff over the Intracoastal Waterway. For visitors, the star attraction out here is the remains of **Wormsloe Plantation** (7601 Skidaway Rd., 912/353-3023, www.gastateparks.org/info/wormsloe), with a beautiful, 1.5-mile live-oak avenue leading to the tabby ruins. This Colonial estate was owned and constructed by Noble Jones, a physician and carpenter who was one of Oglethorpe's first settlers. Jones came to Savannah with the first boatload in 1733 and commanded Marines in charge of Georgia's coastal defense. Jones served as constable, Indian agent, and surveyor. He laid out the outer village of New Ebenezer and the more successful town of Augusta. He also put away his money and saved up to buy a plantation here.

Today you'll see the ruins, a nature trail, and a living-history area that provides costumed re-enactors (during special programs only) exhibiting the crafts and skills that the people used to survive (and in Jones's case, prosper greatly) on the 18th-century Georgian frontier.

Open Tues.–Sat. 9 AM–5 PM, Sun. 2–5:30 PM. Admission is $4 adults, $3.50 seniors, $2.50 kids 6 to 18, free for those 5 and under. To get here, head out on Skidaway Road from downtown Savannah.

MUSEUMS, HISTORY, AND ART
Savannah History Museum

Set inside the same old railroad building (303 Martin Luther King Jr. Blvd., 912/651-6825, www.chsgeorgia.org) as the Savannah Visitors Information Center, this museum is not overly impressive but still a good first stop to get you oriented. They have plenty of interesting historical photographs to view and artifacts both large and small (including an 1890 locomotive)

© SEAN SLINSKY

Savannah's Temple Mickve Israel is the only gothic synagogue in the country.

dating from pre-Colonial times through World War II and even into the *Forrest Gump* era.

The famous "box of chocolates" bench, whipped up out of fiberglass by the props crew for the scenes shot in Chippewa Square, was taken back to Hollywood when filming was finished. Only after the movie became a major hit and a tourist draw for Savannah did the city think to ask for one of the benches; when they got it, the bench came here to the museum, where you can see it, as well as a replica of the "Bird Girl" statue that used to stand in Bonaventure Cemetery, famous for its appearance on the cover of John Berendt's blockbuster book, *Midnight in the Garden of Good and Evil*, which also became a film in 1997.

Speaking of movies, the museum's in-house film, *Savannah the Survivor*, on the city's founding is informative, if a little heavy-handed in its politics; after incorrectly asserting that James Oglethorpe banned slavery in Savannah purely out of concern for the town's white inhabitants (and not, as Oglethorpe's letters show, at least partly out of his compassion for slavery's Afri-

can victims), it concludes with Oglethorpe, the imaginary narrator, performing a *mea culpa* for not properly celebrating diversity, 1990s style, in 1733. Open Mon.–Fri. 8:30 AM–5:30 PM, Sat.–Sun. 9 AM–5 PM. Admission is $4 adults, $3.50 seniors and military, $3 kids 6 to 11, and free for those under 6.

Mighty Eighth Air Force Heritage Museum

Located off I-95 off Exit 102 in Pooler, this museum (912/748-8888, www.mightyeighth.org) is a must for aviation buffs. Planes on display include a Messerschmitt Komet, an F-4 Phantom, a MiG 17 Fresco, and a B-47, among others. Open daily 9 AM–5 PM; admission is $12, discounts available.

First African Baptist Church

I suspect I'm not the only American child who felt a twinge of disappointment when he learned that the famous Underground Railway of the antebellum South did not involve an actual subterranean train system chugging (very quietly) with its carloads of escaping slaves north to the free states.

Of course, life along the real Underground Railroad was far more compelling—and dangerous—than my childhood conceptions allowed. The First African Baptist Church (23 Montgomery St., 912/233-2244, www.oldest-blackchurch.org) was on the Railway, a network of safe houses where escaped slaves could hide before being spirited north to the next link in the chain. Church members told whites and other outsiders that the holes forming a unique diamond-shaped pattern in the floor were a traditional African design; they were actually airholes for the freedom-seeking slaves the church hid downstairs. The artistic touches inside the church point to the African births of many in the church's first generation; the 1859 structure was largely built by slaves and for slaves, after the slaves had finished their day's work. The congregation these slaves formed has met continuously since that first meeting, making them the oldest African American congregation in the United States.

Cathedral of Saint John the Baptist

This Gothic cathedral on Lafayette Square (222 E. Harris St., 912/233-4709, www.savannahcathedral.org) was Flannery O'Connor's first church, although you won't find that fact commemorated anywhere in the building. The present cathedral dates to the 1870s, but French refugees from a Haitian revolt formed the congregation in the 1790s. Before that, many of them had been nobility in France, and they had avoided beheading by fleeing the French Revolution, which began in 1789. Perhaps it's no coincidence then, that Jesus's decapitated cousin, John the Baptist, was chosen as the church's patron.

The church was originally part of the Charleston diocese, but in 1850 it became a cathedral, the mother church of the Diocese of Savannah, which at the time included all of the Catholics in Georgia and most of the ones in Florida—a grand total of about 5,500 parishioners. The present cathedral was originally dedicated to "Our Lady of Perpetual Help," but by 1883, they changed the name back to the traditional John the Baptist. The cathedral nearly burned down completely in 1898, but by 1900 it was open again. The stained-glass windows, created in Innsbruck, were installed in 1904; the murals were added in 1912. More recently, a two-year project completed in 2000 replaced the slate roof, restored the interior, and removed and cleaned the stained-glass windows.

The inside of the cathedral feels like a bit of Old Europe. If you're here at Christmas, be sure to stop in to see the elaborate—and I mean *elaborate*— nativity set, which includes scores of human and animal characters (although only one baby Jesus) and waterfalls. Not that the year-round artwork is shabby. The Stations of the Cross (the small, three-dimensional frescos depicting Jesus's arrest, trial, beatings, and crucifixion) were carved in Bavaria. Although they were painted white to resemble marble in the 1950s, the restorations returned these intricate vignettes to their multicolored, original appearance. The baptismal font near the entrance was carved in Carrara, Italy.

Second African Baptist Church

Before he gave his famous "I Have a Dream" speech in Washington, a Southern Baptist

---

THE FLIPSIDE OF "JINGLE BELLS"

James Pierpoint (1822–1893), in addition to penning the cheerful Christmas classic "Jingle Bells," wrote several popular songs in the style of Stephen Foster. Although his family came from Boston, he came to Savannah in 1852 to serve as organist at the Savannah Unitarian Church, where his brother was pastor. After his wife died in 1856, Pierpoint married into Savannah society by wedding the daughter of Thomas Purse, one of Savannah's mayors during the War Between the States. When the war came, the Unitarian songster took up arms with the 1st Georgia Calvary and did his bit for homeland defense by penning such passionate songs as "Strike for the South" and 1861's "We Conquer or Die":

The war drum is boasting, "Prepare for the fight,"
The stern bigot Northman exults in his might.
Gird on your bright weapons your foemen are nigh,
And this be our watchword, "We conquer or die;"
And this is our watchword, "We conquer or die. ... "
Go forth in the pathway our forefathers trod;
We too fight for freedom. Our Captain is God.
Their blood in our veins with the honors we vie;
Theirs too was the watchword, "We conquer or die."
Theirs too was the watchword, "We conquer or die."

preacher named Martin Luther King Jr. tried out the sermon on the congregation here (123 Houston St., 912/233-6163). Nearly 100 years earlier, General W. T. Sherman and Secretary of War Edwin Stanton had spoken of a different, but related dream when they read, on the steps out front, Sherman's famous Field Order No. 15, offering freed slave families 40 acres of Sea Island land for the duration of the war. The Second African Baptist Church was founded in 1802, as the congregation at the First African Baptist Church began to overflow its building.

Telfair Academy of Arts and Sciences

The oldest public art museum in the South, the Telfair (121 Barnard St., 912/232-1177, www.telfair.org) was designed and built in 1818 by William Jay on the site of the royal governor's old residence. The mansion, a National Historic Landmark building, is worth a visit because it contains many Telfair family furnishings in two period rooms. In 1886, the museum added a large wing, which now houses American and European art. The latest addition—The Jepson Center for the Arts—opened in early 2006, and features major traveling exhibits and permanent galleries showcasing Southern and African American artwork. A shop, an interactive art gallery for kids, and a café are also planned. Open Mon. noon–5 PM, Tues.–Sat. 10 AM–5 PM, Sun. 1–5 PM. Admission is $8 adults, $7 seniors, $2 students, $1 kids 6–11, free for those under 6.

Tybee Island Light Station and Museum/Fort Screven

Fort Screven was one of the last coastal artillery batteries ever constructed along the East Coast of the United States. Built in 1875, it served through World War I, although it never saw a battle. Today the worthwhile museum, set in a fort building, displays Colonial and pre-Colonial artifacts in one vault. The lighthouse station (30 Meddin Dr., 912/786-5801, www.tybeelighthouse.org; open Wed.–Mon. 9 AM–5:30 PM; $6 adults, $5 seniors and children 6–17, those under 6 free) un-

derwent a long-term restoration project that finished in 2004, and the lighthouse and its related outbuildings, like the head keeper's cottage and summer kitchen house, are huge Tybee draws.

Ships of the Sea Maritime Museum

Set in the William Jay–designed, 1819 William Scarbrough House (41 Martin Luther King Jr. Blvd.; 912/232-1511, www.shipsofthesea.org), the museum holds a large collection of ship models and artifacts that help bring to life the past 2,000 years of nautical history, with a special focus on seacraft connected to the port city of Savannah.

The choice of this house, which contains the largest oasis garden in the city, is fitting: Scarborough (1776–1838) was a principle investor in the building of the *Savannah,* the first steam-powered craft to cross the Atlantic, and you'll see a model of that interesting hybrid of sail and paddle wheel here. Another display documents the history of the Savannah-based Ocean Steamship Company, which operated from 1872 to 1942, connecting Savannah with New York and Boston. Other displays chronicle the lives of sailors all around the world, including displays on navigation, shipbuilding, and on-board recreation. Open Tues.–Sat. 10 AM–5 PM. Admission is $7 adults, $5 seniors and students, free for kids 7 and under.

Andrew Low House

A Scotland-born cotton merchant who moved to Savannah in the 1830s, Andrew Low had by 1848 socked away enough money to build the Italianate and Greek Revival Andrew Low House (329 Abercorn St., 912/233-6854, www.andrewlowhouse.com) on Lafayette Square. Unfortunately, Low's four-year-old son died before he could move in, and his wife Sarah died a few months later. Low was lonely for years, but with his money came power and prestige; Low played host to *Vanity Fair* author William Makepeace Thackery in 1856 and to General Robert E. Lee in 1870. His son William MacKay Low married the eccentric Juliette Magill "Daisy" Gordon in 1886, and the couple lived, childless, in this house for as long as William (whom she called "Billow," a play on his name) could stand it. He left for another woman but died before Daisy could get a formal divorce. It didn't matter anyway: His mistress got most of the money.

Daisy Low lived here when she founded the Girl Scouts of the United States of America in 1912. It's a must-see house museum. Open Mon.–Wed., Fri., and Sat. 10 AM–4:30 PM; Sun. noon–4:30 PM. Admission is $8 adults, $4.50 for Girl Scouts and kids 12 and under.

Bethesda Home for Boys

The nation's oldest existing children's home (9520 Ferguson Ave., 912/351-2040, www.bethesdahomeforboys.org) was a sort of Colonial-era Boys Town, founded in 1740 by Anglican minister George Whitefield and philanthropist James Habersham. Bethesda (the name means "House of Mercy") continues today as a "structure-providing" residential facility for boys. In addition to the lane of live oaks and the mix of modern and historic buildings along the Moon River, sites include 19th-century structures and the 1925 Whitefield Chapel—featuring movable pews.

Benjamin Franklin was among those who contributed to the work done here by Whitefield and others. Over the years, roughly 10,000 children have called Bethesda home. The museum and office are open Mon.–Fri. 9 AM–5 PM, but you can come here anytime before dusk to see the grounds or visit the chapel.

Flannery O'Connor Childhood Home Museum

I have found that anything that comes out of the South is going to be called grotesque by the Northern reader, unless it is grotesque, in which case it is going to be called realistic.

– Flannery O'Connor, "Some Aspects of the Grotesque in Southern Fiction"

A relatively (for Savannah) modest stucco affair (207 E. Charlton St., 912/233-6014) on Lafayette Square, Flannery O'Connor's childhood home is an understated and underdeveloped attraction, mainly because it is underfunded. More on that as follows.

Young Flannery lived here from her birth in 1925 until moving to Milledgeville, Georgia, in 1938 when she was 12 years old. O'Connor used to attend church at the parochial school beside St. John's Cathedral on the other side of Lafayette Square, although the feisty only child got into trouble and ended up attending another parochial school across town. She raised chickens here, and even taught one of them to walk backward. A newsreel company came down from New York and did a story on her, and for several weeks, Americans across the country watched young Flannery O'Connor and her walking chicken before the main feature. O'Connor jokingly described this as the greatest honor she'd ever received.

© SEAN SLINSKY

Flannery O'Connor spent her early childhood in Savannah; tour her home on Lafayette Square.

SHERMAN, STANTON, FORTY ACRES, AND A MULE

Secretary of War Edwin Stanton made a special trip to Savannah while Sherman was there, anxious to find out whether Sherman was onboard with the Republicans' political agenda as regarded the "Negroes." He knew that Sherman had not been eager to take on black troops or to allow large convoys of freed slaves to follow his men, and he wanted to make sure that African Americans were pleased with his conduct. One of Sherman's generals was rumored to be a Democrat and "hostile to the Negro." Stanton believed that the desperate Confederacy might soon emancipate and arm its slaves against the North, and the Secretary of War wanted Sherman's smoldering path across Georgia to become a highway for escaping slaves, and wanted Savannah to be their great refuge.

Stanton's reasons were also political. The Republicans, unknown to anybody else, planned to give the newly emancipated slaves of the South the vote, and by doing so, hoped to politically dominate the South, which since Andrew Jackson's day had voted solidly Democratic. But first, they needed to make certain that they won and kept the goodwill of the black population.

At Stanton's request, Sherman arranged a meeting upstairs at the Green House between the Secretary, himself, and 20 African American leaders, mostly Baptist and Methodist ministers. Stanton interviewed the leaders. When asked their preference, the clergymen said that they would rather live in all-black colonies by themselves rather than side-by-side with whites because prejudice in the South ran deep and would undoubtedly take years to overcome. According to Sherman's account, when asked their opinion on the enlistment of black troops for the Union, the black leaders politely suggested that the Union should stop forcing freed slaves into serving as manual laborers for the U.S. Army. Furthermore, at least one minister suggested that making blacks into soldiers didn't seem to be strengthening the Union Army much, since for every African American who was given a uniform, a white draftee was allowed to stay home. (Indeed, part of the strategy of allowing more whites to stay home while black men did the fighting was to help quell the North's draft riots of previous years.)

Then Sherman was asked to excuse himself from the room, and Stanton solicited the leaders for the "feeling of the colored people" toward Sherman. They praised the general, reporting that he had treated them with the

---

The house is owned by a small, local nonprofit group of Savannah literary folk who lead tours that now include the restored bedroom floor, answer questions, and sell O'Connor books. While the group plans to restore the entire place, when I last visited, author/docent/Armstrong Professor Carl Weeks told me that the organization was still renting out the upper floor as a source of income.

If you're an O'Connor fan, you might consider contributing to this worthwhile project via the O'Connor Home Restoration Fund (912/727-2690). The organization holds a Fall and Spring Reading Series, normally held at 3 PM on Sunday afternoons. Open Sat.–Sun. 1–4 PM; special tours by appointment. Admission is $5.

◖ Old Fort Jackson

Originally built to guard a Colonial-era deepwater port on the Savannah River, Fort Jackson (1 Fort Jackson Rd., 912/232-3945, www.chsgeorgia.org) stands three miles from downtown. The current brick fort was built in fits and starts between 1809 and 1842, seeing service in the War of 1812 and later (of course) in the War Between the States. It's a worthwhile visit with a theater presentation and several displays, including one on the desperation-forged ironclad, the CSS *Georgia*. Come June 15 to August 15 for daily cannon firings. Open daily 9 AM–5 PM. Admission is $4 adults, $3 seniors and students, free for kids under six.

utmost respect, and that they had complete confidence in him.

Sufficiently convinced that Sherman had satisfactory political views, Stanton asked him to draft an order regarding the treatment of the freedmen, and Sherman did, writing the famous Order No. 15, on January 16, 1865. In it, he first granted the black leaders' request and argued that former slaves could not be subjected to forced military service except by the written orders of the highest military authorities and/or the president himself. He also set aside the Sea Islands south of Charleston to temporarily establish the sort of all-black colonies the leaders had desired, forbidding whites to live there. He ordered that every "respectable" black family would be granted

> a plot of not more than forty acres of tillable ground, and, when it borders on some water-channel. . . not more than eight-hundred feet water-front. . .

From this clause, the phrase "Forty Acres and a Mule" has derived. According to Sherman himself, however, this order was never intended to provide permanent land grants to the freed slaves, but rather, as Sherman explained in his *Autobiography,* "to make temporary provisions for the freedmen and their families during the rest of the war, or until Congress should take action."

Within nine months, President Andrew Johnson – normally no friend of the aristocrat, but attempting to follow Lincoln's Reconstruction policies in the face of stiff Radical Republican opposition – gave the island lands back to their prewar owners; however, without field crews, there wasn't much the destitute owners could do with the land. Land prices sat at around two dollars an acre, and for this, even former slaves were soon able to purchase small farms' worth of plantation land. Some of these families continue to farm the islands, even today.

Stanton left for Washington shortly after the meeting, but the incident gave Sherman a dislike for Stanton that lasted the rest of his life. In his *Autobiography,* he wrote:

> The idea that such men should have been permitted to hang around Mr. Lincoln, to torture his life by suspicions of the officers who were toiling with the single purpose to bring the war to a successful end, and thereby to liberate all slaves, is a fair illustration of the influences that poison a political capital.

◖ Fort Pulaski National Monument

Maybe it's the moat, but Fort Pulaski (Hwy. 80 E, 912/786-5787, www.nps.gov/fopu) just looks Old World. And perhaps it's no surprise; the fort's original designer, General Simon Bernard, was a veteran of Napoleon's staff. Although Bernard died before the conflagration, every other Army engineer who worked on Pulaski ended up as either a Union or Confederate general, including young Robert E. Lee, who came to Fort Pulaski fresh from West Point. Open daily Memorial Day to Labor Day, 9 AM–7 PM, and 9 AM–5 PM otherwise. Admission is $3, free for those 15 and under.

Fort Morris State Historic Site

Built to protect the Colonial port of Sunbury from British invasion during the American Revolution, Fort Morris was built and garrisoned in 1776. The British came calling in November 1778, demanding the fort's surrender. Patriot Colonel John McIntosh is said to have answered back, "Come and take it!" The redcoats thought about it and decided to head back to Florida to get more troops for what promised to be a bloody encounter. A month and a half later, they returned with a huge number of men and guns and began to bombard the fort. The patriots saw the Brits' point of view and surrendered. Thirtysomething years later, the British came by again, but Fort Morris, now renamed Fort Defiance, stood tall against the British and stopped their advance.

Today, the 70-acre Fort Morris site (912/884-5999) features a visitors center (with the requisite, informative historical film), picnic tables, bird-watching on the Colonial Coast Birding Trail, and a one-mile nature trail. To get there from I-95, take Exit 76 and follow the brown Liberty Trail signs to the Island Parkway and then Fort Morris Road. Open Tues.–Sat. 9 AM–5 PM, Sun. 2–5:30 PM. Admission ranges $1.50–2.

Christ Church Savannah (Episcopal)

Christ Church (28 Bull St., 912/232-4131, www.christchurchsavannah.org) held its first service on February 12, 1733, underneath the oaks on the banks of the Savannah. Oglethorpe set aside a lot on Johnson Square for the building and it went up quickly. The current building, dating from 1838, is the fourth one to stand at the same spot. John and Charles Wesley came here early in the first years, but Charles—who eventually wrote hundreds of beloved hymns, including "Hark! The Herald Angels Sing"—went to Frederica with Oglethorpe to provide spiritual leadership to the settlers there, but Charles and Oglethorpe had a falling out over what Wesley believed were Oglethorpe's adulteries; the former withdrew his statement, but he had never liked the weather anyway, and within five months, he was ready to go home. John stayed, but not much longer. A gossip spread scandalous rumors concerning Wesley's appointments with a young parish girl; though the rumors appear to have been false, Wesley's fall from public esteem was real enough. He ended up departing secretly for England in the company of other Savannah outcasts. Before leaving, however, he spent extensive time with the Congregationalists who had moved down from Dorchester near Charles Town and who would later settle Midway, and was impressed greatly with their attention to their dedicated, methodical praying and Bible readings in their quest to "seek first the Kingdom of God." Many religious scholars believe that Wesley's time with the Dorchester Congregationalists

was important to his later founding the movement that would become Methodism.

George Whitefield, a well-loved pastor who founded the Bethesda Orphanage, served as a priest here for several years. Among many other famous Savannahians, Juliette Gordon Low, founder of the Girl Scouts of America, attended here. In fact, not only was she baptized here and memorialized here, but it was on the steps of Christ Episcopal that Juliette, on her wedding day, was hit in the ear with a grain of rice which deafened her—a chilling tale of the detrimental effects of carbohydrates. Open Wed. and Fri. 10:30 AM–3:30 PM.

Green-Meldrim House

General Sherman was so impressed with this Gothic Revival home that he accepted owner Charles Green's offer to make it his headquarters while in town, rather than taking over a wing of the Pulaski Hotel, as he'd planned. The home (14 W. Macon St., 912/233-3845) is now the parish house for St. John's Episcopal Church. Docents lead tours, which run about 20 minutes long. Open Tues., Thurs., and Fri. 10 AM–4 PM; and Sat. 10 AM–1 PM; except religious holidays. Tours are $5 for adults, $3 for children.

Roundhouse Railroad Museum

This museum, at 601 West Harris Street, 912/651-6823, is set in the oldest antebellum railroad manufacturing and repair facility in the United States. If those words strike joy into your heart, then you'd better head over here, as well should anyone with children of the Thomas the Tank Engine mind-set. Here they'll see restored diesel locomotives and street cars, an antebellum blacksmith shop where 14 kilns ran for 100 years, and the oldest portable steam engine in the country. Join the Coastal Railroad Buffs Thursday nights as they operate their model trains. Open daily 9 AM–5 PM. Admission is $5 adults; $4 seniors, kids, students, and military; free for those under six.

Isaiah Davenport House

Located on Columbia Square, this period-furnished Federal home (324 E. State St.,

912/236-8097, www.davenportsavga.com) is a popular landmark in Savannah. Much of the home's fame comes from the fact that the Davenport House was the one that was about to be torn down in 1955 when a group of residents stepped forward and stopped the demolition, marking the first in a long run of victories for Savannah's preservationists. In 2005 the home won the Preserve America Award from the President. Open Mon.–Sat. 10 AM–4 PM, Sun. 1–4 PM. Admission $7 adults, $3.50 students and those 18 and under.

Juliette Gordon Low National Girl Scout Center, a.k.a. "The Birthplace"

Back in the 1950s, when many Savannahians believed that Yankees would never be interested in their grand old houses, reflective as they were of Savannah's isolated, turned-inward history, and soiled by their births in a cotton economy stained by the sweat of slaves, they always knew that "The Birthplace" was their ace in the hole: Savannah's nationally significant, noncontroversial historical site. Sure enough, this house (10 E. Ogelthorpe Ave., 912/233-4501) became Savannah's first National Historic Landmark in 1965. Of course, Low, who was born here in 1860, went on to found the Girl Scouts of America in 1912 while living over on Lafayette Square at the Andrew Low House. The National Society of the Colonial Dames of Georgia has restored the Birthplace, which is now owned and operated by the Girl Scouts of the U.S.A. as a memorial and as a program center for its members. Furnishings meant to reflect the way it looked on Juliette Gordon Low's 1886 wedding day, which according to some estimates was just about the last happy day Low and her husband William enjoyed. The home is worth a tour for the Victorian furnishings. Open Mon.–Sat. 10 AM–4 PM, Sun. 11 AM–4 PM; closed Wed. Sept.–Feb. Admission is $8 adults, $7 for ages 5–20.

King-Tisdell Cottage

This home (514 E. Huntingdon St., 912/234-8000, www.kingtisdell.org) now houses an African American museum, one stop on the **Negro Heritage Trail Tour** that takes in 17 different African American sites of historical interest. To venture inside, you must take the bus tour that leaves from the Savannah Visitors Information Center (301 Martin Luther King Jr. Blvd.) Mon.–Sat. at noon and 2 PM. (Call for reservations. Tours are $19 for adults, $10 for kids, and free for those under 10.)

THE TELEGRAM

In his *Autobiography*, Sherman recalled that within hours of settling into his quarters at the Green House on December 22, 1864, Massachusetts-born A. G. Browne, a U.S. Treasury agent for the Department of the South, appeared at Sherman's door, ready to claim possession, in the name of the Treasury Department, of all the cotton, rice, buildings, weapons, and other items that Sherman's army had captured. Sherman refused to turn over the goods, feeling that he and his men had "fairly earned them." Then Browne, who Sherman describes as "a shrewd, clever Yankee," told the general that a ship was just about to sail north, and that if she had good weather off the Hatteras coast, the ship might just reach Fort Monroe by Christmas. Browne suggested that Sherman might want to send a note on the ship to be passed to the telegraph office at Fort Monroe and passed electronically to the president, who "peculiarly enjoyed such pleasantry." Sherman agreed, and wrote on a slip of paper the following word, immortal in the hearts of Savannahians:

> To His Excellency President Lincoln, Washington, D.C.: I beg to present you as a Christmas-gift the city of Savannah, with one hundred and fifty heavy guns and plenty of ammunition, also about twenty-five thousand bales of cotton. W. T. Sherman, Major-General

The message actually reached Lincoln on Christmas Eve, and was extensively published in newspapers both North and South.

The foundation that runs the cottage also oversees the **Beach Institute** (502 E. Harris St., 912/234-8000, www.kingtisdell.org/beachinst), which was founded in 1867 by the Freedman's Bureau as a school for freed slaves. In the beginning, there were more than 600 students, and tuition cost $1. The institute is now a series of galleries, with the work of famed Savannah folk artist Ulysses Davis on permanent show, among other revolving exhibits. Open Tues.–Sat. noon–5 PM.

Oatland Island Education Center

Laced with well-marked nature trails and devoted to wildlife conservation, the Oatland Island preserve (11 Sandtown Rd., 912/898-3980, www.oatlandisland.org) offers visitors the chance to view the coast's indigenous animals on their own home turf. Tours and special programs are listed on the website. Open Mon.–Fri. 9 AM–4 PM, Sat. 10 AM–4 PM. Admission is $3.

Old Cotton Exchange

At Drayton and Bay streets, this 1887 structure served as the center of economic activity in Savannah; if cotton was Kkng, then the Old Cotton Exchange was its castle. The price of tea in China might not matter to most Americans, but people all over the world were affected by the price of cotton in Savannah.

◖ Telfair's Owens-Thomas House

Located on Oglethorpe Square, the tabby 1819 Owens-Thomas House (124 Abercorn St., 912/233-9743, www.telfair.org) is a favorite of many locals; many architectural historians consider this home to be the greatest example of the Regency style in the entire country. Upstairs, a bridge connects two wings of the house. Lafayette, upon his triumphant tour of the States in 1825, addressed the people of Savannah from a balcony on the side of the house. (Later, Lafayette Square was named in his honor.) In back you'll see some of the earliest intact urban slave quarters in the South, complete with original "haint-blue" paint and furnishings. Open Mon. noon–5 PM, Tues.–Sat. 10 AM–5 PM, Sun. 1–

5 PM. Admission is $8 adults, $7 seniors, $2 students, $1 kids 6–11, free for those under 6.

Ralph Mark Gilbert Civil Rights Museum

Named in honor of Dr. Ralph Mark Gilbert, called by many "Savannah's father of the Civil Rights movement," the museum (460 Martin Luther King Jr. Blvd., 912/231-8900) chronicles the journey of Savannah's African American community from slavery to the modern day. Displays inside include a large catalog of historical photos and interactive exhibits. Open Mon.–Fri. 9 AM–5 PM. Admission is $4 adults, $3 seniors, $2 students and children.

◖ Bonaventure Cemetery

Located east of town on Bonaventure Road, Bonaventure Cemetery (912/651-6843) is the site where the famous "Bird Girl" statue featured on the cover of *Midnight in the Garden of Good and Evil* was shot by photographer Jack Leigh. The statue is long gone, however; the family who owned it had to remove it to save it from vandalism (you'll find a replica in the Museum of Savannah), along with a print of the original photo and a document explaining the origin of the photo.

Although the scales have been removed, the Bonaventure Cemetery is a unique and worthwhile visit; while staying in Savannah at the end of his March across Georgia, Sherman regarded the oak-shaded landscape as the only worthwhile site outside of the town itself. The land here, a high-water mark of moss-covered oaks, camellias, and azaleas, was originally a plantation owned by a Colonel Mulryne in the earliest years of the colony. It burned to the ground one night during a dinner party and became a cemetery in the 1860s, when cemeteries were good business. Today, residents include songwriter Johnny Mercer, poet Conrad Aiken, and Noble Jones, owner of Wormsloe Plantation.

COLLEGES
Georgia Southern University

The largest college in the Savannah region is 16,000-student Georgia Southern University,

SHERMAN: NOT OVERLY IMPRESSED

A cherished Savannah legend has it that the reason Union General William Tecumseh Sherman didn't burn Savannah was that he found it, "too beautiful to burn." But that's giving both Savannah's antebellum allure and Sherman's troops' aesthetic sensitivity too much credit. First of all, his troops burned many beautiful cities, including Columbia, South Carolina, and Atlanta, Georgia, both of which were known as beautiful cities before the war. And shortly after leaving Savannah, Sherman's men used the striking cedar **Church of the Holy Apostles,** in Barnwell, South Carolina, as a stable for their animals, employing its imported medieval stone baptismal font as a watering trough. These were not aesthetes.

In fact, Sherman himself had visited Savannah earlier in his career, as a lieutenant stationed at Fort Moultrie near Charleston, and even upon his return, his response to the town's charms were singularly lukewarm. In his *Autobiography*, he writes:

The city of Savannah was an old place, and usually accounted a handsome one. Its... streets and parks were lined with the handsomest shade-trees of which I
have knowledge... and these certainly entitled Savannah to its reputation as a handsome town more than the houses, which, though comfortable, would hardly make a display on Fifth Avenue or the Boulevard Haussmann of Paris.

So why didn't Sherman's men burn Savannah? Sherman states in his autobiography that his purpose while in Savannah was to establish a base for ground operations into South Carolina, to establish a temporary settlement of freedmen on the Sea Islands, and possibly to ship himself and most of his troops north to Virginia where Grant wanted them. None of these needs would have been satisfied by burning Savannah.

His men would burn Columbia, the capital of South Carolina, a few weeks later; Sherman claimed that this act helped expedite the end of the war by destroying Carolinian morale. But by the time they reached Savannah, Sherman's troops had already taken the heart out of Georgia by burning its commercial center, Atlanta. Just as he had spared Savannah, he spared Charleston – because he didn't see any reason to burn it.

one hour west of Savannah in Statesboro. In town, **Armstrong Atlantic State University** (11935 Abercorn St., 912/927-5277, www.armstrong.edu), part of the University of Georgia system, offers undergraduate and graduate degrees in more than 75 majors.

Savannah College of Art and Design (SCAD)

The largest art school in the United States, Savannah College of Art and Design (SCAD) (342 Bull St., 912/525-5100, www.scad.edu), has a much more profound effect on the downtown, largely because SCAD seems to *own* downtown, or much of it. This school costs nearly $7,000 a quarter, so while many of the 7,000 students here have artistic talent, all of them have money (or scholarships). Although many native Savan-

nahians weren't too happy about the idea of a bunch of wealthy bohemians planting themselves downtown, the students have come to be well regarded by most residents.

The students have brought the town a lot of vitality, economic and otherwise. They've also brought some good (if not necessarily regionally sensitive) taste and added a lot to the community by buying up old White Elephant buildings, restoring them, and using them to meet various institutional needs. The school preps students for careers in fine arts, design, and architecture with both undergraduate and graduate degrees. They operate the stately Gryphon Tea Room on Bull Street. But the most important thing they add for most visitors is the **Jen Library** (201 E. Broughton St., 912/525-4700), where with a photo ID you can get a visitor's pass for free, which entitles you to in-house use of the library (no checking things out) and use of the library's computers, which provide access to the Internet. SCAD students have priority, of course, but unless it's Finals Week, you should be fine. Be sure to head to the back of the first floor to take a look at the 12-by-10-foot video wall that flashes images of college events and student work. Open every night until 1 AM.

Savannah State University

With 2,800 students and 173 acres of campus, four-year Savannah State University (3219 College St., 912/356-2186, www.savstate.edu) was founded in 1890 as one of the original Negro Land-Grant Colleges in 1890, making it Georgia's first public institution of higher learning for blacks. Originally called The Georgia Industrial College for Colored Youths, the nature of the institution has changed from a technical school to a liberal arts college to a university, but the student body has remained almost entirely African American.

Savannah Technical College (STC)

Although a cluster of other tiny schools with student bodies of fewer than 1,000 students operate in Savannah, the only other sizable school is 4,000-student Savannah Technical College (STC) (5717 White Bluff Rd., 912/443-5700, www.savannah.tech.edu), offering associate degrees and diploma and certificate programs in 50 fields. At one-eighteenth the price of SCAD, which mainly caters to non-Georgians, STC serves the needs of local residents.

SKIDAWAY ISLAND

To get to Skidaway, take I-16 to Savannah, and Exit 164A onto I-516, which runs into De-Renne Avenue. Turn right on Waters Avenue, and go straight to Diamond Causeway.

Skidaway Island State Park

Although it's home to a large gated community with six private golf courses on-site, the public parts of Skidaway are still a favorite getaway for nature-minded Savannahians, especially 588-acre Skidaway Island State Park (52 Diamond Causeway, 912/598-2300), which borders the Skidaway Narrows stretch of the Intracoastal Waterway. You can hike two nature trails through marshes, beneath huge live oaks, towering longleaf pines, and cabbage palmettos. Wildlife includes shorebirds, such rare migrating birds as the painted bunting, deer, and raccoon. The park's one-mile Sandpiper Nature Trail is disabled-accessible, but the viewing towers are not.

If you're here in fall, winter, or spring, camping at Skidaway (88 camping sites) offers a neat chance to combine the urban adventures of downtown Savannah with a little one-on-one time with coastal Georgia. If you're here in the summer, battling the humidity and gnats, you may well wish you'd paid for a motel.

Marine Extension Service Aquarium

The University of Georgia's Marine Extension Service Aquarium (10 Ocean Science Circle, 912/598-2453, www.uga.edu/aquarium), offers a no-nonsense exhibit of local marine life, including prehistoric coastal artifacts, plus nature trails, and a shop. Tours of the Skidaway Institute—devoted to studying local sea life—are available. Open Mon.–Fri. 9 AM–4 PM, Sat. noon.–5 PM. Admission is $2 adults, $1 seniors and children.

Entertainment and Events

FESTIVALS

Georgia Historical Society's Georgia Day Celebration (912/651-2125, www.georgiahistory.com) commemorates Oglethorpe's founding of the state in February. The two-week festival early in the month includes reenactments, a processional parade down Bull Street, and events at Wormsloe Plantation, where living-history displays are held.

In mid-February, the Shamro-centric city warms up for March by holding the **Savannah Irish Festival** (912/232-3448, www.savannahirish.org) at the Savannah Civic Center at Liberty and Montgomery streets. This is more about authentic Irish roots, families, dances, songs, dishes, and crafts than the party-'til-you-taste-cobblestone spirit that occasionally possesses the March event.

The **Savannah Music Festival** (912/234-3378, www.savannahmusicfestival.org) takes place the last two weeks in March. The lineup spans music of the Deep South to chamber music to international fare and focuses on musical performances at numerous venues throughout the historic district. The American Traditions Competitions invites blues, Broadway, country, folk, gospel, and jazz performers. Winners collectively take in more than $30,000. Past judges have included Shirley Jones, of *Music Man* and *Partridge Family* fame.

St. Patrick's Day is one of Savannah's "High Holidays." Savannahians like to say that their parade is America's second-largest St. Patrick's Day parade in the country and that New York's parade is America's second *best.* Rooms book up well in advance, the fountains are dyed green, and some 250,000 out-of-towners descend on the city to hoist green beers, eat corned beef and green grits, and generally act out the stereotype Know-Nothings held about the Irish Menace back in the mid-1800s. It's hard to imagine any other American group allowing, nay, *encouraging* this sort of mockery. Surely the persecuted immigrants fleeing the potato famine in the 1840s would be amazed to hear the owners of today's Savannah pubs boldly claiming to be just a wee bit more authentically Irish than the others.

The **Savannah Tour of Homes and Gardens** (912/234-8054, www.savannahtourofhomes.org) takes place in March, as it has since 1935. Self-guided tours ($35) and special events focus on the historic district, and let your peek inside some of the area's most grand residences. Begun in 1974, the Garden Club of Savannah's **N.O.G.S. (North of Gaston Street) Tour of Hidden Gardens** (912/961-4805) takes place each April. The walking tour include behind-the-scenes access to eight walled gardens—different ones each year. Hostesses at each lush garden point out the plants, fountains, statues, and blooms that highlight their different spaces. Tickets ($30, proceeds given to charities) also include an afternoon tea.

SCAD holds a free **Sidewalk Art Festival** in Forsyth Park (912/525-5225,

historic Lucas Theatre for the Arts

© SEAN SLINSKY

www.scad.edu/saf) in April; and the **Savannah Film Festival** (912/525-5050, www.scad.edu/filmfest) in late October, with independent and other films shown in venues throughout the city. Also in the fall, the **Savannah Jazz Festival** (912/232-2222, www.coastaljazz.com) takes place September at Forsyth Park, and features international and local acts that appeal to everyone from kids to blues enthusiasts. Later, in October, the **Savannah Folk Music Festival** (912/786-6953, www.savannahfolk.org) takes over the City Market area, and features an old-time country dance, plus concerts in the Roundhouse. The holiday season includes **Santa Cruises** held by River Street Riverboat Company (912/232-6404, www.savannahriverboat.com); and from Thanksgiving to January, **Southern Lights** are in full swing, meaning all the historic squares are lit and decorated.

CONCERT VENUES

The 1,201-seat **Lucas Theatre for the Arts** (912/525-5040, www.lucastheatre.com) is located at Abercorn and Congress streets near Reynolds Square. Built in 1921 during the silent film era as a "movie palace," the Lucas's 40-foot-wide ceiling dome and elaborate interior painting and gold leafing reveal the grandeur of an earlier day. The theater was scheduled for destruction but was saved by preservationists in 1987, although the theater was not ready for the public again until 2000. Today, the Lucas welcomes a diverse slate of performers; recently, Preservation Hall Jazz Band, Merle Haggard, and Eileen Ivers took to the stage.

The SCAD-run **Trustees Theater** (216 E. Broughton St., 912/525-5050, www.trusteestheater.com), brings a variety of acts to town; one recent season included the B-52s, Wilco, Vanessa Carlton, and Ziggy Marley. Tickets run $25 and up. The **Savannah Civic Center** on Liberty at Montgomery Street (301 W. Ogelthorpe Ave., 912/651-6556, www.savannahcivic.com) includes two huge concert venues that draw similarly big-time performers to sold-out crowds.

NIGHTLIFE
Clubs

They may not be *Midnight's* legendary "Lady of 6,000 Songs," but the dueling pianists at **Savannah Smiles Dueling Piano Saloon** (314 Williamson St., 912/527-6453) probably know 3,000 songs between the two of them. This lively, good-humored nightspot sits behind the Quality Inn, just off West Bay Street. It's very popular because the two pianists play a broad variety of familiar rock songs from the 1950s to today. The kitchen serves bar food till 2 AM. You must be 21 to enter. Open Mon.–Sat. 7 PM–3 AM; music begins at 9 PM; closed most Sun.

The Mercury Lounge (125 W. Congress St., 912/447-6952) offers live music most nights and caters to local hipsters who appreciate the 3 AM (Mon.–Sat.) and 2 AM (Sun.) closing times.

Pubs

Savannah features many fine pubs—so many, in fact, that one of the local tour groups offers a pub walk a couple of nights a week. Of all the spots on the Charleston-Savannah coast, the best fish-and-chips may well be those at **Kevin Barry's Irish Pub and Restaurant** (117 W. River St., 912/233-9626). The fish are light, the chips are actually round (like chips, not fries), and there's plenty of good beer to go along with them. This is the sort of place where, as soon as you order the fish, they hand you a bottle of malt vinegar. They know. It's always St. Patrick's Day at Kevin Barry's; the dim, brick-walled pub has live Irish music seven nights a week. Or you can sit upstairs in the glass-enclosed balcony and enjoy a view of the waterfront.

Although it's *only* been around for seven years, **Churchill's** (13 W. Bay St., 912/232-8501, www.thebritishpub.com) reeks of pubbish authenticity with its hand-carved English bar. The Holmes's, owners of this bit of Britain in the midst of Savannah, are, fittingly enough, a Brit and his Savannah-born wife. Not surprisingly, Churchill's has won reader polls as Savannah's Best Pub for several years now. Its authentic British (not Irish) food includes fish-

JOHNNY MERCER: 1909-1976

Born to an old Savannah family and raised in the city, songwriter/singer Johnny Mercer always considered the city his home, even though he lived much of his adult life in New York and Los Angeles. After making it in New York as a songwriter, his fame grew and he starred in his own radio program in the 1940s.

Mercer was popular, but he was even more talented. Because the songs he co-composed (as lyricist) were recorded by different performers in different musical styles, most people don't realize how many hits he had through the years. But pick up a list of Mercer credits, and the dots start to connect: song after song that stands out from its contemporaries for its original, evocative lyrics, and their common thread is Johnny Mercer. "Summer Wind," "Moon River" – they all break through the clichés and create memorable imagery.

One of my favorites is the playful, allusive, and slang-filled "Glow-Worm," recorded most successfully by the Mills Brothers. The lyrics include:

Glow little glow-worm, glow and glimmer.
Swim through the sea of night, little
  swimmer.
Thou aeronautical boll weevil.
Illuminate yon woods primeval.
See how the shadows deep and darken.
You and your chick should get to
  sparkin'.
I got a gal that I love so.
Glow little glow-worm, glow.

If another American Top 40 hit has ever included the terms "primeval" or "aeronautical boll weevil" – much less *both* of them – I am not aware of it. And though Michael Jackson is often kidded for having scored a hit with a ballad to a rat, this is certainly the biggest smash ever written to a creature without eyes.

As anybody who read *Midnight in the Garden of Good and Evil* can tell you, Savannah's favorite son is buried at the Bonaventure Cemetery. The former "Back River" was renamed "Moon River" in his honor.

and-chips, shepherd's pie, bangers and mash, bubble and squeak, and Yorkshire pudding. The Holmes's also offer a wide variety of imported stouts, ciders, and ales on tap. Daily lunch specials start at $5.95.

Set in an 1870s brothel, **The Rail Pub** (405 W. Congress St., 912/238-1311) counts less on tourists and much more on students and other locals, and the prices reflect this fact. Nearby is the certifiably Irish-owned **Finnegan's Wake** (108 W. Congress St., 912/231-8499), just off the City Market, one of the city's most oft-lauded pubs with music. It's worth a visit for its 15 draft beers, darts, pool table, and jukebox.

Bars and Lounges
Pinkie Master's (318 Drayton St., 912/238-0447) may sound like a niche manicurists' studio, but it's one of the town's most venerable drinking establishments. **Notorius** (112 W. Congress St., 912/233-4227) is a low-key,

deco-all-the-way bar in the City Market area. **Venus de Milo** (38 Martin Luther King Jr. Blvd., 912/447-0901, www.venusdemilo.biz) is a swanky wine bar out of the tourist fray.

Brewpubs
The Moon River Brewing Company (21 W. Bay St., 912/447-0943, www.moonriverbrewing.com) offers the usual brewpub food and atmosphere for lunch and dinner. ("Moon River" is of course a local river, which was renamed in honor of local-boy songwriter Johnny Mercer, who penned the big hit, among many others.)

Gay and Lesbian
A popular haunt for gays and lesbians is **Chuck's** (305 W. River St., 912/232-1005). *Midnight's* cross-dressing songstress Lady Chablis still appears at least once a month at **Club One** (1 Jefferson St., 912/232-0200, www.clubone-online.com).

THEATER AND DANCE VENUES

The Savannah Theatre (222 Bull St., 912/233-7764, www.savannahtheatre.com), offers two-hour musical variety productions. Starting in the fall of 2006, the **City Lights Theater Company** (316 E. 55th St., 912/234-9860) resumes its show schedule; check the website for details.

CINEMAS

The restored **Lucas Theatre for the Arts** (32 Abercorn St., 912/525-5040) is the only movie house in the downtown historic district; while it's mainly a special-event location, it does shows films during the local film festival in late October and independent flicks occasionally throughout the rest of the year. Call for details.

For the latest wide releases, head to the Regal Savannah 10 (1132 Shawnee St., 912/927-7700); it's a short drive out of the historic district.

© SEAN SLINSKY

Come during late October for the local film festival, where you can catch indie flicks in restored theaters.

COFFEE SHOPS AND CAFÉS

Savannah has a Starbucks (on Broughton), but don't go there. The only justification for a Starbucks is the lack of quality coffee in a town, or the lack of a nonclassy coffeehouse for those who occasionally tire of sipping their lattes in a patently urban, "alternative" atmosphere, with the surly help and flyers for yoga lessons beneath the counter. But Savannah has a wealth of good coffee places, and most of them offer a classical/jazz atmosphere.

Of them all, perhaps **The Gallery Espresso** (234 Bull St., 912/233-5348, www.galleryespresso.com), is the most congenial. Just take a look around the place: With its low ceiling and fireplaces, this is the sort of location the owners of strip-mall coffeehouses around the country dream about. Owner Judy Davis moved up from Florida to open The Gallery, and she's passionate about her coffee and her coffee-drinking customers; when last I stopped in, she told me she'd lost a little business to the new Starbucks, but she wasn't concerned. After all, she told me, the defectors were mostly "decaf drinkers" anyway—they weren't serious about their coffee. The joe is strong and good, and since your barista is likely to be an art student, you may well receive the comeliest mochaccino you've ever seen. A wide variety of teas are also available. Open Mon.–Thurs. 7:30 AM–midnight, Fri. till 1 AM, Sat. 8 AM–1 AM, Sun. till midnight.

Down on Johnson Square along Bull Street is the **Savannah Coffee House Café** (7 E. Congress St., 912/232-5282), where they roast their own beans and don't sell jazz CDs or board games. It's a good, serious place, popular with young professionals, and with not-so-young professionals as well. If you can, grab the couch facing the plate-glass window that looks out on the square. My wife—who knows her joe—calls this the best (i.e., most potent) coffee in town. Open Mon.–Fri. 6:30 AM–5 PM, Sat.–Sun. 8 AM–4 PM.

Finally, **The Sentient Bean** (13 E. Park Ave., 912/232-4447, www.sentientbean.com), located on the south end of Forsyth Park beside the Brighter Day health-food store, markets itself towards the retro-60s crowd, serving up Fair Trade Organic coffee, as well as light lunches and baked goods. Nice people, nice location, and nice outdoor dining. Open daily 7:30 AM–10 PM.

Tearooms

"Taking tea" has become a popular in Savannah. The ◖ **Gryphon Tea** (337 Bull St., 912/525-5880), on the ꞏꞏꞏꞏꞏer of Bull and Charlton streets, is actually run by SCAD in a high-ceilinged old pharmacy, and most of the workers are SCAD students. The Gryphon's high style (it's a *tearoom*, after all, not a coffeehouse) is a nice variation from the usual bohemian motif. Fine desserts and good coffee are served in a memorable atmosphere, with a proper afternoon tea service offered at 4:30. Open weekdays 8:30 AM–6 PM, Sat. 10 AM–6 PM.

The Tea Room (7 E. Broughton St., 912/239-9690, www.thetearoomsavannah.com) offers a full lunch with finger sandwiches, quiche, and sweets. Afternoon teas are 2:30–4 PM (reservations suggested), and lunch runs 11:30 AM–4 PM.

Shopping

Savannah's shopping scene spreads throughout downtown, but can be narrowed to a few areas. The more touristy spots are centered around the **City Market** (912/232-4903, www.savannahcitymarket.com) at Jefferson and West St. Julian streets and **River Street** by the water. A mix of consignment shops and mainstream clothing stores (Banana Republic, etc.) are mixed with home-goods stores on Broughton Street, for a few blocks both east and west off Bull Street. Throughout the historic district, on the squares, and along the streets that also shoot off Bull Street, you find bookstores, home-accessory shops, and galleries. As for antiques and home goods, the design district is along Whitaker Street, in between Charlton Lane and Gaston Street. Of those areas, here are some favorites.

Artists' Galleries

SCAD operates nearly a dozen galleries throughout downtown, featuring displays in many different media; all exhibits are free. All of the galleries enjoy their share of truly inspired work, but if your time is limited, be aware that **Shop SCAD** (340 Bull St., 912/525-5180), **Pinnacle Gallery** (320 E. Liberty St., 912/525-4950), and Red Gallery (201. E. Broughton St., 912/525-4735) are all SCAD-related and considered the most prestigious.

The **City Market Art Center** (309 W. Saint Julian St., 912/234-2327), features several working studios and galleries. And of special interest to *Midnight* fans is the **Jack Leigh Gallery** (132 E. Oglethorpe Ave., 912/234-6449, www.jackleigh.com), featuring photographs of the American South by Jack Leigh, who took the famous photo of the "Bird Girl" that graced the cover of John Berendt's best-selling book.

For information on other galleries, stop by one of those listed or visit **The Gallery Espresso** (234 Bull St., 912/233-5348, www.galleryespresso.com) for handout directories.

Home and Garden

@home (7 W. York St., 912/201-0015) specializes in vintage home, kitchen, baby, and garden goods. That means if you are looking for a baby shower invitations from the 1970s, or if you need an antique porcelain wedding cake topper, or if you must have your kitchen jars smartly labeled "jar," this is the place for you. Another home store riding the chic home stuffs wave is the peppy **One Fish, Two Fish** (401 Whitaker St., 912/447-4600, www.onefishstore.com), where you'll find smart lighting and refurbished furniture, plus locally harvested and handmade Savannah Bee Company products, including divine Tupelo honey and lip balms. If you're near One Fish, visit the **Urban Oasis** (400 Whitaker St., 912/232-9807) for loads of garden decor, like topiaries (dragon-shaped, even), fountains, and imported urns. Just outside the historic district in the up-and-coming scenester neighborhood known as the Starland district, you'll find **Brownesville**

Be sure to visit the cobblestone River Street and get a pecan praline from one of its candy shops.

(2401 Bull St., 912/231-2345), where shabby-chic types get their fix of chandeliers, furniture, china, and trinkets. If you only have time to stray in the City Market area, at least hit **The Paris Market & Brocante** (36 W. Broughton St., 912/232-1500, www.theparismarket.com). There are two floors of everything French, from make-your-own lavender sachets to antique baskets and country furniture pieces. It's a huge place, great for rainy day wandering.

Farmers Market

The **Savannah State Farmers Market** (701 Hwy. 80 W, 912/966-7800), features locally grown fruits and vegetables, wholesale products, and a small restaurant, all open year-round.

Antiques

One of the bigger venues for antiquing is **37th @ Abercorn Antiques and Design** (201 E. 37th St., 912/233-0064). More than 8,000 square feet of booths yields a trove of silver, crystal, clocks, books, estate jewelry, and more. Be sure to check out the courtyard behind the main house, where they have garden items. In the spirit of an antique "village," other structures here contain niche collections of antiques, so don't think you're finished if you've only browsed the main house. Open Mon.–Sat. 10 AM–5 PM, Sun. noon–5 PM.

Right at Factors Walk over River Street, you'll find the 10,000-square-foot **Cobblestone Lane Antiques** (230 W. Bay St., 912/447-0504), where they will ship anything you purchase. Open 10 AM–6 PM daily.

Bookstores

In the City Market area, present-day metaphysical bookstore **Moondance** (306 W. St. Julian St., 912/236-9003, www.moondancecenter.com) occupies an 1880s building that was a gunsmith back in 1884. When the City Market area was revitalized in the 1980s, this shop was one of the first to move in. Find books on finding yourself here. As you wander the square, be sure to spend some time in Savannah favorite **E. Shaver, Bookseller** (326 Bull St., 912/234-7257). The rambling store carries a wealth of

© SEAN SLINSKY

The Book Lady specializes in rare books.

regional titles, in addition to a great general selection that fills its 12 rooms, floor-to-ceiling. A few blocks away, just off Wright Square, is the less-obvious, but no-less-iconic **Book Lady** (17 W. York St., 912/233-3628). Having been in the city since the 1970s, this ol' gal features more than 10,000 used, rare books.

Flea Markets

The biggest flea market in the region, **Keller's Flea Market** (5901 Ogeechee Rd., 912/927-4848, www.ilovefleas.com) charges no admission to visit its more than 500 vendors. Included among the white elephants are fresh produce, antiques, and local crafts. Open Sat.–Sun. 8 AM–6 PM.

Other Shops

Fans of John Berendt's 1994 blockbuster *Midnight in the Garden of Good and Evil* who are looking for a souvenir will find them most everywhere in town, but certainly they'll save time going to **"The Book" Gift Shop** (127 E. Gordon St., 912/233-3867, www.midnightin-savannah.com). The store sells copies of the book (signed and not); recordings of the late Emma Kelly, Savannah's Lady of 6,000 Songs; photos and prints of Mercer House (although Jim William's sister has been trying to stop people from selling images of the house without her permission); and the autobiography of Lady Chablis. The store also stocks items that are not directly related to the story but still related to Savannah, such as prints, silver pieces, and Lowcountry cookbooks. Be sure to check out the small **Midnight Museum.**

Saints and Shamrocks (309 Bull St., 912/233-8858, www.saints-shamrocks.com) is a great place to stop in if you're looking for things Irish or Catholic, including Irish imports, books, music, heraldry items, and the statues and medals you might expect. Open Mon.–Sat. 9:30 AM–5:30 PM.

Specialty Stores

Byrd Cookie Company (6700 Waters Ave., 912/355-1716 or 800/291-2973, www.byrd cookiecompany.com) is the place to go if you got hooked on sweet Lowcountry benne wafers or cheese biscuits while you were touring this region. Open since 1924, the 50,000-square-foot location (a onetime warehouse) is a sprawling place filled with Byrd creations, and loads of other gift-basket gourmet treats. If you can't make it here (10 minutes from the visitors center), get your sweet tooth fix in the candy shops on River Street.

When it's your pooch's turn for a treat, head to **Harry Barker** (411 E. Liberty St., 912/527-2700, www.harrybarker.com). Here, a onetime Ford model and magicians Penn and Teller's fire-eating assistant now sells her gourmet dog snacks and toile doggie beds. Don't laugh—Oprah and Rosie are huge fans, as is *InStyle,* along with scores of other national home magazines.

Sports and Recreation

BEACHES
In general, Savannahians go to **Tybee Island** or **Hilton Head** when they want to go to the beach. The first is your best bet if you're in town and want to see a pristine Southern coastal beach; the second is highly developed but still pretty. Tybee is covered at the end of this chapter, and Hilton Head is covered in the chapter on Beaufort.

IN AND ON THE WATER
Surfing
Surfing's not great around here, but you can find some waves now and again, and with waves come surfers. For more info, check out Tybee Island's **High Tide Surf Shop** (Hwy. 80 E, 912/786-6556).

Kayaking and Canoeing
Paddlers around here usually head up to Hilton Head or the ACE Basin, or down to Darien or the Okefenokee Swamp. But you can also put in at the **Isle of Hope Marina** (50 Bluff Dr., 912/354-8187).

Cruises
The **River Street Riverboat Company** (9 E. River St., 912/232-6404 or 800/786-6404, www.savannahriverboat.com), offers dinner and entertainment cruises aboard two paddle wheelers, the *Savannah River Queen* and the *Georgia Queen,* along with narrated sightseeing cruises. The sightseeing cruise lasts an hour and runs twice a day, daily through the high season and on the weekends during other months. Fare runs $17 for adults. **Dinner Entertainment Cruises** run $44; if you want an evening cruise but want to eat elsewhere, try the **Moonlight Cruise,** which runs 90 minutes and costs just $15, Apr.–Sept. If you're looking for something with cultural oomph, a two-hour **Gospel Dinner Cruise** runs Mon. Apr.–Oct. at 7 PM, fare is $34. Reservations are required. The Company also offers **Saturday Luncheon, Sunday Brunch,** and **"Murder Afloat"** cruises. Call for information.

Dolphin Magic Tours (912/897-4990 or 800/721-1240, www.dolphin-magic.com) depart from River Street, with dolphin-watching/nature tours, and a two-hour narrated tour of River Street, Forts Jackson and Pulaski, Tybee Island, lighthouses, and the Barrier Islands. Prices start at $22 for adults, about half that for children.

GOLF
Golf courses abound in the area, as you might suspect, and include **Bacon Park Golf Course** (1 Shorty Cooper Dr., 912/354-2625, www.baconparkgolf.com), which will run you $30–32; and the **Crosswinds Golf Club** (232 James B. Blackburn Dr., 912/966-1909, www.crosswindsgolf.com), $39 for a round weekdays, $47 on weekends. Perhaps tops in the area is the **Club at Savannah Harbor** (2 Resort Dr., 912/201-2007, www.theclubatsavannahharbor.net), across the river from the city on Hutchison Island, which runs $95 and is open

to the public and Westin resort guests both. For information on Savannah-area golf, contact the **Georgia State Golf Association** (770/955-4272, www.gsga.org). Courses are open early morning till dark daily year-round.

HIKING

Although Savannah is an urbane, walking city, its outskirts offer some good nature hikes as well. **Skidaway State Park** (52 Diamond Causeway, 912/598-2300, www.gastatepark.org) offers two nature trails through marshes, beneath huge live oaks, towering longleaf pines, and cabbage palmettos. Wildlife includes shorebirds, such rare migrating birds as the painted bunting, deer, and raccoon.

The tree-lined **Old Savannah-Tybee Railroad Historic and Scenic Trail,** located on Highway 80 East, is a mostly shaded, 6.5-mile (one-way) trail that follows the roadbed of the railroad that hauled beachgoers from Savannah to Tybee in the late 1800s and early 1900s. Today the ties and rails are gone, replaced by crushed stone. This trail is good for hiking, biking, or jogging and offers pretty views of the Savannah River's south channel. Wildlife includes alligators, box turtles, brown pelicans, and red-tailed hawks. **Oatland Island Preserve** (11 Sandtown Rd., 912/898-3980, www.oatlandisland.org) has well-marked trails that also offer opportunities for wildlife viewing.

BIKING

Perhaps the best trip in the Savannah area is just a long ride along the hard-packed sands of Tybee Island. But there's also a nice bike trail leading from Fort Pulaski: the **Old Savannah-Tybee Railroad Historic and Scenic Trail** located on Highway 80 East. For details, see the *Hiking* section.

TENNIS

The Westin Golf Resort & Spa (1 Resort Dr., 912/201-2000, www.westinsavannah.com)

across the river has courts for guests; others are welcome to use several public courts in and around Savannah. Closest to downtown you'll find four free lighted courts at **Forsyth Park** (912/351-3850) at Gaston and Drayton streets. There are nine courts ($3) at **Daffin Park** (1001 E. Victory Dr., 912/351-3850), although only three are lit at night. Farther out, **Bacon Park** (6262 Skidaway Rd., 912/351-3850), has 14 courts ($3), all lighted; and 2 courts (free) are available between 3rd and 4th streets on Butler Avenue over at **Tybee Island Memorial Park** (800/868-2322).

PROFESSIONAL SPORTS
Baseball

The City of Savannah got its first team in 1903; Babe Ruth, Shoeless Joe Jackson, and Jackie Robinson all barnstormed at Grayson Stadium, built in 1941. It's big for a single-A ballpark, at 5,000 seats—and it can look a little empty at times because the average crowd for the **Savannah Sand Gnats** (1401 E. Victory Dr., 912/351-9150, www.sandgnats.com) averages only around 1,500 people per game, but don't let that stop you. The Gnats have played at Grayson Stadium in Daffin Park since 1996. Their mascot is Gnate the Gnat. Their season is 140 games long, so Gnats season appropriately stretches from April through September. The Gnats, a Washington Nationals affiliate, generally field a strong squad in the storied South Atlantic, or "Sallie" League. One of the teams they tend to beat is the Charleston River Dogs.

Incidentally, although no one's ever been accosted by an actual River Dog at a Charleston game, in Savannah you'd best bring your Skin-So-Soft or other repellent because you'll find plenty of genuine gnats abuzz here on a warm summer night. Tickets run $6–9.50 with discounts for seniors, children, and members of the military. Parking is free.

SAVANNAH AND VICINITY

Accommodations

Savannah is its historic downtowns and its riverfront. Don't stay anywhere else. One exception: If you're going to be splitting your time between the beach and the streets, you might choose a spot on Tybee Island. All accommodations listed here are located in the historic district.

$100 and Under

The **Days Inn** (201 W. Bay St., 912/236-4440 or 800/469-6130, www.daysinn.com) is probably the best bet for a reasonably priced stay in the historic district. Rooms facing the busy boulevard offer river views along with the traffic noise. Non–street-facing rooms will offer more quiet. Rates run $89–185.

$100-$150

In the "For-this-money-why-not-pick-a-bed-and-breakfast?" category is the **Best Western Savannah Historic District** (412 W. Bay St., 912/233-1011, www.bw.historicsavannah.com). For some people the answer is, "Because we want a pool." And the location is attractive—right on top of River Street's action. Rates run $99–159.

$150 and Higher

The **Mulberry** (601 E. Bay St., 912/238-1200 or 877/468-1200, www.savannahhotel.com), which is affiliated with Holiday Inn but a different animal entirely, is set in what was once a cavernous brick livery stable down by the river, and which later became (in many adult Savannahians' lifetimes) the local Coca-Cola bottling plant—second largest in the world, after the original in Atlanta. This is a nice location, just slightly out of the thick of things at Washington Square. Rates run $150–250.

The towering **DeSoto Hilton** (15 E. Liberty St., 912/232-9000 or 800/426-8483, www.desotohilton.com), with its good location and Hilton consistency, is a preferable option to being shut out of the historic district entirely on a busy weekend, but ultimately, Sa-

vannah is not a high-rise town; it's much better to look up into the historic district's wonderful facades, rather than down over its rooftops. Rates run $109–219.

On Lafayette Square, the **Suites on Lafayette** (201 E. Charlton St., 912/233-7815, www.suitesonlafayette.com) run about $175 per night for 2 people in high season, but because some of the suites can sleep as many as 10 people ($600), this could be the cheapest thing going downtown. Special rates are available for families, groups, and longer stays.

(**Marshall House** (123 E. Broughton St., 912/644-7896 or 800/589-6304, www.marshallhouse.com) was built as a hotel in 1851. When this stretch of Broughton went downhill in the late 1940s and 1950s, the hotel closed. Therefore, after a multimillion-dollar renovation, the recent reopening of the Marshall portended good news for the rest of this stretch of Broughton, which is still in the process of regeneration. Rates start at $150.

With a great central location, the Marshall is a fine stay if you'd like something historic, with period furnishings, but want more privacy than that found at some B&Bs. Certainly, at the Marshall, you are in the middle of it all. If you have a second-floor street-side room, your room comes with a balcony overlooking thriving Broughton Street. While the street-side rooms can be loud for some tastes, the rooms facing the interior courtyard (where continental breakfast is served daily) enjoy a serene view. Be sure to see the painting in the courtyard commemorating General Sherman's signing of Field Order No. 15.

Located on tranquil Oglethorpe Square beside the Owens-Thomas House, (**The President's Quarters Inn and Guesthouse** (225 E. President St., 912/233-1600 or 800/233-1776, www.presidentsquarters.com) never really served as quarters to a president, but back in the days when this house belonged to the Confederate General Andrew Lawton, it did play host to Robert E. Lee's daughter,

SAVANNAH ACCOMMODATIONS AND FOOD

Savannah   River

0
0   200 m

W FACTORS WALK

WILLIAMSON ST

KEVIN BARRY'S

RIVER   ST

E FACTORS WALK

SHRIMP FACTORY

BEST WESTERN

SAVANNAH SMILES

BARNARD RAMP

MOON RIVER BREWING CO

RIVER STREET INN

E BAY   ST

Emmet Park

THE MULBERRY

W BAY   ST

CLUB ONE

DAYS INN

CHURCHILL'S

THE OLDE PINK HOUSE

THE PIRATE'S HOUSE/HANNAH'S EAST

W BROAD

W BRYAN ST

VINNIE VAN-GO-GOS

Ellis Square

SAPPHIRE GRILL

Johnson Square

E BRYAN ST

Reynolds Square

Warren Square

Washington Square

Franklin Square

CITY MARKET

NOTORIOUS

THE LADY AND SONS

SAVANNAH COFFEE ROASTERS

PLANTERS INN

W CONGRESS ST

E CONGRESS   ST

VENUS DE MILO

THE RAIL PUB

BISTRO SAVANNAH

MERCURY LOUNGE

FINNEGAN'S WAKE

IL PASTICCIO

45 BISTRO

E BROUGHTON ST

W BROUGHTON ST

THE TEA ROOM

MARSHALL HOUSE

E BROUGHTON LN

Liberty Square

W STATE   ST

Telfair Square

Wright Square

E PRESIDENT ST

Oglethorpe Square

Columbia Square

E STATE   ST

Greene Square

ANN

MARTIN LUTHER KING JR BLVD

W YORK   ST

E YORK   ST

THE PRESIDENT'S QUARTERS INN AND GUESTHOUSE

OGLETHORPE AVE

W OGLETHORPE AVE

JEFFERSON ST

BARNARD ST

WHITAKER ST

DRAYTON

E OGLETHORPE   AVE

PRICE

HOUSTON

TURNER   ST

Elbert Square

CIVIC CENTER

W HULL   ST

Orleans Square

Chippewa Square

ABERCORN

COLONIAL PARK CEMETERY

E HULL   ST

Crawford Square

W PERRY   ST

E PERRY   ST

LOUISVILLE RD

W LIBERTY ST

SOHO CAFÉ

GALLERY ESPRESSO

LINCOLN

HABERSHAM

E LIBERTY ST

MADISON SQUARE

DESOTO HILTON

PINKIE MASTER'S

W HARRIS   ST

Pulaski Square

E HARRIS   ST

HAMILTON-TURNER HOUSE

Troup Square

E MACON ST

W CHARLTON ST

W CHARLTON LN

GRYPHON TEA ROOM

LAFAYETTE SQUARE

SUITES ON LAFAYETTE

FIREFLY CAFÉ

E CHARLTON ST

E CHARLTON LN

W JONES ST

E JONES ST

MRS WILKES' BOARDING HOUSE

CLARY'S CAFÉ

E TAYLOR ST

W TAYLOR   ST

Chatham Square

Monterey Square

Calhoun Square

E WAYNE ST

Whitefield Square

W GORDON ST

E GORDON ST

W ALICE   ST

E ALICE   ST

W GASTON ST

E GASTON   ST

16

16

MONTGOMERY ST

TATTNALL ST

W HUNTINGDON ST

FORSYTH PARK

DRAYTON

ABERCORN

E HUNTINGDON ST

W HALL   ST

E HALL   ST

© AVALON TRAVEL PUBLISHING, INC.

who was in town accompanying her ailing father on his trip to visit his own father's grave on Cumberland Island. She wrote her mother on April 3, 1870, that, "the Lawtons are as kind as possible, [and] wanted papa to stay here, but Mr. Andrew Lowe [sic] had arranged to take him to his house at bed-time," and had in so doing deprived her father of the alternating, nightlong serenades of two bands that showed up outside, thinking the former general was there.

Possibly to protect the frail Lee, Lawton did nothing to discourage their misunderstanding, telling the crowd simply that Lee had "retired from fatigue," without telling them that he was in fact retired over at Andrew Low's house. The former general wrote his wife that because Low's house was "partially dismantled" and because Low lived alone, Lee was having "a quiet stay" there and was "very comfortable." The general didn't like being separated from his daughter, however, who had become ill herself, but though the two had

Built in 1873, the Hamilton-Turner house is now a charming inn.

offers to stay at the homes of several other prominent citizens, he deemed it "awkward to change," and they stayed separated for the duration of their stay in town, even when they returned after a brief sojourn to Cumberland and Jacksonville.

But separated from her family or not, Agnes Lee was treated like a Kennedy child in Boston, and though she was ill while here, she seems to have enjoyed her visit immensely. From the house's parlor, she wrote, to her mother, "I wish you could see a large marble table in the parlour, where I am writing, with a pyramid of jasmine in the center and four large plates full at the corners, almost covering the square, all sent me Saturday."

In 1987, the four-story town houses were restored as The President's Quarters, and fortunately, since the Andrew Low House is now a museum, you won't have to worry about your traveling companion being carted away to spend the night over there. Owner Raymond Clawsons's inn features 19 stately, ornately decorated rooms, each named for a U.S. president. This can raise some intriguing questions for the historically minded: for instance, whether guests in the Grover Cleveland room can book for two nonconsecutive nights. Although other rooms feature either a queen or king bed, many with poster beds, the room named for the last true Victorian-era president, William McKinley, fittingly features two doubles. Rooms include working fireplaces, refrigerators, TVs, VCRs, and desks with Internet hookups. Each suite in the three-bedroom guesthouse features an oversized hot tub. Breakfast is served, weather permitting, in the courtyard. Children are not only welcome, but under age 10, they stay for free. Rates run $137–225.

The 18-room ◖ **Hamilton-Turner Inn** (330 Abercorn St., 912/233-1833, www.hamilton-turnerinn.com), has a pleasant surprise for fans of Southern Literature. Not only is this the home formerly owned by Nancy Hillis, "Mandy" of John Berendt's *Midnight in the Garden of Good and Evil*, but it's also located a stone's throw from Flannery O'Connor's Childhood Home on Lafayette Square and stands between O'Connor's home and the beautiful, sonorous (when the bells are ringing) St. John the Baptist Catholic Church, where O'Connor attended as a young girl. Of course, the home figures into the Savannahian imagination of a later writer, John Berendt, who used the home as a setting in *Midnight*.

One of the nation's best examples of a Second French Empire Victorian home, the Hamilton-Turner was built originally for jeweler and onetime Charleston mayor Samuel Pugh Hamilton in 1873. There is a complimentary full breakfasts in the sunny dining room, wine and hors d'oeuvres, and a turndown service. Rates run $175–350.

The 60-room **Planters Inn on Reynolds Square** (29 Abercorn St., 912/232-5678, www.savannahplantersinn.com) stands next to the Pink House, on the site of the first parsonage of John Wesley, the founder of Methodism. It partially consists of the former John Wesley Hotel, which the Planters Inn folks proclaim served as "Savannah's premier brothel." English breakfasts are served and evenings bring wine tastings in the lobby. Rooms include period Baker furnishings, four-poster rice beds,

private baths, and in-room coffeemakers. Dinner room service is available 5–10 PM from the Olde Pink House, and there is free valet parking. Rates run $199–325.

The 86-room **River Street Inn** (124 E. Bay St., 912/234-6400 or 800/253-4229, www.riverstreetinn.com) is another quality lodging within walking distance of everything downtown…and within earshot of the traffic unless you choose a room in back. The 1817 building is on the National Register of Historic Places. In the evenings, guests are welcomed to an evening wine reception, Mon.–Sat., which includes hors d'oeuvres, a glass of wine, and an informative talk by the inn's resident historian. Rates run $149–275.

Across the river is the 403-room **Westin Savannah Harbor Golf Resort & Spa** (1 Resort Dr., 912/201-2000, www.westinsavannah.com), which offers golf, tennis, exercise facilities, pools, a spa, and a restaurant for its guests, who are mainly conventioneers. Rates run $149–299. The free-for-guests boat taxi across to River Street actually makes it a pretty handy place to stay, although the taxis stop running at 10:30 PM nightly.

Food

SAVANNAH PROPER
Seafood and Lowcountry Cuisine

The Pirates' House (20 E. Broad St., 912/233-5757, www.pirateshouse.com), is where you'll want to head if you have a child with you. The "house" is actually a collection of old buildings cobbled together over the centuries, beginning with 1734, when the brick building that now makes up a small dining room was the house for the gardener of the Trustees' Garden, an experimental garden from which Georgia's first peaches took root (literally). Open daily for lunch and dinner.

In the 1750s, the experimenting was over and this plot on the river and on the outskirts of town became home to an inn for sailors. Soon pirates infested the area. Rumors spread

of tunnels (which have been uncovered) being used to carry drunken patrons out to the ships of shorthanded sea captains, where they'd awaken, on their way halfway across the world. One such legend of the house tells of a Savannah constable who stopped in for a couple of drinks and ended up spending two years sailing around the world, trying to get back to Savannah.

It is said that events that took place here served as inspiration for elements of Robert Louis Stevenson's *Treasure Island*. In the story, Captain Flint dies upstairs in this house with his reliable mate Billy Bones at his side.

The tunnels leading to the river still run below the labyrinthine rooms of the house, although nobody who works in the restaurant seems much interested in poking around down there. What brings people here nowadays is the hearty if not gourmet luncheon buffet in the Buccaneer Room; a steal at $13, with children half price. The room is flanked on either side by holes leading down to the tunnels, and one stairway has a stuffed pirate who talks when he's a-mind to—corny but a definite delight for kids.

◖ **The Olde Pink House** (23 Abercorn St., 912/232-4286) features catch-of-the-day fish, crispy scored flounder with apricot glaze ($23), blue-crab-stuffed grouper ($23), and several other fine appetizers and foods all with a Southern flare. Open seven nights a week for "Elegant Southern Dining," the Pink House is a landmark in town and has been since the 1700s. The Planters Tavern in the house is a popular nightspot, with torch singers and a jazz piano. Open nightly for dinner.

Down on the river, **The Shrimp Factory** (313 E. River St., 912/236-4229, www.the-shrimpfactory.com) is set in an old cotton-and-resin warehouse built in the 1820s, and open for lunch ($12 on average) and dinner ($22 on average) daily except Sundays. With plenty of nonseafood fare, too, it's a good spot for casual dinner and good views of the river and passing ships.

For something much closer to the spirit of the Gourmet Channel, **Bistro Savannah** (309 W. Congress St., 912/233-6266), at the Market, has been called "Georgia's #1 Seafood Restaurant" by the Zagat Survey. It's a fine restaurant, not unlike upscale bistros you'd find in New York or Los Angeles. The food is exquisite if smallish; the crispy scored flounder with apricot shallot glaze ($22.95) is beloved by locals, as are the garlic sautéed mussels and asparagus with pepper cream and creamy risotto ($14.95). If you're not in the mood for seafood, steaks provide alternatives. Open nightly for dinner.

In the early 1980s, when Southern food was getting a nouveau spin and accepted as its own fine dining genre, ◖ **Elizabeth on 37th** (105 E. 37th St., 912/236-5547, www.elizabeth-on37th.com) was a forerunner of the move-

ment. Today, the restaurant's a grand dame of an institution with a national following. Set in a 1900 Greek Revival mansion just south of the traditional historic district, the restaurant seats guests in rooms filled with cozy white-linen covered tables and antique chairs. Favorites are Lowcountry standards with a kick: Southern fried grits with shrimp, country ham, and red-eye gravy; a mustard barbecue turnover; spicy red rice with local shrimp, and clams, sausage, and okra, for instance. Entrées range $25–32. Open nightly 6–10 PM.

Contemporary

For one of the best fancier meals in Savannah these days, head to ◖ **Sapphire Grill** (110 W. Congress St., 912/443-9962, www.sapphire-grill.com). In the midst of the City Market and lodged between two bars, it's easy to pass it up as another tourist spot. But don't. Sure the setting's hip and stylish, with its mosaic artwork, bare brick walls, and swanky ebony bar where martinis are the hit of the moment, but the substantive menu wins out as the real star. Here are some headliners: arugula and chevre ginger grits; jumbo lump crab cakes with greens and caper aioli and lobster oil; rosemary and shallot–spiked Colorado lamb lollipops with golden potato sage pancakes, rutabaga puree, and cranberry oil; benne en-crusted local black grouper with vinegar-spiked jasmine rice, melted leek and heirloom tomatoes, and sweet soy and preserved lemon. The offerings are fusion in the truest sense, with French-tinged gourmet rendered from local flavors. Entrées range $23–33. Open nightly Mon.–Sat.

◖ **45 Bistro** (123 E. Broughton St., 912/234-3111, www.themarshallhouse.com) is in the bottom floor of the Marshall House bed-and-breakfast, one of the best places to stay in town. Given the inn's high-caliber ranking and white-glove service, it only makes sense the accompanying restaurant would be on par. Expect an elegant setting with fireplaces and a publike bar, and a staff that is more about being friendly than putting on airs. As for the food? Try the minted confit of lamb shank with fennel, tomato, and shallots over risotto with grated block parmigiano-reggiano ($20); the "crisp" lasagna with jumbo scallops, wilted spinach, mascarpone cheese, and spicy ragu ($22); or the Black Angus filet mignon, seared au poivre with gorgonzola gratinée pomme frites, arugula, and a tarragon roasted aioli ($32). Entrées range $15–28. Open nightly Mon.–Sat.

Italian

Fine dining has not only infiltrated the City Market area, but it's spread to Broughton Street as well. One of the better restaurants in town is here, and happens to be Italian and owned by a Sicilian expat. People come to **Il Pasticcio** (2 E. Broughton St., 912/231-8888) as much for the scene (youngish hipsters) and setting (cool and mod) as they do for the food, but the latter still delivers and then some. The chef, another Italian who learned to cook from his family, earned the place a top 10 ranking from *USA Today;* try his favorite: the grilled beef and gorgonzola fillet. Entrées range $14–35. Open nightly for dinner.

On the dining with kids (or with shallow pockets) front, try **Vinnie VanGoGos** (317 W. Bryan St., 912/233-6394, www.vinnievangogo.com) on the Market for the best pizza in town. If you're too whooped to make it there, they can deliver to downtown hotels and inns. Open for dinner nightly (till 1 AM Fri. and Sat.), and for both lunch and dinner Sat. and Sun.

Cafés

If course a quaint town would have its share of quaint cafés. If you're wandering the historic district and are near Troup Square, try the tiny neighborhood **Firefly Café** (321 Habersham St., 912/234-1971) for breakfast or lunch. The crab-and-spinach omelet with hollandaise is a great start to a day of exploring, as is a stack of blueberry corn pancakes. At lunch, the Cajunspiced mac-and-cheese with chicken and broccoli fills you up nicely, and the cranberry pecan spinach salad with jicama, raisins, goat cheese, candied pecans, and cranberry vinaigrette satisfies lightweights. Entrées average $13, but breakfast, salads, and sandwiches are all under

$10. Open Mon.–Sat. for breakfast, l dinner; Sun. for brunch only.

The reigning place in town for lun. **Soho South Café** (12 W. Liberty St., 912/233-1633, www.sohocafe.com), at Liberty and Bull streets in the historic district. Locals come to the café, with its funky art, books, and indoor umbrella-topped tables, for the fresh fare: hearty and huge salads (the blackened tuna nicoise is great); inventive sandwiches (Mom's meat loaf on a kaiser roll with Russian dressing and fixings and the smoked ham, brie, and apples in a baguette with Dijonnaise both rock); and daily quiches. Dinner dishes are just as tasty (featuring Southern favorites like shrimp and grits, and jumbo crab cakes), though the scene is much more subdued and prices comparable to finer restaurants in the area. Lunch entrées range $6–10. Open for lunch Mon.–Sat.; dinner Tues.–Sat.; and brunch Sun.

Steak and Ribs

While Sapphire Grill, 45 Bistro, and Il Pasticcio all offer top steaks in linen settings, sometimes you want to head where they specialize in serving meat eaters. If that sounds like you, try the longtime Savannah landmark, **Johnny Harris Restaurant** (1651 E. Victory Dr., 912/354-7810), where you can get certified Angus beef, barbecue, chicken, and seafood for about $10 to $15 an entrée. Open for lunch and dinner Mon.–Sat.

Barbecue

Johnny Harris has some of the best 'cue in town; and it's also good at the Pirate's House, and other Southern-style cookeries, **Walls' BBQ** (515 E. York La., 912/232-9754) is devoted to the stuff. Expect no frills here, but you'll get the genuine article. Cash only. Open Thurs.–Sat. 11 AM–9 PM.

Southern Home Cooking

The most famous Southern food is served for lunch in the basement at **Mrs. Wilkes' Boarding House** (107 W. Jones St., 912/232-5997, www.mrswilkes.com), including

Southern chicken biscuits and vegetables all passed around tables family-style. There's no sign, but it's an institution with tourists and locals alike, so you shouldn't have any trouble finding the front door. Bring cash, average meals are $13. Open Mon.–Fri. 11 AM–2 PM.

The Lady and Sons (102 W. Congress St., 912/233-2600, www.ladyandsons.com), has been open down on the Market since 1989. Run by Paula Deen and her sons Bobby and Jamie, this place has been acclaimed everywhere from *USA Today* to *Good Morning America.* And since Paula began hosting her Food Network show in recent years, the place has been packed, as are the cooking classes she offers. The restaurant's buffet reads like a crash course in Southern cuisine, loaded with fried chicken, beef and cabbage, collards, black-eyed peas, and other top-of-the-line confections of the former Confederacy. You can also order an entrée here: the Savannah blue crab, BBQ shrimp and grits, and grouper are all popular. Open Mon.–Sat. 11 AM–3 PM

for lunch, from 5 PM for dinner; Sun. 11 AM–5 PM only.

Diner Food

After its supporting role in *Midnight,* humble little **Clary's Café** (404 Abercorn St., 912/233-0402), spawned a second location, but the one on Abercorn Street is the original that opened back in 1903. Sit at the counter for the best experience, and get the fresh, homemade Kosher hash or country fired steak with gravy, grits, and biscuits for breakfast, or anything flame-broiled off the grill for lunch. Everything's under $10. Open for breakfast and lunch only.

At the Savannah Visitors Information Center and Savannah Museum, the **Whistle Stop Café** (303 Martin Luther King Jr. Blvd., 912/651-3656) delights kids because it's set in an old dining railcar. The simple but decent food, including some very tasty fried chicken, can come in handy after a morning trip to the museum. Open for breakfast and lunch daily.

Information and Services

GETTING THERE
Airlines
Savannah/Hilton Head International Airport (400 Airways Ave., 912/964-0514, www.savannahairport.com) receives flights from AirTran (800/247-8726, airtran.com), American Eagle (800/433-7300, www.aa.com), Continental Express (800/525-0280, www.continental.com), Delta (800/221-1212, www.delta.com), Independence Air (800/359-3594, www.flyi.com), Northwest, United Express (800/241-6522, www.ual.com), and US Airways (800/428-4322, www.usairways.com). Shuttles and taxis are available from the airport to downtown hotels.

Bus
If you're riding the Joe and Ratso Trail, you'll come into Savannah via **Greyhound Bus**

Lines (610 Oglethorpe Ave., 912/232-2135, www.greyhound.com).

Rail
Assuming that **Amtrak** (2611 Seaboard Coastline Dr., 912/234-2611, www.amtrak.com) is still afloat by the time you read this, Savannah will no doubt still be a prime stop, a favorite layover for those traveling between New York and Miami aboard the *Silver Star, Palmetto,* and *Silver Meteor.*

GETTING AROUND
I've said it elsewhere: This is a walking town. Unless physical limitations keep you from walking, you really should take in the town by walking it. Even late at night, you're likely safe from unsavory types as long as you're not walking alone. Be sure to wear comfortable shoes, and although I've never tried it, I would

© SEAN SLINSKY

To get the lay of the land in Savannah, take a trolley from the visitors center.

imagine that walking the cobblestones of River Street would be more challenging than pleasant in high heels.

If you've walked your feet into submission, you might want to call **Savannah Pedicab** (912/232-7900, www.savannahpedicab.com), which provides tip-only, radio-dispatched service in minutes to your location in the historic district. They also rent bikes for downtown use.

CAT
The **Chatham Area Transit (CAT)** (912/233-5767, www.catchacat.org) runs buses and trolleys seven days a week, although the schedule is much lighter on Sundays. Stops include the Savannah Visitors Information Center, so if you would like, you can park your car there and explore without having to brave driving Savannah's challenging squares.

The green, trolleylike CAT Shuttle is a free public shuttle for visitors and residents alike, serving the historic district only with 30 stops in that area. It connects to most CAT routes,

for which you will need to pay $1. Children shorter than 41 inches tall can ride for free. Be sure to pick up a current CAT schedule from the Savannah Visitors Information Center (301 Martin Luther King Jr. Blvd., 912/944-0455, www.savannahvisit.com).

By Boat
The Savannah Belles Ferry offers passenger ferries from River Street to Hutchinson Island, home of the Westin resort. Round-trip fare costs $1. Ferries depart every 30 minutes from the City Hall dock and land at the Trade Center, adjacent to the Westin. This is a nice, cheap way to view the city from the water. Service operates 7:30 AM–10:30 PM.

Taxis
Taxis are another way to get around, especially late at night or in the rain. Local outfits include **Toucan Taxi and Shuttle Services** (912/233-3700).

Rental Cars
You'll find a lot of the car rental places down at the airport, of course; many of them offer discounts on the weekends. **Enterprise** (800/261-7331, www.enterprise.com) has an in-town location (7510 White Bluff Rd., 912/355-6622) and an airport location (912/964-0171). I've had good experience getting good rates by booking (slightly) ahead with Priceline.com. If you can, save money on your rate and then splurge and get a convertible for riding out under the oaks to Tybee Island.

ORGANIZED TOURS
Walking Tours
Plantation Carriage Company and Tours (219 W. Bryan St., Ste. 303, 912/233-0119), offers group walking tours (adults, $15) of the historic district. Call for reservations. **The Savannah Walks** (912/238-9255 or 888/728-9255, www.savannahwalks.com), offers 90-minute *Ghost Tours* departing from the center of Johnson Square at 5:30 and 7:30 PM year-round, with a 9:30 PM tour in high-season; $14 adults. Jonathan Stalcup, a SCAD grad, puts

his architecture degree to use by leading Architectural Tours of Savannah (912/604-6354, ·www.architecturalsavannah.com), which cover design and urban planning by foot. The tours are based on themes (Colonial to contemporary; antebellum and Victorian; and Lit City—a nighttime tour that looks at how electricity changed the town) leave daily from various points in Savannah. Tickets are $20 adults, $10 students. Reservations are required.

Carriage Tours

Carriage Tours of Savannah (912/236-6756) located at the City Market offers hourlong (or nearly so) narrated tours of the historic district in an open-air, horse-drawn carriage. During daylight hours they offer a historical tour; at night they offer a popular ghost tour. Rates are adults, $19; kids (5–11), $8; free for those under 5. Private carriages for two cost $85 per hour. The **Plantation Carriage Company** (219 W. Bryan St., Ste. 303, 912/201-0001), is another option. Their 50-minute tours depart from the City Market on Jefferson Street every 20 minutes; adults, $19; kids $8. Reservations aren't necessary

Minibus Tours

The enterprising **Plantation Carriage Company** (219 W. Bryan St., Ste. 303, 912/236-4331) also offers narrated, air-conditioned bus tours. They offer two standards: the **Julep & Jasmine Tour,** which runs 2.5 hours, costs $18, and includes admission into two historic sites; and the popular, shorter **Behind the Door** tour, which includes admission into one historic site.

Finally, their **Low Country Tour** provides an informative look at Savannah beyond the historic district, including a visit to the Bethesda Orphanage, Wormsloe, and Bonaventure Cemetery. This wide-ranging tour is for groups only and reservations are required.

Also popular are **Pat Tuttle's Tours** (135 Bull St., 912/233-1776, www.pattuttle.com). A native Savannahian, her **Savannah by the Book Tour** is tops. The 2.5-hour van tour costs $22 and shows you many of the locations

featured in *Midnight,* including Bonaventure Cemetery.

Another locally owned and operated group, **Old Savannah Tours** (912/234-8128 or 800/517-9007, www.oldsavannahtours.com) offers a variety of vehicles—trolleys, buses, limos, minivans—and several tours, including a Paula Deen culinary tour (with lunch), and tours off to Fort Pulaski and Tybee Island.

National tour companies **Trolley Tours** (912/233-0083, www.historictours.com) and **Gray Line Tours** (912/234-8687, www.graylineofsavannah.com) also run popular "Book," ghost, and Lowcountry tours on wheels, along with in-town tours: adults, about $20; kids, about $10. For an additional charge ($1), many of the bus companies offer on-and-off service, allowing you to hop off the tour at any location that catches your interest, and then hop on again later. Some people like the freedom of this option, although for first-timers I'd suggest sticking with the tour all the way through, first thing after arriving downtown. Then, once you have your bearings and an idea of where you want to go, you can walk or take the local CAT (912/233-5767, www.catchacat.org) bus to get from site to site.

Members of the **Congregation Mickve Israel** (20 E. Gordon St., 912/233-1547, www.mickveisrael.org) lead Jewish-history tours of Savannah, including their famous Gothic temple, the only one of its kind in the country. These tours are specially arranged through the synagogue; contact Temple Mickve Israel for more rates and other details.

The **Negro Heritage Trail Tour** leaves from the Savannah Visitors Information Center (301 Martin Luther King Jr. Blvd.), but is operated by the King-Tisdell Cottage Foundation (514 E. Huntingdon St., 912/234-8000, www.kingstisdell.org). Tours are Mon.–Sat. noon and 2 PM. Call for reservations. Tours are $19 for adults, $10 for kids, and free for those under 10.

Bike Tours

One of the newer ways to explore the river town is with **Blazing Saddles of Savannah**

(129 Jacquelyn Dr., 912/659-1000). Tour guides provide bikes and helmets, and lead you in and around the city for 1.5-hour rides that cover some of the more typical and off-the-path sights. If you want to get the lay of the land it's a great alternative to hopping on a trolley. Rates are $15 per person.

INFORMATION AND SERVICES
Tourist Offices and Visitors Centers
Set right at the end of I-16 to catch new-comers before they have time to get lost, the **Savannah Visitors Information Center** (301 Martin Luther King Jr. Blvd., 912/944-0455, www.savannahvisit.com) was formerly home of Georgia's first railroad, the Central of Geor-gia, built in response to Charleston's, which was the first regular railroad in the nation. The **Savannah Area Convention and Visitors Bureau** (101 E. Bay St., 912/644-6401 or 877/728-2662, www.sav-visit.com) has a help-ful office at downtown and a suboffice (1 River St., 912/651-6662) near the Hyatt. On Tybee Island, stop by at the Visitor Information Cen-ter (at Campbell and Hwy. 80, 912/786-5444, www.tybeevisit.com).

Hospitals, Police, Emergencies
Major area medical facilities include tops-in-the-region 530-bed **Memorial Health University Medical Center** (4700 Waters Ave., 912/350-8000, www.memorialhealth.com), which includes the region's only Level 1 trauma center and a Mother-and-Infants Clinic;

WHEN SHERMAN MARCHED DOWN TO THE SEA (1865)

To R. W. Shields, Esq.

Our campfires shone bright on the mountains,
That frown'd on the river below;
While we stood by our guns in the morning,
And eagerly watched for the foe;
When a horseman rode out of the darkness
That hung over mountain and tree,
And shouted "Boys! up and be ready,
For Sherman will march to the sea."

Then cheer upon cheer for bold Sherman
Went up from each valley and glen,
And the bugles re-echoed the music
That rose from the lips of the men—
For we knew that the stars in our banners
More bright in their splendor would be,
And the blessings from Northland would greet us
When Sherman march'd down to the sea.

Then forward boys; forward to battle,
We march'd on our wearysome way,
And we storm'd the wild hills of Resaca,
God bless those who fell on that day!
Then Kenesaw, dark in its glory

Frown'd down on the flag of the free
But the East and the West bore our standard
When Sherman marched down to the sea.

Still onward we pressed till our banners
Swept out from the Atlanta's grim walls,
And the blood of the patriot dampened
The soil where the traitor's flag falls;
But we paused not to weep for the fallen,
Who slept by each river and tree,
Yet we twined that a wreath of the laurel,
And Sherman marched down to the sea.

Proud, proud was our army that morning,
That stood by the cypress and pine,
Then Sheman said, "Boys you are weary,
This day fair Savannah is mine!"
Then sang we a song for our chieftain,
That echoed o'er river and sea.
And the stars on our banners shone brighter,
When Sherman marched down to the sea.

Words by Adjutant Samuel Hawkins
Marshall Byers of the 5th Iowa Cavalry,
at Columbia, S.C.
Music composed by Edward Mack,
1826-1882

335-bed **Candler Hospital** (5353 Reynolds St., 912/819-6000, www.sjchs.org); and 305-bed **St. Joseph's Hospital** (11705 Mercy Blvd., 912/819-4100). If you're not sure you need to go in, give **Memorial's Nurse One** a call at 912/350-9355. If you're not sure where to go, give **St. Joseph's Care Call Center** a call at 912/819-3360.

For emergencies, dial 911. On Tybee Island, call 912/786-5600 for police, or 912/786-5440 for the Coast Guard.

Post Office

You'll find a **post office** (118 Barnard St., 912/232-2601) downtown on Telfair Square.

Public Libraries

The **Live Oak Public Libraries** (www.liveo-akpl.org) serve Savannah with two locations downtown: the main branch (2002 Bull St., 912/652-3600), and the smaller Ola Wyeth branch (4 E. Bay St., 912/232-5488). Tybee Island has a branch as well (405 Butler Ave., 912/786-7733).

Newspapers

The **Savannah Morning News** (912/236-9511, www.savannahnow.com) is Savannah's chief newspaper, and on weekends it puts out an entertainment section that will tell you what's going on in town. **Connect Savannah** (912/231-0250, www.connectsavannah.com) is Savannah's free entertainment weekly, replacing *Creative Loafing*. This is the place to find a slightly more "alternative" look at the entertainment scene.

Beyond Savannah

◖ TYBEE ISLAND

Although it somewhat shares duties with Hilton Head and Skidaway, Tybee is Savannah's beach. In fact, many called Tybee "Savannah Beach." As an urban beach, it's about as far from Savannah as Charleston is from Isle of Palms, Sullivan's Island, or Folly Beach. And like those beaches, Tybee's isolated, island feel is enhanced by the 20-minute drive (in good traffic) from Savannah. Although many island residents (those who haven't retired yet) commute to Savannah five days a week, Tybee still feels detached, and this otherly feeling has attracted millionaire home buyers, including celebs who have helped push land prices out of reach for the most of the masses. On the way to the island, you'll likely flinch as you pass an out-of-place (and controversial) multistory condominium complex on the right, perched on the banks of the creek with a rooftop pool and a view of the marshes.

On the island proper, the "beachy" action (including the fishing pier) centers on 16th Street. Every Savannahian whose childhood began since World War II can remember visiting the tacky yet venerable **T. S. Chu's Department Store** (6 Tybrisa St., 912/786-4561) for flip-flops, sunglasses, and other beach-town curio, along with fishing supplies, hardware, and housewares.

Head to the north or south ends of the island for a quieter visit, although once you're too far on either side, inlet currents make the waters too dangerous to swim. Stay at one of several quiet bed-and-breakfasts offering quiet porches beneath the palms and explore **North Beach**, which features old Fort Screven, a row of old officer's houses and the **Tybee Light Station and Museum** (30 Meddin Dr., 912/786-5801, www.tybeelighthouse.org; open Wed.–Mon. 9 AM–5:30 PM; $6 adults, $5 seniors and children 6–17, those under 6 free). The museum is set in an 1897 coastal artillery battery and specializes in local history. To get to Tybee Island, head east on East Bay or Liberty Street and look for Highway 80.

Recreation

Logging beach hours and exploring the outdoors is the main pastime for those vacation-

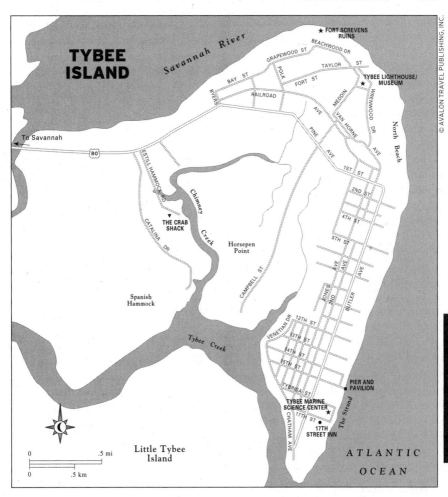

TYBEE ISLAND

To Savannah

THE CRAB SHACK

Horsepen Point

Spanish Hammock

Chimney Creek

Tybee Creek

Little Tybee Island

FORT SCREVENS RUINS

BEACHWOOD DR

GRAPEWOOD ST

TAYLOR ST

TYBEE LIGHTHOUSE/ MUSEUM

BAY ST

POLK

FORT ST

RAILROAD

MEDDIN AVE

VAN HORNE AVE

WRENWOOD DR

North Beach

BYERS

PINE AVE

1ST ST

2ND ST

4TH ST

5TH ST

JONES AVE

2ND AVE

BUTLER AVE

CAMPBELL ST

12TH ST

13TH ST

14TH ST

15TH ST

VENETIAN DR

TYBRISA ST

PIER AND PAVILION

TYBEE MARINE SCIENCE CENTER

17TH ST

17TH STREET INN

CHATHAM AVE

The Strand

ESTILL HAMMOCK RD

CATALINA DR

ATLANTIC OCEAN

0   .5 mi
0   .5 km

ing at Tybee. Rent bikes for $10 a day or $50 a week from **Pack Rat Bicycle Shop** (1405 Butler Ave., 912/786-4013). Visit the **Tybee Island Marine Science Center** (1510 Strand, 912/786-5917) near the base of the pier at 14th Street for kids' summer sea camps, beach walks, and the touch tank with loads of critters. Open Mon.–Sat. 9 A.M.–4 P.M., Sun. 1–4 P.M. Winter open weekdays only. Admission $1.

Take one of the many available nature tours. Some of the best include the crabbing and cast-net shrimping outings from **Sundial Nature Tours** (142 Pelican Dr., 912/786-9470 or 866/786-3283, www.sundialcharters.net). They also lead shelling tours, barrier island hikes, swims, and camping trips, plus fossil hunts, and dolphin-watching boat rides. Rates range $110–180 per boat (up to six people), and drop considerably in the off-season. Those into birding and wildlife who want to explore black-water rivers lined with cypress and tupelo trees and wander through salt marshes

© SEAN SLINSKY

Built in 1875, the recently restored Tybee Island Lighthouse is next to Fort Screven.

should try **Wilderness Southeast Coastal Expeditions** (912/897-5108, www.wilderness-southeast.org). Leading tours since 1973, the guides know their stuff. Rates vary greatly depending on the tour, and whether you walk, canoe, or motor along. Contact the group for more information. To explore the area by sea kayak, **Sea Kayak Georgia** (1102 Hwy. 80, 912/786-8732, www.seakayakgeorgia.com) leads tours that range from $55 for a three-hour jaunt to $500 for a four-day overnight expedition. Ask about their bed-and-breakfast tours. To rent your own kayak or surfboard, and for lessons, contact **North Island Surf and Kayak** (1C Old Tybee Rd., 912/786-4000, www.northislandkayak.com).

Accommodations

It used to be that the one dependable stay out here was the Desoto Beach Hotel, a 1938 tile-roofed hotel that was a little rough around the edges but that was a favorite for generations of Tybee visitors. Time, weather, and bull-dozers got the best of the Old Desoto. The

new **DeSoto Beach Hotel: Oceanfront** (212 Butler Ave., 912/786-4542 or 877/786-4542, www.desotobeachhotel.com), evinces little interest in the sacredness of its name and its location in the hearts of Tybee long-timers. The lodging advertises itself as the "Newest Beachfront Hotel on Tybee Island!" and plays a continuous loop of Marley's "Jammin'!" on its website. High-season rates begin at $145.

If your vision of a beach holiday focuses less on rocking chairs beneath the palmettos and more on tans, bikinis, and volleyball nets, try the $130–160 **Ocean Plaza Beach Resort** (15th St. and Oceanfront, 912/786-7777 or 800/215-6370, www.oceanplaza.com). It's right on the sand, right beside 16th Street, and complete with pools and a popular on-site rooftop restaurant featuring outstanding ocean views. The $125–175 **17th Street Inn** (12 17th Pl., 912/786-0607, www.tybeeinn.com), will put you about as close as a body can get to the action on 16th Street, unless you're sleeping in the gutter (it's been done). For something cheaper (from $109) and farther from the beach, try the

Sand Castle Inn (1402 Butler Ave., 912/786-4576, www.sandcastle-inn.com).

Run by innkeeper Ann Last, the circa-1898 **Savannah Beach Inn Bed and Breakfast** (21 Officers Row, 800/844-1398, www.savannah-beachinn.com), used to serve as officers' quarters for personnel stationed at Fort Screven. The gracious old home with its deep porches is on the National Register of Historic Places, but more important, it's just across the street from the beach, offering ocean views. Rates during peak season start around $160. Rooms include a private bath, cable TV, and phone, and some have a fireplace, soaking tub or spa, canopy bed, and/or ocean view. Gourmet breakfast is served, and murder mystery weekends and Wednesday sunset cruises are offered.

The pleasant **Tybee Island Inn** (24 Van Horn St., 912/786-9255, www.tybeeisland-inn.com), is another possibility for a relaxing island holiday. The restored circa-1902 property is also on the National Register, situated one block from the beach with no major roads to cross. All rooms have private baths; some offer a private deck, porch access, or garden tub. Rates run upward of $129 in high season.

Another quiet stay (for $135–209) on the island's historic north end is **Lighthouse Inn Bed & Breakfast** (16 Meddin Dr., 912/786-0901 or 866/786-0901, www.tybeebb.com), where rocking chairs and homemade biscuits in the morning make things cozy.

Rental Houses, Condos, and Cottages

Of course, the way most people stay on Tybee is in a rental home or cottage. To line up one of these, contact **Private Island Rentals** (1 Causton Bluff Plantation Dr., 912/233-7766, www.oceanfrontcottage.com); **Solomon Properties** (912/786-5466 or 888/756-2694, www.solomonproperties.com); **South Beach Ocean Front Condominium Rentals** (2 17th St., Unit 4, 912/786-0586 or 800/565-0107, tybeecondos.com); **Tybee Beach Vacation Rental and Property Management** (802 1st St., Tybee Island, 912/786-8805, www.renttybee.com); or **Tybee Cottages, Inc.** (1310 Jones Ave., 912/786-6746 or 877/524-9819, www.tybeecottages.com).

For a quaint, two-bedroom house painted in cheery coastal colors, try **The Catfish Cottage** (1304 Jones St., 912/441-4407, www.thesavannahguide.com/catfishcottage). Built in the 1940s, it has a screened-in front porch, immaculate and smartly furnished rooms, a six-person hot tub, two outdoor showers, and is a five-minute walk from the pier and beach. Rates at the gay-friendly cottage range $120–155 daily.

Food

The Crab Shack (40 Espill Hammock Rd., 912/786-9857, www.thecrabshack.com) on Chimney Creek on Tybee Island is a must-visit for Savannah visitors. The Shack has been out here for a while now and, perched as it is on a sandy bank beneath the oaks and above the salt marshes, it is the very sort of place that places like Charleston's Crab Shacks mean to recall. This place is extremely casual; the decor is late-20th-century plywood; the music is Jimmy Buffett. Sit inside or out, although inside is just a screened in—plasticked in, in winter—porch; a fire's always burning outside, and at night the trees are lit up with Christmas lights. The food is casual and incredibly fresh. Go—it's one of the Savannah region's most memorable restaurants, thanks to the food, the setting, and the gators out front. (Lunch and dinner daily, average entrée prices around $15.)

Just as colorful, but even more casual, is the **North Beach Grill** (41A Meddin Dr., 912/786-9003, www.northbeachgrill.com). In the shadow of the island lighthouse, you could easily pass over this place as a graffiti-covered shack, but don't. To miss out on this part of the island would be to miss a quintessential Tybee hangout. For as casual as the place is, it's also got some of the best food on the island, not to mention a wicked margarita and loaded (or unloaded) frozen lemonade. The menu's tinged with Caribbean flavors (jerk chicken and pork, conch fritters, plantains and salsa), but not limited to it. Try the roasted duck

© SEAN SLINSKY

Drive out to The Crab Shack on Tybee Island to eat outside on the marshfront decks.

leg, duck fricassée, Thai tuna, or even the hot dogs and you'll be surprised at the gourmet renderings. Open for lunch and dinner daily. Entrées are mostly less than $10. If you're here during the day, come back at night for the bar scene. A similarly laid-back dive with loads of heart and locals, **Huc-a-Poo's Bites and Booze** (912/786-5900) is even more of a shack than the grill. The menu's a fun read *and* eat with $6 wraps (try the Biz Mark E: grilled chicken, cheese, romaine or spinach, tomatoes, and house dressing); the $5 Hellicat Hotdog (with chili, cheese, mustard, ketchup, and chips); and the $15 specialty pizzas (the Honkey rules: garlic spread, with basil, spinach, black olives, and red onions). Open Mon.–Fri. 4 PM–midnight, Sat.–Sun. 11 AM–midnight. Definitely stick around for the late-night mellow.

For finer dining (translation: where you need to wear more than a bathing suit and T-shirt), visit **Tango** (1106 Hwy. 80, 912/786-8264, www.tangotybee.com), where the chef keeps racking up best of awards for his world-tropical dishes, like the West Indies–inspired ginger-brown sugar pork tenderloin with Tango jerk barbecue sauce and mango chutney ($17); the Barbadian bouillabaisse with seafood, garlic, herbs, and tomatoes, topped with mussels and crispy calamari ($20); or the Indonesian gado-gado bowl with chicken or shrimp in rice, veggies, and peanut sauce, with sweet soy, cilantro, peanuts, and "O-rings" ($13–17). Set in blink-and-you-disregard-it building on the way onto the island, its interiors are as zesty as the menu, with bright umbrellas and wafting fabric curtains throughout. Open for dinner Wed.–Mon. 6–10 PM, and Sun. for brunch 11 AM–2 PM.

Just across the highway from Tango is **George's** (1105 E. Hwy. 80, 912/786-9730, www.northbeachgrill.com), the *very* grown-up brother restaurant to North Beach Grill. Come here for an extensive wine list, extra fork and glass settings, and a menu that makes it the most downtown of the Tybee lot. Try the pan-sautéed grouper over bamboo rice with Asian slaw and curry ($26); grilled rack of lamb with spinach, olives, and mushrooms tossed with Israeli couscous on apricot-fig chutney ($24–34, half of full rack). Open for dinner Tues.–Sun.

Dolphin Reef Oceanfront Restaurant (15th St., 912/786-8400, www.oceanplaza.com) sits atop the Ocean Plaza Beach Resort, and offers a hard-to-beat ocean view. Come here for breakfast at sunrise. Breakfast runs about $6.50 on average, $11.95 for steak and eggs; lunch averages $6.50; dinner entrées run about $20.

FORT MCALLISTER STATE PARK

The 1,724-acre site of Fort McAllister State Park (912/727-2339), sits on the southern bank of the Great Ogeechee River in the former Colonial town of Sunbury and is home to one of the Confederacy's best-preserved earthwork fortifications. Because its sand berms simply tumbled back into place after each cannon blast—unlike the shattering brick walls of Fort Pulaski—Fort McAllister didn't fall until December 13, 1864, when Sherman finally took the fort in a fixed bayonet charge, a bloody and fittingly dramatic conclusion to his infamous March to the Sea.

But McAllister didn't go easy. In fact, the fort had already fended off a brutal March 1863 Union bombardment, during which the only casualty was the company's mascot, a house cat (duly noted in the fort's log). When Fort McAllister finally did fall in 1864, the Union fleet was able to sail clear up to Savannah, providing supplies to Sherman's troops and eliminating their need to expend men elsewhere to keep supply lines open.

Granted, while earthwork fortifications may have lasted better than many of their brick counterparts, they don't always prove quite as dramatic as historic sites, but McAllister has been nicely restored. The fort is worth a visit or a stay over at one of its 64 car-camping sites. If you want to get away a bit, try its primitive campsite. The park also features a small Civil War museum, boat ramps and a dock, and 4.3 miles worth of trails. You can also rent canoes and kayaks here. Call to reserve a fort tour. To get there from I-95, take Exit 90 and head east for 10 miles on Spur 144.

OSSABAW ISLAND

Tabby slave quarters from Ossabaw's plantation years still stand on the island, but perhaps this 25,000-acre island's most exciting history began in 1976, when, after years as a private hunting club, it was designated Georgia's first Heritage Preserve. Today the largely closed-to-the-public island features nine miles of pristine beaches. Alligators, beavers, and minks share the island with wood storks, bald eagles, and feral pigs. The good news is that not only does the Ossabaw Foundation lead programs for naturalists and artists, but boaters can also use the beaches to the high-water mark without a permit. Bradley Point on Ossabaw Sound is a popular landing spot.

BRUNSWICK AND THE GOLDEN ISLES

When the Spanish used the term Golden Isles, they referred to the amber waves of marsh grass on St. Simons, Little Saint Simons, Jekyll, and Sea islands. Although some today use the term to refer to as many as 11 islands along the Georgia coast, most islanders use the term to refer only to the 4 islands. This is the definition I'll use, although this chapter covers not only the Golden Isles but also the stretch southward to the Cumberland Sound (with a brief trip across the Florida border to Fernandina), northward to the mainland town of Darien, and westward into the lush Okefenokee Swamp.

As is the case throughout most of the Sea Island Coast, the bulk (but not all) of known history is found along the mainland. Darien, founded by James Oglethorpe and stocked with Highland Scots ready to fight the Spanish, is the state's second-oldest planned community, after Savannah. Today, it continues as a fishing village but is best known to the average traveler for its outlet shops on I-95. Historic Brunswick serves as the gateway to the Golden Isles, but the shrimping town—the second-largest city along the Georgia coast—is a worthwhile, low-key destination in its own right.

Each of the Golden Isles has its own flavor. By far, St. Simons offers the most restaurants, nightclubs, and shops. Jekyll Island offers the historic Jekyll Island Club Hotel and several family-oriented beaches. Little Saint Simons and Sea Island, although largely undeveloped, both offer wide beaches and unique, old-style resort lodging.

© SEAN SLINSKY

PLANNING YOUR TIME

If you're heading to this part of the Georgia-Florida coastline, most likely you're not looking to rush anywhere and you hope to avoid a crowd wherever you land. For starters, pick your Golden Isle of choice: **St. Simons** for its family-friendly feel, with the pier and village area; **Jekyll** for its long beaches, tame camping grounds, and its historic hotel and old mansions; **Sea Island** for the swanky Cloister and its exclusive, upscale resort-island feel; or **Little St. Simons,** for its remote, undeveloped offerings—a luxe lodge surrounded only by nature and water. No matter where you pick you'll get Southern hospitality, fresh local seafood, and gorgeous live oaks at every turn.

Coming or going, head to **Brunswick** for a peek at Savannah's Southern cousin, laid out in 1771, and pillage its bountiful antique shops along Gloucester and Newcastle streets. If you've got the time, continue south for an outdoor camping adventure, spent either with the wild horses on the virtually undeveloped and thoroughly protected **Cumberland Island National Seashore,** or with the gators in the vast maze of waters and bobbing islands known as the **Okefenokee Swamp.**

HISTORY

Archaeology points to human habitation long before the arrival of the Spanish in the 1500s. Early island dwellers fished, traded with other tribes from as far away as Lake Superior, and built shell mounds at Gascoigne Bluff and Cannon's Point on St. Simons and near the Hampton River on the northeast end of Sea Island. Finds during large-scale Works Progress Administration (WPA) excavations during the Depression uncovered some 150 Native American burial sites, including one of a presumably much-revered individual buried with an apron of strung olive shell beads. Researchers shipped many of the artifacts uncovered in these digs to the Smithsonian in Washington, but you'll find some worthwhile displays in local museums.

A branch of the Creek family, the Guale people lived on the islands when the Spanish arrived. Although Desoto and some 600 men had trekked through Georgia in early 1540, the trip convinced the Spanish that no gold fields, much less *cities* of gold, were forthcoming. Consequently the Spanish soon lost interest in immediately settling North America because all of the gold seemed to be southward.

Jean Ribaut's establishment of a French Huguenot colony near modern-day Jacksonville in 1564 made the Spanish reconsider. After all, control of the coast was essential if they wanted to protect their galleons loaded with South American gold as they cruised up the Gulf Stream on their way to the strong winds that would sweep them home to Spain. Unless they wanted their treasures looted by the likes of Britain's Sir Francis Drake, the Spanish needed to establish and maintain a strong foothold on the American East Coast.

As a first step, an expedition led by Pedro Menendez de Avila slaughtered Ribaut's Protestant colony along the shores of St. John's River. Menendez also reinforced the base at St. Augustine and sent out Spanish Jesuit priests (and later, the Franciscans) to spread Roman Catholicism to the Native Americans by planting missions in or near each of the larger coastal Indian villages. Reaching from southern Florida as far north as modern-day Port Royal, South Carolina, more than 70 Catholic missions eventually took root. Indians were taught new farming methods as well as Christian doctrine. Small contingents of Spanish soldiers accompanied each missionary as a sort of rudimentary police force.

By 1570, the village of Santa Elena, on Parris Island near modern-day Beaufort, South Carolina, flourished as the capital of all La Florida Province. Even after a 1576 raid by Drake sent the Santa Elenans packing to the safety of St. Augustine, Spain still considered all of modern-day Georgia, South Carolina, and North Carolina to be her rightful domain, but since nobody else was actively attempting to settle the area, Spain spent the late 16th and early 17th centuries fortifying St. Augustine against the British.

And the British were coming. By 1670, England had established Charles Town (Charleston),

HIGHLIGHTS

◖ **Brunswick's Old Town National Register District:** Downtown Brunswick is getting a new life as its Newcastle and Gloucester streets are filled with the area's best antique shops and a host of restaurants, set in a charming portside setting with roots back to the 1770s (page 206).

◖ **The Village:** The quiet Golden Isle of St. Simons still charms in a distinctly Southern way, thanks to its old fishing pier—the social hub at sunset—and collection of locally owned long-standing village area shops, restaurants, and pubs (page 210).

◖ **Jekyll Island Club Hotel:** This Golden Isle was once the playground for the Rockefellers and their ilk; visit their onetime-club–turned–hotel and its surrounding historic district to see how America's barons used to entertain themselves (page 221).

◖ **Cumberland Island National Seashore:** Take the ferry to this protected and nearly undeveloped island, home to wild horses, armadillos, deer, and a wide spectrum of Sea Island flora. Overnight here and you'll see how life on a barrier island once was (page 230).

◖ **Okefenokee Swamp:** To truly get away from it all—except gators, cypress trees, waterfowl, and a maze of swamp rivers, lakes, and ponds—head to this refuge for a canoe trip or overnight camping (page 233).

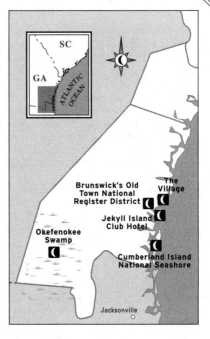

LOOK FOR ◖ TO FIND THE BEST SIGHTS, ACTIVITIES, DINING AND LODGING.

and in 1721, the Crown, having finally taken royal control of Carolina from its ineffective lords proprietors, established Fort King George, near modern-day Darien, manned by a garrison of "invalids"—debilitated soldiers from England—and led by South Carolina's Indian war veteran, "Tuscarora Jack" Barnwell. By 1728, the fort was evacuated for the one at Port Royal, which was easier to defend and closer to the growing town of Beaufort.

In 1733, James Oglethorpe founded Savannah as a self-sustaining, nonmilitary buffer for Charles Town. The new town grew so quickly that within a few years Oglethorpe turned south, now worried about creating a buffer for Savannah. In 1736, he established some 177 Scotch Highlanders at the southern edge of the English-American frontier in what is now Darien. Six years later, Oglethorpe and his men turned back a Spanish attack on St. Simons Island, in the Battle of Bloody Marsh. Because it ended Spanish attempts at possession north of Florida, assuring English dominance in North America, this little-known battle is arguably one of the most important in American history.

During the American Revolution, many Georgians fled south into northern Florida

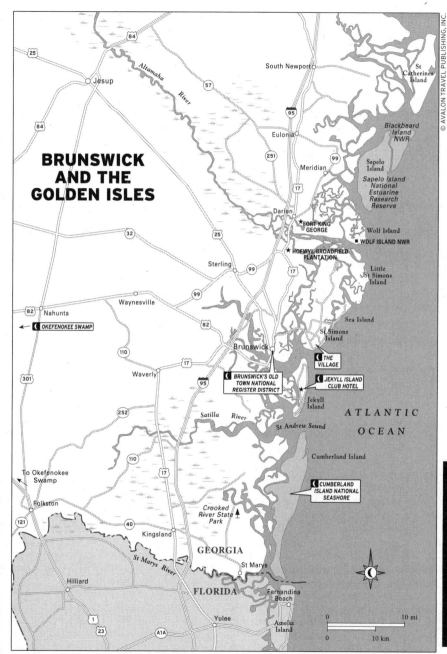

© AVALON TRAVEL PUBLISHING, INC.

BRUNSWICK AND THE GOLDEN ISLES

Jesup

Altamaha River

South Newport

St Catherines Island

Eulonia

Blackbeard Island NWR

Meridian

Sapelo Island

Sapelo Island National Estuarine Research Reserve

Darien

★ FORT KING GEORGE

Wolf Island

■ WOLF ISLAND NWR

★ HOFWYL-BROADFIELD PLANTATION

Sterling

Little St Simons Island

Waynesville

Sea Island

Nahunta

◄ OKEFENOKEE SWAMP

St Simons Island

Brunswick

THE VILLAGE

BRUNSWICK'S OLD TOWN NATIONAL REGISTER DISTRICT

JEKYLL ISLAND CLUB HOTEL

Waverly

Jekyll Island

ATLANTIC OCEAN

Satilla River

St Andrew Sound

Cumberland Island

To Okefenokee Swamp

CUMBERLAND ISLAND NATIONAL SEASHORE

Folkston

Crooked River State Park

Kingsland

GEORGIA

St Marys River

St Marys

FLORIDA

Fernandina Beach

Hilliard

Yulee

Amelia Island

0   10 mi

0   10 km

MARSHES OF GLYNN

*By a world of marsh that borders a world
of sea.
Sinuous southward and sinuous north-
ward the shimmering band
Of the sand-beach fastens the fringe of
the marsh to the folds of the land.
The world lies east: how ample, the marsh
and the sea and the sky!
A league and a league of marsh-grass,
waist-high, broad in the blade,
Green, and all of a height, and unflecked
with a light or a shade,
Stretch leisurely off, in a pleasant plain,
To the terminal blue of the main.
Oh, what is abroad in the marsh and the
terminal sea?
Somehow my soul seems suddenly free*

*From the weighing of fate and the sad
discussion of sin,
By the length and the breadth and the
sweep of the marshes of Glynn
Ye marshes, how candid and simple and
nothing-withholding and free
Ye publish yourselves to the sky and offer
yourselves to the sea!
Tolerant plains, that suffer the sea and
the rains and the sun,
Ye spread and span like the catholic man
who hath mightily won
God out of knowledge and good out of
infinite pain
And sight out of blindness and purity out
of a stain.*

–Sidney Lanier, 1870

to escape British persecution. After the American Revolution, Florida, which had been a base of British operations, transferred back into Spanish hands, and the former American patriot refugees trickled back into the St. Marys and Brunswick areas, where they resettled. Soon, long-staple (or "Sea Island") cotton became the area's prime crop and the key to wealth for the many island plantation owners. Because cotton farming was a labor-intensive process, more slaves than ever were brought to the region.

The (after 1809) illegal and largely unpopular slave trade continued all the way up to the War Between the States along the Golden Isle plantations. During the war, Confederates quickly gave up the idea of holding fortified St. Simons Island. As they evacuated in late 1861, they destroyed the old St. Simons Lighthouse, hoping to make things more difficult for Union ships along the coast. As men up and down the sparsely populated coastline marched off to join the Confederate Army, the towns along the coast fell to the Union with ease. In Federal hands for most of the war, southeast

Georgians could at least take solace in knowing that Camden County's own General William Hardee and his mightily outnumbered army was irritating Sherman's troops—if not exactly repelling them—with skirmish after skirmish along the Northerners' flaming trail through Georgia and the Carolinas.

Sherman temporarily gave freed slaves custody of the Sea Islands immediately after the Union took possession of Savannah. Freed slave Tunis Campbell declared himself governor of the new Black Republic, but President Andrew Johnson returned the land to its former owners after the war.

In 1868, a pair of former slaves on St. Simons gave birth to Robert Abbott, who, at age 27, moved to Chicago to found the *Chicago Defender*, the nation's first black newspaper and an important voice for civil rights in the first quarter of the 20th century.

While Robert Abbott was a young boy playing and working on St. Simons Island, across the water in Brunswick, tubercular Confederate veteran and former POW poet Sidney Lanier stayed with his wife's family in Brunswick.

The salt air was good for him, and he felt especially good when he'd ride in his carriage by himself and stop at the edge of the broad, vast marshes. While doing this, he was inspired to write his most famous poem, "The Marshes of Glynn."

As the Industrial Revolution powered up, the enormous amounts of money made in the Northern states, coupled with the continued economic devastation in the South, brought Northerners south to exploit the cheap vacation spot. Sometimes the wealthy would buy up entire islands for themselves as retreats for hunting and fishing. In 1886, a group of multimillionaires purchased Jekyll Island and formed the Jekyll Island Club. For the next 55 years, the club's power and wealth would shape local life, providing plentiful service jobs for locals. The Jekyll Island Club held an estimated one-sixth of the world's wealth at one point.

A devastating hurricane, the "Big Blow of '98," flooded the Brunswick coast under up to 12 feet of water, killing 179 people. But this slowed down the area's popularity as a resort area only for a season or two. By 1908, timber mogul Philip Berolzheimer had purchased Little Saint Simons Island as a private hunting and fishing preserve, and in the 1920s Howard E. Coffin, inventor of the Hudson automobile, built The Cloister, a fantastic luxury hotel on Sea Island. The causeway connecting the mainland and St. Simons opened on July 11, 1924, making the island accessible to the middle class far more than before, and allowing for building up St. Simons' commercial district.

German submarine activity off the coast during World War II closed down the Jekyll Island Club, even as it brought new life to Brunswick, which helped the Allied effort by constructing 99 447-foot "Liberty ships" in just two years to replace those lost to Axis torpedoes. A new naval air station was erected in Brunswick as part of a coast-wide system, and blimps flew from Brunswick over the sea lanes, searching for German U-boats. By war's end, Brunswick's blimps had escorted more than 98,000 craft safely across this stretch of the coast without losing a single ship or aircraft.

In more recent years, as Atlanta has grown a large upper class in search of second homes, and as the federal interstate system has brought most of the East Coast within a day's drive of the Golden Isles, tourism and real estate have joined shrimping and lumber as major industries in the region.

Brunswick

Brunswick is a shrimping town. It may be, logistically, the "Gateway to the Golden Isles," and it may be that John Villani named it as one of the *Top 100 Small Art Towns in America,* but if you really want to understand Brunswick, get down to the docks on Bay Street around 3 PM and watch the local fishermen unloading the day's glistening catch.

That's not to say Brunswick doesn't have more to it than that. First off, Brunswick's great claim to fame is that it is the birthplace of "Brunswick Stew," that tomato-based side dish that has graced many a plate of barbecue across the South. (True, by some accounts the first potful was actually brewed on St. Simons, but it's called *Brunswick* stew, after all.) The town honors this important identity with the annual Brunswick Stewbilee each year.

Even so, Brunswick doesn't take itself too seriously. Sure, it's a Colonial town, begun just four years before the opening gunshots of the American Revolution by no less than Georgia founder James Oglethorpe, and named for Braunsweig, Germany, ancestral home of King George II. In the early days, Brunswick's potential for growth seemed almost unlimited. By 1789, President George Washington named it as one of the new nation's top five most important ports. Even the devastating "Big Blow of 1898," which put downtown under six feet of water, didn't dampen

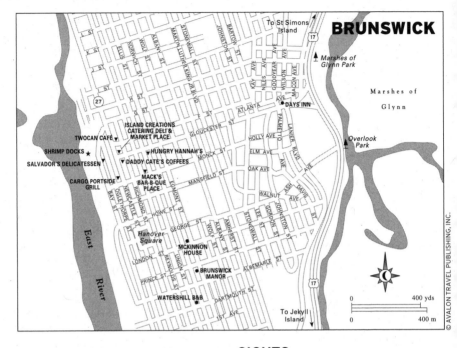

BRUNSWICK

To St Simons Island

Marshes of Glynn Park

Marshes of Glynn

DAYS INN

Overlook Park

ISLAND CREATIONS CATERING DELI & MARKET PLACE

TWOCAN CAFÉ

SHRIMP DOCKS

SALVADOR'S DELICATESSEN

HUNGRY HANNAH'S

DADDY CATE'S COFFEES

CARGO PORTSIDE GRILL

MACK'S BAR-B-QUE PLACE

Hanover Square

MCKINNON HOUSE

BRUNSWICK MANOR

WATERSHILL B&B

East River

To Jekyll Island

0   400 yds
0   400 m

© AVALON TRAVEL PUBLISHING, INC.

Brunswick's spirits. As late as 1907, town officials were declaring that Brunswick was ready to explode and take its place beside the Savannahs and Charlestons of the world.

It didn't happen. But the many ornate homes and quaint cottages erected during the town's boom in the late 19th and early 20th centuries did contribute a Victorian charm to the town. And now, a minor rebirth is taking place most evidently along Newcastle Street, a walkable, riverfront brick "Main Street," which features a couple of good restaurants, a handful of great shops, and an active community calendar.

The **Farmers Market** (1327 Union St., 912/262-6665), held every Tuesday, Thursday, and Saturday 7 AM–5 PM at Mary Ross Waterfront Park, where Gloucester hits Bay Street, brings a lot of life to the area as well. You'll find not only fresh fruits and vegetables here—a nice thing to have around the beach house if you're heading out to one of the islands—but also antiques, arts and crafts, and other flea market flotsam.

SIGHTS
◖ Brunswick's Old Town National Register District
Brunswick's Old Town National Register District, contained by H Street, Newcastle Street, First Avenue, and Martin Luther King Jr. Boulevard, is the section of town General James Oglethorpe laid out into a grid of streets and squares in 1771. Unlike Savannah, Brunswick didn't rename its streets to "Americanize" them after the American Revolution, which is why you'll still see street names like "Prince," "Gloucester," "Hanover," and "Halifax" on the street corners. Even Union Street, which a person might reasonably (but mistakenly) attribute to the Reconstruction days, was actually named during British rule to celebrate the uniting of England and Scotland.

In the aftermath of several catastrophes, including the "Big Blow of 1898," those Brunswickians who were able to rebuild often rebuilt in the styles of the day, including Victorian, as evidenced by the homes here. Architectural historians consider the **Mahoney-McGarvey House** (1709 Reynolds St.), opposite the courthouse, an important example of Carpenter Gothic architecture, and the **Glynn Academy** (1001 Mansfield St.), the second-oldest public school in Georgia, as two of Brunswick's most notable buildings. The recently restored 1889 **Old City Hall** (1229 Newcastle St., 912/265-4032) is also worth a look.

Hofwyl-Broadfield Plantation State Historic Site

North of Brunswick on Highway 17 (but south of Darien), you'll come across the Hofwyl-Broadfield Plantation State Historic Site (5556 Hwy. 17 N, 912/264-7333), an 1807 rice plantation complex. Here, William Brailsford of Charleston bought land and created a rice plantation amid the cypress swamps. By the time Brailsford and his son-in-law James M. Troup were done, they owned 7,300 acres, 357 slaves, and several homes.

The War Between the States brought a halt to all this feudal splendor, and by 1915, Brailsford's descendants turned their rice plantation into a dairy, which lasted less than 30 years. Fortunately, Orphelia Troup Dent donated the plantation and various period furnishings to the state in 1973. This is neither the grandest plantation you'll find nor the oldest, but it is one of the most representative of its time and place. The parks open Tues.–Sat. 9 AM–5 PM, Sun. 2–5:30 PM. The last tour of the day is given at 4 PM. To get there, look for the signs between Darien and Brunswick on Highway 17, or take I-95 Exit 42 and head one mile east. Admission is $5 adults, $4.50 seniors, $2.50 kids 6–18, and free for those under 6.

SHOPPING

Take Gloucester Street to Newcastle Street to get to the main shops. Two of the best are **Hattie's** (1527 Newcastle St., 912/554-8677), a terrific bookstore for kids and adults, and **The Market on Newcastle** (1624 Newcastle St., 912/554-7909), home to piles upon piles of cool home goods, gift books, cards, furniture, stationery, and knickknacks, lots with a French flair.

Off Newcastle, the bounty of Brunswick's shopping is its antique malls. With the largest selection in the Golden Isles area and the best prices, too, it's a hunt-and-bargain heaven. The best collection of former warehouses loaded to the rafters is the trifecta at the corner of Gloucester Street and Martin Luther King Jr. Boulevard. There, you'll find **Piddlers** (1505 Martin Luther King Jr. Blvd., 912/265-0890); **Victorian Place** (1412 Gloucester St., 912/265-3175); and **Rags & Riches** (1503 Gloucester St., 912/261-0771). There are other worthwhile shops along Newcastle and Gloucester streets, so let your schedule and eye guide you. Get beyond the shabby look of the buildings and you'll score some of the best finds in the region.

ACCOMMODATIONS
Less Than $50

In the few-frills department, the **Palms Motel** (2715 Glynn Ave./Hwy. 17, 912/265-8825, $49) offers 32 rooms, a pool, and microwaves (in most rooms).

© SEAN SLINSKY

For the best steals and deals, head to Brunswick for the region's top antique shops.

For $20 a night and $15 each night thereafter, you can get a one-of-a-kind experience by staying in one of the tree houses at **The Hostel in the Forest** (mile marker 11, Hwy. 82, 912/264-9738, www.foresthostel.com), about 10 minutes west of town. Started in 1975, it's much more than your typical hostel, thanks to its glass house (for meditation, yoga, writing), sweat lodge, and labyrinth walk. You can canoe in the lake, hang out on the floating dock, swim in a spring-fed pool, and hike two miles of trails. Come for a retreat to commune with nature, as quiet hour begins at 11 PM, and excessive drinking is not permitted. Reservations are required, and pets and children are not allowed.

$50-100

Downtown you'll find the **Brunswick Manor** (825 Egmont St., 912/265-6889, www.brunswickmanor.com, $95–100). The 19th-century bed-and-breakfast offers four rooms featuring Victorian decor, a hot tub, full breakfast, and afternoon refreshments. The Victorian **McKinnon House** (1001 Egmont St., 912/261-9100, www.mckinnonhousebandb.com, $100 on average) offers three rooms in a Queen Anne–style home, featuring elegant furnishings. A "gourmet" breakfast is served, along with afternoon refreshments. No smoking is allowed indoors.

If you're traveling with children or simply looking for something less personal, the **Days Inn** (2307 Gloucester St., 912/265-8830, www.the.daysinn.com) downtown features 95 rooms for $53–85. Free continental breakfast is available, and the hotel is located right across from a playground, a public tennis court, and an exercise court. Farther out by I-95 is the **Quality Inn** (125 Venture Dr., 888/394-8495, www.qualityinnbrunswick.com, $80), with 83 rooms, 50 cottages, and 52 suites.

$100-150

The **WatersHill Bed and Breakfast** (728 Union St., 912/264-4262, www.watershill.com, $85–115) features five "old South" furnished rooms and landscaped gardens with a pond in back, home to the home's guardian goldfish, Esther and Fernando. Weather permitting, you can take your continental breakfast on the veranda. Bicycles are available for use.

FOOD
Breakfast and Lunch

Lunchtime offers a few possibilities. For the best paninis (with caramelized onions and sautéed peppers), and terrific sauces like jalepeño mayo, and tomato-pesto cream), try **Island Creations Catering Deli & Market Place** (1430 Newcastle St., 912/264-9899). Sandwiches average $7. To have a white-linen experience, visit **Twocan Café** (1618 Newcastle St., 912/280-0899, www.twocancafe.com) for crab cakes, shrimp and fish, salads, pimiento cheese, and fried green tomatoes. Average prices are $8. Open for lunch Mon.–Sat. For the complete opposite experience, **Willie's Wee-Nee Wagon** (3599 Altama Ave., 912/264-1146) serves the much-lauded Willie Burger. For some time, Willie's has offered $500 to anybody who can find a better pork chop sandwich, and nobody has collected the prize. Expect to pay $2 for a hotdog, $5 for a burger, $5 for a steak.

Barbecue

Talk to local Brunswickians, and a handful of names get the raves when it comes to BBQ. Walk from the historic district to locally renowned **Mack's Bar-B-Que Place** (1402 Reynolds St., 912/264-1065), or check out **Sonny's Real Pit Bar-B-Q** (5328 New Jesup Hwy., I-95 Exit 36B, 912/264-9184). **❰ The Georgia Pig** (912/264-6664) is a great place to hit on the way in off I-95 Exit 29 at Highway 17. Apparently unfazed by the demise of his own kin, the pig serves up pulled pork, ribs, beef, and sausage for dinner and lunch, every day of the week. For $10 and under, get a platter or BBQ sandwich at any of these.

Seafood and Southern Cooking

The **❰ Cargo Portside Grill** (1423 Newcastle St., 912/267-7330, www.cargoportsidegrill.com) is powered by a former Atlanta owner who serves its award-winning crab

BRUNSWICK STEW

Brunswick Stew most often plays Festus to barbecue's Marshal Dillon, but it has also been known to consort with fried shrimp and other dishes. Done wrong, it tastes like clumpy tomato-based barbecue sauce; done right it's a Sea Island classic. Here's how to do it right:

Ingredients:
3-lb. chicken
1 lb. lean beef
1 lb. lean pork
3 medium onions, chopped

Place meat in large pot. Season with salt and pepper. Add onions and cover with water. Cook for several hours, until the meat falls from the bones. Remove from heat and allow to cool. Shred the (cooled) meat and return it to the stock. Then add:

4 16-oz. cans of tomatoes
5 teaspoons of Worcestershire sauce
21 oz. (1½ bottles) of ketchup
1 tablespoon of Tabasco
2 bay leaves
6 oz. of chili sauce
½ teaspoon of dry mustard
½ stick of butter
Cook this for an hour. Stir it occasionally. After an hour, add:

3 small diced Irish potatoes
32 oz. of small butter beans or lima beans
32 oz. of cream-style corn
15 oz. of small English peas

Cook slowly until thick.

© SEAN SLINSKY

Brunswick stew is celebrated in Brunswick during the annual cook-off festival.

cakes, seafood, salads, and cuts of meat. It's one of the best restaurants in the Golden Isles area. The flash-fried catfish has a sesame crust, and is served in cherry miso sauce and jalepeño tartar, with jicama and snow pea slaw, and sticky rice. Try the Georgia peach pound cake for dessert—it's grilled warm in butter, then drizzled with Jack Daniels caramel sauce, topped toasted pecans, and served with a scoop of vanilla ice cream. Entrées average $20. Open Tues.–Sat., dinner only.

For something authentically Southern, head out of Brunswick, north on Highway 17 or I-95 until you hit Route 57 at Eulonia. Take it toward Townsend, and at the Sapelo River you'll come to **Pelican Point Restaurant and Lounge** (Sapelo Dr., 912/832-4295, www.pelicanpointseafood.com), favored by many locals as the best seafood in the area. They open at 5 PM daily (Sun. at noon) when the boats come in, so you know the fish and shrimp are fresh. The place also offers a beautiful view of the river. Entreés range $16–24; the buffet is $24.

For something closer in to Brunswick, you might try **Mudcat Charlie's** (250 Ricefield Way, 912/261-0055) at Highway 17 and Two-Way Fish Camp. Come prepared for fresh fish and better-than-average steaks. Lunch averages $7, dinner averages $15. Open daily for lunch and dinner.

INFORMATION

If you're traveling I-95, you'll come to **Brunswick-Golden Isles Visitors Center** outposts between Exits 38, 36, and 29, where attendants can make reservations for you. If you're already in town, head over to the main center (2000 Glynn Ave., 912/264-5337)

for maps, coupons, and information. The **Brunswick and the Golden Isles of Georgia Convention and Visitors Bureau** operates out of the Brunswick-Golden Isles Chamber of Commerce (4 Glynn Ave., 912/265-0620 or 800/933-2627, www.bgivb.com), near the St. Simons Causeway in Brunswick. You can also get maps and pamphlets in any one of their three welcome centers: on St. Simons (in Neptune Park in the Village), on I-95 South (between Exits 42 and 38), or in Brunswick, at the corner of Glynn Avenue and the St. Simons Island/F. J. Torras Causeway. You'll also find a visitors center (901 Downing Musgrove Causeway, 877/453-5955, www.jekyllisland.com) specific to Jekyll Island just after your cross the causeway and come onto the island.

St. Simons Island

Although nobody would ever confuse it for Hilton Head, much less Myrtle Beach or Fort Lauderdale, St. Simons is known as the commercial Golden Isle. If you're looking to stay at the beach and want to be able to walk or bike to a host of restaurants, bars, and shops, this is where you want to go.

The British first occupied the island in their attempt to stem Spanish expansion north from Florida. The island was home to two forts, Fort St. Simons on the south end of the island—where the lighthouse now stands—and Fort Frederica, at the island's northern end. A road, generally following today's Frederica road, cut six miles through the dense, marshy woods to connect the two.

In addition to the important English-Spanish Battle of Bloody Marsh, St. Simons has witnessed other history as well. The oak trees used to build the famous frigate the USS *Constitution*—more famous as "Old Ironsides"—were harvested here and loaded into ships at Gascoigne Bluff (to your left as you enter the island), in the last decade of the 18th century. In fact, after the cotton plantations were destroyed after the Civil War, lumber got St. Simons' residents through the latter part of the 19th century.

Before long, people began to settle the island in earnest, and ferry service ran between Brunswick and St. Simons. The area near where the ferry used to land at the southern end of the island built up into what is called "The Village" today, and it's here that you'll find many of the island's restaurants and most of its charm.

SIGHTS
◖ The Village

The heart of St. Simons centers on The Village, which includes a horseshoe of longtime local stores (a hardware shop, a toy store, and used-book store included), a handful of laid-back, local-flavored restaurants, **The Pier** (a popular public fishing and strolling spot), and the **St. Simons Island Lighthouse.** Here's where families come during the summer after a day on the beach to play a round of minigolf, enjoy a scoop of ice cream, and watch the sunset.

St. Simons Island Lighthouse

The 104-foot lighthouse (101 12th St., 912/638-4666, www.saintsimonslighthouse.org), built

BRUNSWICK AND ST SIMONS ISLAND

© AVALON TRAVEL PUBLISHING, INC.

THE CLOISTER

Sea Island

SEA ISLAND DR

FORT FREDERICA NATIONAL MONUMENT

CHRIST CHURCH

FREDERICA RD

SEA ISLAND RD

Dunbar Creek

BLOODY MARSH NATIONAL MONUMENT

East Beach

Massengale Park

OCEAN BLVD

SEAWATCH

THE KING & PRINCE HOTEL

SEA GATE INN

DEMERE RD

LIGHTHOUSE

ATLANTIC OCEAN

Frederica River

St Simons Island

FREDERICA RD

DEMERE RD

KINGS WAY

EPWORTH BY THE SEA

QUEEN'S COURT

VILLAGE INN AND PUB

ST SIMONS INN

THE LODGE AT SEA ISLAND

THE VILLAGE

PIER

VISITORS CENTER

St Simons Sound

Jekyll Island

Lanier Island

ST SIMONS CAUSEWAY

Mackay River

Back River

To Darien

1 mi

1 km

0

F J TORRAS CAUSEWAY

Marshes of Glynn Park

Overlook Park

US 17

OCEAN HWY

Brunswick

ALTAMA AVE

4TH ST

MLK JR BLVD

GLOUCESTER ST

ALBEMARLE ST

BAY ST

GLYNN AVE

4TH AVE

US 17

EGMONT ST

NEWCASTLE ST

US 25

4TH ST

To Jekyll Island

Brunswick River

Brunswick

SEE "BRUNSWICK" MAP

BRUNSWICK AND THE GOLDEN ISLES

© SEAN SLINSKY

Find the oldest church (1888) on St. Simons at Epworth By The Sea, a present-day Methodist retreat with low-priced accommodations for visitors of any denomination.

in 1872 and photogenic as ever, is a St. Simons landmark, and yep, you can climb up to the top. This is the second lighthouse to grace the site; the first was erected in 1810 on the site of the former Fort St. Simons, which used to anchor the southern half of the island for the British. In 1742, the Spanish captured this fort, which was much larger than Fort Frederica on the north end, and the British survivors fled to Fort Frederica, where they joined the troops garrisoned there. The combined groups of Englishmen then marched south to ambush the encamped Spanish mid-island at Bloody Marsh, forcing the Spanish out of Georgia for good. The Lighthouse Museum next door doubles as a gift shop for the Coastal Georgia Historical Society. Both museum and lighthouse are open Mon.–Sat. 10 AM–5 PM, Sun. 1:30–5 PM. Rates are $5 adults, $2.50 kids 6–11, free for those under 6.

Fort Frederica National Historical Site

Founded by Oglethorpe in 1736 as a fortress

to hold the southern edge of the English frontier against the Spanish, **Fort Frederica** (6515 Frederica Rd., 912/638-3639, www.nps.gov/fofr) was originally settled with 44 men and 72 women and children. The fort's name came from Prince Frederick, son of King George II. England considered Fort Frederica so strategically important that the Crown built the most expensive British fort in all of North America here to provide seaward protection against Spanish attack on Savannah, just as Darien helped protect along the mainland. That first year, Anglican ministers (and founders of Methodism) John and Charles Wesley visited and held services for Fort Frederica residents under the oaks on Frederica Road at the modern-day site of Christ Church.

The town's residents lived right in the shadow of the fort, but most also owned 50 acres in the surrounding countryside, which they farmed. By the early 1740s, Frederica was home to some 500 citizens. In 1742, Spanish troops did attack, but the English defeated them in what is known as the Battle of Bloody Marsh. This turned back the Spanish for good, securing the eastern American seaboard for British colonization.

In fact, the English success at Bloody Marsh spelled the end for Fort Frederica. With the Spanish threat eliminated, Oglethorpe left for England in 1743, and within six years, Fort Frederica's regiment was formally disbanded. With all the soldiers gone, the local shops soon closed, and before long, Frederica was a ghost town.

It's a stirring feeling, walking in this deserted place where so much human life was lived out, now bled of its cooking smells and voices. Before you tour the site, be sure to take in the dated, but still interesting film at the visitors center to help prime your imagination and bring the tabby foundations and ruins to life. On the fort's well-marked grounds, you can walk right down Frederica Town's Broad Street, past numerous interpretive plaques and building foundations, to the partially standing fort, whose guns used to point into the river below. The barracks, to your right as you face the river, have probably survived best.

On the park's grounds, you can also see a monument to the parents and aunts of black newspaperman Robert S. Abbott, founder of the *Chicago Defender*, who returned in the 1930s to the place of his birth (and his ancestors' former enslavement) to build this obelisk. Park open daily 9 AM–5 PM. Admission is $5 per vehicle or $3 per biker or walker.

Bloody Marsh Battle Site

A detached extension of the Fort Frederica National Monument, this site (in the 1800 block of Demere Rd., 912/638-3639, www.nps.gov) marks the spot where, in 1742, an outnumbered but proactive band of British fighting men left their well-fortified fort and ambushed Spanish troops, who had stacked their arms in a pile and were waiting to attack the English the following morning. The routed Spaniards left, burning what they could on the way back to St. Augustine. The Battle of Bloody Marsh thwarted Spain's last attempt to control the east coast of North America. The free site offers a visitors center. Open daily 9 AM–4 PM.

Slave Houses

In the 1850s, some 14 plantations did a mean business on St. Simons, employing the services of thousands of slaves. As with most slave dwellings, most of the island's field slave cabins have long since burned or rotted away; however, you can see two of the house slave cabins on Gascoigne Bluff, one at the intersection of Frederica and Demere roads, and one at The Methodist Center, Epworth By The Sea (100 Arthur J. Moore Dr., 912/638-8688, www.epworthbythesea.org), on the north end of the island.

The Beach

Because Sea Island and Little Saint Simons Island crowd in front of so much of it, not much of St. Simons actually faces the Atlantic Ocean. The stretch that does is called **St. Simons Beach** or **Massengale Park** (Ocean Blvd., 912/265-0620), and features several miles of oceanfront, picnic tables, and public bathrooms. Open daily 6 AM–10:30 PM.

ENTERTAINMENT AND EVENTS
Nightlife

If you want to dance on St. Simons Island, head over to **Ziggy Mahoney's**, located inside Bennie's Red Barn Restaurant (5514 Frederica Rd. N, 912/634-0999), which features a diverse blend of live music Thurs.–Sat. Doors open at 8 PM, and the music starts at 9 PM. **Rafters Blues and Raw Bar** (315½ Mallory

---

THE THWARTED PARADISE OF CHRISTIAN PRIBER

Fort Frederica was where they brought Christian Priber, a German utopian philosopher who sold all his worldly possessions and disappeared, only to resurface 500 miles away in eastern Tennessee, where he attempted to establish a community based on the idea that all men were (some 41 years before Jefferson would coin the phrase) created equal. Priber's kingdom allowed for no slavery, and tolerated "all crimes. . . excepted murder and idleness." He became something of a legend to the British settlers along the Georgia and Carolina coasts, as traders returned from their meetings with the Native Americans and told of the educated white man who had formed something he was calling the "Republic of Paradise."

Unfortunately for Priber and his followers, Priber's tendency to undermine British authority – and his friendliness to French settlers – brought him into disfavor with Oglethorpe and other British leaders. Oglethorpe's men captured Priber as the leader was traveling to present-day Alabama to unite all Southern Native Americans against the British. He was taken back to Frederica and imprisoned for the rest of his life, which wasn't long.

THE LEGEND OF THE IGBO

In May 1803, a group of Igbo (pronounced "eebo") tribesmen, captured in what's now Nigeria, found themselves prisoners on a ship smuggling fresh African slaves into Georgia. The Igbo successfully mutinied, brought the ship to shore, and marched into a nearby creek, chanting a hymn to Chukwu, the Igbo creator-god, whom they trusted to keep them safe. Many of them drowned, but slaveholders brought the survivors to Cannon's Point Plantation on St. Simons Island, and to Sapelo Island, and the story they told became a local folk legend. Even today, it's said that the spirits of the Igbo still haunt the waters of Dunbar Creek.

St., 912/634-9755, www.raftersblues.com) down in the village features live music (blues, usually) Wed.–Sat.

SHOPPING

Undoubtedly the best place to shop on St. Simons is the village area around the pier. Here you find a small-town mix of longtime local shops that have survived the development-induced decimation that plagues so much of the Sea Island Coast. Your best bet is to park and wander the "U" of stores that surround the pier. As for standout stores, here's a rundown. Buy crabbing and fishing gear from the village hardware shop, **J.C. Strother & Co.** (221 Mallory St., 912/638-8601), which has been in the same spot since 1930, or rent it from **St. Simons Bait & Tackle** (121 Mallory St., 912/634-1888). Buy used, new, and rare hardbacks at **Beachview Books** (215 Mallory St., 912/638-7282), which has been rooted in the same spot since 1977. They also have paperback beach reads, and regional books. Pop into **Frederica Station** (209 Mallory St., 912/638-9400) for souvenirs and random beach gifts. And **Just for Funn Toys** (205 Mallory St., 912/638-3866) has the best toy selection in town. Explore the other stores and you'll find loads of clothing shops (from tourist Ts to fine men's and women's wear), a shell store, and a place that sells the requisite beach-town hermit crabs.

Elsewhere on the island, the Red Fern Village shopping center is a series of one-story, porch-hung buildings with locally owned stores selling artwork, gifts, antiques, clothing, and more just north of the intersection of Federica and Demere roads. You'll find another shopping enclave at the intersection of Sea Island Causeway and Frederica Road with a similar mix of stores.

The two best stand-alone antique shops with booths are **1610 Frederica Antiques** (1610 Frederica Rd., 912/634-1610) and the **Village Mews** (504 Beachview Dr., 912/634-1235).

SPORTS AND RECREATION
Biking

Rent bikes from **Wheel Fun** (www.wheelfun.com); with two locations, one on St. Simons (532 Ocean Blvd, 912/634-0606), and one on Jekyll (60 S. Beachview, 912/635-9801), and options like four-person surreys, coupes, slingshots, choppers, they've got the best offerings in town. (They also rent beach umbrellas, chairs, sand toys, boogie boards, and regular bikes). Open daily 9 AM–sunset.

Diving

Divers (or those who want lessons) should contact the **Island Dive Center** (101 Marina Dr., 912/638-6590, www.islanddivecenter.com) at the Golden Isles Marina on the St. Simons Causeway.

Kayaking and Canoeing

Barry's Beach Service (420 Arnold Rd., 912/638-8053) rents kayaks and offers tours, as does **Ocean Motion Surf Co.** (1300 Ocean Blvd., 912/638-5225). **Southeast Adventure Outfitters** (www.southeastadventure.com) offers rentals and books fall overnight camping trips from its two locations—St. Simons in the Village (313 Mallory St., 912/638-6732), and Brunswick (1200 Glynn Ave., 912/265-5292).

Sailing

Barry's Beach Service (420 Arnold Rd., 912/638-8053) offers sailboat rentals. If you want somebody else to do the tacking, you can charter a sailboat with the **Dunbar Sales** (206 Marina Dr., 912/638-8573, www.dunbaryachts.com) based at the Golden Isles Marina on the St. Simons Island Causeway.

Fishing

Anglers who arrive in the area sans seacraft will find more than 20 charter boat outfits in the Golden Isles region. Offshore boats commonly bring in barracuda, dolphin fish, grouper, jacks, mackerel, marlin, sailfish, sea bass, shark, snapper, and tuna, among others. Call **Golden Isles Charter Fishing Association** (206 Marina Dr., 912/638-7673) at the Golden Isles Marina on the St. Simons Island Causeway, or the **Jekyll Marina** (1 Harbor Rd., Jekyll Island, 912/635-3137). Both can connect you with several experienced fishing charter captains and their craft.

You can fish from the beach along stretches of St. Simons and Jekyll Island. Piers, which are good for float fishing, bottom fishing, and crabbing, are at St. Simons in the Village area and on Jekyll at the north end by the Clam Creek picnic area.

You'll find trout, bass, and flounder from inland piers below the bridge on St. Simons Island Causeway, at Blythe Island Regional Park, and on the Jekyll Island Causeway, near the bridge. And you're free to fish from most of the area's bridges. If a bridge is off-limits, signs will tell you so.

All fishing and crabbing requires state fishing licenses ($3–7) are available at local hardware and fishing supply stores.

Tours

Take a boating nature tour of the salt marshes with **Captain Jeanne or Captain Jim** (912/638-9354, www.marshtours.com), who have been leading groups around the Golden Isles since 1986. Tours are $40 per person, for 4–6 people. Cap and Catherine Fendig lead **Dolphin Tours** (912/638-5678, www.stain-simonstransit.com) around the area, and to Sapelo Island as well. Tours are $20 adults, and $10 children 10 and under.

To learn a little island lore, talk a **Ghost Walk of St. Simons** (912/638-2756, www.ghost-walksofstsimons.com). Rates are $12 adults, $6 kids 12 and under.

ACCOMMODATIONS

Unless you're here primarily to play golf (and possibly even then), the places you'll want to stay on St. Simons are in the charming village at the island's southern tip, with all the shops and restaurants right outside your door, or on the beachfront along Ocean Boulevard. If you're not staying in either one of these memorable locations, you may as well stay in Brunswick. True, you can save a little money by staying in one of the chains at St. Simons Plantation Village or on Frederica Road, but at this point you're going to have to drive to get to the beach anyway, so you may as well stay just over the bridge in Brunswick where it's possible to get rooms for $45 in high season, and where, for the $129 it would cost you to stay at a Hampton Inn on the island, you can stay at a real, historic Brunswick bed-and-breakfast.

$50-100

The exception to this rule is the unique and relatively thrifty **Epworth By The Sea** (100 Arthur Moore Dr., 912/638-8688, www.epworthbythe-sea.org), a Methodist retreat center founded in 1950 that's also open to the general public. Epworth offers 10 motels (not motel rooms, 10 *motels*), and 12 "family apartments." All told, the camp can accommodate up to 1,000 persons at a time. All rooms are individually climate-controlled, and although it doesn't face the ocean, Epworth overlooks the Frederica River and the Sydney Lanier Marshes of Glynn.

The center is named for Epworth, England, childhood home of John and Charles Wesley, founders of Methodism. It's run by the mainstream-to-left South Georgia Conference of the United Methodist Church, and although on-site alcohol and smoking is forbidden, if that doesn't bother you, a stay here will be pretty much like a stay at any other waterfront motel on the island, only cheaper, and with cafeteria-style meals available ($6.25 breakfast, $8.50 lunch, $10.25 dinner).

The center also features a small museum covering Methodist and local history, as well as an athletic field, two river fishing piers, a swimming pool, covered basketball courts, tennis courts, and a beautiful wedding chapel—the oldest standing church on the island (1888). Also on the grounds is a restored tabby slave cabin. If you're coming with a group of 10 or more, you can also reserve time on the camp's extensive ropes course ($22–35, depending on the height and duration), the sort of climbing/swinging/repelling gauntlet that corporate executives and juvenile offenders often endure as a team-building exercise and that might be a memorable experience if you have some friends or family members game to do it. Finally, the center also serves as an Elder Hostel; seniors should call for special rates. Year-round room rates range from $65 for the older, inland rooms to $100 for a spot in the recently added lodge that features private balconies that overlook the water.

Queen's Court (437 Kings Way, 912/638-8459, www.queenscourtmotel.com) is the place to be if you want to stay in the village but want to pay less than $100 per night. The classic old motor court offers 23 rooms for around $56 year-round, near the beach and still within walking distance of the village. The relatively new but quaint 34-room **St. Simons Inn by the Lighthouse** (609 Beachview Dr., 912/638-1101, www.stsimonsinn.com), offers rooms for about $62 in the village, close to all the shops and restaurants, and within view of the lighthouse (you may need to close your blinds). Microwaves and refrigerators are included in each room. Complimentary continental breakfast is served daily.

$100-250

Over on Ocean Boulevard, the **Sea Gate Inn** (1014 Ocean Blvd., 912/638-8661 or 800/562-8812, www.seagateinn.com, $70–125) offers 48 rooms and a pool. This is not a resort hotel, but it is convenient and comfortable. You'll choose between a stay at the Ocean House (facing the ocean) or the Pool House (you guessed it), but both are an easy walk to the water. One feature that might work if you're traveling with a group is to get adjoining rooms, which provides a full kitchen. Pets are allowed for a $10 fee.

The ◖ **Village Inn and Pub** (500 Mallory St., 912/634-6056 or 888/635-6111, www.villageinnandpub.com) is within walking distance of the Pier and lighthouse, and is an enclave of little stucco buildings centered around a small swimming pool. With shell paths, and tiny balconies, it's pretty quaint, and has the most amenities for the best price in its location. There's a complimentary continental breakfast and bar, as well. Rates range $130–220 for a high-season deluxe bedroom.

$250 and Higher

Near the top of the list on St. Simons is the ◖ **King and Prince Beach & Golf Resort** (201 Arnold Rd., 912/638-3631 or 800/342-0212, www.kingandprince.com), a historic hotel on the National Register of Historic Places. Prices run $100–500, more for villas. Amenities include an indoor pool, four outdoor ocean-side pools, and a hot tub. The resort also offers a restaurant known for its seafood, steaks, and Friday-night seafood buffet in the summer, and its weekly Sunday brunch.

At the *top* of the list is **The Lodge at Sea Island Golf Club** (100 Retreat Ave., 912/638-3611 or 800/732-4752, www.seaisland.com), opened in 2001 by the folks who brought you nearby Sea Island's The Cloister. Just to the right of the St. Simons Village pier as you face the water, it's meant to mimic the extravagant haunts of the Gilded Age's nouveau riche tycoons. The five-star lodge includes, among all the other amenities, personal butlers for its guests. The $500–1,000 rooms all feature water or golf views, and, one hopes, some really, really, really comfortable beds.

Vacation Rentals

If you're coming for a week or more, one possibility might be to rent a property like the **Shipwatch Condominiums** (1524 Wood Ave., 912/638-5455 or 888/315-6060, www.resortqueststsimons.com), which offers 30 two-bedroom condos for about $1,400 a week, in-season. Contact **Resort Quest St. Simons** (1440 Ocean Blvd., 912/638-5455 or 888/315-6060, www.resortqueststsimons.com) which has condos and houses for weekly and monthly rentals.

FOOD
Seafood

Just about every restaurant around here sells fresh seafood of some sort, so be sure to check out the following sections even if you definitely have shrimp on your mind. Close to the pier is the **Blue Water Bistro** (115 Mallory St., 912/638-7007), offering seafood and all the major meats. Entrées average $11. Open for dinner only, Mon.–Sat.

Also in the village on St. Simons is ◖ **Barbara-Jean's Restaurant and Bar** (214 Mallory St., 912/634-6500, www.barbara-jeans.com), a great seafood restaurant that makes perhaps the best spicy she-crab soup I've tasted in Georgia. They're known for the soup and their all-crab crab cakes, but they offer a complete country-meets-the-sea menu. This place is bright, friendly, and normally pretty busy. Average $7 for sandwiches and up to $20 for a loaded seafood platter, with plenty of choices for $10. Open after 11 AM daily.

Other seafood fans in the village turn to **Mullet Bay** (512 Ocean Blvd., 912/634-9977, www.mulletbayrestaurant.com), serving shrimp and oyster po'boys, and seafood platters ($11–19), along with salads and even a handful of seafood pastas. Open at 11:30 AM daily.

Although it's a little farther out, ◖ **The Crab Trap** (1209 Ocean Blvd., 912/638-3552, www.saintsimons.com/crabtrap) is well worth the short ride away from the village area. The Trap offers bowls of "Rock'em Sock'em Rock Shrimp" ($6.75), and, in general, a local-flavored, deep-fried-with-hush-puppies menu. Think shrimp- and crab-shell refuse holes in wooden tables, paper menus, and families waiting in line to get a spot and you've got the idea. Open nightly 5–10 PM.

Gnat's Landing (310 Red Fern Village, 912/638-7378) is a little shack of a place over in the Redfern Village shops off Fort Frederica Road. Part laid-back bar, and all-laid back restaurant, it's a great stop for lunch if you're shopping in the area. The gumbo, fish sandwiches, and seafood po'boys, with a side of cheese grits or crunchy sweet slaw are all darn good. Gumbo goes for $4–6, sandwiches are about $8, seafood platters average $15. Open for lunch and dinner nightly.

For those who prefer their fish raw as opposed to fried, there's a sushi bar that's got promising all over it: **Ni Koi** (3415 Frederica Rd., 912/634-2564) is tucked away in the back of Plantation Place shops, but worth the hunt. Hip trappings, cool fish sculptures, and a down-to-earth staff and owner only compliment the menu. While there's a full sushi bar with standard favorites, the entrées are also enticing. Start with the spicy seaweed salad and then try the Ni Koi tuna—panko crusted Ahi tuna with and Asian shiitake slaw. Prices average $16 for main dishes, are $2 per piece of Nigiri sushi, and about $6 per Maki sushi roll. Open for dinner Tues.–Sun.

Steaks and Southern Cooking

◖ **Bennie's Red Barn** (5514 Frederica Rd. N, 912/638-2844, www.benniesredbarn.com), is another old locals' favorite, one that has been around on the other side of the island since 1954, cooking steaks over a wood fire and serving fresh seafood. They serve conch fritters ($5.95), crab au gratin ($14.95), and New York strip steaks ($21.95). Open daily at 6 PM.

The Fourth of May Café and Deli (444 Ocean Blvd., 912/638-5444) features fried, grilled, and blackened seafood, Southern-style vegetables, and a full deli. The date in the restaurant's name, which sends many first-timers wracking their brains for historical significance, celebrates the fact that the restaurant's original three owners all shared the same birthday. Prices range $7 for a big breakfast to $13 for dinner.

◖ **Halyard's** (600 Sea Island Rd., 912/638-9100, www.halyardrestaurant.com) is probably the finest dining experience on the island, and serves its spin on seafood, steaks, and produce with a contemporary flair and a hint of a Southern accent. Grouper is wrapped in bacon, served with horseradish mashed potatoes, watercress, pistachio, and a blueberry; the pork tenderloin is glazed jerk style, over black beans and rice with a mango South Carolina peach chutney. Start with their grilled sausage appetizer, and a bowl of the blue-crab soup. Entrées average $23. Open Mon.–Sat. for dinner.

Barbecue

The **Beachcomber BBQ & Grill** (319 Arnold Rd., 912/634-5699) is easy to miss, as it's barely more than a two-room shack with a screened-in front porch tacked onto the front. But locals and tourists-in-the know seek it out (partly by following the smoke), as it's the most bare-bones authentic barbecue experience on the island. The meat varies (pork, beef, chicken), but the best is the pork, of course. Sides include the regulars (baked beans, slaw, potato salad, fries), and they sell tea, soda, and beer, too. Eat in or take out a family-size portion (pork's $10 per pound, sides go for $3.75 a pint). In-house meals (meat and sides) are just under $8. Open daily for lunch and dinner.

Pigtales Bar-B-Q (122 Longview Center, 912/634-6022) is run by a fellow named "Boomer" and a spin-off from Sweet Mama's (see *Breakfast*), so it maybe be the newest 'cue contender in town, but it's already got a lot going for it. Just beside the Redfern Village shops, it's another great spot for lunch if you're in the area. A barbecue sandwich runs $5, and a plate with seasoned fries and homemade potato salad is $8. Open for breakfast and lunch Mon.–Sat.

Breakfast

Dressner's Village Café (223 Mallory St., 912/634-1217) has the best little breakfast in the village area, though The Fourth of May Café and Deli also serves up some nice fare. Head to the latter if you want to eat outside, and to Dressner's for their creaky floors, tin roof, and cozy quarters. The biscuits here are made from scratch, making the biscuits and gravy special ($2) pretty terrific. Otherwise

think country breakfast (pancakes, home fries and grits, bacon, sausage, cured ham, and eggs every way). One omelet's more than $5, everything else is about $3. Open Mon.–Fri. 7:30 AM–2:30 PM, Sat.–Sun. 8 AM–2:30 PM, and Thurs.–Sat. 5:30–8:30 PM, as well. (Breakfast is only offered during morning breakfast hours.)

For a fast, late breakfast, head to either **Sweet Mama's** (1201 Ocean Blvd., 912/638-9011 or 122 Longview Center, 912/634-6022) location and grab a buttermilk biscuit sandwich, or their $0.50 pork pops (biscuit with cheese, bacon, and sausage). If you're heading to the beach, ask for sandwich to go, and make sure to get a cake bar, too. Breakfast averages about $1, lunch $4. Open Mon.–Thurs. 10 AM–6 PM, Fri.–Sat. 10 AM–9 PM.

Mexican

If St. Simons' Battle of Bloody Marsh had gone the other way, this is how Lowcountry Georgian Cuisine might taste today. A link of the local chain **El Potro Mexican Restaurant** (2205 Demere Rd., 912/634-0703) features fajitas, enchiladas, and all their compadres. Not a bad choice, and it's the best Mexican food in the area. Entrées average $10.

Dessert

In the Redfern Village shopping area is the **Monkey Love Dessert Bar & Gallery** (256 Redfern Village, 921/638-8400, www.monkey-lovefessi.com), where you'll find off-the-wall local art (for sale), chairs sized for grown-ups and kids, occasional live music, and WiFi. Oh, and you'll also score the usual coffee and tea drinks, and the very *unusual* desserts: monkey poop and dookie bars, for instance. The treats are chocolate-covered concoctions of graham crackers, marshmallows, nuts, and more. Most all the treats are less than $3. Open Mon.–Sat. 8 AM–10 PM.

INFORMATION AND SERVICES

The **Brunswick and the Golden Isles of Georgia Convention and Visitors Bureau** operates out of the Brunswick-Golden Isles Chamber of Commerce (4 Glynn Ave., 912/265-0620 or 800/933-2627, www.bgivb.com), near the St. Simons Causeway in Brunswick. Get maps and pamphlets in any one of their three welcome centers on St. Simons (in Neptune Park in the Village), on I-95 South (between Exits 42 and 38), or in Brunswick, at the corner of Glynn Avenue and the St. Simons Island/F. J. Torras Causeway. You'll also find a visitors center specific to Jekyll Island on the Jekyll (Downing Musgrove) Causeway.

LITTLE SAINT SIMONS

One of the last privately owned barrier islands along the Georgia Coast, Little Saint Simons is accessible only by boat. If you're staying here, you'll be staying at ◖ **The Lodge on Little St. Simons Island** (912/638-7472, www.littlessi.com), the only accommodation going. In 2000, the resort received the *Condé Nast Traveler* Reader's Choice Award for "Best Small Hotel in North America." A stay here allows you the opportunity to share an entire 10,000-acre island with just 30 other guests—about as much tropical seclusion as you can hope for without having to appear on a reality-based TV show. The price per night is about what you'd expect: $600 for a double room, meals included.

SEA ISLAND

Formerly home to a Spanish-style mission before the British victory at Bloody Marsh over on St. Simons, Sea Island lay flat as a tortilla after the Civil War destroyed its plantations and loggers unburdened the island of its trees during the rough Reconstruction years. Eventually, the pines grew back, and then the hardwoods, and Yankees with guns and spare time came down here to shoot the wildlife. Finally, in the 1920s, Howard Coffin, inventor of the Hudson automobile, bought the old Retreat Plantation and five miles of Atlantic coastline and built the Spanish-styled resort, The Cloister, which opened to acclaim in 1928. Having weathered the Depression, World War II, and a few hurricanes, ◖ **The Cloister** (100 1st St., Sea Island, 800/732-4752, www.seaisland.com) continues to wow vacationers today with posh rooms, attentive service, first-class meals, and an extensive list of amenities, which include a host of planned activities, lakes, horseback riding, and extensive bird-watching opportunities. And then, there's the private beach. Rooms run more than $600 per night for two, double-occupancy.

At press time, The Cloister was undergoing a *massive*, multiyear overhaul. In fact, the main hotel and enclave was torn down and is being rebuilt. The nearby villas and other units, and the amenities (like the spa and island activities) are still up-and-running. The reconstructed hotel should begin opening in staggered stages in early 2006. Check the hotel website for progress, as all signs point to even more luxury and poshness than before.

Jekyll Island

Jekyll Island was less settled by Georgia's original inhabitants than St. Simons and some of the other Sea Islands. Some of the first Spanish explorers report that the Guale who lived on surrounding islands used Jekyll as a hunting island, and hadn't even come up with a name for the place; others report that they called it "Ospo," which is the name the Spaniards used for as long as they controlled the island. They planted a mission here, the tabby San Buenaventura, around 1566, and helped the Indians by introducing them to new farming methods and tools, including the hoe. In 1680, the British, avenging Spanish attacks on Charles Town, attacked the island. They destroyed the mission and drove off its inhabitants, both Spanish and Native American.

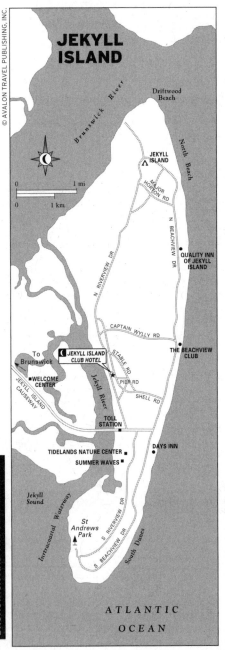

The British didn't resettle the island, however, for many years, which made it a fine spot for pirates looking for a place to hide out and hunt between raids. As is alleged about nearly every other island along the southeast seaboard, Edward "Blackbeard" Teach is said to have buried some treasure on Jekyll Island. If you're ever in the Jekyll woods and come upon a copper hook stuck into a massive live oak, follow the direction that the hook is pointing to find the spot where the treasure lies. Once you find the treasure, contact me, the author, care of Avalon Travel Publishing.

When the British arrived in 1736 to establish a tabby outpost here, they changed the name to Jekyll Island to honor one of Georgia's English sponsors, Sir Joseph Jekyll. One of Oglethorpe's officers, William Horton, established a plantation here, which was later burned by the Spanish, then rebuilt. Perhaps in honor of all those thirsty pirates who had once dwelt here, Georgians built the colony's first brewery here from tabby, and grew the rye for the beer right here on the island. After the Spanish threat disappeared in the 1740s, cotton and indigo plantations began to grow here.

The millionaires began arriving in 1886. After the Revolution, French-American patriot Poulain duBignon had purchased the island and, several generations later, his descendant Josephine duBignon married a New Yorker named Newton Finney. Finney became a financial and social success, and he began to boast to his wealthy Northern friends about the lush vegetation and plentiful game on his wife's family island down in Georgia. The New York financiers took the train down and enjoyed a hunting trip there, and, as friends are wont to do after a successful trip, decided to buy the island for themselves. They paid $125,000 to the duBignon family and began building the clubhouse and the mansions that they called "cottages." Most of them lived here at most from New Year's until Easter each year. Most of the tycoons used to ride down from the North in their plush private cars and then ride a steamer to the island. Others docked their yachts at the

© SEAN SLINSKY

The Jekyll Island Club Hotel was built in 1888, when America's Gilded Age was in full swing.

boathouse dock or anchored in the channel if their crafts were too large and took smaller boats to the dock.

In 1947, after German subs offshore shut down the club during World War II, the state of Georgia purchased the island for $675,000 and made it a state park, under the authority of the Jekyll Island Authority. Consequently, although several hotels and other businesses operate on Jekyll Island, their owners must lease the land from the Authority.

You'll need $3 to gain entry to Jekyll Island; it's not an entrance fee, it's a "parking fee." If you can convince them you'll keep your car moving at all times, maybe you can talk your way out of it; otherwise, come prepared. For more information on Jekyll (like its many festivals), contact the **Jekyll Island Convention and Visitors Bureau** (1 Beachview Dr., 877/453-5955, www.jekyllisland.com), or visit the welcome center (901 Downing Musgrove Causeway), which you pass just as you come onto the island.

SIGHTS
◖ Jekyll Island Club Hotel

The island's star attractions are its historic district (a modest collection of 100-year-old summer homes and services buildings), plus the real gem: the Jekyll Island Club Hotel (371 Riverview Dr., 912/635-2600 or 800/535-9547, www.jekyllclub.com), which opened in 1888, at the height of the Gilded Age. Rarely has so much power been concentrated in such a small place. During any given winter, families worth a collective one-sixth of the world's wealth might have stayed here. The Federal Reserve was formulated, so they say, in a smoky gentleman's meeting in the clubhouse. The hotel's guest rooms once housed Rockefellers and Vanderbilts.

When German U-boats started prowling around along the coast, it was suddenly clear to club members how juicy a target they were making themselves, congregating like this. It was deemed wise to disband the club for the duration. By the end of the war, the members had grown fond of new vacation spots, and the club never reopened. The state of Georgia purchased the island and made it a state park, but the Jekyll Island Club's buildings lay dormant until a vigorous restoration in 1986.

With heart pine floors, ornate woodwork, leaded art glass, and fireplaces everywhere you look, the clubhouse is a rare chance to live the way the tycoons lived, if only for a night or two—and best of all, without their worries. Of course there's a beautiful, nearly Olympic-size, marsh-front pool here, but what makes the club is the croquet course. Get out there with your spats and straw hat, and suddenly you're waiting for Jay Gatsby to bound out from around an oak with an affable, "Hello, old sport."

SHOPPING

Jekyll island is for beaching and kicking back, but not the place to shop, as the pickings are pretty nonexistent. Still, though, you can pick up a souvenir at the **Jekyll Books at the Old Infirmary** (101 Old Plantation Rd, 912/635-3077, www.jekyllbooks.com), particularly if you're looking for books on local lore. You'll find a handful of antiques at **Yesteryear** (271 Riverview Dr., 912/635-3443) in the Jekyll Island Club Hotel.

SPORTS AND RECREATION
Horse Riding and Carriages
Victoria's Carriages & Trail Rides (Island History Center, 912/635-9500) gives carriage tours of the historic district on Jekyll, and leads trail ride through the maritime forest and along the beach. Closed Sun.

Biking
Wheel Fun (60 S. Beachview Dr., 912/635-9801, www.wheelfun.com) rents bikes and surreys, great for exploring an island crisscrossed with separate bicycle paths that wind through gorgeous settings. They also rent other beach gear, like chairs and umbrellas. For a bike (and jogging) map, ask your hotel, or find them in the Jekyll Island Hotel check-in lounge.

Water Park
Summer Waves (210 Riverview Dr., 912/635-2074, www.summerwaves) water park is on the southern end of Jekyll. Tickets are about $15 per day. Closed from after Labor Day weekend until Memorial Day weekend.

Tours
Dolphin Tours (912/638-5678, www.saintsimonstransit.com) leads boat rides around Jekyll. And naturalists from the **Tidelands Nature Center** (100 S. Riverview Dr., 912/635-5032, www.tidelands4h.org) lead a variety of marsh, beach, and maritime forest walks.
   The Jekyll Island History Center (100 Stable Rd., 912/635-4036) leads tram tours of the historical district; the Passport to the Century tour includes entry to two cottages.

ACCOMMODATIONS
Unless you're purely at Jekyll Island to catch rays and waves and check out the babes (and if you are, you're probably over at St. Simons, anyway), try to stay at the Jekyll Island Club Hotel. Nearly all of the island's other lodgings are essentially big, beachfront (or across-the-road) behemoths, and these types of stays are as common as fiddler crabs along the Southern coast; you can find essentially the same thing at Nags Head, Myrtle Beach, Tybee Island, or Jacksonville. Even if you're not wowed by the indulgences of the very rich, a stay at the Club Hotel is—for most of us—a chance to experience a foreign culture and an opportunity to live, for a moment, in the remnants of a bygone era. If you can swing it, you'll likely remember your stay at the Club Hotel for many years to come.

$100-150
Smallest on the island is the two-story, 38-room **The Beachview Club** (721 N. Beachview Dr., 912/635-2256 or 800/299-2228, www.beachviewclub.com, $89–169), situated amid live oaks and featuring good views of the Atlantic. The 71-room **Quality Inn of Jekyll Island** (700 N. Beachview Dr., 912/635-2202 or 800/281-4446, www.jekylislandquality.com), which stands across Beachview Drive from the beach, has rooms starting at $119 in the high season. The **Days Inn** (60 S. Beachview Dr., 912/635-9800, www.daysinn.com) is also right on the beach and definitely one of the best spots for service, cleanliness, and location. High-season rooms start at $119, but call at the last minute, and you can score deals as low as $89.

$150 and Higher
Founded as an exclusive retreat for the wealthiest members of American society, 🄲 **Jekyll Island Club Hotel** (371 Riverview Dr., 912/635-2600 or 800/535-9547, www.jekyllclub.com), hasn't completely forgotten its roots, with room prices starting at $139, but what you'll get for your money is a memorable stay. The main clubhouse is excellent, a recipient of Mobile Four-Star and AAA Four-Diamond awards, and the newer Crane and Cherokee Cottages are beautiful restorations of former millionaires' winter homes. The Spanish-styled, 13-room Crane Cottage is my favorite, built in 1917, with a beautiful, tranquil courtyard (where meals are served). The hotel

also features Victorian teas served daily, a pool bar, carriage rides, horseback riding, a private beach pavilion for guests, and children's programs (seasonal).

Packages, particularly in the off-season, can include meals in the hotel dining rooms (a bed-and-breakfast package in the off-season runs for $178 for two, double occupancy). When you work in the cost of two meals at a local restaurant (and eating here, you're eating at the best on the island, anyway), it's not a bad deal.

Camping

Jekyll Island Campground (1197 Riverview Dr., 912/635-3021 or 866/658-3021, www.jekyllisland.com) is at the north end of the island and has primitive campsites, full-hookup sites, and room for RVs. It's deluxe camping, with water, laundry, showers, propane, phones, a computer room, and a well-stocked general store. (Some sites are handicap accessible). Set under a live-oak canopy, right on the island network of walking and bike paths, and just across the street from a fishing pier and waterfront picnic area, it's tops.

FOOD

You'll find three of Jekyll's most memorable restaurant experiences right where you might expect, on the grounds of the Jekyll Island Club Hotel. For the height of old-school romance, make reservations for dinner by fire and candlelight at ◖ **The Grand Dining Room** (371 Riverview Dr., 912/635-2818); jackets preferred for men at dinner. Or if you would like to save money and still enjoy the high-end ambience, stop by for breakfast (casual dress), when they open the shutters on the banks of windows and the room is flooded with glorious morning light. Breakfast and lunch average $10, dinner about $25–30. Open for breakfast, lunch, and dinner daily.

Perhaps even more romantic, **The Courtyard at Crane** (375 Riverview Dr., 912/635-2600) at the Crane Cottage features Mediterranean cuisine in a quaint courtyard under the stars. Call ahead to make

Latitude 31 is home of the best peach margaritas on the island.

sure it's open because private parties often book it up. Lunch runs about $8–12, dinner $18–28. Open for lunch daily, and dinner Sun.–Thurs. Finally, **Latitude 31** (1 Pier Rd., 912/635-3800, www.latitude-31.com) at the Jekyll Wharf across from the Jekyll Island Club, offers you the chance to dress casually while enjoying—and paying for—a fine dining experience, plus an excellent view of the marshes. Lunch and dinner entrees range $15–20. Open for lunch and dinner Tues.–Sun.

SeaJays Waterfront Café and Pub (1 Harbor Rd., 912/635-3200, www.seajays.com) in the Jekyll Island Marina to the right of the bridge as you enter the island, is a different animal. It has good food, live music Thurs.–Sat. after 7 PM, and it's aimed at Parrotheads. Lunches are inexpensive and focus on sandwiches and salads; dinners (including an "all you care to eat" shrimp boil buffet for $14.95) are good but not remarkable; the prices are not remarkably cheap. They have a nice waterfront deck, however, and if you're staying in the Jekyll Island Club, the Buffett tunes and tie-dye-wearing musicians provide a nice break from formality. Plus, the Kentucky bourbon pecan pie and key lime pie are impeccable. Open daily for lunch and dinner.

If you're looking for breakfast, try the baked goods at **Café Solterra** (371 Riverview Dr., 912/635-2600), which is on the Jekyll Island Club grounds in the main hotel building.

North of Brunswick

DARIEN

Darien packs a lot of history into its diminutive borders. Remember the scene in *Glory,* where the 54th Massachusetts was used to burn and loot a Southern town? That was Darien they were burning. Even so, most American's didn't hear about the town of Darien until Melissa Fay Greene's 1991 nonfiction book, *Praying for Sheetrock,* which detailed life here before desegregation.

British settlers came down to this area as early as 1721, when they established Fort King George as the southern outpost of the British Empire in North America, a garrison to stop attacks against Charles Town. The fort was originally built by men under Colonel John "Tuscarora Jack" Barnwell, who lived at the fort for seven years, battling Spanish and Indian attackers and suffering dreadfully from disease. In 1728, they abandoned the fort, but Oglethorpe, now attempting to protect the new town of Savannah, brought 177 tough-as-nails Scottish Highlanders to settle a town at the site in 1736. Thus, Darien was the second town planned in Georgia. The Highlanders originally called the town *New Iverness,* but, as a reminder of their mission and precarious situation, renamed the town in honor of a previous Highlander settlement in Panama, which had been wiped out by Spanish soldiers in 1697.

When it was founded, Darien's location at the mouth of the Altamaha River placed it at the southernmost tip of the original land grant given to the Georgia Board of Trustees. As with many towns in this area, Darien saw its best days during the lumber boom of the late 1800s and early 1900s, when the town, which was located conveniently at the mouth of the

woods, traversing the Altmaha River, kept several sawmills running and loaded up as many as 30 ships daily for export. Most of its classic Victorian homes were built during this time.

Today, Darien Riverfront Park offers a public boardwalk and docks for fishing and boating.

Fort King George

If your visit to Fort Frederica left you wishing you could see what it looked like before the walls came down, head to Fort King George (1600 Wayne St., 912/437-4770), the first English fort built in Georgia. The fort's palisaded earthworks still exist, and the fort's three-story blockhouse has been rebuilt on its original foundation in accordance with old drawings and plans. Interpreters in handmade period costumes engage in living-history demonstrations, reenact battles, and help explain the ways of days gone by. (The fort is open year-round Tues.–Sat. 9 AM–5 PM, Sun. 2–5:30 PM. Find it three miles east of Exit 49 off I-95.)

Sapelo Island National Estuarine Research Reserve

Darien is also known as the gateway to pristine Sapelo Island National Estuarine Research Reserve (912/485-2251, www.sapeloneer.org) a 6,110-acre reserve—the fourth largest along the Georgia Coast—featuring upland forests, salt marsh, and dunes.

Head to the Sapelo Island Visitors Center (Rte. 1, Box 1500, Darien, 912/437-3224, www.sapeloislandneer.org/visitor_center) on the mainland at the tiny town of Meridian, eight miles east of Darien on Highway 99, and you'll find displays detailing the natural and cultural histories of Sapelo. The center is open Tues.–Fri. 7:30 AM–5:30 PM, Sat.

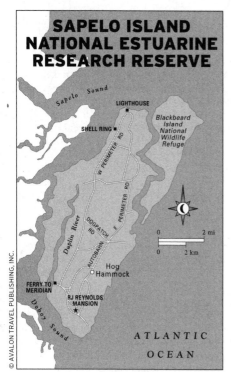

SAPELO ISLAND NATIONAL ESTUARINE RESEARCH RESERVE

© AVALON TRAVEL PUBLISHING, INC.

8 AM–5:30 PM, Sun. 1–5 PM. You can take a ferry from here across the water to the island itself. Sapelo lures about 10,000 visitors a year with its compelling mix of attractions: a brick lighthouse built in 1820 and restored in 1998); a 4,500-year-old Indian shell ring; a small, traditional Gullah/Geechee community (Hog Hammock, population 60); and the South End House, aka R. J. Reynolds Mansion.

To visit, you'll need to take a guided tour with the Georgia Department of Natural Resources. Your tour begins with a half-hour ride to the island aboard the 65-foot *Annemarie*. Group tours are offered Wed. (and Fri. June–Labor Day); they depart at 8:30 AM, return at 12:30 PM, and include a visit to the R. J. Reynolds Mansion. Sat. trips run 9 AM–1 PM and include a tour of the lighthouse. Reservations are required. Tours cost $10, adults, $6, kids 6–18, free for those under 6. On the last

Tues. of every month Mar.–Oct., a special "extended" tour allows you to stay 8:30 AM–3 PM. Individual tours are also offered.

To get to the Sapelo Island Visitors Center, head east off Highway 17 onto Highway 99 for eight miles until you come to Meridian, where you'll find signs for the Sapelo Island National Estuarine Research Reserve.

The Ridge

After you leave Darien, but before you get to Meridian on Highway 99, you'll come to Ridgeville, locally called The Ridge, a bluff overlooking Doboy Sound, where many of the local 19th-century elite—timber barons and harbor pilots, mainly—built their houses high above the water to catch the breezes and escape malaria.

Accommodations and Food

It's possible to stay on Sapelo Island at the antebellum **R. J. Reynolds Mansion** (www.reynolds-onsapelo.com) or at the **Pioneer Campground** near the beach (www.gastateparks.org), but these stays are mainly designed for groups and arranged through the **Sapelo Island National Estuarine Research Reserve** (912/485-2299 or 800/864-7275, www.sapeloneer.org). Some of the private residents of Hog Hammock rent out rooms in trailers and lodges for overnight visitors for less than $100 per couple: call Nancy and Caesar Banks (912/485-2277, www.sapeloweekender.com); or Cornelia and Julius Bailey (912/485-2206), for more information. If you're staying with Hog Hammock residents, you'll be allowed onto the island ferry any day of the week. There are no restaurants or markets on the island, so food arrangements are made with hosts, or you bring your own groceries.

Over in Darien, Jeff and Kelly Spratt, with their kids Hannah and Hank, host **Open Gates Bed and Breakfast** (301 Franklin St., Darien, 912/437-6895, www.opengatesbnb.com), an 1876 frame house on historic Vernon Square. Period antiques fill each of the five guest rooms, and the yard includes a garden, fountain, and swimming pool. Both elder Spratts hold an MS in biology and are involved with wildlife conservation. That means they can answer your questions about local species and good birding spots, that the home's cypress-paneled library features a broad selection of field guides, and that they offer kayak and boat tours of the Altamaha River. But it doesn't mean they can't cook: they serve a full-sized breakfast featuring local shrimp and grits, fresh fruit, and homemade biscuits. In the evenings, they serve wine and cheese.

For good fresh local seafood, the best is still north on Highway 17 or I-95 until you hit Route 57 at Eulonia, where you'll find the riverfront **Pelican Point Restaurant and Lounge** (Sapelo Dr., 912/832-4295, www.pelicanpointseafood.com) and its fresh out-of-the-nets fare. Open 5 PM daily (Sun. at noon).

Information and Tours

For information and the latest tour and charter leads on Darien, Sapelo Island, and Fort King George, contact the **McIntosh County Chamber of Commerce** (105 Fort King George Dr., 912/437-6684, www.mcintoshcounty.com).

Longtime resident James Morrison leads his **Guided Tours of Historic Darien and Coastal McIntosh Co.** (912/437-6808, hjmorrison@aol.com) throughout the area, and offers biking and boating options.

MIDWAY

When they felt that their settlement at Dorchester, near Charles Town, was getting crowded, the children and grandchildren of the independent-minded Congregationalists who had moved down from Massachusetts to settle the burg in the 1690s moved farther down the coast, 30 miles south of Savannah, into the scantily settled region on the Southern frontier. They named the community "Midway" to denote its location smack dab between Savannah and the Highlander community of Darien.

Hardworking and smart with their money, the settlers of Midway cultivated rice and indigo and founded satellite communities

throughout the St. John's Parish. Economically and politically, they dominated the parish.

As the Revolution drew near, St. John's Parish tried to stir up the rest of Georgia to join the movement for independence, but their cries for liberty fell on deaf ears. When Georgia failed to send representatives to the First Continental Congress and stalled at sending them to the second, St. John's Parish sent Dr. Lyman Hall as its own delegate, after first attempting to be annexed to South Carolina.

Two of Georgia's three signers of the Declaration of Independence, Hall and Button Gwinnett, came from St. John's Parish. In 1777, St. John's combined with St. Andrew's and St. James' parishes to become Liberty County.

A battle took place here in Midway in 1778; the British burned Midway's church and several houses and other buildings. In 1792, the present church was completed.

Today, the **Midway Museum** (Hwy. 17, Midway, 912/884-5837), is set in a raised cottage-style home modeled after those that stood in the area in the 18th century. Displays include period furnishings and items related to the original Congregationalists who moved here and the liberty-loving people who descended from them. Hours are Tues.–Sat. 10 AM–4 PM, Sun. 2–4 PM. Rates are $5 adults, $4 seniors, $2 students. Find it one mile north of the intersection of Highway 17 and Highway 84.

ST. CATHERINES ISLAND

With 11 miles of Atlantic Ocean beach, St. Catherines would be any developer's dream come true. Thankfully, this one got away from them; the island is owned and managed by *The St. Catherines Island Foundation* (St. Catherine's Island, 912/884-5002) in cooperation with the Georgia Department of Natural Resources, Georgia Southern Universities, and others. Because the island was apparently formed in two different geologic periods, St. Catherine's features several interesting features, including a 22-foot bluff on the northern end of the island. The New York Zoological Society established its Rare Animal Survival Center here in 1974 and has experimented with breeding gazelles, lemurs, Madagascar turtles, zebras, and other exotic species.

Before the island was preserved, it was a plantation owned by Declaration of Independence signer Button Gwinnett, who was one of the few signers to be killed in a duel. Before the British arrived, the Spanish operated the Santa Catalina de Guale mission here, the most important mission in the region, largely because it was set in what was the Guale Indians' capital. The mission's foundations have been discovered, and other archaeological work has been undertaken on Colonial and pre-Colonial sites.

Because Georgia beaches are all public property to the high-water mark, no one can stop you from using the pristine beaches here, but above the high-water mark, access is by invitation only. The Nature Conservancy (912/437-2161) runs rare group trips out here, available after an application process.

South of Brunswick

ST. MARYS

It's hard to call a town that *Money* branded as "America's #1 Hottest Little Boomtown" "undiscovered," but St. Marys definitely has that feel to it. The *Money* criteria emphasized the amount of good-paying jobs in the region—at the Kings Bay Naval Submarine Base and the Gilman Paper Company—but retiring baby boomers who don't plan to work another day in their lives are beginning to collect down here as well. Those coming down include the standard Northerners moving purely for the weather, retired Navy officers returning to a fondly remembered point of assignment, and the "boat people," folks who discovered St. Marys via the Intracoastal Waterway. Some stopped here repeatedly before deciding to make this their permanent home; others docked, had a couple of drinks at the Riverview Hotel on Osborne Street, and decided they'd finally found their own private Margaritaville.

Founded in 1787, St. Marys, in its early years, served as the United States's only eastern seaport south of Savannah. Consequently, the town grew quickly. By 1850, St. Marys claimed a county courthouse, five churches, three schools, and nine dry goods stores. Things slowed down a bit after the War Between the States, but when the railroad came in 1906, it gave residents of St. Marys a chance to sell their shrimp inland and gave local interests the chance to mill and ship some of the Georgia pine from points west. From this latter opportunity, The Gilman Paper Company, which is now the Durango-Georgia Paper Company, soon became a dominant employer in the region. The arrival of the Kings Bay Naval Submarine Base in the 1970s brought nearly 9,000 jobs to the area, and the area has continued to grow since then.

The population of Camden County, which includes St. Marys, scenic Kingsland, and Woodbine, has soared in recent decades, from 13,371 in 1980 to 43,664 in 2000. After the last census, both St. Marys and Kingsland were named among Georgia's fastest-growing cities. Nonetheless, after visiting Charleston and Savannah, where plaques seem to document something every 10 feet, St. Marys is refreshingly un-self-conscious. The town is quaint, but not metaquaint. Its charm still largely derives from its native personality, rather than from its making itself over for tourists. St. Marys' historic district contains dozens of historic structures and—if you don't count the Oak Grove Cemetery (1780) and the tabby ruins (1770?)—the oldest structure dates to 1801. But most folks here think more in terms of recent history, who lived there in 1990, not 1820. I asked the longtime owner of a house reputed to have been pocked from a cannonball in the War of 1812, and whereas a home owner in Savannah or Charleston could probably have produced a brochure on the question, she

© SEAN SLINSKY

Shrimping still plays a role in the economies of small towns like St. Marys.

merely shrugged and said that sure, she knew where the mark was—in the window frame of her bottom floor—but she couldn't remember if the British or Northerners had done it.

St. Marys may be a small Southern town, but it's still a port town and a military town—meaning, of course, that it likes its parties. In February they celebrate Mardi Gras with a parade and festival; July Fourth there's the classic small-town Independence Day Celebration; in October the big Rock Shrimp Festival takes over; and there are various holiday events at the end of the year, like the Candlelit Tour of Homes on the second weekend in December. Contact the visitors center for detailed dates and more.

St. Marys is a quirky, personable town of countless beguiling stories: Like that of Jerry, who earned a Ph.D. in Chemistry at Ohio State and then returned to St. Marys to operate the old Riverview Hotel, just as his aunts had done before him. His long term as mayor just came naturally. Or that of Jan and Alf, the British couple who arrived here via the Intracoastal

Waterway and decided to settle. Then there's the anticlimactic story told by Mamie, who in the early 1960s took part in a civil-rights sit-in up at a Kingsland diner. The diner's staff ignored them, and Mamie and the protesters eventually left.

And then there's the local millionaire Warren Bailey, owner of the local phone company, who passed away without heirs and donated $60 million to the local Methodist Church. The shocked Methodists built St. Marys an assisted living center, and then, realizing that the deceased church member could have just as easily—but for the grace of God—been a Lutheran or Baptist, generously donated large sums to each of the town's other congregations.

Perhaps the most evocative St. Marys' story concerns a local girl, daughter of a widow, who was taken under the wing and groomed as a fashion model by St. Marys lumber baron Howard Gilman. After a promising start on the Road to Super-Modeldom, one day at a New York City photo shoot she did the inexplicable—she quit. She decided she didn't want to be a model anymore. She wanted to go home to St. Marys, and she did. Last time I was down there, her mother was planning her wedding at the Howard Gilman Waterfront Park, near the spot where her parents had married on the deck of a boat on the sound, 20-some years earlier.

Jacksonville oozes closer to St. Marys every day. People in St. Marys are not above driving down to the city to shop at Costco and Sam's Club. And workers in Jacksonville have increasingly begun using St. Marys' new world-class golf developments as a bedroom community to the Florida city. But even if St. Marys is pretty enough to turn the heads of the *Money* crowd, this humble little port town knows who it is.

St. Marys Convention and Visitors Bureau

The historic district stretches from St. Marys Street at the waterfront, roughly to about Norris Street, and this is where you'll want to stay and explore when you visit. St. Marys Convention and Visitors Bureau (406 Osborne St., 912/882-4000 or 800/868-8687, www.stmaryswelcome.com) makes a good first stop. Ask an attendant for a printed tour guide and map on local attractions and lodging.

Orange Hall House Museum

Although St. Marys has several buildings of local historic significance—you can pick up a walking-tour map at the convention and visitors bureau—tourist mostly consider it a gateway to Cumberland Island National Seashore, as it's where you catch the ferry over to the refuge. Still, one home worth definitely worth checking out is the Orange Hall House Museum (311 Osbourne St., 912/576-3644, www.orangehall.org), a classic Greek Revival mansion built in the 1820s for the family of the pastor of the Presbyterian church across Conyers Street. Hours are Mon. by appointment, Tues.–Sat. 9 AM–4 PM, Sun. 1–4 PM. Admission is $3 adults, $1 children.

St. Marys Submarine Museum

St. Marys Submarine Museum (102 St. Marys St., 912/882-2782, www.stmaryssubmuseum.com) honors the participation of the nearby Kings Bay Naval Submarine Base. The museum has an extensive collection of models, relics, and photos, and allows visitors to peer into a periscope that takes in downtown St. Marys and the waterfront. Open Tues.–Sat. 10 AM–4 PM, Sun. 1–5 PM. Admission is $4 adults, $3 seniors and kids 6–18, free for those under 6 and those over 99. Discounts for military.

Crooked River State Park

Crooked River State Park (6222 Charlie Smith Sr. Hwy., 912/882-5256) is a favorite place to start paddling trips. The 500-acre site includes 62 tent and RV sites ($20–22) and 11 cottages ($85–110), as well as a nature center. To get there from I-95, head eight miles east of Exit 3. An interesting historical site off Crooked River Road is the McIntosh Sugar Works mill, built of tabby in 1825 and used as a starch factory during the War Between the States. President Calvin Coolidge visited the site in the 1920s.

Recreation

Next door to the Riverview Hotel is **Up The Creek Xpeditions** (111 Osborne St., 912/882-0911, www.upthecreektrips.com), where you'll find a friendly crew, an extensive selection of rentals, guided tours, and prices that are generally more reasonable than those found on St. Simons or across the Sound in Fernandina. For a 3.5- to 4.5-hour kayak tour, prices run $50 per person. Beginners and children are welcome. Or if you're game, recreational kayaks run $30 per day, rentals run $40 per day ($45 for tandems), which includes all equipment. Shuttles and trailer rentals are available, too.

Accommodations

Former mayor Jerry Brandon and his wife Gaila own both the **Riverview Hotel** (105 Osbourne St., 912/882-3242, www.riverviewhotelstmarys.com), which Brandon's great aunts once ran, and **The Goodbread House Bed and Breakfast** (209 Osbourne St. 912/882-1872, www.goodbreadhouse.com), where Brandon's great aunt used to live. Also in the downtown

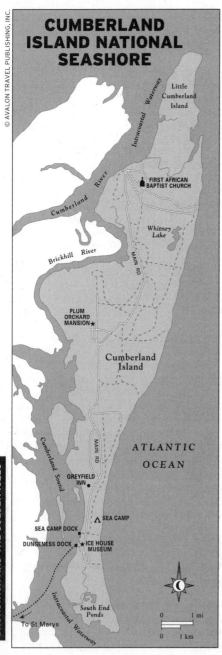

CUMBERLAND ISLAND NATIONAL SEASHORE

© AVALON TRAVEL PUBLISHING, INC.

Little Cumberland Island

Intracoastal Waterway

Cumberland River

FIRST AFRICAN BAPTIST CHURCH

Whitney Lake

Brickhill River

MAIN RD

PLUM ORCHARD MANSION ★

Cumberland Island

Cumberland Sound

MAIN RD

ATLANTIC OCEAN

GREYFIELD INN

△ SEA CAMP

SEA CAMP DOCK

DUNGENESS DOCK ★ ICE HOUSE MUSEUM

Intracoastal Waterway

South End Ponds

To St Marys

0   1 mi

0   1 km

district, **Emma's Bed and Breakfast** (300 W. Conyers St., 912/882-4199, www.emmasbed-andbreakfast.com) and the **Spencer House Inn Bed & Breakfast** (200 Osborne St., 912/882-1872, www.spencerhouseinn.com) offer friendly, historic rooms in the historic district. Rates range from $60 for Riverview Hotel rooms, to $100–185 at the inns.

Food

Lang's Marina Restaurant (307 W. St. Marys St., 912/882-4432) serves lunch Tues.–Fri. and dinner Wed.–Sat. after 5 PM. Most of the fish, shrimp, and blue crabs are pulled right from the waters around St. Marys, and Lang's gets most locals' vote as the best seafood in town. Prices average $8 for lunch, $15 for dinner.

The restaurant in the Riverview Hotel is now called **Seagle's Waterfront Café** (105 Osborne St., 912/882-3242, www.riverviewho-telstmarys.com). The only food available to nonguests is a lunch buffet, $7 weekdays, $9 on weekends.

Some argue that **Trolley's** (104 W. St. Marys St., 912/882-1525), the place around the corner, serves the best seafood in town. Meals average $10 for lunch or dinner.

◖ CUMBERLAND ISLAND NATIONAL SEASHORE

The **Cumberland Island National Seashore Reserve Visitors Center** (107 St. W. Marys St., 912/882-4335, www.nps.gov/cuis/) sends two ferries a day from St. Marys waterfront to the island, blessed with 17.5 miles of sugar-white beaches, scores of trails, maritime forests, ruins, and wild inhabitants including horses, sea turtles, armadillos, and more. While there is a small visitors center, icehouse museum, and a ranger-lead a tour ($6) of the Carnegie's 1898 Plum Orchard Mansion (the second and fourth Sunday of each month), the main event remains the island's raw landscape. Day hikers and camping backpackers must bring whatever they need—gear, water, and food included—and take any refuse to the mainland, as the preserve is serious about maintaining its pristine state. Boat trips are $15 adults, $12

© SEAN SLINSKY

Catch the ferry to the Cumberland Island National Seashore from tiny St. Marys in Georgia's southernmost coastal corner.

seniors, and $10 kids 12 and under. There is also $4 island-use fee. Cars and bikes are not permitted on the ferry, but you can rent bikes once you are on Cumberland. Campers opt for the **Sea Camp** area ($4), with its restrooms, cold showers, and water, or primitive back-country sites ($2). Reservations are required (877/860-6787).

Although Uncle Sam owns and administers most of the island, Cumberland is also home to a few private residences and the **❮ Greyfield Inn** (P.O. Box 900, 904/261-6408, www.grey-fieldinn.com), a 300-acre Carnegie estate that became an inn in 1962 is still owned by the family. The Greyfield has been ranked as one of America's "Top 10 Romantic Inns." Room rates start at $350 per night, and include meals on the American plan (dinners require jackets for men), round-trip ferry from Fernandina, Florida, unlimited use of bicycles and beach gear, and naturalist-led tours of the island. If you're visiting Fernandina, you can make reservations for a meal at the inn Mon.–Thurs. (six people maximum) and see the island that way.

The late JFK Jr. and his bride were married on Cumberland, at a tiny, unassuming church where slaves once worshipped. Before that, Robert E. Lee used to make pilgrimages to Cumberland to visit the grave of his father, Revolutionary War Hero "Lighthorse Harry" Lee, who died here while visiting an old friend in 1818. Years after his son's death, the elder Lee was reinterred in Virginia, beside his son's grave.

FERNANDINA, FLORIDA

As long as you're down this far south, you may as well slip down to Amelia Island, just off the coast of Florida, and its chief community, Fernandina, a historic waterfront community more akin to St. Marys or St. Simons than it is to Cocoa Beach.

No fewer than eight different flags have flown over the island: the French (1562–1565), Spanish (1565–1763), English (1763–1783), Spanish again (1784–1824), St. George's Green Cross (1817, filibuster Sir Gregor MacGregor's family flag), the Mexican revolutionary flag (also 1817, a wild year), the American flag (1818–1861), the Confederate flag (1861–1862), and the current American (1861–present).

Now that everyone's pretty confident that the United States will hold power in Fernandina for a little while, the town has grown into a charming vacation town on the order of St. Simons. In the town's glory days, 1875–1910, steamers from New York used to bring guests directly from the East River to the town's tourist hotels. Much of the historic downtown you see today dates to that heady period. After this, development picked up farther south along the coast, and Fernandina's day in the spotlight ended.

Today, the area retains a Victorian charm. Other than the beach, people come here to visit the downtown antique shops and restaurants, to visit **Fort Clinch** (2601 Atlantic Ave., Fernandina Beach, 904/277-7274), which never saw battle but is nonetheless now a state park, and to see the lighthouse from afar, since it's on private land and inaccessible to visitors. Another worthwhile stop on this history-thick island is the **Amelia Island Museum of History** (233 S. 3rd St., 904/261-7378, www.ameliaisland.org), housed in what was once the Nassau County jailhouse. Here, costumed interpreters and docents lead visitors through the island's past, including the Spanish mission, Native American, and Civil War periods. Open Mon.–Sat. 10 AM–4 PM, Sun. 1–4 PM, closed holidays. Admission is $5 adults, $3 kids. The museum offers a ghost walk Fri. nights at 6 PM, plus a guided walk of the 50-block historic district, which leaves from the railroad depot (101 Centre St.) at 3:30 PM Fri.–Sat. Call to arrange special off-time tours.

Accommodations

Of the thousands of aging tourist hotels up and down the length of Florida, the decidedly well-aged 1859 **Florida House** (22 S. 3rd St., 904/261-3300, www.floridahouseinn.com), outdodders all the rest. The venerable old railroad hotel still takes in visitors just as it did back in James Buchanan's day. A night in one of the 18 rooms here runs $149–169 and includes breakfast, plus scooter or bike rental.

For something nearer the beach, try **Best Western Inn at Amelia Island** (2707 Sadler Rd., 904/277-2300, www.bestwesternameliaisland.com) for about $100 a night. The inn offers lighted tennis courts, an Olympic-size pool, a hot tub, and an ocean, thoughtfully installed just a short walk away.

The historic 1895 **Bailey House** (28 S. 7th St., 800/251-5390, www.bailey-house.com) offers rooms ($149–209) and breakfasts downtown in an attractive, peak-roofed Victorian.

Food

One of the chief reasons to visit Fernandina is the dining. The following restaurants represent only a sampling of what's available, but they're some of the best.

For a truly memorable experience, make reservations ahead, take the Greyfield Inn ferry from Fernandina to Cumberland Island, and eat a meal at Cumberland Island's **Greyfield Inn** (P.O. Box 900, Cumberland Island, 904/261-6408, www.greyfieldinn.com), which is regularly cited as one of America's most romantic inns. The price is $118 for the boatride, house tour, three-course dinner, hors d'oeuvres, and nonalcoholic drinks. Price includes tax, but alcoholic drinks are extra.

In Fernandina proper, on the pricey end you'll find the **Beech Street Grill** (801 Beech St., Fernandina Beach, 904/277-3662, www.beech streetgrill.com). Set in the two-story 1889 Captain Bell House, Beech Street is the real thing: For years, *Wine Spectator* has repeatedly given the restaurant its Award of Excellence. Try the macadamia nut–crusted Mayport scamp grouper over dirty rice with tropical fruit salsa ($27). Dinner nightly from 6 PM; reservations are recommended. Live piano music is played upstairs, Thurs.–Sat. evenings.

For something far more filling and equally as memorable, if not as blatantly epicurean (or expensive), try the **The Marti Room** (22 S. 3rd St., Fernandina Beach, 904/261-3300, www.floridahouseinn.com). The Sunshine State's oldest tourist hotel offers Southern fried chicken, pork chops, fish, and other seafood;

Sundays means meals are served boarding-house style on huge tables. Meals range $7–10, breakfast at the low end, dinner at the high end. Open for breakfast, lunch, and dinner, Tues.–Sat. and Sun. for brunch.

At the **Le Clos Café-Restaurant Provençal** (20 S. 2nd St., Fernandina Beach, 904/261-8100, www.leclos.com), Le Cordon Bleu–trained chef Katherine Ewing wields impeccable credentials, including past training at Paris's Ritz Hotel. Her Provençal menu includes fresh fish and seafood and braised lamb, all served by candlelight. Call ahead to reserve a table in this 1906 cottage. Entrées average $25. Dinner only; closed Sun.

At the other end of the dining spectrum, **T-Ray's Burger Station** (202 S. 8th St., Fernandina Beach, 904/261-6310), inside the Exxon station, turns out one mean burger, which locals have voted T-Ray's tops on the beach. T-Ray's also serves grilled chicken, homemade banana pudding, breakfasts, and french fries. Expect to pay less than $10 for a meal. Open Mon.–Fri. 7:30 AM–2:30 PM; Sat. 8 AM–1 PM.

Speaking of local favorites, **Moon River Pizza** (925 S. 14th St., 904/321-3400) dishes out the best pizza on Amelia Island—the menu here includes nearly two dozen topping choices. Prices are $3.50 per slice, $11 per pie on average. Open for lunch and dinner; closed Sun. **O'Kane's Irish Pub** 318 Center St., Fernandina Beach, 904/261-1000, has won the Jacksonville paper's Best of Jax Award for Best Neighborhood Bar on the island. Set in a 19th-century building, this is the real thing—the kind of place all those McPubs on the pads in the strip malls are trying to replicate. No real surprises: The beer selection is to be expected, and the food in back includes fish-and-chips and Irish potato soup in sourdough bread bowls, a great warm meal on a foggy day at the beach. Like any good Irish pub, O'Kane's is family-friendly during the day. Meals average $7 for lunch, $11 for dinner. Open daily; live music Thurs.–Sat.

For coffee, **Amelia Island Gourmet Coffee & Ice Cream** (207 Centre St., 904/321-2111) offers coffees, breakfast sandwiches, muffins, bagels, cheesecakes, and other baked goods, as well as deli sandwiches for lunch. They serve beer and wine as well. Meals range $4–6 for breakfast and lunch. Open Sun.–Thurs. 7 AM–9 PM; Fri.–Sat. 7 AM–10 PM.

◖ OKEFENOKEE SWAMP

Some non-Southerners are surprised to find a place like the Okefenokee in Georgia, rather than down in southern Florida. But the 500,000-acre Okefenokee is not only a bona fide black-water swamp, it is also the largest swamp along the entire Atlantic coastline.

What makes a swamp? Think of it as something like the waterway equivalent to an aneurysm. The Suwannee River (that of Stephen Foster "Way Down Upon the" fame) originates in the Okefenokee and, like any sensible river, attempts to push its way eastward, to the Atlantic. But then it hits a long, elevated section called Trail Ridge, which for centuries now has been playing goal line defense and succeeding, blocking nearly all drainage to the Atlantic. Turned away, the black waters of the Suwannee back up, flooding the area's "prairies" (water-collecting depressions) and then gradually meandering southwestward to the Gulf of Mexico. A second river, the St. Mary's, is more headstrong and craftier. It hits Trail Ridge, drops south from the southern end of the refuge, cuts east around the ridge's southern tip, then back north, and then east again and into the Cumberland Sound, reaching the ocean between the goalposts of St. Marys and Fernandina. This shrewd move by the St. Mary's River creates Georgia and Florida's unorthodox, U-shaped border.

Despite these rivers' best efforts, only about 20 percent of the swamp's water ends up draining anywhere, which is why it's a swamp. Most of the water around here ends up in the root systems of oaks, pitcher plants, and other thirsty flora, or laid out flat in the shimmering black prairies, slowly evaporating into the saunalike air.

The Seminoles called this the "land of the trembling earth" because methane gas, created by submerged branches, leaves, and other

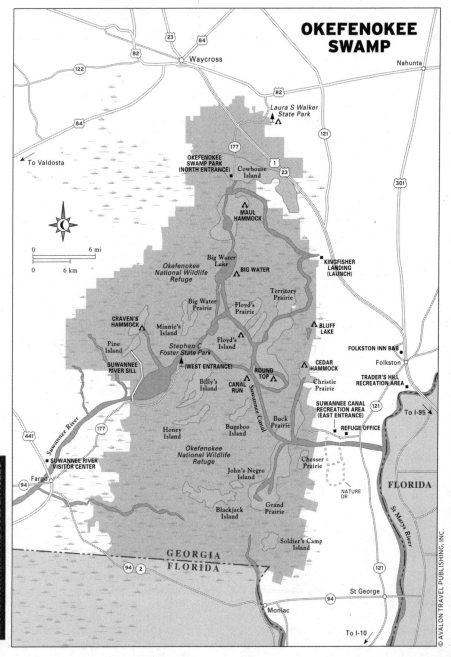

organic matter, bubbled up and stirred the floating sod. Plants don't grow any thicker than they do in the Okefenokee, and it's rare you'll find blacker water. The rivers and prairies of the swamp teem with more than 40 varieties of fish, including bass, bluegill, catfish, and warmouth perch. Alligators and Florida cottonmouth snakes abound as well, as do canebrake and diamondback rattlesnakes.

Besides the gators and snakes, armadillos, black bear, bobcats, flying squirrels, possum, raccoons, turtles, and three trillion mosquitoes and white flies (bring repellent) all dwell in this amazing, verdant region, along with more than 220 varieties of birds, including egrets, bald eagles, ospreys, green-winged teals, purple martins, and the endangered, red-cockaded woodpecker. Walt Kelly's creation from the comics, the humble possum Pogo, also lives here, a fact you'll find hard to forget in area gift shops.

More than 300 wildflowers bloom in the Okefenokee, making spring a particularly pretty time of year here. Trees and shrubs include the Allegheny chinkapin, American holly, bald cypress, black cherry, black tupelo, chinaberry, dogwood, Eastern redwood, live oak, loblolly pine, longleaf pine, pecan, pond cypress, pond pine, slash pine, red bay, Southern magnolia, swamp bay, sweet bay, sweet gum, sycamore, water oak, and white oak.

Although the entire swamp area is encompassed by the Okefenokee National Wildlife Refuge, two parks inside the refuge's eastern perimeter serve the needs of visitors: the Okefenokee Swamp Park, and Suwannee Canal Recreation Area.

Okefenokee National Wildlife Refuge

Sure, the wood cutouts of Pogo Possum are a little cheesy, but if you've only got one day to visit the swamp, and/or if you're with kids, let the guides at **Okefenokee Swamp Park** (5700 Okefenokee Swamp Park Rd., 912/283-0583, www.okeswamp.com) show you around. The nonprofit Swamp Park includes a guided boat tour, a 1.5-mile train ride, exhibits, a video,

the use of walkways and an observation tower, a serpentarium, and a visit to Pioneer Island, site of a re-created swamp homestead. There's also a souvenir shop and a barbecue shack. If the water's high enough, canoe rentals and extended boat tours ($16–20) are available. To get there, you'll need to drive for about one hour after leaving Highway 17 for Highway 82 West, and then take Route 177, which will dead-end into the park. Admission is $12 adults, $11 seniors and kids 5–11, free for those under 5. Open daily 9 AM–5:30 PM.

On the west side of the refuge, **The Suwannee Canal Recreation Area Visitor Center** (Rte. 2, 12 miles southwest of Folkston, 912/496-7836), is the closest entrance near St. Marys (via Rtes. 40/121). It affords an explorer's look deep into the swamp's wonders, and features an elevated (and thus dry) boardwalk with a viewing tower, 10 miles of hiking trails, a helpful visitors center with interpretive exhibits, plus Chesser Island, which includes a photogenic, restored swamp homestead. **Okefenokee Adventures** (912/496-7156, www.okefenokeeadventures.com) staffs the visitors center and operates guided water tours, rents bikes, canoes, and motorboats to both daytime visitors and overnight campers from its outfitter business next door. You can buy swamp gear and gifts in their small shop, and light meals (some vegetarian offerings) in the café. The outpost is open daily, sunrise–7:30 PM. Mar. 1–Oct. 31; sunrise–5:30 PM otherwise. Admission is $5 per car.

GETTING THERE AND AROUND

Several airports are convenient to Brunswick, the Golden Isles, and the Okefenokee Swamp region. Forty-five minutes south of Brunswick, and closest to the Okefenokee, the Jacksonville International Airport (904/741-4902, www.jaa.org) hosts 14 different airlines, including discounters Airtran and Independence Air. **Savannah/Hilton Head International Airport** (400 Airways Ave., 912/964-0514, www.savannahairport.com), 1.5 hours north of Brunswick, receives flights

BRUNSWICK AND THE GOLDEN ISLES

from AirTran, American Eagle, Continental Express, Delta, Delta Connection, Independence Air, Northwest, United Express, and US Airways. Brunswick Golden Isles Airport (500 Connole St., Brunswick, 912/265-2070, www.glynncountyairports.com) is served by Atlantic Southeast Airlines, which connects with Delta. Car rental (a necessity) is offered at the airports; try **Avis** (800/230-4898, www.avis.com); **Enterprise**(www.enterprise.com, 800/261-7331), or **Hertz** (800/652-3131, www.hertz.com). Brunswick is roughly one hour north of Jacksonville and one hour south of Savannah on I-95 and Highway 17.

Boaters are fond of the area, located as it is on the Intracoastal Waterway. The region features more than 14 full-service marinas; contact the **Brunswick and the Golden Isles of Georgia Convention and Visitors Bureau** (4 Glynn Ave., 912/265-0620 or 800/933-2627, www.bgivb.com) for a current directory.

BACKGROUND

The Land

The Sea Islands

The Sea Islands, or barrier islands, cover the entire stretch from Charleston to the Florida border. The biggest is Hilton Head Island, the largest Sea Island south of New Jersey. Euro-Americans have inhabited some of them, such as Sullivan's and Edisto islands, for centuries; others, including Hilton Head, Kiawah, and Sea Island, saw duty as plantation lands, then as poor farming communities, before adorning themselves in tile-roofed villas and putting greens in the 1960s and 1970s. Still others, such as Seabrook and Fripp islands (home of novelist Pat Conroy), are just now being dragged down the path of Disneyfication. Prime pristine island experiences include Hunting, Bull, Ossabaw, and Blackbeard islands, which are protected by law from the developers' axes.

Black Rivers

As opposed to the large rivers draining the Piedmont region, Lowcountry-born black rivers form at a much lower elevation, normally at the foot of the sand hills in the center of the state's coastal plain. As a result, the larger rivers carry sedimentary loads and are often colored a milky reddish-yellow (about the color of coffee with a lot of cream), while the slower,

© SEAN SLINSKY

SOUTH CAROLINA SYMBOLS AND EMBLEMS

Animal: white-tailed deer
Beverage: milk
Bird: Carolina wren
Butterfly: tiger swallowtail
Dance: the shag
Dog: Boykin spaniel
Fish: striped bass
Flower: yellow jassmine
Folk dance: square dance
Fruit: peach

Gem: amethyst
Insect: praying mantis
Reptile: loggerhead turtle
Shell: lettered olive
Songs: "Carolina" and "South Carolina on My Mind"
Stone: blue granite
Tree: palmetto
Wild game bird: wild turkey

non–sediment-carrying Lowcountry rivers receive their coloring exclusively from the tannic acid that emanates from the decaying coastal plain trees and tree roots along their shores. The color of these rivers is black—about that of thin, unadulterated coffee.

The Edisto River is the longest black-water river in the world. It combines with other, smaller rivers such as the Ashley and Combahee, to drain about 20 percent of South Carolina. Although large, sediment-carrying rivers like the Cooper and Savannah tend to drop their loads right at a river's end, creating river deltas, black rivers, with their slight but steady water flow and very little sediment, dig estuaries and deep embayments, such as Charleston Harbor and Port Royal Sound near Beaufort.

The Suwannee River (of Stephen Foster fame) originates in the Okefenokee Swamp west of Brunswick, but because Trail Ridge hems in nearly all drainage toward the Atlantic, the black waters of the Suwannee meander southwesterly, to the Gulf of Mexico. Another river, the St. Mary's, drops south from the southern end of the refuge and serves as Georgia and Florida's unorthodox, U-shaped border before finally making it to the ocean at St. Marys and Fernandina.

The Intracoastal Waterway

The Intracoastal Waterway slides down the inside of the Sea Island Coast, inside of barrier islands, down rivers, and through man-made canals. Running from Norfolk, Virginia to Miami, Florida, the waterway allows boaters to travel up and down the East Coast without worrying about storm waters or the Gulf Stream's prevailing northerly current.

CLIMATE

Carolina is in the spring a paradise, in the summer a hell, and in the autumn a hospital.

– Colonial American saying

First-time visitors to the American South always comment on how green everything is. The South in general, and the Sea Island Coast in particular, is a very damp place. Even the hottest day of the year might have a rain shower. In fact, some parts of Carolina receive as much as 81 inches of rain annually (most of Hawaii gets only 45 inches). The statewide average in both Georgia and South Carolina is around 49 inches of rain annually.

One thing that many non-Southerners don't realize is that summer is the rainy season in the South. Convectional rain comes on humid days in the summer. As the sun heats the earth, the earth in turn warms the air layers just above it. Pretty soon you've got convection currents—movements of warmed air pushing its way upward through cooler air. Eventually, this rising moisture reaches an elevation where it begins to cool and condense, creating cumulus clouds. As the clouds thicken and continue to cool, they create the dark thunderclouds that send picnickers and beachgoers scurrying for cover.

In a land this humid, every sunny day holds a chance for "scattered showers." Bring an umbrella; if you're camping, consider tarping your tent and gear before leaving for any long hike; you don't want to return to a soggy sleeping bag and waterlogged supplies. If you get hit by a particularly heavy storm while driving, do what the locals do: pull off under an overpass and wait it out. These types of heavy torrents don't usually last more than a few minutes. As one Carolinian said: "When God wants to show off like that, I pull over and let Him do it."

As opposed to convectional precipitation, which is always a warm-weather phenomenon, frontal precipitation nearly always takes place during the winter. Frontal precipitation also differs in its general lack of drama; instead of a rapidly forming and short-lived torrent, it normally takes the form of a steady rain or drizzle, with little or no lightning and thunder. It almost always means chilly—and sometimes polar—air masses, but most cold fronts coming down from the north are diverted by the Blue Ridge Mountains. Warm air from the Caribbean often can keep the thermostat at a bearably warm level in the winter.

Frontal precipitation brings what little snow comes to the Sea Island Coast. Charleston has received snow in the past, but if you're only heading to the Lowcountry, you can feel safe leaving your snowshoes home.

Hurricanes

Floyd. Hugo. Hazel. It seems as if every generation of Sea Islanders has its own Day 1, its own hurricane from which to date the events of their lives. As in, "Our Honda's only a couple years old, but we've had that old truck since before Hugo." Dealing with the damage of hurricanes is seen as part of life. In 1991, I had the following conversation:

ME: So Hugo really gave you a hard time, eh?
MOUNT PLEASANT SHOP OWNER: Oh no. The fellow down the street, his place got ruined. Terrible—nothing left. But other than losing the roof, we-all here didn't have any damage.
ME: Other than *losing the roof?*

Hurricanes have undoubtedly struck the Sea Island Coast ever since there *was* a Sea Island Coast, but the first one recorded in history books hit in late 1561, when three of four Spanish ships set on settling the Port Royal region were lost. Twenty-six men drowned.

In 1686, a hurricane blasted the same section of coastline, just in time to stop a marauding army of Spaniards who had already slaughtered the Scottish settlement in Beaufort and were mauling their way to Charleston.

GEORGIA SYMBOLS AND EMBLEMS

Bird: brown thrasher
Butterfly: tiger swallowtail
Crop: peanut
Fish: largemouth bass
Flower: Cherokee rose
Folk dance: square dance
Fruit: peach
Insect: honeybee
Marine mammal: right whale

Motto: "Wisdom, Justice, and Moderation"
Possum: Pogo possum
Reptile: gopher tortoise
Shell: knobbed whelk
Song: "Georgia on My Mind"
Tree: live oak
Vegetable: Vidalia sweet onion
Wildflower: azalea

Three more hurricanes hit the coast in the first half of the 18th century without causing too much damage, but a 1752 hurricane nailed Charleston dead center, hurling harbor ships into city streets, flattening homes and trees, and killing at least 28 people.

In 1885, just as South Carolina was shaking off the bonds of Reconstruction and attempting to salvage its economy, a 125-mph hurricane smashed into Charleston, killing 21 people and damaging or destroying 9 of every 10 homes in the city.

And then the fun really began. On August 23, 1893, a hurricane swept up from Savannah through Charleston and the Sea Islands, killing at least 1,000 people. Another devastating hurricane followed the same October. The "Big Blow of '98" flooded the Brunswick coast under up to 12 feet of water, killing 179 people. Others wreaked havoc in 1894, 1906, 1910, and 1911.

Hazel of 1954, Hugo of 1989, and Bertha, Fran, Dennis, and Floyd in the late 1990s are the hurricanes that stick out in the minds of many living Sea Islanders. Hazel killed 95 people from South Carolina to New York, not to mention perhaps as many as 1,000 in Haiti and an additional 78 in Canada. It sent 90-mph winds as far west as Raleigh. And then things were relatively quiet—for a while. Almost every year came watches, with occasional small strikes. But this lull in mother nature's war with humanity allowed for a huge buildup along most of the Sea Island Coast.

Which, of course, just set up more pins for Hurricane Hugo to knock over. Hugo blew into the region in 1989, featuring 135-mph winds and a 20-foot storm surge into Bull's Bay, north of Charleston—the highest storm surge in U.S. history. Hugo claimed 79 people overall (49 in the United States), but although it slammed through the antiquated, heavily populated Charleston area, only 17 people died in South Carolina.

Huge tides and brutal winds tore down electrical lines, wrenched bridges from pilings, and tossed about trawlers and yachts. Hugo destroyed more than six billion board-feet of timber, flattening more than 70 percent of the 250,000-acre Francis Marion National Forest, north of Charleston. Several lesser hurricanes hit the coast between 1989 and 1996.

Nearly every year brings two or three hurricane watches, but this doesn't keep people from building expensive multimillion-dollar homes right on the waterfront. And why should it? The Housing and Urban Development Act of 1968 (amended in 1969 and 1972) made federal flood insurance available to home owners and developers, subsidized by taxpayer money. Thus after each hurricane, home owners and developers replace the old rambling beach houses of yesteryear with beachfront mansions on stilts.

Earthquakes, Too?

It's August 31, 1886, a warm St. Louis evening on the banks of the Mississippi River. You stand on the silent dock, awaiting the whistle of a steamboat, but hear only the sounds of cicadas drifting out over the silent brown water. And then the surface of the river ripples. The dock quivers, drops you to your knees. What could it be? Then the movement's over and you rise again, thankful the earthquake was minor. But 1,000 miles away, near the quake's epicenter, all hell has broken loose in Charleston. Buildings 200 years old have crumbled; brick facades topple forward onto passersby in the street.

All those retaining bolts you see in old Charleston buildings aren't there for hurricanes. The 1886 quake here did more damage than Sherman. After "The Shake," Charleston home owners inserted long rods between the walls of their houses to brace them. You can still see the unique plates today.

Experts estimate that the 1886 quake ran a 7.7 on the Richter scale and a 10 on the 12-point Mercalli scale of earthquake intensity. It left 60–92 dead (accounts vary) and caused an estimated $23 million in damage. Savannah felt the quake, too, to a lesser degree. Families slept in the squares for weeks.

Theoretically at least, another quake is always lurking. Even today, more than 100 years later, the Sea Island region is rated as a major earthquake risk area, based almost entirely on the 1886 incident and the 351 smaller jolts that followed over the next 27 years.

Flora and Fauna

For the following information I owe much to Audubon International; to the fine *Landscape Restoration Handbook,* by Donald F. Harker, Gary Libby, Kay Harker, Sherri Evans, and Marc Evans; and to horticulturalist George Sigalas III.

LOWCOUNTRY FLORA
Coastal Vegetation
Among the native vegetation you'll see along the coast are the South Carolina state tree, the cabbage palmetto *(Sabal palmetto),* along with dwarf palmetto *(Sabal minor)* and the groundsel bush *(Baccharis halimifolia),* covered with what look like tiny white paintbrushes in late summer and fall. You'll also see grand live oak *(Quercus virginica)* and laurel oak *(Quercus laurifolia)* shading the coastal cities.

Many of these trees hang thick with Spanish moss *(Tillandsia usneoides),* which is not, as many people believe, parasitic. Instead, it's an epiphyte, similar to bromeliads and orchids. These plants obtain their nutrients from the air, not from their host plants. Many oaks are also adorned with resurrection fern *(Polypodium polypodioides),* which looks shriveled up and often blends in with the bark of the tree it is climbing. When it rains, however, the fern unfolds, and its dark green fronds glisten like green strands of jewels.

Sea oats *(Uniola paniculata)* grow among the sand dunes on the coast. Waving in the ocean breezes, they look like something out of a scenic calendar. State laws now protect the sea oats because of their important role in reducing sea erosion.

Freshwater Marsh
The Southeast has many freshwater marshes, characteristically thick with rushes, sedges, grasses, and cattails. Many of the marshes and associated swamps were diked, impounded, and converted to rice fields during the 18th and 19th centuries; today many of these impoundments provide habitat for waterfowl. Charac-

teristic plant species include swamp sawgrass *(Cladium mariscus),* spike-rush, bulrush, duckpotato, cordgrass, cattail, wild rice *(Zizania aquatica),* southern wax myrtle *(Myrica cerifera),* and bald cypress *(Taxodium distichum).*

Southern Floodplain Forest
Southern floodplain forest occurs throughout the coastal plain along large and medium-size rivers. A large part of the floodplain lies saturated during the winter and spring, about 20–30 percent of the year. In these areas you'll find abundant amounts of laurel oak and probably willow oak *(Quercus phellos),* sweet gum *(Liquidambar sturaciflua),* green ash *(Fraxinus pennsylvanica),* and tulip tree *(Liriodendron tulipifera)* as well.

In higher areas on the coastal plain, swamp chestnut oak *(Quercus michauxii)* and cherry-bark

© SEAN SLINSKY

Spring and summer finds this corner of the Southeast exploding with colorful blooms like this hydrangea.

KUDZU: THE VINE THAT ATE THE SOUTH

Although Asians have harvested kudzu for more than 2,000 years – using it for medicinal teas, cloth, paper, and as a baking starch and thickening agent – the fast-growing vine wasn't introduced to the United States until it appeared at the Philadelphia Centennial Exposition of 1876. Southern farmers really first became acquainted with it when they visited the Japanese pavilion at the New Orleans Exposition of 1884-1886. For some 50 years afterward, although some visionaries proclaimed the vine as the long-awaited economic savior of the South, most Southerners thought of it largely as a garden ornamental. They called it "porch vine" because many used it to climb trellises and provide shade for swings.

After the boll weevil infestation of the 1920s wiped out Georgia and Carolina cotton crops, and as years of single-crop farming began to take their toll on the soils of the South, the U.S. Department of Agriculture under Franklin D. Roosevelt imported vast amounts of kudzu from Japan, and the Civilian Conservation Corps planted some 50,000 acres of the vine for erosion control and soil restoration. Down-and-out farmers could make as much as $8 an acre planting kudzu, and in the midst of the Depression, few could refuse the offer.

And that was the last time many of those acres saw sunlight. The problem, it seems, is that kudzu's insect nemeses had no interest in immigrating to America along with the vine, so kudzu actually grew better in the United States than in Asia – often a foot or more a day. Soon, kudzu had covered fences, old cars, and small houses. It swallowed whole trees, depriving their leaves of sunlight and killing them. And this all happened at about the time that many farmers realized that loblolly pine timber, not kudzu, could bring them back to prosperity.

Today, a wiser Department of Agriculture categorizes kudzu as a weed. Millions of dollars are spent each year trying to eradicate the stubborn vine, whose roots survive the South's mild frosts and most available herbicides. Some say it covers more than two million acres across the South.

Read any Southern newspaper long enough and you'll run across a dozen varieties of the same story: *Kudzu May Contain Cure for X.* Nobody can believe that the plant could be as annoying as it is without also providing some major benefit to humanity. One thing we do know for sure: as a member of the bean family (*Fabaceae*), kudzu's roots contain bacteria that fix atmospheric nitrogen and thus help increase soil fertility.

And Southerners know how to make the best of things. Up in Walhalla, South Carolina, Nancy Basket creates kudzu paper and then uses it in multicolored collages celebrating rural life and Native American themes. Others weave thick baskets from the mighty vine. Some farmers have experimented with grazing goats and other livestock on kudzu, which not only provides free food for the animals but also seems to be one of the few dependable ways to constrain the plant.

Although there may be less kudzu in Georgia and South Carolina than there was a few years ago, don't worry – you'll still find kudzu all across the Sea Island Coast, climbing and covering trees, inching toward the edge of the road. It's everywhere. Are you parked on a Lowcountry roadside as you're reading this? Reach over, open your glove box, and you'll probably find some kudzu.

If you'd like to find out more about the vine that ate the South, go to the website www.cptr.ua.edu/kudzu.html, which will in turn lead you to several other sites dealing with the vine. A documentary, *The Amazing Story of Kudzu,* has been distributed to public TV stations nationwide, so watch your local listings to see when it might be broadcast in your town. Or you can purchase a copy of the video by calling 800/463-8825. Tapes run about $21.

oak *(Quercus pagoda)* dominate; in lower areas, you're more likely to find bald cypress, water tupelo *(Nyssa aquatica),* and swamp tupelo *(Nyssa biflora),* along with southern magnolia *(Magnolia grandiflora),* American beautyberry *(Callicarpa americana),* common papaw *(Asimina triloba),* southern wax myrtle, dwarf palmetto, trumpet creeper *(Campsis radicans),* groundsel bush, Virginia sweetspire *(Itea virginica),* cinnamon fern *(Osmunda cinnamomea),* sensitive fern *(Onoclea sensibilis),* and the carnivorous pitcher plant.

MAMMALS

Scientists have claimed that in ancient days great bison, camels, and even elephants roamed the Sea Island Coast, but you won't find any there today; however, you may well see raccoons, badgers, beavers, possums, and a variety of squirrels, although you'll need a flashlight to catch the nocturnal flying squirrel. River otters, beavers, and the seldom-seen bobcat also dwell in the forests, as does the rare red fox, which is currently being reintroduced into the Francis Marion National Forest north of Charleston.

Ocean mammals include the playful bottlenosed dolphin and the rare, gentle manatee, which attempts to dwell peacefully in the coastal inlets but often ends up playing speed bump to the many leisure craft swarming the waters.

AQUATIC LIFE

The Sea Island Coast's diverse waters provide a correspondingly wide variety of fish and other sea life. The tidal rivers and inlets teem with flounder, sea bass, croaker, drum, and spot. Deep-sea fishing, particularly as you head out toward the Gulf Stream, includes bluefish, striper, flounder, drum, Spanish and king mackerel, cobia, amberjack, shad, and marlin, to name only a few.

Other sea life includes numerous types of jellyfish, starfish, conch (pronounced "conk" hereabouts), sand dollars, sea turtles, numerous species of shark (many of them edible), rays, shrimp, and Atlantic blue crabs. You'll also find oyster beds along the coast, although

most of these are no longer safe for consumption because of pollution.

REPTILES AND AMPHIBIANS

Water brown snakes often grow as long as four feet. You'll find them all along the coastal plain. Water browns are also tree-climbers; sometimes you'll see them enjoying the sun on tree limbs overhanging rivers, streams, and swamps. They feed mainly on catfish. In blackwater swamps you'll find black swamp snakes, which are usually just over a foot long.

But these aren't the kinds of snakes most visitors have on their minds when they're hiking in the South. South Carolina, after all, leads the nation in its variety of poisonous snakes, housing six different slithering creatures that can bring on trouble with a bite: the copperhead, the canebrake rattlesnake, the eastern diamondback rattlesnake, the pygmy rattlesnake, the cottonmouth (water moccasin), and the eastern coral snake. Fortunately, none of these animals is aggressive toward humans; you'll probably never even see one while visiting. If you do, just stay away from them. Most snakebites occur when someone is picking up or otherwise intentionally disturbing a snake.

BIRDS

Along the Sea Island Coast, bird-watchers have spotted more than 400 different species—over 45 percent of the bird species found on the continent. Along the coasts, look for various wading birds, shorebirds, the wood stork, the swallow-tailed kite, the brown pelican, the marsh hen, the painted bunting, the seaside sparrow, migrant ducks and waterfowl, the black-necked stilt, the white ibis, the marsh wren, the rare reddish egret and Eurasian collared doves, and the yellow-crowned night heron. Popular birding sites include Cape Romain National Wildlife Refuge, Francis Marion National Forest, including the Swamp Fox section of the Palmetto Trail starting in McClellanville, Magnolia Plantation and Gardens (near Charleston), ACE Basin National Wildlife Refuge, Edisto Island State Park, the National Audubon Society's Francis Beidler

© SEAN SLINSKY

The Sea Island coast is a main thoroughfare for migratory birds and a year-round home to scores of waterfowl.

Forest Sanctuary, Pinckney Island National Wildlife Refuge, near Hilton Head; Savannah National Wildlife Refuge, near Hardeeville, Wassaw National Wildlife Refuge, Ossabaw Island Heritage Preserve, Blackbeard Island and Sapelo Island National Estuarine Sanctuary, Wolf Island National Wildlife Refuge and Wilderness Area, Jekyll Island, and Cumberland Island National Seashore.

INSECTS

The members of the Sea Island Coast's vast insect population that you'll want to know about include fireflies, mosquitoes, and no-see-ums. The first of these are an exotic sight for those who haven't seen them before; people traveling with kids might want to ask around to find out where they can hope to spot some fireflies at sundown.

Don't worry about where to find mosquitoes and no-see-ums—they'll find you. If you're visiting between spring and late fall and plan to spend any time outdoors, bring insect repellent.

ENVIRONMENTAL ISSUES

As opposed to, say, most parts of California, where landscapers must intentionally plant grass and trees—along with artificial watering systems—the Sea Island Coast is so fertile that at times it seems that if you don't hack nature back, it might swallow you up. Farmers complain about "wet" summers here. Grass grows to the edge of the highways. Pine trees grow everywhere they haven't been cut down, and kudzu grows over everything not in motion.

Consequently, although there have always been some farsighted environmentalists in the region, many Sea Islanders have been slow to see a need for conserving natural resources and preserving places of wild scenic beauty. A common Carolina practice when building a home, for instance, is to (1) clear-cut the entire property of native scrub pine; (2) build the home; and (3) plant a lawn, along with a few nursery-bought oaks or willows for shade.

But this view of nature-as-adversary is slowly changing. With the arrival of so many emigrants and tourists from denuded areas, the

Carolinas have of late come to see the beauty that some residents had taken for granted. Of course, some native Carolinians and Georgians—not uncommonly those who bear long-held deeds to now-developable land—complain that activists who have so recently arrived from bombed-out northern climes have no business preaching the gospel of conservation in their new home. Fortunately, many native Sea Islanders have noticed the declining quality of life and are just as eager, if not *more* eager, than the transplants to keep chaos out of the order of nature.

The popularity of Adopt-a-Highway programs, the increased traffic to North and South Carolina's excellent state parks, and the huge number of Carolinians and Georgians from industry, government, and the private sector currently pitching in to build South Carolina's Palmetto Trail—a hike/bike path across the entire state—are all signs boding well for the future of the Carolinas' remaining wilderness.

Perhaps the darkest cloud over the coasts is the need to slow suburban sprawl. The population boom of recent years has been one thing. The tendency of these migrating Northerners (and inland Southerners) is to purchase large lots on cul-de-sac–gnarled "plantations" in huge, often upscale developments that attempt to create an exclusive community within, or slightly outside, established communities. Around Charleston, South Carolina, for instance, forecasters estimate that if trends continue, by 2030, developers will have beaten 500 square miles of currently rural land into suburbia, creating a 247 percent increase in suburban land area to handle a population increase

of only 49 percent, and destroying the ambience of the Lowcountry forever.

Fortunately, forward-thinking, community-minded South Carolinians and Georgians are taking a stand. Responding to its population surge, Charleston County has moved toward open space zoning (or clustering), which allows development while eliminating as little farmland, timberland, and open space as possible. Communities with open-space zoning allow landowners to subdivide into smaller lots, but only if they permanently protect 50 percent or more of the original parcel from development. Or they offer all developers the right to build more houses than normal, but only if they cluster the structures instead of building on large lots.

The idea of "clustering" has industrial applications, too. In the late 1990s, the South Sea Island Coastal Conservation League and Charleston Mayor Joe Riley called for establishing greenbelts around Lowcountry urban areas, and several Lowcountry General Plans began to require industry clustering. By locating industries near each other (to preserve natural space), planners hope to encourage plants to use each other's waste products in their own manufacturing, whenever possible.

In addition to development regulation, some Carolinians are encouraging outright preservation. In 1997, for instance, South Carolina Senator Arthur Ravenel helped to get acres in Georgetown, Horry, and Marion counties established as the Waccamaw National Wildlife Refuge. Another positive sign is the arrival of traditional neighborhood developments (TNDs) on St. Helena Island, Daniel Island, and in Mount Pleasant, Manteo, and elsewhere.

History

Much of the early history of South Carolina and Georgia centers along the coasts where European settlers first landed and prospered. In fact, the very first European colony in North America nestled, if briefly, in the Carolina-Georgia region. Historians disagree as to its precise location, but they agree that it was either near modern-day Georgetown, South Carolina; St. Marys, Georgia; or Wilmington, North Carolina.

Because Colonial North America was a virgin land rich in raw materials coveted by Europeans, the most prosperous communities were port cities like Charleston, Beaufort, Savannah, and Brunswick. And because the coastal South, particularly Charleston and Savannah, held special sway in antebellum Southern politics, the coasts witnessed many events of national and even world significance. The first major American victory in the American Revolution took place at Sullivan's Island, near Charleston. The Americans' most lopsided defeat took place at the Battle of Savannah. After the war, the cotton gin was invented on a Savannah-area plantation. Most of America's African slaves entered the country through Charleston. The world's first regular railroad chugged off to the Augusta area from Charleston. The first transatlantic steamship was built and sailed from Savannah. The War Between the States began in Charleston, and Sherman's March to the Sea ended in Savannah.

History buffs—or those just looking for enough "cultural value" to justify their beachfront indulgences—will find the Charleston-Georgia coast a rewarding place to visit.

Many fine books have been written on the history of South Carolina and Georgia. The following section is particularly indebted to Walter Edgar's *South Carolina: A History,* Preston Russell and Barbara Hines's highly readable *Savannah: A History of Her People Since 1733.* Robert E. Lee's autobiography and William T. Sherman's *Memoirs* also provide telling glances of the region in the days leading up to and following the Civil War.

FIRST ARRIVALS

Estimates vary on the number of Native Americans who lived along the Southern coast at the point of first European contact; what's certain is that European diseases tore at the indigenous population from the very start. By the time the British arrived to settle the region in earnest, disease spread from the initial Spanish explorers, and failed Spanish settlements of the 16th and 17th centuries had already cut the local population in half. By the time of the American Revolution, the indigenous population was a small fraction of its former size. Today, the number of Native Americans along the Charleston and Georgia coasts is in the hundreds.

If these people had only known that they would end up lumped for all eternity into a dimly lit category called "prehistory," they no doubt would have kept better notes for posterity. What many scientists theorize based on the little existing evidence is that migrating peoples reached the South Carolina and Georgia territories some 15,000 years ago. This was still at the end of the Ice Age, but they found megafauna such as mammoth, mastodon, and great bison. All we know about these early people is that they made primitive tools and hunted.

Toward the end of the Pleistocene epoch, the Paleo-Indian appeared, which is to say, descendants of the same Indians, but with better tools. The culture, which was primarily defined by its use of Clovis points used on spears, spread apparently from the Great Plains toward the Atlantic. The Paleo-Indians were the first great big-game hunters of South Carolina and Georgia. They went after mammoth and mastodon; one of their tricks was to burn the marsh or woods, driving the animals that hid within to slaughter. They may have also added some gathering to their prodigious hunting efforts.

When the Ice Age finally ended, South Carolina and Georgia's physical environment went through some predictably large changes in the region's flora and fauna. The early Americans adapted to these changes, creating a society fed on fish, shellfish, small mammals, and fowl. With the greater abundance of game, and the resulting leisure time, you might think that a "high" culture would have developed at this point, but the living was so easy, and apparently the existing philosophies were so comfortable, that little change is noticeable in the artifacts of these cultures, although they're separated by thousands of years.

During this Archaic period, Native Americans apparently spent spring and summer near a major body of water—a river, marsh, or the Atlantic; shell middens and shell rings on Edisto, Jekyll, and other islands identify these sites. The people would move to higher regions to hunt white-tailed deer in the fall, returning to their waterside digs for the winter. Trade may have also begun during this period: Tools made of Piedmont materials have been found along the coast; coastal plain materials have been found at Archaic sites in the mountains.

Pottery that some experts date to between 2500 BC and 1000 BC first appeared along the Savannah River around the time Moses and the Israelites were waiting for a ferry on the shore of the Red Sea. Archaeologists have found these simple ceramics around the shell middens along the coast.

During the late Archaic period, domestication of such plants as beans, squash, sunflowers, and sumpweed began, although apparently corn was not a big crop in the Southeast until much later.

During the Woodland period from 1000 BC to AD 1000, Native Americans began to rely increasingly on agriculture. Farming both permitted and required a less mobile lifestyle, which in turn gave rise to further development of ceramics (now that nobody had to lug the

SPAIN'S FIRST COLONIZATION EFFORT

Close your eyes. Imagine you're the first European to set foot in South Carolina. It's 1526: There are no paramedics a phone call away, not even a bottle of peroxide in the ship's doctor's cupboard. The scariest beasts you've ever seen – giant armor-covered, man-eating, lizardlike monsters – cruise the inlets, waiting to tear off an arm idly draped over the gunwales. Beyond the quicksand on shore, deadly water moccasins swim the rivers, ready to strike. There are mosquitoes and no-see-ums, humidity and malaria. And no beach music, she-crab soup, or hot boiled peanuts to balance things out.

Had it been me rather than Spaniard Francisco Gordillo to land first in South Carolina, I might have taken a quick look around and headed back across to Spain for some hot paella. But history is not made by people who head back for paella. Gordillo and, later, 500 Spaniards under commander Lucas Vasquez de Ayllon, came, saw, and colonized.

Ayllon had gathered up about 500 men, women, and children from Santo Domingo in the modern-day Dominican Republic for the colonization effort. Ayllon sailed back to the region the natives called Chicora, establishing San Miguel – the first European settlement in what would become the United States. No one knows precisely where San Miguel was located. Many suspect it may have been in Winyah Bay, although some argue that it was near the Savannah River, and others somewhere in Georgia.

Wherever it was, things didn't work out according to plan. They had landed in August; by mid-October, the visionary Ayllon was dead. His successor proved to have the leadership ability of a mime in a school for the blind. After a relatively hard Carolina winter, lethal Indian attacks and disease had killed 7 out of every 10 colonists before a year had passed. The Spaniards decided that San Miguel was really a better name for a beer than a city, and they sailed back to Santo Domingo.

THE FRENCH THREAT

Having cast anchor, the captain with his soldiers went on shore, and he himself went first on land; where he found the place as pleasant as was possible, for it was all covered with mighty, high oaks and infinite stores of cedars... smelling so sweetly, that the very fragrant odor made the place seem exceedingly pleasant. As we passed through these woods we saw nothing but turkey cocks flying through the forests; partridges, gray and red, little different from ours, but chiefly in bigness. We heard also within the woods the voices of stags, bears, lusernes [lynx], leopards, and divers other sorts of beasts unknown to us.

René Goulaine de Laudonnière, a French colonizer who accompanied Jean Ribaut on the first French expedition to Spanish "Florida" in 1562, describing Port Royal

After the failed colonization effort of 1526, the Spaniards pretty much kept themselves busy with a whole New World to rape and pillage, and pretty much ignored the Carolinas. Explorer de Soto passed through in 1540, but it wasn't until 1558 that King Philip II, noticing the hated French eyeing the region, decided it was time to establish a permanent presence in "Florida."

An expedition headed up from Vera Cruz back to the Santa Elena region, near modern-day Beaufort, South Carolina. Its leader Villafañe arrived in Port Royal Sound on May 27, 1561. He sailed up the river but found nothing that interested him, so he sailed northward as far as Cape Hatteras, where a number of troubles sent him foundering back to Santo Domingo.

What Villafañe had seen in his travels convinced Philip II that there was no true French threat, so he put settlement of the region on the back burner, which appears to have been precisely what the French had been waiting for. The very next year, France sent Jean Ribaut, leading a group of French Protestants – Huguenots – who were looking for a place to practice their faith without persecution.

Ribaut and 150 faithful, including a Calvinist minister, first reached North America at the site of Saint Augustine and turned north until they arrived in the Santa Elena area and founded a small colony on what's now called Parris Island in Port Royal – site of present-day Parris Island Marine Base. When Ribaut sailed to France and was kept from returning immediately, however, the men left behind grew restless, built a ship (the first built in America for transatlantic travel), and sailed back to France. When Ribaut finally returned to "Spanish Florida" with reinforcements, not only were his men gone, but the Spanish were

pots from mountains to sea anymore) and permanent structures. Being tied to one area also meant that hunters needed to be able to kill more of an area's available wildlife instead of moving on to easier pickings elsewhere; to that end, the bow and arrow, which was developed around this time, came in handy.

The Mississippian period (named because this type of culture seems to have first appeared in the middle Mississippi Valley region) was a time of great advances. Cultural nuances such as ritual burial practices, platform mounds, and a hierarchical structure organized under village chiefs suggest a so-

phisticated religio-sociopolitical system. Just over the South Carolina–Georgia border, near Macon, you can find temple pyramids. Along South Carolina and Georgia's fall line, in the decades after AD 1150 or so, as the French were constructing Chartres Cathedral, Mississippians were battling their way eastward into the pristine world of the well-established Woodland Indians.

Because the Mississippians were an unwelcome, invading force, their early sites in the state feature encircling palisades—defensive structures for protecting themselves against the hostile Woodland peoples. Eventually, the back. Ribaut and his men surrendered to the Spaniards and were executed.

The Spaniards' take-no-prisoners attitude toward the French Protestants revealed their newborn seriousness about settling the east coast of North America quickly, before another European power did. In 1566, Philip II established a chain of Spanish forts along the coasts of Florida, Georgia, and South Carolina. Fort San Felipe – named after the same physician-saint for whom their king was named – was built that April on what's now called Parris Island. The Spanish left 110 men to garrison the fort and sent one soldier with each local Indian chief to help spread Catholicism. Soon, the fort was reinforced with another 300 men under Captain Juan Pardo.

That November, Pardo was sent inland from San Felipe with the order to explore and conquer the land clear from there to Mexico, establishing an overland route to the silver mine of western Mexico. Pardo marched upland to the east of the Savannah, stopping by Cofitachiqui. At the foot of the mountains, Pardo and his men built a blockhouse for safety before moving on. By the time he had reached Wateree, a messenger reached him with orders to return to San Felipe. Pardo did so, leaving behind four soldiers and a priest to begin the job of evangelization.

Pardo marched west again the following September, establishing various garrisons and reaching as far as present-day Alabama before returning back to San Felipe. Indians destroyed the small forts soon afterward, massacring the men who were left behind to guard them.

Two years later, Jesuit priests arrived, and an earnest effort was made to found a true settlement there on Parris Island. The village of Santa Elena flourished, becoming the capital of all La Florida Province. Unfortunately, Spain could not effectively defend her far-off colony; the inhabitants had to flee to St. Augustine in 1576 to escape hostile Indians, who burned the vacated buildings. The Spanish returned the following year to rebuild the town and build San Marcos, a new, stronger fort, on the same site. But in 1587, when the English sea captain Sir Francis Drake swept down the South Atlantic Coast to harass Spanish settlements, the people of Santa Elena decided to cast their lots with their countrymates in Saint Augustine, leaving South Carolina for the final time.

Only a handful of Spanish friars, devoted to their work among the Indians, were left behind. Even after a 1597 massacre by Indians, which only one friar living above the present-day Georgia-Florida border survived, the Jesuits continued their work in the region that includes South Carolina. They established several missions at San Felipe, on the mouth of the South Edisto, on the Ashepoo, and on St. Catherine's Island. The last of these survived 10 years into the British Colonial period, finally disappearing in 1680.

Mississippians, and the Mississippian way of life, won out.

Mississippians tended to plant their crops in the rich bottomlands beside rivers, building their villages up on the bluffs overlooking them. One of the best—and only—descriptions of one of these "towns" comes from Hernando de Soto. When de Soto explored western Georgia and South Carolina in 1540 (on his way to discovering the Mississippi River), he encountered Cofitachequi, an important Mississippian town on the banks of the Wateree River in today's Kershaw County, South Carolina. Ruled by a female chief, Cofitachequi consisted of temple mounds and several rectangular, wattle-and-daub, thatched-roof houses, with storehouses of clothing, thread, deerskins, and pearls.

The pearls suggest that the good folks of Cofitachequi traded with coastal Indians—an interpretation that is further bolstered by the fact that they were well versed in the existence of the Spanish, whose only other presence in the region had been established 14 years earlier, on the coast, at the failed colony of San Miguel de Gualdape.

All the Native Americans who dwelt in South Carolina and Georgia at the time of the

European invasion derived from Iroquoian, Siouan, Algonquian, and Muskogean language groups. Northeast of the Catawba-Santee waterway lived the numerous Siouan tribes, the southern portion of the Sioux nation extending to the Potomac River near what would later become Washington, D.C. At the coast, where the living was easy, tribes tended to be small but plentiful: the Combahee, Edisto, Kiawah, Etiwan, Wando, Waccamaw, and Yamacraw. The fewer tribes of the Upcountry (e.g., the Cherokee, Lumbee, and Creek) were larger and stronger.

For instance, the most powerful tribe, the Cherokee, ruled a 40,000-square-mile region—the northwestern third of modern-day South Carolina and North Carolina—although they were constantly at battle with the more warlike Creeks and the Chickasaws of northern Mississippi and western Tennessee, and the Choctaw in the southern Mississippi region. Only with the Cherokees' help during the Yamassee Wars did the Carolinian colony survive.

In the early 1700s, the Yamassee Indians, who had clashed with the Spanish in modern-day Georgia, moved up into the Sea Islands around Beaufort after receiving the go-ahead from British colonials in Charles Town, who were glad to have them as buffers against the Spanish. Although the Yamassee soon struck out against encroaching settlers, leading to the bloody Yamassee Wars, the British were still worried enough about the Spanish that when the small Yamacraw tribe asked to be allowed to settle on a river bluff south of Beaufort, permission was granted. A few years later, the Yamacraw leader Tomochichi would agree to share their bluff with James Oglethorpe and the first settlers of what was to become Savannah.

South Carolinian and Georgian Indians contributed many things to the Carolinian way of life, most notably place-names. Whether you're sunning on Ossabaw Island, surfing off Kiawah Island, watching a Warriors game at Wando High School, fishing the Altamaha River, or doing time in Pee Dee Federal Penitentiary, take time to reflect on the Native Americans who gave the name to your location. Also, the next time you sit down to a plate of grits or *barbacoa* (barbecue), thank those who first developed them.

SOUTH CAROLINA'S BRITISH PROPRIETARY PERIOD

Although the 16th century brought a handful of reconnaissance missions and attempts at colonization by Spain and France, the Spanish and the French had nearly all disappeared by the turn of the following century. Except for a handful of Spanish Franciscans manning the missions along the Golden Isles and as far north as Port Royal, South Carolina was left again to the indigenous Americans.

But this didn't mean that Europeans had forgotten about the Southeast coast. By the second quarter of the 17th century, Spain's power had declined to the point where British monarch Charles I began to assert England's historic claims to the coast, founded on the discoveries of the Cabots. The king was prompted by his need to do something with the French Huguenots who had taken refuge in already overcrowded England. In 1629, he granted his attorney general, Sir Robert Heath, a charter to everything between latitudes 36 and 31 degrees (more or less from the present-day Georgia–Florida line to the North Carolina–Virginia line) and all the way west to the Pacific. In the charter, Charles lists the name of the region as "Carolana," a transmogrification of "Charles." Despite one failed attempt (the famed *Mayflower* miscalculated and landed its French Huguenot passengers in Virginia), no one ever settled in Carolina or Georgia under the Heath Charter.

Establishment of the Lords Proprietors

While the Heath Charter was gathering dust, Cromwell and the Puritans beheaded Charles I and took control of England. Upon Cromwell's death, Charles II was restored to the throne, largely as a result of the efforts of the English nobility. The king was short of funds but wanted to show his gratitude to his allies, so in

1663 he regranted most of the Heath Charter lands to a group of eight noblemen: his cousin Edward, the Earl of Clarendon; his cousin and counselor George Monck, the Duke of Albemarle; William, the Earl of Craven; Lord John Berkeley; Anthony Ashley-Cooper; Sir George Carteret; Sir John Colleton; and Sir William Berkeley. This grant was expanded in 1665 into an even larger swath encompassing everything from 65 miles north of St. Augustine to the bottom of Virginia.

Of course, the successors of Robert Heath had a legal right to Carolina (Charles II had changed the "a" to an "i"). To mollify them, the king promised future lands, which eventually turned out to be 100,000 acres in interior New York. The original grants were made null and void, and Carolina thereby gained eight lords proprietors.

The term "lords proprietors" does a good job of explaining both the nobles' roles and their motives in the early settlement of Carolina. As lords, they had penultimate say over what life would be like for settlers in this new land. As proprietors, they had an almost purely financial interest in the venture. Certainly none of them came to Carolina to live. The weaknesses inherent in this government-by-the-preoccupied were to become soon apparent.

British Settlement of *La Florida* Begins

Perhaps the first problem the proprietors faced was the defiant attitudes of the settlers who since at least 1657 had been trickling down from the thriving colony at Jamestown, Virginia, and purchasing land from the Native Americans around the Albemarle sound at the mouth of the Chowan River in modern-day North Carolina. Unlike later settlers, these first Albemarle settlers had lived—and due to fuzzy boundaries between Virginia and Carolina, emigrated believing they would continue to live—under Crown authority. For all its faults, Royal Colonial Rule meant that the colony received the attention of the Crown and his underlings—full-time governing professionals with extensive financial resources. These ex-Virginians tired quickly of the all-too-often amateurish, vacillating, talk-to-me-next-month governing style of the proprietors.

The king had his suspicions about the proprietors' ability, and so they set off to prove themselves able governors. First, they divided Carolina into three counties: "Albemarle," "Clarendon," which stretched south from the Chowan river to the Cape Fear Valley, and "Craven," which covered the area south of Cape Romaine, south of present-day Georgetown, and including present-day Charleston. The Carolina lands outside these counties, which, on paper, extended westward to the Pacific Ocean, could be settled later, as circumstances permitted.

The Barbadians

The lands are laden with large tall oaks, walnut and bays, except facing on the sea, it is most pines tall and good. . . The Indians plant in the worst land because they cannot cut down the timber on the best, and yet have plenty of corn, pompions, water-melons, and muskmelons. . . two or three crops of corn a year as the Indians themselves inform us. The country abounds with grapes, large figs, and peaches; the woods with dear, conies, turkeys, quails, curlews, plovers, teal, herons; and as the Indians say, in winter with swans, geese, cranes, duck and mallard, and innumerable other waterfowls, whose names we know not, which lie in the rivers, marshes, and on the sands. There are oysters in abundance, with a great store of mussels; a sort of fair crabs, and a round shell-fish called horse-feet. The rivers are stored plentifully with fish that we saw leap and play.

– William Hilton, A True Relation of a Voyage Upon Discovery of Part of the Coast of Florida, 1664

After assigning the Albemarle a governor in October 1664, the proprietors went about spurring on the establishment of the two counties to the south. Happily, some settlers from the successful British colony of Barbados showed interest in exchanging the West Indies' hurricanes, tropical illnesses, unbearable humidity, and already overcrowded conditions for the chance to settle Carolina. The lords sent the self-named "Barbados Adventurers" an enthusiastic letter promising to assist them "by all way and means," and asking them to spread the word about Carolina among their planter neighbors.

The influence these Barbadians and other planters from the West Indies would eventually have over the structure and flavor of coastal Carolina culture is hard to overstate. With them they brought the socially stratified European feudalism upon which the Carolina Lowcountry was founded; their experience raising rice largely determined the economy of South Carolina's Lowcountry through the Civil War; and their preference for West African slave labor would shape Carolina society into the 21st century.

In 1663, the overeager Barbadians had sent William Hilton sailing along the Carolina coast, looking for a good site for settlement, but other than his discovery and naming of Hilton Head Island, nothing much had come of the expedition. In the fall of 1665, Barbadians established "Charles Town" in the short-lived County of Clarendon at the mouth of the Cape Faire (now "Fear") River. Before long, things in the first "Charles Town" began to resemble a particularly hard-edged episode of *Survivor*. Shipwreck, dissension, Indian trouble, and other problems distressed the settlement, although its population rose to 800 before residents finally abandoned shore and headed for the ships again. Before they did, they sent an exploratory mission captained by Robert Sandford southward to explore the Port Royal area. There, Sandford visited with the friendly Edisto Indians. When the ship left to return to Cape Faire, Dr. Henry Woodward stayed behind to explore the interior and study the native languages. When Sandford returned to the failing settlement at Clarendon, he added to the general discontent with glowing reports of the Port Royal region down in Craven County, which was as yet unsettled.

The Treacherous First Passage

Port Royal became the new focal point for the proprietors and for their Barbadian clients. Advertisements and pamphlets in England proclaimed the glories of Carolina, and recruitment rolls began to fill with adventurous and sometimes desperate men and women of all circumstances.

After many, many delays, in August 1669 the first three ships (the *Mayflowers* of South Carolina, more or less), named *Carolina, Port Royal,* and *Albemarle,* sailed from England to Barbados, arriving in late fall. Actually, the *Albemarle* turned out to be the *Santa Maria* of the journey—it sank off Barbados. After gathering up proprietor-prescribed farming supplies, the *Carolina* and *Port Royal* set sail again, with the sloop *Three Brothers* replacing the *Albemarle.* Not long afterward, the ships were separated by a storm. The *Port Royal* drifted, lost, for six weeks (running out of drinking water in the process) before finally wrecking in the Bahamas. Although 44 persons made it safely to shore, many of them died before the captain was able to build a new vessel to get them to the nearest settlement. On the new craft, the survivors reached New Providence, where the captain hired another boat that took most of the passengers to Bermuda. There, they caught up with the *Carolina.*

In Bermuda, an 80-year-old Puritan Bermudan colonist, Colonel William Sayle, was named governor of the settlement in the south part of Carolina. Under Sayle, the colonists finally reached Port Royal on March 15, 1670. As Nicholas Carteret reported, the Indians who greeted the settlers on shore made fires and approached them,

whooping in their own tongue and manner, making signs also where we should best land, and when we came ashore they stroked us on the shoulders with their hands, saying "Bony Conraro, Angles," knowing us to be English by our color.

These Indians spoke broken Spanish—a grim reminder that Spain still considered Carolina its land. The main Spanish base, in St. Augustine, was not all that far away.

Running across overgrown remnants of Spanish forts on Santa Elena island and remembering the not-so-long-ago Spanish massacre of a French colony there no doubt made the English reconsider the wisdom of settling at the hard-to-defend Port Royal. Neither did the Edistoes seem thrilled to have the English as neighbors. Fortunately for the Brits, the *cassique* (chief) of the Kiawah Indians, who lived farther north along the coast, arrived to invite them to settle among his people, in exchange for help in beating back the ever-threatening Spanish and their Westo Indian allies.

The settlers agreed to the terms and sailed for the region now called West Ashley, just south of Charleston Peninsula. There, in early April at Albemarle Point on the shores of the Ashley (the site of present-day Charles Towne Landing), they founded Charles Town. The name honored their king.

On May 23, the *Three Brothers* struggled into Charles Town Bay, minus 11 or 12 of its passengers, who had gone ashore for water and provisions at St. Catherine's Island, Georgia, and run into Indians allied with the Spanish. In fact, of the several hundred who had begun the journey from England or Barbados, only 148 survivors stepped ashore at Charles Town Landing; 3 were African slaves.

Carving Out a Home

The settlers immediately set about protecting themselves against the Spanish and their Indian allies, and not a moment too soon. In August, the Spanish at St. Augustine sent forth Indians to destroy Charles Town. Fortunately, Dr. Henry Woodward, who had been left behind by Sandford four years earlier, was now able to help. When the Spanish and Indian aggressors arrived, Woodward had just returned from a diplomatic journey throughout the region, in which he had convinced the Lowcountry's many small tribes to unite with the English into a single, powerful defense league against the hated Spanish.

Facing the united tribes and a British militia well warned of its coming, the arriving Spanish and Westoes decided they didn't really want to attack after all. The Spaniards went back to St. Augustine and decided to get serious about making that a permanent, well-fortified city.

CAROLINA BLOSSOMS

By the following February, 86 Barbadians had joined the Charles Town settlement. Shortly after that, steady old Governor Sayle died, replaced by the temporary Governor Joseph West, one of the state's most capable Colonial-era leaders. On September 1, 1671, Barbadian Governor Sir John Yeamans showed up with nearly 50 more Barbadians. Yeamans eventually replaced West as governor.

In their earliest days, the economies of both the Albemarle and Charles Town communities depended largely on trade with the Indians. To coax the continent's furs from the indigenous peoples, traders went deep into the territory—some as far as the Mississippi River—bearing metal tools, weapons, and other things for which the Native Americans were willing to trade pelts.

This same sort of trade was taking place up in Albemarle, but the lack of a deepwater port kept large ships from being able to haul the riches back to England. So while the Albemarle remained small, unprofitable, and unruly, "Carolina"—as the proprietors now referred to the Charles Town region—grew quickly in population and prosperity. By 1700, it was inarguably the crown jewel of England's North American colonies; however, with so much land and a crop system that required a great amount of labor, the bulk of South Carolina's first immigrants came as indentured servants or slaves to work for those Barbadians who were already building plantations among the coastal Sea Islands and up the rivers. Because they could legally be kept as slaves for life, and because many of them had experience growing rice back in their native country, West Africans were the preferred import.

Yet while the traders were penetrating the interior as they bartered with the Indians, the sheer logistics of the growing plantation economy meant that planters had to spread out. In *South Carolina: A Geography*, Charles Kovacik and John Winberry estimate that even as late as 1715, 90 percent of South Carolina's European/African population lived within 30 miles

PIRATES OF THE CAROLINAS

South Carolina drew a line in the seashells against piracy as early as the 1680s, when Charles Town colonists hung pirates at the mouth of Charles Town Harbor as a warning to others to keep out. But the poorer people of North Carolina – with less to lose and more to gain from the free-spending, goods-dealing buccaneers – tolerated a certain amount of piracy. Pirates even worked hand-in-hand with corrupt government officials, including Governor Charles Eden. Edward "Blackbeard" Teach, one of the most notorious pirates of all time, frequented Beaufort, selling his stolen wares openly on the wharves of Bath. In 1718, Blackbeard's and Charles Vane's crews held a large, festive "saturnalia," considered one of the largest pirate gatherings ever held in North America.

Many pirates were originally legitimate sailors who had been encouraged by their mother countries to attack, loot, and commandeer ships owned by competing imperialist nations. These "privateers" were paid with whatever they stole, so, in fact, the European governments themselves educated a generation of sailors about the joys available to those who combined a little avarice with their violence. When the War of Spanish Succession ended in 1714, it left a lot of well-trained sea robbers out of work. To no one's surprise, most privateers simply kept doing what they had been doing – now without official sanction – and became pirates.

In 1717, Blackbeard anchored just outside Charles Town Harbor. When a ship stopped to await a pilot boat to lead it through the shoals and into the docks, the pirates pounced. When the pilot boat arrived, they grabbed that, too. Then they proceeded to rob the next seven or eight ships that came along – ships carrying materials the young colony needed to survive.

Finally, Blackbeard grabbed a ship with several Carolina notables on it. He sent messengers ashore to tell the Charles Townians that he was holding their neighbors hostage and would kill them unless he received a shipment of medicine. Given the alternative, the people of Charles Town coughed up the requested provisions. The passengers were released – robbed to their skivvies, but alive.

South Carolina's Governor Robert Johnson complained to the lords proprietors, who took a deep breath, rolled up their puffy sleeves, and... rang for another snifter of brandy. To their credit, the English government, realizing their role in creating this predicament, and the difficulty of actually rounding up all these scurvy bilge rats and swinging them from the nearest yardarm, at least tried to help. In September 1718, the royal government offered amnesty for any piracy committed before the previous January. Many pirates took advantage of the opportunity to wipe their records clean, hoping to begin new, reasonably upstanding lives.

After the halfhearted pirates took an early retirement, the meaner, saltier pirates pulled out all the stops, repeatedly blocking Charles Town harbor, capturing every ship that attempted to land there. Pirate captain Charles Vane looted a slave ship of much of its human cargo just outside the harbor (the poor Africans were no doubt resold elsewhere), looted another craft from Boston, and then accosted four more ships trying to slip out. Then word came that yet another pirate ship was barreling down the coast, headed for Charles Town.

THE CITIZENS' REVENGE

Johnson and the rest of the colony had just about had it. With no one to turn to, the South Carolinians resolved to help themselves. Johnson put Colonel William Rhett in charge of two of Charles Town. The danger from the Spanish and Westoes was simply too great for most would-be pioneers to venture farther afield.

Those whites who did live out on the plantations lived largely among their own slaves, with African American bond servants outnumbering free persons often as much as 10 to 1 in some districts. The voices of whites who warned that planters were setting themselves up for an insurrection were lost amid the clinking of gold in the planters' coffers. The Barbadians had turned a wild land into a boom economy

sloops and a force of 130 men. The sloops took off south after Vane, but to no avail. Still itching for a fight, they tacked northward and sailed past Charles Town toward Cape Fear, in search of the pirates who were rumored to be on the way. They arrived at sunset and espied in the dying light the masts of the infamous pirate Stede Bonnet, commanding an eight-gun sloop, the *Royal James*, and two unarmed trading vessels – recently acquired prizes.

Both groups of men spent the hot, salty August night in the cramped cabins of their respective sloops, preparing for battle at sunrise. At first light, Bonnet raised anchor; Rhett gave chase, but in the excitement – and with all parties in unfamiliar waters – both Bonnet and the two Carolina ships ran upon shoals, fixing the three ships in a kind of still-life chase scene. One of the Carolina ships was stuck out of firing range of the pirates, but Rhett's ship was mired within musket range (in 1718, that was not very far away).

In a straight-out cannonfest, the better-armed Carolina boat could have won the day handily. But then the tide turned – or ebbed. Rhett's ship, the *Henry*, tilted sharply toward Bonnet's ship, as if to say, "Here, let me help you shoot my crew." At the same time, the *Henry*'s guns were now pointing at water – good for bagging porpoises, but completely useless against the pirates. The men on deck scrambled for their lives, most diving into the hold, others crumpling as the shots found them. For six straight hours, the pirate guns pounded the *Henry*. Except for the wounded and dying above decks, the Carolinians huddled down below, praying, no doubt, for high tide. Both crews knew that if Rhett's men could withstand the barrage until the tide came back in, the first ship to rise off its shoal would have the other at its mercy.

The tide came in. Slowly, the battered *Henry* tilted upright, and slowly her guns rose... until they pointed straight at the side of the *Royal James*. The Carolinians staggered from the dank hold of the ship where they'd spent the most harrowing day of their lives, and, standing amid the bodies of 10 shipmates, prepared to board the pirate's ship. Rhett promised to intercede for Bonnet with the governor if Bonnet allowed the Carolinians to board without further bloodshed. With five men already dead and two mortally wounded, Bonnet raised a white flag.

Rhett brought his prisoners back to Charles Town, where 22 of them were executed. Bonnet managed to escape, but was recaptured and sentenced to death. Remembering his promise, Rhett made a passionate plea for the pirate's life, even offering to sail Bonnet to England to personally plead his case before the king, but Johnson demurred. On December 10, 1718, Bonnet was hanged.

THE PIRATE ERA ENDS

Immediately following the capture of Bonnet, another two pirate ships – commanded by a Captain Worley – set up right outside Charles Town harbor. Rhett, who was angry at having had his word violated by the governor, refused to take part in any further action against the pirates. So the governor himself decided to lead the operation. Outfitting four vessels with 70 concealed guns, Johnson deliberately sailed into Worley's trap. When Worley fired, Johnson's men returned fire. The shocked pirates tried to escape, but after a four-hour flight and fight, both pirate ships were sunk. Most hands were saved long enough to be hanged. Only a few days later, on November 22, 1718, Blackbeard was killed in battle off Virginia's Ocracoke Island, marking the end of the Pirate Era.

before, and they were certain that slavery was the way to do it.

The proprietors, who were all for government by the elite, were not too concerned about the explosion of slavery in Carolina. Neither were the royals, because slavery was still legal in the British empire. What concerned them was Carolina's exports: Carolinian rice (and, after 1740, indigo) was extremely valuable to the empire; in the 1730s, England even made a point of settling Georgia to act as a buffer zone between the prized plantations of Carolina and the Spanish at St. Augustine.

By 1680 Charles Town settlers had decided that the Albemarle Point spot was too unhealthful and hard to defend; some settlers began moving north to Oyster Point, site of the present-day Charleston Battery. The white-shell point at the end of a narrow-necked peninsula was much easier to defend; there was no question about which direction a ground attack might come from, and anybody attacking from the harbor would be visible a long ways off. In May 1680, the lords proprietors instructed the governor and his council to resettle Charles Town at Oyster Point. It really *was* a better spot. Because it was low on the peninsula, coastal planters both north and south of the town could easily transport their goods to Charleston's port using tidal creeks.

Fortunately for the colony, accepted standards for political stability were low in the 17th century, and new colonists continued to arrive, rebellions or not. Boatloads of French Huguenot Protestants began arriving in 1680; France's 1685 repeal of religious freedoms for non-Catholics accelerated this process.

By now, the Spanish had agreed to stop harassing the English settlement at Charles Town, and they forbade any further encroachment to the south. In 1684, a group of Scottish religious dissenters had tried to start up a community at Port Royal, but Floridian Spanish raided it and, with their Creek allies, slaughtered most of the residents. In 1686, 100 Spanish, free blacks, and Indians landed at Edisto Island and broke into Governor Joseph Morton's house, stealing his valuables and kidnapping and then murdering his brother-in-law. They also kidnapped/liberated/stole 13 of Morton's slaves. Although the Spanish offered liberty to escaped English slaves, two of them escaped and returned to their master.

The concept of the Carolinas as two distinct entities, north and south, and not one or three, had begun to take root. By 1695, Charles Town's citizens (or rather, their slaves) had built thick stone walls and six bastions, making the city into an armed fortress. By 1702, England was embroiled in Queen Anne's War with France and Spain. Because the French were now in the Mississippi Valley to the west, and the Spanish in Florida to the south, the penned-in Carolinians decided to be proactive and attack the Spanish stronghold of St. Augustine. Although Moore's men were able to clean out smaller Spanish settlements between the rival capitals, the War of Augustino ended in failure.

The following year, brave settlers on the southern side of Charles Town established the town of Beaufort at the location of the massacred Scottish settlement of Stuart Town. Although settlement continued to accelerate, the first part of the 18th century brought numerous problems to the coast—pirates and the Tuscarora and Yamassee wars principal among them. In each case, when the colonists pleaded with England for help, the proprietors took a deep breath, rolled up their puffy sleeves, and. . . did nothing.

THE YAMASSEE WAR

The Carolina settlers suffered from animosities with the indigenous peoples as early as 1671, when they declared open war on the Kussoes, a Lowcountry tribe who had been stealing corn from the settlers' public holds—and whom they believed to be in league with the Spanish. But by and large, Carolina's Indians and settlers got along in an interdependent fashion, as Charles Town merchants sold and shipped the furs that traders acquired farther upstate. Unfortunately, the men who lived among and traded with the various indigenous tribes, as one settler admitted, "were not (generally) men of the best morals." Many tended to cheat the Indians in financial dealings and were known to seduce Indian women and use violence against the men. Against the pleas of the village chiefs, they continued to sell whiskey to the men of the tribe. And worst, perhaps, was the fact that traders—against the wisdom of most other Carolinians—liked to extend credit to the Indians, allowing them to run up cumulative tabs as high as an estimated 50,000 pounds sterling. Even if they forgave the Europeans' other harassments, the Indians had a strong financial motive for throwing off the strangling yoke of the English.

On top of all this, some of the Lowcountry tribes were concerned about squatters who had begun encroaching on land they hadn't first purchased from the Indians. So universal in fact was Indian resentment against them that one tribe—some suspect the Upcountry Creek, although most believe it to have been the Lowcountry Yamassee—went about spreading word of an upcoming intertribal massacre of the traders and the rest of the non-Indians in Carolina. Odds are that the Spanish, who were always trying to present themselves as the Indians' true friend, egged on the violence.

Initial Violence

In 1715, some settlers in the Port Royal area heard from Indian friends that such a plot was taking shape, especially among the local Yamassees, a tribe who had moved up from the Spanish-held Georgia coast with the Carolinians' permission in the 1680s and settled on and near Coosawhatchie Island. The planters were well aware of the unscrupulousness of many traders—something like the used-car salesmen of the Colonial era—and promptly sent a delegation to the Yamassee town of Pocotaligo to promise redress of their grievances and let them know that the governor was on the way to negotiate treaties with them. On April 14, the Yamassee welcomed the Carolina diplomats, received their message, fed them dinner, and then, the following dawn, murdered most of them. A few were taken prisoner. Among these were Indian agent Thomas

Nairne, whom they subsequently burned at the stake in a prolonged torture that took several days. All told, the Yamassee killed somewhere around 90 settlers who were living with them at Pocotaligo. Then they moved on to Port Royal, where they killed 100 more whites and Africans.

The First Stage

South Carolina Governor Charles Craven was en route to the Yamassee negotiations when word of the slaughter reached him. He immediately called out the meager state militia and, leading the troops himself, attacked in retaliation. He stopped them at the Stono River, and sent a company of riflemen up by water to Port Royal, from which they sailed up the river to Pocotaligo and destroyed the town.

When Craven had sent the delegation to Pocotaligo, he'd also dispatched messengers to each of the other tribes supposedly involved in the conspiracy, sending conciliatory messages, along with pleas for help in standing against the Yamassee. One by one, each of Craven's messengers drifted back into camp with grim news: their assigned tribe had massacred every or nearly every white man, woman, and child among them.

Although an estimated 16 Indian nations, reaching as far as present-day Alabama, began the war as part of a coalition with the Yamassee and Creeks, most of these tribes were more concerned with exacting vengeance on the scurrilous traders than with wholesale genocide. Given the overwhelming ratio of Native Americans to Europeans and Africans, only the humanity of these reluctant warriors spared the Carolinians from complete annihilation.

After the first wave of killing, frightened settlers came fleeing to the walled city of Charleston. One thing Carolina had on its side was a shrewd governor. Craven realized quickly that this was not going to be a brief campaign. He also knew well that once the initial excitement had died down and the most obvious threat had passed, his untrained militiamen were going to want to head back home—and that this was just what the Indians would be waiting for. To prevent this, he declared martial law and ordered militia deserters put to death. He also sent messengers to the other colonies and to England pleading for assistance.

By June 6, Craven and an army of 250 Carolinian militiamen and Native Americans, in cooperation with another party of men led by Colonel Robert Barnwell (who sailed south past Beaufort and approached from the rear), decisively defeated the Yamassee at Pocotaligo, at the head of the Cumbahee (Salkehatchie) River.

The Second Stage

Now the Cheraws and Creeks grew more aggressive in the north, marching southeast toward Charles Town. North Carolina's Colonel Maurice Moore headed down with a small army to help, and Craven and his militia marched north to join them. But no sooner had Craven and his now-700-man militia crossed the Santee River than a party of 700 Native Americans attacked European settlements from the south, pouring across the Edisto River and burning and slaying their way up the coast until only a few miles stood between them and the cowering city of Charles Town. Fortunately for the Holy City, when word came that Craven was returning, the Indians retreated.

In fact, the number of men who could legally take up arms to defend the colony—white men, free blacks, and loyal Native Americans—stood at only 1,400–1,500, and men not yet burned out of their homes were understandably torn between staying to support and defend their houses and families and joining the militia to battle the aggressors directly elsewhere. The Indians numbered an estimated 15,000. The Colonial Assembly voted to raise a "standing army" of 1,200 men, to include 600 white Carolinians, 100 Virginian mercenaries, 100 loyal Indians, and (here you can hear the collective "gulp!" of Lowcountry planters) 400 African Americans or other slaves. The move to arm the African American slaves—who, their advocates noted, were just as concerned about their families' safety as anyone else—was a wise one, although it understandably made a lot of slave owners nervous.

Craven sent agents to Virginia, New York, and Boston to get men, guns, and ammunition. Virginia, which was by far the strongest colony and most able to help, was making a fortune while South Carolina was preoccupied and unable to trade with the Indians. Finally, Virginia Governor Alexander Spotswood convinced his stingy burgesses to send 130 men. The burgesses agreed but demanded that South Carolina send up 130 African American slave women to take these men's places at their jobs.

Virginia dragged its gutters to come up with its 130 men, many of them derelicts and malcontents whom they were just as glad to get out of the state. South Carolina knew it shouldn't look a gift horse in the mouth, but it also realized that to take the 130 women Virginia wanted away from their slave husbands for a prolonged period was a good way to start a slave insurrection. Wisely, South Carolina never made good on its part of the deal.

Up in New York, the governor of New York and New Jersey attempted to get the Seneca Indians to come down and help fight on the side of the English, but they proved unwilling. Most colonies were hesitant to send along their best fighting men when, for all they knew, a riot might break out among Indians in their own region. To forestall this eventuality, the British government sent along 1,000 muskets, 600 pistols, 2,000 grenades, and 201 barrels of gunpowder, but no soldiers.

The lords proprietors (in some cases the heirs of the original grantee) helped very little at all. They provided some money but weren't able to ship any arms or ammunition. The British Parliament told them to hand over the province if they couldn't defend it; the lords told the king he could buy the property if he wanted, but that they would never give it up without getting paid the fair price. Just what the "fair price" for a colony full of butchered colonists and their slaves was, the lords did not say. So, while the Carolinians sweated and looked longingly eastward for their deliverance, a debate arose in England about what the proper price of South Carolina should be, and about whether England really needed a colony in Carolina after all.

The Cherokee to the Rescue

Fortunately for the Carolinians, their salvation didn't depend on the actions in England. In truth, it rested in another nation, just a few hundred miles away. North Carolina's Colonel Maurice Moore took 300 men up the eastern side of the Savannah River and into the homeland of the Lower Cherokee peoples. The Cherokee were old trading partners with the British, and aside from murdering a few corrupt traders, they had taken no part in the violence thus far. They wavered back and forth between remaining neutral and joining the British to help them defeat the other tribes. If the Cherokees helped the English and the English won, the Cherokees would be in a great position to demand land rights they coveted. And if they did *not* help the English and the Creek and Yamassee—the Cherokees' longtime adversaries—won, the Cherokees would probably be the coalition's next target. In fact, though, this was true whether or not the Cherokees helped the English. So it was ultimately in the Cherokees' best interest to protect their trading partners.

Finally, an incident between the Cherokees and the envoys sent by the nearby Creeks, who wanted to murder the English in the woods on the way back to Charleston, decided the issue. On January 27, 1716, the red "war stick" was sent throughout the Cherokee villages to announce that the Cherokees would fight on the side of the English.

A Hostile Peace

This Cherokee/Carolinian combination was unstoppable, and the other tribes knew it. Most of them quickly made peace upon the Cherokees' arrival. The Lower Creeks bolted from their Georgia homes and fled clear to the Chattahoochee River. The Cherokees also put an end to the Cheraws' bartering for guns with Virginia traders.

Knowing the war was essentially won, Craven sailed that April for the mother country,

leaving Colonel Robert Daniel to serve as governor in his stead. Isolated killings of settlers continued for another year or so, but by the summer of 1717 even these had tapered off to a prewar level. All told, 400 settlers had been killed during battle, many of them in the initial ambushes. History doesn't record how many Native Americans died, but the number was horrendous. The once-great Yamassee tribe was devastated, and its members drifted south, eventually becoming part of the hodgepodge Seminole people. South Carolina, which had generally tried to help the "loyal" tribes get along, was now confronted with the threat of a united Indian coalition attacking them. From now on, the Carolinians' theory was divide and rule.

Perhaps the most profound result of the Yamassee War was the way it proved the lords proprietors' inability, or unwillingness, to protect the lives and livelihoods of those to whose labor they owed much of their wealth. When the colonists had come to them for help, the proprietors had passed the sixpence. Although they certainly didn't mean to do it, the proprietors convinced the Carolinian settlers that they didn't need lords proprietors at all.

"DOWN WITH THE LORDS, UP WITH THE KING!"

By 1719, it was time for a revolution, South Carolina style. It was a very polite and orderly revolution. Everyone said "please," "thank you," and "yes, ma'am." No one was killed. In a sense, the South Carolina Revolution of 1719 was the opposite of the Revolution of 1776. Colonists in 1776 tended to feel some fidelity to the distant King George, even while hating the governors and soldiers he had installed over them. But the Revolutionists of 1719—which, again, unlike 1776, included just about everyone—respected proprietary governor Robert Johnson, who had, after all, just saved Charles Town from the pirates. But Johnson wasn't popular enough to atone for the sins of the lords proprietors back home. In November 1719, Carolina elected James Moore as governor and sent an emissary to England to ask the king to make Carolina a royal province with a royal governor and direct recourse to the English government.

The royal government, which had interest in Carolina's exports and realized that the lords proprietors were not up to the task of protecting the colony, agreed. While this was all being worked out, South Carolina was a self-ruling nation for two years. At the end of this time, Carolinians elected Robert Johnson—the old proprietary governor—as the first royal governor.

Now that the boundaries of South Carolina were more or less defined (although disputes with Georgia over the exact border extended into the 1980s), Johnson set about trying to encourage settlement in the western frontier—both to make Charles Town's shipping more profitable and to provide a buffer against whomever might next want to cause the Carolinians grief. The western frontier at this point meant just about everything beyond the coastal inlets and river mouths.

Johnson also wanted to protect Charles Town and Beaufort from the Spanish and Indians to the south. In 1721, he established a fort manned with British pensioners and by Tuscarora Jack Barnwell on the Altamaha River near present-day Darien. When the small Yamacraw tribe, who had made a lot of enemies fighting for the British during the Yamassee War, asked if they could relocate on British turf, Johnson told them they could relocate south of the Savannah River. The Yamacraw wanted to be as close as possible to the military might of the British and they picked the best, safest site they could find, a spot on the southern bank of the Savannah River, which gave them freshwater and fish. Their spot was also on a bluff, which cut down on the bugs and allowed them to spot any waterborne enemies while they were still a long ways off.

Oglethorpe and the Georgia Pioneers

Of course, Charles Town and the Crown were never really comfortable with the Yamacraw arrangement. After all, another "friendly" tribe, the Yamassee, had just spearheaded a war

that had slaughtered 400 Carolinian settlers. What the English really wanted as a buffer for Charles Town was a strong British city. And then along came James Oglethorpe.

Oglethorpe was a 33-year-old English parliamentarian. Although he came from a privileged family in Godalming, Surrey, he was not exactly your average English parliamentarian. For starters, before taking office, he had spent time in prison for stabbing a man to death in a drunken barroom fight. This brief experience in prison (power and privilege shortening his sentence to five months) gave him an understanding of the less-privileged that most of his peers lacked. After taking office, however, he spent six years of mediocrity in London. Then a young writer friend, Robert Castell, failed in publishing a book, dropped into debt, and was thrown into London's Fleet Street debtor's prison. Quickly, Oglethorpe had come to grasp the corruption of the system, in which debtors were charged exorbitant lodging fees for their squalid quarters, even as they attempted to work their way out of debt. Castell contracted smallpox after arrival and died a short time afterward.

Oglethorpe immediately sought to reform English prisons, but the changes that came were too slow and ultimately too ineffective. Soon, the new Parliament prison reform group began to envision a better system. One thing that was needed was jobs that would allow the poor to escape their station rather than falling into debt. Oglethorpe and the others envisioned the "New World" as a place where overpopulated Englanders could start anew. To sell the idea, he promoted the notion that, as he wrote in his promotional journal, "England will grow Rich by sending her Poor Abroad," asserting that the land south of Carolina was eager to grow mulberry trees, and hence, silk, for British settlers. In fact, the early symbol for the colony was a maple leaf with a silkworm and cocoon, along with the altruistic motto, *Not for Ourselves, But for Others.*

This suited King George II just fine. After all, he already wanted to settle the area as a buffer for Spain, and Oglethorpe's mulberry idea would help England to become less dependent on silk from the hated French. Oglethorpe also promised to provide for the resettlement of the oppressed Protestants of Germany, which—given that George II was more German than English—was not only a benevolent but also a shrewd idea. King George appointed Oglethorpe and 21 other Parliament members as trustees of the Georgia Settlement. Of these, Oglethorpe was the only one to ever live in the colony.

Coming to Georgia

The king signed Georgia's charter in April 1732, and the next months were busy ones. More than 600 people applied to be allowed into the colony, and only 114 were chosen. Oglethorpe thoroughly planned each element of the new settlement, including laying out the town's grid, which featured easily defendable wards centered on common squares. He also created statutes forbidding the presence of Roman Catholics, slaves, lawyers, and hard liquor in the colony.

The reason for banning Catholics was easy to understand: Both Spain and France had designs on the region, and both were Catholic nations. Oglethorpe and others feared that a Catholic Georgian might feel a first loyalty to other Catholics. The trustees and Oglethorpe agreed that slaves must be banned for several reasons, not the least of which was the hypocrisy of slavery in a humanitarian colony. Oglethorpe wrote:

> If we allow slaves we act against the very principles by which we associated together, which was to relieve the distressed. Whereas now we should occasion the misery of thousands in Africa. . . and bring into perpetual slavery the poor people who now live free there.

The trustees worried that slaveholding would lead to idleness on the part of the owners. Because the settlers were all impoverished to begin with, Oglethorpe deemed it wise to keep them busy.

Lawyers were banned because they were seen as an agent of corruption in the English legal system. If any man needed to appear in court, he could "represent his own Cause, as in old times in England," as Oglethorpe put it. Finally, the reasons for banning hard liquor were similar to those for banning slavery. Life would be hard enough without lawyers and drunkenness. Oglethorpe did, however, allow wine and beer. He was said to enjoy a quaff as much as the next man and brought 20 tons of beer across with the first settlers.

The *Anne* raised its anchor at Gravesend, England, in November 17, 1732. At the last minute Oglethorpe decided that he would go along—the only trustee to do so. He immediately became the leader of the group, and although he had no formal authority, the settlers treated him as the leader, calling him "Father Oglethorpe." The *Anne* sailed uneventfully across the Atlantic to Carolina. Oddly, not one of the settlers had been pulled from, or had ever spent time in, a debtor's prison. It may have been that some imprisoned debtors tried to join the expedition but were held back by their creditors who, after all, had been stern enough to throw them into debtor's prison in the first place. Yet although there were no debtors, Georgia's first settlers were very poor, and in this sense, Oglethorpe was working proactively in the interest of the downtrodden, giving them a chance to prosper before the cycle of poverty led them to the doorway of the debtor's prison.

The 35 original families sailed across the Atlantic, the men drilling in the use of muskets, bayonets, and swords on the journey across. They stopped at Charles Town, where Oglethorpe went ashore for supplies, then on to Beaufort, where everyone got off the ship. Meanwhile, Oglethorpe and a scouting party, aided by Charles Townian and future South Carolina Governor William Bull, headed up the inland waterways to Tybee Island, Oglethorpe's original choice for the site of the new town.

The island, it turned out, was mostly marshes; Oglethorpe said it wouldn't work.

Bull remarked that there was a nice spot on a bluff about 12 miles up the river, but the Yamacraw Indians had settled there. They were a small tribe, however, and friendly to the British. Oglethorpe reasoned that if the Native Americans, who knew the region, had chosen the bluff, it was probably a good spot. The party headed up the river.

The Yamacraw welcomed them with open arms, although not from completely altruistic motives. After relocating to the region, the Yamacraw found themselves amid a coastline full of Creek who were allied with the Spanish and antagonistic to the smaller tribe. Having the British on their side would help the Yamacraw, and so their chieftain Tomochichi welcomed them and agreed to let them build on a section of the bluff. Later, friendly treaties ceded the entire coastline to the English, except for St. Catherine's, Sapelo, and Ossabaw islands, which were to remain forever Indian.

Colonial Belle

Savannah became Georgia's first city, named—so most historians agree—after the Spanish word for the river, *Sabina,* or for the savanna grasses all around the area.

The bans against slavery, rum, lawyers, and Catholics fell one by one. Almost from the first, colonists had sent petitions to England to try to remove the ban against slavery. Although Oglethorpe had early on dismissed their protests, noting that "The Idle ones are indeed for Negroes," the ban against slaves faced several challenges. First, the English did not have enough warm bodies to perform the work necessary to make the Georgia wilderness into a profitable region. Oglethorpe himself had borrowed South Carolinian slaves to perform the onerous work of clearing the town site, although he had quickly sent them back when the job was through. Second, toiling Georgians had only to look across the Savannah River to South Carolina to see other colonists getting rich quick through the use of African slaves, and Georgians needed only to abandon Savannah, cross the river, and buy land there to take part in that bonanza. Even still, the trustees held out until

1750—just three years before the end of the trustee period—before formally removing the ban against slavery. Three years later, the population of Georgia was one-third slave.

The ban against rum had lasted only until 1742; John Musgrove, a trader who had moved down from Charles Town and had actually been with Tomochichi when he first greeted Oglethorpe at the bluff, had tempted settlers and Native Americans alike with the demon drink, and many had succumbed. Beer-drinking James Oglethorpe was convinced that rum was largely responsible for the strange fevers that killed 1 in 10 of the colonists in the first summer. He petitioned his fellow trustees in 1738 for more beer because he believed that the presence of beer—and its cheaper price—kept the colonists from turning to rum. By 1742, however, Oglethorpe had turned his focus to the new settlement at Frederica. Savannahians convinced the other trustees that the ineffective ban wasn't stopping rum drinking anyway, and the ban was removed.

Even quicker to go was the ban against Catholics; just six months after the town's founding, a boatload of Portuguese Jewish refugees washed up in Savannah; one of them happened to be a doctor, Samuel Nunes Ribeiro, and because fevers had already killed the town's only physician, Nunes and the rest were gladly welcomed. Oglethorpe credited Nunes's treatment of victims with saving the colony.

In 1736, Oglethorpe established 177 Scotch Highlanders at the southern edge of the English-American frontier in what is now Darien. Six years later, Oglethorpe and his men turned back a Spanish attack on St. Simons Island, in the Battle of Bloody Marsh. Because it ended Spanish attempts at possession north of Florida, ensuring English dominance in North America, historians consider this little-known battle one of the most important in American, and even world, history.

As the threat of hostile Spanish and Native Americans decreased, inland settlements blossomed, many of them settled by various ethnic and/or religious groups. Whatever surplus the Upcountry residents did create was likely to be shipped out through Charleston or Savannah. Consequently, the coastal region grew richer and richer.

In fact, no other English colony enjoyed the amount of wealth now concentrated in the South Carolina Lowcountry. Plantations generated more than one million British pounds annually, allowing planters to hire private tutors for their children and to send their sons to England for further education. These well-educated planters' sons, who were familiar with, but not unduly impressed by the subtleties of English law, would eventually lead the charge for the colony's independence from the mother country.

Of course, if only a handful of elites had wanted revolution, the Revolution would never have taken place. But while the wealthy were essentially being raised to lead, the colony's constant battles with Indians, the French, and the Spanish were enhancing the average colonist's feelings of military competence and independence.

"DOWN WITH THE KING, UP WITH LIBERTY!"
Prerevolutionary Agitations

At first glance, most tidewater South Carolinians and Georgians had little reason to want to go to war with England. As British colonists, coastal Georgians and South Carolinians had prospered more than any other; however, the Lowcountry elites had ruled the colony for so long that when an impoverished Crown began taxing the American colonies to raise revenues, the rulers felt put upon. To protest the Stamp Act, South Carolina sent wealthy rice planter Thomas Lynch, 26-year-old lawyer John Rutledge, and Christopher Gadsden to the Stamp Act Congress, held in New York in 1765. Historians commonly group the hotheaded Gadsden—leader of Charles Town's pro-Independence "Liberty Boys" (akin to Boston's Sons of Liberty)—together with Massachusetts' James Otis and Patrick Henry as one of the three prime agitators for American independence. Gadsden designed the famous "Don't Tread on Me" flag, which was first

hoisted on John Paul "I Have Not Yet Begun to Fight" Jones's *Alfred* on December 3, 1775. The flag features a rattlesnake with 13 rattles, each representing an American colony.

Georgia's popular South Carolina–born governor James Wright convinced the colony's leaders to stay home from the Stamp Act Congress, and soon Carolinians were publicly criticizing the "weak and unpatriotic Georgians who refused to join in support of the fight for American freedom," and threatening to stop trade with Savannah. South of Savannah, the little Puritan town of Midway was the birthplace of Georgia patriotism; its citizens threatened and even tried to secede from Georgia and join their fellow liberty lovers in South Carolina.

But if Savannah's masses had not yet turned against the Crown, several discontented men began meeting at Peter Tondee's Tavern at Broughton and Whitaker streets, calling themselves the local chapter of the "Liberty Boys." They donned Liberty stocking caps, gathered to decry their mistreatment over steins of grog, and by the time of the American Revolution, would number in the hundreds. They even tried to seize the stamps when they landed in Savannah but were turned back by the muskets of Wright's soldiers.

Although England repealed the Stamp Act in 1766, the 1767 Townsend Acts laid new taxes on glass, wine, oil, paper, tea, and other goods. In South Carolina, Gadsden led the opposition. Even the Georgia Assembly, meeting in Savannah, drew the line at implementing the 1765 Quartering Act, which forced colonists to pay for quartering soldiers that England sent to watch over them. Even when the British removed the taxes from everything except tea, Charles Townians mirrored their Bostonian brethren by holding a tea party, dumping a shipment into the Cooper River. Other shipments, although allowed to land, were left to rot in Charles Town storehouses.

One year later, Benjamin Franklin was planning to head to London to try to intercede on behalf of his native Pennsylvania. Having been previously moved to contribute to Savannah's

Bethesda Orphanage and having sponsored a printing business in Charles Town, Franklin offered to represent Georgia's interests in London as well. When delegates from the colonies (except Georgia, which still refused to send any) came together for the First Continental Congress in 1774, five South Carolinians, including the three who had represented the colony in the Stamp Act Congress, headed for Philadelphia, and South Carolinian Henry Middleton served as president for part of the Congress. The following January, after being disbanded by Royal Governor William Campbell, the South Carolina Colonial assembly re-formed as the extralegal Provincial Congress. During this and subsequent meetings, in June 1775 and March 1776, the South Carolinians created a temporary government to rule until the colony ironed things out with England. Henry Laurens and, later, John Rutledge were voted "president" (de facto governor) of the state.

Unfortunately for the Revolutionaries, not all Georgians and Carolinians believed it practical or even moral to separate from the British government. Many of these loyalists—or "Tories"—came from the western parts of the colonies, where domination by the elitist Savannah and Charles Town planter class in an unsupervised new government sounded worse than continued subservience to the British Crown. In South Carolina, in order to win over converts to the "American Cause," Judge William Henry Drayton and the Reverend William Tennent were sent into the backcountry to evangelize for the Lowcountry's General Committee and Provincial Congress. They met with limited success.

By 1774, Georgia's patriots were in open revolt. Their highest-ranking political leader, Johnathan Bryan, was pressured to resign from the legislature. When English ships closed Boston's port as punishment for the Boston Tea Party, Savannah's Liberty Boys sent more than 500 barrels of rice to feed the suffering Bostonians and express their solidarity.

In July 1775, 102 delegates meeting at the second Provincial Congress at Tondee's Tavern sent a petition to the king, asking him to control his oppressive parliament, and declaring that in the meantime, "a civil war in America" had already begun.

Georgia Governor Wright dissolved the Colonial assembly to try to give everyone a chance to cool off, but when he tried to reconvene them, the members refused to come. In September 1775, the Royal Governor William Campbell dissolved what would be South Carolina's last-ever Royal Assembly, and, declaring, "I never will return to Charleston till I can support the King's authority, and protect his faithful and loyal subjects," was rowed out to the safety of the British warship *Tamar* in Charleston Harbor.

Violence Erupts

The popular consciousness has so intertwined the American South with the Civil War that it's often forgotten that the Revolution was also fought down here. It's said that history is written by the victor, and in an odd way, the North's triumph in the Civil War long gave Northern academia—centered in Boston, the self-proclaimed "Athens of America"—the job of telling the whole American story. And in the Northern version, the Revolutionary battles fought in New England and thereabouts are given all the emphasis. As a result, many people are surprised to find out that South Carolina and Georgia were the site of any Revolutionary action at all. They're even more surprised when (and if) they learn that 137 significant Revolutionary battles were fought within South Carolina's borders—more than in any other state.

On November 19, 1775, revolutionists (or "Whigs") fought loyalist forces in the old western Cherokee lands at Ninety Six, spilling the first South Carolinian blood of the war. Colonel Richard Richardson rushed a large party of Whigs Upcountry to squelch the uprisings there and to assert the power of the Revolutionary General Committee over the entire colony.

The "South First" Strategy, Part I

With war erupting in and around Boston, the British decided that their best strategy was to take advantage of the strong loyalist support in the Southern colonies, beginning a military drive from Charleston that might sweep through the Upcountry, then on through North Carolina and Virginia, gathering men along the way with whom to take on Washington in the North.

When the South Carolinians under William Moultrie brought the British Navy a stunning defeat at the battle of Sullivan's Island in late June 1776, they gave the American army its first major victory. When the news reached the Colonial delegates up in Philadelphia a few days later, it emboldened them to write up and sign a Declaration of Independence from England. The Sullivan's Island debacle also caused the British to rethink their strategy, and they abandoned the South for nearly three years.

Other Events

Late but not too late, Georgia had elected representatives to the Second Continental Congress, who headed north to join the Congress in Philadelphia, which was already in progress. Months later, when the first copy of the Declaration of Independence came to Savannah, one of the places it was read aloud was, fittingly, by the Liberty Pole in front of Tondee's Tavern. Archibald Bulloch, ancestor of Theodore Roosevelt, was elected the state's first governor. Unfortunately, he died mysteriously after a month in office. Declaration of Independence signer Button Gwinnett took office temporarily.

The British, having failed to establish a beachhead at Charles Town, sent troops south to Florida as a staging area for attacks on Georgia and Carolina. Savannah prepared for attack by putting Darien's Scottish military leader Colonel Lachlan McIntosh, a veteran of the Battle of Bloody Marsh, in charge of nearly 300 men. Then it proactively sent troops south to attack the British at their camps in Florida, but as with Oglethorpe's failed attack decades earlier, the troops failed miserably in the Florida swamps. McIntosh and Gwinnett differed as to who bore responsibility for the debacle; Gwinnett—who hadn't been chosen to serve a complete term as governor—challenged

McIntosh to a duel. McIntosh and Gwinnett wounded each other in the leg, but Gwinnett's wound, after a weekend of suffering, ended in death. McIntosh decided to leave for the north to serve under George Washington.

The "South First" Strategy, Part II

By 1778, the British had seen enough success up north to attempt the 1776 south-to-north strategy a second time. With George Washington's troops now mired down in the North, the idea was to sandwich them by pushing troops up from the south while Washington tried to defend himself to the north.

British troops sailed up to Savannah from St. Augustine, Florida. Led by a local slave they had bribed, they snuck around the patriots' fortress through a little-used marsh path and easily took the town. Governor Wright was restored to power. Shortly thereafter, the British took Beaufort as well.

In October 1779, French, American, and Irish forces put Savannah under bombardment in a prolonged attempt to retake the town, but when British Colonel John Mailand hurried south from Beaufort and snuck 800 British by the Americans in the fog, the king's troops were strengthened to the point of invulnerability. When the pro-Colonials finally launched their clumsily coordinated ground assault, they charged to their slaughter.

By 1780, the British were back on Charles Town's doorstep, landing on John's Island, from where they moved across to James Island and attacked Charles Town. After a two-month siege, General Benjamin Lincoln (who had failed in the attempt to reclaim Savannah, and had now foolishly allowed his army to get bottled up on the Charles Town peninsula) was forced to surrender his men—practically every Continental soldier in the Carolinas—to British General Clinton. An army of Continentals under General Gates marched into the state to try to reclaim it for the patriots, but it suffered a devastating defeat at Camden.

This was the low point for the Carolina Revolutionaries. The fence-sitting Carolinians who had finally been persuaded to take the independent government seriously now rubbed their eyes and once again proclaimed allegiance to the king. Even Henry Middleton, onetime president of the First Continental Congress, was forced as a prisoner at Charles Town to take an oath of allegiance to the Crown.

On June 4, 1780, General Henry Clinton gloated:

> With the greatest pleasure I further report. . . that the inhabitants form every quarter reparit to the detachments of the army, and to this garrison (Charlestown) to declare their allegiance to the king, and to offer their services in arms for the support of the Government. In many instances they have brought in as prisoners their former oppressors or leaders, and I may venture to assert, that there are few men in South Carolina who are not either our prisoners or in arms with us.

Unfortunately for Clinton, South Carolina President John Rutledge was one of the "few men" still on the loose. Lincoln had begged Rutledge and the rest of the state's council to leave Charles Town while there was still time, and they had. Although Georgia's dispersed patriots didn't cause much trouble until Mad Anthony Wayne liberated the area in 1782, South Carolina was a different story. Patriot Governor Rutledge moved to and fro about the state, encouraging the patriots, printing up proclamations and other state papers on a printing press he had taken with him, and sending letter after letter demanding that the Continental Congress send the Continental Army for the relief of South Carolina.

Clinton's understanding of South Carolina was that it was an essentially loyalist colony that had been bullied into Revolutionary actions by a small minority of rabble-rousers. Certainly, this was the way the loyalists had presented things. Consequently, Clinton's idea was to increase the British presence over the entire state and win back the confidence of the moderates so that they, too, would want to fight for the British in the long-planned Northern push.

Clinton's idea of turning the Southern militia into loyalists willing to shoot their former comrades might have been a bit dubious, but Clinton's public relations skills were even more so. Rather than spending money on extra arms and soldiers, the British would have been wise now to simply hire a few spin-doctors. Instead, Clinton and his men proceeded to do everything they could to turn the Carolinians against them.

How to Lose Friends and Alienate People

The first thing that made erstwhile loyalists blink was Clinton's sending Lieutenant Colonel Banastre Tarleton after Colonel Buford and his body of Virginia patriots. Buford had raced south with the intention of defending Charles Town, but he turned back when he realized that they had arrived too late. Tarleton was unwilling to let the rebels escape back to the North, however, and gave chase. He caught up with them on May 29, near the present town of Lancaster. The Americans were told to surrender but refused. Soon, they found themselves attacked furiously by the British. Realizing quickly that they had no chance of victory or escape, the Americans finally threw down their arms and begged for quarter, but the British ignored their pleas, butchering the unarmed Americans. Of 350 rebels, only 30 escaped capture, wounding, or death. For the rest of the war, Southern patriots would charge at their British enemies to the cry of "Tarleton's quarter!" (i.e., "Take no prisoners!").

The second major British blunder was Clinton's revocation of the Carolinians' paroles. To gain leverage in the battle for the hearts and minds of the Carolinians, he reneged on the paroles of Carolinians who had surrendered with the understanding that if they did not actively seek to harass the British government, the British would leave them alone. Clinton's June 3 proclamation notified all prisoners of war that they might have to choose between taking arms up against their fellow Americans or being considered traitors to the Crown. This understandably rankled many of the militiamen, whose pride was already bruised by defeat. Many of them reasoned that if they were going to have to take the chance of getting shot again, they might as well fight for the side they wanted to win.

The third mistake the British made was in harassing the invalid wife and burning the Stateburg home of a rather inconsequential colonel named Thomas Sumter. In his fury at this outrage, "The Gamecock" became one of the fiercest and most devastating guerrilla leaders of the war.

Other Carolinian Whigs took matters into their own hands as well. The Lowcountry partisans fighting under Francis "The Swamp Fox" Marion and the Upcountry partisans fighting under Andrew Pickens (whose home had also been burned) plagued British troops with guerrilla warfare in the swamps, woods, and mountains of the state.

The Tide Turns in the Upcountry

At Kings Mountain on October 7, 1780, British Major Patrick Ferguson and his body of American loyalists were attacked on a hilltop by a body of Carolinians under Pickens. This major victory for the patriots, particularly because it was won by militiamen and not trained Continentals, provided a great swing of momentum for the fence-sitting Uplanders who had grown tired of British brutality. Because of this victory, it is considered by some to be the turning point of the Revolution, especially because it forced General Cornwallis to split his troops, sending Lieutenant Colonel Banastre "No Quarter" Tarleton into the South Carolina Upcountry to win the area back for the British. This division of his forces made it impossible for Cornwallis to move on his plan for a major push north because that plan required a loyalist body of troops to stay behind and keep the peace in the Carolinas.

Finally, that December, General Nathanael Greene arrived with an army of Continental troops. Once Greene heard of Tarleton's ap-

proach, he sent General Daniel Morgan and his backwoodsmen thundering over the Appalachians to stop him. On January 17, 1781, at a natural enclosure that was being used as a cow pen, the two forces met.

Pickens and his guerrillas joined up with Morgan just before the battle. Morgan felt they were still too weak to take on Tarleton's trained troops and, in order to secure a chance of retreat, wanted to cross a river that would have separated them from the British. Pickens convinced him to stay on the British side of the river, so that they would have to fight it out. And fight they did, in what some military historians consider to be the best-planned battle of the entire war. The patriots devastated the redcoats, and later victories at Hobkirk's Hill and Eutaw Springs further weakened the Brits. In December 1782, the British evacuated Charles Town. Shortly thereafter, jubilant residents changed the name to "Charleston," merely because to their ears it sounded somehow "less British."

One historian notes that some 137 battles, actions, and engagements between the British/Tories/Indians and the American patriots in South Carolina were fought by South Carolinians *alone*. Despite the version presented in U.S. history textbooks, no other state endured as much bloodshed, sacrifice, and suffering during the Revolution as South Carolina.

Writing the U.S. Constitution

In all of those famous paintings of the Founding Fathers, South Carolinians make up a lot of the faces you see behind Washington, Jefferson, Franklin, and the other big names. In 1787, John Rutledge, Charles Pinckney, Charles Cotesworth Pinckney, and Pierce Butler headed up to Philadelphia, where the Constitutional Convention was cobbling together the Constitution. Just 30 years old, Charles Pinckney had long been a critic of the weak Articles of Confederation. Although wealthy by birth and quite the epicurean, Pinckney became the leader of democracy in the state; he was even considered something of a turncoat to his fellow elites. On May 29, 1787, he presented the Convention with a detailed outline that ended up as perhaps the primary template for the U.S. Constitution. John Rutledge also gave valuable input. Ominously, Pierce Butler's sole contribution was the clause for the return of fugitive slaves.

As before the war, Georgia's involvement took second place to South Carolina's. So dominant was Carolina, in fact, that it nearly succeeded in annexing Georgia as its rightful property, citing the former colony's original charter boundaries. Georgia survived as a separate entity, however. Both states ratified the Federal (and Federalist-leaning) Constitution in 1787.

EARLY ANTEBELLUM OLD SOUTH (1790–1827)

As the nation's southern frontier, Georgia had a lot of good, unoccupied land, especially now that a lot of loyalist plantation owners had vacated their homes. General Nathanael Greene and Mad Anthony Wayne were both awarded plantations. The 44-year-old Greene died of sunstroke only three years after taking possession of the Mulberry plantation, leaving his vivacious young widow, Caty, to raise four children.

In 1785, Georgia honored Benjamin Franklin's prewar assistance by naming the state's new public university "Franklin College." The school, built in the new piedmont town of Athens, was the first state college in the nation, and would later change its name to the University of Georgia.

In 1786, pressure from the rapidly developing Upcountry caused Georgia to relocate its capital in Augusta; that same year, South Carolinians voted to relocate their state capital to the planned sandhills town of Columbia, which would also be home to the state's university. In 1790, however, when South Carolina's capital formally moved from Charleston to Columbia, Charleston didn't let go of all of its power that easily; some state offices remained in the Holy City until 1865. The Lowcountry and Upcountry even had separate treasury offices, with separate treasurers.

© SEAN SLINSKY

Charleston was the center for slave trade during pre-Civil War times; The Old Slave Mart on Chalmers Street was just one of many such auction houses in the neighborhood.

In 1800, South Carolina's Santee Canal, connecting the Santee and Cooper rivers, was completed, making it possible to transport people and goods directly from the new capital to Charleston. In 1801, Columbia's South Carolina College (now the University of South Carolina) was chartered.

The widow of Nathanael Greene, the thirtysomething, blunt-talking Caty Greene, inadvertently changed the course of the world when she met 27-year-old Eli Whitney, who had come south from New Haven, Connecticut, to teach school, but had found the job gone when he arrived. Greene convinced Whitney to stay in town a while, living out on Mulberry Plantation, and tutoring her four children. Whitney became interested in the problems cotton farmers had in removing the seeds from cotton bolls, particularly form those of the short-staple cotton grown in the Upcountry. His subsequent invention of the cotton gin made Lowcountry, "long-staple" cotton even more profitable and enabled Upcountry farmers to finally take part in the cotton bonanza. Now short-staple cotton couldn't be grown quickly enough. For the first time, Upcountry Georgia and South Carolina landowners had the chance to escape subsistence-level farming and make their fortunes. Unfortunately, cotton plantations required great numbers of workers, so Upcountry planters began importing large numbers of African and African American men and women as slaves. Now with its own wealthy planter class, and with a common interest in protecting the institution of slavery against Northern "do-gooders," the Upcountry began to work alongside the Lowcountry more than it had before. Nonetheless, slaveholding in the Upcountry never reached anything like the level in the Lowcountry.

As the cotton boom exploded, Charleston and Savannah profited the most as port towns. Savannah alone exported 90,000 bales of cotton in 1820—90 times more than before the advent of the cotton gin.

Resentment of the North

In 1811, British ships plundered American ships, inspiring the South's outraged "War Hawk" representatives to push Congress into declaring the War of 1812. During the war, tariffs on exported goods were raised to support America's military efforts, but afterward, Northern lawmakers continued to vote for higher and higher levies on exports and imports. These surcharges mainly punished the South for selling its goods in Europe instead of in the North. Not surprisingly, laws also forced the South to buy its manufactured goods from the North.

Concluding that they were at the hot end of the poker, many South Carolinians began to talk of seceding from the union to operate as an independent state with trade laws tailored to its own best interests. Even South Carolina–born vice president John C. Calhoun, who had begun as a Federalist favoring a strong centralized government, began to doubt the wisdom of this vision as he saw the rights of his home state trampled for the "good" of the more powerful North; however, he also saw the political dangers of dissolving South Carolina's union with the other states.

Meanwhile, both Charleston and Savannah were becoming chief American cities; both were among the 20 largest cities by 1820. In 1819, the SS *Savannah,* the first steam-powered transoceanic ship in the world, set off from Savannah for England. It reached Liverpool in a world-record 29 days and 11 hours. A few years later, Charlestonians would build the world's first regularly running railroad from their city to the east side of the Savannah River across from Augusta, in a successful attempt to get back the business of South Carolina farmers who had taken to shipping their crops out along the Savannah River, and hence, through Charleston's rival port, Savannah. Soon afterward, ever-competitive Savannah built its own railroad.

The Nullification Crisis

In 1828, Calhoun decided on the doctrine he would espouse for the rest of his life—the primacy of "states' rights." He believed that constitutionally, the state government of each state had more power within that state than the Federal government. Consequently, if a state deemed it necessary, it had the right to "nullify" any Federal law within its state boundaries.

To most South Carolinians, this sounded like a sensible compromise. Some in the state, however—such as Joel R. Poinsett (for whom the poinsettia and Poinsett State Park are named), novelist William Gilmore Simms, and James L. Petigru—believed that while a state had the full right to secede from the Union if it chose, it had no right, as long as it remained a part of the Union, to nullify a Federal law (this same theory has been codified by millions of parents of teenagers as the "as long as you're sleeping under my roof" law).

Not surprisingly, the Federal government saw the whole idea of nullification as an attack on its powers, and when, in 1832, South Carolina's houses quickly "nullified" the hated federally mandated tariffs, President Andrew Jackson (ironically, South Carolina's only native-born president) declared this an act of rebellion and ordered U.S. warships to South Carolina to enforce the law.

In December 1832, Calhoun resigned as Jackson's vice president (making him the only vice president to resign until Spiro Agnew, some 150 years later) so that he could become a senator and stop South Carolina's destructive run toward secession, while solving the problems that had so inflamed his fellow Carolinians.

Fortunately, before Federal forces arrived at Charleston, Calhoun and Henry Clay agreed on a compromise tariff that would lower rates over 10 years. The passage of this tariff pacified everyone just enough to prevent immediate armed conflict. But the debate between the relative importance of states' rights versus Federal power became a dividing line between the North—whose majority position gave it power over Federal decisions—and the South, which, because it featured a different economy and social structure from the North, knew that it would rarely be in the majority opinion on a Federal vote.

The Abolitionist Movement and Southern Response

By this time, the fact that most of the slaves in the Northern states had been freed made it much easier for Northerners to be intolerant toward the sins of their Southern neighbors. Most abolitionists were Christians who saw the protection of African Americans, along with any other unfortunates, as a God-given responsibility. Southern slaveholders—most of them at least nominally Christian, and many quite devout—generally saw their opponents as dangerous, self-righteous meddlers who would be better off tending to their own sins than passing judgment on the choices of others.

The journal of Mary Boykin Chesnut, a native of Camden, South Carolina, and the daughter, granddaughter, and great-granddaughter of plantation slave owners, shows how one Southern woman perceived the similarities and differences between abolitionists and slave owners. Except for a small group of Southern extremists, both sides agreed that the slave trade was immoral and should remain illegal. The question, then, was how best to treat the African Americans already in the country. On one side of the issue, she writes, lay the abolitionists, in "nice New England homes. . . shut up in libraries," writing books or editing newspapers for profit—abolitionist books and tracts sold extremely well in the 1850s and early 1860s. "What self-denial do they practice?" she asks her journal. "It is the cheapest philanthropy trade in the world—easy. Easy as setting John Brown to come down here and cut our throats in Christ's name."

As for Southerners, she argues, "We [are] not as much of heathens down here as our enlightened enemies think. Their philanthropy is cheap. There are as noble, pure lives here as there—and a great deal more of self-sacrifice." Plantation masters and mistresses, she points out, had been "educated at Northern schools mostly—read the same books as their Northern condemners, the same daily newspapers, the same Bible—have the same ideas of right and wrong—are highbred, lovely, good, pious—doing their duty as they conceive it."

Many pro-slavery apologists argued that Northerners had no place in the debate over the morality of slavery because they could not own slaves and would therefore not suffer

SLAVE HOUSES

It can strike the visitor as a sort of conspiracy, a further indignity to the memory of the enslaved: *After keeping millions of African Americans in bondage for more than 200 years*, the thought goes, *white Southerners have proceeded to eliminate nearly every single one of their homes.*

Certainly, Euro-Americans might have saved more slave cabins as a living memorial to the victims of American slavery. For that matter, more ex-slaves who resettled some of the lands might have saved them as well. And surely it's puzzling that the white Northerners who bought up entire plantations after the Civil War wouldn't have preserved more slave cabins as dirt-floored reminders of the North's moral high ground in the clash.

No doubt, slavery was a sore point with everyone involved in the post-Civil War South. To freed slaves, who, bound or not, had grown up and struggled so long in slave cabins, the meager structures might have held some sentimental attachment, but it seems instead that they were seen as an enigma, a too-real reminder of where their white neighbors believed they belonged. Those who could afford to do so bought their way out of their old shacks and into recently vacated "white" houses. Some packed up wagons and headed west or north, out of the region entirely. But the slave street's virtual disappearance from the Southern landscape seems to owe more to routine practicalities than to anything else.

Unlike other buildings on the plantation, the cramped wooden slave cabins – as opposed to the Big Houses, or masters' mansions – simply had no attraction or practical use for the owners of the former plantations, who as often as not were Northerners who had moved south to upgrade, not downgrade, their lifestyles. The former slave cabins were generally left to rot, or fell victim to fire. The same fate befell nearly every home belonging to poor and working-class whites of the same period. Generally, only the better-made, better-preserved mansions survived – and not many of those, either.

Fortunately, some slave quarters did survive. The elites of slave society, house slaves – cooks, drivers, butlers, nurses, personal attendants – normally lived very close to the master's home for convenience's sake, and therefore, plantation owners tended to construct their houses of nonflammable brick or tabby. After Emancipation, many of these brick slave houses survived the hurricanes that blasted their clapboard brethren halfway to Raleigh, not to mention the fires that burned more than one slave street to cinders. Because these houses were sturdy and located near the main house, they were sometimes preserved by their postwar owners for storage or as quarters for hired servants.

Throughout the early-20th-century development of the Sea Islands, reminders of the "romantic" antebellum period came to be greatly prized landscape elements to many a Northerner's winter retreat in "Old Dixie." You can see some of the house slave cabins at numerous places along the Sea Island Coast, including at places where they outlived the Big Houses themselves, such as Boone Hall Plantation in Mount Pleasant and at two different locations on St. Simons Island.

© SEAN SLINSKY

Slave cabins, like this one outside Charleston, show just how dire living conditions were for African Americans during plantation days.

the societal impacts that manumission would mean to the South.

The crux of the slavery debate lay in the question of the extent of the humanity of slaves. Slaveholders contented themselves that Africans, while admittedly sharing many traits of human beings, were somehow less than fully human, which made the slaves' own views about their enslavement unworthy of consideration. Many believed that blacks were on their *way* to becoming "elevated" as a race but needed close interaction with whites (even at gunpoint) to help them along. Hence, Columbia-area plantation mistress Keziah Goodwyn Hopkins Brevard could, on the brink of the War Between the States, write: "Those who have come & have had kind masters have been blest—had they been left to this day on Africa's sands there would have been one trouble after another for them—it is only in favoured spots *now* that they are safe from war & slavery in their own country."

The effect of real and threatened bloody slave rebellions, such as the Vesey Plot of 1822 and John Brown's massacre at Harper's Ferry in 1859, embarrassed more moderate abolitionists into silence, particularly in the South. Pro-slavery Southerners perceived these isolated incidents as indicative of the "true" ends and means of all abolitionists, inflaming and galvanizing Southerners into a reactionary anti-abolitionist stance that effectively ended reasoned debate on the issue. To most abolitionists, the question was one of man's duty to respect other human beings as children of God; to many Southerners, it was a question of—to use modern terminology—"choice"; slave owner or not, they didn't want anybody taking away their legal right to own slaves. That feared "somebody" would be the U.S. government, ruled by a majority of non-slaveholding states. Gradually, as the 19th century pressed on, Southerners realized that as a perennial minority faction, their only hope for self-determination on the slavery issue was to ensure continued state autonomy, hence the "states rights" argument—defending a state's right to determine what was best for its own people.

Brevard wrote in her journal, "cut throat Abolitionists—I will not call them neighbours—not [sic] they are the selfish & envious. . . not a grain of Christ's charity in their whole body."

The Cult of Slavery: Slavery as Intrinsically Good

Carolinians had earlier tolerated slavery more or less as a necessary evil. But largely in reaction to the continual sparring with abolitionists, in the last decades before the Civil War many people in the Carolinas reached a new height of sophistry—proclaiming slavery to be a positive good, a benefit to the enslaved, and a proper response to the "natural" differences between whites and blacks. Apologists such as Thomas Harper argued that the wage-employee system of the North was irresponsible, and more exploitative than slavery itself. The Southern slaveholder, after all, paid room and board for a slave even when the slave was too young, too sick, or too old to work. Meanwhile, the Northern capitalist paid his wage earners only for the hours they worked; when they were sick, or when they got too old, or when a new technology came along that they were not trained for, the wage payer could fire the employees, and his responsibility for their welfare was considered finished. (Some historians argue that the average slave was actually paid 90 percent of his or her life's earnings by the time of death.) Virginian George Fitzhugh, in such 1850s titles as *Sociology for the South* and *Cannibals All!*, argued that slavery, being the most humane and efficient system, was destined to regain its popularity throughout the world.

So avid had this defense of the indefensible become that by 1856, South Carolina Governor James Hopkins Adams recommended a resumption of the Foreign Slave Trade. A powerful minority of slaveholders always looking for ways to get the rest of the state behind them had begun arguing that every white man should be legally required to become the owner of at least one slave, a measure that would give every male citizen an interest in the issue as well as instilling the sense of responsibility that they believed slave owning engendered.

Even the Charleston *Mercury,* though, which had long agitated for secession, denounced the return to the slave trade as cruel and divisive. Nonetheless, Carolinians were embittered by the North's refusal to enforce the Fugitive Slave law. Consequently, in 1858 and 1859, several newly captured slaves were imported into the state at Charleston, in violation of Federal law. Federal officials in Charleston—Southerners themselves—looked the other way.

Free Blacks and the Vesey Plot

Since Colonial times, South Carolina had always been home to a sizable population of free blacks, many of them descended from mulattoes freed by their white father/owners. Others had been freed because of faithful service or by buying themselves free with portions of their earnings they had been allowed to keep. As long as there had been free blacks, free blacks had made the white population nervous.

In 1822, free-black craftsman and preacher Denmark Vesey was convicted and hanged for having masterminded a plan for slaves and free blacks to overthrow Charlestonian whites. Afterward, whites established curfews and forbade assembly of large numbers of African Americans. Forbidden, too, was the education of slaves, although this seems to have been widely flouted. Because the mere presence of free blacks was seen as dangerous, South Carolina leaders also made it illegal for slaveholders to free their slaves without a special decree from the state legislature.

Like Denmark Vesey, many of South Carolina's free blacks lived in Charleston, where their own subculture—with its own caste system—had developed. Charleston free blacks performed more than 50 different occupations, some as artisans. Some African Americans, such as Sumter cotton-gin maker William Ellison, amassed great fortunes—and did so in the same fashion that most wealthy whites had: through the labor of black slaves. In fact, historian Richard Rollins estimates that a full 25 percent of all free Southern blacks legally owned slaves. Some were family members purchased by free blacks, but most were purchased to act as the owners' servants or workers. Opinions vary about whether slaves could normally expect better treatment from a black owner than from a white one. Some free blacks, wanting to demonstrate their fitness to join "white" society, probably felt a special pressure to exert their authority over their slaves. Doubtless, the relative happiness of a slave owned by an African American depended on the character of the individual owner.

The Mexican War (1846)

The war with Mexico affected the Carolinas considerably. For coastal Carolinians, what was at stake was the acquisition of additional lands open to slavery—and hence more representation in the U.S. Congress by slaveholding states. South Carolina's enthusiastic involvement in the undertaking reflected both her regional leadership and her military self-assuredness. Under Pierce M. Butler, J. P. Dickinson, and A. H. Gladden, the Palmetto Regiment's palmetto flag entered Mexico City before any other flag. South Carolina's fighting prowess was once again proven in battle, but, largely because of disease, of 1,100 South Carolinian volunteers who fought in the war, only 300 returned alive.

Even with its much smaller population, the South as a whole, in fact, sent and suffered the loss of more soldiers, furnishing 43,232 men in the Mexican War while the North, whose pundits had disapproved of the effort, sent along only 22,136 troops. Hence, the Wilmot Proviso, a proposal by a Pennsylvanian legislator to ban slavery within all territory acquired as a result of the Mexican War, struck Carolinians as extremely unjust: Southerners who had risked their lives to win over the New Southwest were now being told they could not expect to bring their "property" with them if they settled there. John C. Calhoun attempted to rally the rest of the slaveholding states to oppose Wilmot's plan as yet another effort to tighten the noose around slavery's neck. The Southern-led Senate blocked the bill.

But the question of how to handle the issue of slavery in the new and future acquisitions of an expanding nation was now out in the open. The issues raised by the acquisition of the American West in the Mexican War made plain to Northerners and Southerners their different visions of America's future, and hence accelerated the nation's tailspin toward civil war. In the North, many of those willing to tolerate the cancer of slavery in those states that already practiced it could not with good conscience watch it spread to new lands beneath the shadow of the Stars and Stripes. The South, which had held a hope that territorial expansion and the spread of slavery might allow the South to ascend again to equality or even dominance in national politics, finally had to confront the fact that the North would never willingly allow this to happen. As long as the South remained in the Union, it would always be the oppressed agricultural (and, hence, to Southern perceptions, slaveholding) region, with its interests continually overlooked for the interests of the industrialized North. South Carolinians had been telling the rest of the South this since the Nullification Crisis 20 years before.

Eruption of Secessionism and the Descent into War

Few coastal Southern whites saw general emancipation as an option. If blacks—the vast numerical majority in most parts of the state—were freed, whites feared the "Africanization" of their cherished society and culture, as they had seen happen after slave revolutions in some areas of the West Indies.

Carolinian leaders had long divided up between devoted Unionists, who opposed any sort of secession, and those who believed that secession was a state's right. Calhoun proposed that Congress could not exclude slavery from the territories and that a territory, when it became a state, should be allowed to choose which type of economy it wanted—free labor or slave. But after Calhoun's death in 1850, South Carolina was left without a leader great enough, both in character and in national standing, to stave off the more militant Carolinian factions' desire to secede immediately.

"THE WAR FOR SOUTHERN INDEPENDENCE"

In 1850 and 1851 South Carolina nearly seceded from the Union all by its lonesome. Andrew Pickens Butler, considered by historian Nathaniel Stephenson to be "perhaps the ablest South Carolinian then living," argued against fiery Charleston publisher Robert Barnwell Rhett, who advocated immediate and, if necessary, independent secession. Butler won that battle, but Rhett outlived him. By 1860, no strong personality in South Carolina was Rhett's equal.

Several historians argue that South Carolina's "states' rights" demand to be recognized as an independent, autonomous entity was not simply a rationalization for slavery but rather a protest integral to its nature and understanding of itself. As Stephenson wrote:

> In South Carolina all things conspired to uphold and strengthen the sense of the State as an object of veneration, as something over and above the mere social order, as the sacred embodiment of the ideals of the community. Thus it is fair to say that what has animated the heroic little countries of the Old World – Switzerland and Serbia and ever-glorious Belgium – with their passion to remain themselves, animated South Carolina in 1861. Just as Serbia was willing to fight to the death rather than merge her identity in the mosaic of the Austrian Empire, so this little American community saw nothing of happiness in any future that did not secure its virtual independence.

When Lincoln was elected, several conventions around the Deep South organized to discuss their options. Had the previous (and first-ever) Republican Presidential candidate, Savannah-born and Charleston-schooled John C. Fremont, won, possibly Southerners would have given him a chance, despite his avowed abolitionist stance. But they wouldn't, couldn't trust Lincoln, a Northerner by birth, whose choice for running mate was Maine's polemic abolitionist senator Hannibal Hamlin, and whose cabinet selections included anti-slavery radical William Seward of New York as Secretary of State. Even still, Georgian Unionist Alexander H. Stephens fought against secession until the bitter end, when he finally joined the Confederacy, accepted a post as Jefferson Davis's vice president (mollifying the South's many moderates), and gave an ill-chosen, oversimplified, and oft-quoted speech at the Athenaeum on Bull Street in Savannah, in which he stated that the Confederacy's "cornerstone. . . rests upon the great truth, that the Negro is not equal to the white man; that slavery—subordination to the superior race—is his natural and normal condition." Though racism was rampant in the Confederacy, it was nearly as common—some would say more so—north of the Mason-Dixon Line. A broader reading of statements by Confederate soldiers and leaders suggests that most Southerners ultimately favored secession because they resented Northern domination of American politics and desired regional autonomy, which was patently impossible if they remained in the Union. The chief reason that most Southerners *fought* was simply because they had been invaded.

Nonetheless, Northern abolitionist newspapers seized on Stephens's quote and used it to further justify the Federal invasion of the South. They asserted that the primary purpose of the war was not the vanquishing of a minority American province seeking political independence, thereby weakening the rest of the Union both economically and militarily, but was rather the beneficent alleviation of slavery against a cruel, morally corrupt people singularly bent on defending the "peculiar institution."

South Carolina's assembly met first, at Columbia on December 17, 1860. States with strong pro-secession movements like Alabama and Mississippi sent delegates to the convention, where they advised the Carolinians to "take the lead and secede at once."

Thus it was that on December 20, 1860, South Carolinians in Charleston (where the convention had moved following an outbreak

LEE ON SAVANNAH

The start of the War Between the States saw General Robert E. Lee in charge of the coastal defenses near Charleston, Savannah (where he had been stationed as a young engineer in the 1830s), and as far down as Amelia Island in Florida. Not long after Federal troops landed on Hilton Head Island to establish a base there, they began working their way south to Savannah.

On November 22, 1861, Lee wrote to his daughter Anne, expressing his concerns:

This is my second visit to Savannah. I have been down the coast to Amelia Island to examine the defenses. They are poor indeed, and I have laid off work enough to employ our people a month. I hope our enemy will be polite enough to wait for us. It is difficult to get our people to realize their position.

Lee frantically attempted to stir Savannahians and their slaves to building defenses, but found it hard-going. In his March 2, 1862 letter to a daughter, Lee writes:

I trust that a merciful God will arouse us to a sense of our danger....Our people have not been earnest enough, have thought too much of themselves and their ease....This is not the way to accomplish our independence.

Lee explains that in the past four months he has done everything possible "with our small means and slow workmen," to defend the cities and coast, but confidence still eludes him. Finally, Lee puts his finger on what would be the chief deciding factor in the war – sheer numbers. Ominously, he writes:

Against ordinary numbers we are pretty strong, but against the hosts our enemies seem able to bring everywhere there is no calculating.

of smallpox in Columbia) voted to secede from the Union. The hot-blooded delegate from Edisto Island declared that if South Carolina didn't secede, Edisto Island would secede all by itself.

Six days later, on the day after Christmas, Major Robert Anderson, commander of the U.S. garrisons in Charleston, withdrew his men against orders into the island fortress of Fort Sumter, in the midst of Charleston Harbor. South Carolina militia swarmed over the abandoned mainland batteries and trained their guns on the island. Sumter was the key position to preventing a sea invasion of Charleston, so Carolina could not afford to allow the Federals to remain there indefinitely. Rumors spread that Yankee forces were on their way down to seize the port city, making the locals even itchier to get their own troops behind Sumter's guns.

Meanwhile, the secessionists' plan worked. Mississippi seceded only a few weeks after South Carolina, and the rest of the lower South followed. On January 3, 1861, Savannahians stormed Fort Pulaski and took the Federal fort for the Confederacy, two weeks before Georgia had even voted to secede. Because only two caretakers, one of whom would later join the Confederacy, had manned the fort, this hardly ranks as a major military action. Even so, proud Georgians are arguably correct in labeling this episode as the first hostile action of the war.

Six days later, on January 9, 1861, the U.S. ship *Star of the West* approached to reprovision the soldiers in Fort Sumter, and two Citadel cadets fired what some (particularly Citadel alumni) consider to be the first shot of the War Between the States, a cannon shot that was meant to warn the vessel off. One of the ship's officers quipped: "The people of Charleston pride themselves on their hospitality. They gave us several balls before we landed."

On January 19, Georgia joined her mentor state (and a handful of others) in the Confederacy. On February 4, a congress of Southern states met in Montgomery, Alabama, and approved a new constitution, which prohibited the African slave trade among other things.

So excited was Florence-born bard Henry Timrod that he was moved to write what many consider to be his greatest poem, "Ethnogenesis," in honor of the convention, which includes the hopeful lines:

> HATH not the morning dawned with added light?
>
> And shall not evening call another star Out of the infinite regions of the night,
>
> To mark this day in Heaven? At last, we are
>
> A nation among nations; and thee world
>
> Shall soon behold in many a distant port Another flag unfurled!

Unfortunately for Timrod, Lincoln argued that the United States were "one nation, *indivisible*," and denied the Southern states' right to secede. It looked as if a war were imminent. Virginia, which had not yet seceded, called for a peace conference, and North Carolina—similarly uncommitted—sent delegates. But it didn't matter anyway; Washington ignored the suggestions the conference came up with. Even the best efforts of reasonable minds couldn't pierce the accumulated bitterness on both sides of the Mason-Dixon line.

Anticipating the battles to come, Timrod wrote:

> We shall not shrink, my brothers, but go forth
>
> To meet them, marshalled by the Lord of Hosts,
>
> And overshadowed by the mighty ghosts Of Moultrie and of Eutaw – who shall foil
>
> Auxiliars such as these?

All eyes remained focused on Fort Sumter, but for the rest of the month, nothing happened. Finally, Virginian orator Roger Pryor barreled into Charleston, proclaiming that the only way to get Old Dominion to join the Confederacy—and thus bring along the other border states—was for South Carolina to instigate war with the United States. The obvious place to start was right in the midst of Charleston Harbor.

On March 15, North Carolina Senator Thomas L. Clingman and Senator Stephen A. Douglas proposed evacuating nearly all the forts in the seceded states, including Fort Sumter in Charleston, thinking—rightly—that this would defuse the most obvious flash points for confrontation between Federals and local secessionists, allowing time for peaceable discussion of the issues. It was rumored that Lincoln planned to carry out this idea, although his old Illinois enemy Douglas had proposed it. Then, unexpectedly, he sent Federal ships to Charleston to reprovision the soldiers in Fort Sumter, which led Charlestonians to fire the first shot of the war.

On April 10, the *Mercury* reprinted stories from New York papers that told of a naval expedition sent southward toward Charleston. The Carolinians could wait no longer if they hoped to take the fort without having to take on the U.S. Navy at the same time. Some 6,000 men were now stationed around the rim of the harbor, ready to take on the 60 men in Fort Sumter. At 4:30 AM on April 12, after days of intense negotiations, and with Union ships just outside the harbor, the firing began. Thirty-four hours later, Anderson's men raised the white flag and were allowed to leave the fort with colors flying and drums beating, saluting the U.S. flag with a 50-gun salute before taking it down. During this salute, one of the guns exploded, killing a young soldier—the only casualty of the bombardment and the first casualty of the war.

Again, South Carolina's instigation persuaded others to join the Confederacy: Virginia, Arkansas, North Carolina, and Tennessee—now certain that Lincoln meant to use force to keep their fellow Southern states under Federal rule—seceded, one by one.

In truth, the outgunned, outmanned, and virtually Navy-less South had no chance against the North. Federal ships sailed south, sealing off one important port after another. As early as November 1861, Union troops occupied Hilton Head and other Sea Islands in the Beaufort area, establishing an important base for the ships and men who would stymie the important ports at Charleston and Savannah. When the plantation owners—many of them already off with the Confederate Army elsewhere—fled the area, the Sea Island slaves became the first "freedmen" of the war, and the Sea Islands became the laboratory for Northern plans to educate African Americans for their eventual role as full American citizens.

On March 2, 1862, General Robert E. Lee, in charge of coastal defenses in the Lowcountry, wrote his daughter from Savannah, reporting:

> They have worked their way across the marshes, with their dredges, under cover of their gunboats, to the Savannah River, about Fort Pulaski. I presume they will endeavor to reduce the fort and thus open a way for their vessels up the river. But we have an interior line they must force before reaching the city. It is on this line we are working, slowly to my anxious mind, but as fast as I can drive them.

Lee's fears were well founded, but so was his focus on "the line." Although Federal ships quickly shut off the harbor and made use of the Savannah River below town, the invaders stopped there. Savannah itself remained in Confederate hands until Sherman arrived two and a half years later. What the Federals *could not* do was take Charleston or Savannah, and this fact allowed blockade runners to bring in needed supplies to the Southern armies, protracting America's bloodiest war by several years.

Despite South Carolina's important role in the start of the war, and the long, unsuccessful attempt by Federals to take Charleston from 1863 onward, few military engagements occurred within the Palmetto State's borders until 1865, when Sherman's Army, having already completed its infamous March to the Sea in Savannah, marched north to Columbia and leveled most of the town, as well as several towns along the way and afterward.

South Carolina lost 12,922 men to the war—23 percent of its white male population of fighting age, and the highest percentage of any state in the nation. Georgia lost more men but fewer per capita. Nonetheless, both states lost many promising young men to the graveyards, which would contribute to the region's postwar woes.

Sherman's 1864–1865 march through Georgia and the Carolinas resulted in the burning of Atlanta, Columbia, and numerous other towns, but most coastal towns were spared. Nonetheless, poverty would mark the region for generations to come.

Sherman had marched down to Savannah from Atlanta with the intent of destroying all of Lee's supply lines and railroads, essentially cutting the South in half. When Fort McAllister fell on December 13, 1864, the Union fleet was able to sail clear up to Savannah, providing supplies to Sherman's troops and eliminating their need to keep supply lines open. But in early December, as he neared his ultimate objective—Savannah—Sherman got bad news from his superior officer, Ulysses S Grant, who was having trouble in Virginia with Lee and wanted Sherman and most of his men to head up to Virginia immediately:

> My idea now is that you establish a base on the sea-coast, fortify and leave in it all your artillery and cavalry, and enough infantry to protect them, and at the same time so threaten the interior that the militia of the South will have to be kept at home. With the balance of your command, come here by water with all dispatch. Select yourself the officer to leave in command, but you I want in person.

Before leaving, Sherman wanted to complete what he'd set out to do, and yet to his frustration, Savannah, under command of Confederate General William Hardee, refused to surrender. Sherman sent him a harsh note on December 17, asserting that he was able to reach downtown Savannah with his artillery and that further resistance was useless, concluding:

> I am therefore justified in demanding the surrender of the city of Savannah. . . .Should I be forced to resort to assault, or the slower and surer process of starvation, I shall then feel justified in resorting to the harshest measures, and shall make little effort to restrain my army – burning to avenge the national wrong which they attach to Savannah and other large cities which have been so prominent in dragging our country into civil war.

Of course, Sherman knew that Hardee knew what had happened in Atlanta; his choice of the verb "burning" to describe his men's thirst for vengeance was not an accident. Nonetheless, Hardee was unfazed. He wrote back on the same day, explaining to Sherman:

> The position of your forces is, at the nearest point, at least four miles from the heart of the city. That and the interior line are both intact. . . .Your demand for the surrender of Savannah and its dependent forts is refused.

On December 18, Sherman received Hardee's letter and sent Grant copies of both his and Hardee's letters, and wrote Grant:

> I still hope that events will give me time to take Savannah, even if I have to assault with some loss. . . .With Savannah in our possession. . . we can punish South Carolina as she deserves.

Sherman knew an assault would be bloody, and decided to try one more time to seal off the city and spur on a surrender, or at least to be certain that when the assault began, Hardee could not escape. Knowing Hardee might try to get his men across a pontoon bridge to the East, Sherman put an underling in charge of preparing for the assault while he himself went by boat to regional Federal Headquarters on Hilton Head to try to request a detachment to intercept them. A storm delayed his return.

By the time he returned late on December 21, he found that Union skirmishers had noticed that the city seemed to be empty of Hardee's 15,000 troops and that the Union troops had been able to march into town unaccosted. On the morning of December 22, Sherman rode down Bull Street to the customs house. There, he climbed to the top of the roof to look around, and reported:

The navy-yard, and the wreck of the iron-clad ram Savannah, were still smoldering, but all else looked quiet enough.

Afterward, Sherman rode to the Pulaski Hotel on Broughton Street, where he had stayed decades earlier as a young soldier stationed at Charleston. Although he planned to requisition an entire wing of the hotel for his headquarters, an Englishman, Charles Green, came in and said he wanted to offer his house, completely furnished, as Sherman's headquarters. One of Sherman's staff generals had told Green that Sherman would probably want his house to use, and he wanted the General to know that this was fine with him. Sherman was concerned that staying in a private dwelling might cause friction with the locals, but Green was more concerned that any lack of hospitality might mean the city's doom, and insisted. Sherman visited the house, accepted the offer, and stayed there for his entire time in Savannah, deeming it, "a most excellent house. . . in all respects."

Sherman quickly went on establishing norms for life under the Federal military. The mayor, whom Sherman regarded as "completely subjugated," was allowed to convene the City Council to take charge of most civic functions, although all were warned that they must remain subordinate to the military authority. About 200 Savannahians—most with husbands, fathers, and sons still wearing gray—refused to live under Yankee rule and were delivered to Confederate authorities in Charleston.

On January 16, 1865, Sherman penned the famous Field Order No. 15. In it, he set aside the Sea Islands south of Charleston to establish, temporarily, the sorts of black-only colonies the African American leaders had desired, forbidding whites to live there. The order granted every freed "respectable" African American family, for the duration of the war, a 40-acre plot of land on the Sea Islands south of Charleston and north of the St. Mary's River. Tradesmen and personal servants were allowed to remain in Savannah and Brunswick as required by their jobs.

The Fall of Charleston

On February 21, 1865, with the Confederate forces finally evacuated from Charleston, the black 55th Massachusetts Regiment marched through the city. To most of the white citizens—those few who hadn't fled—this must have looked like Armageddon. To the African Americans of the city, however, it was the Day of Jubilee. As one of the regiment's colonels recalled:

*Men and women crowded to shake hands with men and officers. . . .On through the streets of the rebel city passed the column, on through the chief seat of that slave power, tottering to fall. Its walls rung to the chorus of manly voices singing "John Brown," "Babylon is Falling," and the "Battle-Cry of Freedom." It's hard to conceive of how **unbelievable** Emancipation must have seemed for these men and women people born into slavery.*

At a ceremony at which the U.S. flag was once again raised over Fort Sumter, former fort commander Robert Anderson was joined on the platform by two men: escaped Beaufort slave and African American Union hero Robert Smalls, and the son of Denmark Vesey.

RECONSTRUCTION

Within nine months after Sherman wrote the famous Field Order No. 15, President Andrew Johnson gave the islands back to their pre-war owners; however, land prices had sunk to around two dollars per acre, and for this, many former slaves were able to purchase small farms. Other former rice plantations were drained and developed for industry. Although they had long made up the majority of the Southern coast's population, African Americans played a promi-nent role in governing the region for the first time when Federal troops occupied the states from 1866 to 1877.

And so it was that Savannah suffered rela-tively little from the Civil War, but it would suffer from Reconstruction, beginning with a major fire that claimed scores of blocks downtown. As early as January 1865, Sher-man himself complained about the hosts of Northerners filtering down to exploit the de-feated South.

In South Carolina, despite the anti-North-ern fury of their prewar and wartime politics, most Carolinians, including South Carolina's opinion maker, Wade Hampton III, believed that white Carolinians would do well to accept President Andrew Johnson's generous terms for reentry to full participation in the Union. When the powerful "radical" anti-Southern Congress seized control of the Reconstruction process, however, things got harder for white Southerners.

The idea of these Republicans was to es-tablish a solidly Republican South by con-vincing blacks to vote Republican and then keeping former Confederates from voting for as long as possible. Northern "carpetbaggers" formed "Union" or "Loyal" leagues to regis-ter African Americans as Republican voters after 1866. No doubt some of the Union and Loyal league members were truly motivated by a desire to improve the African Americans' sta-tion in life, but Southern Democrats saw this registration program as a manipulative politi-cal move. The subsequent domination of the generally uneducated freeperson population by Republican political bosses—and the rampant graft and corruption of Republican officials in the South—would be remembered bitterly by white Southerners.

Both South Carolina and Georgia's fed-erally mandated new Constitutions of 1868 brought democratic reforms, but by now most whites viewed the Republican government as representative of black interests only and were largely unsupportive. Laws forbidding former Confederates (virtually the entire native-white male population) from bearing arms only exac-erbated the tensions, especially in South Caro-lina, as rifle-bearing black militia units began drilling in the streets.

Added to the brewing interracial animos-ity was many whites' sense that their former slaves had betrayed them. Before the war, most slaveholders had convinced themselves that they were treating their slaves well and had thus earned their slaves' loyalty. Under-standably, most slaves had been happy to give their masters the impression that they were, indeed, devoted to the household. Hence, when the Union Army rolled in and slaves deserted by the thousands (although many did not), slaveholders took it as a personal affront. Mary Jones, a Savannah slave owner, complained about the disappearance of an-other worker: "My life long. . . I have been laboring and caring for them, and since the war have labored with all my might to sup-ply their wants, and expended everything I had upon their support. . . and this is their return."

And thus went Reconstruction in the Caro-linas: the black population scrambled to enjoy and preserve its new rights while the white population attempted to claw its way back to the top of the social ladder by denying blacks those same rights.

Perhaps predictably, Ku Klux Klan raids began shortly thereafter, terrorizing blacks and black sympathizers in an attempt to reestablish white supremacy. In Savannah, bills appeared around town before the April 1868 elections, threatening Republican leaders and candidates with death. Area blacks replied with a defiant handbill, reading:

Take Notice K.K.K. And all BADMEN of the City of Savannah, who now THREATEN the LIVES of all the LEADERS and NOMINEES of the Republican Party, and the President and Members of the Union League of America. If you Strike a Blow, the Man or Men will be followed, and the house in which he or they takes shelter, will be burned to the ground. TAKE HEED! MARK WELL!! Members of the Union. Rally! Rally!! Rally!!! For God, Life and Liberty!!!

To their credit, most of the region's "better element" showed little tolerance for Klan-like violence, especially when undertaken anonymously, and largely squelched the movement locally after a few years. In 1876, after a deadlocked gubernatorial election that was rife with voter intimidation and ballot box stuffing—and was finally decided through a political deal with handlers of President Rutherford B. Hayes (who needed their support in his own convoluted "victory" over Samuel Tilden)—South Carolina elected former Confederate General Wade Hampton as their governor. The state would not elect another Republican governor for 99 years.

In April 1877, President Hayes—in fulfillment of the deal worked out up in Washington—withdrew Federal troops from South Carolina and Georgia and other Southern states, leaving it in the hands of white political leaders. Thus was begun the "solid South" stronghold of Democratic power for many years. The normal American two-party system was thrown off balance because the Democratic Party, in those years, was the "white" party in the South, and whites successfully kept blacks away from the ballot boxes through various Jim Crow laws.

THE NEW SOUTH

Savannah bounced back from the war more quickly than did Charleston. Its white population also regained control of the state legislature and governor's mansion earlier (both by 1872). At first, after Sherman gave his approval, Savannah had thrived from the sales and shipment of cotton stores, which had been stockpiled around the state for safekeeping during the war years. Following the predictable sag in the years immediately following, cotton again regained its prominence in the local economy; by 1872 the city built its Cotton Exchange on Bay Street, where cotton "factors" (brokers) did business in an arena akin to Chicago's "Pit" or New York's Wall Street. Although both Savannah and Charleston began to exploit the local pine trees to create turpentine and rosin as naval stores (Charleston also mined its phosphates), cotton was still king in the coastal South.

In 1886, Atlanta newspaper publisher Henry W. Grady, speaking before a New York audience, proclaimed his vision of a "New South" (i.e., a South based on the Northern economic model). By now, the idea had already struck some enterprising Southerners that all that cotton they were sending North at cut rates could be processed just as well down South. By the end of the 19th century, the textile industry was exploding across both Georgia and South Carolina, but particularly in their upstates, with their powerful turbine-turning rivers.

For whites, anyway, things were looking up. In 1902, South Carolina hosted the Charleston Exposition, drawing visitors from around the world, hoping to impress on them the idea that the state was on the rebound. On April 9, President Theodore Roosevelt—whose mother had attended school in Columbia—even made an appearance, smoothing over the still-simmering animosities between North and South by declaring:

The wounds left by the great Civil War. . . have healed. . . .The devotion, the self-sacrifice, the steadfast resolution and lofty daring, the high devotion to the right as each man saw it. . . all these qualities of the men and women of the early sixties now shine luminous and brilliant before our eyes, while the mists of anger and hatred that once dimmed them have passed away forever.

Northerners had long made this kind of reconciliatory talk—the sort of easy generosity possible to the victor, especially if the victor needs the loser's cooperation to have a successful economy. But now—in economics, if not in civil liberties—the South truly did seem to be improving.

Unfortunately, the invasion of the boll weevil, beginning in 1919, destroyed the cotton crop, which, although it hadn't paid well since before the Civil War, was nonetheless the primary crop in Georgia and South Carolina. Thus, just as they were coming out of the post–Civil War slump, the cotton states led the nation's topple into the Great Depression. Blacks and low-income whites left the states in droves for factory jobs up north. Only the establishment and expansion of military bases during World War II, as well as domestic and foreign investment in manufacturing in more recent decades, have revitalized the states.

DESEGREGATION

Compared to hot spots such as Mississippi and Alabama, desegregation went relatively smoothly during the 1950s and 1960s in coastal Georgia and South Carolina.

The states' universities began integrating in the early 1960s. When Clemson was forced to allow Harvey Gantt into its classes in 1962, making it the first public college in South Carolina to be integrated, word went out from influential whites that no violence or otherwise unseemly behavior would be tolerated. Gantt's entrance into school there went without incident. Gantt himself had his own explanation for this: "If you can't appeal to the morals of a South Carolinian," he said, "you can appeal to his manners."

Another front of the civil-rights battle revolved around voting rights, which had been largely denied blacks in both states since the 1890s. The flight of African Americans to the north during Jim Crow left few counties with black majorities. Nonetheless, African American legislators, mayors, and judges began to win elections.

Blacks, who tended to be poorer than whites, favored the Democratic Party, with its greater funding of social programs. Whereas the Southern Democratic party had long been the "white man's" party, during the Kennedy/Johnson years conservative Southern Democrats found themselves unwelcome in their own party.

Since the early 1970s, as the economy of the Carolina and Georgia up-countries have grown, more and more folks from places like Atlanta, Augusta, Greenville, and Columbia have bought second homes along the Southern coast. Simultaneously, more and more non-Southerners have discovered the region, and many of them have chosen to move down permanently, as the nation's collective memories of race riots and lynchings in the South continue to dim. In recent years, many descendants of black Carolinians and Georgians who moved out of the South during the Jim Crow years have moved back.

Culture

THE PEOPLE

Despite all its physical beauty, despite its music, its food, and the salty scent of the coastal marshes, the very best thing about the Sea Island region is its people. Remove Georgians and Carolinians from the Sea Island Coast, replace them with New Yorkers, give it five years, and what would you have? Miami.

Make no mistake: the people make the Sea Island Coast the unique place it is. Despite Charlestonians' and Savannahians' legendary pridefulness, by and large people around here are a meek lot, humbled by the mistakes of their past in a way that Northerners and Westerners are not.

Unless they leave home, Southerners cannot escape their past: A white Middleton may

© SEAN SLINSKY

Some of the region's older post offices are as historic as they are utilitarian.

well share a classroom with two black Middletons, likely descendants of his great-great-great-grandfather's slaves—and possibly distant cousins.

A lot of Southerners see Northerners as the finger-pointing husbands who quit cheating on their wives and immediately became crusaders against adultery. Westerners are the husbands who ditched their wives and kids and headed to the coast with their secretaries. Southerners are the husbands who have been caught in the act, been half-forgiven, and now live on in a town where—no matter what other accomplishments they may muster—their sin will never be forgotten. Because of this, white Carolinians tend to evince an odd mixture of defensiveness, good nature, and perhaps a little more understanding of human nature than other folks. Perhaps because so much of their history has been spent withstanding the tugs and blows of other regions that commanded them to change, Carolinians are none too quick to equate change with progress, which, granted, can make them

a bit slow to acknowledge even a good change when it comes about.

In a speech to the Georgia Writer's Association, Savannah-born author Flannery O'Connor once pointed to what she believed made Southerners different from their fellow Americans:

> We have had our Fall. We have gone into the modern world with an inburnt knowledge of human limitations and with a sense of mystery which could not have developed in our first state of innocence – as it has not sufficiently developed in the rest of our country.

Southerners' understanding of people as intrinsically flawed creatures also makes them value traditions and manners more than many—for in a culture where human nature is seen as inherently flawed, "self-expression" and "doing what you feel" are not necessarily good things. To Southerners, some parts of the self are, well, just selfish.

Hence, Charlestonians and Savannahians use ritualized courtesies copiously to smooth out the rough edges of humanity. They are taught to say "yes, ma'am," "no, sir," "please," and "thank you," whether or not their inner children feel like it.

Attitude Toward Tourists

One of the most charming things about people on the Sea Island Coast, particularly outside of Charleston and Savannah, is how they're nearly always genuinely surprised to hear that non-Southerners have bothered to come all this way just to see their little state. They know that the Sea Island Coast is a gem, but want to know how you found out about it. Most people around here are proud of where they live and are usually happy to show you around.

Southern Subtleties

You and your travel companion meet a nice Charleston couple, who invite you to their home for dinner. You eat, you adjourn to the porch for beverages, and then you sit around, talking. It gets a little late, but your hosts seem so eager to continue the conversation that you linger. It gets later. You really *should* go, but as you rise, your hosts offer another round of drinks. Finally, you decide you must go. You leave, while your hosts openly grieve your departure. You're begged to return again when "y'all can stay a little longer."

What average unsuspecting non-Southerners don't realize is that they have just committed a major faux pas. Although you of course had no way of knowing it, your hosts were ready for you to leave right after dessert, but they

---

FAMOUS NATIVES OF THE SEA ISLAND COAST

ARTS AND LITERATURE
Conrad Aiken, poet, novelist
Hervey Allen (Charleston), author of *Anthony Adverse*
Pat Conroy (Beaufort), best-selling author of *The Prince of Tides, Beach Music, The Great Santini, Lords of Discipline*, and others
Dubose Heyward (Charleston), author of *Porgy* (basis of subsequent Gershwin opera *Porgy and Bess*)
Flannery O'Connor, short story writer, novelist

MOVIES AND TELEVISION
Helen Chandler (Charleston), actress, Bela Lugosi's *Dracula*
Stanley Donen (Charleston), director, *Singin' in the Rain* and many other films
Thomas Gibson (Charleston), actor, television's *Chicago Hope, Dharma and Greg*
Stacy Keach (Savannah), actor, television's *Mike Hammer*

MUSIC
Mike Curb (Savannah), songwriter, producer, performer
Johnny Mercer (Savannah), songwriter
John Phillips (Parris Island), guitarist, songwriter, leader of Mamas and Papas
Darius Rucker (Charleston), singer, Hootie and the Blowfish

POLITICS
John C. Fremont (Savannah), explorer, military leader, U.S. Presidential candidate
Charles Pinckney (Charleston), framer of U.S. Constitution
Henry Martyn Robert (Roberts), protocol expert, author of *Robert's Rules of Order*

SCIENCE
Alexander Garden (Charleston), Colonial-era botanist (the gardenia is named in his honor)
Joel Poinsett (Charleston), former U.S. ambassador to Mexico (the poinsettia is named in his honor)

SPORTS
Bucky Dent (Savannah), Yankee shortstop
Joe Frazier (Beaufort), former heavyweight boxing champion

offered drinks on the porch only because you showed no signs of leaving, and they wanted to be polite.

So what's the rule of thumb when visiting with Southerners you don't know very well? Leave about when you first suspect you should, only an hour earlier.

LANGUAGE

One of the things outsiders often notice about Southerners is the Southern way with figurative language. To some degree this is derived from the strong Biblical tradition of the region; for centuries, Southern evangelical Christians have naturally striven to illustrate the intangibles of life with easy-to-visualize parables, following the example of Jesus, who used illustrations drawn from situations familiar to his unschooled 1st-century audiences (e.g., a shepherd's concern for his sheep, wheat planted among briars, a disobedient son returning home) to explain complex theological doctrines.

Hence, if you're butting into a conflict between two Carolinians, you may be reminded that "y'all don't have a dog in this fight." If you think a person is smart just because he went to school, you're forgetting that "living in a garage don't make you a Ford." My favorite saying, although I only heard it once, describes a thoughtful person who, apparently, was "sweeter than sugar cubes in syrup." Makes you want to brush just hearing it.

Folks around here don't think or figure, they "reckon." They don't get ready, they "fix," as in, "I'm fixin' to head into Charleston." They don't push buttons, they "mash" them. They "cut" lights on and off, "carry" people around in their cars (e.g., "I need to *carry* Miss Sharon to the store"), accomplish urgent tasks in a "skinny minute," and push shopping "buggies" around the Winn-Dixie. If a Carolinian or Georgian is a stranger to a subject, she "doesn't know 'boo'" about it. If she's never met you before, she doesn't know you from "Adam's house cat." If she *does* know you and sees you, she won't just hug you, she'll "hug your neck." And if someone down here says

he really needs to "take a powder," it probably just means he has a headache and is taking a dose of Goody's powder (a regional remedy—essentially crushed aspirin). If he tells you he's "like to pass out," it means he's very tired, not drunk. Carolinians and Georgians never pop in to say "hello" or "hi"—they stop by to say "hey." In fact, you'll rarely hear "hi" in public—it's usually "hey."

Fairly well known is the preference for "y'all," or the more formal "you-all." (Some argue that "y'all" is actually more politically correct than the Yankee "you guys," since it's not gender-exclusive.) It's usually the first linguistic nuance you'll pick up when you're in the region, and it's one of the hardest for displaced Southerners to mask when they're outside of Dixie. It just sounds friendlier.

You may also hear (usually) white coastal males call each other "Bo," the way males in other American subcultures might call one another "Buddy," "Homes," or "Dude": "Hey, Bo, can I borrow your johnboat?" "Sure, Bo."

Pronunciation counts, too. Although there's not the space to go into all the regional variations, just remember that no one watches television down here; they watch "the TEE-vee." And cautious Georgians and Carolinians buy "IN-surance" on their house, which will pay for the family to stay in a "HO-tel" if the house burns down.

Terms of Address

One of the most admirable qualities of Southern culture is its resistance to the Cult of Youth. The South is a place where it's not against the law to get old (see Thurmond, Senator Strom). Here, age is generally still respected, and one way of showing and reinforcing this deference is the customary way of referring to elders as "ma'am" and "sir." For example:

"Excuse me, ma'am, but could you tell me where to find the trailhead?"

"Didn't y'all see the sign back aways? Where the two magnolias used to be?"

"No, ma'am."

Granted, there is some classism involved. Bosses and the wealthy tend to hear themselves addressed as "sir" or "ma'am" more often than, say, gardeners or house cleaners. "Aunt" and "uncle" were once familiar terms used by whites toward elder African Americans, but you'll only hear this—if at all—among the oldest generations.

Note that visitors don't *have* to say "ma'am" and "sir"—Southerners expect non-Southerners to be ill-mannered, anyway—but doing so might help you blend in a little better.

Children address adults normally with "Mr.," "Miss," or "Mrs." attached to either the adult's first name or last name. Family friends or other adult friends are often addressed by the first name, preceded by either Mr. or Miss—whether or not the woman in question is married. Hence, to our friends' children, my wife and I became "Miss Kristin and Mr. Mike." It's much more genuine than the automatic uncle or aunt status some parents elsewhere are always trying to confer upon you. It's a typically Carolinian compromise, reinforcing societal roles and responsibilities by keeping the generations separate, yet also encouraging intimacy with first names.

Note, too, that, even if you're an adult, if a large age difference exists between you and another (older) person, it's still proper to address elders as Mr., Ms., Mrs., or Miss; among the 20 fairly bohemian graduate English students in James Dickey's Poetry Workshop at the University of South Carolina, I never heard one of us address him (even in private) as anything but "Mr. Dickey."

BEACH MUSIC

Outside the South, beach music is one of the least-known and least-understood musical genres in America. Part of the confusion lies with those who assume that the term "beach music" refers to the California vocal surf music of the Beach Boys and Jan and Dean. Carolina beach music is a whole different animal, popular on a whole different coast. One main difference is that it is not primarily music featuring lyrics about the beach or developed to capture the rhythms of the ocean (as instrumental

West Coast surf music was), nor is it necessarily written and performed by Carolinian or even Southern artists. Some of beach music's greatest stars have probably never known that they were making "beach music" at all.

Beach music is blues music; most of the early performers of beach music were black. All that was needed was an easy-flowing song with four beats to the measure, about 120 beats per minute. Songs like the Drifters' "Under the Boardwalk," the Tams' "What Kinda Fool Do You Think I Am?" and Maurice Williams and the Zodiacs' "Stay" became beach classics. Perhaps the "Johnny B. Goode" for beach music is the Dominoes "Sixty-Minute Man."

If people found that a jukebox song was good to shag to—even if recorded and/or lyrically set hundreds of miles from the Strand (e.g., Bob and Earl's "Harlem Shuffle")—it quickly became absorbed as part of the canon of beach music. Later, in the late 1960s, 1970s, and 1980s, a few regional groups began to record songs that lyrically celebrated the beach music/shagging subculture, including The Embers' anthemic "I Love Beach Music" and General Johnson and Chairmen of the Board's "Carolina Girls."

Of all of the beach-specific songs, the most popular outside the beach music subculture has been the Tams' "There Ain't Nothing Like Shagging," which surprised everyone when it raced up into the top 20 on the British pop charts in the mid-1980s. And then everyone remembered what "shagging" means in British English and got over their surprise.

Today, any song with the right beat, whether it's country-and-western, gospel, blues, or rock, can make the beach music charts. Such diverse acts as The Cherry Poppin' Daddies, John Fogerty, Tracy Chapman, Alabama, and Patty LaBelle have shared the charts. You'll find shagging nightclubs in almost any good-sized coastal town throughout the South.

You'll also find almost every other kind of live music on the Southeast coast, from blues to church-bell choirs to reggae. Check the local listings in whatever town you're visiting.

ESSENTIALS

Recreation

The Sea Island Coast has a reputation, whether down in Charleston, or on the Golden Isles, for a certain languidness. And this sort of graciousness (and, okay, slowness) of living certainly does still exist along the coast. All the water around here, however, has also attracted a lot of active types from other areas—people who didn't just happen to be born here, but who have chosen to live here, and who are paying far too much for their house with private boat ramp access and a jogging path to just sit on the screened porch, sip sweet tea, and look at the view. They're anxious to paddle, windsurf, waterski, scuba dive, bike, in-line skate, and fish every last inch of the Sea Island Coast.

These work hard–play hard sorts—and their time-on-my-hands snowbird brethren—have created a massive entertainment-and-recreation industry on the Sea Island Coast, providing far more recreational opportunities than you'll find anywhere else in the state.

OCEAN SPORTS
Surfing

Yes, Southerners surf. Towns like Folly Beach and St. Simon's Island host a full-blown surf subculture as well. The enthusiasm for the sport runs much higher than the waves, in fact.

© SEAN SLINSKY

The single best, most dependable surf spot in the Charleston area, if not in the entire region, is Folly Beach, where the state's surfing championships take place every year. If the waves are small everywhere else, they tend to still be decent here. And if they're good everywhere else, they'll be pounding here. Of course, if the swell's good, it's also going to be crowded, and while the localism among area surfers is nowhere near Hawaii or California levels, you might want to let the tube-starved locals enjoy themselves. At press time, Folly was undergoing a beach renourishment project that was adversely affecting its surf, but locals hold out hope it's just a temporary setback. To get to Folly, take Highway 17 south of Charleston, then take Highway 171 (Folly Beach Road) until it dead-ends at the Holiday Inn. Turn left at East Ashley Avenue and keep going to get to some of the best spots, like the famed **Washout.**

Another popular spot at Folly is at **10th Street,** where the swells and the crowds are less intense than those along East Ashely. Beside the Holiday Inn at East Atlantic Avenue, the **Edwin S. Taylor Fishing Pier** (101 E. Artic Ave., Folly, 843/588-3474, www.folly-fishingpier.com) stretches far into the water, and creates better (cleaner and longer) rides than elsewhere. But play smart: Surf within 200 feet of the pier and you'll get ticketed.

On the other side of Charleston, Isle of Palms (IOP) and Sullivan's Island both offer a few more wave-riding opps. At IOP, try anywhere from 25th Avenue on down to the Wild Dunes Resort. When the wind's a northeaster, try Sully's, especially Station 22. Dubbed **Bert's,** in honor of the venerable bar out here on Middle Street, it's one of the best places to surf at low tide.

McKevlin's Surf Shop (8 Center St., Folly, 843/588-2247, www.mckevlins.com) has been based on Folly since 1965 and is *the* place for pros and newbies alike. They have a 24-hour surf report (843/588-2261). Charleston's newspaper, *The Post and Courier,* maintains the **InfoLine Surf Report** (843/937-6000, ext. 7873), and updates it throughout the day as well.

In the Savannah area, the best spot is Tybee Island, on the north end, at Fort Screven. For information on Tybee Island surf conditions, check out the **High Tide Surf Shop** (Hwy. 80 E, 912/786-6556). In the southern part of the Georgia Coast, it's all river mouths and sandbars; you may as well head down to Jacksonville to surf the pier.

Other Water Sports

Sailing, parasailing, windsurfing, and **kiteboarding** are all popular along the Sea Island Coast, especially around Charleston's Isle of Palms and Sullivan's Island, and down around Hilton Head. On the Golden Isles, you'll see some action as well. The offerings run deep, so check specific chapters for the best outfitters and more info.

Diving

The coast's long history of shipwrecks makes the waters offshore a virtual wonderland for divers. If you're here in the winter, though, rough,

© SEAN SLINSKY

Windsurfing and kiteboarding are top-draw watersports along the Sea Island coast.

cold waters can make offshore diving pretty inhospitable between October and May.

But people dive in the historic rivers and sounds year-round; one Lowcountry favorite is the Cooper River, which is filled with fossilized giant shark's teeth, bones, and mammal teeth, as well as Colonial and prehistoric artifacts. Expect water temperatures in the 50s. Off Brunswick, Gray's Reef is another popular dive. See individual destination chapters for outfitters.

CANOEING AND KAYAKING

The Sea Island Coast is a paddler's paradise, lacking only challenging mountain white water to complement the peaceful black-water rivers, swamps, sounds, and inlets that are teaming with wildlife and are challenging Atlantic beach paddles.

Mount Pleasant–based **Coastal Expeditions** (514-B Mill St., 843/884-7684, www.coastalexpeditions.com) can set up a sea-kayak trip to the uninhabited, well-regulated **Bull Island** just north of Charleston. If you're a nature lover, it may well be the best experience of your Lowcountry visit, including fantastic scenery and birding.

In the Lowcountry between Charleston and Hilton Head you'll find the **Edisto River Canoe & Kayak Trail,** which takes in some 56 peaceful Lowcountry miles along the Edisto River. You'll find guided canoe and kayak tours of the ACE Basin National Wildlife Refuge and the Edisto River Canoe and Kayak Trail offered by scores of outfitters along the coast. To dig in on your own, check in with the folks at the Edisto River Canoe & Kayak Trail Commission (P.O. Box 881, Walterboro, SC, 29488, 843/549-5591, www.edistoriver.org). Their website offers local maps and more.

In the Savannah area, a good place for canoeists and kayakers to put in is the **Isle of Hope Marina** (50 Bluff Dr., 912/354-8187). Down on the Golden Isles, the better outfitters rent kayaks and offer tours of the local waterways, as well as for paddles in the Okefenokee Swamp, and even up toward Savannah. See the *Brunswick* chapter for information.

Paddling is the best way to wander the swamps, rivers, and marshes of the Sea Island coast.

© SEAN SLINSKY

FISHING

The person who invents the all-in-one driving iron and fishing pole will make a quick fortune on the Sea Island Coast—beyond golfing, Carolinians like most to fish.

The Sea Island Coast features Gulf Stream fishing for amberjack, marlin, sailfish, tuna, dolphin, and wahoo. Closer in, you can still hope to land mackerel, blackfin tuna, cobia, and shark. Surf, pier, and jetty fishing include channel bass, Spanish mackerel, shark, flounder, croakers, and whiting. You'll find more than 30 public and private piers jutting from the shore into the waters of this part of the Atlantic. More than 20 charter boat outfits in the Golden Isles region alone help offshore anglers hook barracuda, dolphin fish, grouper, jacks, mackerel, marlin, sailfish, sea bass, shark, snapper, and tuna, among others.

Fishing types not up for boating are still in luck, as you can cast from the beach along on St. Simons Island and Jekyll Island, and from most of the local ocean piers, and bridges, too. While charter captains typically handle the paperwork for their guests, individual license information varies from state to state. In South Carolina, contact the **South Carolina Department of Natural Resources** (P.O. Box 167, Columbia, SC 29202, www.dnr.state.sc.us, 803/734-3886 or 888/434-7472). SCDNR's massive website, the **Great Lodge** (www.greatlodge.com), also covers licensing details. For saltwater fishing in Georgia, contact the **Georgia Department of Natural Resources Coastal Resources Division** (One Conservation Way, Ste. 300, Brunswick, GA, 31520-8687 or 912/264-7218, www.gofish.com).

SHRIMPING

For shrimping, you'll need a cast net and an ice chest (or some saltwater). A cast net is round, with weights all along the rim; you throw a cast net somewhat the way you would throw a Frisbee, although in truth it flies closer to the way an uncooked pizza would, which is one way of saying this might take you a little practice.

© SEAN SLINSKY

Fishing from bridges is allowed, but you generally need a fishing license.

But what's a half hour or hour's practice when it teaches you how to catch shrimp?

After you've thrown a perfect loop—so that the net hits the water as a circle, its weights bringing the net down in a perfect dome over the unsuspecting shrimp—wait for the weights to hit the bottom. This is something you just have to sense because you can't see or feel it. Now jerk on the center line that draws the weights together, closing the bottom of the dome into a sphere and trapping the shrimp.

You can rent a small johnboat or outboard, or you can throw from some inlet bridges; it's up to you, but most people seem to feel that ebb tide is the time to throw because this is when the shrimp, who spend high tide spread out and frolicking in the marsh grasses, are the most concentrated in the creek beds. Cast your net toward the side of a waterway, just on the edge of the grasses, and you may well snag some of these mobile crustaceans. Local hardware stores and some angler outfitting stores carry the nets, and some offer lessons—formal and informal.

CRABBING

Crabbing has to be one of the easiest ways to catch some of the best food found in the ocean. Sure, you can charter your boats far out to sea, slaphappy on Dramamine, but you'll find *me* in the shallows with a bucket, a string, a sinker, a net, and some ripe chicken backs. That's pretty much all you need to land a good supper's worth of blue crab in South Carolina.

1. Tie the string to a piece of chicken and the sinker.
2. Wade out in the water about waist high.
3. Hold onto one end of the string and drop the chicken and sinker into the water.
4. Wait for the crabs to come scuttling over for supper.
5. When you feel a tug on the chicken, pull up on the string and swoop beneath the crab with your net.
6. Call me; invite me over for dinner.

A few rules here:

ALLIGATORS VS. SHARKS

If you're from an area free of sharks and alligators, you may wonder about the wisdom of sharing the Sea Islands' waters with them.

Consider the facts: From 1976 to 1995, of the millions who flocked to the islands' surf and sounds, alligators attacked just six of them, and sharks sunk their teeth into nine others.

So which is worse – a gator attack or a shark attack? Based on statistics compiled on attacks in six states, neither is as lethal as you might expect. If you get attacked by an alligator, you've still got a 96.6 percent chance of walking away – or at least hopping away – from the encounter. And a full 98 percent of shark attack victims live to tell the tale.

Some say surviving a shark or alligator bite is like buying real estate: It's all about location.

- If the crabs have yellow eggs (roe) on the underside, the law requires you to toss them back.
- If the crab is less than five inches wide across its back, you'll need to toss it back, too.
- Drop the "lucky" ones who pass these two tests into an ice chest and keep them cold until you cook them.
- Of course, some people, particularly up around the Outer Banks, prefer to fish with crab pots. This is a less interactive—you bait the pots and return later to see what you've caught—but more time-efficient way to catch crabs. You can get crab pots at a number of hardware stores and fishing shops.

HUNTING

For many Carolinians, a crisp fall day just isn't complete without heading out into the woods to go hunting. Few instincts seem to be as ingrained in humans as the instinct to hunt prey, and the activity ("sport" seems somewhat misleading—as if the animals had to kick in a league fee to join the fun) has a long history in the South, and in the cultures from which modern-day Southerners descend.

Hunters can find white-tailed deer, wild turkey, ruffed grouse, quail, squirrels, and other small mammals in national and state forests, national wildlife refuges, and wildlife management areas. Get the specifics on hunting from the **South Carolina Department of Natural Resources** (P.O. Box 167, Columbia,

SC 29202, 803/734-3886 or 888/434-7472, www.dnr.state.sc.us). Licenses can be bought by calling the SCDNR's toll-free number, or by visiting **Great Lodge** (www.greatlodge.com), their licensing website. For Georgia, call the **Georgia Department of Natural Resources Wildlife Resources Division** (2070 Hwy. 278 SE, Social Circle, GA 30025-4711, 888/748-6887, www.gadnr.org or www.georgiawildlife.com).

HIKING, BACKPACKING, AND BIKING

The coasts of South Carolina and Georgia feature several excellent hiking trails. Although it won't help your wildlife-viewing any, during hunting season try to wear some fluorescent orange. Better yet, you'll find plenty of great trails in hunting-free state parks and nature preserves to keep you busy until the smoke clears at the end of hunting season. Just to be safe, however, it won't hurt to wear some orange here also to keep safe against poachers. If you're hiking with a dog, make sure Fido's wearing some orange, too.

Some Notable Trails

In South Carolina, you'll find the **Swamp Fox Trail** north of Charleston. Passing through the former gator-infested haunts of Revolutionary guerilla leader Francis Marion (the area is now part of Francis Marion National Forest), the Swamp Fox is also the easternmost leg of the Lowcountry-to-Upcountry **Palmetto Trail.**

South of Charleston, the **Edisto Nature Trail** is right off Highway 17 South just in Jacksonborough, and provides a short (one-mile) walk through cypress swamp and a former barge canal. A spur trail leads to a prehistoric Native American shell mound. Finally, down near Beaufort, the **Hunting Island State Park Trails** provide 6.5 miles of hiking through pine and palmetto-forested island land, with lots of wildlife viewing.

Laced with well-marked hiking trails and devoted to wildlife conservation, the **Oatland Island Education Center** near Savannah offers the chance to view coastal wildlife in action. **Skidaway State Park** offers two nature trails through marshes, oaks, pines, and cabbage palmettos. Wildlife includes shorebirds, rare migrating birds, deer, and raccoon.

Farther south and inland, the **Suwannee Canal Recreation Area** provides four miles of hiking trails through the Okefenokee Swamp.

The **South Carolina State Trails Program** (South Carolina Department of Parks, Recreation and Tourism, 1205 Pendleton St., Columbia, SC 29201, 803/734-0173, www.sctrails.net) can school you on the best trails in the state, and offers superior maps and info on each on their website. **Georgia Trails** (georgiatrails.com), a commercial group, offers the best info for that neck of the woods. For more information, consult regional chapters for more specifics.

TENNIS

The top spots for tennis along the Sea Island Coast would have to be at Hilton Head Island and the Isle of Palms, plus in the Golden Isles, all of which are home to world-class tennis resorts. See individual regional chapters for specific resorts and public courts.

As for watching tennis, the **Family Circle Tennis Center Cup** (161 Seven Farms Dr., Charleston, 843/856-7900 or 800/677-2293, www.familycirclecup.com), one of the country's top professional women's tennis tournaments on the Corel WTA Tour, takes place in early April on Charleston's Daniel Island. High-caliber pros like the Williams sisters, Jennifer Capriati, and Anna Kournikova typically draw the big crowds.

GOLF

The Sea Island Coast features hundreds of opportunities for golfing, but the South Carolina Coast is clearly center stage. With the help of veteran duffer Kendall Buckendahl of Mount Pleasant, here's a rundown of Carolina's finest:

Classic Courses

In its 2004 Course Rankings, *Golf Magazine* ranked three Lowcountry and Golden Isles greens in its Top 100 courses. **Kiawah Island Golf Resort** (12 Kiawah Beach Dr., Kiawah Island, 843/768-2121 or 800/254-2924, www.kiawahgolf.com) and its Ocean Course came in eighth. **Sea Island Golf Club** (100 Retreat Ave, St. Simons Island, 912/638-5118, www.seaisland.com) Seaside Course ranked 17th. And **Sea Pines Resort** (32 Greenwood Dr., Hilton Head Island, 800/925-4653, www.seapines.com) followed close behind, with its Harbour Town Golf Links Course coming in at 19.

Other Stellar Courses

In a 2004–2005 poll, the magazine ranked those resorts, plus South Carolina's **Wild Dunes Resort** (5757 Palmetto Dr., Isle of Palms, 843/886-2113, www.wilddunes.com) and **Palmetto Dunes** (P.O. Box 5606, Hilton Head Island, 843/785-1161 or 800/845-6130, www.palmettodunes.com) in the country's top 50 golf resorts.

Values

If you want to golf inexpensively, keep a couple of things in mind. One is the time of year. Spring and fall are high season, and "high season" equals "high prices." Other values come from areas that have resorts close by, such as Hilton Head and Charleston. The well-cared-for courses at the resorts force the public courses in the surrounding area to upgrade their grounds for competition's sake; the value comes from not having to pay the resort's high prices for a resort-grade course.

In the Charleston area, **Charleston National Country Club** (1360 National Dr., 843/884-4653, www.charlestonnational-golf.com), as well as **Dunes West Golf Club** (3535 Wando Plantation Way, 843/856-9000, www.duneswestgolfclub.com), **Coosaw Creek** (4210 Club Course Dr., 843/767-9000, www.coosawcreek.com), and **Crowfield Golf and Country Club** (300 Hamlet Circle, 843/764-4618, www.crowfieldgolf.com) all have great layouts and cost less than $100 to play, even in the high season. On **Hilton Head Island** a couple of names that stand out value-wise include **Shipyard Plantation Golf Club** (45 Shipyard Dr., 843/686-8802, www.hilton-headgolf.com) and **Pintail Creek Golf Club** (Pintail Creek Dr., 843/784-2426).

You might also head two hours north of Charleston to Myrtle Beach. Go in the winter and dead of summer for great price specials. The Grand Strand offers the highest concentration of golf courses in the country. It is really *the* golf destination of the South, if not the nation.

Of course, the Georgia Coast has its courses, too, including the 63-hole **Jekyll Island Golf Club** (322 Captain Wylly Rd., Jekyll Island, 912/635-2368, www.jekyllisland.com) and the **Sea Palms Golf & Tennis Resort** (5445 Fort Frederica Rd., St. Simons, 800/841-6268, www.seapalms.com) on St. Simons.

South Carolina offers an excellent booklet, the *South Carolina Golf Guide,* which is published annually; pick one up at one of the state's visitors centers, or call 800/682-5553 for a copy. The **Georgia State Golf Association** (121 Village Pkwy., Bldg. 3, Marietta, 770/955-4272 or 800/949-4742, www.gsga.org) has an online guide, and suggests duffers call for more information for Georgia courses.

SPECTATOR SPORTS
Football
Although courted by the Carolina Panthers, Jacksonville Jaguars, and Atlanta Falcons, along the Southeast Coast, *college* football still dominates the popular imagination. Even people who never got around to completing eighth grade take intercollegiate ball very seriously.

How seriously? Consider South Carolina. If football is a religion, then South Carolina is Northern Ireland. The chief denominations? USC Gamecockism vs. Clemson Tigerism. True believers of either faith can live anywhere in the state, although loyalties grow predictably fiercer near the home coliseums. Signs of devotion can include anything from class rings and ball caps to 40-foot motor homes painted with tiger paws. Yes, other South Carolina colleges have notable football programs, but that doesn't mean you can answer "Wofford" when asked who you're *for* on USC/Clemson game day. In and south of Savannah, the big game is the Georgia-Florida game; one of Savannah's "high holidays," according to *Midnight in the Garden of Good and Evil*'s Joe Odom.

The biggest, most competitive football actually played on the Carolina coast is probably down at the **Citadel Military College** (171 Moultrie St., 843/953-6726, 800/868-DAWG, or 800/868-3294,www.citadel.edu), although **Charleston Southern University** (9200 University Blvd., North Charleston, 843/863-7000, www.charlestonsouthern.edu) has been building its program as of late. Getting tickets to a Citadel contest, with its ferociously active alumni base, can be a challenge, but check the sports page in whatever town you're in, and if it's pigskin season you'll find a college playing somewhere nearby.

Minor League Baseball
It's hard for a lot of fans to take major-league baseball seriously these days; it's hard to see much drama in a game when you're looking out at a diamond full of players who, win or lose, are cumulatively worth more than the GM Board of Directors. If you've grown weary of high ticket prices and multimillionaire players, be sure to catch a minor-league game while you're in state. Watching these 18- and 19-year-olds—who are being paid less than a middle manager at Hardee's—battle it out for a chance at the bigs just might help you

remember why you fell in love with the game in the first place.

The Sea Island Coast is blessed with *two* single-A baseball teams. Northernmost are the **RiverDogs** (360 Fishburne St., 843/577-3647, www.riverdogs.com), who compete in the venerable South Atlantic (or "Sallie") League. They play in Joseph P. Riley Stadium, colloquially known as "The Joe," and named after Charleston's longtime, and as of this writing, current mayor. Overlooking the Ashley River, this classy ballpark was created by the same people who created nostalgic Camden Yards in Baltimore. The 5,549 seats—legion for a single-A field—go for $4–8.

Also battling in the Sallie league are the **Savannah Sand Gnats** (1401 E. Victory Dr., 912/351-9150, www.sandgnats.com), who have played at Grayson Stadium in Daffin Park since 1996. The team is a Washington National affiliate.

Professional Soccer

The **Charleston Battery** (1990 Daniel Island Dr., Daniel Island, 843/971-4625, www.charlestonbattery.com) has played in the Holy City since 1993 when the team joined the neophyte U.S. Indoor Soccer League (USISL), which is now a conglomeration of nearly 150 teams in five separate leagues. The Battery has placed toward the top of their division every year since 1994, including winning the USISL finals in 1996. After that they moved to the newly form A-League—the United Soccer League—where they have remained competitive, winning the Atlantic Division in 2000. Very popular among Charlestonians, the team plays about 20 games a year in the 5,600-seat Blackbaud Stadium, located right off the Mark Clark Expressway (I-126), 843/740-7787. Tickets range $8–10. Be sure to bring the kids (under 16 years) to the park up to an hour before game time, when the FunZone, an "interactive soccer theme park" (which overstates it a bit) is open, including a soccer bounce, various games, a playground, and a picnic area.

Minor League Hockey

Charleston's **South Carolina Stingrays** (3300 W. Montague Ave., Ste. B302, North Charleston, 843/744-2248, www.stingrayshockey.com), affiliated with the Washington Capitals in the NHL and the Hershey Bears in the AHL, have done battle at the North Charleston Coliseum since first skating their way into the hearts of Charlestonians in 1993.

Food

SEAFOOD

Along the coast, seafood is king. Shrimp are everywhere; you can catch them yourself or buy them right off the boats or nearly as fresh from coastal supermarkets. Ditto for the Carolina soft-shell crab, which is used mainly for crab cakes and she-crab soup (along the coast, you'll find lots of places serving crab legs, but these are from imported Alaskan king and Dungeness crabs). The most common way to eat shrimp or fish is to deep-fry it, but grilling has become common as well.

CLASSIC CAROLINA EATS
Barbecue

My brother George, who lives not far over the border in Athens, Georgia, told me recently that he and his wife had become vegetarians. I asked him if he was going to have a hard time giving up barbecue. He reminded me that in the South, barbecue is a vegetable.

People have various theories as to how to spot a good barbecue joint. Some say that the presence of a pig anywhere on the sign is a good omen. Others claim that anyplace that is open more than three days a week (normally

BARBECUE AND HOME-COOKED SUPPER

Down in this neck of the woods, Southerners still fry everything – our chicken, our seafood, our hush puppies, and even grits – and no one even calls it soul food, it's just old-school Southern. While "nouveau Lowcountry" restaurants are well and good for those interested in linen tablecloths, everyone in these parts is still attached to their favorite buffet and paper-basket dives. Locals are particularly passionate about sticking to bacon-seasoned greens, and a menu where mac-and-cheese counts as a vegetable. And they are dead serious about whether their barbecue is pulled or chopped, and sweetened with the state's signature honey mustard sauce or soused in vinegar like they do north in Tarheel country. To take a waistline-be-damned trip around the area, check out the listings in each chapter for barbecue and Lowcountry home-style fare. And bring the antacids.

© SEAN SLINSKY

Barbecue is the fifth food group in the South featured here at the Georgia Pig restaurant.

Thursday through Saturday) should be avoided like a Danish pizza parlor. I would add only the following amendment: the fewer windows, the better.

The ideal barbecue joint is built of bricks or cinder blocks, usually on a country road where police cruise-bys are weekly events (unless it's mealtime) and where security alarms would only irritate the possums. Hence, most barbecue owners seem to figure, no windows,

no hassle. And who needs windows, anyway? Eating barbecue is a serious business—you're not here to admire the scenery.

There are exceptions to the rule. I have even once or twice been into a decent barbecue joint with both windows *and* central air-conditioning—but somehow, it felt like camping on Astroturf.

Now the question comes—what is barbecue? The answer varies across the country: In

ANITA'S BANANA PUDDING

Banana pudding is a classic Southern dessert – served with vanilla wafers but without airs. Its cool, creamy sweetness is just perfect after a hot plate of food on a steamy day. Most barbecue places and home cooking restaurants make a good pudding, and really, it's hard to make one wrong. What separates great banana pudding from lesser forms is the use of real banana slices and the distribution of vanilla wafers *throughout,* rather than merely scattering them *atop* the pudding. Try this recipe from a friend of mine, a native of Duplin County. Though true purists would claim that starting with homemade custard (instead of instant pudding) will knock the taste up yet another notch, in my experience, banana pudding doesn't get much better than Anita's.

One 14-oz. can sweetened condensed milk
1½ cups cold water
1 pkg. instant banana-flavored pudding
1 pint heavy whipping cream
2 tablespoons sugar
36 vanilla wafers
3 large bananas
lemon juice to taste

1. Whisk condensed milk and water. Add pudding mix. Beat. Chill 15 minutes.
2. Whip whipping cream until stiff. Add sugar and whip 30 seconds more. Fold into chilled pudding.
3. Layer 12 wafers, one banana, and one-third of the pudding. Repeat twice more. Chill 4-6 hours minimum.

the West, "barbecue" is something you do, not something you eat. You barbecue some ribs or steaks. To tell a Nevadan you're going to eat some "barbecue" is like telling them you're going to eat some "fried." In the Midwest and Texas, "barbecued" is an adjective and usually comes before "ribs." Most parts of the deep South agree that "barbecue" (the noun) refers to smoked shredded or pulled pork. Where they can't agree is on how that pork should be dressed.

There are three main camps on this issue in the Sea Island Coast: the vinegar-based camp, the tomato-based camp, and the mustard-based camp. The vinegar-based variety was historically probably the most common along the coast; however, the coast has served as a vacation spot for so many inland Georgians and Carolinians for so long that you'll find a good mix of styles along it. My own preference is for the mustard-based sauces you'll find in the various Dukes and Bessenger-family barbecues along the South Carolina coast, but you'll find some great barbecues of every denomination (and some that have mastered more than one style) from Charleston to the Florida line.

Meats

You'll want to try slaw burgers and pimento cheeseburgers, regional variations on the American artery-clogging favorite. Slaw dogs are simply hot dogs with coleslaw on top; you'll also find chili slaw dogs offered at many stands. Fried chicken is sold everywhere, from gas stations to Chinese restaurants to drive-up carhop restaurants. And most of it is good.

Fried chicken livers are offered at most places that sell fried chicken. If you've always publicly admired Native Americans for using up every bit of the animals they killed, here's a chance to walk your talk. And of course, chitlins will give you another such chance. These are the deep-fried small intestines of a pig.

Side Dishes

Biscuits stand as an integral element of Southern country cooking. One surprising place where you'll find good biscuits is at Hardee's, but maybe that shouldn't be surprising because Hardee's was founded in the Carolinas.

Folks trying to eat healthfully in the region are sometimes stymied by the tendency of Southerners toward stewed vegetables, including spinach, okra, and collard greens, throwing in a slab of fatback for good flavor, and fried vegetables, which again seems to miss the point of eating vegetables entirely. But in the case of okra, perhaps it's an improvement.

Grits have become something like the official food of the South. Grits are made from corn or hominy. Most Northerners would mistake them for Cream of Wheat, but you shouldn't put sugar and cinnamon on them. The proper way to eat this plain-tasting food is with butter and salt and pepper—or Texas Pete's—and/or mixed in with eggs, ham, and whatever else is on your plate.

Finally, no trip to the South would be complete without a helping of black-eyed peas. These are actually beans, not peas—they're called cowpeas in other parts of the country—and they're not particularly tasty. If they were, you wouldn't have to come to the South (or to a Northern "soul food" restaurant) to eat them. They became popular Southern food items because, like collards, they were easy to grow and cheap to buy down here, in a region that only recently has recovered from the Civil War.

Hot Boiled Peanuts

Take raw, unshelled peanuts. Add water and salt. Boil for about a decade. Now you have hot boiled peanuts, often spelled "hot boil p-nuts" on roadside signs and pronounced "hot bowled peanuts" down here. If you've never heard of them, they sound almost unimaginable. If you've never eaten them before, they taste a little bit like salted peas. But if you've eaten a handful of them, you're probably hooked for life.

You can find hot boiled peanuts for sale in many convenience stores—usually in a brown paper bag enclosed in a zip-type resealable bag—outside many Wal-Marts, in front of a flea market, or, best of all, at roadside and at minor-league baseball games.

Soul Food

With African Americans making up nearly 50 percent of the population in many sections of the Carolina coast, you might think there'd be more "soul food" or African American restaurants. The truth of course is that much of the food you'll find in a soul-food restaurant

---

KRISTY-MARIE'S LOWCOUNTRY BOIL

Lowcountry Boil, aka "Frogmore Stew," aka "Beaufort Stew," is about as Lowcountry as you can get. It's also a very simple meal to make. Kristy-Marie's tangy version, which she readily admits she cribbed off a local cooking show and a box of Old Bay, but which a number of veteran Lowcountry shrimpers have pronounced the best they've eaten. What I like about it is the chicken broth (used rather than plain water) and the fact that she peels the shrimp before cooking. Some insist that this takes away some of the flavor, and if you want absolute authenticity, you can leave the peeling for later. But I sure enjoy not having to fiddle around peeling the slippery, hot shrimp when I'm hungry.

½ lb. smoked kielbasa per person, cut into 1–1½ inch slices

½ lb shrimp peeled and deveined per person
2-3 new potatoes per person, quartered
One large bunch celery, cut up into 1½-inch chunks
1 large yellow onion, cut into eighths
1 box Old Bay crab and shrimp boil
6 cups chicken broth
2 cups water

Bring chicken broth and water to a boil in a large stockpot. Add Old Bay seasoning, potatoes, celery, onion, and kielbasa. Boil five to seven minutes or until celery, onion, and potato are soft. Turn heat down to medium. Add shrimp. Cook the shrimp for *only three minutes* – just until it turns pink. Serve immediately, otherwise the shrimp will turn rubbery. Serves four. If you have more than four people, just adjust the last five ingredients accordingly.

up in New York City is called "country cooking" down here.

BEVERAGES
Tea

The terms "sweet tea" and "ice tea" (no "d") are nearly synonymous here. At some restaurants, it's served as a matter of course, like coffee at a truck-stop diner. The sugar in sweet tea is added while the water's still hot, which allows the sugar to melt and blend more fully into the drink. If you're at a restaurant, particularly in the country, and you want unsweetened tea, ask for it (quietly) and hope they have it.

SOUTHERN RESTAURANT CHAINS
Waffle House

Each of the 1,470 locations of this chain (www.wafflehouse.com) is nearly identical: stools, bright yellow and imitation wood Formica, appalling coffee, a sizzling grill, an order-shouting staff, and a jukebox. A patron of the Waffle House in Orangeburg could easily walk into one in Biloxi, Mississippi, blindfolded, sit down, order, play the jukebox, and pay the bill without taking the blindfold off. But the Waffle House serves the needs of Southerners so perfectly that it somehow transcends its chain status.

Founded in an Atlanta suburb in 1955—the same year Disneyland opened and the same year Savannahians saved their first historic house—the Waffle House calls itself "America's Place to Eat, America's Place to Work." I've never worked at a Waffle House, other than doing some writing at one, but it does seem to be the one inescapable dining experience in the South. Because it's so common, and because it's so *available* (open 24 hours every day except Thanksgiving and Christmas), it's become an icon of the South. So beloved is it that the Internet contains several nonofficial Waffle House sites.

The chain boasts of being the world's leading server of waffles, omelets, raisin toast, grits, and apple butter. It's also the only place in the world where the jukeboxes play such specially recorded songs as "Waffle Doo-Wop" and

"Good Food Fast," along with standard oldies and country selections.

Try the pork chops and eggs with hash browns and raisin toast. Bert's Chili is also pretty good. Or just order some hash browns with tomatoes, "scattered, smothered, covered, chunked, topped, and diced."

Cracker Barrel

Don't dare let it keep you away from the mom-and-pop restaurants in town, but if you're out on the interstate and in a hurry, or in dire need of a pullover, this chain (www.crackerbarrel.com) is a safe bet for good country cooking. With rocking chairs out front, a fireplace burning, and old-timey photos on the wall, Cracker Barrels feature a warm ambience that makes an hour's meal seem like a genuine break away from the highway.

Founded in 1969 in Lebanon, Tennessee, each restaurant contains a gift shop featuring regional knickknacks reflecting the South in general and often the restaurant's location in particular.

Hardee's

Hardee's (www.hardees.com) was founded in 1960 in Greenville, North Carolina, and today the chain has nearly 3,000 locations. Hardee's is usually the first chain restaurant to infect a small Southern town, opening the way for Ronald McDonald and the rest of the coven.

Some time back, the folks at a consumer magazine rated the fast-food mongers of America and named Hardee's food No. 2 among all major fast-food chains. It used to be that the main item worth getting here was the breakfast sandwiches made with fresh biscuits. A few years back, Carl Karcher Enterprises, owner of the Carl's Jr. chain on the West Coast, purchased Hardee's, and while they unfortunately changed the retro NASCAR-style logo to a new mainstreamed star, they added their headline-grabbing Angus Thickburgers.

Chick-fil-A

Don't call it "Chick feela"; it's pronounced "chick fih-LAY." This is the largest privately owned restaurant chain (www.chickfila.com) in America. Georgia's Truett Cathy founded his first restaurant back in 1946; today the company operates nearly 1,200 restaurants, and in 2004, raked in nearly $1.74 billion. You'll see one in nearly every mall in South Carolina and Georgia, as Cathy pioneered the idea of fast-food restaurants in malls. The food doesn't do much for me, but obviously somebody likes it: Fans laud the seasoned boneless chicken breast sandwich and lemonade. Closed on Sunday to allow workers to go to church and spend time with their families, Chick-fil-A remains a true Southern phenomenon.

Bojangles' Famous Chicken 'n Biscuits

The dirty rice and Cajun chicken make this Tennessee-based chain (www.bojangles.com) a cut above the rest. The chicken biscuits and spicy, battered fries have been known to undo fans.

BUYING GROCERIES
Farmers Markets

With all the agriculture in the area, most towns in South Carolina have some sort of farmers market. Where possible, I've mentioned them in the description of the town. But if you have a certain town in mind, call its chamber of commerce.

Charleston's Farmers Market (843/724-7305, www.ci.charleston.sc.us) takes place every Saturday at the intersection of Marion Square, March–December. **Mount Pleasant's Farmers Market** (645 Coleman Blvd., Mount Pleasant, 843/884-8517, www.townofmount-pleasant.com) is open every Tuesday April–October.

Down in Savannah, the **Savannah State Farmers Market** (701 Hwy. 80 W, 912/966-7800), is open year-round.

Supermarket Chains

Piggly Wiggly (www.pigglywiggly.com) was the world's first true self-service grocery store, and was founded in 1916 by a Memphis, Tennessee, entrepreneur named Clarence Saunders

(who later went on to pioneer—unsuccessfully—the world's first completely automated store). Where did the name "Piggly Wiggly" come from? Nobody knows. When people used to ask Saunders, he would answer, "So people will ask that very question."

Do note that although the Piggly Wiggly logo looks a lot like Porky Pig wearing a butcher's hat, Piggly predates Porky by 20 years or so. Today there are more than 600 Piggly Wiggly stores stretching from Texas north to Wisconsin, south to Florida, and north to Virginia. You'll find one or two in every decent-sized South Carolina town. The Piggly Wiggly store brand is usually a good way to save money, especially on their barbecue sauces and peanut butter.

Winn-Dixie (www.winndixie.com) sounds like a political statement, but the name actually refers to the 1955 merger of the Winn & Lovett stores from Florida and Georgia, and the Dixie Home Stores of the Carolinas. Now with 587 stores in 14 states in the Bahamas, and in the

From early spring to well into the fall, farmers markets are essential stops for locals to get fresh vegetables.

Sunbelt, Winn-Dixie is building several Marketplace Stores, with delis and ATM machines and such, but the chain is struggling to stay afloat.

The new kid on the Southern grocery chain block, North Carolina's **Food Lion** (www.foodlion.com), got a lot of bad press a few years back when ABC's television newsmagazine *20/20* sent an undercover reporter to work at one of their stores and exposed some shoddy food-handling practices, including a tendency to relabel outdated meats. Despite successful countersuits that challenged the network's methods, the chain has been troubled since then, although individual locations can be quite good. I don't recommend the Food Lion brand foods, however; they're nothing special.

Kroger (www.kroger.com) stores are a part of a Cincinnati-based chain, but because they're so plentiful in larger South Carolina cities, and because their superstores are often the most comprehensive supermarkets available (including, in many cases, ATM machines), you might want to use them if you're shopping for food while on the road or while staying at a rental.

If you find a **Publix** (www.publix.com) in your travels, you've likely stumbled on a clean, well-lighted place with good produce and fish.

Harris Teeter (www.harristeeter.com) is probably the high-end choice for groceries. There's a great one located in an old warehouse on East Bay Street in Charleston; for seeing how even chain stores can blend successfully into their environment, it's worth checking out.

Getting There and Around

BY CAR

Several interstates crisscross the Carolinas, making the states quite easy to get to from almost anywhere east of the Mississippi. The coasts have always been just a bit trickier, but not along the Sea Island Coast, where I-95 starts a half hour away from Charleston and veers ever closer to the old Coastal Highway, Highway 17, finally entwining with it below Savannah.

Of course, from New York and other parts north, just head south on I-95 (following the historic Fort Lauderdale Trail blazed by generations of spring breakers). To get to Charleston you'll want to take I-26 east.

From Atlanta, just head either northeast on I-85 until you cross I-40, then head east, or head west on I-20 until you get to Columbia, South Carolina, then head east to Charleston. Another worthwhile route from Atlanta, although infinitely more time-consuming, is to take the Atlanta Highway (Highway 29) due east through the scenic Piedmont towns of northeast Georgia, including Athens, where if you're lucky you'll run across a member of R.E.M. or the B-52s.

But as I say, this is the slower, two-lane route, which stops numerous times in small towns all the way across the Piedmont. It's scenic, but don't say I didn't warn you.

If you're up in Charlotte, either catch I-85 and head east until you hit I-40, then head to Wilmington, or take I-77 due south to Columbia, and then on to Charleston on I-26. Unless you're planning to hole up in downtown Charleston, or in a resort like Hilton Head that bustles with hotel trams, you'll want a car. Despite all its development, the Sea Island Coast remains rural enough that the best way to explore it is still by automobile.

Rentals

You'll find locations for all the major car rental chains throughout the Sea Island Coast and especially around its airports. Contact these agencies for information: **Alamo** (800/327-9633, www.alamo.com); **Avis** (800/831-2847, www.avis.com); **Budget** (800/527-0700, www.budget.com); **Enterprise** (800/325-8007, www.enterprise.com); or **Hertz** (800/654-3131, www.hertz.com).

© SEAN SLINSKY

Buses and trolleys operate in downtown Savannah and Charleston, rendering cars unnecessary if you're sticking to the historic districts.

Americans drive on the right side of the road, the way God intended. If you forget and drive on the left side of the road, other drivers will remind you by driving straight toward you and blaring their horns. A driver's license serves as indispensable identification. In America, you need a driver's license for everything from cashing a check to renting movies.

A driver must be 25 years old, and have both a valid driver's license and a major credit card to rent a car. You will have the chance to buy insurance coverage for the car and yourself; unless your policy back home covers you, you'll want to go ahead and get some now. It's illegal to drive without at least liability coverage in the United States.

Travelers from outside the United States must carry an International Driver's Permit as well as a current valid license from their home country.

Note: It's illegal in both South Carolina and Georgia to drive while drinking alcoholic beverages or while under the influence of alcohol.

BY AIR

Charleston and Savannah have fairly large airports, although you'll probably need to stop in Atlanta first. If you'll be in the Golden Isles or St. Marys region, try the Jacksonville, Florida, airport as well. If you're hunting for cheap tickets and don't mind a few extra miles on the rental car, check out flights into Columbia or Greenville, South Carolina, or Charlotte, North Carolina.

BY TRAIN

Most sizable towns in South Carolina and Georgia are served by Amtrak (800/872-7245, www.amtrak.com). Train ticket prices can rival those of airline tickets, and the times can even be less convenient, so shop around before committing. Contact Amtrak for reservations and schedule information.

BY BUS

Most all Southern towns, sizable or not, are served by Greyhound Bus Lines (800/231-2222, www.greyhound.com). Contact them for reservations and schedule information.

BY BOAT

For the nautically endowed—those who own boats—the Carolinas are very accessible. The Atlantic Intracoastal Waterway is a 1,095-mile nautical pathway that stretches from Norfolk, Virginia, south to Miami, Florida, and passes behind the coastal islands of North and South Carolina. Get nautical maps free online from National Oceanic Atmospheric Administration (NOAA) (http://chartmaker.ncd.noaa.gov/). To learn what marinas are along the way and the amenities they offer, check out the Intracoastal Waterways Facilities Guide (www.cruise-guides.com/iwfg); or contact area visitors centers and the regional chapters.

VISAS AND OFFICIALDOM
Entry Requirements
Non-U.S. citizens will need the following for entry to the country:

· Valid passport from a recognized country.

- A valid visa or a visa waiver.
- Round-trip or return ticket, or proof of sufficient funds to support yourself during your visit and to afford a return ticket. You may be required to purchase a return ticket at the airport before you are given a visa, or you may have to show proof of a return ticket when you are actually applying.

Since September 11, 2001, entry requirements and regulations have become more strict than ever. To be on the safest side, contact your nearest U.S. Embassy for specifics related to your situation. Otherwise, the following organizations have helpful, detailed online information: **United States Immigration and Citizenship Services** (www.uscis.gov); the **U.S. Customs and Border Patrol** (www.cbp.gov); and the **U.S. Department of State** (www.travel.state.gov).

Passports

Passports are the most common type of travel document used as proof of your identity when crossing an international border. A passport is required for travel into the United States and even for air travel within the country.

It is always easier to travel with a passport than to try to get by with some other type of photo identification.

If you don't already have a passport, you should start the process for acquiring one as soon as possible. Make sure that it is valid for at least six months, preferably a year, after you plan to return home. If the passport issued to you by the government in your country expires while you are in the United States, you will have to contact an embassy or consulate of your home country to renew it. U.S. passport offices do not provide services to holders of non-U.S. passports.

For extended stays, bring your birth certificate, extra passport photos, and even a photocopy of the original passport. This will help speed the process of replacing a lost or expired passport. If your passport is stolen, report it to the police immediately and get a copy of the police report, or at least record the important details contained in it (e.g., name and title of the officer, the police precinct number, the file number). This should also help in replacing your passport.

Visas

Visas are documents, usually a stamp in your passport, that are issued by the government of the country you want to visit. Visas are a precondition for being admitted to a country, but they are not a guarantee of entry. The rules for acquiring a visa are arbitrary and occasionally strict, but if you plan ahead and follow the rules to the letter, you shouldn't run into any problems.

Twenty-seven countries (mostly European) participate in the Visa Waiver Pilot Program with the United States. Check with a U.S. Embassy or consulate to find out if your country is included in the program. Otherwise, you are required to have a visa. You should always be courteous and respectful to consular, immigration, and customs authorities. If you are applying for a tourist visa to the United States, you

© SEAN SLINSKY

Bring about $10 for a rickshaw ride in Charleston.

will be required to appear in person at a U.S. consulate or embassy for an interview, as well as meet certain other requirements, including proof that you have a return ticket.

Make sure to find out what the current visa requirements are for travel or if your country is "officially recognized" by the U.S. government. Visa requirements can change at any time, without notice. If you have already bought nonrefundable air tickets and are denied entry, you'll be out of luck.

For visa information, call **United Stated Department of Visa Services** (202/663-1225, www.travel.state.gov/visa).

State Border Crossings

Part of the evidence that South Carolina, Georgia, and the rest of the Confederacy lost the argument over state sovereignty is the ease with which one can travel between American states. The only restrictions you're likely to encounter involve transporting certain plants or produce across state lines, or transporting illegal substances or guns across state lines.

Border authorities sometimes forbid produce and plants from entering a state because the flora may contain pests or diseases that are harmful to the native plants or agricultural products of the state. In some cases, if you are carrying produce in your car and are stopped at a state border, you will be asked to dispose of the produce.

Generally forbidden substances include illegal drugs, explosives, or dangerous chemicals. In most states, transporting illegal drugs across the state line increases the legal penalty for possession from a misdemeanor to a felony.

Many counties also have laws governing the amount of alcohol and number of cartons of cigarettes you can bring across their border. If a county border is also a state border and you are carrying alcohol or cigarettes into that county, check its laws concerning alcohol and cigarettes. A pack of cigarettes and a bottle of beer are not cause for legal action, unless the beer is open. A carton of cigarettes and a bottle of whiskey might raise a few eyebrows, but shouldn't cause you any trouble. Twenty car-

tons of cigarettes and a case of whiskey will get you into trouble in many counties.

If you are carrying a gun, you must have a valid permit. Check with the embassy or consulate where you got your passport if you plan to buy and carry a gun while traveling in the United States, and understand that foreign visitors requesting information regarding firearms will be viewed with some suspicion.

Note: In 1996, it became legal in South Carolina for a citizen who has taken a safety course to carry a concealed weapon. Consequently, as you pass through many business doorways, you'll see signs forbidding concealed weapons while on the owner's private property. Don't let these signs make you think that everyone in South Carolina is packing heat. The number of people requesting such permits is low indeed. But if you are, you'll need to unpack it; remove the cartridges and put it somewhere where it can't be stolen.

TIPS FOR TRAVELERS
Travel with Children

South Carolina and Georgia are very much family-oriented states. Many parks feature wide, family-size swings; nearly every community event includes children's activities; and most resorts provide thorough programs for youngsters. The only places where children are unwelcome are in nightclubs and bars (obviously), in South Carolina gambling parlors (no big loss), and in many bed-and-breakfasts. Still, the region seems to have a higher percentage of "children-welcome" B&Bs than most others. Where possible, I've noted whenever establishments have stated a preference.

One nice thing about automobile travel along the Sea Island Coast is that everything in the region is so close together that you'll rarely find yourself driving very long without the opportunity to stop and let the kids get out and burn off some energy. The enclosed playgrounds now popular at Chick-fil-A, McDonald's, and some of their competitors make pretty handy pit stops, even on a rainy day.

Women Travelers

I've never been a woman, despite what my football coach used to yell, so I've asked my wife, Kristin, to help with this section:

Most women find themselves treated especially politely in the Carolinas. Doors will be opened and bus seats offered. There are, however, areas that are still considered male domains—the same places, generally, that are considered male domains throughout most of the Western world—honky-tonk bars, hunting clubs, golf clubs (some of them), billiards parlors, and sports bars. A woman is in no particular danger in most of these places, but her presence there may be interpreted as a desire for male companionship.

Women traveling alone should be aware of their surroundings. When you head for your car, carry your keys in hand and get to and into the car quickly. Drive with your doors locked and your windows rolled up.

If possible, carry a cellular phone; otherwise, a breakdown on the highway will leave you waiting and hoping the first motorist to stop for assistance has good motives.

People impersonating police officers commit a sizable number of crimes each year. If you're pulled over by an unmarked vehicle, especially at night, don't open your car door or window more than a crack, and then only to demand that a marked patrol car be called. This is well within your rights.

No matter how authentic the uniform looks, demand to see the marked car. If the officer can't produce a black-and-white, move on. Don't hand over your license, which gives your name and address. If you feel suspicious, ask the officer to follow you to a more-populated, better-lit area.

Gay and Lesbian Travelers

In recent decades, American gays and lesbians have begun to enjoy an increase in tolerance toward same-sex couples. Along the Sea Island Coast, larger cities like Savannah and Charleston have their share of gay hangouts and nightclubs, many of them private clubs that require a nominal "membership fee" for admittance. In other areas, gay and lesbian travelers not wanting to draw attention to themselves generally respect the local mores and avoid public displays of affection.

Travelers with Disabilities

Although all of the region's new public buildings provide facilities and access for the physically disabled, many historic structures and sites have been hard-pressed to do the same.

A PRONOUNCING GAZETTEER OF SEA ISLAND NAMES

With so many newcomers arriving along the coast, some of the following names now enjoy multiple pronunciations. Use the ones below and you should have no trouble:

Beaufort (SC): BYOO-fort
Blenheim: BLEN-um
Broughton: BROTT-un
Charleston: CHAWRL-stun
Colleton: COL-ton
Congaree: CON-guh-REE
Edisto: ED-i-STOE
Fernandina: FUR-nen-DEE-nuh
Guale: WALL-ee

Kiawah: KEE-a-wuh
Pocotaligo: POKE-uh-tuh-LEE-go
Saluda: suh-LOO-duh
Santee: san-TEE
Savannah: suh-VAN-uh
Sherman: SAY-tun
St. Helena: saint HELL-en-uh
St. Simons: saynt-SY-mons
Tybee: TY-bee
Wadmalaw: wahd-MALL-ah
Wando: WAHN-doh
Yamassee (tribe, war): YAM-uh-see
Yemasee (town): YEM-uh-see

Throughout this book, I've tried to note attractions that may pose special difficulties for the disabled, as well as those that specifically define themselves as wheelchair accessible. If you're uncertain about the accessibility of a specific attraction, be sure to call ahead.

Churches

Visiting the Southeast without attending a church service is like going to Thailand and not visiting a temple. Church life and the spiritual life (and sometimes the two intersect) are of major importance to most South Carolinians, and it would be hard to get any real grasp on the culture without passing between the white pillars and taking a spot in the pew.

If you're seeking a representative experience, then in the Lowcountry you might want to visit one of Charleston's enormous Episcopalian cathedrals or attend synagogue at America's first reformed temple. Or visit the region's fastest-growing church, Seacoast Community Church in Mount Pleasant, a "seeker" church that began with a marketing survey of the East Cooper area and today packs in several thousand people each Sunday.

In Savannah, the historic Christ Episcopal Church is where the brothers Wesley once preached and is home to the oldest congregation in Georgia. The First African Baptist Church (which has better music) is home to the oldest African American congregation in the United States. The beautiful First Presbyterian Church downtown not only features sonorous bells, but the congregation was once pastored by Woodrow Wilson's father-in-law.

Of course, for every large, celebrity church, a couple hundred humble congregations of every stripe meet each Sunday. To get a truly representative feel for the spiritual tempo of the Sea Island Coast, you might be best off pulling out a Yellow Pages, picking a church that catches your eye, and attending a service.

Compared to most parts of the country, Southern churches are still fairly dressy: Most women wear dresses or pantsuits (most Southern women, visiting a new church, wear a dress or skirt just to play it safe); men wear slacks, shirts, and ties, and often jackets. The general philosophy behind all this finery runs something like this: "You'd dress up to go ask some fellow at the bank for a loan, so doesn't God deserve the same respect?" (Whether it's respectful to treat God as though he thinks as superficially as the average loan officer is another question.) Fortunately, dress is generally more casual along the coasts, and even more so in nondenominational churches. At some, shorts and T-shirts are quite acceptable attire.

With the exception of most Pentecostal and Charismatic congregations, few services are significantly integrated—reminding one of Martin Luther King's quote about Sunday morning being the most segregated hours in America; however, very few congregations will object to the presence of friendly, respectful visitors of a different race, and most will be quite happy to have you there.

JEWISH HISTORY

When **Kahal Kadosh Beth Elohim** (90 Hasell St., 843/723-1090, www.kkbe.org) began services in English in 1841, Charleston became the birthplace of Reform Judaism. Today, the city is home to America's fourth-oldest Jewish congregation, and Jewish tour guides tell visitors that past residents started the country's oldest Jewish charity organization and that they established the first Hebrew Orphanage in the early 1800s. Book time with Janice Kahn for the **Chai Y'all Tour** (843/556-0664), which that covers the rich legacy that Jewish settlers – and their descendants – have left. Savannah is similarly significant for Jewish history, and claims the **Temple Mickve Israel** (20 E. Gordon St., 912/233-1547, www.mickveisrael.org), the only Gothic-style temple in the country. Its congregation (the third oldest in the country) leads customized Jewish-themed tours of the city, and every October hosts the Jewish Food Festival, where, they say, you can try the South's *other* soul food.

Health and Safety

HEALTH MAINTENANCE
Insect Repellent

Unless you're planning to spend all of your time on city streets, you'll want insect repellent while you're here. The two critters that will trouble you most are no-see-ums (particularly at the coast) and mosquitoes. "No-see-ums" are tiny gnats that bite as if it's personal. The best way to fight them seems to be with Avon's Skin-So-Soft. Wear a hat because they'll bite your scalp as well.

Mosquitoes are pleasant companions by comparison, but in swamps and salt marshes they can quickly turn a day hike into a personal purgatory. Skin-So-Soft works with them as well, and so does Deep Woods Off and most Cutter products.

Sunscreens

Southern summers can be particularly deceiving; although it's hot, the gray sky overhead can lull you into thinking that your skin's not taking a beating from ultraviolet rays, but it is. To ward off skin cancer, premature wrinkles, and sunburn, use sunscreens with an SPF rating of 15 or more—higher for those with fair skin.

Adjusting to the Humidity

Stepping off a plane into the middle of summer in this region can just about knock you out. If you live in a less-humid area and your plans along the Sea Island Coast include a lot of physical activity, try to give yourself a day or two to acclimate.

Local Doctors

Georgia and South Carolina have no dearth of qualified physicians for those with the money to pay for them. Neither are these states short of walk-in medical clinics where you can stop in without an appointment. Check the local phone book under "Physicians" to find the address and phone number of physicians in your area, or stop into a shop, explain your situation to a clerk, and ask for a recommendation.

VACCINATIONS

The United States currently has no vaccination requirements for any international traveler. Check with the U.S. embassy or consulate in your country and request an update on this information before you leave.

The International Health Regulations (IHR) adopted by the **World Health Organization (WHO)** (www.who.int/en) state that countries may require an International Certificate of Vaccination (ICV) against yellow fever. An ICV can also be required if you are traveling from an infected area. For current information, contact the WHO or the **Centers for Disease Control and Prevention (CDC)** (www.cdc.gov.travel/vaccinat).

NATURAL HAZARDS

For all its natural beauty, the South does seem to have more than its share of natural hazards—from alligators and poisonous snakes to hurricanes and jellyfish. But 99 percent of the time these hazards can be avoided with a little foresight and caution.

Lightning Storms

Sociologists throw around a lot of reasons for the fervent spirituality of many Carolinians, but one overlooked cause may be the prayer-inspiring lightning storms. When the sheet lightning flares across the sky like a flickering fluorescent bar, and the bolts are blasting transformers to either side of the road, even a trip to the local package store can quickly turn into a religious experience.

For instance, in a 32-year stretch from 1959 to 1990, 228 Carolinians met their maker via lightning—one person zapped to Beulah Land every month and a half. And this is only counting fatalities—859 people took a bolt during that same 32-year stretch, to varying effect.

It really does happen. So if you're out on the trail or the golf course when a storm rolls in, seek shelter, although not under a tree because the tree is likely to get hit, in which case you don't want to be anywhere around it. Electrocution is rarely worth risking, especially since the average summer convectional storm will be over in less than an hour anyway. Go find a cup of coffee somewhere and enjoy the show from safety.

If you're indoors, do as most folks around here do: They won't talk on a phone (although cordless phones are okay) or use plumbing when a storm is striking around them because both phone lines and water can serve as conduits. Several urban legends revolve around a man/woman using the toilet during a lightning storm; ask almost anyone down here, and he or she can fill in the details.

Hurricanes

Hurricanes—and, more commonly, the threat of hurricanes—are simply a fact of life in the Sea Island Coast. Annually, Charleston's *The Post and Courier* (www.charleston.net) includes a pre–hurricane season insert, providing informative articles that help Carolinians understand and survive these storms. Local news teams run ads boasting of their prophetic capabilities, and supermarkets like Piggly Wiggly buy full-page ads to proclaim themselves "Your Hurricane Stock-Up Store."

Pay attention to the public warnings on the radio and television when you're in the state, especially during hurricane season, June to October. The mildest warning is a **Small Craft Advisory,** issued when strong winds—up to 38 mph—strike the coastal waters. This is not the day to rent or charter a fishing boat. Next up is a **Gale Warning,** issued when winds reach 39–54 mph. A **Storm Warning** means winds 55–73 mph. **Hurricane Watches** are issued when hurricane conditions are a real possibility and may threaten coastal or inland areas within 36 hours. A **Hurricane Warning** means a hurricane is expected to hit an area within 24 hours. If you're visiting the coast and a Hurricane Warning is issued, it's time to consider visiting the Carolinas' historic interior for a few days. One way to stay ahead of the game—or to put off a visit if you haven't left

home yet—is to check the National Weather Service's **National Hurricane Center** (www.nhc.noaa.gov) website, or with a Lowcountry news station, like Charleston's CBS affiliate, which runs its own online hurricane center (www.hurricane.wcsc.com).

The two things you *don't* want to do are panic or ignore the warnings. If an evacuation is called, you'll hear about it on the radio and TV. But by this point, you as a traveler should be gone already. Save the spot in the relief shelter for a local resident. Get thee to the Upcountry.

Snakebites

No other region offers the variety of poisonous snakes found in Georgia and the Carolinas. A full six different snakes can make your life complicated here, but even the outdoorsiest visitor is unlikely to come across any of them on a visit.

The **copperhead** averages around 2–3 feet long and normally lives in damp woods, mountainous regions, or in the high ground in swampy areas, which is to say you'll find it all through the Sea Island Coast.

Canebrake or **timber rattlesnakes** are also found throughout the state, usually in deciduous forests or swamps on high ground. These snakes average 3–4 feet in length and can even reach 5 feet.

The **eastern diamondback rattlesnake** runs 3–6 feet and up, with a basic dark brown color and brown/yellow diamonds. It mostly keeps to the woods of the Lowcountry.

The **pygmy rattlesnake** is rare and only reaches a bit over a foot long. You'll find them in all but the highest lands of the Carolinas. They're dull gray with brown splotches on the back and sides.

The **cottonmouth** or **water moccasin** thrives in wetland areas of the coastal plain.

The beautiful black, red, and yellow **eastern coral snake** is rare, found in woods and fields.

Bring a **snake kit,** wear leather boots to protect your ankles, and watch where you step. Here's the good news: Poisonous snakes bite several thousand people each year, but fewer than 10 die in the United States annually.

More good news: In most cases, snakebite is preventable. More than 50 percent of poisonous snakebites take place after the victim has seen the snake and had the chance to get away. In fact, most victims are bitten in the attempt to pick up a poisonous snake, harass it, or kill it. The point is simple enough: Keep your eyes open when in the woods and stay away from any snake that you're not absolutely certain is nonpoisonous.

If a snake bites you or somebody in your party, try not to panic. Even if the snake is poisonous, odds are nearly even that it was a "dry" bite—meaning that no poison was injected into the victim. Nonetheless, don't allow the victim to engage in strenuous physical activity because this will get the heart pumping faster, thus spreading the poison quicker. Try to safely identify the breed of snake if it's possible and if it doesn't take too long to do it. Get the victim to the nearest hospital or emergency medical facility as soon as possible.

If local doctors are unsure of the correct snakebite serum to use to treat the bite, tell them to contact the regional Poison Information Center.

Yellow Jackets

To avoid most stinging insects, the place to start is in your clothing—bright colors attract, dark ones don't. If you notice yellow jackets about and you're drinking or eating something, be sure to keep checking the food or drink (soda cans are notorious) to make sure no yellow jacket has snuck aboard.

Yellow-jacket stings are painful, not unlike being burned by a just-extinguished match. But the real danger comes in when people have allergic reactions. How can you tell if you're having an allergic reaction? A good rule of thumb is that as long as the reaction is around the site of the bite, you can assume it's a local reaction and needs to be treated with something like an antihistamine and maybe a little topical steroid, if anything. But if you get bitten or stung by an insect and you develop symptoms

elsewhere on your body, those are signs of an allergic reaction; in this case, you need to see a doctor.

Some of the signs of an allergic reaction are hives; swelling of the lips, tongue, eyelids, and internal organs; blocked airways; shock; and low blood pressure. If you're headed in this direction, your doctor will probably administer an EpiPen injection, which contain epinephrine and quickly reduce the symptoms of an allergic reaction.

Fire Ants

These ants are extremely aggressive when protecting their nests; if you inadvertently knock over a mound, don't stand around apologizing too long or you may soon find yourself covered with stinging ants. Stings can cause a severe reaction and even death. Watch for their domed mounds, commonly at least 15 inches wide at the base and about 6 inches high, usually found in damp areas—which includes almost all of the American South—particularly under trees, in lawns, or in flower beds.

Winged fire ants originated in South America and first appeared on U.S. soil in Mobile, Alabama, in 1918. Since then they've spread like the kudzu of the animal kingdom to 11 Southern states, including the Carolinas, and in the last half of the 1990s made their appearance in Southern California—about the same time as Krispy Kreme doughnuts.

You'll find numerous chemical treatments for ant mounds in any grocery store or hardware store. Some swear that pouring boiling water into the top of an ant mound will do the trick, without harming the local water supply.

Fire ant bites leave a sterile pustule. The urge to scratch or pop the pustule is very tempting, but try not to do it. Scratching or picking at a bite until it becomes open allows it to get infected. If you're allergic to fire ants, wear shoes and socks; don't go outside barefoot or in sandals.

Jellyfish

If stung by a jellyfish, clean the area carefully. If you have tentacles still stuck to the wound area, don't just pull them off with your hand because they may still have venom sacs attached. Instead, use a credit card to scrape parallel with the skin, pushing the tentacles off sideways. Try not to break any of the venom sacs.

For pain relief, try meat tenderizer, a baking soda–and–water paste, or vinegar. Jellyfish stings rarely cause allergic reactions, but when they do, they can include hives, itching, and swelling on parts of the body that weren't stung. If any of these symptoms occurs, get to an emergency room.

Stingrays

Stingray wounds are much more rare than jellyfish stings, but they happen. To avoid them, shuffle your feet as you walk in the water.

If you do happen to step on a stingray, it will let you know—it'll swing its mace of a tail around and send you hopping back to shore. Most stingray victims get it on the foot or ankle.

One treatment is to submerge the wound in the hottest water you can stand for 20 or 30 minutes. This seems to neutralize the poison. Most people enjoy noticeable relief within a few hours. Even so, if you've danced with a stingray and come away stung, you should still see a doctor because you may need an antibiotic if the sting gets infected.

Sharks

Sharks in Carolina waters usually attack 1–3 people each year. A few years back, the number shot up above 10, mostly in the Grand Strand, which should put to rest those charges of Myrtle Beach visitors having bad taste.

The odds of being bitten are still incredibly low. To make them lower, the experts say:

- Swim in groups, preferably composed of people better tasting than you are.
- Don't swim too far out: If you see sharks, you want to be close to shore so you can get out fast.
- Avoid swimming in the late afternoon, at night, or in the early morning. This is when sharks feed the most.

- Lose the flashy jewelry. Sharks can't see well in the murky waters, but they'll see the glitter from that belly ring of yours.

Another thing to remember is that sharks don't watch movies, so they don't know that they're supposed to stick their dorsal fins up out of the water as they cruise toward the beach. Most sharks near the shore usually swim on the bottom, so their victims have no advance warning.

Although the whole U.S. East Coast may see only 40 shark attacks a year (and few if any of these fatal), the number of incidents has been increasing over the past 15 years, presumably because more folks than ever are hitting the surf. Along the East Coast, practically all shark attacks are "hit-and-run strikes" by black-tipped or spinner sharks, usually no more than six feet long. The shark bites, realizes that the victim tastes bad, and releases. Most bite victims bleed but don't lose any actual tissue.

Of course, sometimes sharks do kill people, as evidenced by deadly attacks in Florida and North Carolina during the much-hyped "Summer of the Shark" 2001, which technically ended on Labor Day but was completely forgotten by September 12th. Nonetheless, fatal shark attacks do occur in these waters. But vengeance is certainly ours: While sharks kill about 100 people a year worldwide, humans kill some 100 million sharks annually, to the point where even the population of Great Whites—that most fearsome of shark predators—is being threatened.

Poison Ivy

If you've been exposed to poison ivy, you have two or three hours to wash it off and avoid a breakout. If you are out and about and can't take a shower, rubbing the skin with alcohol—even beer—will often help. What you *don't* want to do is touch the unwashed, exposed part of your body with any other part, thus spreading the irritating serum.

Giardia

Ironically, one of the smallest critters in the state causes much more cumulative discomfort across the state than any other. Although a lake or stream may appear clean, think twice before taking a sip. You're risking a debilitating sickness by drinking untreated water. The protozoan *Giardia duodenalis* is found in freshwater throughout the state, spread by both humans and animals. Although curable with prescription drugs, giardia's no fun—unless bloating, cramps, and diarrhea are your idea of a good time. Carry safe drinking water on any trip. If your canteen's dry, boiling creek or lake water will kill giardia and other harmful organisms. Some hikers prefer to use water filters made by companies like Mountain Safety Research and Pur, which can be purchased for about $60–140 at most backpacking stores; however, cheaper filters may allow the tiny giardia protozoan (as small as 0.2 microns) to pass through. Even the best filters may not always filter out other, smaller organisms. Traditional purifying chemicals like chlorine and iodine are unreliable, taste foul, and can be unhealthful. Boiling is really your best bet.

Unfortunately, it's also possible to get giardia while bathing; be careful not to swallow water while swimming in freshwater; men with mustaches should carefully dry them after leaving the water.

Lyme Disease

Lyme disease is caused by a bacteria transmitted to humans through the bite of the deer tick. Not all ticks carry the disease, but infection rates in certain areas can be quite high. Don't assume that because you are not in a high-infection area you cannot get Lyme disease. Most cases have been reported in the Northeast and upper Midwest, but an increasing number of cases are being seen in Southeast states. If you are bitten by a tick anywhere in the United States, you should get checked for Lyme disease. The disease can be detected by a blood test, and early treatment can cure the disease or lessen the severity of later symptoms.

An early symptom of Lyme disease is a red, circular rash in the area of the bite that usually develops a few days to a few weeks after being bitten. Other symptoms can include flulike symptoms, headache, stiff neck, fever, and muscle aches. Sometimes these symptoms will not show up for months. If any of these symptoms appear, even if you don't remember being bitten by a tick, have a doctor check you. Early detection of Lyme disease provides excellent opportunity for treatment (largely with antibiotics).

The three types of ticks known to carry Lyme disease (not necessarily every individual) are the deer tick (most common) in the Northeast and north-central United States, the lone star tick in the South, and the California black-legged tick in the West. If you are bitten by any tick, save the body for later identification if at all possible.

Remove a tick as soon as possible after being bitten. The best way is to grab the tick as close to your skin as possible with a pair of tweezers. The longer a tick has been on your body, the deeper it will bite you to find more blood. The closer to its head you can grab it, the less chance that its mouth parts or head will break off in the wound. If you can't get the whole thing out, go see a doctor. Clean the wound with antiseptic and cover it to avoid infection.

CRIME

The Sea Island Coast's crime statistics aren't overly high, relative to some other regions in the United States, but of course, when it's late at night and you're on a dicey side of town, this doesn't mean much. A friend of mine from Orangeburg says his father gave him three rules for staying safe, and they seem worth repeating:

- Nothing good ever happens after 1 AM.
- Don't carry more than you're willing to lose.
- There's safety in numbers.

Most Charleston bars close at 2 AM; Savannah's close at 3 AM. After last call in each city, the streets become populated with drunk folk and those who prey upon them. So rule No. 2 is an important one. If you can't immediately hand over your wallet to a robber and know you'll be all right, then you need to go through your wallet and remove the "valuable" contents. Rule No. 3 also makes sense. Single people get robbed more often than couples, who get robbed more often than trios, who get robbed more often than quartets, and so on. The bigger the crowd, the better the odds.

In Charleston a few years back, a trio of young men on bicycles held up at gunpoint a Georgia tourist walking with a woman. It was after 1 AM. The man refused to give his wallet to the kids, and one of them shot him dead before they rode off into the darkness. Police who responded to the scene found several thousand dollars in the victim's wallet.

How to Protect Yourself

- Don't carry too much money. How much is too much? Too much is so much that you won't gladly give over your wallet to get a robber to leave you and your travel companions alone.

- Don't give carjackers time to size you up. Walk to your car quickly, with your keys in your hand; get in, lock the doors, start up, and drive off. Fix your hair and/or makeup while you're at a stoplight, like a good American.

- When driving, particularly in urban areas, keep your doors locked and your windows rolled up. Carjackers are generally not the hardest-working individuals you'll ever run across—they're watching for an *easy* mark.

- Keep your wallet or purse out of sight when you're driving.

- If you're involved in an accident that seems suspicious, signal to the other driver to follow you and then drive to a better-lit, more populated area. A common ploy for carjackers is to bump their victims from behind and then rob them as they get out to inspect the damage to their car.

- If you're traveling with children and get carjacked, tell the carjacker you've got a child in back and ask if you can take him or her out. Many times the carjacker, who doesn't want to add a kidnapping charge to all the others he's racking up, will let you get the child out.

- Park in a central, well-lit area. In downtown Charleston and Savannah, for instance, you might consider using one of the paid lots, which normally have some sort of supervision. Be aware, though: Sometimes the attendant leaves at sunset, which might leave your car unattended in a dark, deserted parking lot until 2 AM. Ask the attendant how late the car will be supervised.

- When in public, wear your money and/or purse close to your body and keep wallets in your front pocket. This will make it harder for pickpockets and purse snatchers to rob you undetected.

- If you're driving a rental car, make sure there are no identifying markers. Travelers have, in some places in the United States—Florida, most famously—become targets. If certain items indicate that your car is rented (e.g., license-plate frames emblazoned with the name of the company), ask the folks at the rental office if you can remove them while you have the car in your possession.

OTHER ISSUES
Racism

People have found many excuses for not loving each other throughout the centuries; one of the most common is racism. Members of every imaginable race and combination of races live in the Carolinas, but the vast majority—more than 95 percent—consider themselves either "white" or "black." And of course, most of the racial tension in the Carolinas has traditionally existed between these two groups.

Most of what passes for racism in the Carolinas is, instead, largely "classism." What appears as white/black animosity is disguised class hatred: In the most common scenario, "racist" whites attribute to blacks all the traits historically attributed to anyone at the bottom of the social ladder—laziness, low intelligence, dishonesty, envy, criminal habits, and reproductive irresponsibility. "Racist" blacks, on the other hand, attribute to whites all of the traits underclasses generally hang on an upper class: greed, snobbery, condescension, lack of compassion, hedonism, shallowness, spiritual vacuousness, clubbishness. In each case, the "racist" person is probably right to oppose the values they attribute to people they dislike. Where they err is in attributing these values to members of a given race.

If you're "white" or "black," it's possible you'll feel some hostility from "the other" while visiting the Carolinas. If you are part of an interracial couple, you'll possibly experience some disapproving looks from members of both races, especially as you venture into the country or into the more homogeneous neighborhoods of the major cities. (If you're a nonblack person of color, and far from any large town, you may find people scratching their heads, wondering how you ever ended up in these parts.)

To an amazing degree, a smile and eye contact break down the walls that most people put up between strangers of the "other" race and their better selves. Your goal is to show them that you're an exception, that you don't carry the attitudes they expect to find in someone with your pigmentation. If this doesn't work, the best thing to do is to cut your losses and move on.

Drugs

Neither South Carolina nor Georgia is known for its tolerant attitude toward illicit drugs or for the comfortable nature of its jails. Possession and sale of marijuana are illegal here, as are all the usual mind-altering substances.

Sexually Transmitted Diseases

AIDS is alive and well along the Sea Island Coast, as are numerous other debilitating sexually transmitted diseases (STDs), including a couple of flavors of hepatitis and genital herpes. The safest thing to do is to not share hypodermic needles and not have sex with anyone you haven't screened first. If a person tells you he or she is HIV-negative, make sure the person hasn't had sex with another partner since that last screening. And since there's a six-month window during which someone who has contracted HIV may still show negative in an HIV test, to be safe you need to know that a person didn't have sex for six months *before* the screening (although some people with HIV have tested negative as late as five years after contracting the virus).

If, given the irresistible attractiveness of Georgians and Carolinians, celibacy seems an impossible task, you should reduce the risk by using a latex condom, although these tear easily.

Information and Services

MONEY

The U.S. dollar is divided into 100 cents. Paper notes include $1, $2, $5, $10, $20, and $100; the $2 bill is rarely seen but perfectly legal. Coin denominations are 1 cent (penny), 5 cents (nickel), 10 cents (dime), 25 cents (quarter), 50 cents (the rare half dollar), and the $1 coin (even more rare). Unfortunately, many counterfeit bills are in circulation, usually hundreds or twenties.

In the late 1990s, the old $100, $50, and $20 bills were replaced with new bills featuring much larger portraits on the front side. Tens and fives soon followed. If you're handed one of the earlier forms of bills, rest assured that they're still accepted as legal tender.

Banks

It's best to carry traveler's checks in U.S. dollar denominations. Most businesses and tourist-related services accept traveler's checks. Only in very small towns will you run into problems with traveler's checks or exchanging foreign money. The solution? Drive to a larger town. It's not a very big state.

Most major banks in big cities are open 9 AM–5 PM. Hours for branches in smaller towns vary. Banks are usually closed on Saturday, Sunday, and most national and some religious holidays; however, some larger banks open for limited hours on Saturday, frequently 9 AM–1 PM. Branch offices are becoming more omnipresent in the United States, popping up in grocery stores and shopping malls across the state, but typically only major commercial banks have the ability to exchange foreign currency. Although banks are your best bet, other good places to obtain U.S. dollars include international airports and American Express offices. Check the local Yellow Pages for addresses and phone numbers. Many banks have toll-free numbers answered by an automated voice, which gives options for various numbers. Stay on the line or press the appropriate number to speak to a human.

Most businesses accept major credit cards (i.e., MasterCard, Visa, and American Express). On occasion, in very small towns and rural areas, cash (US$) will be the only accepted form of money. It's also possible to get cash advances from your credit card at automated-teller machines (ATMs). ATMs are ubiquitous in the United States. You'll see them in grocery stores, shopping malls, sometimes at festivals or fairs, sporting events, street corners, and, of course, at most banks. In Charleston, the police department got proactive about the number of incidents occurring around ATMs and installed one inside the lobby of the police building.

In many supermarkets, it's now possible to pay for your groceries with a credit card or a debit card, which deducts the amount directly from your checking or savings account. This method often incurs a small transaction fee; check with your bank for details. For you to use ATMs and debit cards, your bank must be affiliated with one of the several ATM networks. The most common affiliations are Star, Cirrus, Plus, and Interlink.

Taxes

In Charleston, except to pay 6.5 percent sales tax in stores, 8.5 percent in restaurants, and 12.5 percent for lodging. In Savannah, sales tax is 6 percent at stores and restaurants, and 12 percent for lodging.

Tipping

It's standard to tip your food server 15 percent of the bill for acceptable service. If you're at a breakfast place, where the bills are lower but the staff is often just as hardworking as those at more expensive dinner spots, you may wish to tip at least 20 percent. Never tip the regular amount to reward rude or inattentive service; it only encourages more of the same.

Tip airport skycaps $1 a bag; the same for hotel bellhops.

COMMUNICATIONS AND MEDIA
Postal Services

Sending mail from the United States to anywhere in the world is pretty easy. Almost every town and city that you are likely to visit has at least one post office or a local business that acts as the local post office. In larger cities you'll also find the major international delivery companies (UPS, Federal Express, and so on). The U.S. Postal Service and the delivery companies will also ship packages for you to many foreign countries. Charges are based on weight. At publication, a standard U.S. postal stamp costs $0.39. The delivery companies and the postal service offer next-day and two-day service to almost anywhere in the world.

If you plan to receive mail in the United States, make sure that the person sending mail addresses the envelope with your name exactly as it appears on your passport. This will help to avoid any questions about whether the mail is yours. You can also have mail delivered to your hotel. Make sure to provide the person sending you mail with the correct address. Also request that the person sending you mail print or type your address on the envelope to avoid any confusion that might arise because of worldwide differences in writing styles.

Always attach postage yourself to ensure that the proper amount is used.

When shipping large parcels overseas, it's best to pack the item(s) yourself or oversee the job. There are many packaging stores in the United States, offering boxes in various sizes, as well as tape and other packaging material. Many of these stores double as a post office or pickup/drop-off spot for the large delivery companies.

Unfortunately, although the U.S. Postal Service likes to cite Herodotus's quote, "Neither

FESTIVALS AND EVENTS

Nothing makes the delights of a small town (or even a bigger city) more accessible than a public festival, and the Sea Island Coast offers bushels of them – the following list represents only a sampling.

If you're planning to visit a region, check ahead of time with the respective tourism department or chamber of commerce on upcoming events.

JANUARY

Lowcountry Oyster Festival (Charleston, 843/577-4030, www.charlestonrestaurant-association.com). Features buckets of oysters, live music, kids' events, and a shucking contest.

FEBRUARY

Lowcountry Blues Bash (Charleston, 843/762-9125, www.bluesbash.com). A 10-day music festival featuring more than 50 acts playing everything from Urban to Delta.

Georgia Historical Society's Georgia Day Celebration (Savannah, 912/651-2125, www.georgiahistory.com) commemorates the founding of the state with reenactments, a parade downtown, and events at Wormsloe Plantation.

Savannah Irish Festival (Savannah, 912/232-3448, www.savannahirish.org) Irish roots, families, dances, songs, dishes, and crafts. Held at the Savannah Civic Center at Liberty and Montgomery streets.

Mardi Gras (St. Marys, 912/882-4000 or 800/868-8687, www.stmaryswelcome.com). It won't make you forget your last Fat Tuesday in New Orleans (if you remember it), but there's nothing like watching a spunky little town get down.

MARCH

Edisto Indian Cultural Festival (Ladson, 843/871-2126, www.powwows.com). Held just north of Charleston, celebrates Native American culture with lots of authentic dance demonstrations, as well as dance and craft competitions.

Annual Festival of Houses and Gardens (Charleston, 843/722-3405, www.historic-charleston.org). For more than 50 years, this festival has allowed common folk to tour the port city's most fabulous historic manses and private gardens, thanks to the Historic Charleston Foundation. Throw in some oyster roasts and you've got yourself a quintessential Charleston experience. Includes walking tours, lectures, dinners, and more.

Spring Tours (Beaufort, 843/522-1712, www.sthelenas1712.org). This self-guided tour showcases beautiful Lowcountry homes and plantations – a 50-year tradition.

St. Patrick's Day Celebrations (Savannah, 912/944-0455, www.savannahvisit.com). The biggest party in the South this side of Mardi Gras is held when more than 400,000 temporary Irish men and women pour into the city to watch the nation's second-largest parade, drink green beer, and enjoy authentic Irish foods and music.

Savannah Tour of Homes and Gardens (Savannah, 912/234-8054, www.savannahtourofhomes.org). The Garden Club of Savannah sponsors this tour, which takes place in March, as it has since 1934.

APRIL

Blessing of the Fleet and Seafood Festival (Mount Pleasant, 843/849-2061, www.townofmountpleasant.com). Combines seafood, crafts, and entertainment – simply shrimpalicious.

N.O.G.S. (North of Gaston Street) Tour of Hidden Gardens (Savannah, 912/961-4805). Begun in 1974, the Garden Club of Savannah holds this event each April. The walking tour includes eight walled gardens. Hostesses point out the plants, fountains, statues, and blooms that highlight their gardens.

MAY

Shakespeare Festival (Savannah, 912/234-9860, www.savannahga.gov). The Bard holds court in one of the Savannah's many parks.

Gullah Festival (Beaufort, 843/525-0628, www.gullahfestival.net). A cultural event featuring storytelling, fine art, dance, music, and special events in celebration of the cultural traditions of the Sea Islands.

Spoleto Festival USA (Charleston, 843/722-2764 or 843/579-3100, www.spoletousa .org). From late-May to mid-June, more than 130 dance, music, and theater performances by international and nationally renowned artists take over the city. Offerings include everything from avant-garde renditions of classics to premieres and traditional performances. Opera, ballet, modern dance, chamber music, marionettes, jazz, old-fashioned circuses, and much, much more for every age, every palette. One-of-a-kind experience, especially with Charleston as the backdrop. Absolutely not to be missed.

Piccolo Spoleto (Charleston, 843/724-7305, www.piccolospoleto.com). The City of Charleston's partner festival to Spoleto. Piccolo shows run during the same time as Spoleto, but leans toward nominal ticket prices and scores of free events. Includes stand-up comedy, gospel music, outdoor concerts, open-air art shows, independent theater productions, flea circuses, and loads more.

JUNE

Spoleto Festival USA and Piccolo Spoleto (Charleston, see above) continue into the first weeks of June.

JULY

Patriots Point Independence Day Blast (Charleston, 843/884-2727, www.patriotspoint.org). Because it was the headquarters of Revolutionary activity in the South, Charleston's a fitting place to spend the Fourth. Look for live music and fireworks over the harbor, with Patriots Point putting on a daylong celebration that anchors the city's main light show.

Fourth of July on the Waterfront (Savannah, 912/234-0295, www.riverstreetsavannah. com). Riverfront arts, crafts, and food festival that culminates with fireworks over the water.

Small-town Fourth of July Festivals (Various, but including Beaufort, Saint Mary's,

St. Simons, Sullivan's Island, Tybee Island). If you happen to find yourself in the area on the 4th of July, try to take in some of the friendly atmosphere, music, food, and fireworks over water.

AUGUST

Tybee Island Beach Music Festival (Tybee, 912/786-5444 or 800/868-2322, www .tybeeislandfestival.com). Two days of shag dancing tunes and local seafood.

Rockville Regatta (Rockville, 843/559-1410). This quiet, tiny waterfront village (about 40 minutes outside Charleston) has hosted this raucous regatta since 1890. More than 100 racing boats, more than 100 spectator boats.

SEPTEMBER

MOJA Arts Festival (Charleston, 843/724-7305, www.mojafestival.com). Music, arts, food, and lectures focused on Charleston and Lowcountry African American history.

Scottish Games and Highland Gathering (Charleston, 843/529-1020, www.charlestonscots.com). Held at beautiful Tara-esque Boone Hall Plantation, this is a gathering of the kilts that includes medieval competitions, Scottish dancing, and, yes, bagpipes.

Savannah Jazz Festival (Savannah, 912/232-2222, www.coastaljazz.com). In Forsyth Park, features international and local acts that span jazz to blues.

OCTOBER

Rock Shrimp Festival (Saint Marys, 912/882-4000 or 800/868-8687, www .stmaryswelcome.com). Strap on a bib and put your cardiologist on alert. The seafood flies fast and furious, but really it's just another excuse for St. Mary's to have a street party.

Oktoberfest (Savannah, 912/234-0295, www.riverstreetsavannah.com). Oompahpah bands, beer, arts and crafts, bratwurst, plus weiner-dog races at River Street.

Annual Fall Candlelight Tours of Homes and Gardens (Charleston, 843/722-4630,

(continued on next page)

FESTIVALS AND EVENS (continued)

www.preservationsociety.org). Six weeks of touring the city's finest historical and most exclusive properties, sponsored by the Preservation Society of Charleston.

Fall Festival of Homes and History (Beaufort, 803/379-6335, www.historic-beaufort.org). Historic Beaufort Foundation leads visitors on home tours throughout the historic waterfront neighborhood and offers related lectures.

Savannah Film Festival (Savannah, 912/525-5050, www.scad.edu/filmfest). Eight days of indie films shown throughout the city, at the historic Lucas Theatre and elsewhere. Animation, shorts, student films, documentaries, lectures, and more.

NOVEMBER

Holiday Festival of Lights (Charleston, 843/795-7275, www.holidayfestivaloflights.com). Head over to James Island County Park at night to drive through a wonderland of miniature light displays. Christmas gift shops, concessions area with hot chocolate. November through New Year's; admission $10 per car.

Heritage Days Celebration (St. Helena Island, 843/838-2432, www.penncenter.com).

Three days of African American Sea Island culture at the Historic Penn Center. Crafts, music, food, and more.

DECEMBER

Christmas/Holiday Parades (Various). You'll find these in many of the small towns along the coast, always in the first half of the month.

Holiday Boat Parades (Charleston, Savannah). Locals deck boats out in lights and parade before the cities' waterfronts, usually followed by with fireworks. Pack a Thermos of hot chocolate and bring a blanket. Call the local Chambers of Commerce or CVBs for information.

First Night (Charleston, 843/724-7305, www.ci.charleston.sc.us). Ring in the new year with an alcohol-free street celebration. Fireworks replace the giant ball they have up north. Call for information about First Night Charleston.

New Year's Bluegrass Festival (Jekyll Island Convention Center, Jekyll Island, 877/453-5955, www.jekyllisland.com). Features live music from local and regional acts, New Year's Eve and the day before. Bring your instrument and jam with others.

---

snow, nor rain, nor heat, nor night stays these couriers from the swift completion of their appointed rounds," you'll find that just about any old bank holiday—even Columbus Day—will stay these couriers. Post offices will also close, and any mail you've already sent off will sit for a full day, so be prepared.

Telephones

Public phones are widely available on street corners and outside convenience stores and gas stations. They are maintained by a variety of private companies, which may sometimes charge more than the usual fee of $0.35. Use any combination of coins; however, in the case of a 35-cent local call, if you use two quarters, change will not be provided. Dialing directions are usu-

ally provided on the face of the phone, but when in doubt simply dial "0" for an operator, who will direct your call for an added charge of one to three dollars. To place a local or long-distance call, simply dial the number and an automated voice will tell you how much money to deposit. When using a calling card billed to your home account, dial "0" plus the number (including area code) you're calling. You'll hear a tone, then often a voice prompting you to enter your calling card number and Personal Identification Number (PIN). For universal calling cards, follow the instructions provided on the back of the card or dial "0" for operator assistance.

Prepaid calling cards are the most hassle-free method of making long-distance calls, short of carrying around a cell phone. If you purchase a $10 card, you are given $10 of long-distance credit to spend. You can spend it all on one call, or more likely on a series of calls throughout your trip. Best of all, if you lose your card—unlike some other calling cards that give access to your account with your phone company—you can't lose more than the $10 you spent on it. Stores like Kroger, Wal-Mart, convenience stores, and some gas stations sell prepaid calling cards.

Phone books are generally available at public phone booths and normally cover everything within the local area code, although frequently they are vandalized. Besides containing phone listings, phone books also carry maps to the local area, zip codes and post offices, information on public transportation systems, and a listing of community services and events.

In an emergency when an ambulance, firefighters, or police are required, you can dial 911 and be instantly connected with an emergency switchboard; otherwise dial "0" for the operator. When you dial 911, your number and address are displayed on a viewing screen, enabling the authorities to locate you, even if you don't know where exactly you are.

The area code for the entire South Carolina Lowcountry is 843. The area code for the entire Georgia Coast is 912. The area code for Fernandina and Amelia Island, Florida, is 904.

Internet Access

After a brief heyday, pure Internet cafés are few and far between anymore along the coast; however, they are listed where they can be found. Now WiFi (wireless free Internet) is offered at loads of coffeehouses. Many public libraries boast Internet access: SCAD's **Jen Library** (201 E. Broughton St., 912/525-4700, www.scad.edu/jenlibrary) in Savannah; and the **Charleston County Public Library Main Branch** (68 Calhoun St., 843/805-6801, www.ccpl.org). Most hotels (and scores of bed-and-breakfasts) offer separate modem lines, or at least modem hookups that use your room phone line.

Newspapers

Nearly any Sea Island Coast town of any size has its own newspaper; reading these can give you a good feel for the pace of life in a town. Along the South Carolina Coast, Charleston's *The Post and Courier* (www.charleston.net) is well thought of and well read. The *Savannah Morning News* (www.savannahnow.com) is the paper of record for Savannah and the Beaufort–Hilton Head region, as well as points south.

You'll also find *USA Today* all around the region. The *New York Times* is available in the business districts of major cities.

Radio

In most of the Sea Island Coast, you'll find a wide variety of music, with a heavy emphasis on country but liberal dosings of urban, metal, and pop stations. Contemporary Christian rock music stations have popped up in a couple of the bigger cities. As usual, nearly everywhere in the state, the left end of the FM dial is where you'll find gospel stations and the Georgia or South Carolina Public Radio/NPR affiliate, where faithful listeners will find *All Things Considered, Prairie Home Companion,* and *Car Talk,* along with local shows, a few of which highlight regional music.

The AM dial contains gospel music and preaching, country music, some local news and talk shows, and the sonic strip mall that is American syndicated talk radio today.

TOURIST INFORMATION
Statewide Offices

The **Georgia Department of Economic Development** (75 5th St. NW, Ste. 1200 Atlanta, 800/847-4842, www.georgiaonmymind.org) has a wealth of tourism information for visitors. In South Carolina, contact the **South Carolina Department of Parks, Recreation and Tourism** (1205 Pendleton St., Columbia, 803/734-1700, www.discoversouthcarolina.com) to request a copy of the free, helpful, and up-to-date *South Carolina Travel Guide,* which includes a travel map of the state and other materials.

Welcome Centers

If you're driving into the area, be sure to stop at one of Georgia's and/or South Carolina's many welcome centers along the major highways at the state borders, as well as one in the middle of South Carolina on I-95 in Santee. The folks at these offices are generally knowledgeable about the states' recreational opportunities and can help you plan to get the most possible from your stay on the Carolina coast. They also dispense free maps and about a zillion pamphlets from every region of the state. They can even help you set up tee times.

LIBRARIES

You'll find either a college or public library in almost every good-sized town along the Sea Island Coast. The **Charleston County Public Library Main Branch** (68 Calhoun St., 843/805-6801, www.ccpl.org) has a fine selection of books, DVDs, CDs, and more. Probably the coolest little library in the region is the **Edgar Allan Poe Library** (843/883-3914, 1921 I'On Ave., www.ccpl.org), built into an old fort bunker on Sullivan's Island.

The **Live Oak Public Libraries** (www.liveoakpl.org) operate in Savannah and have two downtown locations: the main branch (2002 Bull St., 912/652-3600), and the smaller Ola Wyeth branch (4 E. Bay St., 912/232-5488). Tybee Island's branch (405 Butler Ave., 912/786-7733) serves that area. SCAD's **Jen Library** (201 E. Broughton St., 912/525-4700, www.scad.edu/jenlibrary) is also open to visitors.

Bring a photo ID to any library you visit. You'll find these and other libraries listed in the appropriate destination chapters.

ODDS AND ENDS
Photo Etiquette

You will see quaint homes along the coast. You will want to take pictures of them. If you're in downtown Charleston or Savannah, and the house is one of the famous old Charleston or Savannah houses along The Battery or on Rainbow Row or on one of the squares, then go ahead and snap away. If you're up in a tiny Albemarle town and you want to take a picture of a private citizen's house, then you might try to get permission first. It's not really a legal requirement, just a courtesy, but courtesy goes a long way down here.

Some of the savvy basket-weaving Gullah women you'll see in Charleston and along Highway 17 in Mount Pleasant will charge you $5 or more to take their picture.

Camping Gear

With rain showers so unpredictable, particularly in summer, you'll want a tarp over your tent as well as beneath it. If you're car camping, consider a screen canopy, inside of which you'll be able to sip your hot cocoa without enduring mosquito and no-see-um bites. If you'll be hiking long distances from civilization and transportation to a doctor, then bring a snakebite kit.

WEIGHTS AND MEASURES

Georgia and South Carolina, like all other states in the United States, do not use the metric system. For help converting weights, distances, and temperatures, see the table at the back of this book.

Electricity

Despite what Hollywood may have led you to believe, it's rare to find anywhere in the South that doesn't vibrate with electrical power. Electrical outlets in the United States run on a 110- or 120-volt AC. Most plugs are either two flat prongs or two flat and one round. Adapters for 220-volt appliances are available in hardware or electronic stores.

Time Zone

Georgia and South Carolina rest within the Eastern time zone, the same one used by New York City, Boston, and Florida. It is three hours ahead of Los Angeles.

RESOURCES

Suggested Reading

Battaile, Andrew Chandler, Arthur W. Bergernon Jr., et. al. *Black Southerners in Gray: Essays on Afro-Americans in Confederate Armies.* Edited by Richard Rollins. Redondo Beach, CA: Rank and File, 1994. Fascinating studies on this little-known minority group in the Civil War.

Berendt, John. *Midnight in the Garden of Good and Evil: A Savannah Story.* New York: Vintage, 1994. If you haven't read it, you should, in part because it captures an amazing amount of Savannah's quirky charm in its pages, and in part because "the Book"'s massive success has shaped the way Savannah defines itself.

Bodie, Idella. *South Carolina Women.* Orangeburg, SC: Sandlapper Publishing, 1991. Stories of notable female Gamecocks.

Bryan, Bo. *Shag: The Legendary Dance of the South.* Beaufort, SC: Foundation Books, 1995. The single best reference on the dance and the surrounding subculture.

Dickey, Christopher. *Summer of Deliverance: A Memoir of Father and Son.* New York: Simon and Schuster, 1998. A heart-wrenching and insightful look at the rough-edged career of the late James Dickey—poet, novelist, screenwriter, critic, and longtime USC professor.

Edgar, Walter. *South Carolina: A History.* Columbia: University of South Carolina Press, 1998. A long-needed 700-page comprehensive history by a longtime Carolina scholar.

Farrant, Don W. *The Lure and Lore of the Golden Isles: The Magical Heritage of Georgia's Outerbanks.* Nashville, TN: Rutledge Hill, 1993. A diverse grouping of lively, true stories from along the southern Georgia Coast.

Federal Works Project. *South Carolina: A Guide to the Palmetto State.* 1941. The definitive old-time guide, created during the WPA years.

Freeman, Ron. *Savannah: People, Places, & Events.* Savannah: Freeman, 1997. Savannah native Ron Freeman has written and self-published perhaps the best short history of the city and its most famous people.

Gale, Jack. *Same Time, Same Station.* Palm City, FL: Gala Publishers, 1999. Great anecdotes of the days of early rock-and-roll radio in the Carolinas.

Hudson, Charles, and Carmen Chaves Tesser, eds. *Forgotten Centuries: The Indians and Europeans in the American South, 1521–1704.* Athens: University of Georgia Press, 1994.

Hurmence, Belinda, ed. *Before Freedom, When I Can Just Remember: Twenty-seven Oral Histories of Former South Carolina Slaves.* Winston-Salem, NC: John F. Blair, 1989. Absolutely fascinating accounts of life under slavery and during Reconstruction.

Jones-Jackson, Patricia. *When Roots Die: Endangered Traditions on the Sea Islands.* Athens: University of Georgia Press, 1987.

Kovacik, Charles F., and John J. Winberry. *South Carolina: A Geography.* Boulder, CO:

Westview Press, 1987. Reprinted by University of South Carolina Press in 1989 as *South Carolina: The Making of a Landscape*. The definitive look at the various geographies of the state.

Lippy, Charles H., ed. *Religion in South Carolina*. Columbia: University of South Carolina Press, 1993. Fourteen essays shed light on the tangle of denominations that make up organized religion in South Carolina.

Martin, Floride Milner. *A Chronological Survey of South Carolina Literature*. Self-published. A representative sampling of the state's literature, from early explorer records to present-day Carolinian authors.

McCloud, Barry. *Definitive Country: The Ultimate Encyclopedia of Country Music and Its Performers*, New York: Berkley, 1995. A wonderful reference for the student of country music.

O'Connor, Flannery. *Collected Works*. Edited by Sally Fitzgerald. New York: Library of America, 1988. Everything this Savannah-born writer penned, from her short stories to her two novels and letters, assembled and notated by her longtime friend and editor.

Pinckney, Elise, ed. *Letterbook of Eliza Lucas Pinckney, 1739–1762*. Chapel Hill: University of North Carolina Press, 1972. Along with Mary Chesnut, the indigo pioneer Pinckney is one of South Carolina's most interesting women.

Powers, Bernard E., Jr. *Black Charlestonians: A Social History: 1822–1885*. Fayetteville: University of Arkansas, 1994. A much-needed accounting-for of the important contributions of the black citizens—slave and free—to one of the most important Southern cities of the 19th century.

Rhyne, Nancy. *Carolina Seashells*. Orangeburg, SC: Sandlapper Publishing, 1989. Learn to know your conch from your limpet.

Rhyne, Nancy. *Chronicles of the South Carolina Sea Islands*. Winston-Salem, NC: John E.

Blair, 1998. Colorful tales from a cherished local storyteller and folklorist.

Russell, Preston, and Barbara Hines. *Savannah: A History of Her People Since 1733*. Savannah: Beil, 1992. A lively, captivating, well-illustrated read through Savannah's past.

Simpson, Lewis P. *Mind and the American Civil War*. Baton Rouge: Louisiana State University, 1989. Studies American history's foremost conflict in terms of the collision of two distinct philosophies and the cultures that spawned from them.

Smith, Reed. *Gullah*. Edisto Island, SC: Edisto Island Historical Preservation Society, 1926. Reprinted 1993. Somewhat dated but still informative look at Gullah speech.

Starobin, Robert S., ed. *Denmark Vesey: The Slave Conspiracy of 1822*. Englewood Cliffs, NJ: Prentice Hall, 1970. A collection of essays and original documents pertaining to the aborted revolt.

Wallace, David Duncan. *South Carolina: A Short History 1520–1948*. Chapel Hill: University of North Carolina Press, 1951. Until Walter Edgar's book, this was the most recent large work on the entire state. Still worth reading for its compelling storytelling.

Weeks, Carl Solana. *Savannah in the time of Peter Tondee*. Columbia, SC: Summerhouse Press, 1997. Insightful, novelistic exploration of Savannah's Colonial and Revolutionary periods, told through the story of Liberty Boy tavern keeper Peter Tondee. Author Weeks is a Tondee descendent.

Wood, Virginia Steele, and Mary R. Bullard, eds. *Journal of a Visit to the Georgia Islands of St. Catherines, Green, Ossabaw, Sapelo, St. Simons, Jekyll, and Cumberland, with Comments on the Florida Islands of Amelia, Talbot, and St. George, in 1753*. Macon, GA: Mercer University, 1996. With a subtitle like that, I don't need to describe it much. The journal's author, apparently, was early Georgia settler Jonathan Bryan.

Woodward, C. Vann, ed. *Mary Chesnut's Civil War.* New Haven, CT: Yale, 1982. The Pulitzer Prize–winning collection of letters by a witty, shrewd eyewitness to the inner workings of the Confederacy.

Internet Resources

GENERAL INFORMATION
Charleston Area Convention & Visitors Bureau
www.charlestoncvb.com
Home base for the Charleston Area Convention and Visitors' Bureau. An excellent resource.

Savannah Convention & Visitors Bureau
www.savcvb.com
The above site's sister-in-arms in Savannah.

NEWSPAPERS
Beaufort Gazette
www.beaufortgazette.com
Beaufort's daily paper, online.

The Brunswick News
www.thebrunswicknews.com
The *Brunswick Newspaper* online. Provides coverage of Brunswick and the Golden Isles.

Tribune & Georgian
www.tribune-georgian.com
Home of the Camden County *Tribune-Georgian,* local paper for St. Marys and vicinity.

The Post and Courier
www.charleston.net
The Charleston *Post and Courier* online. Includes a special section on the recovery of the CSS *Hunley* and the building of the new bridge.

The Island Packet
www.islandpacket.com
Hilton Head's daily paper, online.

SavannahNOW
www.savannah.net
The *Savannah Daily News,* online.

RADIO
Unfortunately, recent lawsuits by ad firms have stopped and reversed the proliferation of online local radio programming, which would have enabled you to listen to Sea Island radio stations live, from anywhere on Earth. All the parties involved—broadcasters, advertisers, advertising companies—are trying to work out some sort of arrangement that will enable broadcasts to resume, to everyone's benefit (including us listeners). In the meantime, the Charleston RiverDogs continue to broadcast their games live—muting out the commercials, and you can also hear older broadcasts at the site below:

ReelRadio
www.airchecks.com
Hear radio broadcasts from the 1950s to 1990s from Savannah and Jacksonville stations, and from other stations all around the country.

PARKS AND RECREATION
National Parks Service
www.nps.gov
National Parks Service site includes information on all Federal lands in the region, including Fort Sumter, Fort Moultrie, Fort Pulaski, and Cumberland Island.

South Carolina State Trails Program
www.sctrails.net
South Carolina State Trails Program online: the best trails and maps for the entire state.

South Carolina State Parks
www.southcarolinaparks.com
All the specs and contact info for parks in the Palmetto state.

Georgia State Parks and Historic Sites
www.gastateparks.org
Everything about Georgia's state parks online.

Reserve America
www.reserveamerica.com
To book a state park campsite or cabin in South Carolina.

Great Lodge
www.greatlodge.com
All about hunting and fishing in South Carolina, plus license info.

South Carolina Aquarium
www.scaquarium.org
The official site for the South Carolina Aquarium in Charleston. Worth checking for their hotel/aquarium packages.

SPORTS TEAMS
Charleston RiverDogs
www.riverdogs.com
Online information and ticket sales on Charleston's minor-league baseball team. Online radio broadcasts of games.

Savannah Sand Gnats
www.sandgnats.com
The lowdown on Savannah's minor-league baseball team.

Charleston Stingrays
www.stingrayshockey.com
Home page and online ticket sales for the Charleston Stingrays.

Charleston Battery
www.charlestonbattery.com
Info and online ticket sales for the Charleston Battery, the only professional soccer team on the Sea Island Coast.

SURF CONDITIONS
Surfline
www.surfline.com
Current conditions at Folly Beach.

High Tide Surf Shop
www.hightidesurfshop.com
Current conditions at Tybee Island.

Index

CHURCHES AND PLACES OF WORSHIP

MUSEUMS

Amelia Island Museum of History: 232
American Military Museum: 59
Avery Research Center for African American History and Culture: 58-59
Beaufort Museum: 120
Charleston Museum: 57
Children's Museum of the Lowcountry: 57
Citadel Museum: 63
Coastal Discovery Museum: 136
Colleton Museum: 146
Confederate Museum: 45, 58
Congressional Medal of Honor Museum: 59-60
Edisto Island Museum: 110
Flannery O'Connor Childhood Home Museum: 167-168
Gallery Chuma/African American Art Gallery: 129
Gibbes Museum of Art: 58

John Mark Verdier House Museum: 121
Mercer House Museum: 160
Midway Museum: 226
Mighty Eighth Air Force Museum: 164
Old Slave Mart Museum: 47
Orange Hall House Museum: 229
Parris Island Museum: 131-132
Pauline Pratt Webel Museum: 148
Ralph Mark Gilbert Civil Rights Museum: 172
Red Piano Too Art Gallery: 126, 129
Roundhouse Railroad Museum: 170
Savannah History Museum: 163-164
Ships of the Sea Maritime Museum: 166
Slave Relic Museum: 146
St. Marys Submarine Museum: 229
Summerville-Dorchester Museum: 109
Tybee Island Light Station and Museum: 166, 194
York W. Bailey Museum: 127, 129

nature preserves: Audubon Newhall Preserve 135; Crooked River State Park 229; Cumberland Island National Seashore 230-231; Ernest F. Hollings ACE Basin National Wildlife Refuge 145; Oatland Island Education Center 172; 233-235; Pinckney Island National Wildlife Refuge 136; Sapelo Island National Estuarine Research Reserve 224-225; Savannah National Wildlife Refuge 147; Skidaway Island State Park 174; St. Catherines Island 226-227; Wassaw National Wildlife Refuge 163
Negro Heritage Trail Tour: 171
New Year's Bluegrass Festival: 316
Newpoint: 128-130
newspapers: 107, 194, 317, 321
nightlife: see entertainment
N.O.G.S. Tour of Hidden Gardens: 175, 314
no-see-ums: 306
North Beach: 194
North Charleston Performing Arts Center: 69

O

O'Connor, Flannery: 160, 167-168, 283, 284
Oatland Island Education Center: 172, 292
Oatland Island Preserve: 183
Odom, Joe: 179
Oglethorpe, James: 260-262

Oglethorpe Square: 160-161
Okefenokee National Wildlife Refuge: 235
Okefenokee Swamp: 233-235; map 234
Okefenokee Swamp Park: 235
Oktoberfest: 315
Old Bluffton: 143-145
Old City Market: 42, 45
Old Cotton Exchange: 172
Olde Pink House: 161
Old Exchange and Provost Dungeon: 48
Old Fort Jackson: 168
Old Powder Magazine: 45
Old Savannah-Tybee Railroad Historic and Scenic Trail: 183
Old Slave Mart Museum: 47
Old Zion Cemetery: 135-136
Orange Hall House Museum: 229
Orleans Square: 161
Osceola: 67-68
Osprey Pond Trail: 136
Ossabow Island: 199
Owens-Thomas House: 160-161, 172

PQ

packing: 17
Palmetto Dunes: 138, 292
Palmetto Islands County Park: 56
Palmetto Trail: 80, 291

Acknowledgments

Thanks to Jean Berler for her tireless, thorough fact-checking and can-do spirit; Sean Slinsky for his photographic talents and road warrior stamina; my friends for their local secrets and constant cheerleading; and my family for celebrating and supporting their freelance adventure-hound.

www.moon.com

For helpful advice on planning a trip, visit www.moon.com for the **TRAVEL PLANNER** and get access to useful travel strategies and valuable information about great places to visit. When you travel with Moon, expect an experience that is uncommon and truly unique.

MAP SYMBOLS

▦▦▦ Expressway	◖ Highlight	✕ Airfield	⚑ Golf Course	
▦▦ Primary Road	○ City/Town	✈ Airport	℗ Parking Area	
▦ Secondary Road	◉ State Capital	▲ Mountain	▲ Archaeological Site	
▪▪▪ Unpaved Road	⊛ National Capital	✛ Unique Natural Feature	⛪ Church	
▪▪ Trail	★ Point of Interest		⛽ Gas Station	
▪▪▪ Ferry	• Accommodation	⚐ Waterfall	◌ Glacier	
┼┼ Railroad	▼ Restaurant/Bar	▲ Park	Mangrove	
▨ Pedestrian Walkway	▪ Other Location	⊡ Trailhead	Reef	
▨▨ Stairs	Λ Campground	⛷ Skiing Area	▨ Swamp	

CONVERSION TABLES

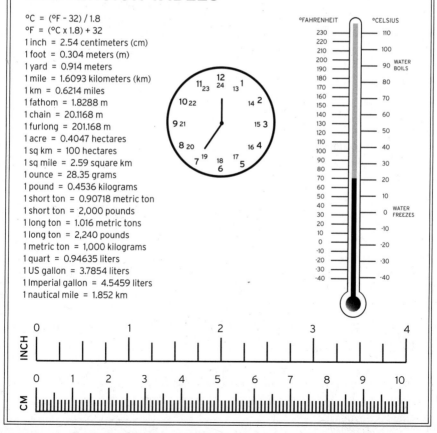

°C = (°F - 32) / 1.8
°F = (°C x 1.8) + 32
1 inch = 2.54 centimeters (cm)
1 foot = 0.304 meters (m)
1 yard = 0.914 meters
1 mile = 1.6093 kilometers (km)
1 km = 0.6214 miles
1 fathom = 1.8288 m
1 chain = 20.1168 m
1 furlong = 201.168 m
1 acre = 0.4047 hectares
1 sq km = 100 hectares
1 sq mile = 2.59 square km
1 ounce = 28.35 grams
1 pound = 0.4536 kilograms
1 short ton = 0.90718 metric ton
1 short ton = 2,000 pounds
1 long ton = 1.016 metric tons
1 long ton = 2,240 pounds
1 metric ton = 1,000 kilograms
1 quart = 0.94635 liters
1 US gallon = 3.7854 liters
1 Imperial gallon = 4.5459 liters
1 nautical mile = 1.852 km

MOON CHARLESTON & SAVANNAH

Avalon Travel Publishing
1400 65th Street, Suite 250
Emeryville, CA 94608, USA
www.moon.com

Editors: Kay Elliott, Chris Jones
Series Manager: Kathryn Ettinger
Acquisitions Manager: Rebecca K. Browning
Copy Editor: Gerardyne Madigan
Graphics Coordinator: Stefano Boni
Production Coordinators: Jacob Goolkasian,
    Karen Heithecker
Cover & Interior Designer: Gerilyn Attebery
Map Editor: Kevin Anglin
Cartographers: Kat Smith, Kat Bennett,
    Mike Morgenfeld
Indexer: Deana Shields

ISBN-10: 1-56691-752-2
ISBN-13: 978-1-56691-752-0
ISSN: 1539-1027

Printing History
1st Edition – 2002
2nd Edition – May 2006
5 4 3 2

Text © 2006 by Mike Sigalas.
Maps © 2006 by Avalon Travel Publishing, Inc.
All rights reserved.

Some photos and illustrations are used by permission
and are the property of the original copyright owners.

Front cover photo: © Sean Slinsky, Angel Oak, John's
Island, Charleston County

Title page photo: © Sean Slinsky, carriage tour
through The Battery, Charleston

Printed in Canada by Transcontinental

KEEPING CURRENT

If you have a favorite gem you'd like to see included in the next edition, or see anything
that needs updating, clarification, or correction, please drop us a line. Send your comments via email to feedback@moon.com, or use the address above.